MARGINAL
NATIVES

CONTRIBUTORS

Morris Freilich
NORTHEASTERN UNIVERSITY

Nancie L. Solien González
UNIVERSITY OF IOWA

John Gulick
UNIVERSITY OF NORTH CAROLINA
AT CHAPEL HILL

John J. Honigmann
UNIVERSITY OF NORTH CAROLINA
AT CHAPEL HILL

Robert J. Maxwell
PHILADELPHIA GERIATRICS CENTER

Pertti J. Pelto
UNIVERSITY OF CONNECTICUT

Melvin L. Perlman
UNIVERSITY OF CALIFORNIA
AT BERKELEY

William B. Schwab
TEMPLE UNIVERSITY

Norman E. Whitten, Jr.
WASHINGTON UNIVERSITY

Aram A. Yengoyan
UNIVERSITY OF MICHIGAN

MARGINAL NATIVES

ANTHROPOLOGISTS AT WORK

Morris Freilich

EDITOR
Department of Sociology
and Anthropology
Northeastern University

Harper & Row, Publishers
New York, Evanston, and London

MARGINAL NATIVES: Anthropologists at Work
Copyright © 1970 by *Morris Freilich*

LIBRARY OF CONGRESS CATALOG CARD NUMBER: 76-91252

CONTENTS

PREFACE

The Marginal Man
is "one whom fate
has condemned to live
in two societies
and in two,
not merely different,
but antagonistic cultures."

Stonequist (1937)

The anthropologist has been a marginal man for most of anthropology's history. Regardless of time, place, or people present, he almost invariably "came on" as marginal to society. To members of his family he was "the strange one" who was more interested in primitive rituals (like how to make rain by dancing) than modern rituals (like how to make money by singing). To the neighbors his entrance into the community was a traumatic experience. He arrived with digging sticks, broken bits of pottery, masks, apelike heads of prehistoric men, and naked figurines. Once in, he held strange parties at which he offered his guests unsightly morsels, queer liquids that burned the stomach, and weird noises called "primitive music." At the university he was the professor who taught those wild courses on "Sex and

Magic Everywhere," and who attracted a following of disheveled students. Or were they really students? One could never be sure; perhaps they were informants brought back from some primitive tribe.

To social scientists who had a general idea of the nature of anthropology, the anthropologist was an object of ambivalent feelings. On the one hand, he had lots of interesting data always good for comic relief during a serious lecture; on the other hand, this cross-cultural researcher was intellectually perverse. He ceaselessly spoke of "what the data indicate" in ways unflattering to his audience. Social scientists were informed that their generalizations, looked at from a cross-cultural perspective, accounted for but 1 percent of the variance, although their theories did help to explain *some* of the behavior of freshmen students in nonsectarian liberal-arts colleges located in the urban centers of North America.

As the anthropologist found his way around to different departments, he informed geographers that geographic determinism was not a viable theoretical framework, no matter what Huntington had said, notified historians that history "existed" before writing, and suggested to psychiatrists that they take less seriously the Oedipus story and its Freudian interpretations. To their chagrin these latter gentlemen learned that all five-year-old boys do not hate their fathers; that indeed some "normal" kids, in the Trobriand Islands and elsewhere, loved their fathers and for some enigmatic reason hated their Mother's brothers. Economists were saddened to hear that "economic man," already considered quite sick by some, had, in actuality, "died."

Today, the anthropologist is still a marginal man, particularly in the field. At home, he is (almost) a solid citizen. The research method he fathered—participant observation—has been emulated far and wide, even by such rivals as sociologists. And his writings are being read by young and old, intellectuals and dilettantes. Anthropology has come of age; anthropologists have arrived. It is now possible to answer the old question of some students with a positive, "Yes! One can be an anthropologist and eat regularly!"

Anthropologists have been discovered by the students. The English literature-oriented co-ed is now reading *Patterns of Culture* and loving it. The brilliant senior once ready to set the world on fire via a doctorate in physics is thinking of a good graduate program with research opportunities in Africa, or perhaps Southeast Asia, or Latin America. Even the average student finds it necessary to take an anthropology course or two, for how else will he learn "in" terms like *potlatch* and *fête* and put-downs like, "Having met you, I better understand the mentality of Australopithecus." Some students are currently developing such a passion for this discipline that they have demanded extra ethnography courses.

The remarkable growth of cultural anthropology, particularly in the last decade, is due to many factors, including (1) the fact that, due to the revolutionary changes in transportation and communication technology, the lives of peoples all over the world have become more familiar, meaningful, and important to us; (2) the growing importance of such related disciplines as sociology, psychology, economics, and political science, and the realization by many that effective work in these sciences is greatly helped by some knowledge of cultural anthropology; and (3) the growing realization that the natural sciences cannot solve the major problems of the modern world: wars, racial and ethnic conflicts, crime, poverty, and overpopulation.

As more and more students become involved in collecting cross-cultural ethnographic data, and as such information progressively becomes more important both as a basis for scientific generalizations and as a guide for social planning and political action, it becomes the duty of professional anthropologists to see that data collection follows rigorous, scientifically sound procedures. Unfortunately, sound research methods have not been adequately developed in anthropology. The novice, off to live among "primitive" peoples for the first time, has often been dispatched with minimal training and a "sink-or-swim" philosophy.

In order to develop a rational and comprehensive program in anthropological research, it is necessary to discover how such research has been done in the past by anthropologists working in every part of the world. The contributors to this book are anthropologists truly interested in field research. Their interest goes far beyond the mechanics of research: they wish to share their experiences so that life-in-the-field will lose some of its mystery and apprehension. Each informant is a well-trained and experienced field worker. Each has successfully passed through the two *rites-de-passage* required of the professional anthropological researcher: *academic competence,* measured by graduate degrees, and *research competence,* measured by his survival and his return with valuable data. To achieve success in both these areas requires a unique mixture of talents: an ability for introvertive, ivory-tower scholarship, and an ability for extrovertive field work.

Contributors were sent an outline suggesting that each chapter be presented in three parts: Project 1, Project 2, and Comparisons. It was also suggested that the description of each project be structurally similar, with sections discussing (1)

Problem, Theory, Research Design, (2) Passive or Adaptational Research, (3) Active Research, and (4) Summary and Evaluation.

Each contributor was thus asked to think of field research as work involving two distinguishable stages: (1) adapting to a novel environment, and (2) solving a research problem. Each stage was described as having a major goal and a number of related problems. The problems of one stage did not disappear in the next stage; rather they assumed different meanings. For example, a major problem of the passive-research stage is "getting and maintaining rapport." Clearly, this problem exists throughout the research period, but in the active-research stage, maintaining and developing rapport becomes of greater importance than "getting" rapport.

Within the limits of this general structure, the contributors freely wrote what they did, thought, felt, and believed. Within the limits of accurate first-level interpretation, I have summarized some of the information presented by contributors and have gone on to derive generalizations, models, research strategies, and orientations for which the contributors are not responsible.

The essays that follow indicate the stylistic differences in anthropological research. Such differences are due in part to differences in the anthropologists' age and personality, the research sites worked in, and the problems around which data collection was oriented. However, additional and important differences stem from the paucity of theory directly relevant to anthropological research. These essays thus show the creative and bold attempts of individual anthropologists, working with a minimum of guidelines, to solve research problems.

A preface is a ritual and traditional one that ends with grateful acknowledgments. This book, while not traditional in many respects, does toe the line on ritual when gratitude is involved. I thank the contributors for their readiness to enter this "public confessional" and thereby help disperse the myths of life-in-the-field. It takes special people with a very special type of courage to allow an unknown public to look in on intimate and personal matters pertaining to life with the natives.

A host of colleagues and students are thanked for their comments, criticisms, and suggestions, all of which have improved this book. In particular I must identify and thank a good friend and renowned colleague, Rose Laub Coser, for considerable and challenging comments on various drafts of my work.

I thank a number of students for their committed assistance in the pragmatics of typing, proofing, and bibliographical work, in particular, Elizabeth Grady, Brenda A. Newman, Inez Middleton, and Evelyn Hulda Barchi. Carol Lynn Wodinsky is thanked for her considerable labors on the pragmatics of a field project (Appendix).

Finally, I owe my family a deep debt of gratitude: my wife, Natalie Asch Freilich, for listening to endless hours of field-work talk and for bouncing back with psychological information of such high caliber that it found its way into this text; my sons, Harold Aaron and Steven Phillip, for listening to methodological arguments and staying neutral and sane: and my extended family, for graciously accepting my temporary disappearance from social life.

M.F.

Boston

FIELD WORK:
AN INTRODUCTION[1]

Morris Freilich

When an anthropologist speaks of "going into the field to do field work," the field refers to the place where the group he plans to study resides, and field work includes living as well as working in this place. The culture being researched is assumed to go through all of its major temporal variations in one year, so the anthropologist generally remains in the field for at least that long. Although anthropologists use a number of methods to collect data, the basic method associated with field work is *participant observation*. This means observing the behavior of a group while participating in its community life.

[1] The writer is much indebted to Rose Coser, Pertti Pelto, Norman Whitten, Munro Edmonson, and Robert Maxwell for critical and constructive comments on an earlier version of this essay.

The field anthropologist attempts to become part of the culture he is studying. Depending on his personality, the peculiarities of the group being studied, and contingent factors operating at the time of the study—wars, revolutions, prosperity, famine—the anthropologist acts in one of a variety of possible stylistic modes. At one extreme, he may "go native," in which case his speech, dress, eating and sleeping habits, interactions, social relations, and personal identification all begin to approximate community norms. Or, at the other end of this role-playing continuum, he may become a "privileged stranger," a stranger with rights to live for an extensive period in the community, to question community members extensively, and to record what he observes and hears. More often, the anthropologist's role is somewhere in between "native" and "privileged stranger."

Irrespective of what role he assumes, the anthropologist remains a *marginal man* in the community, an outsider. No matter how skilled he is in the native tongue, how nimble in handling strange social relationships, how artistic in performing social and religious rituals, and how attached he is to local beliefs, goals, and values, the anthropologist rarely deludes himself into thinking that many community members really regard him as one of them. This is true even when he gets "adopted," as I was by the Mohawk steel workers. It was true for me even when Trinidadian peasants asked the clearly rhetorical question, "Mr. Morris, you one of us, yes?"[2]

The role of marginal native is not an easy one to play, for the real natives are often suspicious of the anthropologist. Although his credentials appear legitimate, his goals honorable, and his behavior friendly, his work is of a kind that few, if any, have ever heard of before. At best he is a collector of *loshon hora* (literally, evil talk or gossip), as one of my informants put it. At worst he must be lying, for the question remains: Who could be paying him to collect information on land holdings, economic behavior, kinship relations, sex and mating practices, religion and magic?

The real natives quickly develop their own explanations for the sudden entrance of a stranger into their community life. Mohawk steel workers, for example, thought I was some kind of scholarly tramp looking for a home, since I was constantly sitting

2 Most people in Anamat, Trinidad, called me "Mr. Morris." I interpreted the "Morris" as a sign of friendship, and the "Mr." as indicating some respect for my position of high status in the community. The concept of "high-status friend" (Freilich, 1964) appears to describe well both the position I attained in the community and its functional meaning. Unlike Norman Whitten (p. 349), I made no attempt to influence the natives in their way of addressing me. There is probably no one correct way to deal with this matter.

in "their" bar, without displaying any interest in finding a job. Trinidadian peasants thought I was an income-tax spy, a reasonable deduction, since I set up residence in a government-owned building (a dilapidated former schoolhouse) shortly after the passage of an income-tax bill.

The belief that the anthropologist is some kind of spy—that he is not what he pretends to be and that he is gathering information for some purpose harmful to the community—is quite common. Many Nova Scotian Negroes thought the Whittens were spies; two Samoan women spread rumors of Robert Maxwell's "spying" activities; some of the Toro of Uganda thought that Melvin Perlman was a government tax spy; Mandaya cultivators were concerned that the data Aram Yengoyan was collecting would be used to increase their taxes. Some Oshogbo initially viewed William Schwab as a potential tax collector, or as a harbinger of the white man's imponderable laws; and the Slave and Cree Indians thought that John Honigmann was spying on a U.S. military air base. The anthropologist must counter these and other false beliefs of the natives with information that truthfully describes his work, yet "makes sense" to the highly pragmatic natives. With the help of a few special informants, the marginal native gets to know some of the stories that are being circulated about him and discovers what description of cultural anthropology and of a cultural anthropologist will be convincing to them. Out of this knowledge he is able to construct a "story" that the natives find believable. For example, I described my interest in modern Mohawks as part of a fascination for Iroquois history and for the way of life of the descendants of the great warriors of old. In Trinidad, I defined myself as a student of tropical agriculture and related cultural practices.

An educational role—student, teacher, professor, scholar, writer—is one that an anthropologist frequently finds useful in order to describe himself and his activities. The teacher role was so used by Nancie Gonzáles among the Cakchiquel Indians, by Robert Maxwell among the Samoans, and by Norman Whitten in Nova Scotia. In Tripoli, John Gulick presented himself as a "professor-scholar-writer," a role similar to that used by Melvin Perlman among the Toro. These and other role descriptions that anthropologists use do not immediately convince all the natives that the anthropologist can be trusted with personal information. At times the anthropologist has little control over his role assignment. For example, among the Oshogbo, William Schwab was assigned a quasi-political role, and in Gwelo he could not escape the Africans' image of every white man as an "inimical authority." However, presenting one's self and one's project in ways meaningful and flattering to the people being studied, and in a friendly and humble manner, will generally provide the anthropologist with a number of informants who will be willing to work with him. As Pertti Pelto points out, many of these initial collaborators are, like the anthropologist himself, marginal members of the system being researched.

Despite the many problems of the role of marginal native, this role permits an intensive involvement with community members and maximum opportunities for participant observation. Participant observation is a method to which anthropologists are intellectually and emotionally attached: they believe in its efficacy, they like to use it, and they enjoy discussing it with colleagues and students. Strangely enough, they are often loath to write about it in a personal way. That is, they only rarely publish accounts of their own experiences as participant observers. The method of participant observation is anthropology's special contribution to the study of man. The dearth of published descriptions of field experiences and methods used by anthropologists in various parts of the globe is, therefore, quite an enigma. My interest in this puzzle is not solely a matter of intellectual curiosity. Solving this enigma will, I maintain, produce a deeper understanding of the nature of field work and will thus lead to superior field research.

My explanation for this enigma is complex. It includes several interrelated, casual "variables," referred to respectively as (1) field-work culture, (2) problems of field research, (3) common self-evaluations of anthropological researchers, and (4) unwillingness to present a "true" self to an "unknown" public. Each of these variables will be briefly discussed below.

FIELD-WORK CULTURE

Anthropological field work in its modern form—carried out by a social or cultural anthropologist, who lives with the natives, speaks their language, and, to a certain extent, practices their culture—is a relatively new phenomenon.[3] Its roots, however,

---

[3] British and U.S. anthropologists who study on-going social systems do much the same thing, but use different terminology to describe it. The British say they engage in *social anthropology*, an activity that focuses on the social relations of primitive and complex societies. The Americans think of themselves as students of culture, focusing on the goals, values, beliefs, symbols, and rituals of primitive and complex societies. They thus define

lie deep in history in the first-hand reports of historians, explorers, travelers, fur traders, missionaries, and others whose interests or vocations have led them to reside among peoples with "strange customs." The data provided by these amateur ethnographers are not uniformly valid: some writings are moralistic or fanciful accounts of "life among the savages"; others are factual descriptions of native life. Irrespective of their validity, many of these reports are rambling and poorly organized. The writers, possessing neither specialized theoretical terms nor systematic theory, were guided by popular opinion coupled with personal interest.[4]

The nineteenth-century scholars who were interested in "primitive" societies used these data to develop universalistic generalizations concerning man's history and the nature of primitive culture.[5] The fact that such data were used extensively and often uncritically by scholars is itself a phenomenon that requires much explanation. Suffice it to say that these men were children of the Enlightenment. Behind them stood the remarkable achievements of Kepler (1571–1630), Galileo (1564–1642), and Newton (1642–1727), scholars who formulated principles of great generality and predictive power and freed their intellectual offspring from the dogmas of the Middle Ages. Behind them too stood the British empiricists John Locke (1632–1704), George Berkeley (1685–1753), and David Hartley (1705–1757), the Scottish moral philosophers David Hume (1711–1776), Adam

---

their field as *cultural anthropology*. Since it is impossible to study social relations without studying culture at the same time and vice versa, the distinction between social and cultural anthropology is purely academic. For a different view see E. E. Evans-Pritchard, *Social Anthropology and Other Essays*, New York, Free Press, 1964.

[4] Evans-Pritchard has pointed out that no one sees reality without some kind of "theoretical frame." "The student [of anthropology] makes his observations to answer questions arising out of the generalizations of specialized opinion, and the layman makes his to answer questions arising out of the generalizations of popular opinion. Both have theories, the one systematic and the other popular." (1964:65)

[5] The word *primitive* as used in such contexts as "primitive society," "primitive culture," and "primitive man" is a rather unfortunate term that is now deeply embedded in anthropological terminology. It does not mean inferior, of lower quality, or anything else that suggests a position subordinate to "civilized" or "advanced" society, culture, and man. Nor does the word *primitive* group social systems and individuals into a homogeneous class of phenomena. In its modern usage the term *primitive society* refers to social systems that are generally small in scale (with regard to size of territory inhabited, number of members, and range of social contacts) and lack a written history, a complex technology, and a highly specialized economy. Further, in primitive societies, familial ties and kinship relations are generally the focus of much social action. Anthropologists often place quotation marks around the term to indicate its specialized meaning; they also use as synonyms the terms *tribal, nonliterate*, and *preliterate*, none of which really describe these systems very adequately.

Smith (1723–1790), Thomas Reid (1710–1796), and Dugald Stewart (1753–1828), and, in France, Montesquieu, the Encyclopaedists, the Physiocrats, and Saint-Simon (1760–1825). These philosophers rejected Cartesian notions of innate ideas and focused on sense experience. They believed in the possibility of a science of society (called "sociology" by Saint-Simon's famous disciple, Auguste Comte) and in societies as natural systems with functionally interdependent parts. These systems, they believed, must be studied empirically and inductively. In these men strong beliefs in the "environmental determinism" of social life, in progress and the ultimate perfectability of man, were aligned with a strong interest in formulating general principles about man and society.

The intellectual climate seemed to be right for the creation of a science of man. Unfortunately, most of the nineteenth-century scholars who were interested in such an endeavor set out to create, instead, a history of mankind. Furthermore, perhaps because they were eager to emulate the achievements of the physical scientists, the fathers of anthropology were in a great hurry to generalize. Given the sparsity of data on primitive man, the poor quality of much of these data, the frequent labeling of almost all non-Western cultures as "savage" or "primitive," the generally accepted (although dubious) proposition that living primitives represent prior cultural stages of all mankind, and the scholars' inexperience in handling anthropological data, it is understandable that most anthropological generalizations of the nineteenth century can hardly be described as "science." They are more accurately "creative speculations."[6]

These speculations on the origins and history of man were often presented scientifically. Data were analyzed within a theoretical framework—evolutionary change and progress—and logical reasoning was used to buttress the conclusion reached. Using scientific models, Gustav Klemm (1802–1867), J. J. Bachofen (1815–1887), Lewis Henry Morgan (1818–1881), Theodor Waitz

---

[6] The lack of sophistication in handling ethnographic materials continued in the early twentieth century and is well exemplified in the writings of Edward Westermarck. In R. H. Lowie's words, "The profusion of Westermarck's documents has blinded some critics to his amazingly uncritical use of them. Not only are there inconsistencies . . . but bad, good, and indifferent sources are cited indiscriminately. . . . In short, Westermarck neither appraises his evidence discriminatingly nor becomes absorbed in his cultural phenomena." (1937:98–99) Marvin Harris describes other scholars of this same period in equally unflattering terms. Comparing these men with Franz Boas, he writes, "[T]here was nothing illusory about the shoddy standards of his contemporaries . . . [many of whom] were temperamentally unsuited to scientific discipline. It was an age in which the license to generalize on the basis of fragmentary evidence was claimed by second- and third-rate people." (1968:253–254)

(1821–1864), Adolf Bastian (1826–1905), and John McLennan (1827–1881), among others, fitted the available data into a variety of conjectural histories. Working with great energy, enthusiasm, and imagination, these scholars and some of their contemporaries developed what I have called the "rubber-data" stage of anthropology, a period when the information available was both "stretchable" and "stretched."[7]

To judge the scholars of the rubber-data stage too harshly would be to ignore their important contributions. As they struggled to make sense of the available information on primitive societies, they developed some categories and concepts that are now basic to anthropological thinking. In their arguments concerning the nature of "savage" life and in their passionate defense of a particular scheme of evolution, they gave meaning to barren data. The intellectual excitement they generated captivated many brilliant minds for service in the development of a discipline yet in its infancy. Finally, the scholars of the rubber-data stage created the conditions necessary for the development of a science of man. That is, they brought to the study of primitive societies an interest that underlies all scientific endeavor: *an interest in making generalizations whose claims to "correctness" are linked to empirical data.* Very clearly, these scholars laid the foundations for modern anthropology.

Factors conducive to the development of a more scientific discipline were present even during the rubber-data stage. First, many of the scholars of this period themselves took a critical view of the type of data that was being used for generalizations. As early as 1859 Herbert Spencer delineated the type of data that is necessary in order to understand "how a nation has grown and organized itself."

---

[7] The aptness of this label is attested to by the following statements of Lowie and Evans-Pritchard: "Able travelers mingled fancy with observation, indulged in the superficial psychologizing that duped Klemm and otherwise twisted the facts from initial bias." (Lowie, 1937:70) The missionaries and administrators, although frequently "men of greater culture than the gentlemen of fortune of earlier times" (Evans-Pritchard, 1964:67) were themselves often far from objective in describing primitive society and culture. Their data was therefore also to some extent a "twisting of the facts."

By the time the synthesizers had added their own interpretations and had completed their attempts to fit the data into preconceived theories of evolution and progress, descriptions of primitive society were far removed from the reality being depicted. Thus, Sir John Lubbock, an eminent prehistorian, could conclude from his readings that the Andaman Islanders have no sense of shame and have many habits that resemble "those of the beasts," that the Greenlanders, Iroquois, and Fuegians have no religion, and that almost invariably "savages are cruel." (1872:430–570) And Lowie could write of Morgan's *Ancient Society*, "the total picture of ancient society that resulted was curiously distorted." (1937:57)

. . . an account of its government; with as little as may be of gossip about the men who officered it, and as much as possible about the structure, principles, methods, prejudices, corruptions, etc., which it exhibited. . . . Let us of course also have a parallel description of the ecclesiastic government . . . of the control exercised by class over class, as displayed in social observances—in titles, salutations, and forms of address. Let us know, too, what were all the other customs which regulated the popular life out-of-doors, including those concerning the relations of parents to children . . . [and of the] superstitions . . . the division of labor . . . the connection between employers and employed; what were the agencies for distributing commodities; what were the means of communication; what was the circulating medium. Accompanying all of which should be given an account of the industrial arts technically considered . . . the intellectual condition of the nation . . . the degree of aesthetic culture . . . a sketch of the daily lives of the people—their food, their homes and their amusements. And lastly, to connect the whole, should be exhibited the morals, theoretical and practical, of all classes as indicated in their laws habits, proverbs deeds. (1876: iv–vi)[8]

In line with this, Lewis Morgan and James Frazer tried to obtain superior data by using a "mailed questionnaire" technique: they asked missionaries, traders, and consular agents who were living among primitive peoples to describe the cultural practices of their hosts. In addition Morgan did his own field work for some of his writings, thus exemplifying the potential benefits of this activity for anthropology.

Second, the functional thinking that pervaded evolutionary treatises (Freilich, 1967) set up its own demands for data collection. In the words of E. E. Evans-Pritchard,

But once it was accepted that a custom is more or less meaningless when taken out of its social context it became apparent both that comprehensive and detailed studies of primitive peoples in every aspect of their social life would have to be undertaken, and that they could only be undertaken by professional social anthropologists who were aware of the theoretical problems in the subject, had in mind the kind of information required for the solution of them, and were alone able to put themselves in the position where it could be acquired. (1964:55)

---

[8] With the aid of three assistants, Spencer began a work in 1870 that was to provide summaries of existing knowledge on a great variety of sociocultural systems. Under the title *Descriptive Sociology* the following volumes were published during the period 1873–1934: (I) *English;* (II) *Ancient Mexicans, Central Americans, Chibchans, Ancient Peruvians;* (III) *Types of Lowest Races, Negritto and Malayo-Polynesian Races;* (IV) *African Races;* (V) *Asiatic Races;* (VI) *North and South American Races;* (VII) *Hebrews and Phoenicians;* (VIII) *French;* (IX) *Chinese;* (X) *Hellenic Greeks;* (XI) *Ancient Egyptians;* (XII) *Hellenistic Greeks;* (XIII) *Mesopotamia;* (XIV) *African Races;* and (XV) *Ancient Romans.*

Third, the scholars of the rubber-data stage did not write solely on evolution. Some of their works were very much concerned with specific subareas in sociocultural life, and such writings did much to stimulate future research by anthropologists concerned with collecting specific data. For example, the works of Waitz and others on primitive mentality were later used as a base for systematic research by W. H. R. Rivers among the Torres Straits Islanders, Morgan's writings on kinship developed the field of comparative kinship studies and sent several generations of anthropologists into the field to collect kinship data, and Frazer's notions of primitive magic, science, and religion challenged many anthropologists to do in-depth studies on these and related phenomena.

Fourth, the writings of Charles Darwin (among others) demonstrated the value of careful empirical studies of phenomena in their natural environment. As Darwin's work was followed up by prehistorians whose careful and persistent research uncovered evidence of the Iron, Bronze, and Stone ages, considerable pressure was exerted on anthropologists to make analogous contributions through research with living aborigines. As R. H. Lowie notes (1937:22), "prehistory proved evolution by the rigorous technique of geological stratigraphy at a time when ethnographers were still groping for proper methods of investigating living aborigines. No wonder that ethnographers leaned heavily on the staff of archaeology."

Fifth, the times produced a number of great men, among the most influential of whom was Edward B. Tylor (1832–1917). With a strong sense of probability, Tylor spurned data that many of his contemporaries found acceptable, assembled a vast mass of authentic data, derived concepts therefrom, and defined terms critical to the new discipline: *culture, religion, local exogamy, teknonymy, cross-cousin marriage.* By emphasizing the importance of weighing the evidence, Tylor provided a model for future theorists and thus helped steer anthropology in the direction of science.

It is beyond the scope of this essay to discuss further the many scholars, events, and convergent trends whose work and influence led to the demise of the rubber-data stage of anthropology. Suffice it to say that by the time the nineteenth century had passed so had the rubber-data stage.[9] Twentieth-century an-

---

[9] According to Sol Tax, between 1860 and 1890 cultural anthropology had grown "from nothing to maturity" (1955:466). I would say, rather, that during the period 1860–1900 cultural anthropology grew from "infancy" to "childhood." By 1900 Boas' expeditions to Baffin Island and British Columbia and the British expeditions to Torres Straits had been completed. Such investigations took anthropology out of its "infancy," but hardly represented

thropologists have assumed the duties—with their concomitant pains and pleasures—of collecting ethnographic data and have given more and more thought to the validity of ethnographic descriptions and to the degree of fit between such information and the generalizations and theories that continue to develop.

To guide them in their field work, the anthropological researchers of the early 1900s could refer to various models. There was Morgan's field work among the Iroquois, which led to his book *League of the Ho-de-no-saunee, or Iroquois* (1851), and his expeditions through Kansas and Nebraska, to Hudson's Bay, to the Rocky Mountains, and up the Missouri as part of his study of comparative kinship structures. There were the works of such pioneer ethnographers as Henry Schoolcraft, one of the founders of the American Ethnological Society, W. H. Holmes, Otis T. Mason, Alice Fletcher, and James Mooney. There were the ethnographic descriptions of Henry Callaway, R. H. Codrington, H. A. Junod, B. Spencer, and F. J. Gillen, the work of Franz Boas in Baffin Land (1883–1884) and in British Columbia (started in 1886), and the British expeditions to the Torres Straits regions of the Pacific in 1898 and 1899 by A. C. Haddon, W. H. R. Rivers, and Seligman and associates. Anthropologists who had themselves done field work and who had a university base were able to impart to their students the importance of this activity and some of the basic problems associated with reaching its goals. These teachings fell on receptive ears and, often, on brilliant minds. As students became researchers and teachers and as their students in turn continued to file into the ranks of professional anthropology, a culture of field work slowly developed. Before presenting my description of this culture, let me, at the risk of sounding like a page out of the Old Testament, list some of the people who helped develop this tradition.

A. C. Haddon and W. H. R. Rivers trained A. R. Radcliffe-Brown, whose study *The Andaman Islanders* (1922) represents a landmark in ethnographic achievement. This was the first attempt by a social anthropologist to describe the social life of a primitive society in such a manner as to represent a test of current theory of primitive society. Seligman helped train Bronislaw Malinowski, the first anthropologist to conduct a long and intensive field study through the native language. Malinowski

---

the labors of a mature science. For further discussions on this and related topics, see Sol Tax, "From Lafitau to Radcliffe-Brown: A Short History of the Study of Social Organization," in *Social Anthropology of North American Tribes*, ed. F. Eggan, Chicago, University of Chicago Press, 1955, pp. 445–481, and Marvin Harris, *The Rise of Anthropological Theory*, New York, Crowell, 1968, particularly pp. 142–216.

trained Raymond Firth, Evans-Pritchard, Hortense Powder-maker, Isaac Schapera, and S. F. Nadel, among others, who in turn have trained many well-respected and renowned anthropologists.

Franz Boas, and the anthropologists who studied with him, set the tone for the development of cultural anthropology in America. Included among those who took a degree with Boas at Columbia are A. L. Kroeber, Albert B. Lewis, William Jones, R. H. Lowie, A. A. Goldenweiser, Paul Radin, E. Sapir, F. C. Cole, L. Spier, Ruth Benedict, M. J. Herskovits, Margaret Mead, G. Herzog, Jules Henry, and M. F. Ashley-Montagu. Among others who spent some time studying with Boas or doing research under his guidance were R. B. Dixon, Clark Wissler, J. A. Mason, J. R. Swanton, and Ralph Linton.[10]

The modern masters—Boas, Radcliffe-Brown, Malinowski—taught much that was similar, but they differentially emphasized given aspects of field work. Boas taught that a field study should include a "thoroughgoing description of all cultural data . . . House types, basketry, social structure, beliefs, and tales must all be registered faithfully and with the fullest detail possible." (Lowie, 1937:131) Further, like Malinowski, on the other side of the Atlantic, Boas insisted that a command of the aboriginal language was a requisite for effective data collection.

From Radcliffe-Brown came the emphasis on studying social relations and attempting to show their harmonious equilibrium: their function for the system (i.e., structural-functionalism). From Malinowski came the insistence that intensive involvements with the (real) natives in terms of their culture was a necessity in field work. He stressed that such research would enable the investigator to demonstrate that man (even in "savage" societies) was not a puppet on cultural strings, but a decision-maker who at times opted to go against cultural rules and to accept the sanctions such behavior called forth. He argued that without an intensive involvement with the native it is not possible to understand local meanings, functions, and structures.

Through the sharing of a common publication language—English—and through other communications between the modern masters and their students, a common information pool developed

---

[10] Others include L. E. W. Benedict, T. Waterman, H. K. Haeberlin, M. W. Beckwith, Manuel Gamio, Louis R. Sullivan, G. Reichard, I. G. Carter, Erna Gunther, Erich F. Schmidt, Ruth Bunzel, T. M. Durlach, R. Sawtell, Anita Brenner, H. A. Carey, R. F. Fortune, M. C. Jacobs, Frederica De Laguna, E. Phelps, M. J. Andrade, B. W. Aginsky, E. G. Aginsky, Marcus Goldstein, E. A. Kennard, C. A. Lewis, Ruth Underhill, and William Whitman, III.

for British and American anthropologists concerning the nature and goals of field work. This information pool can be referred to as field-work culture.

Field-work culture—particularly in its early developmental stage—stressed goals rather than the means (methods) of attaining them. The reasons for this are as follows. First, statements concerning what needs to be done logically precede statements describing *how to do it,* but anthropologists had had too few field-work experiences to be able to formulate such a description. Second, the interests of many early anthropological field workers were focused on the collection of cultural data—beliefs, values, rituals—rather than data on social relations—roles, relationships, rights, and duties. Cultural data are of much greater variety than data on social relations, and it was thus assumed that getting such very "different" data from societies around the world required a host of different procedures, methods, and approaches. Not only were cultures considered to be very different from each other, but it was widely believed that, when all the "parts" of a particular culture were "put together," they became a unique system, each system requiring a unique methodological set for obtaining rapport and collecting data. Third, there was no general agreement that anthropology was a science (a few anthropologists still say it is not), and this lack of consensus was not conducive to an emphasis on methods. Men of such widely different backgrounds as Evans-Pritchard and Lowie argued for a "common-sense" approach to field work, an approach that lets the culture under investigation be the guide for both what to study and how to study it (Lowie, 1937; Evans-Pritchard, 1964).

Fourth, there was, particularly in America, the strong influence of Franz Boas, whose disciples had one major goal: to get data. As M. Smith, himself a student of Boas, put it: "Boas' emphasis on systematic fieldwork led to the collection of whatever data became available. . . . [There was here] a fascination in following the details of a subject just for its intrinsic interest." (1959:54) [11] Fifth, in the early years of field work, a curious relationship developed between the anthropologist and the tribes

---

[11] It might be said that Boas' teachings helped cultural anthropology change from a rubber-data stage into a holy-data stage. In the words of Marvin Harris (1968:257), "Unprecedented also was the precise quality of Boas' devotion to the collection of facts. There is a strong puritan element in his outlook. For him, science was very much a sacred enterprise. Those who rushed to conclusions without proper attention to facts were in effect desecrating a temple." This influence of Boas, while undeniable, is still somewhat strange, since in some of his own work he developed problems that were so sharply defined as to allow for solutions through ethnographic research. See Lowie's chapter on Boas in *The History of Ethnological Theory* (1937).

he studied that in some ways is analogous to the relationship between many psychotherapists and their patients. Anthropologists became "possessive" of their tribes, and the "my tribe" or "my people" approach to field work was a strong factor in holding back replications of given field studies. Since no anthropologist was supposed to study someone else's tribe (just as no psychotherapist is supposed to treat another's patient), and since it was believed that each tribe was unique and required unique approaches, what was the point of describing one's methodology and the various environmental facts that in part were responsible for it? Further, what one does with one's tribe (or one's patient) is a personal matter not "decently" discussed at length. A lack of regular discussions of these "private" matters functioned to keep methodology an underdeveloped phenomenon in field work.[12]

Sixth, ethnographies existed that were written by laymen. Since some of these were and still are considered excellent, the professional anthropological field worker could argue, "Why should I worry about methods? I'm already 'ahead' of these laymen of good judgment and keen sensibilities, and unlike them, I know much ethnography and some theory."

Seventh, anthropologists were constantly adding to their field-work goals. Due either to the influences of books and articles or to the direct requests of colleagues, teachers, and high-status friends, anthropologists collected an ever-increasing variety of "data." They looked for and stored local plants, herbs, leaves, and roots; they took head measurements; they recorded dreams; they administered various psychological tests; and they observed and recorded the activities of young children (Powdermaker, 1967, particularly pp. 96–97). In thus carrying out the cross-cultural work of the botanist, physical anthropologist, and psychologist the goals of the field worker ever increased and took much time and energy away from methodological concerns.

Finally, the above factors and their consequences—a lack of emphasis on methodological procedures and a sparsity of guides for field work—forced the anthropologist to resort to his own

---

[12] The public nature of all aspects of a scientific project is considered basic to modern science. It is interesting that as both cultural anthropology and psychotherapy are becoming more scientific, these public "broadcasts" are becoming more common and more complete. In anthropology we now have such writings on field-work experiences as Gerald Berreman's *Behind Many Masks* (1962), Hortense Powdermaker's *Stranger and Friend* (1967), and Bronislaw Malinowski's diary materials (1967). In the literature of psychotherapy it is becoming more common for a therapist to describe precisely what, when, how, and why given techniques are used. Some clinicians even permit others to observe the actual process of therapy, either directly or through tape and/or films. See John G. Watkins, "Psychotherapeutic Methods," in *Handbook of Clinical Psychology*, ed. B. B. Wolman, New York, McGraw-Hill, 1965, pp. 1143–1167.

devices in solving field problems. In a process that is often seen in cultural systems and that helps to explain many cultural complexes, this behavior developed its own rationalizations. That is, *a necessity was transformed into a virtue.* The good professional came to be one who went into a "mysterious" situation (the field), gained rapport through a likeable personality and an imaginative mind, and collected valid data through hard work and creative thinking. The researcher was regarded as a creative problem solver, and the field as a place full of unpredictable situations. The result was that few anthropologists attempted to develop sophisticated field-work procedures, for within this framework such attempts appeared foolish. After all, how can one program the unpredictable?

Field-work culture—a system of implicit and explicit rules for field work—developed over time under the influence of a complex set of factors: the excitement and optimism of the Enlightenment, the work of amateur ethnographers, the creative hypotheses of "rubber-data" professionals, the work of sister-disciplines, the scarcity of professional ethnographers, the presence of a variety of types of great men, and the novel nature of field work itself. These and related variables developed field-work culture into a system that has much in common with other cultural systems. It includes methods for selecting new members and for achieving rank and status. Moral and ethical rules exist and function as both community solidifiers and guides for behavior. Science, magic, art, and economics are all to be found in this cultural system. And, though this characteristic is somewhat underplayed in the current neo-functionalist era of anthropology, field-work culture has as many inconsistencies and incongruities as any other ongoing and viable system. Let me illustrate this with a brief description of two complexes within field-work culture that taken together provide considerable inconsistencies. I will refer to these respectively as the "field-work mystique" and "field work as science."

When anthropologists get together and discuss field work, something happens to the immediate environment. The term *field work* is so packed with meanings, highly prized sentiments, and basic beliefs that its powers to influence anthropologists border on the magical. The term conjures up happy thoughts, pleasant memories, and exciting expectations. That the term should have these powers is not surprising, for it belongs to a category of terms describable as "environmental transformers." Among other environmental transformers are the terms *fête* and *puja.* At the mention of *fête* the faces of Trinidadian Negroes take on an ecstatic glow. *Fêtes* represent the good life, when one is living in a truly meaningful way. In Hindu Indian culture, the term *puja* designates good living. At a *puja,* or family prayer meeting, a man is surrounded by his family as he sits facing the *pundit,* whose prayers will assure the future well being of all who participate.

For the young graduate student preparing for his first field trip, field work represents mystery, opportunity, and excitement. Field work is also a trial through battle in a war for which the novice has little preparation. The student knows that this is a challenge he will have to face, a major *rite de passage* that will provide him with the opportunity to prove his ability, courage, and temperamental suitability for the profession. He knows that, in doing field work and in working with the ethnographic data he will collect, a number of transformations will occur. Basic anthropological concepts—culture, community, family, values— for which he previously demanded unique operational definitions will become "understood." By living in a strange cultural tradition he will somehow learn what culture "really means." By living among strangers whose good will is a requisite for survival, he will somehow learn to achieve enough rapport to collect personal information concerning sex, family, education, economy, polity, and religion. By attempting to change his "raw" field notes into artistic and anthropologically meaningful essays, he will some- how learn to analyze and draw generalizations from ethnographic materials. No specific techniques exist to help the young eth- nographer transform a group of hostile natives into friendly informants; no specific and operationally useful rules exist for obtaining valid data; no program exists for translating raw data into information that is meaningful for anthropological analysis; and no specific techniques exist for drawing predictive general- izations from such information. Much like the *rites de passage* of many primitive societies, success in field work is more a func- tion of personal ability than of previous training in specific tech- niques. Success in field work proclaims manhood and generates a major transformation: a student of culture becomes an anthro- pologist. Along with this new title come the rights of a real marginal native: to have one's "own" tribe and to be considered a specialist of an ethnographic area (i.e., the continent in which the tribe resides). The young anthropologist also becomes the owner of his own data bank, which can be used for teaching and for publications.

The mystique of field work—the magical properties of the term, the mysterious aspects of the work involved, the wonderful transformations that occur through living and working "in the field"—never disappears. Although field work develops more profound and subtle meanings after many field trips, its magic and mystery somehow remain. The field stands forever as a direct challenge to one's ability to be a real marginal native. Time and again I have heard experienced anthropologists—respected for their many successful field trips and publications—speak eagerly of plans for yet another field project. In their eagerness far more was involved than the added prestige they expected through the collection of new data and further publications. They were interested in reaffirming their right to be considered real, working anthropologists. Much like the knights of old who periodically had to legitimatize their status by yet another involvement in mortal combat, the anthropologist must periodically return to the "combat" of field work, so as to demonstrate that he is still an effective professional. The first field trip provides membership in the anthropological fraternity, but those who rest on the laurels of their *rite de passage* research become marginal members of this fellowship. To have status of a full participating member—a first-class anthropologist—one must think constantly of the next field trip, plan for it, and periodically carry out the plans. Field trips subsequent to the initial trip are thus *status-maintenance rites* and, I would claim, purification rites. An individual who decides to become an anthropologist enters into this profession with a variety of conscious and subconscious motives. Those motives that are more idealistic and more noble are reinforced through graduate training, and the anthropologist's personal involvement with them reaches a peak during his first field trip. After a period back in his own comfortable and materialistic world, the anthropologist may forget some of the important goals that drew him into this discipline. A return to the field thus functions as an intellectual, emotional, and spiritual "cleansing."

Each field trip is thus, in part, both a mystical experience and a sacred ritual. Somehow important data are collected, and somehow desirable transformations occur. The techniques for reaching desired goals have been set down by the modern masters (the "High Priests") and their disciples; they are thus susceptible to little critical evaluation. If traditional techniques are followed, the desired goals will be reached. If traditional techniques do not produce success, then it is the person, not the tradition, that is at fault. Success is assured for the ethnographer who is in a state of anthropological "grace"—with sincerity of purpose, emotional maturity, adaptability, sensitivity, friendliness, honesty, and a readiness to sustain much physical and psychological discomfort. Given the very general methodological guidelines that tradition provides we can better appreciate Lowie's ideas of a good ethnographer (1937:6) : "It is when a talent for observation accompanies both protracted residence and contact with professional ethnography that we obtain such superb results as mark the work of Snr. Nimuendaju."

The field-work mystique—field work as a "mystery" to be solved by doggedly following tradition and being of right character and personality—exists alongside a complex based on a very different set of principles. This complex, here designated "field work as science," includes a slowly expanding pool of information that instructs the field worker to do the following: (1) to gain knowledge of the language of "his tribe"; (2) to read up on all available ethnographic accounts of the area in which his research is planned; (3) to use the general methods of observation and participation, special informants, and informal and formal interviews; (4) to collect life histories and genealogies; (5) to check frequently on the reliability of both given bits of information and of information sources; (6) to develop controls for generalizations by designing studies such as "natural experiments" (Freilich, 1963); (7) to develop a host of related techniques for gathering, storing, retrieving, and analyzing data; (8) to develop programs for efficient use of time in the field; (9) to be concerned with reciprocities in field work (i.e., what informants can and do get in return for providing valid data); and (10) to use some of the research designs, techniques, and methods that have been developed by sister sciences such as sociology and psychology.

All anthropologists are commited to *some* aspects of the field-work-as-science complex, and most of them are also strongly attached to the field-work mystique. Somehow, these two somewhat contradictory complexes remain part of the field-work culture.

In summary, in this century field work developed a tradition or culture that guided (and continues to guide) both the training of anthropologists and the activities of field workers. Field-work culture, a system where goals rather than means are emphasized, includes mystical notions and "sacred" beliefs, as well as methodological and theoretical concerns related to "science." The underemphasis on science, the focus on goals, ritualism, and artistry have all functioned jointly to keep discussions on methodology to a minimum.

LIFE IN THE FIELD

Anthropologists have regularly left for field trips with only a scant knowledge of what awaits them and how best to achieve their research goals. Life in the field is rarely free of problems. Many of these problems are novel and difficult to handle, and the anthropologist often solves them in ways that are far from satisfactory. A second explanation for the dearth of published accounts of field experiences is, then, that such works would have to reveal the anthropologist's ineffectiveness or inefficiency in dealing with such problems. This explanation, which is supported by discussions with colleagues, friends, and students, general readings in anthropological literature, and my own field work with Mohawks, Trinidadians, schizophrenics, Hasidim, and rural Missourians, needs considerable explication.[13] Such an explication is attempted in the analysis that follows, which could be labeled the "natural history of a field project."

Traditional anthropological field work includes two distinguishable although overlapping stages. The first stage is primarily an adaptation period when the anthropologist must learn how to survive physically, psychologically, and morally in a strange setting. The second stage consists of the anthropologist's attempts to obtain the data pertinent to his research problem. The adaptation period involves activities that I will call *passive research*, and the second period involves activities that I will call *active research*.

Passive research is difficult for both the experienced researcher and the novice. The anthropologist generally arrives in the field with a broadly defined problem and a limited budget. Traditionally, the "field" is in some far-off place and involves groups about which little is known. When this is the case, the researcher is often wise to allow the field experience itself to guide him in formulating specific research problems. A strategy that is often used is to begin a project with a problem of wide generality. This strategy produces meaningful research problems and provides the anthropologist with a considerable work load. The researcher's limited budget means that he can rarely afford to pay for all the assistance he needs, so he must collect most data by himself. Working long hours, and often seven days a week, he is well aware of the size of his task and the brief time allotted for it, and thus he often begrudges the time he must spend in "passive" research.

The passive-research period is, however, the time when the anthropologist's efforts serve to solve basic field problems. It is

---

[13] The study in Missouri attempted to arrive at what I have called *mental-health culture*. In this study involving thirty-four rural communities, a mixture of anthropological and sociological methods were used. Ministers and medical doctors living in the communities were used as special informants on matters relating to local beliefs, values, and attitudes concerning mental health and mental illness. Similar data were collected in a much more "sociological" manner from representative household heads. For a summary of the initial findings of this research, see *Mental Health Culture in Rural Missouri*, St. Louis, The Social Science Institute, 1967.

during this period that he learns to restructure his views of social and cultural reality. To attain maximum rapport, he learns that he must accept the community's definitions of cultural reality. At the very least, he must learn to act *as if* the community's cultural world is a reasonable alternative to his own. During the passive-research period the anthropologist occupies the status of an insufficiently socialized child: he frequently acts inappropriately by community standards, and he receives negative sanctions for doing so. As he learns more and more about the culture of the community, two different and often incompatible sets of values govern many of his social interactions: those of his own culture—the *culture of orientation*—and those of his community's culture—the *native culture*. As the anthropologist attempts to develop a set of norms that integrates the culture of orientation with the native culture, he discovers that successful field work frequently requires *replacing* old cultural rules rather than integrating them with new ones, and this discovery often results in considerable internal conflicts.

The situation is exacerbated by the fact that the anthropologist is actually dealing with three, rather than two, cultures during this research stage: the culture of orientation, the native culture, and the field-work culture. While the latter should ideally provide many rules for learning the native culture, it actually lays down only a few and very general guides. Further, the difficulty of knowing how, when, and if to follow even these few guides in particular situations increases the problems of passive research. So the field anthropologist discovers rather quickly that he must work out his own research program and develop styles of work suitable both to the native culture and to his own personality. The novice, who is forced to rely heavily on his common sense, finds all too often that what is common sense in his culture of orientation is nonsense in the native culture. The more experienced field worker is in a superior position, for some of his problems are quite similar to those he faced in previous field sites. However, even anthropologists on their third and fourth field trips encounter novel problems requiring creative on-the-spot solutions.

The anthropologist deals with at least four types of problems while doing passive research: (1) physical survival, (2) psychological comfort, (3) everyday pragmatics, and (4) moral dilemmas.[14] The problems of physical survival are considerable in

---

[14] Like many other problems of passive research, these are present during the active-research stage also. However, by that time the anthropologist can deal with them more effectively due to his understanding of native culture.

most field-work situations; they are particularly difficult to handle in primitive societies. Finding a suitable dwelling, a steady and "interesting" supply of food, keeping either warm enough or cool enough for comfort and good health, and protecting oneself and one's possessions are problems not easily solved. Among the Mandaya in the Philippines, Aram Yengoyan was fortunate to have an abandoned dwelling "loaned" to him. His food, however, had to be transported by horseback and human carriers, and catsup became a necessity to mask the other food he had to eat. The problems of physical survival are aggravated when climatic conditions are difficult. John Honigmann, for example, had to allot a considerable portion of his field work time to collect and cut wood and to carefully nurse the stove in his cabin during his research among the Kaska Indians. Low temperatures and nearly constant winds caused the Honigmanns considerable problems in Baffin Island too. And although Professor Honigmann spent much time dressing for the cold, he suffered several mild cases of frostbite during his work with the Frobisher Bay Eskimos. In Ecuador, Norman Whitten developed a series of light fevers and intestinal problems and lost about twenty pounds. In Samoa, Robert Maxwell suffered from infected mosquito bites that left his body flecked with white spots and for two months he had an eye infection that kept his lids swollen and inflamed. Melvin Perlman and his wife contracted malaria while living among the Toro, and William Schwab, while working with the Oshogbo, also became quite ill with malaria.

The problems of physical survival, if unsolved, may lead to death and, if poorly solved, to physical sickness. The problems of psychological comfort, if unsolved, could lead to insanity and, if poorly solved, to periods of deep depression, anxiety, or related psychological states. The kinds of efforts needed to make a good psychological adaptation to field work are suggested in Napoleon Chagnon's description of the scene he encountered upon his arrival among the Yanomamö Indians in Venezuela.

> The excitement of meeting my first Indians was almost unbearable as I duck-waddled through the low passage into the village clearing. I looked up and gasped when I saw a dozen burley, naked, filthy, hideous men staring at us down the shafts of their drawn arrows! Immense wads of green tobacco were stuck between their lower teeth and lips making them look even more hideous, and strands of dark-green slime dripped from their noses. My next discovery was that there were a dozen or so vicious underfed dogs snapping at my legs. . . . Then the stench of decaying vegetation and filth struck me and I almost got sick. I was horrified.

This situation, described in Chagnon's *Yanomamö: The Fierce People* (1968), is an extreme one. The typical situation is much easier on the researcher's psyche, although it presents a considerable number of psychological problems. For example, Honigmann describes his short stay among the Slave and Cree Indians as a "dreadful seven weeks" that included "loneliness occasioned by separation from my family, claustrophobic fear of isolation brought on by the flooded rivers, and . . . interpreter and informant problems." Gulick, too, found the separation from his family a heavy burden, and Yengoyan speaks of the need he had to get away from the field to maintain his sanity. Maxwell speaks of a need to leave his village periodically to communicate with the Samoan élite, a need he could not meet, since, as he puts it, "The élite were so clean cut, and they placed so much stock in appearance that I found it embarrassing to present myself to them." In *Stranger and Friend,* Hortense Powdermaker writes of the times when she was "totally fed up with life and with native life" (1967:100), a psychological state I experienced during my research with Mohawk Indians and Trinidadian peasants.

Problems of "everyday pragmatics" include (1) *how to program one's time in the field:* when to get up, when to eat, when to sleep, when to relax, when to look for informants, when to allow informants to visit, and when to write up field notes; (2) *where to "hang out" during the quiet times of field work:* the docks, men's houses, gambling places, local rum shops, bars, other native spots; (3) *how quickly to accept and reciprocate friendly overtures from natives:* to get intimate quickly with community members who show obvious signs of desiring such a friendship, or to discover first how marginal these would-be friends are and what the other natives think of them; (4) *how to handle local commerce (if such exists):* where to purchase food, liquor, other consumable supplies, and hardware items, how to select a store for shopping, and how to allocate one's purchases among several stores; (5) *what exchange "currency" to use as payment for services rendered:* whether to pay informants, provide them with valued goods (cigarettes, liquor, food), offer them valued services (help in the fields, help with housebuilding, rides, the use of equipment, or use a combination of "payments"; (6) *how to deal with local "con men,"* i.e., people who want to "borrow" money or sell things the anthropologist doesn't need; and (7) *how to handle community schisms.* Almost invariably, the anthropologist will find himself in the midst of some kind of community conflict based on ethnicity, race, caste, or class. What kinds of roles can he play that will both enable him to maintain the respect of the natives and allow him to keep his own self-respect?

The following passage describing my field work in Trinidad highlights some of the problems of "everyday pragmatics":

Shortly after arriving in Anamat, Trinidad, I entered a general store in an area called "The Village." I introduced myself to the proprietor (Bram, an Indian in his fifties), who agreed to cash checks for me (a small one first, followed by larger amounts), to send orders up to my house, and to order special things for me from Port-of-Spain. For several weeks Bram was my sole Anamatian supplier, although I was aware that other stores like his existed in Anamat. I was happy with Bram's services and according to our cook—a daughter of a local peasant farmer, and an extremely bright woman—rightfully so. I was not being overcharged for anything, and I received services not generally afforded Anamatians. I never thought to ask her what in retrospect appears to be a most obvious question: What do the Anamatians think of Bram? Do they like him? Quite accidentally I discovered that I was losing rapport with both Indian and Negro informants because of my business relations with Bram, a man who was disliked by many of the community. My situation with the Indians was aggravated by the fact that another local and general store was owned and run by Maj, a man who belonged to the most prestigious Indian family in Anamat. For a variety of reasons I did not think it wise to immediately change my buying habits in a drastic fashion. Instead I slowly began to divide my purchases between the stores of Bram and Maj.

I had developed the habit of "hanging around" the post office when I had nothing else to do. Mr. Rapas, an Indian who had been introduced to me by the school teacher, was often to be found there. Rapas and I soon became quite friendly. We bought each other cold drinks while waiting for the postmaster to sort out the mail (the post office doubled as a "parlor," a general store, and a rum shop), and we exchanged house visits. I was later to discover that many of my initial problems with some members of the community stemmed from my habit of loafing at the post office (considered a lower-class hang out), and from my friendship with Rapas. Because of his constant fights with his brothers and his mother, Rapas was generally avoided by the prestigious Indians of Anamat. He was also disliked by most of the Negro peasants.

The moral dilemmas of field work arise when the anthropologist must decide whether to continue acting in the role of anthropologist—marginal native—or whether to temporarily assume the role of "real native"—an individual who can behave in ways he thinks "right," "just," and "human." The marginal native observes, listens, copies behavioral modes, feels, thinks, and records. The real native is often in a situation where his moral training or personal feelings incline him toward *active intervention*. Irrespective of the influences that lead the anthropologist to play the role of "real" native and irrespective of the effects on field work of playing this role, the practice raises several moral questions: Does the anthropologist have the right to interfere with the way of life of a community? Does his "contract" with the natives—in which he is alowed to live and work in the community in return for documenting their way of life, aiding in world peace, and so forth—allow or prohibit periodic attempts to intervene in the community life of the real natives? These are questions that plague both the novice and the experienced researcher. My own handling of one situation may throw additional light on the dimensions of this dilemma.

A Negro friend—who was also a good informant—came to my house one day, specifically to invite me to attend a "curing" session for his brother. The event was scheduled to begin around midnight, and was expected to continue until the early hours of the following morning. My friend's brother was described as a "wild man" who was always insulting people, who was not willing to work, and who repeatedly ran off into the woods and disappeared for days. My informant had been saving his money for nearly two years to pay for the services of an Obeah man (the charge was $300!). Through contacts (which he declined to discuss) he had found a "bush doctor, a great Obeah man," in Port-of-Spain, who had a fine reputation for treating people like his brother. The treatment, I was told, would include tying the patient to a tree, drenching him alternately with cold and hot water, beating him, and chanting secret "prayers." My dilemma—to stick to the role of anthropologist, show up with a camera and notebook and get a complete record of an interesting event, or to be a humanist, and try to save my friend from wasting his hard-earned savings and his brother from useless suffering—was "solved" by giving myself a short vacation. I invited my friend to have lunch with me and made my pitch. I argued eloquently against the value of using "doctors" who did not really understand what was actually mental illness and not a spell cast by another Obeah man. I offered to help him get psychiatric help for his brother in Port-of-Spain. As I kept talking and replenishing his glass with rum, his resistance to my arguments slowly faded. Finally, my friend was convinced. He promised to call the whole thing off. Satiated with food and somewhat high, he left to get a message off to the "doctor" about his change of plans. I sat a while gloating over the success of my strategy: alcohol mixed with reason.

The next day another informant told me of an interesting event that had taken place during the night. He was surprised that I had not been there so that I could learn "the way we do things for people who are crazy in the head." As the informant walked off I began to brood on the wisdom of "attacking" a curing-complex that in its own way (as a form of shock therapy) might be just as effective (or just as ineffective) as the psychiatric treatment I believed in. I remained in a depressed state for the rest of the day, alternatively worried about my interference, and upset by its failure.

Theoretically, optimal solutions exist for all passive-research problems, but the anthropologist is rarely lucky enough to hit on them. His major fear is that a particular solution will hinder his field work, will hurt his public image in the community, will force him to lose rapport with his informants, and will cut him off from given types of data. Such a fear is quite realistic.

As problems follow each other in rapid succession, and as some attempted solutions fail, the anthropologist develops strong doubts about his ability to conclude the project successfully. He is concerned about the passage of time and dissatisfied with his image in the community and with his relations with the real natives. The passive-research stage thus tends to be an emotionally painful time, marked with periods of anxiety and depression. Feelings experienced during psychotherapy are not significantly different from those the researcher develops while adapting to a native culture. Both the patient and the anthropologist have strong feelings of personal inadequacy, and both must look deeply into themselves and learn to change well-integrated behavior patterns, beliefs, values, and emotions. These highly personal experiences are not easily revealed to an impersonal public in cold print. If they are communicated at all, it is to long-time associates and friends "who understand." Even then, alcohol is often required to loosen the anthropologist's tongue on these sensitive topics.

It is important to emphasize that during the passive-research stage some information is gained relative to the project's end. As the anthropologist solves his adaptive problems—finding a site for his tent or finding a hut or house in which to live, stocking his new home with utensils, arranging for a regular food supply, acquiring efficiency in a "strange" language, hiring help, learning how to get around with ease (how to paddle a canoe, ski, handle a machete, or drive on the "wrong" side of the road), learning the route to central meeting places, and developing rapport—he is gathering much information about the native culture. However, at this stage, the information is often too novel and traveling toward him at too fast a rate and in too great a volume to be adequately decoded. Some of this information is received on a cerebral level, some gets picked up on a subconscious level, and some is completely missed. Thus, although the researcher has some general knowledge of the native culture at the conclusion of his passive research, he has little data of whose validity he is certain.

Once he has obtained shelter, developed a system for feeding himself, gained some rapport, learned to communicate, and learned the rituals for different types of encounters, the anthropologist systematically begins to collect the data for his research problem: he embarks on *active research*. The good personal feelings that were anticipated when passive research terminated actually occur, but only for short and infrequent periods. Active research rarely follows the ideal patterns described in textbooks on scientific method. The information the anthropologist obtained while doing passive research often indicates that some of his previously made plans either cannot be used or will not work. For example, a strict sampling may not be possible if local customs prohibit him from interviewing particular people or groups; if the subject matter central to the project's goals is too sensitive to be researched, due to the internal problems of the system being studied; or if important informants do not cooperate with the researcher because of his nationality, race, sex, or religious affiliation. If these or other obstacles arise, the anthropologist often has to give up an artistic and scientifically sound research design—one in which much hard work has been invested—for a less sophisticated but more practical project. Such changes are rarely made easily or without considerable pain.

Often, part of the suffering that occurs at these times is due to the anthropologist's unawareness that his colleagues are facing the same kinds of problems. This ignorance leads him to believe that his difficulties are due to his personal inadequacies. Isolated from the physical and psychological benefits of his culture of orientation, and away from family, friends, and colleagues, he has frequently lacked the comforting knowledge that, in field work, we are all "in the same boat."

Traditional anthropological research had as its goal the complete description of a way of life. Unfortunately, little consensus exists among professional anthropologists as to what a "complete" description of a culture is. To operationalize the term adequately one needs a theory of culture presented in language that is meaningful to the field anthropologist, but such a theory of culture currently does not exist. Working without one, the field worker who is engaged in a traditional study has few guides for deciding what data are relevant, marginal, or irrelevant for a given subject. Without a formal model, which would set the boundaries for data collection, the typical field study has no logical end.[15] A common cry of the anthropological field worker is:

---

[15] Margaret Mead has described this situation as follows: "The anthropological approach is to go into primitive societies without any too specific theories and ask instead open-ended exploratory questions. How do male

"I could have gone on and on, there was so much to be done." The logical question, but one rarely asked, is: "If I had as much time as I desired, how would I know when the study was completed?" Hence, when the time comes for the anthropologist to leave the field, he has a strong sense of "unfinished business."

In sum, the many problems faced in the field, the poor solutions used to solve some of them, the dissatisfactions with an uncompleted task, and a lack of knowledge of the similar plight of other field workers often lead the anthropologist to leave the field with an unduly harsh evaluation of his own performance. He blames himself for the generality of his research problem—forgetting the sparse data he had with which to develop a more complex design. He is upset by the length of time it took to achieve enough rapport to begin active research—forgetting the many novel rapport problems he had to face. He chastises himself for having spent some time away from his field site—forgetting the physical and emotional states that prompted his flight, and the recuperative value of such holidays. Often reasoning in terms of Protestant-ethic values, he wrongly believes that with harder work and less time "wasted" for "fun," he could have accomplished a much more successful project.[16]

Upon his return from the field, the anthropologist busies himself analyzing and writing up his field notes. When he is finally ready to publish his work, he generally presents the central focus of the study as a thesis, a monograph, or a book, and writes up the other data for scholarly journals. At this time one might assume that his data on field experiences and methods would be brought together and handled in a manner analogous to other data collected during field work, but generally this does *not* occur. Although field-work culture stresses the importance of sharing ethnographic data with the anthropological community as soon as it can be analyzed and written up, it has traditionally provided only minimal encouragement to publish on

---

babies and female babies learn their social roles in different societies? What types of behavior have some societies classified as male, what as female? What behaviors have they failed to treat as sex-typed? How like have some societies felt males and females to be—and how unlike? . . . how different peoples expect infants to behave, how they use the difference in sex to define difference in role, and how they succeed in evoking the expected responses." *Male and Female: A Study of the Sexes in a Changing World,* New York, William Morrow, 1949 Ch. 2.

[16] This point is well illustrated by Malinowski's diary materials. For example, Malinowski was upset that he did not work hard enough, and that women excited him: "I turn in too late, I get up at irregular hours. Too little time is devoted to observation, contact with the natives, too much to barren collecting of information. I rest too frequently. . . . I must never let myself become aware of the fact that other women have bodies, that they copulate." (1947:247–249)

methods and field experiences. Lacking such encouragement and often unaware that the "goofs" of other anthropologists are as many and as serious as his own, the researcher delays writing up these painful experiences. These delays are often life-long and most understandable.[17] One resists publishing material that appears to document one's inadequacies in the field, particularly since competence in field work is considered the mark of a real professional.

An institution that probably contributes to the lengthening of these delays is the "bull session" on field work that often takes place at anthropological conferences. After a day of listening to and presenting scholarly papers, anthropologists generally get together at little parties where the talk frequently turns to field work. In an atmosphere made cheerful by alcohol, and often in the presence of envious graduate students yet without field experiences, these discussions of life in the field almost invariably omit certain kinds of information. Much time is spent presenting bits of data that throw new light on a given theoretical problem or that make a traditionally accepted ethnographic description either doubtful or in need of some revision, and considerable time is spent recalling the "joys" of field work. Happy solutions to field-work problems, prestigious meetings with high-status officials—chiefs, tribal leaders, and the government élite—and wonderful parties with exotic food and entertainment are discussed at length, but it is rare indeed to hear a speaker describe the emotional pains of field work, especially those of the early "culture shock" period. Rarely mentioned are anthropologist's anxious attempts to act appropriately when he knew little of the native culture, the emotional pressures to act in terms of the culture of orientation, when reason and training dictated that he act in terms of the native culture, the depressing times when the project seemed destined to fail, the loneliness when communication with the natives was at a low point, and the craving for familiar sights, sounds, and faces.

What happens to these memories of pain, anxiety, and sorrow? Anthropologists, either consciously or unconsciously, attempt to forget the more stressful and unhappy times of field work. Such attempts are facilitated by and indeed casually related to a number of phenomena. First, anthropologists are dedi-

---

[17] Professor Powdermaker writes that when many of her contemporaries heard about her book *Stranger and Friend* they claimed that they too had often thought of doing such work (i.e., one describing in an intimate fashion the experiences of field work). Since Professor Powdermaker's contemporaries began their research careers in the exciting days when the masters were teaching anthropology, these scholars have already delayed quite a while.

cated to field work; they consider it both a mission and a privileged duty. It is understandable, therefore, that the memories that surround field work should be selectively weighted toward the pleasant. Second, the meaning, sentiments, and feelings conjured up by the term *field work* are such that unpleasantness is not easily linked to it. As highly selective recollections are shared with colleagues, friends, and students, positive and pleasant meanings are reinforced, and the magical qualities of the term are strengthened. Third, by maintaining and developing the fiction of the pure joys of field work, the anthropologist can conveniently repress some of the misinterpretations he has made of his own field-work performances. That is, since he often believes that many of his field problems are signs of personal incompetence, since he has much other evidence of his competence as a field worker, and since he would rather believe the positive "data," a useful bit of self-deception is to forget the bad times. By such mental manipulation a number of elements of field-work culture can remain in equilibrium: (1) in the field the anthropologist can continue to attribute many of his problems and errors to personal inadequacies; (2) after leaving the field he can continue to forget field problems, aided both by the tradition of not writing up field experiences and by discussions centering on the "joys" of field work; and (3) by maintaining an image of himself as a good field worker and of the field as an exciting and pleasant place, he can continue to plan future field trips with self-confidence and happy anticipations.

The forgetting process is probably far more complex than this, and it probably is closely related to the personality of the anthropologist and the degree to which he is able to practice self-deception. However, I submit that such forgetting occurs with considerable regularity and contributes greatly to the dearth of writings on field experiences. To summarize, the following "variables" jointly function to inhibit the writing up of field experiences and methods: field-work culture, problems encountered in the field, the habit of defining many field problems as a function of personal inadequacies, and the repressing of painful times and events in the field.

But why, you may ask, is there also a shortage of published accounts describing the happy events of field work? Why are descriptions of the latter by and large limited to bull-session discussions? Precisely what do anthropologists find enjoyable about field work, and why are these pleasures rarely shared with the scientific community?

It is difficult to present a list of experiences related to field work that *all* anthropologists will describe as joyful and pleasant. Obviously, many such phenomena are matters of personal taste and are related to the different personalities and backgrounds of field workers. However, some phenomena exist that most anthropologists would probably describe as pleasurable and personally rewarding. Among these I would isolate (1) the professional and personal "stock taking" that accompanies the planning stage of a new project; (2) the excitement of field preparations and early field-work experiences; (3) the intellectual challenge of field work; and (4) the opportunity it offers to escape from normal routines, i.e., to change one's life-style.

Life in the field shows strong discontinuities with life in one's culture of orientation. New field projects thus become "time markers" in the life of the anthropologist: they close one period and herald the start of another, and they present the anthropologist with an opportunity to review his basic ideas, beliefs, values, and goals, a mental exercise that is personally very satisfying. This review is also useful for field work, for it helps the anthropologist to develop a project that *really* interests him by incorporating theories and methods that he has come to believe in. Further, it brings to a more conscious level the self-doubts and fears that accompany new challenges, allowing them to be handled more rationally and thus more effectively.

Preparations for field work invariably generate considerable excitement. A combination of real and unreal anticipations, hurried attempts to complete travel arrangements, "goodbye" parties, and attempts to contact scholars familiar with the culture to which one is bound all put the researcher into a state of euphoria.

The intellectual challenge of cross-cultural research is also a source of considerable personal and professional satisfaction. In finding solutions to the many problems that field work provides, the anthropologist's analytical and creative powers are often taxed. The joys experienced in solving vexing field problems are later relived when the data are being analyzed. The data analysis and synthesis necessitate a rethinking of current anthropological theory. Often this leads one to develop new categories and theoretical modifications that better explain the findings of the study. In brief, the challenges found at every stage of a field project, and the solutions developed around them, provide the anthropologist with considerable satisfactions. The latter increase as the researcher publishes and otherwise communicates his findings and as he receives valuable feedback from his peers and students.

Finally, field work provides a kind of "escape" from normal routines. In attempting to carve out some kind of consistent set of behavior linking together the culture of orientation, the field-work culture, and the native culture, the anthropologist develops new roles and new routines that provide him with an opportunity to be himself or, better, his selves. A discussion of the pleasures of field work of necessity becomes a discussion of the type of person who seeks and enjoys such pleasures. The anthropologist is often a person with idealistic beliefs about man's ability to improve his way of life, with romantic notions concerning the good human relations and noble goals of primitive societies, and with strong humanistic feelings for people of all races and cultures. He also has a strong belief in the mission of anthropology: to collect data from fast-disappearing primitive societies, to get laymen to understand the relativity of culture, so that prejudice is given no basis in fact, and to communicate ideas about the basic dignity of man.

Many anthropologists traditionally have shown a disdain for the comforts of modern Western societies and a disregard for the findings of modern medical research, at least as they apply to many health problems in the field, yet these same anthropologists are deeply interested in the problems of the modern world. Convinced that cultural anthropology has much to offer in easing race relations, ethnic conflicts, and world tensions, some anthropologists have recently attempted to maximize their contributions by following ever more strictly the dictates of the scientific method.

This portrait of the anthropologist as an idealist, romantic, humanist, scientist, adventurer, and man with a mission is not easily presented to an impersonal public. Indeed, it is not easily acceptable to the anthropologist himself! These various traits rarely "sit well" in one body. If he thinks of himself primarily as a scientist, the anthropologist may well be unhappy with the "impurity" of his motives for doing anthropology. That is, he may not realize that an individual must have a rather complex set of motives to leave the comforts of understood environments for the world of native cultures. The more he thinks about the experiences of field work—both the pleasant and the painful ones—the more he is forced to look into himself in order to understand his reactions to the various field situations he encounters. This kind of self-analysis is not easy, and if accomplished, the findings are not easily communicated via the cold and impersonal media of the printed page. The anthropologist who plays "center stage" in a "strange" society for a year or more is reluctant to present his real self (or selves) to members of his culture of orientation.[18]

---

[18] It is interesting to compare my portrait of a typical field worker with Evans-Pritchard's description of the qualities that make for a perfect field worker (1964:82): "To succeed [in field work] a man must be able

WHITHER FIELD-WORK CULTURE?

The consequences of anthropologists' reluctance to publish their field experiences and their widespread disinterest in developing a systematic methodology for field work are quite serious for a discipline generally classified as a science. It has meant that for many anthropologists, and for most anthropological graduate students, field work is still a venture into a mysterious world: rules for survival, for work, and for play are both sparse and very general.[19] If field experiences were shared, many common errors could be avoided, and many successful strategies, methods, and ways of coping emulated.

The anthropologist experienced in field work has much valuable information to share. With every field trip he learns to work more effectively and more efficiently. He learns how to obtain rapport faster, how to avoid with less embarrassment and difficulty excessive involvement with marginal members of the community, how to better utilize his personality for the project's ends, how to better understand his own particular tendencies to misinterpret some kinds of phenomena, and, by paying more careful and studied attention at these times, how to achieve greater objectivity in his research. He learns to develop more and better field tests to validate given conclusions, and to discover quicker ways of finding situations where data flow freely and better means of avoiding situations that produce little information relative to the time and energy invested. His reactions to an informant's communication signals and symbols are more often correct. He is better able to decode signs of boredom, fatigue, resistance, hostility, and cooperation. He learns to avoid

---

to abandon himself without reserve, and he must also have intuitive powers . . . ability, special training, and love of a careful scholarship . . . the imaginative insight of the artist which is required in interpretation of what is observed, and the literary skill necessary to translate a foreign culture into the language of one's own. . . . he must have in addition to a wide knowledge of anthropology, a feeling for form and pattern, and a touch of genius."

19 Learning a native culture is still, for many anthropologists, a procedure not unlike seducing a woman. Success is made more probable if one knows the language, if he is passionately attached to his goal, if he has the charm and style to gain good rapport, if effective use is made of special informants, and if the project is vigorously pursued with a high investment of time and energy. Questions concerning very specific techniques, operationally described, are rather indecent.

hasty interpretations. He learns how to broadcast his project in ways that the natives find more understandable and acceptable. He learns to estimate more accurately when to arrive at functions and when to leave, when he is being used as the group's goat, and when his work is being taken seriously. He is able to predict with greater accuracy how he is likely to react to given field situations: what kinds of field experiences he will find enjoyable and what kinds of situations will make him anxious or depressed. These kinds of understandings are vital for effective field work; put to use regularly they also make for more efficient field work.

The average graduate student leaving on his first field assignment knows little about these matters. The prospect of the mysterious "field" makes him quite apprehensive, and he is anxious to pick up any bit of information he can get to make his assignment more predictable. Gerald Berreman makes this point very clearly (1962:3) :

> Not so many years ago, when a group of us were preparing to leave the relative security of the teaching assistant's room for the entirely mysterious world of the "field," we went to one of our teachers and asked him to tell us what it was like. We also expressed some doubts about our capacity to carry on "field work" in spite of the steady diet of ethnographies which for months had been ours. . . . the council fell rather short of our expectations, not because we had wanted solemn warnings about unlikely diseases or sanitation problems, but because we had wanted to know "what it is like" rather than "how to do it."

In anthropological field work a close relation exists between the questions "what is it like?" and "how do you do it?" What it is like includes feelings of frustration, fears, hopes, isolation, exciting "on-stage" performances, euphoric heights, and deep depressions, and these feelings must be understood both for the anthropologist's psychological comfort and for effective research. Learning to understand them is a basic part of "how to do it," for in anthropological research the field worker is not just a dogged follower of an artistic research design; he is not a puppet programmed to follow automatically a plan of research operations; he is not just the bearer of research tools; he is not just a "reader" of questions found on questionnaires; and he is not just a dispenser of printed schedules. He is the *project:* his actions will make the field trip either a success or a failure. What he does in the field will tend either to attract or to repel information. He is the information absorber, the information analyzer, the information synthesizer, and the information interpreter.

The flow of information toward the field worker—its frequency, amount, and validity—depends to a large extent on his image in the community. Are his "on-stage" performances consistent? Are they honest? Are his beliefs in racial and cultural democracy sincere? Is private information safe with him? Is it rewarding to treat him as a friend? These and similar questions are silently, but regularly, put to the anthropologist by his informants. The answers informants receive come in large part from the anthropologist's actions while in the community. His public image becomes either that of an individual who should be avoided, one with whom only brief discussions are wise, or one with whom it is rewarding to converse at great length. The information the anthropologist receives can be totally false, slightly misrepresented, the very bare facts, or facts and interpretations presented as completely and as honestly as possible. The nature of the information he receives depends largely on his public image. A favorable public image requires some "impression management"—a process much facilitated if the anthropologist is emotionally calm and if he has an understanding of his mental states. Such self-knowledge also helps to develop the kind of rapport necessary for receiving complete and honest data. As information of various kinds flows toward the anthropologist, it is his internal states that by and large determine how it is received. That is, such data are caught, fumbled, dropped, or completely missed, largely depending on the state of the marginal native's psyche. If the anthropologist is constantly plagued by fears, anxieties, and desires to please everyone at all times, much information will either pass him by or will be completely misunderstood.

As the raw data are analyzed, synthesized, and interpreted, errors made during data collection can be highly magnified, partly because anthropology currently lacks well-developed, formalized methods for decoding field-work information. The analysis and synthesis of the data are very much at the mercy of the individual researcher, and the anthropologist with psychological problems and little insight concerning them produces analyses that are quite suspect. His final presentation of findings merits investigation: Were the natives really that paranoid? Or is the paranoia more in the researcher than in the cultural world he is depicting? Were the natives really that angry, anxious, hostile, and megalomanic? Or were these traits more a part of the basic personality of the researcher than of the culture he studied?

The point is, the critical tool in anthropological research is the researcher himself. This is why it is so important that he be ready to meet the many challenges of his work. To prepare well-fashioned field workers a pool of information and training programs are needed that will permit the following kinds of questions to be answered: (1) What is it like in the field? (2) How is field work done by experienced anthropologists? (3) How *should* field work be done? (4) How am I, the novice preparing for a first field trip, likely to perform in the field?

A discussion of how field work should be done and how to gather the kind of information that will permit a novice to make good predictions about his future performances in the field is delayed for the final chapter of this book. Here I am concerned with how to make field work a more public experience. It seems clear that field work will become more public only if individual anthropologists are ready to make it so. The gaining of much more data on *what it's like* and *how it's done* requires answers to a very basic question: Why should the field worker present his real selves—his problems, mistakes, and satisfactions—to an impersonal public? My answer is, because he will find it "pays" to do so. I believe it is demonstrable that the net benefits from such writings (the positive feedback *minus* any negative sanctions) are greater than the net benefits from following present field-work culture.

What predictable reciprocities are there to tempt a field worker to relive his field experiences for thousands of readers? What kind of "compensations" can marginal natives hope to receive for the time-consuming and difficult introspective work necessary to transform field notes on methods and experiences into meaningful essays on life in the field? Two kinds of "payments" will be forthcoming from such efforts. First, writings that demand deep introspective thought will help the anthropologist to achieve a superior knowledge of himself, a deeper and more objective self-awareness. As he relives fearful, stressful, and tension-creating field experiences, he will get deeper insights into his fears and anxieties. Second, not only will this superior understanding of himself better enable him to handle similar field situations in the future, but verbalizing painful times of the past actually reduces the fears that may have generated them in the first place.[20] Writing on field experiences thus represents a kind of self-analysis: an analysis of internal mental states focused around experiences in the field. By getting to understand his field-work fears and anxieties, the anthropologist may be able to handle situations previously considered difficult. In brief, at the very least, such writings will permit the researcher to relive fearful times "on paper" and make his future

---

[20] Systematic desensitization as a therapeutic method is well described by Joseph Wolpe in his paper "The Experimental Foundations of Some New Psychotherapeutic Methods," in *Experimental Foundations of Clinical Psychology*, ed. Arthur J. Bachrach, New York, Basic Books, 1962, especially pp. 564–566.

adaptations to analogous situations more effective. At best, such situations will no longer be conceived as fearful. In either case superior field adaptations will result.[21]

The benefits of this focused self-analysis are far greater than merely reducing the problems in the field. As previously indicated, the internal mental state of the anthropologist is a prime determinant of his presentation-of-self in his research community. His presentation-of-self leads to a public image that attracts or repels valid data. Indirectly, therefore, the anthropologist's internal mental state greatly affects the nature of the messages that are "sent" to him. Further, his internal mental state is an important determinant of what happens to the data that are sent: how much of it he "receives," what meanings he gives to it, and the closeness of fit between the "meanings" informants intend and the "meanings" the anthropologist decodes. In short, other things being equal, the greater the reality-orientation of the anthropologist, the more likely that his raw data and his interpretations are valid. Hence, anything that tends to increase the field worker's reality-orientation makes him a superior field worker.[22] Once field workers realize that writing about their life and work in the field increases their reality-orientation, they will write more on these phenomena.

The long-term benefit of such writings is the development of an ever-widening pool of information on field experiences and practices. This matter has already been discussed and needs but a brief review. Personal field-work errors will become under-

---

[21] Often a researcher with some insight can reinterpret a troublesome situation to his advantage. For example, after several very difficult weeks at the beginning of one of my field trips, I fell into a state of deep depression. A psychotherapist, after a few sessions, pinpointed my anxieties by asking me the following question: "Do you want to do a good project, or do you want all your informants to like and admire you?" It soon became clear that I wanted both "instant" popularity with the natives and the satisfaction of doing a good project. I somehow learned to accept my position in the community as that of a marginal native who in time could develop enough rapport with the real natives to complete the project successfully. I was helped to reinterpret a situation—the passive-research period—that I had successfully adapted to in several previous projects. I might well have been spared this depressing period had I previously written up my field experiences.

[22] This argument provides support for the belief held by many social scientists that some kind of psychotherapy is a valuable adjunct to other forms of field-work training. Margaret Mead has for a long time been a vigorous proponent of this position. It has also received published support by Hortense Powdermaker, Herbert Gans, and Morris and Charlotte Schwartz. The Schwartzes discuss the possible harmful influences of one's feelings toward the informants and their culture and conclude, "Only by increasing awareness of his own feelings and their effects will the researcher be able to counteract their destroying influence." See "Problems in Participant Observation," *American Journal of Sociology*, LX:4:343–353.

stood for what they usually are—the common experiences of researchers working in strange and minimally understood environments. Self-castigations for poor decision-making in the field and the concomitant effects of such self-blame—a lowering of self-confidence and the development of a cycle in which foolish mistakes keep increasing due to increasing concerns with one's performances—will by and large disappear. The mistakes will also decrease because the researcher will be constantly learning from the field experiences of others. The constantly increasing pool of information on field experiences and methods will enable anthropologists to develop a sophisticated set of methods, strategies, and theories for use in field research. Field work culture can, in this manner, evolve from a system that includes magic and mysticism to one firmly rooted in science and its methodology.

In summary, the sparsity of writings on anthropological field methods and field experiences is explained by, first, a field-work culture that underemphasizes methodology and supports private rather than public communications of field experiences, and, second, the "rewards" field workers receive for keeping their errors and their personalities hidden and for maintaining a romantic attachment to the field-work mystique. It is suggested that anthropologists will receive valuable personal and professional rewards by writing on their field-work methods and experiences. I would add that irrespective of the benefits that individual anthropologists will get from such writing, they have a duty to their discipline to make field experiences public information, for it is only through a regular sharing of field methods and experience that anthropology can develop a truly scientific methodology. As Joseph McGrath reminds us (1964:534):

> Differences in research methodology *do* make a difference in the yield of research . . . . When we choose one methodology over others . . . , we are thereby affecting the kinds and amount of information which we can obtain from results of that study . . . . It follows that we should choose the methodology that we will use in a given case on the basis of the kinds of information we are seeking (i.e., the nature of the problem we are studying), and we should choose so as to maximize the amount of information which we will gain about that problem . . . . When we choose our methodology for reasons of personal preference, familiarity, or operational expediency, we are changing the nature of the problem about which we will gain information, as well as altering the amount of information which we can gain from our study.

Differences in research methodology do make a difference in the research yield. To take a hard line, the meaning of data is intrinsically connected to the manner in which they are collected. It is clearly of critical importance that anthropologists state fully, frankly, and unapologetically what they do, and when, how, and why they do it. The gains from such expositions will be high: the data from anthropological research will be more understandable, the methods available for anthropological research will be better and more widely understood, and individual anthropologists will more objectively do their work, due to a superior reality-orientation. Taken together, this will mean that anthropological field work will be able to evolve from an art only slightly touched by science into a science that permits its practitioners ample opportunities for artistic expression.

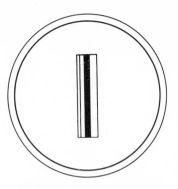

FIELD WORK IN TWO NORTHERN CANADIAN COMMUNITIES

John J. Honigmann

In this chapter I shall describe how ethnographic knowledge is
acquired in the field. Using two cases from my own experience,
my study of the Kaska Indians of British Columbia in 1944 and
1945 (here regarded as a single field trip), and my study in 1963
of the Eskimo in Frobisher Bay, Baffin Island, I shall examine
some of the conditions that affect the field worker in his search
for knowledge. The study of the Kaska was one of my earliest
experiences in ethnography; the study of the Frobisher Bay
Eskimo is my most recent and my major field work.[1]

---

[1] For published information on Kaska Indians and the region they inhabit
see J. Honigmann, 1943–1944, 1946, 1947a, 1947b, 1949, 1954, 1966b, and
J. Honigmann and I. Honigmann, 1944, 1947. Frobisher work has been
written up in J. Honigmann and I. Honigmann, 1965a, 1965b, 1965c, and
1965d. See also J. Honigmann, 1966b.

My sources for what happened among the Kaska Indians roughly a quarter of a century ago consist, in addition to my field notes, of two journals, one from June 16, 1944, the day I arrived in Lower Post, British Columbia, to September 15, 1944, where occurs the terse entry: "Rain. Packing." and one from June 9, 1945, to December 25, 1945. Other sources are a collection of photographs, data pertaining to several major informants, especially notes of incidental encounters and lengthy interviews with them, miscellaneous material such as expense vouchers, and correspondence dating from before entering the field to after leaving. I also drew on my memory and the memory of my wife and fellow anthropologist, Irma Honigmann, who, preoccupied with the care of two small children (a boy and an infant girl), had relatively little time to help me in my research.

In Frobisher Bay I did not keep a journal (except during a two-week camping trip), nor did I write up my field notes as formally as I had in 1944 and 1945, when I recorded my observations on 4″ × 5″ slips of paper and categorized each slip according to the advice in George P. Murdock's manual called *Outline of Cultural Materials*. In 1963 I employed an 8″ × 12″ loose-leaf notebook and reserved certain pages for major topics in which I was interested (change, children, communication, cooperatives, dances, employment, interpersonal relations, law, leadership, marriage, personality, and recreation). I recorded each day's encounters and the information derived from them in informal, journal-like style. In the margins of each page I noted further categories for cross-referencing, categories I then carried over to an index volume. (The system of indexing turned out to be more refined and detailed than I required.) Before writing this chapter I also consulted my large collection of photographs from Baffin Island to refresh my memory, and I again drew on the recollections of Irma Honigmann, who this time was able to play an active part in research. Finally, I consulted correspondence, tabulations, expense vouchers, maps, and other materials dating from the period of field work itself or before, and from the time when we were analyzing data.

PART I: THE KASKA INDIANS

Problem, Theory, and Research Design

Correspondence with the Hudson's Bay Company in Edmonton and northern British Columbia combined with reading completed while I was a member of Cornelius Osgood's seminar at Yale University on northern North America initially familiarized me with the Kaska Indians of British Columbia. As a first-year graduate student, my knowledge of the northern tier of the continent was limited, and until this time I had never contemplated doing field work in the boreal forest. In April, 1943, I asked Professor Osgood to finance ninety days of field research during the coming summer at McDame Creek or Watson Lake, British Columbia, two locations where these very poorly known Indians could still be found. I pointed out that my trips could take advantage of the recently opened Alaska Highway through British Columbia. I proposed to concentrate on Northwest Coast influences in Kaska culture (suggesting the possibility that diffusion had emanated from the Tlingit and Tahltan Indians), while reconstructing the aboriginal culture of one or more Kaska bands and studying the present-day operation of the culture in the light of the historic past. I cited Diamond Jenness's *The Sekani Indians of British Columbia* as a model that I would attempt to emulate. More specifically, I promised to devote attention to several topics that interested me, including aggression and its social control (I was resolutely pacifist during that wartime period), the potlach (provided any traces of it could be uncovered), and the extent of polyandry. I wished also to explore the prospects for obtaining life-history data among the Kaska, an interest doubtlessly reflecting the degree to which I had been impressed by Leo Simmons' recently published *Sun Chief* (the comprehensive life history of a Hopi Indian).

From a fund established by Mr. and Mrs. William A. Castleton, Professor Osgood provided $750 for the trip (I had requested $620), of which I actually spent $680, but in 1943 I never reached the Kaska. When hitchhiking brought me to the vicinity of Fort Nelson, British Columbia, I learned that heavy rain and spring runoff in the Rockies had washed out a part of the new highway. Panicking at the delay that I feared would defeat my summer plans, I promptly crossed the river to the Fort Nelson trading post and began field work with the Slave and Cree Indians who made that their summer home. A dreadful seven weeks followed, marked by loneliness occasioned by separation from my family, claustrophobic fear of isolation brought on by the flooded river, and what I have since learned to be not unusual interpreter and informant problems. The men I sought to work with showed up once or twice and thereafter proved difficult to get hold of. Later I discovered that my stay had been clouded by the Eurocanadian inhabitants' unshakable suspicion that I was an enemy agent primarily interested in spying on the large, new U.S. military air base located across the river. It surprises me to think that I secured enough material by questioning and observation during those seven weeks to be able, the following academic year, to write a monograph about the Fort Nelson Slave (Honigmann, 1946a). The trip also helped forge my omniverous style of data collection, in which I assume nearly everything I observe to be ethnographic grist, likely to be worthy of at least descriptive mention in a monograph and perhaps of even more significant use in making historical or psychological analyses and perceiving configuration emphases in a culture. When in later years I studied cultures considerably more elaborate than a northern trading post, I became somewhat more selective in what I recorded, but I have never wholly abandoned my receptivity to ethnographic stimuli nor ceased to encourage the same trait in graduate students.

In 1944, thanks again to Professor Osgood's interest, I received $950 for nother attempt to study the Kaska. This time I listed among my aims attention to ethos, the character or tone that distinguishes one group from another, a subject on which I planned to write my doctoral dissertation. In 1945, another grant of $1500 (augmented by $111 when I ran short of funds) enabled me to spend six months in northern British Columbia. My intention to study ethos did not materialize in 1944, mainly because I did not know how to analyze that phenomenon from the kind of data I industriously collected. I spent most of my time with English-speaking Indian informants doing what my proposal called "functional reconstruction" (Honigmann, 1954), as opposed to "historical reconstruction," a term that has always, for me, connoted a narrative history rather than a synchronic picture of a bygone way of life.

My serious work on ethos, including an objective method for abstracting it from the contemporary culture, began the following year. As I later pointed out (Honigmann, 1949:18–26), my approach was to begin by observing overt behavior (acts, verbalizations, the manufacture and use of artifacts, and artifacts themselves) that would provide insight into people's underlying motives. When I observed something that I could not explain by an already inferred motive, I expanded either the motive's definition or the stock of motives. I did not coin motives rashly, however, as I assumed that only a small stock of basic or dominant motives would be necessary to account for a culture's ethos. Thus I anticipated the model that Clyde Kluckhohn (1949:208) subsequently sketched in his distinction between peripheral and nuclear areas of personality. My method and theory made me attentive to anything that would yield a picture of the emotional system of the Indians.

In 1944 and 1945, I also collected material on sorcery, because I had read reports of such behavior among the Kaska, inquired about the distribution of the bands, because Osgood had impressed me with his interest in the problem of band distribution, and sought information about vocabulary, a task for which I had little training and less aptitude. Because I believed that my interest in the Indians' psychological system required me to grasp their whole culture whether the behavior or artifacts I observed were immediately emotion-revealing or not, I collected data on everything I observed. The result was that I could and did compile a full-scale ethnography of the living culture. In order to sensitize myself to a large range of observational material in the field, I regularly consulted the early edition of the forementioned *Outline of Cultural Materials*, which Murdock later told me he had never intended as a field guide.

My problem among the Kaska did not specify that I formally sample individuals or bands. In retrospect, I am sure that the Upper Liard River Indians engrossed most of my time and attention, and they are probably disproportionately represented in the data from which I abstracted the Kaska ethos. I did not consider nonresident Tahltan and other non-Kaska visitors to Lower Post, but I did include some individuals who, although not born in Kaska territory, made that country their home.

Passive or Adaptational Research

The environment of the group being researched. Geographical factors influenced my ethnographic work in Lower Post and further up the Liard. The Indians in these areas live cut off from the rest of Canada except for thin lines of communication provided by the Indian agent, traders, missionaries, and schooling for a few young men. Their relative isolation in a northern forest setting, marked by an extremely low population (less than one person per square mile), helped the Kaska to maintain those traits that flaunted the wider society's values and gave the community its disintegrative character. Leighton (1959:319) cites a "weak and fragmented network of communication" as indicative of social disintegration. I believe I follow his reasoning when I point out that geographic marginality reduces the possibility of shared sentiments and blocks sympathetic identification with groups lying beyond the isolated community's frontiers (Wilson and Wilson, 1945:26–27).

Field work involved more than data collection, for I had to provide for my family's and my own essential needs and auxiliary comforts in the field. If my work was to be effective, my family and I had to adapt our living to the character of the geographical setting, both in summer and winter. I have never found insects to be as difficult a side of Subarctic living as have some writers, but perhaps I have simply been fortunate in having avoided the worst places. I do remember feeling thoroughly uncomfortable on hot summer days. I find heat in northern Canada to be intolerable, though it is actually perfectly consistent with a continental climate, which is also marked by plunging mercury in winter. In the far north, the arrival of winter meant that I had to reserve a considerable portion of my time to collect and cut wood. My log cabin stood at the edge of a small settlement of log houses and log-walled tent frames and about a hundred feet from the nearest residence (see Figure 5A in Honigmann, 1949: 90). Our stove had to be carefully nursed, for if it went out in daytime, the cold could become very uncomfortable before it was relighted. Each evening a supply of kindling had to be cut and laid ready, in order to start a fire quickly in the morning. The chimney had to be watched lest it get red hot and set on fire the dry logs of the cabin in which we lived, and the cabin walls had to be chinked with moss. The water hole in the river had to be kept open, but the other families in the community helped, of course, to do this, though I recall the hole once froze over and required much hard chopping with an ax to reopen. The cold drove us to make our trips into the bush for toileting short ones, accomplished with minimal exposure.

Many features of northern Athapaskan Indian culture—snowshoeing, ice-chopping, dog-driving, wood-cutting, and warm dress, among others—represent adaptations to the region's rigorous climate. Though I traveled with the people on one-day hunting trips and on trips to the trading post in December, my ethnographic notes of the outdoor winter activities of the Kaska are quite sparse. In winter in that land one is confined for the most part to one's cabin. Circumstances are not conducive to writing outdoors during the short days of that season or at night in a trap-line cabin or a crowded tent pitched on the trail, nor did I seek out opportunities for winter trips. The onset of winter along the Upper Liard considerably limited my opportunities to observe people. As a result, I began to depend much more exclusively on talking to informants in my home or theirs, and data came to consist primarily of verbal statements of a kind I prized for the psychological insights they furnished. Indoor confinement also gave me time to analyze a large fund of already accumulated data and to outline the dominant features of Kaska personality that I later published.

Northwestern Canada had geopolitical importance during World War II. Construction and maintenance of the Alaska Highway as well as of a nearby military airfield demanded the presence of a large foreign population. Though I started field work among the Kaska when they were surrounded by many foreign influences, they did not appreciably alter their annual cycle. The large fur resources in their country combined with the high prices then being paid in the world's pelt markets did not inspire them to substitute wage labor for trapping. Practically nobody remained in Lower Post once autumn began, and even in summer I encountered no Indian who sought employment.

Entry and initial copings. My field work among the Kaska was the most personally satisfying and ethnographically productive I have ever conducted. Both my wife and I were caught up in another culture as we never have been again. In terms of the larger Canadian society's social norms it happened to be a "delinquent culture" (by which I mean that the young people zestfully pursued activities that they knew were contrary to the larger society's norms and laws, see Honigmann, 1966b), but this hardly detracted from our ability to identify with many of its values; perhaps it even added to the flavor of the life we enjoyed. Although I never acquired even reasonable competence in the Athapaskan language, the pidgin I learned from the Indians made it possible to communicate with them on nearly any topic. Thanks to that tool plus the good rapport my family and I established, especially with a considerable number of young people, I learned more about the less apparent aspects of the culture than I later did in Attawapiskat with the Cree Indians, although I had an interpreter and I was able to speak Cree sufficiently for certain purposes. My success among the Kaska reflects my then current standards of ethnography. I had only two previous experiences by which I could measure my achievements, my work among the Fort Nelson Slave Indians and two weeks of work the same summer (1943) with one informant and an interpreter on the Sarsi Indian Reserve near Calgary, Alberta. Although the Kaska were an emotionally reserved people, I found them easy to get along with. There were times, however, when my wife and I deliberately had to cut down on our participation in the culture; for example, we declined to practice wife exchange, and, soon after our arrival in the small, isolated settlement above Lower Post where we proposed to spend the fall and early winter, we began to shun the drinking parties whose aggressive outbreaks had begun to worry us. Fortunately, the makings for their brew soon ran out, and the parties ceased.

In retrospect, I am always surprised at the way I was able to achieve rapport with unmarried adolescent men as well as with mature men. Similarly, my wife maintained a number of close relationships with both girls and married women. It is possible that the Indians accepted us so easily because they identified us with the area's Eurocanadian trappers, with whom they were accustomed to interact on equal standards, rather than with the police or Hudson's Bay Company, with whom their relations tended to be more formal. Our own Eurocanadian friendships did in fact tend to center in the former rather than the latter category. Being from the United States, we must also have been identified with the U.S. troops who were stationed along the Alaska Highway and who visited the town, sometimes with alcohol and the makings for home brew and sometimes in search of sexual partners. A few soldiers found Lower Post attractive enough to visit regularly. They quickly appraised the community as one of nearly unlimited libidinous gratification and little order or constraint, an image that some of the younger Indians and white trappers delightedly cultivated. "It's a haywire outfit and a haywire town, and if you stick around much longer you'll become haywire too," was an often-heard comment. Something of the same spirit is also expressed in a verse written by John Dall, a local white trapper:

> Where maidens of the forest
> In traders' shacks unlace.
> Where free love does flourish
> and virtue is a sin,
> Where hair tonic and lemon extract
> Are sold for Holland Gin,
> There is a trappers' paradise.
> So no more I'll ramble round;
> I'll build myself a cabin
> Close to the Lower Post
>
> . . . .
> Where they potlatch dusky maidens
> When the daylight fades away.

In the summer of 1944, I carried out my field work from a rented, single-room cabin located near the Alaska Highway. A number of new buildings were going up nearby, and the settlement's center seemed to be shifting. Lower Post, instead of being oriented primarily to the river, was becoming mainly dependent on the new road for a much-increased flow of supplies and visitors. The population, including white and Indian trappers and their families together with the police and other permanent residents, did not exceed about 250 persons, of whom 175 were Kaska Indians. At the start of my second season's work in 1945 I moved into a vacant store that stood in the settlement's former center, a stone's throw away from the riverbank. In mid-August of that year we moved our quarters from Lower Post to a popular Indian camping ground near where the highway crosses a bridge, a few miles above the settlement. Two weeks later, crowded by winter supplies and a mass of bedding—our own and our Indian companions'—we began a slow boat journey up the Liard River to the matrifocal extended family's winter settlement, where we proposed to spend autumn and part of the winter. This settlement consisted of a couple, their two married daughters, the in-marrying husbands, unmarried children, and the mother and grandmother of one in-marrying spouse. We occupied our one-room log cabin until December 10, when we undertook the journey back to Lower Post, the children bundled in a toboggan and my wife and I on snowshoes.

Our winter location, with its eight related adults and six children, provided a good opportunity to get to know people closely and to observe interaction in much less distracting circumstances than in Lower Post. There we received artificial kin statuses, my wife being added to the four true or half-sisters living in the band, and I joining two young in-marrying men as their brother-in-law. In the twilight and cold of winter, we, like the Indians, became anxious as we saw our larder swiftly running down without sufficient game coming in to assure either a rich, varied, or dependable diet. We wished to try to leave the settlement several weeks before our scheduled departure date, but the young men who were to guide us had other responsibilities trapping and hunting and so frustrated our plans. We did not suffer painfully from the cold or in our accommodations. The Indians had sold us proper moccasins, with duffel to go inside, and we had bought warm winter garments. The four of us slept in a large wooden bunk that we had constructed with our hosts' assistance, hewing the green pine into large slabs of lumber. I sometimes slept with my woolen cap on for added protection, for the house was icy when the fire went out and the outdoor temperature dropped to 30 and 40 degrees below zero Fahrenheit. We treated the cold with due respect, as we had been warned to do.

The particular setting an ethnographer works in, together with his informants and the actions he observes, prescribe what he learns, much as do the documents from which an historian draws material. But the ethnographer has an advantage, for, given time, money, energy, and inclination, he often can more readily expand the sample from which he derives information. Spending about three months with only one kinship group and a single band of Kaska Indians determined the range of data available to me. To have repeated a stay of such length with other families drawn from other regions and bands would have been costly, particularly in time, but might have provided additional facts. Of course, two summers in Lower Post had also increased my knowledge of Kaska life, but summer, when the several bands come together, is a time heavily devoted to recreation and sociability. It allows unrelated people to meet one another for sexual encounters, and it also exposes the Indians to the anxiety that certain kinds of sociability, including sex, generate. The use I made of behavior pertaining to sex, drinking, gambling, and other social activities in my monograph *Culture and Ethos of Kaska Society* may have been conditioned by the many opportunities I had to observe such behavior in the trading post, especially with soldiers in the vicinity whose recreational use of the place involved some Kaska girls. I have claimed, however, that ethnography is more complex than simply observing and utilizing sensory impressions that originate in an observer's particular setting. Apart from indicating and adhering to certain settings, ethnography involves the ethnographer's selective perception of his setting as well as the evaluative priorities he attaches to what he perceives. Perception and valuation are active processes rooted in the observer's personality, including the theory to which he is committed. To explain some of the personality factors that motivated me among the Kaska, particularly in Lower Post, I shall try to describe my feelings during field work as well as I can recall (and am willing to report) them.

My stay among the Kaska was, as I said, intensely satisfying. I delighted as much in discovering vestiges of aboriginal Kaska Indian customs as I did in noting contemporary behavior whose significance I have since reanalyzed with the help of the concept of social disintegration (Honigmann, 1966b). For example, I sympathetically viewed the Indians' alienation from the Eurocanadian power structure and standards that conflicted with their own norms. I perceived their loose property norms as a consequence of the conflict between the traditional ideal of sharing and new attitudes arising out of the cash economy. To some extent I shared their positive attitudes toward drinking and regarded as recreational some of its accompanying behaviors. I also accepted permissively the Kaska's sexual behavior, viewing it as indicative of a nonpuritan society which, from the wide arc of human possibilities, had chosen a considerable measure of premarital sexual freedom. In my journal of Saturday, July 8, 1944, I run across this item: ". . . Some kids (girls) 17–18 sent a 10-year-old boy to ask if we wanted something [i.e., sought sexual partners]. The older girls (Stella Wiley's sister and Billy Barre's daughter) were accompanied by the young girls who are always around when illicit sex is being advanced.[2] The same pat-

---

[2] I use here the names I assigned to Kaska individuals in Honigmann, 1949: 27–30. For my generalizations concerning premarital sexuality see *ibid.*, pp. 162–163. The rest of the page from which this excerpt is taken provides a helpful context. I wrote selectively: "There had been talk of a dance

tern was [also] observed at Fort Nelson. The motivation here seems 'fun,' the same motivation that leads to liquor, gambling, and dancing among the Indians. 'Fun' is an important word." The point is that three weeks after my initial arrival I sought to interpret incipient prostitution as "fun," an interpretation that the young Oblate teaching school in Lower Post or the Hudson's Bay Company manager most assuredly did not share. I am not doubting my interpretation or seeking to recast it, but I maintain that it is not the only way in which such aspects of Kaska Indian culture could have been perceived. Instead of striving to appraise the culture as one made up of defensible patterns of behavior, I could have stressed the disorganized character of the Indians' existence. The genesis of such behavior might then have been related to the ravages brought on by the onslaught of another way of life.[3] Perhaps the field trip allowed me, at the age of thirty, to work off unresolved elements of revolt against the conventions of my own culture, or to release other expressive components in my personality. Undoubtedly my attitudes toward sex, drinking, and similar aspects of Kaska life also sprang from the spirit of cultural relativity I had cultivated since first encountering it in 1940. That perspective strongly influenced me to view the Indians' behavior in consistently positive terms (except when it threatened my own safety). Also, my intense interest in psychoanalysis, with which I interpreted many aspects of Kaska culture, not only encouraged me to pay special heed to sexual behavior but also prohibited me from judging Kaska sexuality with moral standards learned in my Catholic childhood.

---

all day—either here or at Watson Lake. Finally about 7:00 [P.M.] all the young people, kids, etc., were hanging around Taku [Trading Company Store] waiting for something to break. The church bell rang but nothing happened except for a boat to come across from the opposite shore with some people who went. . . . Finally N. [a local Eurocanadian] announced he'd drive whoever wanted to go to Watson Lake for the dance. The group electrified, sprang up and debated briefly. . . . We went through town stopping to see if there were any other passengers. Then we started for the 23 mile dusty trip. Time: 10 P.M. . . . When we got there we learned the dance was restricted. . . . Turned around and came back. K [white trapper] said we ought to start a dance ourselves. All agreed but nothing came of it. So we adjourned for a stroll that ended up in C's [Eurocanadian trader's] place for drinks from the bottle they had bought at Watson." Thereafter followed the episode I have reported. The day's entry ends: "Meanwhile the drums were beating across the river . . . indicating gambling in progress [at] 3:30 A.M. . . . dawn was making the moon pale. . . ."

[3] We have recently been told that the impact of Euroamerican culture on Indians, particularly those located on reservations, gives rise to "deculturation" and a way of life resembling the lower-class culture of our cities, including even the latter's earmarks of social disorganization. See James, 1961; Van Stone, 1965:Ch. 9; Stern, 1965:Ch. 18.

My chief pleasure lay in actively participating in the Indians' cultural activities. My journals remind me that I attended practically every dance given in Lower Post. I joined home-brew parties when invited and "crashed" them with Indian companions when not invited. I contributed to a potlatch, helped to set fishnets and repair houses, visited extensively, wore moccasins, and purchased game, fish, and snowshoes. I exchanged gifts with a few Indians at Christmas, wrote letters for friends, and joined in stick gambling. I came to share the Indians' opinions about many things. For example, I resented as strongly as they did the missionary's brash intrusion on a potlatch feast, and I deplored with them the deadness of the post in August, 1944, after many families had departed for the traplines. My journals inform me that at times I assumed more of a leadership role than I was aware of at the time. For example, I was responsible for organizing a dance, and I expressed my opinion on other social plans. My participation involved much of my total being, and departure in both 1944 and 1945 was acutely painful. Nostalgia endured long after I returned to New Haven, and on occasion it still creeps back, especially when I hear such tunes as "Wabash Cannonball" or "Take Me Back to Tulsa," to which we had danced long after an early summer dawn had broken over the Liard.

Active Research

Data-collection techniques. During my first summer in Lower Post, I interviewed relatively mature men representing different Kaska "tribes" (or bands) in order to reconstruct Kaska culture as it had been before exposure to Eurocanadian elements. To guide my research, I referred frequently to the culture traits published by Osgood as appendixes to his Athapaskan studies (e.g., Osgood, 1940:449–458) as well as to an early edition of Murdock's forementioned *Outline of Cultural Materials*. Those tools allowed me to approach each informant with highly specific questions, first soliciting his "yes" or "no" answer regarding particular traits and then probing for further information about how the trait had been patterned. I accepted illustrative case material when an informant offered it, but I did not solicit it as deliberately as I was to do some years later in Attwapiskat with the Cree. During my second year in Lower Post, another type of interviewing served me in my quest for psychological states that I presumed existed beneath the Kaska ethos. I sought persons who would give me life histories and, more ambitiously, would free associate in response to short prompting questions. My object was to get people to verbalize and thereby provide me

with a collection of clues to conscious thoughts and feelings and
—an even more important objective in my method—unconscious
states. I secured a number of short life histories but only one
long series of psychoanalytic-type interviews with a young man.
From men who provided biographical data (I found it harder
to get comparable cooperation from women, who were also less
likely to be able to speak English), I also obtained dreams. I
then probed for associations, asking where and when in his wak-
ing life the dreamer had actually experienced what I regarded
to be a critical element in the dream, or what had happened in
a place occurring prominently in the dream. The associations
helped me to interpret the dream with the aid of psychoanalytic
theory. Frequently, I fed back an interpretation to learn whether
the subject would agree with my decoding of the dream's latent
content, or to see how he would deny my interpretation. The life
history and related interviews were not standardized but varied
somewhat from subject to subject. I always sought to ensure the
subject's privacy, but in winter I occasionally collected dreams
as well as other personal data in my one-room cabin when other
members of my family were present. I conducted a less systematic type of interview about special features of ideational culture,
for example, about the Indians' ethnozoological ideas and their
views about human physiological processes. Twenty-eight adults
and children allowed me to administer Rorschach's inkblot tests
to them. The test's length was irksome to many people, so I
shortened it by combining the inquiry with the initial presentation of the cards, rather than showing the cards a second time.
In my final analysis and report, I did not make as much use of
Rorschach-test results as I had expected I would. Certainly I
did not, as I had intended, employ them to establish the psychological homogeneity of the community (cf. Henry and Spiro,
1953:427; Lindzey, 1961:202). Rorschach results provided one
type of data whose validity I questioned no more or less than I
did my interpretations of the Indians' dreams. In analysis, I
formulated general patterns of personality and ethos, each capable of embracing a variety of data, including observed acts, life-
history materials, dreams, and Rorschach interpretations. My
object being to find patterns, I tried to fit together such data as
dreams of rapelike pursuit of adolescent girls by boys, a woman's
dream of a grizzly bear amplified by other associations, and the
average tendency of my adult Rorschach sample to ignore colored
cards when taking the test. Considered together, such data reveal
a pattern ("dominant motivation") of emotional isolation or,
more specifically, they gave evidence of sexual constriction.

Concerning relatively passive techniques, I have probably

already said enough. While I was among the people, visiting, dancing, walking, working, buying, cooking, drinking, or simply watching, I remained attentive to socially patterned acts, thoughts, feelings, and artifacts, the basic study of Kaska culture. I wrote down what I perceived and inferred, often in people's presence. Occasionally I photographed events of cultural significance. Rarely, or only incidentally, did I observe through other sensory modalities, like smell and touch.

I could not have learned what I did of Kaska culture, ethos, and underlying psychological states without utilizing both an active approach, interviewing and testing, and relatively more passive modes of observation. On the other hand, ethnographic reconstruction clearly depended most heavily on many hours of detailed, patient questioning, but even there I could appreciate largely bygone modes of adaptation better after I saw the Indians hunt, witnessed them traveling in winter, and lived with them in the bush.

Old Man and Nitla: an insight into Kaska personality. In Lower Post I met two men whom I have called Old Man and Nitla whose cooperation and friendship were exceptionally significant. Their relationship with me provided me with many of the insights into Kaska Indian personality that I succeeded in obtaining, for they constituted the principal models of what it meant to be a Kaska male. Without fully comprehending my purpose, they furnished me with many of the clues I needed, clues that later, while formulating Kaska psychodynamics, I sought to check against other data from additional subjects. To have aroused the interest of such willing collaborators, both of whom spoke fair amounts of English and whom I found as congenial as they apparently found me, was a piece of good fortune that I have rarely since had in field work. I recognize the dangerous possibility that I may unknowingly have generalized the idiosyncratic psychological characteristics of these two subjects, ascribing them to the ideal personality system I constructed to account for the Kaska ethos, but I hope that by cross-checking my data I avoided this error. Nevertheless, Old Man and Nitla were *selective* filters of information. By relying on them for assistance, I cut off the possibility of obtaining somewhat different facts from other subjects that might have led me to alter some of the contours of my final analysis. Crises affecting each of these men at the time I knew them also appear in my field notes and have influenced conclusions I drew concerning Kaska Indian social personality in general. Old Man's eyes were giving him difficulty, and he complained much of his handicap. His predicament even entered his dreams, on which I relied heavily for clues to unconscious mentation. Nitla faced a different problem, for he was losing his attractive young wife to his assertive elder brother. He, too, complained much during the many hours when he vented his thoughts and feelings to me. Such idiosyncratic features of behavior alerted me to comparable trends in other people and greatly influenced the importance I came to attach to passive-dependent as well as nonaggressive (or deferent) motives in the social personality.

I have already referred to outsiders, especially soldiers, who happened to be in the area and who provided a stimulus for Indian behavior, encouraging patterns of premarital sexuality, alcoholic drinking, and hostile attitudes toward agents of law enforcement. I did not hesitate to regard such behavior on the part of the Indians as valuable data and have mentioned the significant place that such indicators of socially patterned license occupy in my account of the culture and its personality system. Accidents, in the more literal sense of the word, that happened to me personally or to my family, like a bout of jaundice, are harder to connect with the course of ethnography. I think Abram Kardiner's book *The Psychological Frontiers of Society*, which I read during the summer of 1945, reinforced my determination to attend to unconscious psychological events and in a methodological sense strongly influenced my procedures. Karen Horney's theoretical approach to psychoanalysis, however, had greater relevance for me than Kardiner's theory itself.

Bowing Out

Early in December shortage of food and the relative lack of game made us very impatient to quit the settlement where we had already experienced the onset of a subarctic winter. Finally, after many delays, the southward journey with two dog teams began on December 10. The young married men of the settlement accompanied us in order to transport their first winter furs to the trading post to sell. We arrived at Lower Post on December 14, and spent Christmas there. But few Indians came to town, and so we celebrated the holiday mostly with storemen and local white trappers. On December 26, we boarded the bus that took us to Dawson Creek. In the next eight months, while nostalgia for the North and its people gradually wore off, I wrote up the culture and ethos of the Kaska as a Ph.D. dissertation, which with Wendell Bennett's generous editorial assistance, subsequently became a Yale University Publication in Anthropology.

Summary and Evaluations

My ethnographic standards have remained sufficiently constant during the past twenty years, so that I am still comfortably satisfied with the scope of the ethnography that I covered on my two trips to the Kaska. *Culture and Ethos of Kaska Society,* published in 1949, is, I believe, one of the first monographs to approach the modern culture of an American Indian tribe with the detailed attention that anthropologists in the 1940s reserved for cultures relatively untouched by Western civilization. The book covers technology, social culture (particularly informal interpersonal relations, as I had little interest in formal kinship structure when I wrote it), and beliefs. About a third of the book is concerned with the central problem I went to study, ethos. The other two-thirds are given over to the evidence on which my analysis of the ethos is based. Thanks largely to my confidence in psychoanalytic theory and to the Indians' ability to communicate with me in English, I believe I fulfilled that aspect of my mission satisfactorily. Naturally, in subsequent years I have had second thoughts about both the theoretical tools of analysis and the methodological foundations of my conclusions. For example, I sometimes have second thoughts about the considerable reliance I placed on the Upper Liard Kaska for information and among them to members of a single extended family and its kin. But such evaluation belongs to a longer span of autobiography than this article is intended to cover. In 1954 *The Kaska Indians: An Ethnographic Reconstruction* appeared in print. This monograph, in which I deal more carefully with Kaska tribal divisions, followed largely from work I did during my first summer with the Indians at Lower Post. It provides time depth for the contemporary Kaska, but I am left uneasy by the lack of explicit connection between the aboriginal and contemporary cultures. Kaska Indian acculturation still needs a study that will relate the present to the past and thereby make the culture history more understandable.

PART II: THE FROBISHER BAY ESKIMO

Problem, Theory, and Research Design

In southern Baffin Island, only a few hundred miles from where Franz Boas conducted his pioneer ethnography in 1883–1884, stands a modern town of some 2,000 people, of whom more than

900 are Eskimo who enjoy numerous amenities as a result of having exchanged a life of trapping and hunting for wage labor. What we could learn about the Frobisher Bay community before our arrival impressed my wife and me with its significance, for it seemed to mark a high point in the Eastern Arctic Eskimo's cultural evolution. To a large extent, it was that promised significance that induced us to return north after an absence of eight years.

In those eight years I had not been involved in any research on circumpolar Indians and Eskimo, partly because I felt I had reached a plateau in my development as an ethnologist in that area. I feared that to study yet another trading-post settlement would not present any new intellectual challenges and would result only in my rediscovering largely familiar patterns of life and social organization. Although I spoke of someday revisiting people whom I had already studied, notably the Cree Indians of Attawapiskat in James Bay, the date stood off in the indefinite future. Furthermore, other areas, like Austria, attracted my wife and myself, as much for the more gracious and comfortable level of living possible there as for ethnographic opportunities. My experience in Frobisher Bay in 1963 rekindled my interest in the newly emerging cultures of the Far North, and it also reinforced the conviction, whose beginnings I have traced back to 1943 (Honigmann, 1960b), that the contemporary culture of the Far North is worth studying more than the historic past or the acculturation process by which the past has changed.[4] The decision to investigate synchronically the consequences of town life in Frobisher Bay paid off intellectually. Although it is impossible in such instances to separate other experiences accompanying one's mental growth, I believe the evidence of the Eskimo's adaption to town strongly helped to reorient my thinking about culture change (which had already been deeply affected by Margaret Mead's evidence from Manus), stress, and community development (cf. Honigmann, 1966a). Most importantly, it led me to de-emphasize the importance of enduring motives in behavior and encouraged me to view the situation as an important, if variable, source of action.

I would probably never have conducted field research in Frobisher Bay were it not for the suggestions of V. F. Valentine, chief of the Northern Co-ordination and Research Centre (NCRC) of Canada's Department of Northern Affairs and Na-

---

[4] Renewed interest led me in 1965 to design a study of several northern towns which I submitted to the National Science Foundation. Funds it has made available have allowed me to send several students to northern towns and enabled my wife and me to visit Inuvik in the Mackenzie Delta for six months in 1967.

tional Resources (now the Department of Indian Affairs and Northern Development). He confronted my wife and myself at a national meeting of the American Anthropological Association in 1961 and asked whether we were prepared to go north again. Our tentative commitment to do so in 1963 set off a correspondence in which Valentine included partly published material that Toshio Yatsushiro (1960) had collected when he was working for NCRC in Frobisher Bay. We tried to suit our interests to those of Valentine's office. Early in 1962, I wrote to him as follows: "As I understand your interests . . . I would make a total community study with emphasis on emerging forms of social organization, including leadership, interest groups, and, perhaps, signs of emerging stratification. I would also give considerable attention to values and attitudes, for example, to relative evaluation of the present situation of the Eskimo compared to the past and to evaluation of administrative procedures. Essentially, however, I would be doing basic rather than applied research, although I expect that a study of this sort would interest administrators considerably." I received my contract in January, 1963, was granted a leave-of-absence from the University of North Carolina, and late in February, my wife and I drove to Montreal. I visited Ottawa briefly, and we then flew nonstop in a DC-4 passenger-freight plane to Frobisher Bay. We arrived early on the cold morning of March 1 and stayed until August 27.

The contract held me to one or two topics that I could not recall ever having verbally committed myself to. However, these specifications were not unattractive, and I was wise enough to know that in ethnology a product somewhat different from the one originally agreed upon with the funding agency is usually accepted.

Before going north I had reformulated my general aims. The two sets of study problems are as follows.

Contract aims

1. Total community study of Frobisher Bay with emphasis on transitional forms of social organization, including leadership patterns, interest groups, and signs of emergent social stratification. Particular attention will be given to values and attitudes, to relative evaluation of the present situation of the Eskimo compared to the past, and to evaluation of administrative procedures.
2. Demographic analysis of the Eskimo population in terms of method of livelihood, income, and expenditure.
3. Examination of drinking patterns with emphasis on age, sex, and economic status of the individuals involved.

4. Analysis of the relationship in different age groups between the drinking behavior and social problems such as poverty, delinquency, crime, sickness, broken homes, etc.
5. Extent and effect of local alcohol production ("home brewing").

Aims as reformulated

1. Patterns of organization extending beyond the family plus the circumstances peculiar to the town setting to which those patterns constitute a response.
2. Attitudes and values directing the Eskimo including the people's interests, their satisfaction or dissatisfaction with life in town, as well as specific circumstances to which their attitudes form a response.
3. Psychodynamic aspects of Eskimo personality.
4. Childrearing, with special attention to circumstances in the towns that have helped to form certain patterns of childrearing.
5. Generally, the aim will be to see Eskimo life as it constitutes a response to the full context of the town.

These objectives, together with other topics contractually assigned by NCRC to Irma Honigmann, constituted the framework of our research in Baffin Island. In her contract, she agreed to collect information relating to Eskimo women, especially their "adjustment to town life and in the Rehabilitation Centre," as well as data concerning "childrearing, the development of values in early life, and personality formation." During the ensuing months we studied behavior that did not clearly fit into any of these topics, but we introduced relevance where possible or else omitted the data from *Eskimo Townsmen* (Honigmann and Honigmann, 1965b).

Valentine had referred to the Canadian government's activities in the Far North as community development, by that term seeking to link the Frobisher Bay project to a subject to which I had paid some attention in Pakistan and in general writing (Honigmann, 1958, 1960a, 1960b, 1963:357–362; Swezey and Honigmann, 1962). I failed clearly to see the connection until I arrived in Frobisher Bay and perceived the magnitude of the effort being devoted to the Eskimo's modernization (Honigmann, 1966a). I myself did not view my work as an acculturation study, nor as an account of how Eskimo culture had changed. Nevertheless, an abundance of records in the town of Frobisher Bay extended significantly the temporal boundaries of the period that I could "observe." Although my contract envisaged a report "particularly useful in . . . assisting the Department [of Northern Affairs and National Resources] to devise more effective controls over the use of alcoholic beverages" and offering "invaluable guidance for the development of the new town of Frobisher Bay, now under construction, to assist it in functioning successfully as an administrative, school, and medical centre for Baffin Island," I shall probably never know the extent to which our results have been applied, but I strongly suspect that that end will little affect whatever value they represent.

One conspicuous difference between the aims that guided me in my Kaska Indian and Frobisher Bay Eskimo research is that psychological matters played a much more subsidiary role in 1963 than in 1944 and 1945. I had lost some of my enthusiasm for psychological (especially psychoanalytic) theory and for projective tests, like the Rorschach. My attitudes had cooled not because psychological tests and theory have not been productive in cross-cultural research (the history of culture and personality testifies to quite the contrary), but because the kind of analysis to which they lead results in conclusions too far removed from first-order data. Increasingly, I have come to prefer interviewing and observation and to avoid analysis that proceeds to very high levels of abstraction.

Passive or Adaptational Research

The environment of the group being researched. On Baffin Island winter cold restricted us from observing people outdoors, and so we decided to conduct a census, which would give us a reason for entering every home to meet and identify people. The cold resulted in serious rapport-building problems. In other northern places where I have worked, I arrived in summer when the people are readily found out of doors, enabling me to become acquainted with them and to find potential informants. In the summer, tent living further facilitated the process whereby a stranger could to some extent integrate himself into the community. Some of the procedures we followed in Frobisher Bay, especially interviews with key Eurocanadians and lengthy investigation of records, suited both the problem we had selected for study and the special nature of the town's plural social structure, and allowed us as well to carry on productive work, despite the restrictions of the cold season. In August we joined briefly a camp that furnished precisely the opposite conditions. There life was lived much more publicly, even on rainy days. Tents were easier to invade than the homes in town, and we felt generally much more comfortable. Yet information collected during those two weeks proved to be of slight importance in our overall research, for the field season was already too far advanced to capitalize on the rapport we established with our neighbors.

The rocky tundra of the Eastern Arctic, where ice and snow

last long and spring comes late, imposed certain limitations on ethnographic activity. Dressing warmly consumed much time. Many times daily, when entering warm interiors, outer garments and overshoes had to be laboriously peeled off. Outside, my fingers quickly grew numb, even under the woolen finger gloves that I left on after removing my mittens to take notes or use photographic equipment. My fingers often stuck from the cold to the camera's metal parts. I dreaded the wait for a bus on a windy corner or exposing my face to the biting wind, but these are common experiences in the north, and the extent to which they affected the ethnographic process is negligible.

Entry and initial copings. The cold and wind that we encountered on Baffin Island during the final winter months of 1963 troubled us more than the windless cold that eighteen years before had made winter much more pleasant along the Upper Liard. We protected ourselves against the Arctic cold with modern Eskimo-type parkas made of Grenfell cloth and lined with thick wool duffel, but even the parka's generous hood insufficiently protected our faces from the bitter cold wind. As a result, I suffered several mild cases of frostbite during our first two months in Frobisher Bay.

We lived in considerably warmer and more modern quarters than we had in 1944 and 1945, this time renting a three-room house equipped with an automatic oil range, electricity, electric refrigerator, indoor commode, and running water that flowed from a large storage tank. The building was centrally located with respect only to Apex Hill, one of the town's three neighborhoods. In Apex Hill lived 362 Eskimo. Ikhaluit, the neighborhood with the largest concentration of Eskimo (about 500), was three miles away, and we could only visit it periodically. Apex, however, accommodated the rehabilitation center with its 50 to 60 clients, as well as various Department of Northern Affairs shops and garages where many Eskimo worked. Importantly, for our purpose, it housed a number of the most accomplished Eskimo of both sexes, including those families who had formed a housing co-op and bought their own modern, prefabricated homes.

Although these features of the neighborhood provided us with frequent opportunities to observe the most successful, acculturated townsmen, the setting was not too confining to gain information about other Eskimo adjustments. The rehabilitation center with its transient population, many from isolated settlements, showed us a different segment of town life. We also diligently sought to cultivate friendships with families who, despite living in the town, persistently followed land and sea-based careers rather than wage employment. For about two weeks in August we lived under canvas in a camp containing several such families and observed there at first hand the enthusiasm with which men who had jobs returned to the land with their families for summer vacations. Like the small Upper Liard River settlement where we spent the fall and early winter in 1945, the camp constituted a small social network in which we could observe relationships intensively.

In Frobisher Bay there were more than 900 Eurocanadians, many of whom were employed in government agencies and, unless they worked for the DNA, had little contact with the Eskimo. In spring, a heavy influx of construction workers arrived who rubbed shoulders with Eskimo drinkers in the tavern and, of course, sought to meet native girls for sex. Prostitution, however, while it existed, did not flourish. Until July the town included about 200 U.S. Air Force personnel, who made their own drinking and dancing facilities generously available to white townsmen but unapologetically closed to Eskimo. In consequence we stayed away too, except for a single visit. For much the same reason, we did not go to other clubs catering mainly to Eurocanadians and confined our contacts to persons whose positions brought them into regular dealings with Eskimo, who could verbalize official or unofficial attitudes and policies regarding the Inuit, or who could make us aware of roles that particular Eskimo played in the town's social organization.

We arrived in Baffin Island during the winter. There were indoor public recreational events practically every evening of the week, and these we quickly learned to take advantage of. To identify families, homes, and individuals of each of the neighborhoods, we embarked on our household census. We counted heavily on those visits to announce our presence and mission, to invite people to visit us, to gain the confidence of and attract potential informants, and to spot English-speaking people who might be available as assistants, but the visits proved less fruitful than we expected. Visits took us behind the frosted windows of Apex houses and through the huge drifts that almost obscured some of the self-made cabins in Ikhaluit, they provided us with a cross-section view of the community and of the varieties of physical adjustment to town living, they helped us to make a few acquaintances, and, of course, they provided much information. But the invitations we issued during each census call brought few visitors to our home, and the calls we made turned up few potential interpreters and none who subsequently liked his job well enough to remain in it. They brought only a few informants to light. The visits may have announced our presence, but rapport in Frobisher Bay was never as good as it had been among the Kaska or, to take what may be a more meaningful point of comparison, among the Eskimo of Great Whale River where we had done field work in the summers of 1949 and 1950. The language barrier proved to be almost impossible to surmount with the majority of adults in Frobisher Bay. Some people understood English but nearly all refused to speak it. At the same time it was impossible to secure a steady, willing interpreter or satisfactory informant. Apex children and a few from other neighborhoods found our house inviting, and some visited us regularly, but mostly they were too young to serve as informants. We allotted a good deal of time to learning Eskimo, but for this task we also needed that hard-to-find resource, a willing informant. Furthermore, our effort to learn to speak lagged as we faced increasing competition from other duties. In the end we failed to learn enough Eskimo to conduct serious interviews in the language, but we gained more than a superficial knowledge of its structure. We participated in the culture to the extent of attending movies, bingo games, and dances, as well as any meetings of committees or associations that I could get advance word about. We visited a few homes regularly, relying on English-speaking inhabitants to interpret for us or else struggling with our meager knowledge of Eskimo, and we went to the tavern, especially on payday nights, when there was apt to be a good crowd of Eskimo. In time, our active participation increased, perhaps because with the approach of summer, activities we could join also multiplied. We participated briefly in rather mild games of keep-away (see Honigmann, 1962:20), and I became an inexpert umpire for a newly formed softball team. Far too rarely, however, did we simply sit with Eskimo to share their thoughts, amplify what they reported, and learn their reactions to our emerging generalizations. When we did enjoy such ideal informant relationships, it was usually with someone from the Central or Western Arctic, that is, persons who also spoke English readily. Naturally such obstacles disappointed us but, as the following section on techniques employed in field work will indicate, they did not reduce us to inactivity. Many experiences, both social and professional, brought special rewards, and consequently our stay in Frobisher Bay was not unpleasant, but there was not the kind of pleasurable excitement that in Western Canada had come from identifying with the community and participating intensely in the libidinous tenor of its behavior. In Frobisher Bay I danced with my wife, except for old-fashioned group dances, joined no illicit drinking parties, and in the tavern drank carefully and watched the clock in order to have time to catch the last bus back to Apex. Perhaps by the time I reached Frobisher Bay, I had lost some of the adaptability I possessed in my youth, and perhaps this limited the behavior I could adopt in participant observation. Changes that time had wrought in my professional status may also have been a factor, for my age seems to have alienated me from the younger men and women, especially those deviant from the larger society's norms. On the other hand, the Frobisher Bay Eskimo did not, like the Kaska, tend nearly so unanimously to disregard those norms, and as a result, I did not find myself in a position where, in order to identify with the people, I too had to disparage the "foreign" norms and the social pressure accompanying them. The ethnographer who went to Baffin Island in 1963 was not utterly different from the one who had gone to Lower Post in 1944, for I retained a large measure of cultural relativity and permissiveness concerning elements in another way of life (without, however, confusing cultural relativity and moral relativity quite so much as twenty years before). Though I admired the facility with which even the older adults adjusted to the amenities of civilization, and though I was stirred by the rapidity with which even a highly specialized culture could change—at least in its observable aspects—within a single generation, I condemned none of the families who chose to remain aloof from full-fledged town life. In fact, I sympathized deeply with one young man who nativistically wished to return to his former dependence on the land and sea. Those young men who were oriented toward neither land nor town puzzled me most of all (Honigmann and Honigmann, 1965b:247). But I do not claim to understand any Eskimo very well; I returned from Frobisher Bay much less confident about my knowledge of Eskimo motivational life than I had felt about Kaska personality. The reason is twofold. First, the severe language barrier reduced contact with the people, thereby allowing less insight into motivation; second, I deliberately held back from inferring personality dynamics.

Though field work proceeded differently in the two communities, I think it is clear that these differences cannot, without gross oversimplification, be ascribed entirely to my personality or to the problem I sought to investigate. I argued that the work I turned out about the Kaska Indians owed something to the Kaska culture itself, and the same is true of my work with the Eskimo. The ethnographic process in Frobisher Bay was only partly determined by the kind of person I was in 1963. It also owed something to the more organized character of that place, the historical situation it represented for the Eskimo, the character of the Eskimo's response, and to the kind of people the Eskimo are.

Active Research

Data-collection techniques. The longest series of interviews we conducted in Frobisher Bay pertained to the census that we began almost immediately following our arrival. My wife and I followed a set schedule of questions, deviating from it whenever an informant seemed willing to expound on something that interested us. We sought to learn if the interviewee had ever been to the southern part of Canada, we inquired about each informant's schooling and the male household head's employment record, and we asked why and when adults from outlying settlements had originally moved to Frobisher Bay. In some cases we succeeded in discovering parents' employment expectations for their children, informants' views of what they considered good and bad in the town, the extent of their knowledge about the Community Association, the Community Council, the DNA, and the U.S. Air Force (SAC) base, and their views regarding the amount of local fighting and drinking, but these open-end questions proved so fruitless that we abandoned them.

A major crimp in our interviewing plans was that the men were at work during the day, which meant we could talk only to housewives. We originally felt that the men would be more communicative than their wives. Yet when we did interview them they were not notably more helpful. We visited some homes in the early evening, but to transfer census taking entirely from daytime to evening would have cut into what we regarded as strategically important opportunities to interact with the Eskimo at public events. Thus we had to establish priorities with respect to how we allocated our time and energy. We continued censusing as long as home visits produced a steady stream of respondents, by which time we also knew many of the families and the man's employment status. When we stopped, partly because it proved impossible to hold an interpreter or keep one interested in repeatedly asking the same questions, we had covered about 55, 60, and 100 percent respectively of Ikhaluit, Apex Hill, and the air base, the three residential neighborhoods into which Frobisher Bay is divided.

One of our major activities consisted in locating Frobisher Bay's records and copying them (by hand). Such information was often so abundant that we had to institute some kind of systematic sampling or apply a temporal limit beyond which we would not go. Through these records we learned the frequency of employment and the salaries of all Eskimo employed by the Department of Northern Affairs during 1963, the history of the school system and the extracurricular activities instituted by teachers, actual attendance figures of selected school children, earnings from the sale of Eskimo handicrafts, especially carvings and garments, to the government store, and subjects discussed at the last twelve sessions of the Community Council, including clean-up, a curfew for young people, and sexual irregularity leading to illegitimacy. We copied down data on births and marriages, information that threw light on illegitimacy, and historical material of a more general sort, for example, how the Sisi Housing Co-operative began and the controversy stimulated by news that a territorial liquor store would open in Frobisher Bay. We also learned the names of all persons who held permits to buy alcoholic beverages in two different years, as well as the kinds and amounts of beverages permit holders had purchased; all arrests of Eskimo during a twenty-one-month period, together with the disposition of the cases when they reached the courts; financial records of the Apex Hill Community Association; production figures and the financial condition of the Ikhaluit Fishing Cooperative; and selected information on clients in the Rehabilitation Centre.

Arduously we sought out key Eurocanadian officials, like the head of the Department of Transport, who occasionally doubled as a justice of the peace, the vocational-training instructor, the head of the Girl Guides, and the commanding officer of the U.S. Air Force—to hear them describe their roles vis-à-vis the Eskimo, their views of Eskimo's adjustment to town life, and the expectations and policies that both they personally and their organizations officially held toward Eskimo. I soon discovered that these officials talked less frankly in their offices than at a dance, an official reception, or on the bus.

We attempted to interview Eskimo to obtain native ideas on climate, animal life, and what I hoped would be a diverse range of town-connected topics. However, my youthful English-speaking informants proved uncooperative, so I had to abandon the attempt. I usually opened these sessions by asking for "news" of the community, i.e., who had left for hunting, who had returned, who was visiting, who was ill, and other bits of ethnographically significant gossip.[5] After abandoning this type of interview, my wife and I actively undertook quite formal observation, guided by hypotheses or at least by a clear sense of problem, in order to see how certain issues confronting sections of the community would be resolved, by whom, and in what fashion. For example, we watched to discover how young native leadership emerged to resolve the dilemma confronting young people when, first, the dance band refused to play on Saturday nights without a new contract, and then when the Eurocanadian organizer of the Tuesday night dances decided to abandon the project (Honigmann and Honigmann, 1965b:32–41). We watched

---

[5] I had tried this technique with my principal informant in Attawapiskat in 1947–1948, and it had worked fairly well for some items, such as arrivals and departures, but it never brought much news that would make headlines in a daily newspaper or that was ethnographically very revealing.

to see how the Rehabilitation Centre would operate under a new organizational plan, who visited the tavern on payday, and how an unwed mother would be received by her peers following her confinement.

Such observations were very useful for delineating values, patterns of leadership, stresses and strains confronting categories of Eskimo, and the role of certain Eurocanadians in Eskimo affairs. This technique became more effective as we got to know more people and could identify the conflicts, rivalries, ambitions, and abilities that affected their behavior. Photography also came to play a more important role in my Frobisher Bay field work as I got to know people, but I frankly do not think I maximized this technique for ethnographic purposes. Before going to Frobisher Bay I intended to use the camera to secure photographs that would communicate the ethnography rather than serve simply to illustrate it. My sponsors acknowledged the value of this aim and provided an abundant supply of black and white film. I preferred to plan in advance what to photograph and then take several shots of the subject. Even without an advance plan, however, I usually went out each day with either a Miranda DR (35mm, single-lens reflex camera) or Rolleicord (using 120 film) over my shoulder. Though on occasion I kept a record of the exposure, shutter speed, and date of each picture taken, I do not believe such data serve any significant function in the ethnographies where they are provided (cf. Mead, 1956: 473–480). It may well be, however, that possibilities for doing further analysis with my photographic collection are severely limited because I lack a temporal record, such as I have for my field notes.

I mailed exposed film to a reliable processing firm in Montreal, where I opened an account. In addition to fine-grain developing, I requested contact prints of the 35mm rolls as well as small enlargements of those and of the 120-size negatives. I attached the small contact prints to the numbered envelopes used to file and index negatives. By affixing a piece of tracing paper over a small enlargement I could trace the portion that I wanted further enlarged for publication and write on it my instructions to the darkroom worker. I entrusted custom enlarging to students working in my university's photo laboratory. My plan for integrating photographs and manuscript in *Eskimo Townsmen* collapsed, however, when the publisher decided to print the photographs on glossy stock and group them together in various parts of the book. Though he grouped them as close as possible to corresponding textual material, they were not, as I had planned, intimately associated with the text. Contrary to my original hopes, the Frobisher Bay report perpetuates the concept of pictures as a supplementary adjunct to ethnography rather than demonstrating how they might constitute a vital form of data presentation in their own right.

Finally, our modest data bank deserves to be mentioned, because it proved to be of such great value in analysis that I cannot conceive of doing future field work in a large community without a similar system. It consisted simply of entering Eskimo names, or rather their registration or "disc" numbers, in index form in a book. The Eskimo in Frobisher Bay had only begun to heed government suggestions to adopt patronymics; consequently, teachers, administrators, official documents, and even Eurocanadians in casual conversation usually referred to persons by their given name and a registration number. Children could readily provide their number and regularly identified themselves on drawings we asked them to make. Alongside these numbers, I indexed all references to the individuals that I had located in censuses, Yatsushiro's genealogies, police, employment, and historical records, and in my own field notes. Later I used this information to categorize people as leaders, to note the rise and fall of a leader, and to gauge the degree to which status characteristics correlated with particular kinds of behavior.

Among the Kaska, casual conversation constituted informal interviewing inasmuch as it often brought about a divulging of experiences on the part of the Indian, but this approach was possible in Frobisher Bay with only a disappointingly small number of English-speaking Eskimo whose special background made them approachable enough for visiting or led them to chat with us at public events. In Frobisher Bay, therefore, we concentrated on learning as much as we could by studying Eskimo behavior at work, at school, in the tavern, at the Rehabilitation Centre, and especially toward their children. We attached the greatest importance to regularly attending events wherein Eskimo participated. These included church services, a catechism class that met in a private home, and formal meetings of committees and the Community Council, about which it was sometimes difficult to be informed in advance. I attended every court session, sometimes phoning the police station early in the morning to learn if one would be held that day. In the courtroom I kept a full, running record, a feat made easy by the fact that everything was interpreted from Eskimo into English and vice versa. We also attended practically all dances and many bingo parties, and we made several evening visits to the East Coast Lodge, a tavern. Beer and stronger drink relaxed men's and women's guardedness, even inducing them to speak the broken English they knew, so that the lodge proved to be relatively productive of information.

I treated data obtained in Frobisher Bay from records, through interviewing, and especially from observation much the same as I had treated the psychological data obtained among the Kaska. My wife and I followed customary ethnographic procedure, cross-checking one kind of information against another, noting who had said or done what, or what source had reported given facts as we formulated and analyzed descriptive patterns of community behavior. Verification of a generalization (or pattern) lay in the consistency with which information taken from one source corresponded to related information deriving from another source. Compared to my Kaska ethnographies, the published work we produced on Frobisher Bay is heavily concerned with overt behavior and with the physical events of the Eskimo's life. Our use of records allowed much more precise judgments of who did what, with what approximate frequency, and how he was rewarded or punished. Our data bank showed with what frequency activities overlapped in the same persons or in persons holding similar status and also how certain behavior was segregated by status. This degree of precision and the careful identification of behavior by status I regard as significant developments in my career as an ethnographer. They do not, however, adequately compensate for the relatively little information I obtained about people's purposes, attitudes, and feelings.

Accidental events. In the loosely structured societies in the Far North certain culture patterns are noticeably short term or variable, because of their close dependence on the roles that particular individuals happen currently to be playing in the community. The ethnographer who understands this proceeds cautiously, because he cannot regard the function he assigns to a certain pattern as vital when he knows that the pattern may, at a moment's notice, cease or be drastically revised without the people concerned being consulted. If he traces the integration of one institution with other institutions or its relationship to a value orientation or to personality characteristics, he must realize the tenuousness of the relationship. He must realize that the life of the institution may be quickly ended as a result of decisions made by persons other than the Eskimo or Indians with whom he is primarily concerned.

In Lower Post I remained unaware of this feature of northern culture. In the more complex system of Frobisher Bay, however, behavior we observed shortly after our arrival in March, 1963, had drastically altered or ceased by the time we left in August, when new developments were in progress whose course, unfortunately, we could not follow. Hence early in the book that my wife and I wrote about the town, we state that we cannot predict that observers who arrive after us will find all that we have described. My experience in Frobisher Bay, along with study based on reading, shook the theory of culture with which I had theretofore operated and increased my doubts about the usefulness of a theory of motivation for explaining cultural stability or integration. I suspect that the organization of a culture at any moment is fundamentally the product of accident or contingency and that people are capable of more than they attempt or are permitted to venture.[6] To be sure, not everything in Frobisher Bay is in flux. The kin-term system, qualities of interpersonal relations, and some physical features in the town apparently change only imperceptibly from year to year. But it is not to such features that I allude. Rather it is to adult-education classes, dances, Eskimo entreprenurial ventures, co-ops, deliberative councils, a rehabilitation center presenting many chances for Eskimo re-education, and health programs. Incessant change or cultural instability in this heterogeneous community arises partly from the great degree to which activities depend on teachers and administrators who hold power to innovate, and partly from the extent to which Eskimo have been drawn into town life, which makes them dependent on the decisions of the individuals who hold such power.

The persons occupying powerful positions—not merely government personnel but Eskimo as well—are themselves unstable members of the community. They remain for relatively short periods before they are posted elsewhere (their services are in great demand in the north) to be replaced by others with new plans around which the culture reorients itself. The trial-and-error nature of the patterns that Eurocanadians and Eskimo of all walks of life devise in response to the constantly changing situations of an Arctic town also produce instability. There are few established patterns to follow in a rapidly changing, nontraditional community of this type with its strong dependence on the outside world, nor are there many vested interests to protect against change. The unstable nature of Frobisher Bay society confronted us with a constant series of "accidents," events occurring in the system because of current policies, ideals, and interests of the men who at that time were managing the affairs of the town. It was challenging to work in this setting of intense heterogeneity and unpredictability, but it made me uneasy to think that anything we wrote would not serve very well as a map

---

[6] Culture history, I believe, is less a record of necessity working itself out than a sequence of contingencies in which evolutionists or historically minded anthropologists find pattern, impose structure, and discover necessity. See Honigmann, 1963:14–16.

of the culture but only as a historical document or a baseline against which to measure further change.

One accidental factor that helped to channel our attention and limit our interpretations was that we were assigned a house in highly serviced Apex Hill rather than in the less regularly serviced neighborhood of Ikhaluit, with its many homemade cabins. Although this "accident" may have influenced our judgments about the Eskimo community, we tried to be in Ikhaluit at frequent intervals, and we came to regard adjustment to town life in that neighborhood as more similar to adjustment in Apex than the contrasting physical amenities and Eurocanadian stereotypes suggested.

We had early heard unfavorable words about Frobisher Bay and about the Eskimo's disorganization in the town. Those views encouraged me to see my role as partly a corrective one and in writing my account to emphasize qualities of organization and to report evidence of drinking and law-breaking in very specific, measurable terms. Helpful informants were scarce, and there were no Eskimo who were as crucially important to me as Old Man and Nitla were in Kaska. The high prices paid for sealskins in 1963 probably stimulated a number of Eskimo to go hunting more frequently and for longer periods than they otherwise might have, and this may have influenced the degree to which I describe the community as retaining a strong interest in land-and-sea-based Eskimo specialties, although I also have direct statements from informants that point to the same conclusion.

Bowing Out

To allow some time between field work and the resumption of teaching, we decided to leave Frobisher Bay on August 27. Before departing we distributed kitchen supplies and leftover foods to neighbors, visited friends to bid farewell, and discovered anew that leaving the field grows easier with every trip. Perhaps one learns from painful experience not to invest too much emotion in people. At any rate, the ties we had formed with individual Eskimo were weaker than those we had formed with Kaska Indians. On the morning of departure we taxied to the airport, said goodbye there to the acting regional administrator who was busy welcoming new teachers, and boarded the plane south. For the next eight months we worked together nearly every morning analyzing quantitative data and notes and writing about what we had learned. From the data and analyses in the manuscript, which we sent to the Northern Co-ordination and Research Centre for eventual publication, I selected special topics, such as the drinking of alcohol, for submission to various journals.

Summary and Evaluations

In *Eskimo Townsmen* (Honigmann and Honigmann, 1965b), my wife and I speak of the remarkable change that has come over the Eskimo who moved into the town of Frobisher Bay. Although we refer to change, we do not treat it historically by describing the horizon that existed prior to the people's advent in town, because the past was not an object of study in Frobisher Bay. Primarily *Eskimo Townsmen* describes and analyzes the adjustment that Eskimo have made to town life, the culture they are developing with the assistance of Eurocanadian tutors and with the physical facilities, like houses and cars, that the Canadian Government and the larger society provide. I regard Frobisher Bay as one of history's revolutionary experiments in culture change, one still in process, and one that can be much more carefully observed than many an earlier cultural revolution, and I regard *Eskimo Townsmen* partly as a baseline against which further observations of Eskimo in transition to modernity can be aligned and to which my subsequent Arctic field work can be compared.

Comparisons

Eskimo Townsmen is a less comprehensive ethnography than *Culture and Ethos of Kaska Society,* the only product of my Kaska Indian field work with which it should be compared. Its greater selectivity is due partly to the greater wealth of cultural resources available for study in Frobisher Bay, and partly to the different problem that I investigated in Baffin Island.

Table 1 offers another way of classifying general procedures unequally followed in both communities, one that gets somewhat away from the strict dichotomy between active and passive techniques. Participant observation, it will be noted, occurred in both places but took quite different forms. With only a few exceptions, the Eskimo were not prepared to become intensely involved with us, because they had had and would continue to have much exposure to officials and experts who they knew were staying among them for relatively brief periods. They did not expect us to become active in their affairs, but they accepted us as spectators and received us at a table in the tavern or as an occasional dance partner. Six months were not long enough for people of our age to break out of this assigned status. Our position was made very clear at a Saturday night dance just before our departure when the Community Association presented us with a farewell gift accompanied by a warmly gracious speech to which I had to respond. I had not expected such recognition, and for a time I misunderstood the ritual symbolism, wondering if our rapport had suddenly crested. My wife realized that this was exactly the kind of ceremonial gesture we had previously seen one or another organization make when other prominent Eurocanadians departed. It simply indicated the category in which we stood and the respect that some community leaders felt was due to more or less popular persons of official or important status who had interested themselves in Eskimo affairs.

In the foregoing pages I have several times compared certain aspects of my experience in Frobisher Bay to my field work among the Kaska Indians. Rather than repeat those statements, I will try to sum up the contrast sharply. In 1963 a more mature and sophisticated anthropologist worked more industriously and systematically at ethnography but missed the fun of his

Table 1 Major ethnographic procedures
followed among the Kaska Indian and in Frobisher Bay

ACTIVE INTERVIEWING	PARTICIPANT OBSERVATION	RECORD COPYING
In this activity the ethnographer sits with an informant for the purpose of developing information on ethnographically significant points. It was used heavily among the Kaska but only rarely in Frobisher Bay.	The ethnographer collects his data while living and acting certain roles familiar to the community. Among the Kaska I played an active, integral role, contributing to a potlatch, traveling, hunting, joining brew parties, and sharing the Indians' dismay when a Eurocanadian interfered with their activities. In Frobisher Bay participant observation was more passive. Our roles tended more to be those of spectators; the few exceptions to this generalization included selling bingo cards, playing bingo, and umpiring baseball games.	The ethnographer copies documents in order to acquire a corpus of primary data for further analysis. This activity was heavily employed in Frobisher Bay but almost not at all (except for sales slips and an official welfare schedule) while I was among the Kaska.

earlier wholehearted participation in an exciting culture. Although I participated in both cultures and came to like people in both, the difference between the two cases is one of degree. The difference is as much related to the different characters of the two communities and their historical position as it is to changes that had taken place in the anthropologist himself.

COMPARATIVE FIELD TECHNIQUES IN URBAN RESEARCH IN AFRICA

William B. Schwab

Social anthropology is not an experimental science. We cannot tear apart our raw data, build it up, or modify it in any way. Nor can we conduct rigidly controlled scientific experiments that lend themselves to duplication or verification. Far less than in any physical science are we able to approximate an isolated neutral system of relationships and determine its functions. Yet social anthropology strives for a theoretical understanding of human behavior. It sets out to isolate and expose the regularities manifested in social behavior and to present a rational description of these relationships. Thus, it shares a general orientation with those sciences that endeavor to discover and analyze the regularities in nature.

It also shares with the natural sciences many of the same

problems of demonstrating the validity of theory, methods, and reality. One can argue that if there is a trinity in anthropology, it is the relationship of method and theory to the reality of the collected data. The anthropologist must determine whether the data he has collected reflect real behavior in the society he is studying. If the raw data are questionable and if serious doubts develop with regard to their reality, he must re-evaluate his theory and/or his method. Until recently, many anthropologists carried out their research in small-scale communities in which the populations rarely exceeded 2,000 inhabitants. Because the universe under study was small, the anthropologist was often able to establish social relationships with the total population that provided him with a means of checking on his raw data. Many anthropologists tended to ignore theoretical considerations and let the data "speak for itself" in leading the way to theoretical formulations. Some collected data widely, hoping that if sufficient data were collected, the pieces would fall into their respective places, and the raw data would reflect the true real behavior in the society.

Recently anthropologists have begun to make use of more precise methodology and to pay more attention to theoretical implications than they did previously. This has been particularly true with regard to urban or large-scale studies where the communities under investigation have exceeded 5,000 inhabitants. In communities this large, reality is difficult to ascertain, and the universe may not be reflected in the raw data unless precise tools are used. The anthropologist is unable to meet and know all the inhabitants, and individual and institutional behavior is much too vast and complicated for one observer to record. Nevertheless, more precise tools and greater attention to theory can turn a difficult and complex urban field study into a relatively manageable field-research project.

This chapter will compare the methodology employed in two large-scale urban field studies that I carried out in Africa in the 1950s. I have indicated the flaws, difficulties encountered, and the achievements accomplished in both studies. I have made some attempt to assess the implications of the methodology and theory employed in both studies. The first field venture was an analysis of the Yoruba city of Oshogbo in the western provinces of Nigeria. The second project was a study of Gwelo, a Rhodesian city in the high ridge country between Bulawayo and Salisbury. Oshogbo is a mud city of approximately 150,000 inhabitants, and Gwelo is a European-dominated urban center of 32,000 people.

My interest in Africa was stimulated and developed by the professors with whom I studied. After World War II, I was fortunate to work under Dr. Hans Wieschhoff, one of the few out-standing Africanists in America at that time. Dr. Wieschhoff conveyed to me, and to others, his intense interest in Africa and his concern with the lack of behavioral research in Africa. To him, Africa was a scientific enigma that most social scientists, particularly American anthropologists, had ignored. He saw Africa as a land of mystery that had to be scientifically investigated before its people could be properly understood. Africa, to Wieschhoff, was a vast anthropological laboratory from which could be abstracted basic laws and generalities concerning human behavior.

For many years, I had been concerned with the problems of urbanism in America. As my interests in Africa developed, my concern with urbanism shifted to Africa. In 1949 Africa was the least urbanized continent, and few analyses had been made of its urban centers. The British Social Science Research Council was interested in an analysis of a traditional African city, and, when my interests coincided with theirs, our only problem was what city or people to study. At the time, it was apparent to me and other anthropologists that the Yoruba were the most urbanized people in Africa. When I left America for England, I had agreed to conduct an urban study of a Yoruba city in Nigeria. The exact city was to be decided in England in consultation with the British Social Science Research Council, the Nigerian Government, and British anthropologists.

My second field project was partially determined by my first study. I was interested in comparing Oshogbo with other African urban centers, and I sought a city that had been affected by similar factors of change. I was searching also for an African city that had a structural composition different from Oshogbo's and a city that reflected a geographical background and cultural development different from that found in West Africa. For these reasons, I rejected most of the traditional urban centers of East and West Africa. Southern Africa, with its Rhodesian and South African cities, seems to embody the elements of change and structure that I was seeking, but population size, racial conflicts, economic complexities, political tensions, and marked ethnic diversity and heterogeneity forced me to discard this area, too. By elimination, I was left with the Rhodesias from which to select a city for the second project. I felt that my final decision could best be made in London in consultation with British anthropologists, the Rhodes-Livingstone Institute, and officials of the Rhodesian Government.

A number of personal details affected both studies. In the Oshogbo project, I had no children, and my wife participated fully, collecting much of the data pertaining to women. When I undertook the Gwelo project, we had one child, and so my wife was not able to participate as much as she did in Oshogbo. However, the addition of my son did not present any other problems. His activities were carefully supervised by a nursemaid, and he was able to make friends with the children in the neighboring European households. The operation of our household during both projects was taken care of by the servants I employed. The well-being and operational efficiency of most Europeans in the tropics is usually dependent on the competence of their servants, and I was fortunate in being able to employ extremely skillful and loyal Africans whose efficiency made my own life and activities much easier.

Housekeeping details are essential to the successful operation of any anthropological field study, and probably the most important is to locate a place to live. To find permanent living quarters in Oshogbo was difficult, as there were no vacant houses, spare accommodations, or facilities that we could rent. The African population lived in massive mud compounds and were not receptive to European outsiders residing with them and invading their privacy. In small village studies, the community often builds the anthropologist a house, but this is rare in larger, more complex, and more impersonal communities. In Oshogbo, the indigenous leaders were not inclined to either build or loan me a house, since they considered me to be the responsibility of the colonial power, which politically dominated the community. The European population was made up of ten resident colonial and commercial officials, who resided in a small quarter outside the town limits. Even if I had wanted to live in the European section, I would not have been able to, for there were no houses available in the area. The only other accommodation in the town was a "rest house" or small dried-mud catering hotel that had been built by the Colonial Administration within the town to house transient officials. When my wife and I arrived in Oshogbo, we were temporarily assigned quarters in this rest house. Obviously, we had to find some neutral quarters that would not irritate the Africans, would satisfy the Colonial Administration, and would still allow us to observe and participate in the life of the community. After considerable search and consultation, the only possible solution appeared to be the rest house, and the Colonial Administration, at the suggestion of the local District Officer, permanently assigned to us a section of the rest house consisting of three small mud rooms. The quarters were adequate and clean and allowed us to participate, to a limited degree, in town life. Our greatest difficulty was the lack of privacy, as we were constantly under the scrutiny and surveillance of the Africans who lived in the vicinity. Although the quarters were cramped, and at times quite hot, we eventually made them comparatively comfortable and looked upon them as home.

In Gwelo our housing problem was not so complicated. In London we inquired through the Colonial Office and the Rhodesian representative about a house in Gwelo. Since by Rhodesian law we could live only in the European quarter, our problem was much easier to solve than it had been in Oshogbo. After a short wait, the Rhodesian representative in London informed us that a modern European house would be available to us when we arrived in Gwelo five months later. Unlike our quarters in Oshogbo, it was spacious, cool, and pleasant and contained modern water and sanitation facilities.

Most field workers in a tropical climate fall prey to various illnesses. In Oshogbo, I was quite sick with malaria and dysentery, to which our rather primitive quarters and food contributed to some degree. In Gwelo, I was not seriously ill, for our better living conditions helped us remain healthy and possibly more efficient. As important as good living conditions can be, few studies fail because of the lack of them. It is only when ill health and extremely bad living quarters coincide that the field venture is seriously hurt and severe damage is done.

Finally, there is an excitement and sense of adventure and purpose that accompanies the anthropologist's first field venture that is usually missing in later studies. It is his "first love," and although he may be more efficient in later studies and accomplish much more, his first love is rarely ever replaced.

PART I: OSHOGBO, AN URBAN COMMUNITY IN NIGERIA[1]

Problem, Theory, and Research Design

In 1949, I left America for England and Africa, on a British Social Science Research Council grant, to carry out a field study of a Yoruba urban community in Nigeria. The Yoruba people, who have occupied the western section of Nigeria for many centuries, are probably the most urban of all African peoples. They live mainly in large, densely populated, mud cities, which in re-

---

[1] Sections of this chapter were previously published in *Human Organization*, 13:2, and 24:4. The papers were entitled "An Experiment in Methodology in a West African Urban Community," and "Looking Backward: An Apraisal of Two Field Trips."

cent times have ranged from 10,000 inhabitants to well over 150,000. At the time of the study, late 1949 to early 1951, little was known about the Yoruba, as no systematic analytical research had been conducted among them. There existed no pertinent analysis or description of the indigenous social, economic, or political structure of the Yoruba people or their towns. We knew that changes induced by foreign influences since the advent of the British in 1900 had proceeded far and rapidly, but the direction and scope of these changes had not been investigated. My problem was clear: to make an intensive anthropological survey of the social, political, and economic organization of a Yoruba city. What city to study and what methods to employ had still to be determined.

Before going to Nigeria, I spent most of 1949 in London learning Yoruba, perusing the literature and the Colonial Office files for information about the Yoruba, absorbing British anthropological knowledge, and determining the Yoruba city to be studied and the methodological procedures to be pursued in the field. The methodology that finally emerged was to a large extent a result of the many discussions I had with British Africanists in London. It was quite clear from the very start of the research that such traditional anthropological methods as participant observation, interviewing selected informants, collecting case histories and genealogies, and observing group and individual activities, would not be adequate.

The methodological problem was further complicated by factors inherent in Yoruba urban communities. The population size of Yoruba towns, the great variation in behavior and norms, the extensive social differentiation, and the marked heterogeneity indicated the necessity of using some kind of measurement techniques. These critical social conditions suggested that the selection of reliable and representative informants would be crucial to the success of the project and difficult to obtain. It was not only a question of whether an individual or group was typical or atypical and this is difficult in any study, but also the need for selecting informants who would represent the marked diverse social components of a Yoruba community. These four factors, (1) the inherent complexity and size of Yoruba towns, (2) the enormous variation in behavior, (3) the diverse social components, and (4) the need for a sophisticated measurement technique, that necessitated the use of sociological survey methods and sampling techniques. Questionnaires, field guides, random sampling, and other sociological devices had to be employed. We would also need field assistants to help collect the raw data, as one scientific observer would be unable to observe or record the diverse patterns of behavior. It was apparent also that a random-sample census would be necessary to establish a reliable scientific base for the study that could be used as the basis for future research as well.

But there was another factor that had to be considered. Since British contact in 1900, numerous external forces had exerted profound influence on the internal structure of Yoruba communities. For over forty years, European trading concerns, governmental agencies, and missionaries had been active in Yorubaland. New occupations had developed, and the scope of economic mobility, both horizontal and vertical, had widened considerably. As inadequate as our London sources were, they indicated that we would find a marked variation in wealth—an economic continuum in which the polar ends were the rich and poor. Further, both Christianity and Mohammedanism had become intertwined with the indigenous religions to form a new religious base. We could assume also that new political concepts had been introduced and that those previously ineligible for political office had begun to achieve political power.

As a consequence of this increased multiplicity of social patterns and the introduction of new social forces, we expected to find a complexity and diversification not known before. Consequently, we felt the need for some precise scientific methods with which to collect the raw data and to analyze these complex and rapidly changing social relations and institutions. It was my hope that, through sampling and other quantifying devices, we could isolate the various dependent and interdependent social forces that enter into a rapidly changing network of social relationships.

Our emphasis on quantifying devices was not an attempt to reduce social relations to mere statistics, but rather a recognition of the fact that statistics and other quantifying mechanisms when used properly can be excellent scientific tools. Statistical data in itself does not usually provide the theory or conceptual framework, but it can add the substantive flesh to the theoretical skeleton. By this I mean that statistical data when properly collected and analyzed will reinforce or substantiate the researcher's hypothesis or theory. The difficulty that develops is that statistical data can often be analyzed and interpreted in different ways. Thus, it is possible for a scientist to develop support for different theories with the same statistical data, depending on how he manipulates, interprets, or analyzes the data. Nevertheless, there is little doubt that methods that utilize statistical and other mathematical tools tend to yield results that are more invariant with respect to individual observers. They may reveal also complex linkages between variables that otherwise might remain obscure. In addition, statistics may widen the range of our perception and reduce to practicability problems that otherwise could not easily be handled.

At the same time, I wanted information and insights that are not ordinarily amenable to survey and statistical methods. I hoped that by combining survey and statistical methods with traditional anthropological field techniques we would be able to collect data representative of the entire community and at the same time able to provide cultural insights, details, and nuances. The two methods are not incompatible; in principle each should support the other. Our aim was to develop hypotheses through the information obtained from individuals, and to test these hypotheses in the sample survey. In turn, the survey data was to lead us to formulate new questions and make additional interpretations that could be investigated in depth. Thus it was hoped that the pitfalls and the inadequacies of both methods would be avoided.

The problem of selecting a Yoruba city to study was less complex than that of selecting the methodological procedures to be employed in the field. Although reliable Yoruba data were limited in London, we located some material that indicated general population size, social heterogeneity, and tribal subdivisions of Yoruba cities. After much searching and consideration, we selected Oshogbo, which our data indicated would range in population from 75,000 to possibly 125,000 inhabitants. This population range appeared to be typical of the major Yoruba towns and could be studied by a team of ten field assistants. Oshogbo was 200 miles inland, in the center of Yoruba country, and was inhabited by either Oyo or Ilesha peoples, both major tribal subdivisions of the Yoruba. It was a rail and road center, and we assumed it would have the elements of change that we were seeking. Colonial office files indicated that the town was ruled by an educated king who was not hostile to Europeans. Oshogbo appeared to be a typical Yoruba city. When the Nigerian Government, whom we had consulted, suggested Oshogbo as their first choice also, we were ready to begin our study.

In September, 1949, we arrived in Lagos, the capital of Nigeria, after a pleasant voyage down the west coast of Africa. We spent eleven days in Lagos, where we were briefed by colonial officials and interviewed by the governor. We acquired a pickup truck and gathered together the supplies and gear we would need for at least a three-month stay in Oshogbo. During our stay in Lagos, the Nigerian Government agreed to make line maps of Oshogbo from aerial photographs. Our future area sampling was to be based on these maps, which were to be ready in a month's time. Early on the twelfth day we left Lagos for Oshogbo. As we left Lagos, the capital and port city of Nigeria, we were symbolically and realistically cutting our links with the outside world. Once we were in the interior, communications would be difficult, and until stable relationships were established, we would be isolated from the indigenous population.

The anthropologist under the best of circumstances never becomes a fully accepted member of the culture he is studying, nor does he want to become a member. Usually the people look upon him as being outside the indigenous culture and do not expect him to follow their cultural norms, which both protects him and allows him greater freedom of action. However, this situation has its drawbacks for the anthropologist, because he is often emotionally isolated and almost totally dependent on his own internal resources. Most often he is alone in the field; only rarely is he fortunate enough to have a trusted assistant or informant with whom he can discuss his crucial decisions. The anthropologist must scrutinize his own behavior carefully, for incorrect actions and decisions may mar his standing in the community or weaken a favorable image that he has established. The anthropologist always makes mistakes, but the more emotionally secure he is, the less isolated he is, and the more people he can trust, the less is the probability that he will make serious and irrevocable mistakes.

We arrived in Oshogbo two days before the Great Beirum festival, the major holy day of the Moslim religion, and were greeted by the Assistant District Officer, the colonial administrator for the area. He had booked us into the rest house for three days. The information about our study of Oshogbo had not reached him, and he was rather shocked to learn that we would be with him in Oshogbo for the next two years.

Passive or Adaptational Research

There necessarily must be an initial period of orientation and contact in any field trip (Vidich, 1955). This serves many purposes for the anthropologist and for the people he is studying. It enables the researcher to begin to communicate.[2] It permits him to adjust his language and symbolic systems, so that the meanings he assigns to events and questions or answers can approximate those commonly assigned by his respondents. At the same time it enables the people to assign an identity to him. He is fitted into a role that has some meaning within the culture and that provides a basis for reaction. Typically both the image of

---

[2] We are assuming here that the researcher can speak the language of the people or that he is able to communicate through interpreters, administrators, or a common language.

the field worker and his understanding of the symbols and language of the people are continuously redefined during the course of the field work.

In Oshogbo, during the initial period, which lasted for several months, I had four specific goals. The first was to obtain a broad skeletal outline of the underlying principles of the Oshogbo social system. Very little was then known about the Yoruba. At this stage, I was not interested in obtaining detailed or even necessarily precise information. What I sought was a very general understanding of the forms of relationships and patterns of behavior so that I could begin to isolate sets of relationships and attitudes and thus start to ask meaningful questions.

My second goal was a practical one. Social anthropologists require an adequate framework of demographic data, but none was available for Oshogbo. I began, therefore, to make plans for a sample census with the object of obtaining information on age, sex, ethnic composition, kinship and family composition, occupation and income, education, religious affiliation, and other relevant data. Before any statistically reliable census could be undertaken, the area had to be mapped, and so I was fortunate in having been able to persuade the Nigerian Government to take aerial photographs of Oshogbo from which line maps were made. These maps incorporated every building in the community, and the boundaries of every compound and separate building were marked on them.

My third objective was to hire field assistants and gradually introduce them into the community. Initially, we employed ten assistants. The Africans selected had to meet certain minimum requirements. They had to be the equivalent of our high-school graduates, and they had to be bilingual in English and Yoruba. They could not be natives of Oshogbo but had to be Yorubas from neighboring towns. Initially, they were to indicate the boundaries of all the compounds in Oshogbo on the town map and begin to work on the sample census.

The fourth and possibly the most critical goal was to encourage the Oshogbo people to form a favorable image of me as a field worker and to obtain their permission for the studies. I had come to Oshogbo with the active support of the colonial administration, but I assured them that I was not part of the government and not a missionary or a trader, nor did I have any other role with which they were familiar. Despite my self-definition as a research worker only, which of course was entirely alien to them, I believe my initial image was ill-defined and vague, but nevertheless closely associated with government. I believe the people looked on me as a strange and deviant colonial administrator. This image changed during my stay in Oshogbo. Gradually, over time, I became more and more identified as a friend, and eventually I was assigned a quasi-political role and was known as Oyinbo Atoaja (the Oba's white man).[3] Having found a place for me within their own social system, the people could reorient their behavior. With the change in their attitude the quality of data we collected also changed, for the better.

The main problem, however, was to secure the consent of the community for the study and to begin to establish effective rapport with the people. With the support of the Ataoja, the king of Oshogbo, and the Assistant District Officer, the colonial administrator in the area, I was able to hold a number of open meetings attended by the chiefs, educated members of the community, and other influential people. At these meetings I presented the purposes of the study, defined my role as an investigator, and gave the townspeople an opportunity to question me extensively. At each meeting, I was cross-examined extensively. The chiefs and literate members of the community desired to know what material benefits, if any, would accrue to the community as a result of the study. Although I was unable to promise them any positive material results, I was able to point out the intangible benefits of the study: greater community prestige and possible future governmental developments. Once I had convinced the chiefs and other influential members of the community that the study would bring no harm to the community and might be beneficial, their approval was secured. These meetings culminated in a reception in my honor where the chiefs and other influential people publicly promised their support and cooperation in the study.

During this early period, I did not attempt to begin investigations in the town proper until I had the consent of the ruling hierarchy. The approval of the chiefs and the other literate and influential members of the community did not ensure the approval and cooperation of the people, but it was a necessary prerequisite to gaining the confidence of the community at large. Other methods and activities had to be employed to win the support of the people.

With the sanction of the chiefs, I began to move about the town, meeting and talking with as many individuals as possible until I was no longer a stranger to the community. The people were quite willing to talk to me and responded in a friendly

---

[3] "Oba" is a common Yoruba term applied to any paramount chief among the Yoruba. By assigning to me the term of "Oba's white man" the Yoruba were indicating the close and honored relationship that had developed between the king and myself.

manner as long as I refrained from asking personal questions. The educated people and chiefs, who had had extensive contact with governmental and European trading agencies, accepted me as a scientific investigator, but the uneducated viewed any European investigator as a potential tax collector, or as a harbinger of an imponderable law of the "white man," and thus regarded him with distrust and suspicion. These reactions were not entirely baseless, since previous experiences with most Europeans had led to either increased taxes or unwanted laws; the concept of a scientific investigator was alien to them. By assiduously avoiding the role of an investigator at first, and by attempting to establish warm interpersonal relationships with as many diverse individuals as possible, I found I was able to implant a notion of my purpose in the community and to abate their anxieties concerning increased taxes or other evils. Moreover, the approval of the chiefs and literate people, who used their considerable influence and authority on my behalf, helped to mitigate the peoples' fear and apprehensions. Their efforts, together with my own attempts to explain and publicize the study, succeeded in minimizing anxiety to the point where I felt initial work could be attempted. My task was also made easier as I had the active support of the colonial administration and the hospitality and friendliness of the Yoruba people.

When it seemed apparent to me that I was no longer causing suspicion, I began to question and interview the people. Although their fears and distrust of me were diminished at this time, it was not until many months later that their feelings were fully dissipated.

I spent the next several weeks defining my role and purposes and making preliminary studies of the political and historical background of Oshogbo. Historical and political data are usually not difficult to obtain, and the people of Oshogbo were proud of and willing to speak freely about their history and political hierarchy and about family life and economic organization. The main purpose of my inquiries was not to acquire details or even very precise information, but to obtain the general knowledge necessary to initiate a census. Since no reliable records were available, I had to take a sample census to secure basic demographic and other social data. The objectives of the sample census were not to enumerate heads, but rather to obtain information on the characteristics of the community, and to collect reliable and representative data concerning family organization, occupational structure and the religious, educational, and age composition of the community. It was my intention to select from the census a subsample of families on the basis of the economic differentiation of the male heads of household and to subject these families to intensive investigation for the remainder of the study.

The town was divided into four areas, each of which had markedly different social characteristics. The largest section in both population and area was the old city, inhabited mainly by the indigenous Oshogbo Yoruba people, who live in the traditional Yoruba mud compounds. Physically, a compound is a collection of buildings, usually adjacent, with defined and recognized boundries in which a lineage or several lineages live. The average population size of a compound was 150 inhabitants, but some exceeded 500 individuals. We estimated that between 70,000 and 90,000 people lived in the old city, which took in over three-quarters of the town, including 580 compounds, and extended for approximately two miles around the central market. The smallest area was the Hausa quarter, with 42 compounds, located on the northern limits of the city and inhabited only by Hausa traders and cattle dealers. The third area was the commercial district. Lining either side of the main thoroughfare of the town (Station Road) were approximately 250 small trading stores owned or rented by men and women who had left their native towns to settle in Oshogbo. Most of the inhabitants of this area had become permanent settlers in Oshogbo and were making conscious and positive efforts to be incorporated into the social, political, and religious life of the community. Finally, there was the section classified as the Foreign Quarter. It was the home of temporary immigrants: government clerks, employees of European-owned concerns, teachers, and transient laborers. It was the sophisticated quarter of the town where night clubs, dancing, and intellectuality existed. The typical Yoruba compound structure was absent in this quarter, where most houses were "European" mud or stone dwellings. There were 87 dwellings and buildings in this quarter.

In as orderly a geographic fashion as possible, each compound, store, or separate building was assigned a number on the town map, and a list was then compiled of the names and numbers of each. From this list every tenth name was selected in each of the four differentiated areas. The entire population in the various buildings and compounds selected in the sample was to be enumerated. A total of 94 compounds, stores, and buildings were included in the census.

At the start of the survey, I had hoped that it would be possible to employ educated inhabitants of Oshogbo as my field assistants, but it soon became apparent that the townspeople were too involved in local pressures and commitments. Moreover, the prestige that accrued to the field assistants as members of the survey was of considerable significance. Had the assistants been inhabitants of Oshogbo, this prestige could have created significant complications within the internal political structure. Although the assistants I finally obtained were more Westernized in manner and thought than the local townspeople, they were cautioned to adhere constantly to all local customs and traditions.

In order to facilitate the practical operation of the census, as well as for physical expediency, we divided the town arbitrarily into eight geographical zones. At least one field assistant was assigned to each zone. Four weeks before the census began, the field assistants started to contact the residents of the 94 compounds and other buildings that were to be enumerated. We then estimated the population and the religious, occupational, and educational composition of each compound or store, in order to provide some basis for a check on the reliability of the census. The chiefs and other influential people supported the census publicly and the official messengers and bellringers publicized it among the townspeople.

During this four-week contact period, there was little manifestation of the distrust and suspicion that had been evident immediately after my arrival. Initially, all the compounds granted us permission to conduct the census and indicated their willingness to cooperate with us. However, as soon as the practical operation of the census began, opposition to it developed, some of which had not been apparent previously. Much of the opposition can be attributed to factors rooted in the culture of the people, but some was to the methodology we employed. Our sampling techniques, for example, were incomprehensible to the people. The residents of the compounds selected were unable to understand why they had been chosen in preference to neighboring compounds. As a result, they refused at first to cooperate. Moreover, the residents of a compound are a corporate group, and as such they required what is, in effect, the unanimous approval of the group; at times the dissent of only one man was sufficient to block the census. In addition, the men refused to enumerate their wives and children in the compounds. At this point, it became quite apparent that their previously expressed fears of increased taxation and conscription of women and children into labor gangs and armies had not been fully dissipated. There was also a deep-rooted belief that counting one's children would bring them harm. At times, children up to the age of five were frequently omitted from the census as the people did not consider them to be permanent members of the family, since there was such a high mortality rate among young children. We found also that the literate townspeople who had volunteered originally to assist in the census refused to participate, since they were unable to withstand the pressure from some segments of the community who were opposed to the census. In those few cases where the literate townspeople or school children cooperated and provided us with information, they were publicly chastised and accused of being informers by members of their compound.

Many of these difficulties were overcome by repeated visits to the compounds and by enlisting further aid from the chiefs and other influential members of the community. By concentrating our efforts on the influential compounds in the census, we were able to convince them to cooperate and that the census was harmless. They, in turn, often were able to sway the more obstinate and recalcitrant compounds.

There were also two other significant factors that, I think, contributed to the ultimate success of the census. In the first place, I had no official attachment to the Colonial government, and thus the people knew I was not in a position to impose taxes or unwanted laws. Second, the people of Oshogbo knew that I was not a transient and thus could be held accountable for my actions. At the end of ten days of concentrated effort, only two compounds remained recalcitrant, and they were replaced by alternates. Eventually, 6,241 individuals were enumerated in the census.

Active Research

Once social and demographic data were obtained, more intensive work could begin. A subsample of families was selected on the basis of the occupation of the male head. We studied these families intensively for over a year, taking genealogies and case histories of each family and making a detailed examination of its social and economic organization. Our object was to understand the networks of role relationships that linked the members of a family to one another and to the structures of the wider society.

Research was carried out in the main by field assistants directed by questionnaires and field guides. The questionnaires were employed primarily for the collection of quantifiable factual data and were designed to elicit information relating to specific issues. However, after some experience with the questionnaires, it became evident that they were unsatisfactory for any complex situation. In these circumstances, the field assistants used guides suggesting the lines the investigation should follow. The guides formed the basis for qualitative reports.

There were no formal interviewing procedures, and the form of questioning varied from one field assistant to another and often from one family to another. This approach has the possible disadvantage that the data collected may be uneven. On the other hand, it led to the establishment of excellent rapport and probably led eventually to more accurate and complete knowledge. Since all the assistants followed identical guides and questionnaires, it was possible to check on the reliability of the data of one against another. I should like to stress here that much of the success of this aspect of the study depended upon the intelligence, ingenuity, and loyalty of my field assistants, as well as on the continuing cooperation and good will of the people.

During the period that the field assistants worked with their selected families, I used traditional participant-observation methods throughout the community. I collected geographical and historical data, participated in political councils, and observed and took part in religious and other rituals. In my work the representativeness of an informant was not a primary consideration. On the contrary, I made an effort to seek out those who were best informed about a subject in which I was interested or those persons with whom I could develop closer relationships. With some individuals and families the relationships grew into intimate friendships; with others the links were not so close. To the extent permitted by each relationship, I tried to share in the ordinary day-to-day activities of the people and in the nodal events of their lives.

The use of a combination of survey and participant-observation methods in a single study poses three primary questions. How successfully can the methods be combined? In what areas is each most effective? How consistent are the results of different methods? There were areas of inquiry in the Oshogbo study for which one method or the other was obviously better suited. For example, demographic material in a community the size of Oshogbo could not be obtained except by some sort of survey. But most of the areas of inquiry could be approached by using either or both methods. As the study progressed, several facts began to emerge that helped to guide me in making optimum use of the combined methods. It shortly became evident that the formal underlying structural principles of the social system could not easily or economically be obtained through survey procedures. My conceptual models were largely derived from personal observation and inquiry. The data from the survey families served in several ways to correct and elaborate my conceptualizations. They made possible a closer examination of the empirical fit between the actuality of behavior and the formal rules of social life or between what people do and what they say or feel they ought to do. In even the most stable social system, there is an important gap between the formal rules of behavior and the interpretation and manipulation of these rules. In a social system that is undergoing profound changes in its legal and moral precepts and in its forms of behavior, as the Oshogbo system was, there was an even more urgent need to examine the difference between social theory and social reality. Certainly this was possible without using survey methods. But, because survey methods can reach so many people, they yield a greater insight into the range of the variations and changes that are occurring and hence a better understanding of social process.

But survey techniques, though their range is wide, can penetrate only to certain levels. Consider one aspect of the Oshogbo religious system as an example. We learned, through the survey, that 80 percent of the Oshogbo community called themselves Muslim, 13 percent were Christian, and the remainder adhered strictly to traditional religious beliefs and customs. It was also possible through the use of questionnaires or guides to arrive at some understanding of the motivation for the changes in religious affiliation and to assess some of the conflict between traditional and modern religious rules and beliefs. But the more complicated and frequently more obscured reasons for shifting religious affiliation, the uses to which these changes were put, and the ambiguities about religion were best brought into the open by long and informal personal discussions. Further, I doubt if there is any survey method that would show with such startling clarity at least one important aspect of current Yoruba religious belief—the acceptance of inconsistencies—as did the following event. One Friday afternoon I intended to visit the chief priest of a major native cult whose festival had been celebrated the previous day. I arrived at his house as he was leaving to worship in the central mosque. He was a devout Muslim, too!

Occasionally, there were significant incongruities between my conceptions and the data of the field assistants. These could often be reconciled easily, but at times they required additional interpretations, reformulations, or more information to resolve them. Not every inconsistency that arose was or even perhaps could be reconciled, but, with enough insight and information, the two methods led in every important area to basically compatible results.

Inconsistencies and contradictions in the data were also resolved in another way. Each field assistant was assigned twenty families for intensive study in the same geographic area and worked with these families for a period of a year. Thus, the assistant was able to establish contact not only with the compounds in which his designated family units were located, but with other compounds in the area, and was able to draw upon a large segment of the inhabitants of his area for additional information. In this way, the field assistants worked on two levels of investigation. On one level, their research was concerned with family units; on the other level, they were concerned with the dynamics of the wider community. Where contradictions or inconsistencies arose in the analysis of the data collected from the selected family, checks could easily be made in the wider society with different informants, and the reliability of the data could quickly be ascertained.

Interviews, either by myself or my field assistants, were conducted in Yoruba, the indigenous language, but answers to questionnaires and data collected for the reports were recorded by the field assistants in English. Eventually my own rapport and that of my field assistants became sufficiently well developed with the community that we were able frequently to record the answers to the questionnaires at the time of the interview. The consolidation of reports occurred, however, only after many interviews had been completed. The assistants usually visited each of their families at least once a day, collecting their data over a long period of time. Often these visits were of a purely social nature, designed to promote friendly relationships between the assistants and their informants. With these techniques, the field assistants were continually reviewing and checking their collected data.

For many of the problems investigated it was possible to limit the time slice utilized, but in other cases it was necessary to investigate the problem throughout a major portion of the survey. For example, agricultural data were collected on many different occasions, depending on the variations in the farming cycle. On the other hand, it was possible to collect data concerning marriage and divorce rates, diets and birth rates, within a limited period of time. It was necessary to review at least once many of the more fundamental categories—such as kinship, which was operative in many different aspects of the society— so that the additional material accumulated could be synthesized with the earlier date.

The ease with which data were collected varied considerably depending on the social circumstances. I had anticipated resistance from the women, but we soon found that most of them had little hesitation in discussing their lives and social activities. Serious resistance was encountered in the collection of data pertaining to income and expenditures, and in some instances the people were reluctant to discuss certain ritual procedures and illnesses. It was only after we had resided in Oshogbo for a long time that barriers to acquiring this information and other sensitive data were overcome.

In the early phases of the field study, I had hoped that the literate members of the community might supply significant clues to the analysis of the traditional social structure, but with rare exceptions the family studies, and the illiterate informants who had spent most of their lives in Oshogbo, provided more accurate data. In many instances these data contradicted the information gathered from the literate people. Because of the lack of higher educational facilities in Oshogbo and the demands of their professional or commercial activities, most of the literate people had spent many years away from Oshogbo and were not so familiar with the traditional ways of life. Nevertheless, although the literate people were poor informants about traditional Yoruba behavior patterns, they were able to provide valuable information and insights concerning the changing structuralization of the society and the new values and ethics that were developing. Moreover, they were invariably strong supporters of the survey and, at times, provided the necessary help to overcome difficult situations.

As I look back, it is clear to me now that my role in the Oshogbo study assumed almost a dual aspect. In the first instance I was director of the survey and, as such, conducted field work parallel to that of my staff. Second, it was my role to provide those data that could not be obtained by survey methods and without which the structural framework of the wider society could not be formulated. However, a social fact is often not significant in itself, acquiring full meaning only when it is understood in its historical perspective and in its functional and structural relationships to the society. Thus it was also my job to provide the theoretical skeleton and the structural framework upon which all the social facts collected by the team and myself had to hang. It should be realized also that the data collected by me and that of my staff could not be treated as isolated and unconnected entities. Neither sets of data could be considered as complete or separate. They were, in fact, complementary, with the divisions between them somewhat artificial. Each was a stimulus to the other, for it was the data collected by the field assistants that provided the substantiating facts for a continuing sequence of ethnographic hypotheses.

Bowing Out

After reviewing what we had done and checking and rechecking our facts, figures, and theories, we came to the conclusion that the Oshogbo survey had been completed. For over a year and a half we had been living with and observing the people of Oshogbo. Seasonal, ecological, structural, and cultural effects had been studied and noted, and their effect on the changing behavior patterns of the people recorded. Like most other anthropologists on their first field trip, we had exhausted our check lists and believed that we had scrutinized all forms of behavior so that future analysis could be reliably determined. We were aware of the perimeters of behavior and were confident that we could easily ascertain normal and abnormal behavior in the town. It was not until we had left the field that we became cognizant of a number of factors that we had overlooked. Fortunately, they were not crucial factors and were easily remedied.

It was difficult to leave Oshogbo and bring to an end some extremely meaningful relationships. I had learned not only to respect and admire the king, but had developed a warm camaraderie with him that one rarely achieves with another individual. I was his "Oyinbo" or "white man," and he was my "chief clerk." There is no question, at all, in my mind, that much of the success of the Oshogbo study was dependent on the excellent rapport that I had with him. There were others with whom relationships were almost as close: Old Ajayi, the returned soldier, the catholic schoolteacher, the town councilor, and the Ifa priest. Separating from my team of African field assistants was even more difficult, complicated, and beset with emotions. We had worked together as a team for well over a year and a half and had bulit a strong relationship, akin to a father-son relationship. It is interesting to note that all the young Nigerians who worked for me eventually achieved high university degrees, most obtaining Ph.D's. Before I left Oshogbo I had to see that each field assistant was placed in a job commensurate with his talents, education, and desires, for they were dependent on me for their future activities as I had been dependent on them in the Oshogbo study. It was hard to separate, but we celebrated our departure at a small feast in my three-room mud house where we toasted the study.

Our last day in Oshogbo sadly came. The Atoaja arrived at 5:00 A.M., we said goodbye, and with all my field assistants aboard my truck, we drove off to Lagos. A week later we boarded ship for England. The Oshogbo field venture was over.

Summary and Evaluation

The Oshogbo study was a successful field venture, from the point of view of our objectives. Our goal had been an intensive anthropological survey of a changing Yoruba city. We had examined the major social components that determined behavior in Oshogbo, and we could clearly indicate the traditional organization of the city. Briefly, the city could be viewed in terms of three fundamental principles: patrilineal descent, residential association, and political organization. The ultimate judicial and administrative authority was vested in the paramount chief, the Atoaja, who was regarded as the executive head, the supreme adjudicator, the legislator, the ritual leader, and the military commander in chief. Below the paramount chief were a series of hierarchical lines of chiefs, military, administrative, and ritual, to whom the king delegated responsibilities, duties, rights, and privileges. At the base of this essentially pyramidal political structure were the residential units—the compounds. To facilitate administration, the community was divided into somewhat amorphous and mutable clusters of compounds, each administered by a chief. Each compound contained large aggregates of domestic families, often bound by patrilineal ties, that acknowledged the authority and jurisdiction of their senior male. Residence was patrilocal and polygyny the desired marital state. The compound, with a membership varying from 15 to 500 persons, was in a sense the structural epitome of the political organization, and it was in the compound that the matrix of the jural and administrative organization was to be found.

In common with many West African peoples and, indeed, with many other societies outside of West Africa, kinship was the articulating principle of social organization and the primary determinant of behavior in every aspect of social life in Oshogbo. Descent was traced through the patrilineal line; kinsmen sharing common patrilineal ties formed corporate units or lineage groups.

The Yoruba lineage group was the largest group of living agnates to trace descent from a common male ancestor; marriage and sexual relations were forbidden between them. Their lineage was not an agglomerate of undifferentiated individuals, but a highly segmented structure.

Each lineage group, or a large segment of it, shared a common residence, although the limits of lineage and residence units were not necessarily coterminous. Frequently, two or more lineages lived in a single compound or members of a single lineage resided in two or more compounds. Although the lineage as such did not have explicit functions in the political organization, the highest political offices were vested in certain partilineages. The occupation of each male was determined by lineage affiliation, and male members of a lineage followed the same occupation. The vast majority of lineages were engaged in agricultural pursuits, and subsistence cultivation of the soil was the primary means of livelihood of the Oshogbo people, who lived in the town proper and farmed the peripheral lands. Often the farmers made a daily journey to and fro, although during crucial periods of the farming cycle they might remain in temporary shelters on the farms for a period of a fortnight or more. Other male occupations, such as blacksmithing, drumming, and carving, were regulated by the male members of traditionally designated lineages.

All able women in Oshogbo worked, and almost all were petty traders, but a woman's occupation was not, as was the male's, a function of lineage affiliation. The lineage exercised certain rights in real property and inheritance over its members, regulated marriages, and determined the native cult adherence. Patrilineal ancestor worship was a fundamental part of the religious system. The dead were buried beneath the mud floor of the room in which they had lived.

Thus, Oshogbo was a large community characterized by the close integration and interweaving of its social, economic, religious, and political aspects. Limited economic, differentiation and specialization existed and were intimately associated with the lineage structure. Apart from the usual differentiation of social roles, based on sex, age, and economic specialization, individuals were differentiated in accordance with political rank and power. Kin and residential groupings provided additional social differentials.

A number of factors contributed to the successful development of this study, the most important being the operation of the team. The field assistants collected large quantities of scientific data and functioned with a high *esprit de corps*. They were liked by the people and were able to establish an excellent rapport with large segments of the community. The cooperative spirit that pervaded the team permitted checking and comparing of collected data as part of normal procedure. We were also fortunate in the excellent relationships that I was able to develop with the king, who was my major informant, and other key individuals in the community. Without the information and advice that the king and the other key informants gave us, the study might have proceeded at a much slower pace, and our insights into the behavior of the people of Oshogbo might have been reduced. The excellent relationships that existed between the townspeople and myself and the team increased the quality of the data collected and allowed us to rapidly check the data and quickly ascertain reliability. These factors probably outweighed our difficulties and brought about the successful conclusion of the study.

But mistakes we did make, and the most serious was the census. We underestimated the opposition and resistance to the census and obviously missed many clues that would have reduced and possibly eliminated the census conflict. Closer attention to the census opposition, which we were cognizant of, and broader and deeper knowledge of the Yoruba culture might have alerted us earlier to the census difficulties and given us a greater opportunity to nullify the resistance among the people to the census. However, once the people recognized that we were their friends, would cause them no harm, the census conflict was resolved, and we were able to collect data with few difficulties. In the later analysis of Oshogbo, the census, demographic, and other statistical data proved to be extremely useful in understanding Oshogbo.

We also overestimated the reliability and usefulness of the educated people as informants. Many had spent years away from Oshogbo and could be classified as deviants to the traditional culture. We had expected them to give us much more critical aid than they were able to do, but, as I have already indicated, they were extremely useful in our general understanding of Yoruba culture and the town. Finally, it is now clear to us that we attempted too much. Our subject was too broad, our goal too difficult, and we became involved in too many activities. It is possible that we could have penetrated deeper if the scope of the problem had been reduced and our energies channeled into more specific problems.

PART II: GWELO, AN URBAN COMMUNITY IN RHODESIA

Problem, Theory, and Research Design

In 1955 I was awarded a Ford Foundation grant to carry out a study of an urban community in either Northern or Southern Rhodesia. The grant included a three-month stay in England to examine and locate comparative data, contact British anthropologists who had worked in similar areas, and to select the town to be studied. After considerable correspondence with the social scientists of the Rhodes-Livingstone Institute and lengthy discussions with British anthropologists, I decided to study a town in Southern Rhodesia. Few, if any, urban studies had been conducted in Southern Rhodesia, and the Rhodes-Livingstone Institute had carried out considerable urban research in Northern Rhodesia (Zambia), so it seemed logical for me to concentrate on a town in that area. My aim was twofold: to discover the underlying principles of organization and the form and content of the social relationships that make up the social systems of Central African towns, and to shed some light on the complex problems of adaptations, modifications, and changes in the social patterns that have occurred in Africa as a result of Westernization and urbanization. I also wished to select an urban community that was representative of the towns of Southern Rhodesia and generally reflected the over-all pattern of change that was developing in this part of Africa.

Using these objectives as my major criteria, I began to scrutinize the Colonial Office files and other London sources for reliable data on Rhodesian towns. It soon became clear that my choice was restricted to the seven major towns of Rhodesia; Salisbury, Bulawayo, Umtali, Gwelo, Gatooma, Que Que, and Fort Victoria. These towns had been established by Europeans, since cities, large or small, did not exist in the Rhodesias before the advent of European domination and colonization. All the towns were located in the high ridge country and had climates that were extremely agreeable to Europeans. Since we were seeking a comparatively small city with few complexities, Bulawayo and Salisbury were eliminated as too large and too complex. Fort Victoria was excluded as being atypical and Gatooma as lacking the major elements of change we were seeking. Que Que lacked economic diversification, and Umtali was geographically remote with ethnic and economic complexities that could cause difficulties. Gwelo, by elimination, seemed to be our choice, but Gwelo's vital statistics reinforced this decision. The town was not too large, having a population of approximately 25,000 Africans and 7,000 Europeans. It was the commercial and industrial hub for the surrounding farmlands, and Western economic, social, and political forms seemed to provide the basic social matrix. It appeared to be a city of flux and change with a highly migratory and unstable African population and a rapidly developing European core. Our data in London indicated that Gwelo was typical of the Central African towns and appeared to be an excellent choice. When the High Commissioner for the Rhodesias informed us that it was possible for him to rent and reserve a modern house for us in Gwelo, months before we arrived, the selection became final.

With our city chosen, we could turn to a consideration of the methods to be employed in the field. Our field methods were determined by our previous experiences in Oshogbo, our discussions in London, and the working conditions we expected to find in the city of Gwelo. The population of Gwelo was much smaller than Oshogbo, and the town was administered by Europeans, so it appeared that a team of six to eight field assistants would be more than enough to carry out an efficient field study. Although our data indicated that Gwelo would have a more transient African population and be tribally more heterogeneous than Oshogbo, we did not think that these factors would increase the complexity to such an extent that more than eight field assistants would be needed.

As in the Oshogbo study, we planned to employ statistics and questionnaires wherever possible, to use random-sample devices and a sample census, and to pilot-test all questionnaires. We also faced the probability of making our working sample larger than the normal 10 percent. We were quite sure that the high degree of transiency among the Africans would gradually reduce the number of informants we would be able to retain in the study. We assumed that the longer the study ran, the greater would be our loss of informants. This problem could be overcome by making the original sample larger and gradually adding randomly picked new informants as the older informants dropped out. However, after six months of field work, we assumed that a cut-off point would develop, and that it would no longer be feasible or practical to add more informants to the sample. We also intended to base the census and statistics on area sampling, since we knew that line maps of Gwelo and Southern Rhodesia were available.

But other social factors complicated our field methodology. We were quite aware that Central Africa, and particularly Southern Rhodesia, were plural societies characterized by their social conflicts mainly between Europeans and Africans. The Rhodesian towns were created by Europeans, and virtually all power was vested in them. Socially as well as economically, Africans were subject to rules and rigid constraints that had no applicability to the white segment of the population. These barriers could result not only in apathy and frustration, but could engender bitter resentment causing marked cleavages between black and white in all aspects of social life. Most of the African population, by Rhodesian law, lived in segregated areas or locations on the periphery of Gwelo in the periurban area. These locations were built and owned by the European municipality. When an African found a job, he was assigned living quarters in the location by the Office of Native Affairs. The rent that was assigned to each African was paid for him by the European concern that employed him. Loss of a job by an African usually caused his eviction from his quarters on the location. By Rhodesian law only Africans could live in the locations. The exception was the European supervisor who administered the location. Around Gwelo were four African locations and one Coloured location that housed the majority of Africans and Coloured people. Europeans were allowed to live in the municipal township and by law forbidden to live in the African locations. Our original objective was to study a plural society composed of both the African and European cultures. Under these circumstances we assumed that racial difficulties would develop with both the White and African populations. Gwelo was obviously a city of intense racial antagonism, as were all Rhodesian cities, and it did appear that good rapport with one racial group would antagonize the other racial group. While we were still in London, our limited data indicated that initially we would probably receive some cooperation from both major racial groups. We had no method by which we could determine how long this initial or superficial cooperation would last, nor could we determine whether the hostility of either group was sufficient to prevent the study from moving beyond its initial and superficial stages. These were intangibles that could only be answered in the field, and we had no alternative but to assume that we would be able to carry the study to completion and be unmolested by the government, racial groups, or any other unit during our stay in Gwelo.

But we were faced with other difficulties. We were unable to locate in London any maps, statistics, or data about any of the four locations. Thus the decision of which locations to study had to be put off until we arrived in Gwelo, and much of our early specific planning, which usually eases the initial contact period, had to be postponed. However, all general planning could be and was developed to a much greater extent than had been possible in the Oshogbo study. It was quite clear to us, however, that the intangibles in Gwelo could be major obstacles to any depth analysis in Gwelo. The racial antagonisms and conflicts indicated to us that our future in Gwelo was marked with uncertainties and social difficulties.

Passive or Adaptational Research

After a fruitful three months' stay in London, we sailed for South Africa and in early September, 1955, landed in Durban. From Durban we drove via Johannesburg and Bulawayo to Gwelo, where we found a modern European home awaiting us. According to Rhodesian law we could live only in the European areas. We could visit the African locations as much as we desired but not live there. The Director of Native Affairs issued us a pass that permitted us to go back and forth to the location undisturbed by the police or civil administrators.

The initial weeks in Gwelo presented a number of interesting problems. We had some advantages that we had not had in Oshogbo. Available to us were the results of studies of other towns in southern and central Africa that were not unlike Gwelo, and these provided us, in the early phases of the study, with critical insights, essential clues, and bases for comparisons.

We were also operating in a European-imposed economic and social framework with which we were familiar. The Europeans were not a mystery to us, and we could associate with them and gain knowledge of their values and behavior patterns. We were not culturally isolated or cut off from the outside world as we had been in Oshogbo, and as a result initially we had a better understanding of our field situation. These facts and experiences made our initial orientation in Gwelo somewhat easier.

But there were critical problems in Gwelo, too. There was an obvious absence of any traditional organization that tended to structure the social life of the Africans. There were many factors contributing to this. The most important included the ethnic heterogeneity of the African population, its transience and lack of commitment to town life, and the insurmountable barriers to economic and social achievement placed before the Africans by the Europeans. Our initial probing also indicated a paucity of formal associations. In addition, the administration of the location rested exclusively in European hands. In many Rhodesian towns there are African Advisory Boards, which, in principle, help administer the locations. In Gwelo the Board was defunct. Thus there were no formally constituted or acknowledged native authorities through whom the people could be reached and the purposes of the study publicized and explained.

We had already visited the four locations in the Gwelo area and had decided to concentrate on the two largest: Mambo-Monomotapa and Senka. The Mambo-Monomotapa location was built by the municipality and administered by it, but Senka had been constructed by the central government and was controlled by a supervisor appointed by the central government. Senka had a population of approximately 1,500 people and was nine miles from the center of Gwelo, while Mambo-Monomotapa had been built five miles from the city and had more than 9,500 inhabitants. The other two locations appeared to be atypical, one extremely small and too far away to be conveniently worked, and the other inhabited only by railway workers. It was quite obvious, even with the most superficial inquiries and investigations, that Senka and Mambo-Monomotapa were the key locations in the Gwelo area. Neither of these locations had any apparent African leadership or any structure of government.

Our difficulties in publicizing the study and explaining our purposes to the Gwelo community were resolved with the help of the African field assistants whom we hired in the first few weeks we were in Gwelo. Each field assistant had to speak and read English and be conversant with two of the major indigenous tongues, preferably either Shona or Ndebele and Bemba. The two major ethnic groups in Gwelo were the Shona and Ndebele peoples, and knowledge of Bemba would be helpful with immigrants from Northern Rhodesia, present-day Zambia. Since there were few secondary schools in Southern Rhodesia and few graduates of these schools, we were forced to accept men who had graduated from primary schools. This caused difficulties, in the later stages of the study, since with more education the field assistants would have been able to handle the more complex questionnaires more easily and more rapidly.

We were not greatly concerned with the ethnic identity of the field assistants, since tribalism in a culturally heterogeneous community is not usually very significant. When an African comes to an urban community in Central Africa, he must accept the concept of strangers, for he is usually forced to work, associate, and live with people of different tribal groups. Since the African populations of all Central African cities have been reared in their traditional rural villages and have migrated to the urban centers, there was no possibility of hiring field assistants who were Gwelo-born. We received three experienced field assistants, with qualifications similar to the three we hired, from the Rhodes-Livingstone Institute, with whom I had excellent working relationships.[4] Since strangers were accepted in Gwelo, we had no problems in introducing our field assistants into the locations.

Our procedure in publicizing the study was to visit the churches and schools on the locations with the team of African field assistants and explain the study and its purposes. The schoolchildren would usually carry the information about the study to their parents, relatives, and neighbors, and the church members would relate the information to their friends and associates. Notices and stories about the study were placed in the African and European newspapers. Finally we received permission from the municipal authorities to announce our plans about the study over the public-address system, which is an essential feature of most African locations. The information was announced over the public-address system in six different languages for a period of a week, three times daily, allowing us to contact all the different cultural groups in Gwelo. Thus we were able to achieve considerable publicity, and the African populations of both Mambo-Monomotapa and Senka locations quickly learned about the American, his study, and the team of African re-

---

[4] I was fortunate in establishing close working relationships with the Rhodes-Livingstone Institute in the early stages of the Gwelo study that resulted in my being able to borrow three of their field assistants for the duration of the study.

searchers that were working for him. However, because of the absence of any African leadership or any meaningful African social group that might give a stamp of approval to the work, apart from the churches, which were socially isolated from one another, we received no sense of acceptance or consent from any segment of the African community. On the other hand, there was no overt hostility to our proposed work from the Africans so we felt that far more concrete and intensive work could begin.

In the initial phase of the study, which lasted approximately three months, we were able to achieve a number of our objectives. We planned, as we had previously done in Oshogbo, to base our random-sample census on area sampling. In Gwelo, maps of the location were available that listed every structure and assigned to each building or residence a number. The major location, Mambo-Monomotapa, was divided into living quarters for married men accompanied by their wives and children, and residences for single men or men whose wives and children were not with them. The houses in Mambo, the area for married men, were all the same. Each house had four rooms: two bedrooms, a livingroom, kitchen, bath, and lavatory. Each house contained running water, electricity, and a wood stove. In Monomotapa, the main area for single men, the housing structures were quite different. Each structure contained between twenty and forty rooms with central bathing and lavatory facilities. Four men were usually assigned to one room regardless of ethnic origin, education, or work. It was quite possible for men speaking four different languages to share the same room and act toward each other as distinct strangers. Our procedure in Mambo was to include every tenth house in our sample and in Monomotapa to select 10 percent of the rooms in all the structures. All the individuals residing in the selected houses or rooms were included in the census. We divided Mambo-Monomotapa into six separate areas, and each assistant was assigned an area where he worked for the duration of the study. Each assistant was allotted forty rooms or houses to enumerate during the census. During this period of orientation, each field assistant visited his area daily and established relationships with the people to be enumerated and others living in the same area. The objective of each field assistant was to develop rapport with as many informants as possible in his area and thus have a check and comparison on the people included in the sample census. The sample census included 2,500 people.

The census in Gwelo was intended to collect data in depth, and in this sense each interview resembled a case history. We were interested in the entire development of each individual and recorded all data available from birth to the present. We made a complete record of each person's early childhood, education, occupations, marriages, divorces, wives, children, bride-price payments, movements to and from traditional birth place, membership in associations, religion, ethnic status, and kin and village relationships. We intended to collect as much data as we could in the initial interview, but before the census interview took place each field assistant had, at the most, been able to develop only a superficial relationship with his selected informants. Although no deep relationships were established, the census was surprisingly very successful. There was little discernable opposition to it, few recalcitrant informants, and no organized resistance. There were several reasons for this favorable response to the census in Gwelo. The life of an African in Gwelo was regulated and largely determined by a seemingly endless series of forms, questionnaires, and passes. He was accustomed to them and intimidated by them. He saw the census as just one more inevitable and incomprehensible form to which he must submit if he was to remain working in town. He also saw it as an act of a European against which he had no organizations or leaders who might act as a focus for resistance. Had there been, the census might easily have been prevented. In this particular situation, the formlessness of the internal political system in Gwelo was a strong factor in our favor.

Besides taking the census and interviewing informants in the random sample, we also wished to establish a panel group that would operate as a sounding board for us and allow us to test our ideas and hypotheses and review the questionnaires. Immediately upon our arrival in Gwelo, we began to compile a list of the important, respected, rich, successful, and educated Africans. In a short period of time, we had a list of twenty men whom the Africans classified as successful. These men, for the duration of the study, met in my house twice a week and openly discussed a variety of subjects. At the meetings, which usually lasted for three or four hours, we discussed racialism, African migrations, marriage laws, kin groups, ethnic hostilities, budgets, wages, and similar topics. My function was to get the group to start talking and then withdraw, entering again only if there was a lull in the conversation. Usually the conversation was quite heated as the Africans attempted to analyze and explain their behavior and cultural world. Since any subject was permitted, I was unable to record these conversations until after the meeting was over. These discussions could be viewed as revolutionary, antiwhite, and seditious, and even though the Africans trusted me they feared the repercussions if a record of the talks fell into the hands of the white authorities. We also had to be careful not to break any of the racial laws, or the meeting would have been forbidden by the municipal authorities.[5] Probably the most important aspect of the panel board was that it was a check on the data collected by the field assistants and vice versa. Every questionnaire that we used in the field was pretested through the panel, and this enabled us to avoid many mistakes. The panel thus acted as a testing ground for each major questionnaire. Moreover, since we were working on two levels, we were able to see and collect behavioral data that we might otherwise have missed.

It is clear to me now, although I did not realize it at the time, that participation in the panel group conveyed high prestige on its members. It appears that in a cultural atmosphere in which racial stratification is dominant, close association with a member of the dominant racial group may bring to the depressed group greater prestige and higher social status. This kind of social relationship also allows avenues of communication to develop that may result in greater emotional and material benefits for the depressed individuals. If a crisis or critical situation develops, the member of the dominant social group becomes a channel or source that may possibly help to alleviate or reduce the severity of a difficult situation. In Gwelo, this could mean protection from the police, the waiving of minor infractions or misdemeanors, such as improperly made-out passes or breaking the curfew, and the possibility of achieving a more rewarding job. In other words, I became a social mechanism by which the extreme racial laws and prohibitions in Rhodesia could be diffused or blunted. Another reason for the success of the panel group was that we liked each other. I found the Africans to be interesting, and they were curious about an American whose major activity seemed to be associating with Africans.

In Gwelo, as in Oshogbo, the identity assigned to me and the image the people formed of me were of central importance. I wished to develop in the early months of the study good rapport with all sections of the community, but in Gwelo this was difficult, since great hostility and enmity existed between the African and European populations. I immediately disclaimed any any association with the government, which had given its somewhat unenthusiastic acquiescence to the field work, and attempted to identify myself as a research worker and as an American. The success of these efforts was minimal, for the

---

[5] Laws prohibited Africans from drinking alcoholic beverages, being in the municipal township after 6 P.M., and wandering around the city without specific permission between the hours of 6 P.M. and 6 A.M.

Africans saw me—as they see every white man—as an inimical authority. Despite my continuous efforts to modify it, this initial image did not change basically. In retrospect it seems clear that, almost inevitably, this had to be so. In a society in which racial tensions and conflict is the predominant theme underlying all relationships between black and white, it is unrealistic to expect an African to react on any other basis. However, in the early phases of the study, it was our hope that in time the ascription could be changed.

We also had to contend with the European community. In our original plans, we intended to study a plural world, both the African and European cultures. Initially, our relationships with the Europeans were excellent. It was rather easy to make friends, and we quickly had access to documents and people. However, when I indicated to the town council that I intended systematically and scientifically to examine the behavior of the European community, as well as the African, difficulties developed. The Europeans regarded themselves as being the same as any other European or white community and could not understand why I should want to study them. In their view, it was quite proper to analyze the African but not the European world. They saw the study as a threat to their world and as a criticism of their behavior and policies. Despite much discussion and much pleading on my part, the town council refused to cooperate and indicated that the town would not officially sanction the study. They did agree to allow any European who so desired to participate in the study. Needless to say, without the "blessing" of the community most of the Europeans refused to cooperate. We were given access to documents, could delve into the history of the town, peruse maps and study the town layout, but we were refused permission to attend council meetings, examine the files of the department of native affairs, or systematically and randomly interview Europeans. Thus we were forced to alter our plans and to concentrate mainly on a study of the African locations.

Once we began to contact and interview the Africans, a disturbing situation began to develop. My field assistants reported that African policemen were interrogating our African informants after they had completed their interviews with them. The police were trying to discover what information the informants were conveying to us. It was quite obvious to us that if the police continued to interrogate our informants, the study would abruptly end. The Africans would begin to refuse to talk to us, and what little data we received would be unreliable. For the study to continue, the harassment by the police had to end. Since the Gwelo study had the approval of both the British Colonial

Office and the Rhodesian Central Government, it would have been quite awkward and embarrassing for the Gwelo authorities if we were forced to discontinue the study because of overt local hostility to the project. I mentioned this when I met with the head of Rhodesian intelligence in Gwelo to complain about the interrogation of our informants, and he agreed to countermand his original orders and end the harassment.

Nevertheless, the threat of harassment hung over us for the remainder of the study, and our relationships with the European community never became friendly. With the exception of a few close friends and some European informants who were friendly, most Europeans were civil, but basically uncooperative. The study was allowed to continue but without the cooperation or participation of the European population. The European community regarded us, throughout the duration of the study, as a threat to their way of life and they viewed us with hostility.

These initial encounters in Gwelo during the contact period point up two fundamental differences between the Gwelo and Oshogbo studies that greatly affected both field ventures. The first was the more random and unstructured system of social relationships that operated among Gwelo Africans as compared to the highly complex and organized system in Oshogbo. The second was the very minimal amount of racial antagonism in Oshogbo as compared to the deep cleavages and hostilities between blacks and whites that permeated all aspects of life in Gwelo.

Active Research

Our intensive study of Gwelo presented a number of interesting problems, many of which were quite different from those in Oshogbo. In Gwelo there was no institutional focus or principle of organization that provided a common framework for behavior apart from the remote and broad structuring provided by European industries, administration, and social behavior. Our task was to discover the types and channels of social interaction in this community characterized by ethnic heterogeneity, the absence of discrete groups, high mobility, incomplete families, a disproportionate sex ratio, and economic and social barriers of great magnitude.

We selected from the original census a subsample of heads of households based on occupational differentiation and tribal affiliation. The unit picked for intensive study was not necessarily a family, since much of the Gwelo population was composed of single men or men who had left all or part of their families in the reserves. In this part of the study we had two major aims. The first concerned migration, urban and job stability, the composition of urban families, and other relevant socio-demographic data. The circulation between town and reserve and among towns posed a number of problems. Why do people come to town? How long do they stay, and why do they leave? What are the attractions of town life that cause so many men to trek so far? How do factors such as age, education, occupation, and residence of family influence urban stability and commitment? In what explicit ways do the social and economic constraints hamper the development of a stable urban population? What are the pulls toward and pushes from town life that properly belong to the reserve?

The second part of the study dealt with the network of social relationships an African established in town. Because the range of kin present in Gwelo was almost inevitably incomplete and because many of the rights and obligations that give substance to traditional kin bonds were absent, each person had to discover and establish his own set of relevant kin bonds. What, then, were the kinship obligations in Gwelo, and to whom did they extend? To what new uses were kinship bonds put, and in what situations were they recognized?

Tribalism offered another category of interaction that could be drawn upon and put to new uses. All Africans in Gwelo were born and reared in traditional villages. They grew up with people whom they usually knew from birth, and were members of the same tribe. Social relationships were personal, and each individual established and maintained a web of personal ties that was based on traditional life and activities. Strangers and members of different tribes were rare visitors, and few behavior patterns existed to deal with them. The world of a villager was relatively simple and well structured. When a villager migrated to town, however, he had to live in a culturally heterogeneous world and associate with tribal groups that were different from his own. He had to accept strangers and learn how to associate with them without conflict. He had to move and live in a world for which his socialization process and previous experiences had not prepared him. It was this new way of life, how old patterns were changed and new ones accepted, the problems and difficulties that arose with the retention of old patterns, and the manner in which adjustments were made that concerned us.

We were also interested in neighborhood ties, the more formal associational relationships that provided alternative links between people, and the bonds of friendship and work that could rival the claims of kinship. Were new friendships mainly established from work and neighborhood, or were new relationships kept to a minimum by the bonds of kinship and village ties? The new political relationships between Europeans and Africans also interested us. In 1955 racial tensions and conflicts were increasing and were manifested in all aspects of Rhodesian life. It was essential to understand the new attitudes and values that produced these sharp tensions and conflicts and created a highly structured political world.

Finally, we were interested in examining the forms of institutional life that existed in the location. In the villages, the life of an individual was molded by traditional patterns of behavior, and an individual was anchored by many stable institutions. The world of the location was a world of change and a place where traditional institutions were being remodeled or new forms of behavior being created. For example, religion has been one of the cornerstones of traditional behavior in Africa. In the location, religion seems to dominate many aspects of life and, for most of the people, the Christian church appears to be the stable force around which much of their lives is built. It becomes a place of social interaction, where new ideas and concepts are developed, but where stability still exists. The church, for the African appears to be one of the major links between his traditional world and the new changing world of the location. Thus it was our hope that by studying these institutions and relationships we could discover the intersecting networks and new institutions that gave a measure of order and stability to the Gwelo African social system.

To a very large extent, we depended upon questionnaires and interviews by field assistants to provide information in Gwelo. Much of the material was easily adapted to this particular method, but I think we might have achieved more understanding in many areas had we been able to use a less structured interviewing technique, as we had in Oshogbo. Several factors made this virtually impossible. The use of field guides involves repetitive visits and very informal relationships and thus requires that one have informants who are positively involved in the study. This was not true in Gwelo. For the most part our informants were passive. They were willing to answer questions, provided that the interviews were not too lengthy or the questions did not probe sensitive areas. The expectation that in time our relationships might improve and our informants become more responsive was not realized. On the contrary, some informants became less docile and more reluctant to answer any question as the study continued. As the study progressed many came to realize that I had very little, if any, actual authority or power over their lives and that they were not compelled to cooperate with me. At the same time, we were unable to build up a great enough fund of good will upon which to draw. The tensions be-

tween black and white and even between black and black pre-
cluded, I think, the development of relationships that would
permit the kind of intensive questioning that had taken place in
Oshogbo. In addition, less structured field guides also required
field workers who were better trained and more capable than
those available for the Gwelo study. The resistance of our informants and the performance of my assistants necessitated that
I continuously cross-check and test the data, and this made the
use of structured interviews more convenient. We also faced one
other problem in our interviews in Gwelo that did not exist in
Oshogbo. This was a consequence of the residential unstability
of the Gwelo population, which we had anticipated and had
hoped to control. It was our intention to interview the sample
households continuously for a nine-month period, replacing the
drop-outs wherever possible. During this time a not insignificant
number of our informants left Gwelo either to return to the
reserves or go to another town, and we found that many of them
could not be replaced, so that for a portion of our sample the
data are incomplete.

The barriers and reluctance manifested in the interviewing
phase of the Gwelo study were reflected in my own work. The
initial reaction to me, by the Africans, was determined mainly
by the single criterion of my white skin. This reaction was modified but not basically changed during my stay. I was able to form
some relationships that were relatively free of the consciousness
of color, but for the most I remained primarily in the role of a
white man, a role that carried with it a considerable, though in
my case ill-defined, threat. One important consequence of the
almost uniform, although largely passive, antagonism toward
whites was that all black-white relationships had to be maintained on a level that prevented the hostility from erupting into
the open. This limited the type of question I could ask, as well as
the quality of data I could obtain. There were many areas of
Gwelo social life that were accessible to me, but there were others
that remained closed for the duration of the study. The most
notable example was our inability to either visit or study the
beer hall. We were interested in the leisure activities and habits
of the Africans after their work had been completed for the day.
Most Africans, living on the location, relaxed in the beer halls
where only native beer was sold. The beer hall was built and
run by the municipality, and most Africans view it as a black
retreat or sanctuary. Three times I attempted to visit the beer
hall, and on each occasion I was forced to leave. My field assistants were permitted to use the beer hall, but they could not interview anyone there since the Africans clearly indicated that they
would not talk while under the influence of alcohol. The hostility

of the Africans was great enough to block any further attempts to study them in the beer hall.

Furthermore, even when I was permitted to observe social behavior, I usually felt that my presence not only constrained this behavior but altered it. However, I *was* able to form close relationships with the panel group, who met with me regularly. They were a verbal and cooperative group whose insights guided me in formulating hypotheses and questionnaires. Without the help and insights of this group, the study would have been much more difficult to carry out.

The conditions in Gwelo led to a field situation in which my own researches and those of my staff were more independent of one another than they had been in Oshogbo. In many areas we had to depend either on the questionnaires or on my interviews and observations. There was not the continuous feedback between the survey data and my own material that had existed in Oshogbo. Thus in many areas we were not able to obtain the multileveled understanding and additional insights that more integrated methods might have afforded. Nevertheless, the two methods were certainly supplementary and, given the particular circumstances in Gwelo, probably yielded more than either method could have alone.

Bowing Out

In planning the Gwelo study we had allotted a year for field work. Since we were attempting less and were more experienced than in Oshogbo, we had estimated that a year would be sufficient time to carry out the Gwelo study. As the later stages of the study developed, we began to check off completed items and to re-examine our data. After carefully reviewing our work, we came to the conclusion that we had collected more than sufficient material to satisfy the objectives of the study. We could articulate the Gwelo social system and understood the major tenets that controlled behavior on the location. To stay longer would require us to enlarge the scope of the study and redefine our goals. It became clear to us that the study was over; it was time to leave.

There was an even more practical reason for leaving. We had enough funds for one year in the field and to stay longer would have required securing additional funds.

It was not difficult to leave Gwelo. With few exceptions our relationships to both Africans and European were distant and formal, for we had been generally unable to develop close ties or establish intimate friendships. Both the Africans and Europeans viewed us with hostility and as a threat to their existence. We were not accepted or trusted, nor did we trust the Africans or the Europeans. The cultural atmosphere in Rhodesia, with its emphasis on racial conflict and prohibitions against Africans, was a constrained atmosphere in which we had to be very careful not to break any laws and to follow the correct behavior for Europeans. We were constantly being watched. It is not easy to live in a society in which behavior is so restricted and guarded, and we left Gwelo with a sigh of relief, as though a heavy weight had been removed from our chests. We were free once more and could behave without closely guarding our actions.

Most social situations are two-sided, and it was not easy to leave my field assistants, with whom I had established very satisfactory relationships. In these relationships the norms of Gwelo did not prevail, and a healthy bond existed between them and me. During the study, I saw them at least twice a day, and usually more often. When we left, new jobs had to be secured for them, and they had to be protected from any hostility that the study may have engendered against them. We were fortunate in being able to secure fairly safe jobs for three of the assistants, whose new employers had full knowledge of their work with me and felt that it added rather than detracted from their skills. The three field assistants who had been sent to me by the Rhodes-Livingstone Institute decided to return to Lusaka and continue their work with the Institute.

I also had excellent relationships with the members of the panel group. Before leaving Gwelo, my obligation to these men was to safeguard them from possible harassments by the white community in the future. To some extent they were protected by the positions they held, but the white community was fully aware that they met with me regularly. To what extent this was resented was difficult to ascertain, but any extensive relationships between white men and Africans were frowned upon. Again we were fortunate in being able to contact their superiors, who viewed the study and their relationships to me sympathetically.

In the final days of the study an interesting phenomena was brought to my attention by the panel group. At our last session some of the participants indicated to me that I had overlooked a number of individuals whom the African community felt had high status. It had never been our intention to invite *all* the Africans of high status but only a select few. A discussion group becomes unwieldy if it is too large, but some of the men whom we did not invite greatly resented having been overlooked. Apparently, membership in my panel group increased the status of an African, while those who were not included lost prestige in the eyes of the community. If we had acquired this information earlier in the study, we would have taken some action to correct our unintentional oversight.

Another difficult and embarrassing problem confronted us in the last days of the study. Because of the racial situation in Rhodesia and the hostility of the European population to the study, I had refused to grant any newspaper or radio interviews about it. I was concerned that the interviews would be used against the study or against the African people. Nevertheless, I had become quite friendly with a newspaper reporter who persistently pleaded for a story, and a week before we left Gwelo I granted his request. We gave him a carefully worded statement about our results and work, and he promised that it would be published without alterations. We felt that the publicity would be good for us, for our staff, and for future social studies in Rhodesia. We assumed the good faith of the newspaper. When the story was published two days later, it had been modified to support European racial policies in Rhodesia. The reporter apologized and explained that his editor had made the alterations over his objections. Even more embarrassing was the fact that the newspaper would not publish our denials and objections to the story. We had been naive in assuming that we could get a story published in the Rhodesian press that was favorable to the Africans and not to Europeans. Fortunately, the study was over and the harm was not too great. We were able to counteract some of the effect by publishing our original story in the African press.

Finally the end of the Gwelo study came. We had our last farewells in my Gwelo home, and the following day we boarded a train for Beira, a major East African port in Mozambique, and began the long trek home.

Summary and Evaluation

Although the Gwelo study was conducted in a cultural atmosphere marked by extreme racial hostilities and tensions, it was, in my judgment, relatively successful. It is true that we were not able to pursue our original goals, but the limited objectives that we finally achieved produced some rewarding results. We could clearly indicate the behavior of Africans on the location, and we had some knowledge of the problems confronting a plural community as a whole. Briefly, Gwelo was a European community of 7,000 Europeans and 25,000 Africans that had been founded in 1896. Like most of the other towns in Rhodesia, Gwelo was the commercial and industrial hub of the surrounding area. The African populations living on the location in Gwelo were tribally heterogeneous, with the great majority of Africans divided between the Shona (60.5 percent) and Ndebele (13.6 percent) tribes of Rhodesia. There were, however, also Africans from Portuguese East and West Africa, Zambia, South Africa, and Malawi.

The average Central African man is a highly transient and migratory individual. Typically, he leaves his traditional rural village to seek work in European-created industrial towns. Most often he comes alone, leaving his wife and children behind to tend his fields or cattle in his native village. After a considerable period of time in town, he returns to his traditional village, regardless of whether he has accomplished his objective or not. His goals were usually economic. The average African male sets out to seek capital to finance new equipment, to educate his children, and to buy seed, more cattle, or more land. Usually he returns to his village in debt, since living expenses on the locations absorb most of his wages. Eventually, after an undeterminate period in his village, he will return to the same town or even to a different one. This circulation between town and rural areas may continue for the greater part of his life.

There are two other major themes that pervade all aspects of social life in Gwelo. The first is the cleavage between black and white. Each color group forms a stratum in society clearly separated by customary and statutory laws. Virtually all power in the society is in the hands of the Europeans, who control the major mechanisms of coercion, whether they be political, social, religious, or economic. Europeans construct all laws, control the police and armed forces, dominate the expenditure of all funds, indicate who can be educated, and determine, with rare exceptions, what economic pursuits an individual can follow. The only recourse to European domination that the Africans have who reside in the urban location is to leave and return to their traditional villages. Thus, any African migrating to town must accept domination by the white man and be prepared to be coerced into specific areas of behavior.

The second pervasive characteristic of the African community in Gwelo is the discontinuities in the two social systems. With extremely rare exceptions, all Africans are born in their traditional villages and, although the most remote villages in Rhodesia have had some measure of contact with urban industrial patterns and European way of life, the average African male is still primarily a subsistence farmer conforming to traditional patterns of behavior. The essential elements in his social world are familial obligations and personal ties and contacts with his traditional village. When a traditional African man migrates to town, the patterns of urban life are imposed upon him. He must live and work in a world marked by a complex network of strange, unfamiliar, and conflicting relationships and roles. Most often the new network is disturbing and forces him to perform tasks and duties that may be repugnant to his traditional values. To a very large extent, his position in society and his economic and social relationships in the location are now determined by what he does as an individual and not by the traditional groups to which he belongs. His position in the productive system is the critical factor, not kinship, age, and sex, which are usually the major factors determining behavior in traditional structures. He begins to move in a world where relationships tend to be impersonal, amorphous, and transitory. New values and incentives begin to develop that are based on the urban world and have no relationship to the older traditional patterns. Often the new values threaten the old ways of life and are deeply incompatible with traditional social forms. The African stands alone, his old patterns of security are gone, and few counterparts to his traditional security system have developed in his urban world. Thus, when an African migrant comes to the urban world, he enters a social system marked by conflicts and tensions and lacking most traditional forms of security.

Another significant factor in the Gwelo social system is the marked discrimination in roles and occupations between Europeans and Africans. Occupational stereotypes have developed, and by custom and law certain specific categories have been marked off for each color group. Wage differentials are maintained, and professional and managerial roles are virtually barred to Africans. Education for Africans is very limited, but some Africans have received sufficient education to become clerks or schoolteachers with a very narrow range of responsibility and authority. Some commercial traders and skilled artisans have developed among the Africans, but they are allowed to operate only on the location and are not permitted to transact business in Gwelo proper. The vast majority of Africans inhabiting the Gwelo locations are unskilled, illiterate laborers or domestics performing menial, unrewarding tasks for which they receive wages barely sufficient to maintain them in town. Virtually all functionally significant roles are reserved for the white segment of the population.

Although Africans coming to town are forced to accept new patterns of behavior, some of the traditional differentiating characteristics, such as age, sex, kinship, and hereditary political rights, still persist in town, even though they have been greatly modified. Among these, kinship is probably the most important as it still provides some basis for relationships in the Gwelo location. People come to town because their kinsmen are there, and our data indicate that more than 50 percent of the men came to work in Gwelo because a kinsman was already there. A man has the right to seek food, aid, and shelter from his urban kin, and he is rarely refused. Most urban Africans will turn to their kin when such all-important events as death, sickness, marriage, births, loss of a job, and financial embarrassment occur. The importance of kinship is emphasized by the fact that a man in Gwelo almost invariably looks forward to returning to his kin and traditional village permanently. Thus an African in town has divided allegiances, for he must live in the urban world and still accept some of the traditional patterns of behavior that persist in town.

This, then, is Gwelo, a town of conflict and tension. It is a town in which the European dominates, and the African keeps shifting between the urban location and his traditional village. Finally, it is a world of shifting value systems in which the African is creating a new network of social relationships.

In retrospect the relative success of the Gwelo study can be attributed to three factors: the successful operation of the team, the panel group, and my own individual contacts. Although my field assistants had many deficiencies, they also had certain attributes that were an asset in Gwelo. Most important was the fact that we were able to weld them into a team with an *esprit de corps*. As the members of a team they supported each other and helped each other in their work. Although each field assistant worked independently and collected his data separately, they all compared notes and experiences and passed on their accumulated skills, knowledge, and contacts to each other. Sometimes, when the field situation was conducive to it, and the field assistants knew the same informants, they worked together. The assistants were also informants to me and to each other. At times, I discovered significant and key bits of information through the constant discussions and examinations of the data that the team performed as a whole. Each questionnaire was carefully reviewed by the team, and extraneous and faulty probes were eliminated. At our daily meetings a lively discussion took place in which faults were corrected, suggestions made, and new clues passed around. It was this cooperation and exchange of ideas and facts that overcame many of the team's deficiencies.

Nevertheless, the capabilities of the field assistants were limited by their education. They could handle only highly structured questionnaires and were constantly in need of direct supervision. Less structured questionnaires would have created too many difficulties to have been successfully employed by them. It took the field assistants many weeks to complete even the structured questionnaires. Obviously, more educated and talented field assistants would have allowed us to penetrate more deeply and collect more data about the population of Gwelo, but this was not possible at the time of the study. Today, it is conceivable that, in Gwelo, we could hire more educated field assistants and resolve many of these problems.

In many ways, the team of field assistants cannot be separated from the panel group. The panel met at my home, and under my direction they would discuss the problems we were experiencing in the field. They knew the values and problems of their people and often had invaluable suggestions and leads for they possessed insight and knowledge that were quite different from the field assistants' and that often opened up for us new areas of investigations. Although we never attained the flow and feedback of data that we had in Oshogbo, we were able to have considerable exchange of data between the team and the panel group, with me as the intermediary, as little actual contact existed between the field assistants and the panel members. One of the major difficulties in Gwelo was this lack of contact. If we had had more direct communication between the field assistants and the panel group, I think, in retrospect, that we would have achieved greater efficiency and possibly greater depth in the collection of data, even though the panel members perceived my field assistants as Africans with low status. However, I think in time healthy working relationships would have developed between the two groups.

My work was to direct the activities of the team, coordinate and manage the panel group, and collect data from informants. My rapport with the Africans was generally not nearly so good as that of my field assistants, but at times, in difficult situations or with people of high status, I was able to achieve sufficient rapport to collect reliable data. I also collected institutional data by visiting churches, schools, and governmental agencies, where I had less difficulty in establishing rapport. It was also my task to deal with all Europeans, and, fortunately, I was able to develop good rapport with a few Europeans who gave us considerable information on the history, government, demography, and social welfare of Gwelo. Although my activities, at times, were limited and although definite hostility existed toward me, I was still able to overcome many of these difficulties and create a relatively successful study. I have no doubts, however, that if we could have reduced the hostility of both the Europeans and the Africans toward us and created a better image in the society, we would have been able to penetrate deeper into the structure of the society and accumulate more significant data.

Probably the most difficult problem to contend with was the racial conflict between the white and black populations. It affected all aspects of the study and limited my own activities and those of my field assistants. It was quite obvious to us, after the first few months of the study, that neither the European or African populations trusted us. Both perceived us as a threat. It was beyond our powers to affect the racial situation in Rhodesia, nor were there other ways in which we could have reduced the hostility of the two groups toward us. It is interesting that we were able to collect large quantities of data, despite the hostilities.

Because of the transient nature of the African population, many of our informants left Gwelo during the study either to return to their villages or to move on to another town. Although we replaced many of these early drop-outs, we never did develop a satisfactory solution to this problem. Increasing the amount of time allotted to the field work might have alleviated the problem, but the African migratory patterns were an ongoing continuous process. Eventually with rare exception, all Gwelo Africans will leave the location and return to their traditional villages. Consequently, our data are not as complete as they could have been for approximately 15 percent of the sample. Unfortunately, I do not think there is a solution to this type of field problem.

There is one behavioral area where we could have achieved much more than we did, and that is in collecting data on African women. Most of our data on women were collected by men, as I had no female field assistants on my staff, nor were we able to hire any. Data on the personal and sexual behavior patterns of females were secured by my wife, for the women in Gwelo would not talk about their personal and sexual activities to men. An educated African female assistant would have been very helpful and could have collected much more data than we did.

Finally, it should be repeated that the Gwelo study was conducted in an atmosphere of violence, hatred, conflict, and tension. Under the circumstances, we did well, but many of the critical factors were beyond our control.

PART III: COMPARISON OF THE
OSHOGBO AND GWELO STUDIES

In both Oshogbo and Gwelo the aim of our study was twofold: to discover the underlying principles of organization and the form and content of the social relationships that made up the social systems of these towns, and to shed some light on the complex problems of the adaptations, modifications, and changes in social patterns that are occurring throughout Africa today as a result of Westernization and urbanization.

Gwelo and Oshogbo share many common characteristics. Each has a high population density. Oshogbo has a population that exceeds 120,000 Africans. Gwelo, although considerably smaller, numbers about 25,000 Africans and 7,000 whites. The underlying factors causing change in both towns are intrinsically similar and have been grouped under the headings of colonial rule, industrialization, or commerce. Their social systems are characterized by increasing social differentiation and economic diversification and specialization. The introduction of Western institutions and values has given rise to new sets of interests and values that are often deeply incompatible with and threatening to traditional social forms. Thus both Oshogbo and Gwelo are characterized by the existence of contradictory sets of interests and relationships, by the exacerbation of traditional conflicts and the development of new ones, and by many ambiguous choices that may be interpreted and manipulated differently by individuals or groups.

There are also striking differences between Gwelo and Oshogbo. Gwelo, a commercial and industrial hub for the surrounding farmlands, typifies the towns that predominate in central and southern Africa. They were created solely by Europeans and have grown largely in response to the needs of a European market economy (see Schwab, 1961). Western economic, social, and political forms provide the basic social matrix in Gwelo. Oshogbo, on the other hand, was a large, dense, and permanent settlement before European contact. Many of the existing Yoruba towns, including Oshogbo, were probably founded in the eighteenth and nineteenth centuries. Today Oshogbo has an indigenous Yoruba population that is ethnically homogeneous and stable. Although there are some strangers who have migrated to Oshogbo, and others who have left Oshogbo to seek work or education in Ibadan and Lagos, migration plays virtually little or no part in the life of the community. In Gwelo, the African population is tribally heterogeneous, polyglot, migratory, and unstable although most are Shona and Ndebele. Typically, an African leaves his traditional village to seek work in town. After some time in Gwelo, he will return to his village. The circulation between town and rural village may continue for the greater part of a man's life. Unlike Oshogbo, there are only a very few Africans in Gwelo who are committed to town life and regard Gwelo as their home.

Oshogbo is mainly an agriculture community, but the economy in recent years has expanded, new occupations have developed, and there is a new emphasis on a market and impersonal monetary system. The Africans in the Gwelo location participate in a Western economic system mainly as unskilled laborers. When an African migrates to town, the patterns of town life are imposed on him, and he must live and work in a world characterized by unfamiliar and conflicting sets of roles and relationships. The transition from the rural economy to urban industrialism is abrupt, and the African is forced to reject traditional patterns and familial obligations. The African in Oshogbo has a kin-bound social system (see Schwab, 1955) based on segmentary lineages; the rules of kinship regulate and coordinate social behavior in almost all spheres of activity. The centralized administrative and jural authority is composed of a paramount chief (Oba) and a series of lesser administrative and ritual chiefs. Gwelo is controlled by a European minority in whom virtually all power is vested. Every aspect of life, social, economic, and political, is dominated by the cleavages and conflicts between Europeans and Africans. In Oshogbo, the effects of Western industrialized civilization have been less direct and more diluted than in Gwelo. There are no permanent settlers in Oshogbo, and no large-scale alienation of or sale of land to outsiders or Europeans has yet occurred. In Gwelo Europeans own at least 5 percent of the best lands, and fourth-generation Europeans are beginning to exert themselves. Finally, the people of Oshogbo live in a highly complex, organized, and structured system, whereas the Africans of Gwelo are unorganized and have a more random and unstructured system of social relationships.

I think that there is no doubt that the Oshogbo study was more successful than the Gwelo study. Although the methods employed in both studies were quite similar, the range of material covered was wider and we penetrated deeper into basic social processes in Oshogbo. The Oshogbo material is also more valid in the sense that it conforms more closely to social reality. There are many reasons for this. The field assistants in Oshogbo were better educated and more capable. They were able to act independently, handle complex problems, and manage the unexpected. They were capable of developing interviewing techniques and employing complex questionnaires and guides. Eventually they were able to function without direct supervision and gradually developed the ability to recognize what was important and to penetrate beyond the superficial facts and behavior. My field assistants in Gwelo were limited by their education and their command of written languages. Complex interviewing techniques or questionnaires could not be used by them, and they were unable to comprehend the social process to the same extent as my Oshogbo assistants. Also, my Oshogbo assistants were Yoruba and had been reared in the culture they were studying. They spoke the language fluently and understood the shadings and nuances of the culture. It was easy for them to establish rapport and develop relationships with their informants. These relationships deepened over time and resulted in a fuller understanding of behavior than would have been otherwise achieved. Because Gwelo is ethnically heterogeneous, polyglot, and basically European dominated, we could not fully duplicate this field condition there. Nevertheless, at times ethnic ties helped to increase rapport in Gwelo, since half of my team and half of the sample were Shona. But the cultural and racial atmosphere in Gwelo was such that ethnic ties were usually pushed into the background. In fact, the hostilities in Gwelo were great enough to reduce relationships and rapport over time. In many instances, the longer my field assistants continued their relationships with their informants, the less responsive the informants became.

There are other reasons too for the greater success of the Oshogbo study. I think the cooperation I received from the colonial administration in Oshogbo helped facilitate our work. After the initial difficulties of housing, the colonial administration was fully cooperative and put no stumbling blocks in my way. We had no difficulty in securing access to official information, and whenever possible the colonial files were open to our inspection and perusal. In Gwelo the situation was reversed, because the European administration was hostile to us, did not approve of the study, and put obstacles in our way as often as they could. Most of the Europeans were uncooperative, and access to government files and information was difficult. Considering the political and racial circumstances, it is doubtful that we could have improved our rapport with the European community.

Some of the differences in the results of the two studies can be traced to important dissimilarities in the two social systems. The stability and structure of Yoruba society provided an almost built-in analytical framework that made the field work easier. They had not been subject to the massive amounts of Westernization and industrialization that the people in Gwelo had, and the changes that were taking place in Oshogbo were within a social system that had basically remained intact. Gwelo, on the other hand, was characterized by instability, heterogeneity, and the absence of articulating principles of organization. Contrasts between traditional rural life and the industrial modes of town were sharp, and the people were forced into many unfamiliar roles and social situations. In other words, because a man brought many aspects of tribal behavior with him into town, he alternated between urban and tribal forms of behavior according to the social situation that involved him at any given moment. Thus the social system in Gwelo was marked by ambiguity and inconsistency and made for a more difficult field situation.

But most important were the hostility and defenses exhibited by the Gwelo Africans, who feared, hated, and distrusted all white men. The political, social, economic, and religious prohibitions that the Europeans forced on the Africans did not allow them to develop any image of the Europeans other than a hostile one. Under these circumstances, I do not know of any techniques that can clear away such deeply embedded antagonisms, especially when the populations are large. It is conceivable, where populations are small, that time and understanding could reduce the hostilities. By using African field assistants, creating an African panel group, and publicizing the study and the fact that I was an American, we initially assuaged some of their fears and hostilities toward us, but when we continued to question and probe, the basic hostile attitudes and values of the Africans began to re-emerge. In Oshogbo, our rapport deepened with time, and our relationships became friendlier as our stay increased. In Oshogbo, I was the Ataoja's "white man" and he was my "chief clerk." The hostility and fears of the Africans in Gwelo limited the operation of the study and reduced the amount and depth of the data that we could collect. However, it is interesting to note that when we could establish personal relationships, as I did with my field assistants and panel-group members, many of the hostilities and fears evaporated.

Much has been written about the effects on an anthropological study of the attitudes and values of the people among whom the study is undertaken. But what about the effect of the attitudes and values of the anthropologist on the success of the field work? We all admit that the objective anthropologist free from prejudice and preconception is a myth, so, because I suspect that my own reactions played an important if not easily discernible part in the two field studies, I must make some reference to them. I responded to the people in Gwelo very differently from the way I had responded to the Yoruba. A good portion of this difference in feeling can be attributed to the deep and disturbing racial tension in Gwelo. My conscious sympathies were with the Africans, for I was bitterly angry at the degradations and restrictions imposed upon them. At the same time, I was a white man and perforce treated as one by the Africans. This involved more than their restricting my questions and observations. It also involved a subtle personal antagonism, which in turn must have generated feelings of hostility and anger in me. Although I was largely unaware of such feelings while in the field, in retrospect I must question whether my ability to be objective and to gain insights was not in fact hampered by these tensions.

I reacted to other elements in the cultures as well. The Yoruba are a colorful, exuberant people with a great capacity for fun and enjoyment. Their relationships have many dimensions, and their culture has been enriched by its strong traditions, its rituals, and its songs and dances. Little of this ebullience and creativity is evident in Gwelo. Indeed, there were times when I came to think of the Gwelo African community as a kind of Black Necropolis. Some of the inertia and flatness that mark Gwelo is without doubt derived from the repressions of the whites and from the painful adjustments of the Africans to town life. But some of it is simply that the peoples of Gwelo do not have as rich, varied, and enjoyable a culture as the Yoruba. I have no doubt that in both field situations my own personal attitudes and reactions were unconsciously carried over into and affected the research. Thus it is difficult to dismiss them as negligible, even though now I have great difficulty in assessing them.

VILLAGE
AND CITY
FIELD WORK
IN LEBANON

John Gulick

Sometime during the period 1946–1951, when I was an anthropology student (undergraduate and graduate) at Harvard, a visiting anthropologist shocked some of us by declaring that he really hated some of the people among whom he had done field work. Our shocked reaction was the result of what we were being taught explicitly and also implicitly by innuendo: that all cultures are inherently equally lovable and that, if one does not come away from a field trip loving those whom one has studied, one has failed as a field worker and therefore as a true anthropologist.

Since our visitor was unquestionably a "genuine" and accomplished anthropologist, we decided (in those halcyon days of Freudian ethnography) that he must have many unresolved conflicts and problems that had somehow survived the subjective analytic experience of field work. "Be psychoanalyzed before you go," we were advised by another mentor, with little regard to feasibility. If you aren't, the implication seemed to be, you will certainly feel as if you ought to have been before you are through. Some of the recent pronouncements of Lévi-Strauss, and the adulation with which they have been received, suggest that this point of view—equating field work in part with an initiation ordeal and in part with mystical experiences—still has wide currency. The implications of this point of view are as deceptive as the old marriage-manual dogma that a couple who fail to achieve simultaneous orgasms are failures not only personally but also in their "true selves" as man and woman.

When the anthropologist is in the field, field work is his total life. He copes with it by using his whole body and personality in the same way that he copes with life when he is not in the field. This is the fundamental difference between anthropological field research and sociological survey research, which is not only not a total life situation but can even be (and frequently is) done entirely by someone else. Life in the field involves the same emotions as life at home: elation, boredom, embarrassment, contentment, anger, joy, anxiety, and so on. To these are added, however, the necessity of being continually on the alert (of *not* taking one's surroundings and relationships for granted), and the necessity of learning new routines and cues. These necessities are likely to force a heightened awareness of facets of one's personality of which one had not been aware before. This can be an emotionally devastating experience, but it is by no means inevitably so. The emotional and situational factors are so varied and complicated in their relationships that no safe predictions in the abstract can be made on this score.

Why has the performance of this important professional role of the anthropologist been caricatured in terms of either/or emotional extremes and veiled in mystical claptrap? Is it possible that many anthropologists are attracted to the field less out of love for other cultures than out of the feeling of being inadequate in their own? Could it be that many anthropologists are also ambivalent about various aspects of field work, regarding it chiefly as a means to the end of contributing to knowledge, rather than as an end in itself? Could it be that many successful episodes in the field come about through good luck as much as through sophisticated methodology, or that many unsuccessful episodes come about through bad judgment as much as through bad luck?

Indeed, it could be! And once these possibilities are accepted, it is more readily understood why so many anthropologists have been unwilling to be forthright about their field experiences.

Fear of violating the field-work mystique, and of being professionally downgraded because of this, has been a major cause of this lack of honesty, and so the mystique has become self-perpetuating.

This book is an attempt to improve the discipline of anthropology by breaking up this conspiracy of silence. This does not imply, however, that all reticence can go by the board. Field work, being a total life situation, involves some personal reactions that are generally considered to be private. Although much can be done to replace mystique with specific information, there are limits of privacy beyond which most anthropologists (and most people generally) will probably not allow others to intrude. In other words, although we can help each other by sharing our experiences far more than we have in the past, each of us must, ultimately, find his own way.

PART I: VILLAGE FIELD WORK

Problem, Theory, and Research Design

The Arabic-speaking culture of the Middle East had, by 1951, intrigued me to the point of my wishing to study it professionally. This came about through my experiences in the Middle East during World War II and the enthusiasm of one of the very few senior anthropologists, Carleton S. Coon, who was interested in the area's present-day culture. There was very little else upon which to build. What material existed consisted of some out-of-date ethnographies, mostly of nomadic groups whom I knew to be peripheral in fact, though not in reputation, to the mainstream of the culture. Although some socioeconomic monographs existed, many of them substantial but often slanted toward ulterior political aims, there were no intensive community studies of the sort that formed the very foundation of ethnography in other areas, and there were only a few theoretical or problem-oriented anthropological studies. The simple fact was that the contemporary Middle East had been ignored by modern anthropology.

Where and with what problems should I begin? The possible answers were as limitless as the lacunae in Middle Eastern ethnography. In 1949, however, I had written a B.A. honors thesis on the Maronites, a Christian Arab subculture surrounded by Muslims that had adapted itself to the mountainous environment of Lebanon, and this gave me a start (Gulick, 1949). In my thesis, I had had to piece together a composite picture of Maronite family life, kinship, and village structure, for there was no single study that encompassed all of these subjects—either for the Maronites, or for anyone else in the Middle East. The sources indicated in a general way that endogamous patrilineages located primarily in endogamous villages were the rule. The lineages were composed entirely, it seemed, of extended family households. Household, lineage, and village were all described as being cohesive in-groups, each opposed to "outsiders." How, I wondered, could patrilineage endogamy be reconciled with a rule forbidding *bilateral* first-cousin marriages? How, in reality, could household, lineage, and village be cohesive in-groups *simultaneously* for the same individual? How could *all* households consist of extended families at the same time? And how could a system of strong unilineal kin groups be functionally consistent with a system of kinship terms that G. P. Murdock had just christened "Sudanese"? (*Social Structure*, 1949.) I began to suspect that, aside from possible inaccuracies, the various sources expressed idealized norms more than they did generally observable realities. Obviously, only field work could provide answers to these questions.

On the matter of multiple in-groups, my reading of Evans-Pritchard's *The Nuer,* with its concept of balanced antagonisms and related matters, created in my mind an image of a complicated real world of mixed motives and situationally varied cues that was not even hinted at in the literature itself. Here was fascination and challenge combined. In 1951, I proposed to my dissertation committee that I do a village study in Lebanon focused upon these problems. Preferably, it would be a Maronite village, but the particular sect of the village was, as far as I could see, of secondary importance, for the same phenomena were apparently present in all villages, including Muslim ones (except with respect to some details about cousin marriage). The core of my method would be a thorough household survey, establishing the exact composition of each unit and the relationships among them both within the village and outside it.

The committee gave me its blessing, but otherwise I found myself to be on my own. The first reason for this was that the committee, though composed of experts on social structure and complex peasant cultures, did not include anyone with Middle Eastern experiences or interests. In fact, one member of it even exclaimed, *"Lebanon!* What do you want to go to *that* greasy place for?" Second, although four budding young anthropologists of my own age had just returned from field work in Lebanon, they were reticent about their experiences and obviously were not willing to give me entrée into the particular villages they had studied, although they were very generous with the names of other contacts. Third, pressed for funds and concerned (perhaps overly so) about how our three-year-old and one-year-old sons might fare, my wife and I decided that I should go to Lebanon alone. In retrospect, I wish that we had done otherwise. It would be idiotic to claim (as I have heard others claim under similar circumstances) that it would have been a great experience for the children, for they would hardly have remembered it, but the many pains of separation were a burden I could well have done without. Furthermore, I believe that it is very important for anyone, even under "ordinary" circumstances, to have access to at least one other person with whom he can constantly test out his reactions and try out his ideas. If it is important under ordinary circumstances, it is absolutely essential in the field. This other person can be another member of a formal research team, or a spouse, or both, or someone else, but it must be someone who can be completely trusted, emotionally and intellectually, for benevolent candor. (Ten years later, in 1961, when my wife, sons, and daughter went to Lebanon again for field work the validity of these points was amply borne out.)

Passive or Adaptational Research

My original plan was to spend a year in the field, September, 1951, to August, 1952, but red tape about visas and like matters delayed my arrival in Lebanon until the beginning of November. In Beirut, I immediately set out to find and buy a used car, which took some time, and to establish contacts at the American University, using references that had been given to me. From this base, my hope was to establish further contacts who would introduce me into a suitable village.

In regard to selecting a village, one of my acquaintances had said, before I left America, "Well, drive around everywhere you can get to, looking them over. When you find one you like the looks of—especially one with a great view—just move in!" Easier said than done, of course, but although it sounded appealing, it did match my cautious temperament. Had I been a member of a team, as the speaker had been, it might have been different, for a casual, unsponsored entrée into a Lebanese village could have distinct advantages over a formal, sponsored one. The "passive" stage of field work might take longer, but one could hardly start off on a better foot than by saying, "I would like to live in your village for a while because it is so beautiful!"

I quickly discovered that Beirut was full of Lebanese people who had village identities but who were living in the city because village life was, for them, boring and uncomfortable (especially in winter) and unremunerative. My desire to live in a village was thus in a direct countercurrent to the desires of many of my Lebanese acquaintances. To only some of them did the explanation that it was a requirement of my training have much reality. All readily agreed that the Arabs were very badly misunderstood in America. They were, for instance, all regarded as nomads with no fixed abodes, an old romantic notion that happened to fit in well with the aims of Zionist propaganda. Some of my acquaintances assented to the idea that, if more accurate information were made available, it might help to offset these misunderstandings, but what, they asked, is to be learned in villages? Seventy-five percent of the Arabs live in villages, I replied. Yes, they said, but village life does not matter; it is in the cities where our civilization is. Even in this "passive" phase of field work, some of the major conflicts in values and social cleavages in Lebanese culture were having their impact on my plans. I also discovered that none of my contacts at the American University had any suitable Maronite contacts, nor any contacts at the Université St. Joseph, also in Beirut, where there were many Maronites.

A reference to persons in the Catholic and Maronite hierarchy outside of Beirut took me to a village very high in the mountains. The priest received me very kindly, seemed to understand my objectives, and invited me to stay. However, he was not a native of the village and did not know all the families well, and the village, which was often snowbound in the winter, was to a considerable degree depopulated for that season (a common phenomenon). I decided, reluctantly, to keep on looking.

An employee of the American University to whom I had explained my mission some time before then told me that she had mentioned me to a young man from her own Orthodox Christian village who happened to be in town. She said that he was the son of the priest who was a native of the village and would know the kinds of things about families in which I was interested. If I would like to visit the village with him, I would be welcome.

Accordingly, that night we drove to the village, and I spent several days with the young man, his father, mother, and younger brother. A married sister lived in Beirut. The village, which is fully described elsewhere (Gulick, 1955:20–46), is located on the northern coast of Lebanon, about halfway between Beirut and Tripoli. The shoreline at that point consists of eroded layers and big, broken slabs of limestone. A paved highway and a railroad run north-south along the shore, but the land rises almost immediately from the sea in the form of ridges (running east-west) and intervening arroyos. No ground water is available, and the only source of water throughout the year is what is collected in cisterns during the winter rains. Much of the land consists of naked limestone outcrops, but earth has been conserved in some places by means of retaining walls that form terraces. Olives and figs are the main crops. The sparse natural vegetation consists mostly of low, thorny shrubs.

In 1951–1952, the village consisted of a small, subsidiary hamlet on the highway (which has subsequently grown considerably) and a cluster of about a hundred stone houses half a mile inland and up from the hamlet. The main house-cluster consisted of irregular rows of houses at various elevations along the southern slope of a ridge. The top of the house-cluster was on the crest of the ridge 750 feet above sea level, and the lower end of the house-cluster was at about 500 feet. These top and bottom points were about half a mile apart. I lived in the main-house-cluster, but the leader of the faction to which most of my informants were opposed lived in the hamlet on the highway.

The priest did indeed have genealogical information about the village's families, marriages, and occupations. As a priest, it was his business to know these things, but he knew them also by virtue of his being a native of the village. He would be glad to help me, he said, but what was I going to do with the information? I said that I was going to put it into a book whose purpose would be to give people in America a better idea of what life among the Arabs was really like. Whether or not he and the other villagers then believed that I would write such a book, I do not know. There was no reason they should have, except that they knew I was a scholar associated with an institution of high prestige in their culture. I knew that books and a person's associations with books were highly prestigious in these peoples' eyes, but as far as "role-playing" is concerned, it is important to note that it was indeed my intention to write such a book, that subsequently I *did* write it, and after less than four years a copy of it was in their hands. In the Lebanese culture, my role as a scholar was to some degree compatible with the native system of role values, although a social-science study of a village was not. The problem of the anthropologist whose role in the field is not at all conceivable to his informants, and who must therefore define himself in other terms, is obviously different from what mine was.

Because my informants to some extent understood my role, I had one immediate advantage: the period of "passive research" was very short, and I was soon (just after New Year's, 1952) at work with the priest and asking directly for the information I needed.

The priest's family did not have space for me in their two-room house, so I rented a room in a house that would be vacant until the middle of the summer. This was a strictly business arrangement, for I dealt with the owner's brother as agent and there was little haggling, as it was obvious that any sum of money at all would be sheer profit for the owner, who lived in Beirut during the winter.

I took my meals with the priest's family. Hospitality is a matter of great pride among the Arabs. Although there are definite limits to hospitality, more is expected and more is given than in America, especially with regard to food. I had been warned not to make the mistake of trying to pay for what was intended as hospitality, and I was also very conscious of trying to avoid the reputation of Americans as people who thought they could get anything they wanted just by paying for it. But were these meals hospitality or not? I was not sure, and my guess is that the priest's family was not sure either, for though the meals themselves betokened hospitality (for which the host would certainly not ask for payment), the protraction of the service was wholly unprecedented. In any event, neither party was able to suggest that this be made a regular business arrangement, and we entered into the relationship with only my verbal assurances that from time to time I would be pleased to show my gratitude for their generosity. Subsequently, at irregular intervals, I made gifts of money that I felt sure were more than adequate compensation for the food, and at the end I gave them a large polished veneer table that I had had made according to their specifications. Several years later, I learned that they had indeed felt anxious and tense about the whole arrangement and that they would have preferred regular, fixed payments, but apparently they felt unable to raise the issue. At the time, I felt the tension but could not identify its source. This was an instance, I believe, where both the foreigner and the natives were deluded by an ideal norm in the culture, namely that the "spiritual" rewards of hospitality take precedence over fair recompense for services rendered. In practice, the priority of values is the reverse whenever the direct choice must be made.

Active Research

Census and household survey. In establishing a working relationship with the priest, I entered into the active phase of the research. My aims were to obtain, first, a map of the village showing every house (occupied, unoccupied, and ruined—the last being a sign of an emigrated family), second, an exact census of every household, including the name, age, and sex of every occupant, their relationships to each other, any unrelated residents, whether or not spouses were natives of the village, non-resident members of the family and where they were living, occupations of all adults, degree of education of all children, and other details; and third, a genealogy of the families of the village.

The priest had such a genealogy. It was written on a large sheet of paper and was of a style that is standard in Arab culture —present and past, Muslim and Christian. It is a schematic tree and is literally called a tree *(shajarat)*. It shows only males, each represented as a circle (if there is room) with each one's progeny attached as if on stalks. It took some time to decipher the names and to make a version in English with the generations reconciled. I knew that the chart, lacking females, was worthless for any genetic study and that it might be inaccurate in other ways, but it enabled me to begin to piece together the relationships of the twenty-one named lineages in the village. The priest and I worked on this at the same time that we began to work on the census. An individual's lineage name is not ordinarily used in the village, because everyone knows everyone else, and repeatedly I had to remind the priest about it, except when he remembered my interest and supplied the name himself.

For purposes of the census I had prepared some mimeographed forms on legal-size paper. The priest and I usually worked in the evenings, and sometimes in the afternoons, in the reception area of his house. Other family members came and went, sometimes joined us, and, particularly in the evenings, various cronies and other relatives appeared. While we were working, I deliberately left these forms out in the open, so that anyone could see what I was asking and what the priest's answers were, and I let others interject comments or questions. Often these led to long digressions and diverted conversations.

What with the interruptions and variations in mood and my policy of not striving for completion too persistently, all this took a long time. Repeatedly I had to press the priest for specific information on certain individuals, but I did not want to be too persistent. Perseverance is reported not to be a usual characteristic of Arab personality, but through the months, the priest and I persevered together until all 580 residents of the village were recorded in several different ways. Throughout it all, an informal check (but admittedly not a systematic one) was provided by the fact that our discussions were public and that there were many comments and corrections from others.

Meanwhile, one of the villagers who was a trained surveyor was, in company with the mayor, making a cadastral survey of the village. The surveyor made a sketch map of the village—its paths, houses and other buildings—and with it in hand I tramped all over, taking photographs and checking on each structure. Early in this process of checking houses against households, some of the complexities of the ecological realities of the village became evident. In particular, I discovered that many of the households identified with certain houses were absent, in whole or in part, during the winter. This discovery led to a whole line of questioning in regard to occupations and residence elsewhere, to the reasons for and occasions of visits to the village, and to the whole matter of commuting to Beirut and Tripoli. I also discovered that "outsiders," people not on the priest's genealogy, were living in some of the vacated houses. These discoveries introduced many economic factors into the household survey and into the conversations that I recorded in my field notes.

The surveyor was reluctant to talk about land ownership. The mayor himself was also reticent on this subject, although he was vociferous about the necessity of improving the economy of the village itself. He also had a good deal to say about the nefarious influence of Communists, and he made more than one remark about black people. (He had spent several years as an immigrant in Vicksburg, Mississippi.) He said nothing about America's support of Israel, but he did speak disparagingly of the education "for no practical purpose" that seemed to him to be the policy of the American University of Beirut. In contrast, the priest and his friends, with no experience in America, continually badgered me on the matter of Israel and greatly lauded the intellectual importance of the American University. (On the Arab-Israeli question I had to try to defend my country and at the same time acknowledge what I personally felt to have been its excessive zeal in supporting Zionism at the expense of so many Arabs.)

Factions and the role of the ethnographer. I discovered that there were ideological differences of great significance in this village for which I was a sounding board. I do not think that I appreciated their full significance at the time, but I began to realize that the priest and the mayor were members of opposed factions, and that my involvement with one had already gone so far that I did not see how I could make up for it to the other.

This was not a factionalism of simple distinctions between lineages or places of residence, although these factors played some part in the situation, but rather an ideological factionalism. Ideological factionalism, supported by friendships and family ties, and felt to be mortally threatened, can result in a steadfastly defensive possessiveness. Since kinship ties and marriage relationships are properly the province of the priest, and since these were my major interests, too, then my major relationship should be with him. But the priest was also a member of a faction, and as another member of that faction once said to me, "You belong to *us*."

This status of being adopted into a faction was reflected in the names I was given. Some people called me Sayyid John ("Mr. John"), an expression of formal distance. Others called me either John or Hanna, its Arabic equivalent, an expression of familiar equality. But the name by which I was referred to and the one by which, I understand, I am still remembered, was Hanna Khoury. Khoury literally means priest, but it is also a common family name among Lebanese Christians, although it was not the family name of the priest in this village. Normally, in this culture, a person's second name is that of his or her father, or a suitable substitute, while the third name (rarely used) is that of the lineage. I had no lineage affiliation, and though the priest was obviously not my father, I was very clearly identified with him in a style that was compatible with the patterns of the culture.

Techniques. In addition to the census, I kept written field notes on conversations, observations, hunches, and subjective reactions. I found it impossible to separate the recording of "objective data" from the recording of my own reactions and day-by-day activities. One of my professors had advised keeping "field notes" and a "journal" for these dual purposes, but I was not able to separate the two. If one is recording the highlights of a conversation, how does one select those highlights and determine the mood and intent of the informant, especially if the conversation concerns attitudes and values? Is he serious or joking? Is he reiterating stereotypes or expressing a critical judgment? The context of the conversation, including the ethnographer's own state of mind at the time, may provide clues to answers, and these must be recorded along with direct quotations, if the notes are to have any value.

The use of tape recorders does not obviate these problems, except for those ethnographers (if such there be) who keep no records of their field work except tape recordings. As in ordinary life, invaluable information and insights often come to me through some unexpected encounter, and any ethnographer worth his salt must be prepared to cope with such events and write them up effectively. Although I do not deny the value of tape recordings under certain circumstances and for certain kinds of material, I do not believe that they can displace the "old-fashioned" field notes.

I always carried with me a small pocket notebook in which

I jotted down specific information, such as names, dates, and other numerical figures. I also wrote down the spellings of words and names in Arabic, always allowing my informants to see these spellings and therefore anything else that might be on the same page. It always amused them, I think, to see samples of my somewhat clumsy, schoolboyish Arabic characters, but it also pleased them, for one of their assumptions (generally well-founded) is that Americans don't know how to write Arabic.

For the main flow of a conversation, I relied on my memory. I never tried to copy down the other person's discourse, for I knew that to do so would have destroyed not only that particular conversation but very likely the whole relationship as well. I discovered that my own attention span was limited to about an hour and that in longer encounters much was lost as far as my notes were concerned. During the day I would try to retire to my room and record my impressions as soon as possible after a particular event. Often, however, I would have to wait until the evening to do this, and tired though I usually was at the end of the day, I found that it was essential to write the day's notes before going to sleep. If I failed to do this and postponed note writing till the next day, I found that the notes were useless, except insofar as they might contain simple factual information. The subtleties of cues and responses—some of which one can catch in notes if one writes them soon enough—became lost in sleep, and what I wrote the next day was essentially a second-hand account, an oversimplified version, in which the events and my reactions to them were truly blurred.

If one is to catch the immediate realities of life in field notes, one must write them as nearly as possible as one lives the events. They must be raw, fresh, undigested, yet organized enough to be coherent for future reading and analysis. It was and is impossible for me to record field events according to some preconceived system of coded headings for the purpose of facilitating analysis. There is time enough for coding and sorting later on. Impressions, hunches, and "hard" information all should go into the notes together as they come into one's consciousness. Epistemologically, they must not be confused with each other, however, and that is why notes must be recorded promptly.

Note-taking of this kind is difficult and time-consuming. It is also the very essence of real field work. In rereading notes that spanned a period of several months, I have repeatedly discovered discussions of events or ideas that I had completely forgotten, as well as other impressions of phenomena that I subsequently had learned to take for granted and was actually no longer seeing at all.

I wrote my notes on 5″ × 8″ sheets of paper, using a pen,

dating each sheet, and numbering all sheets consecutively. I kept the originals and mailed carbon copies to my adviser at Harvard for safekeeping and for his comments. The previous summer I had been employed by the Harvard "Rimrock" Project to read the field notes of one of the participants, assigning to each paragraph Human Relations Area File code numbers according to the contents. This analysis was intended to facilitate the cross-filing of the notes and the sharing of notes with others.[1] Subsequently, as adviser and critic myself, I have read the field notes of others and, on the basis of these experiences, I think that unless the adviser is also in the field, the usefulness of his comments is rather limited. However, he can comment helpfully on the precision of the recording. For instance, my adviser, in response to my writing that I thought an informant was joking when he said something, would point out that I should also have noted what evidence I had, if any, that the informant was joking.

On the basis of these experiences, I also question both the wisdom and propriety of sharing one's field notes with others, unless, perhaps, the others are simultaneously working in the same locale on coordinated research (although under these circumstances one would expect one's co-workers to be orally sharing their findings and problems). There may be those who record field notes with readers other than themselves in mind, and they may be good field notes, but I know that if I wrote field notes this way I would feel constrained in organization and restricted in expression, and no ethnographer should feel so constrained and restricted.

Extensions of the Field

During the preliminary period of my stay in Lebanon, I had agreed to give a course of lectures on anthropology at the American University of Beirut during the spring semester. I made

---

[1] In the late 1940s and early 1950s, the Harvard Department of Social Relations sponsored a coordinated cooperative research project (now called by the code name "Rimrock") on five different cultures in the Southwest (Mormon, Navaho, Spanish-speaking, Texan, and Zuni). Students and faculty members did field work at the same time, and in order to facilitate communication among them, their field notes were typed on ditto masters, and the contents of each page of notes was analyzed in terms of the inventory of culture content devised by the Human Relations Area Files at New Haven. Each item in the inventory has its own code number, and so each page of notes acquired from one to half a dozen numbers, depending upon how its contents were analyzed. A copy of each page of notes was then filed under every content category involved. A participant in the project would then be able to refer quickly to the numbered headings in the file to see what others besides himself had recorded on a large number of predefined subjects.

this commitment, because I wanted a genuine affiliation with the institution, not a token or merely courtesy one. I also had hoped that my interactions with the students would provide me with an additional dimension of significant contact with Lebanese culture.

When the time came, and as the spring progressed, I found that the teaching itself made greater demands on my energies than I had anticipated. Also, it often removed me from the village, and it undoubtedly slowed down my work there. However, it enabled me to share the commute with many of the villagers, for I often served as a taxi driver and a carrier of messages and packages. My original research design had not envisaged this urban extension of village life, but research in the village had revealed it, and my commitment at the University gave me some first-hand experience with it. In retrospect, I wish that I had concluded my work in the village earlier and turned my attention more fully and systematically to the villagers who were living in the city. The latter, however, were physically dispersed, and at the time, my primary responsibility seemed to be in the village itself.

My students did not become informants, as I had thought they might, but my contact with them was revealing in a number of significant ways. The tensions in their lives, especially those connected with intergenerational conflicts due to revolutionary cultural change, were obvious. Also obvious was the inadequacy, in helping them to identify the sources of their tensions, of their intellectual models and the formal curriculum imposed on them. Arabic intellectual exercises consist of memorizing normative systems of abstractions. The use among Lebanese students of sociology and anthropology textbooks written by and for Americans was, ironically, compatible with these traditional exercises, but not in the least suitable for elucidating local cultural problems. These texts provided normative abstractions to be memorized, but an inductive approach to actual behavioral patterns (or lack of them) was judged unworthy of systematic effort. The Arabs take the same approach to their own language. Only classical, literary Arabic is considered worthy of formal study, though much of it is archaic, whereas the colloquial dialects are academically beneath contempt. The students were not interested in the village materials I attempted to feed into the course; they thought that they knew all about village life, or they had rejected it, or both.

Part of these failures might be attributed to my inexperience and the fact that my field data were incomplete. However, in the intervening years I have discovered that others have had the same experiences, both in the Middle East and in other areas.

The reluctance or inability to distinguish normative patterns from behavioral practices and the great difficulty in generalizing about behavioral practices without parroting normative abstractions appear to be prevalent in many cultures. They constitute barriers to communication not only in field research but also in the transmission of interpretations and conclusions.

Bowing Out

I had originally told the villagers that I would stay only until sometime in the summer, so there was no difficulty in announcing and taking my leave when that time came. I had completed the household survey by the time that I was ready to go, and in that sense I had "finished" my work. Of course, by that time, I was very much aware of the many avenues of inquiry which, ideally, I should be following, or should have followed. Because of this awareness I felt a profound sense of unfinished business.

In saying my goodbyes in the village, I made a special effort to call on everyone with whom I had had contact, even though the contacts had not been frequent or recent. I made a particular point to call on the mayor. At the time, I felt that this was simply a common courtesy that was incumbent upon me, and I still think so. However, according to the oral report on professional ethics presented by Professor Ralph Beals at the Meetings of the American Anthropological Association in November, 1966, such courtesies are apparently not practiced commonly enough by the brethren. Perhaps if they were redefined as "field techniques" they might be taken more seriously.

Summary of Findings and Evaluation of Accomplishments

My publications based on this study provide descriptions of the material culture of the village, which was at that time without piped water or electricity yet was linked rather closely to urban centers through the educational and occupational aspirations of its people. Considerable attention is given in the publications to the decline of farming and the increase of wage labor and white-collar work as substitute means of subsistence, together with the associated commuting and urban-residence patterns.

A major conclusion is that, despite these important socioeconomic changes, loyalty to and identity with large kinship groups, sect, and village as a whole remain essentially intact. Although this conclusion is interpreted in terms of the abstractions of equilibrium theory, it is very similar to more recent findings by others in the same area, particularly in regard to the continuing importance of kinship groups, despite the decline of peasant-type agriculture. Large kinship groups continue to be important because they provide their members with help and security in times of radical change.

My original topic grew, because of the revelations of the household study, to include occupations and the whole urban dimension. I probably could have followed these matters even further than I did. I think also that the younger people became bored with my basic approach, and that I may have missed an opportunity in not trying to get them to talk more about their problems as they saw them, their fears, hopes, and aspirations (or lack of them).

My entrée to the village households was through the priest. If it had been through the mayor, who represented the opposing faction, I might have collected a different order of data on the culture of the village. Once embarked with one faction, however, I do not think that I could have been successful in establishing equivalent contacts with the other without jeopardizing my relationships with the first.

The prospect of my writing a book about them may have led the villagers to withhold certain information or to slant their communications in certain ways. The factional split, its causes, reinforcements, and results, were, I suspect, purposefully minimized on this account. I myself, in fact, contributed to this by never reacting to the personal remarks that were often made. In fact, I sometimes frustrated some people by refusing to state or support the either/or preferences for things and people that were often asserted. In the absence of a "natural" crisis, some other anthropologist might have involved himself in the factional split, risking becoming a target in the hopes of becoming a catalytic agent of actions that might reveal more about the phenomenon. Such involvement might be regarded as sophisticated, gamesmanly field work. I would regard it as unethical, because I do not think that the field worker has the right to interfere in the affairs of the culture he is studying, especially when he himself will not have to live with and bear the consequences of his interference.

I may have defined my role and purposes as unnecessarily narrow and thereby made it difficult for myself to widen my inquiry. Be this as it may, the field work made it difficult for myself to widen my inquiry. Be this as it may, the field work yielded the type of information that I originally had planned to obtain in sufficient amount to permit an analysis along the lines originally projected, and it opened new vistas to me that subsequently led to further research in the area. More immediately, it led to the publication within three years of two papers and a monograph (Gulick, 1953, 1954, 1955).

PART II: CITY FIELD WORK

Problem, Theory, and Research Design

Nine years elapsed before I returned to Lebanon in 1961 for another year of field work, this time in the city. During the intervening period, my interest in Middle Eastern culture did not abate, but I digressed from it to some extent by undertaking the direction of a field-research project among the eastern Cherokee Indians (Gulick, 1960). Simultaneously, my interest in the urban dimensions of culture became more and more focused. I participated in a multidisciplinary study of the cities of the Piedmont Industrial Crescent of North Carolina and acquired some first-hand knowledge of, and experience with, sociological survey techniques (Gulick, 1962; Gulick, Bowerman, and Back, 1962). The popular tendency to equate urban life with impersonal and superficial relationships had a considerable philosophical and theoretical history that was being challenged in a number of quarters (including my own), although social scientists persisted in talking in terms of it. Did they not also *think* in terms of it, despite their disclaimers? The concept of nonpolarized but nevertheless distinctive rural and urban subcultures comprising a more inclusive national culture certainly seemed (and still does seem) worth exploration.

It occurred to me that the impersonal nature of survey research itself might imperceptibly reinforce the old, oversimplified assumptions about urban life in the minds of survey researchers, census-tract analysts, and so forth. As to urban research outside the industrial West, too much of what existed seemed to be a "replication" of methods developed for American cities, and the results were very disappointing.

When undertaking a sociological survey, there is a great temptation to obtain a large amount of data in quick interviews in the belief that there is security in large numbers. It is quite true that the larger the population under research, the larger and more diversified the study samples of it should be. But as an anthropologist, I feel that the advantages of large survey samples are sometimes negated by relying on purely verbal responses and by a lack of concern with the actual environment of the respondents. Ideally, a large, complex system such as the population of a city should be approached through both surveys and the intimate, intensive methods of anthropologists. Such a combination, however, usually calls for a team project. Not wishing to undertake team research in a Middle Eastern city without first having done urban research there myself, I decided to study a Middle Eastern city "anthropologically" and supplement "participant observation" with questionnaires, content analysis of the mass media, and whatever other strategies I could put into operation in the field.

I was already familiar with Lebanese culture, others had done anthropological studies there, and the country was open for social-science research. So I decided to study one of the Lebanese cities. The choice is a narrow one: Beirut or Tripoli. Beirut is entirely too large for one person to tackle meaningfully in a limited time, and besides, some survey studies had already been done there. Beirut is also so heterogenous that, fascinating though they would be, findings on it would very likely not be typical of the Middle East as a whole, and the Social Science Research Council, to which I had applied for financial support, was understandably loath to support research in an "atypical" city. So I chose Tripoli, the second largest city of Lebanon, a stronghold of Muslims, and in this respect, if no other, typical of the Middle East.

The inhabitants of the village that I had studied in 1951–1952 had commuted to both Tripoli and Beirut for work. I had been through Tripoli myself a few times, but had encountered very little published information on it. In fact, many people at first thought I meant the better-known Tripoli in Libya. Those who knew Tripoli in Lebanon described it as provincial and narrow-minded, the site of an oil terminal. Compared to Beirut, Tripoli was the equivalent of Peoria to Chicago, Springfield to Boston, and Fresno to San Francisco. These attitudes, as I eventually encountered them in Beirut, were hardly more tolerant or informed than they had been ten years earlier in regard to villages.

The existing city of Tripoli (not including earlier settlements on the same site) had been in continuous occupation for 770 years and had recently greatly increased in size. I assumed therefore that it probably had two large populations: one with few if any village ties, and another with strong village ties. My research proposal was to compare the two types of population to see what their significant differences and similarities might be. In particular, I proposed to seek comparative information on household structure, occupational patterns, neighborhood relationships, and participation in other types of groups. My plans were to live successively in several different parts of the city so as to check migrant and nonmigrant characteristics, if any, against different environmental factors.

Passive or Adaptational Research

A city the size of Tripoli (about 180,000 people) in a nation the size of Lebanon (about 1.6 million people) is an autonomous entity that can be studied as if it were isolated from the rest of the culture.

Accordingly, as soon as I arrived with my family in Beirut in September, 1961, I began taking field notes on my observations, even though they were not on Tripoli itself. Of particular interest to me were the many changes that had occurred in the intervening years since I had last been in Lebanon, changes to which I eventually became accustomed and of which I would probably have ceased to be aware if I had not made note of them when they were new and striking to me. These changes included increased informality between men and women in public and a far greater number of Western-style commercial enterprises.

I established a home base for my family in Beirut, where the school facilities were suitable for the children, and, as before, made an arrangement with the American University of Beirut to give a seminar in exchange for all the privileges of visiting faculty, including the services of graduate-student assistants in the Sociology and Anthropology Department. I no longer had any illusions about using my students as informants, but I correctly foresaw many advantages in associating myself with the prestigious university.

I decided to play my role—that of a university professor—as straight as possible, even though this role would cut me off from the people of the "culture of poverty," whom Oscar Lewis has studied with such remarkable results. This role, however, would open doors to me that would otherwise be closed, particularly the doors of people who had general information about the city and influence in it. It would probably restrict my informants to "middle-class" people, but I could not be all things to all men in field work any more than I can in life away from the field situation.

I had two references in Tripoli. One, who proved to be very helpful, was a schoolteacher and a life-long friend of a Lebanese-Amercan sociologist whom I knew. The other was a close relative of a person with whom I had become acquainted in America during the previous year. The second reference turned out to be a member of the same small sectarian group as the first, and they were close acquaintances.

One day late in September, I hired a car, went to Tripoli, and sought out the teacher at his school, only to discover that he was still at his summer retreat in the mountains. There he received me very kindly, particularly in response to greetings from the sociologist in America, originally a fellow-villager known to have made a name for himself in the New World. It was helpful in explaining my own mission to be able to say that I was professionally interested in many of the same kinds of information as his sociologist friend was and that I had done a village study in Lebanon ten years previously. Reprints of the papers and a copy of the monograph I had published on the village were available to anyone who was interested in them. I explained my interest in learning more about the relationships between village migrants to the city (of which he was one) and city-dwellers who had no village ties, and I asked him to help me find households in various parts of the city in which I could room and board. He mentioned a couple of possibilities and suggested I look him up in Tripoli later in October when the summer was over.

Meanwhile, I intensified my search in Beirut for sources of information (both written and live) on Tripoli. What I did essentially was to make known among my friends in Beirut the type of information I was looking for, in the hope that eventually some fruitful suggestions would be made, and, indeed, some were. A brief visit to the city (during which the native driver lost his way in the bewildering maze of streets) had reinforced my need for a good, detailed map, but none seemed to be available. Then someone mentioned that a Palestinian city planner who had worked in Tripoli not long before and was now working in another Arab country might be able to help me. I wrote to him and had the good fortune to receive a reply that referred me to a new contact in Tripoli who did eventually provide me with a good map. There were two books on Beirut in print, one socioeconomic and the other urban geographic, but there was nothing of the kind on Tripoli, except for one or two sources that emphasized Tripoli's early architectural monuments. One potential source of information on Tripoli was the Tripolitan students at the American University, but I decided not to approach them until I had much more first-hand knowledge of the city. Because of the dearth of published material, this was not an easy task. No census had even been taken in Lebanon since 1932, and those figures were hopelessly out of date.

The living pattern I had decided upon—a few days in Tripoli alternating with a few days in Beirut—was ideally suited to the wide-net, follow-up-every-lead approach that became indispensable as time went on. For example, since Tripoli was a Muslim city, I wanted to find out if anything remained of the traditional institutional structure of urban Islam on which there was considerable, but extremely dated, literature. What I eventually learned in Tripoli itself led directly to questions on twentieth-century Islamic institutions, especially modern Islamic education, and these questions led me to contacts in Beirut rather than in Tripoli.

In the middle of October, I returned to Tripoli to find a family with whom to live. Two prospects had been found by my primary contact, both of them members of his own sectarian subculture (Christian and definitely a minority group in Tripoli). To each husband and wife I explained my purposes, just as I had to my contact. One of the couples finally decided that they could not accommodate me, because the wife would be out of town during the next few months caring for a married daughter and her first baby. The second couple agreed to provide me with room and board. They had in their apartment a spare bedroom occupied only occasionally by a daughter who was away at college. They were also experienced in this type of arrangement, for during World War II, in another part of Lebanon, they had accommodated British government personnel who were strengthening their command of the Arabic language by living in Lebanese homes.

I had learned a lesson from my previous experience in Lebanon: the room and board arrangement I was making was not a conventional pattern of Lebanese culture, and there was no point in pretending that it was. Accordingly, I suggested paying them a flat weekly fee, an amount that I was sure would more than cover any extra expenses that they might incur on my account. After some discussion, but no haggling, they accepted my suggestion. I also proposed that we initially plan on my staying for five weeks only, as I wished to live in different parts of the city successively. The short-term commitment in itself may well have facilitated the whole arrangement, though it was ostensibly a statement of research strategy.

Toward the end of the five weeks, neither they nor I had said anything about its being time for me to move. Indeed, I had been so busy becoming acquainted with the city, getting introductions to various people, and making initial contacts with them, that I had made no moving plans. My hosts were very helpful, and we were getting along well together. In fact, I did not want to move. Nevertheless, I broached the subject because of our agreement. My hosts said that if I wished to continue to stay on with them, I was most welcome. I felt that they were not being falsely hospitable, and so I accepted their invitation "for a while longer," asking them to assure me that they would tell me if things became unsatisfactory.

During late November and early December, I began to struggle with several questions regarding my course of action. I had good rapport with a number of the members of my hosts' sub-culture. Though they were generally "middle class," they included native Tripolitans and immigrants, elders and adolescents, and professional people who had many pivotal contacts with others in Tripoli. If I were to content myself with them as my base, however, I would be very unlikely to get any direct or intensive information on Muslim family and neighborhood life. Counter-balancing this serious limitation were two other major consider-ations.

First, my own self-generated pressure to live in several parts of the city became greatly lessened once I realized how compact Tripoli was (about 1.5 square miles) and how I was already directly immersing myself in the ambiances of its var-ious sections by walking all through all of them at all times of day. Would finding and getting settled with new hosts in an-other part of town be worth all the trouble? Not, I decided, unless the new hosts belonged to a different subculture, preferably Muslim.

Second, my hosts' subculture was a Christian minority group, many of whose behavioral practices in the domestic and private aspects of life could not automatically be generalized to apply to larger segments of the population. But I did not need to con-centrate my ethnographic work on these particular aspects of culture, nor had I ever intended to limit my study to them. There was much else to be studied: the basic ecology of the city, its growth patterns and commercial structure, the location of its subcultures, its immigrant enclaves, and governmental and sec-tarian institutions, activities, and interrelationships. In addition, there was the entire matter of Tripoli's place in the larger cul-ture. Unless some very much better opportunity arose, I began to think that I would do well to make the most of the base I had already established. As members of a minority, the members of my hosts' subculture had adapted themselves in various ways to Tripoli, and so they were consciously aware of many facets of its culture. Allowing for their sectarian biases, I found some of them to be very informative on many subjects.

Besides all this, I liked my hosts, I was comfortable in their home, and they were apparently comfortable with me. I was beginning to be able to test out hunches in a relaxed, informal manner with them, just as I was already doing, at greater re-move, with my Lebanese friends in Beirut.

As December progressed, I became torn between getting myself into a Muslim household in another part of town, and trying to manage the move without hurting the feelings of my hosts and cutting myself off from their group. I mentioned the possibility of living with a Muslim family to friends of my hosts who had Muslim friends, but I did not pursue the matter, because I sensed that my raising the subject was being taken as a sign of dissatisfaction with my hosts' hospitality (which was far from the truth), rather than as reflecting an impersonal "scientific" procedure. To approach some of the Muslims whom I had met might evoke the same reactions with added complications of intersectarian gossip and backbiting. Even if another suitable family could be found, the costs might cancel out any hoped-for gains.

I was still struggling with these issues at the beginning of January when Lebanese politics decided the matter for me. An attempted *coup d'état* on December 31, 1961, created a state of crisis that continued till the time we were to leave Lebonan for good. Roadblocks, searches, sudden arrests, mass detentions, and rumors of atrocities created an oppressive atmosphere throughout the country. I was obliged to stay in Beirut for the first three weeks of January, during which time I began a systematic survey and analysis of Lebanese magazines and newspapers, which I continued throughout the rest of the project.

When things had cooled down to routine crisis proportions, I returned to Tripoli and discovered that my hosts did not wish to dissociate themselves from me. Americans were not implicated in this particular crisis, but the wariness of the Lebanese among themselves had been greatly intensified, and I had no desire to risk stirring up any further tensions by trying to shift my base of informants from one sect to another. So it was that I remained with my original hosts until my departure in June.

Like any student of Lebanon, I had long been aware of the explicitly sectarian structure of its national social system, but mine had been a rather abstract awareness until I came face to face with it in everyday life. In my initial plans for research in Tripoli, my concentration on the rural-urban frame of references had led me to underestimate the possible effects of sectarian and social-class differences on the issues with which I was concerned. After a few months in Tripoli, I was very much more aware of it.

Active Research

In January, 1962, the "passive phase" of my field work ended with the procedural decision to stay with my hosts. The "active" phase of research, however, had long since begun. The two phases overlapped, and the resulting feedback caused a subtle but important shift in my perception of my field-work role and in my goals. My original plan envisaged intensive ethnographic work on and in two "populations" (native urbanite and migrant). Circumstances did not lead me to any such discrete aggregations, however, but rather to a corporate group whose membership comprised both native urbanites and migrants. With this group as a base, I embarked upon a broad sociocultural analytic inventory of the city. At the Symposium on Urbanization, Annual Meeting of the American Anthropological Association, November, 1966, Peter Gutkind distinguished between microcosmic and macrocosmic studies of cities, emphasizing the usefulness of both. My shift of orientation was, I suppose, from the microcosmic to the macrocosmic. In other words, I went from a concentration in depth on a small segment of the population (relegating the rest of the city to a mere backdrop) to a consideration of all discernible aspects of the city's culture. Since neither kind of study had been done before in Tripoli, either would contribute knowledge and greater understanding of the city.

My key informants were mostly members of the host group, although Muslim informants provided details on Muslim marriage and household composition, physicians and nurses with wide social-class experience related their impressions of different class patterns, business leaders briefed me on commercial conditions and organizations, and various government functionaries provided information on government operations and institutions, etc.

Without disclosing sources and as tactfully as possible, I tested the remarks of one informant against the reactions of others. For example, when one Muslim estimated that 2 percent of the Muslim marriages in Tripoli were polygynous, that the co-wives generally lived in separate establishments, and that the practice was becoming increasingly a lower-class one, I asked other informants to tell me about any specific cases of polygynous marriages with which they were acquainted. In this way I gradually built up a series of native generalizations on many subjects (some factual or purportedly quantitative, others normative or qualitative), backing them up where possible with data on specific cases. Some cases were consistent with the generalizations, others were inconsistent, and others ambiguous. When it was available and relevant, I added documentary evidence on Tripoli (scholarly, journalistic, and official) to this body of information, as well as similar evidence from elsewhere in Lebanon or from other Muslim Arab cities.

Instead of limiting myself to a household, genealogical survey, as I had in my earlier village study, I gathered information from as wide a variety of sources as possible. My organizational frames were (1) the city of Tripoli and any aspect of culture, as anthropologically defined, pertaining to it, and (2) the culture of Lebanon and any generalizations about it that might apply to Tripoli. For example, when a news item or a feature article on Tripoli appeared in a Beirut paper or magazine, I would discuss its contents with Tripolitans to get their reactions. With Tripolitan informants I discussed general articles on Lebanon on such subjects as education, the status of women, or any other subject of current interest to see to what extent they felt the articles were applicable to the city. Conversely, I discussed feature articles in the local Tripoli press with Beirut informants to gain perspective on Tripoli from their point of view. In other words, I attempted to stimulate as much feedback among my various sources and types of information as I could.

I kept field notes on my observations, discursive conversations, and formal interviews in the same way as I had in the village study, except that I more frequently inserted excerpts from and interpretations of published materials. Otherwise, my discussion about note-taking in the village applies equally to my work in Tripoli.

In addition, I built up files of newspaper and magazine clippings and took notes on the numerous mimeographed reports, unpublished theses, and other fugitive sources that came into my hands. The Tripoli telephone directory became a source requiring much investigation after I discovered that from it could be drawn samples indicative of the areal distributions of certain occupations, the relationship of place of work to place of residence, and large, residential kinship clusters.

My informants eventually fell into two types. The regulars were people to whom I could and did repeatedly return without any further explanation of my purposes or presence. Of them, my hosts were, of course, the most regular. Another regular informant was a businessman on whom I dropped in when I saw that he had no customers. A supplier to building contractors, he did not have a steady stream of customers and therefore had time to talk to me. Unlike my hosts, he was a native Tripolitan, not a migrant. The other regulars, all busy people, had to be contacted by telephone or other message when I wanted to see them.

The other type of informant consisted of "specials," with some of whom I had one-shot interviews arranged in advance either for reasons of courtesy or to enable them to prepare certain types of information. Special informants included the mayor, the manager of the city's Muslim endowed properties, and the mufti (nominal head of the Muslims in the city). In Beirut, two of my "specials" were the secretary of the grand mufti of Lebanon and the head of the Muslim educational system (a former Tripolitan). I was not always successful in obtaining information from the special informants, but even when they were evasive the experience in itself was informative in one way or another.

Other special informants, with much persistence on my part over a long period of time, provided data on enrollment figures on the sectarian schools of Tripoli and on the government schools, institutions that were extremely important and intricately involved in the value system and culture-change problems of many people. In this task, whether I used the direct approach or enlisted intermediaries or both, all relationships were focused on a particular, special purpose.

Following the city planner's lead, I eventually got an excellent map of the city that showed all streets and built-up blocks as they had been just before the great spurt of growth that began in 1948. It seemed like miraculously good fortune, too, that superimposed on this map were the outlines of all the planned future streets. With a simplified version of the map that I prepared, I was able to make my own up-to-date map of the built-up parts of the city. It was not easy to acquire the map for it seemed to be regarded by the person I first approached as a classified document. It was only after repeated visits and many assurances that I would not divulge the locations of the as-yet-undeveloped new streets that he gave me a copy of it. Much later, when I was working out the conceptual relationships between the administrative districts and the informal quarters of the city, a higher official gave me an annotated copy of the same map without any "security" cautions whatever. Actually, the map was no more detailed than the street maps one can buy in almost any big-city book store in the United States or Europe, but in Lebanon not only was it not publicly available but it also seemed to be considered something secret. One of my regular informants told me that once, when he had tried to get or see a copy of it, he had been refused. I gathered that difficulties arising out of land speculation were one reason for the generally withholding attitude, but I suspect that there may have been a more deep-seated feeling that surveyed, scale maps, like all kinds of accurate knowledge, are more likely to be used as weapons than as the stuff of neutral enlightenment.

For this same kind of reason, the act of taking down peoples' words as they are spoken, the most elaborated form of which is the questionnaire, was suspect. Questionnaire studies had recently been done in Lebanon, some in an institutional setting, others on the hit-and-run principle in the field. The latter was, and is, repellent to me, and it might have been disastrous to my study in Tripoli, even if I had wanted to undertake it there. The very idea of a questionnaire, as well as the idea of my taking photographs during my wanderings in the city, was horrifying to my regular informants. Long experience with predatory governments has caused Middle Eastern people to resist strongly having their words written down and thus taken out of their control. Furthermore, they have not learned to play the question-and-answer game epitomized in the American questionnaire poll. Sophisticated Middle Easterners feel that the American predilection for taking photographs of them indicates insensitivity and condescension, and they believe that the photographs will be used to show them in an unfavorable light. Less sophisticated people, sometimes including policemen and the military, often seem to regard foreigners' photograph-taking as an act of aggression, and they may respond in kind, so besides disliking questionnaires and photograph-taking, my informants were also apprehensive that any trouble I might get into because of such activities might have repercussions on them.

I recognize the usefulness of questionnaires for some purposes, however, so I constructed one to be taken by the Tripolitan students at the American University of Beirut. My affiliation with the University greatly facilitated the identification and location of these students, of whom there were about sixty. Thirty-five of them (male and female, Christian and Muslim) answered my call. This was in May, after I had had full opportunity to consider what items would be most useful. The questionnaire included an application of two of Kevin Lynch's questions on socially significant visual perceptions of the city, and a long series of questions on village ties, location of relatives and friends, household composition, and social class.[2] Though the sample was small, it nevertheless yielded some very interesting information, much of which was meaningful in terms of other studies as well as to my own.

As a visiting professor at the American University of Beirut, I was affiliated with an institution of considerable interest to some of my informants. In Lebanese culture, a link with someone who has an institutional tie of this kind is automatically regarded as a potential source of special advantage. In a couple of instances, I was asked if it would be possible for me to help

---

[2] Kevin Lynch is a city planner at the Massachusetts Institute of Technology. He has done field rseearch among small samples of inhabitants of Boston, Jersey City, and Los Angeles, asking them what parts or aspects of their cities are important to them, having them draw sketch maps of their cities indicating significant features, and accompanying them on walks during which their verbal reactions to their surroundings were recorded. The results of this study can be found in Lynch's book, *The Image of the City* (1960). In the case of my Tripoli sample, I asked the question about significant parts of the city, and I asked them to draw a sketch map.

influence some decisions that would be beneficial to those making the requests. I knew that I was being put into the role of an intermediary, but I could hardly refuse to help people who were being helpful to me. At the same time, I understood the university system, and I knew that it would have been most inappropriate for me to try to exert any influence on it, even if I had had any, which I did not. What I did was to make some legitimate inquiries at the University, transmit the information to my friends in Tripoli, and volunteer some advice. This was not what was really wanted, but I had at least made a bona fide effort to help. I could have played the expected role and raised their expectations in hopes of a payoff of some sort, but I did not do so, nor would I do so another time if a similar situation ever arose.

As in the case of the village study, "bowing out" posed no particular problems, because I had prepared my informants for it from the beginning, and the concept of my being a temporary visitor with responsibilities elsewhere was entirely comprehensible to them.

An evaluation of the effectiveness of my field techniques must depend on a study of my Tripoli publications (Gulick, 1963a, 1963b, 1965a, 1965b, 1967), and it really should be left to others. I can, however, mention a few matters concerning the outcome of the study. My original research aim, to study two discrete populations in Tripoli (native urban and ex-rural), was not realized for reasons already explained. Instead, my findings on subcultural differences were cast more in terms of sect and social class. In some cases, the boundaries of sect or social class were isomorphic with native urban or ex-rural groups, but this was not true in most cases. The reality was more complex than I had originally envisaged.

As of 1967, my publications on Tripoli constituted the only comprehensive descriptive analysis of a present-day Arab city readily available in print. This analysis includes a thorough physical description of the city that is related to the history of its growth and changes through time. The impact of this manmade environment on some of its inhabitants is also dealt with. Subsistence patterns, in the form of businesses, both traditional and modern, are discussed, as are the governmental institutions of the city viewed locally and from the perspective of the national culture. Major attention is paid to kinship and neighborhood groups, sects and social class, with emphasis on the internal divisiveness manifested in these groups (but generally neglected in most publications on the Middle East, including my own earlier ones). A basic theme in the study is that, although Tripoli is "modernizing" in many respects, the lives of its people have not been impersonalized, and although Tripoli's modernization has not been heavily industrial, there are symptoms of "alienation" among its inhabitants.

COMPARISONS AND CONCLUSIONS

In both studies, my methods were similar in that I relied primarily on my own powers of observation and anthropological skills in eliciting and recording information and feelings from other people. The differences between my methods in the two studies resulted in part from the fact that in Tripoli I was more experienced, more self-confident, and better able to avoid conceptually painting myself into corners merely for the sake of orderly inquiry.

In Tripoli, I had an obviously much larger system to study, and my method of coping with it essentially consisted in making myself the center of a series of communication networks. Tripoli was small enough to be systematically comprehended, once I became familiar with it. Also, like the village, it was virgin territory for anthropological research (or any other kind of social-science research), and I believe the one-man research effort was methodologically justified on this account. To argue that *only* a team project and/or a massive survey is suitable for the study of a population the size of Tripoli's is not valid when nothing systematic is known about that city. Some of the information I laboriously gathered there is of the type that is routinely available, prepackaged as it were, in Western cities, where the random-sample survey has been so much used. Yet, if the time ever comes when both survey research and studies of the Oscar Lewis type are feasible in Middle Eastern cities, I think that the practitioners of these very different methods are likely to continue to talk past and around each other rather than to each other, unless they both can find a way to relate themselves to the same holistic conception of their subject. This conception, so far, seems to have been produced by individual minds. Perhaps computers will make these holistically-thinking minds obsolete, but before they can do so, far more information than is now available will have to be fed into them, at least as far as places like Tripoli are concerned.

It would seem logical to assume that the larger the subject of study, the longer should be the amount of time allowed for it. One could easily illustrate this logic by itemizing the array of specialized studies that, ideally, one "should'" do in Tripoli as opposed to what one "should" do in a village of 500 people. It does not necessarily follow, however, that knowledge and understanding of a culture increase in direct ratio to the amount of time one lives in it, and I became aware of this during my Tripoli study. As I have mentioned before, reviewing my earliest field notes revealed to me how, in only a few months, I had internalized, and become unconscious of, a number of items in the culture, despite the fact that my role was that of observer. I did not cease to be an observer, but I became a specialized one, and adaptation to my surroundings involved routinization, just as does enculturation in general. I was even more impressed with this phenomenon after my encounters with Americans who had lived in Lebanon for many years. As individuals, they did not predictably provide any more (or less) insight than did Lebanese individuals, for they too had been enculturated and, except for isolated incidents, had forgotten the process of enculturation.

A two-year field study *may* be twice as fruitful as a one-year one. It is not the mere time that makes it so, however, but rather the carrying out of successive phases of research that continually requires the anthropologist to reset his sights and take stock of his findings. To do this, regardless of how strong his empathy for his hosts may be, he must to some extent always remain consciously and subjectively what he is objectively: an alien in another culture.

CAKCHIQUELES
AND CARIBS:
THE SOCIAL
CONTEXT
OF FIELD WORK

Nancie L. Solien González

This chapter will compare and contrast four different field-work situations involving two distinct cultures and the variations that may occur due to the nature of the investigator's contact with the natives.[1]

I lived in Santa María, a Cakchiquel-speaking Indian village in Guatemala, for a period of two months in the summer of 1955, during which time I concentrated primarily on recent ac-

[1] The field work was supported in 1955 and 1956–1957 by the Henry L. and Grace Doherty Foundation and by travel assistance from the United Fruit Company. The later research, extending from 1961 to 1964, was carried out while I was employed as research anthropologist by the *Instituto de Nutricion de Centro América y Panama* (INCAP). Grateful acknowledgement is made to all.

culturation in the domestic domain—foods, weaving, gardening, and child-care. Seven years later I returned to the village to do research on a more or less "eight-to-five'" working-day schedule for two or three days a week for about eighteen months. In this later period I studied social structure in relation to beliefs and practices concerning health, nutrition, child-bearing, and child-rearing as part of a larger comparative study involving Guatemalan Indians, Ladinos,[2] and Caribs, both rural and urban.

The second culture is that of the Black Caribs residing in Livingston on the north coast of Guatemala. I spent thirteen months there in 1956–1957 doing a community study that concentrated on the relationships between family and household structure and the economic system. I returned twice to Livingston in 1963 to gather additional data for the comparative study mentioned above. At this time I also collaborated in a study of blood types among the Caribs.

PART I: THE CAKCHIQUELES

Problem, Theory, and Research Design

In the summer of 1955, having completed my master's degree in anthropology, I sought and received a grant from the Henry L. and Grace Doherty Charitable Foundation for two months' field work in Guatemala. I had no particular anthropological reason for choosing this country at this time. I wanted to improve my Spanish and I wished to find out whether I could adapt to the exigencies of field ·work and living in a foreign culture before I went on for a Ph.D. I had already invested in a B.S. and a year's graduate work in nutrition, only to find that I was temperamentally unfitted for the kind of work I had been trained to do—administrative dietetics. If I was to have another disillusionment, I wanted to have it before I went any further in anthropology. I contacted the directors of the Institute de Nutricion de Centro América y Panama (INCAP), and they encouraged me to come to Guatemala.

The Doherty Foundation granted me $500, which I supplemented by persuading the United Fruit Company to give me a free round trip on a passenger freighter sailing the New Or-

---

[2] *Ladinos* are persons of Latin, as opposed to Indian cultural background. Although they are predominantly mestizos racially, this is not their most important identifying feature.

leans–Puerto Barrios route. Upon my arrival in Guatemala I was received warmly by INCAP. Although we had no formal agreement, this organization helped me in making my arrangements. The personal assistance of Dr. Richard Adams, an anthropologist, and his wife Betty, a Guatemalan citizen, was also invaluable. They introduced me to people, helped me arrange inexpensive living quarters in the city, loaned me books and field equipment, gave me counsel and advice, and extended unlimited hospitality to me in their home. I chose the village of Santa Maria largely on the advice of Dr. Adams, who provided me with field notes of his own and of others who had worked in this village at various times previously. Since I had no particular problem to investigate, I was glad to take advantage of this advice, and ended by making a simple analysis of the kinds of changes that had occurred in the few years since INCAP had started its work there.

Environment of the Group Being Researched

Santa Maria is a community of Cakchiquel-speaking Indians in Guatemala's western highlands. It is situated 24 kilometers west of Guatemala City at 6,000 feet above sea level. Although well below the Tropic of Cancer, the temperature is moderated by the altitude. The rainy season lasts from May through October and, although Guatemalans like to say that theirs is the land of eternal spring, foreigners are often tempted to add, "a very early and wet spring." A light jacket was necessary in the evenings and early mornings, and on overcast days I usually wore a sweater all day. In July, when I was there, the actual temperature ranged between 60° and 75° F. during the day, dropping as low as 50° at night.

When I first began field work in Santa Maria in 1955, the population of the village was about 650. In 1962 when I returned, the population had grown through natural increase to 1,053. No new families had made the town their home, and the increase seems to have been due almost exclusively to the lowering of the mortality rate.

The houses of Santa Maria, built of adobe bricks or wattle-and-daub, are set about a central plaza in a grid-iron pattern. Most houses are screened from the street by high adobe walls that enclose the entire yard, within which there may be two or three structures sheltering members of an extended family. Each household is thus ensured of its privacy, and one does not casually intrude without advance warning.

The Indians, using digging sticks, machetes, and hoes, cultivate extensively the surrounding hillsides and valleys. They grow maize and beans for home consumption and vegetables and fruits for sale largely to the non-Indian population in nearby towns and cities. The village has no market of its own, but itinerant peddlers occasionally pass through selling dried shrimp, cheese, bananas, yarn, thread, woven cloth, and other items. When I was there two Ladino-owned *tiendas* (small general stores) sold a variety of candies, spices, staples such as salt, sugar, coffee, and bread, school supplies, and patent and herbal medicines. Two similar smaller stores with a much less varied and plentiful inventory were operated by Indian families. Another Indian operated a meat market, offering beef and occasionally pork about once a week. The supply depended upon the availability of animals. The owner usually purchased one animal at a time, slaughtered it himself, and simply closed up shop when the meat was gone, always the same day the animal was slaughtered.

There were no full-time specialists in the village, although a number of persons had a special skill or enterprise. An Indian from the nearby town of Santiago owned a corn-grinding machine in Santa Maria that was well patronized. One Ladino had a small tavern, patronized occasionally during the week, more so on Saturday evenings, and quite heavily on fiesta days. The customers, almost exclusively men, bought small bottles of local rum there, which they drank off the premises. Indian women also drank this rum on special occasions, but almost always at home.

A few Indian men supplemented their incomes by local carpentry and masonry jobs, and one man (two in 1962) was a curer, using traditional herbal and magical remedies, as well as modern patent medicines. Two midwives attended virtually all the births in the village, although some women sought the assistance of practical nurses who visited the town regularly. A few men occasionally worked outside the town, traveling to the coffee plantations during harvest season, or working on highway construction, but migratory wage labor was not an important source of income for the village as a whole.

Although the Indians kept chickens, ducks, and in a few cases pigs, these were thought of primarily as nest eggs for a rainy day rather than investments for capital gain. They sometimes had the latter function, but this tended to be incidental, and in some cases the keeping of domestic fowls and animals was a losing proposition. No special arts or crafts existed as income resources.

Although there was a Catholic church in Santa Maria, there was no resident priest, and the town's inhabitants maintained the church and its grounds, the saints' statues, and even conducted regular prayer meetings. Two small Protestant congregations also existed; by 1962 they claimed 12 percent of the total population.

A public school offering grades one through six plus preparatory first year of "Castellanización" (teaching of the Spanish language) was a unique feature in a village of Santa Maria's size. A small clinic, maintained by INCAP, offered simple medicines and routine first-aid procedure, its primary interest being health research. This clinic also was a departure from the services usually available in such villages, and Indians from the surrounding area often came into Santa Maria seeking medical assistance from the practical nurses stationed in the village five days a week.[3]

Entry Problems and Initial Copings

On my first visit to Santa Maria, I was accompanied by a professional nutritionist who had carried out dietary surveys there under the auspices of INCAP. Although a native Guatemalan, she was an urban middle-class Ladino with a kindly, but patronizing, attitude toward the Indians there.

Most Ladinos, or persons of Latin-American culture patterns, tend to regard the local Indians as a somewhat inferior species, an attitude that goes back to the Spanish conquest. The Indian is expected to defer to the Ladino in all matters. The more "enlightened" Ladino recognizes that the differences between him and the Indian are cultural, but his behavior toward the other is similar to that shown a child. The fullest description of the interrelationships between Ladinos and Indians is that by Melvin Tumin (1952), but see also Richard Adams (1957).

My guide took me almost immediately to the schoolhouse, where I was introduced to the Ladino teachers who welcomed me politely and enthusiastically. Arrangements were made for me to move into one of the schools' smaller rooms for my two-month stay. The school, in addition to the clinic, was the only structure in the village with running water and toilet facilities, both of which were thought essential for my comfort. Furthermore, there were no empty houses, and I had neither funds nor equipment to establish housekeeping, even had there been such available. The Indians' houses were crowded, and they were not accustomed to accepting boarders—especially foreign women. Although I might have made arrangements to live with a Ladino

---

[3] Since this is not intended to provide a complete description of the culture and history of the highland Indians of Guatemala, the reader is referred to the following works for general background: Tax, 1939; Tax, 1952; Reina, 1966; Wagley, 1949.

family, this alternative was not immediately available, so I accepted the offer made by the teachers and my nutritionist guide without much further consideration. Arrangements were made for me to eat with the family who owned the tavern, which also seemed satisfactory to me at the time. After a casual tour through the village, during which my companion exchanged friendly greetings with many of the Indian women, always introducing me as a "friend of the clinic," we returned to Guatemala City, where I collected my belongings and purchased additional necessary equipment before returning the next day to take up residence.

The following day, a Sunday, a chauffeur employed by IN-CAP drove me to the village in a jeep. He deposited my belongings in the school and left. I then walked around the village, trying to strike up conversations with people in the streets, with women drawing water at the central *pila* (public fountain), and with men lounging on the porch of the municipal office building. I asked about the mayor, expressing a desire to introduce myself to him and explain the purpose of my visit, but I was told that he was absent from the village that day. The previous day I had asked the nutritionist to introduce me to him, but he was working on his *milpa* and did not return before we left. Although the people were polite, they maintained their distance, and I felt very alone and somewhat ill at ease, though not discouraged.

The day appeared to go without serious mishap, but the chauffeur, in a very excited state, returned from Guatemala City that afternoon to inform me that I must vacate the school immediately upon the demand of the mayor. The mayor, apparently, had complained to INCAP about my proposed occupancy of the schoolhouse, because he felt my presence would deprive the local children of the bathing facilities available at the school. The chaffeur, an urbanized nonresident Indian, felt that I should return to the city as it was late and as there appeared to be no place for me to sleep that night. Two Ladino women then stepped forward to offer me a place in their homes, and an argument broke out as to which offer I should accept. At this point, one of the Indian men suggested that I sleep in the clinic, since that building belonged to INCAP with whom they presumed I worked. I quickly made a decision, moved my things into the clinic building, and stayed there for the next two months.

On weeknights I shared the building with two practical nurses who arrived at the clinic on Monday mornings and left on Friday afternoon of each week. Neither objected to the arrangement, which proved to be felicitous and practical for all of us. I assisted in buying and preparing food for the three of us during this period, and in return the girls provided valuable introductions to the townspeople, translations from "Indian" Spanish to my "textbook" Spanish, and friendship and moral support during the first trying days of my first field-work experience. On those nights when the nurses were in the city, I had the privacy to catch up on data recording or simply to relax and plan my next day's activities.

Active Research

Since my primary purpose in undertaking the project in Santa Maria was to gain field-work experience and to improve my Spanish, I contented myself with outlining only the most obvious aspects of community structure, utilizing key informants as well as those data accumulated by previous investigators that were made available to me through INCAP, Richard Adams, and the Instituto Indigenista of Guatemala. I then concentrated on the problem of acculturation in relation to dietary and medical practices and beliefs, with particular attention to the impact of the clinic and the nutrition-research projects that had been conducted in the village during the previous three years.

This topic seemed appropriate, because of my background in nutrition and because of my sex. Nutrition was a topic on which I could rely almost exclusively upon female informants, and during that particular part of the year (July and August) the men were absent from the village most of every day except Sundays. Given the short period of time I had for field work, it was simpler for me as a woman to gain rapport with other women than it might have been for a male investigator on the same topic, so it seemed wise to make an asset of this factor. Also, the topic of diet was relatively neutral, and people were accustomed to being questioned about it.

Data-Getting Techniques

At first I found it difficult to find people to talk with, because, when I approached them in the streets for information, they were usually on their way somewhere or occupied with domestic tasks. I began to spend a great deal of time in the *tiendas,* where I made friends with the owners and later inventoried their stock. When Indian women came in to make purchases, I tried to converse with them, but because they did not waste time lounging around the store, these contacts were limited in usefulness.

I then began to frequent the central *pila* where the women came to do the family washing. Depending upon the amount of their soiled clothing, they spent from thirty minutes to an hour at a time here, and it was possible for them to continue their work while I engaged them in conversation. I soon found, however, that my textbook Spanish—not highly developed conversationally anyway—was inadequate for any but the most fundamental type of communication. Although most of the women spoke Spanish, their pronunciation and grammar were difficult for me to follow, and they frequently misunderstood my halting and stilted phrases. It was clear that if I were to obtain useful data I would have to rely upon Ladino interpreters until I had mastered the Indian's way of speaking Spanish.

The clinic dispensed milk to pregnant and lactating women and preschool children twice a day. Although not all eligible women participated in this program, enough did to make it worth my while to be present at the clinic during those hours when the milk was prepared (from powdered skim milk) and served. The women frequently tarried for a while, enjoying the social aspect of meeting with their friends, and they were relatively at ease in the clinic; also I was able to call upon the practical nurses for aid in translations. The women soon became accustomed to my presence, and some proffered shy invitations to visit them in their homes. I took advantage of these opportunities, at first making "rounds" with the practical nurses who visited households to encourage the women to take part in the milk program, and to advise and assist them in case of illness.

Within a week or ten days, I was able to move freely about the village on my own, and I had established sufficient rapport with several families that I might visit their homes frequently. Children followed me about the streets and delighted in visiting me at the clinic. Sometimes they would take me to their homes, and in several cases I was invited to go along with women and their children when they carried lunches to the men working in the fields. Gradually I began to understand that I had been expelled from the schoolhouse for reasons related to village and national politics, Indian-Ladino relationships, and to the discourtesy of my not having gone through proper channels upon my arrival in the village.

In regard to politics, the village was split by factions, one of which was known as "communist," even though I doubt that anyone then knew what that term implied on an international level. INCAP had first entered the village during the time of Jacobo Arbenz, whose leftist regime was overthrown in 1954. Because of this, INCAP was associated in the minds of the people with that administration. In 1955 it was suddenly brought home to the people that the "communists" had been overthrown, and they were unclear as to what the future of the clinic would be. Some feared to be associated with it; others declined to be friendly because they dissented from the current government's policies.

The schoolhouse had been built by the national government as a normal school, but had recently been converted into a grammar school for the use of the *pueblo*. It was much larger and more elaborate than the school ordinarily found in a village of this size, and the people were, quite properly, proud of it. They resented the idea of a foreigner being billeted there, especially without their knowledge and consent.

Initially I also had some difficulty because the people considered me a medical specialist of some sort and frequently asked me to recommend treatment. I had more knowledge of Western medical practices than they did, and I occasionally made suggestions or referred them to the clinic, but I did so only when I was asked. I explained myself and my purpose in the village as a North American schoolteacher who wished to learn something of their way of life in order to promote international understanding upon my return to my own country. This explanation seemed acceptable to the villagers, and in general I was treated as a somewhat overgrown (I towered above everyone in the village—male and female alike), but well-meaning child who had a lot to learn. I traded recipes and old-wives' tales from the United States for those from the Indians' culture and amused them all with my efforts to grind corn and make tortillas. I spent hours helping the villagers shell corn as we chatted in the afternoons. This was my one domestic accomplishment, for which I paid with blisters and later calluses.

I had contact with the men of the village during the late afternoons and on weekends, but these encounters were formal, circumspect, and few. I eventually did gain the respect and even friendship of several men (including the mayor), but during this first period of field work I associated almost exclusively with women. To the barriers of language, race, ethnic group, and nationality was added that of sex.

The relationships between men and women in this society are accompanied by extreme reserve. This reserve seems related to a general concern with personal privacy that is reflected in many ways, including the high walls surrounding the homes and in a general reluctance to disrobe in the presence of others, including one's spouse. Although crowded conditions in many of the houses make it difficult to maintain complete privacy in the physical sense, modesty and shyness are characteristics highly valued in both men and women. A rigid etiquette circumscribes behavior toward all people in personal matters, but especially toward the opposite sex. Women often refuse to talk with male investigators unless their husbands are present, and sometimes this reluctance extends to women investigators as well. This never happened to me in Santa Maria, but it did once or twice when working in other Indian villages several years later.

My own upbringing, derived from a long line of puritanical New England ancestors, taught me that it was impolite to ask personal questions. "Personal" meant anything relating to home life, sex, finances, religion, disease—in short, many or most of the topics I wished to investigate. In my own society I find it difficult to ask anyone "How much did you pay for it?" or even "How old are you?," and this reluctance carried over into my field work. Coupled with my linguistic inadequacies, this reluctance made it extremely difficult for me to delve into anything but the most superficial matters. I was so reserved that I frequently worried that I might never become a really adequate field worker. I later realized that my initial reserve was interpreted as appropriate behavior and "good manners" in this society, and I now believe it contributed substantially to my final acceptance. I was told, even during this original stay, of a male Guatemalan sociologist who had asked a great many questions concerning relationships between the sexes, and who was deeply resented by the villagers as a result. I myself spoke too freely with one informant about what appeared to be an imminent birth. When I asked her when she expected her baby, she denied being pregnant. The child was born two weeks later. As a single woman without children, this was deemed an inappropriate question for me to ask, and my own grandmother would have agreed, although for different reasons. It was not until my return to the village some seven years later, and by then the mother of two, that I was able to elicit data from a few women concerning sexual activities and childbirth. Even now I would not discuss such subjects with males in this society. In 1955 politics was also a sensitive topic, so soon after the 1954 revolution, and I learned not to discuss the subject except with a very few men whose wives had become my friends.

During this original field stint, I concentrated on visual observation, supplemented by indirect questions on "safe" topics. As the people became more accustomed to my presence, they frequently initiated topics of conversation in which they knew I was interested—specifically diet and child-care. Genealogies were relatively easy to collect through direct questioning, and these enabled me to understand a little of the social structure by observing which people associated with my informants and on what occasions. I was most successful in collecting data concerning the daily round of activities, which I carefully observed, and on the physical structure of the village and its environs. I counted, measured, timed, and photographed incessantly—frequently for no good reason. I collected much useless information and some data that became meaningful only later as I grew to know the culture better.

Research in 1962

My two months in Santa Maria in 1955 went by all too quickly. By the time I left I had been asked to become a sponsor (*madrina*) for a child, and I felt that I had been relatively successful in establishing rapport and securing information on my selected topics. This impression was confirmed when I revisited the village in 1962. I found that my old informants remembered me well—even many whose names I had forgotten. Some youngsters had grown up, married, and now welcomed me into their new households. By this time I had two children of my own, which gave me a new and higher adult status and which aided my investigation of childbearing and childrearing, which were the topics I concentrated on in 1962.

My rather unorthodox field techniques in 1962, necessitated by obligations to my household and family in Guatemala City, yielded results that would have been most difficult or impossible to obtain without an initial residence period. During 1962, when I was actually employed as a research anthropologist by INCAP, I drove to the village three or four days a week, usually arriving shortly after 8 o'clock in the morning and leaving at any time between noon and 5 P.M. I often made arrangements in advance to meet with certain people on succeeding days, which gave my informants an opportunity to prepare themselves for my visits. However, I remained flexible enough to cope with the unexpected. Sometimes informants were not home on the appointed day— either because they had something else they had to do, or because they forgot my appointment. A constant danger in field work under these circumstances is that the investigator may unconsciously impose on informants who are involved in their own domestic tasks. My earlier residence in the village gave me an idea of the daily rhythm of activities, and the people knew that I did not expect them to drop whatever they were doing to devote themselves entirely to me. Ordinarily courtesy dictates that one receive a visitor graciously, providing him with a chair, perhaps a tortilla or a piece of fruit, and one's undivided attention. In Indian villages other than Santa Maria where I also did field work without an earlier period of residence, I found this attitude particularly difficult to overcome, and my home visits were necessarily curtailed by my reluctance to keep the family members from their work.

In addition to scheduled interviews or visits, I made a point of walking around the village, chatting with people on the streets, in the stores, or at the fountain, and catching up on events since my last visit. Usually I would find a friend or acquaintance who would invite me to accompany her home, or I might be hailed from a courtyard as I passed by. Sometimes I might encounter an informant on her way to the bush to cut firewood and I would accompany her, taking the opportunity to talk as we went along.

In Santa Maria there are no restaurants or other commercial resources for securing lunch. Although it would have been possible to arrange with a Ladino woman to eat at her home, I found it more convenient to bring food with me, even though most days I was offered enough by my informants to sustain me. Sometimes I would share what I had with a family, in return for their offers of coffee, a plate of beans, or a few tortillas. In other cases I ate my lunch with the practical nurses at the clinic if they were in town, and sometimes I escaped to the outskirts of the village and picnicked by myself, taking the opportunity to jot down notes on the morning's activities. Children from the village would frequently join me at such times, and I learned much from them also, not only by watching their behavior with one another, but by checking with them data of which I was unsure —identities, residences, names of plants, etc. Since most of these children had attended school, they were more fluent in Spanish than their parents, and I had less difficulty communicating with them. When the men and older boys are working in the fields, it is the custom for wives and daughters to carry their midday meal to them, and the entire family eats in the fields together. Many times the village might be practically deserted at noon, and I would therefore confine my interviewing to older persons, the sick, or Ladinos.

By taking advantage of contacts made seven years earlier, and with my improved Spanish and a series of particular problems to investigate, I was able to collect a large amount of data on my daily visits. However, because I was unable to maintain hour-by-hour or day-by-day continuity, it was difficult, although not impossible, to assess the normality of various occurrences.

This nonresident method of securing data is not unknown in anthropology, but it is probably used less frequently than methods involving the investigator's living in the community. It is also probably considered to be less efficacious than the latter. It need not be so, if the situation is carefully appraised and utilized for all it is worth.

PART II: THE CARIBS

Problem, Theory, and Research Design

After my research among the Cakchiqueles in the summer of 1955 I returned to the United States for further course work and again sought a grant from the Doherty Foundation to return to Guatemala for a full year in 1956–1957. During my first stay in Guatemala, I had learned about the Black Carib culture of the Caribbean coast of Central America and had visited Livingston, the only Carib village in Guatemala. I was impressed by the fact that this culture had never been studied in Guatemala by anthropologists, and I was intrigued by the existence of such an apparently distinct community in this land of Indians and Ladinos. The Guatemalan Caribs seemed to be relatively isolated from other social groups in the country, yet they had strong ties with Caribs in Honduras and British Honduras. I determined to do a community study of Livingston to explore the culture in general and to learn more about how it had maintained its distinctiveness in a foreign environment. At the same time I was interested in studying the relationship of this community to Guatemala as a whole and to other Carib communities in the neighboring countries.

Aside from the general aims stated above, I had no specific problem to investigate and no specific hypothesis to test. The anthropological literature on the Black Caribs was limited, the work of Douglas M. Taylor in British Honduras being the only monograph in existence (1951). My initial objective was simply to describe the community as a whole, but after residing there for several months I became more problem-oriented. It seemed to me, as I studied, that the specific relationship between household structure and the economic patterns was an important key to understanding the position of the community in the broader social context of the nation and the region. This then became my focus, but only after I had been immersed in the culture for some time.

Passive or Adaptational Research

The Black Caribs of Guatemala live primarily in the village of Livingston at the mouth of the Rio Dulce, at one time the primary port and gateway to the interior. Their residence there and in other villages strung out along the Caribbean coast of Central America dates from the turn of the nineteenth century, when they were forcibly deported from the island of St. Vincent in the Lesser Antilles by the British. Although those living in Guatemala, Honduras, and Nicaragua have Spanish surnames, speak Spanish as their second tongue, and belong to the Roman Catholic Church, their culture is composed of a blend of traits inherited from their Carib-Arawak Indian and African ancestors—a combination reflected in the name by which they are known. They also had considerable contact with British and French culture as represented in the general Caribbean area. Black Caribs living in British Honduras usually have Spanish surnames and adhere to Catholicism, but they do not speak Spanish. (See Solien, 1959, and Taylor, 1951.)

The Carib settlements are as close to the sea as possible; often their houses are built just a few yards back of the sandy beach. The climate is tropical—hot and moist. There is no rainy season, for it rains all year round, although July and August are slightly dryer than the other ten months.

Although the Black Caribs still fish and cultivate manioc, their economy today is largely dependent on migratory wage labor. In 1955, Livingston had a total population of about 2,500, of whom 1,800 were Black Carib, according to a census I carried out at that time. The remainder were Guatemalan Ladinos, plus a small colony of East Indians, known locally as "Coolies," and a few Chinese businessmen. The town boasted two schools, several general stores and taverns, a small hotel, a pension, a movie theater, telegraph office, military barracks, an ice plant, and a small generator that provided electricity seven or eight hours a day. Many of the businesses were owned by one enterprising and very wealthy Ladino family who also owned considerable property in Guatemala City, but who preferred to live in Livingston. Some of their interests—the hotel, for instance—were not very profitable, but were maintained in part as hobbies and in part in the hope that someday Livingston might become popular as a resort town. At one time the town had been quite important to the country's interior, but this prominence had declined and almost disappeared with the rise of Puerto Barrios and the building of a railroad line from that city to the capital, Guatemala City.

Livingston stands on a slightly elevated promontory, and thus presents three "faces" to the sea. The main wharf, with its small customs house, is adjacent to the main business section, which stretches along one street from the shore and up a steep hill to a level where most of the Ladinos have their homes. There is no central plaza or square, and the *municipio* offices are somewhat separated from the business section, which is extended, although not dispersed. The military barracks is sharply set apart from the rest of the town, yet it overlooks the sea. The postal and telegraph offices are adjacent to the barracks and the Catholic church is also isolated from the business section and the government buildings. The houses of the Caribs are scattered over a large area in what, at first, appears to be an almost random fashion. Some are oriented to the sea, others are grouped in small compounds, the doors facing inward toward the yard, and others face a street or path. Most yards are unfenced or have only low structures that obstruct neither the view nor access to the yards.

For several generations Black Carib males have left their homes periodically to obtain wage labor up and down the Caribbean coast of Central America. Some have worked aboard ships that have taken them to the United States and to Europe, and many have settled permanently in New York, San Francisco, London, and elsewhere. Basic literacy among males approaches 100 percent, and a large number of women under forty years of age can also read and write. Great emphasis is placed on education in general, particularly on foreign languages. One of my principal informants spoke five languages—Island Carib, Spanish, English, French, and Kekchi (one of the many languages spoken by Indians in Guatemala).

Because the women are often temporarily left alone while the men are away on wage work, their status is extraordinarily high in the culture. They may own property, such as houses and house sites, travel freely according to their own desires, make decisions in regard to domestic matters, and when angry feel free to curse and even strike the men. Many women operate their own small businesses—selling lottery tickets, making and selling various prepared foodstuffs, smuggling, dressmaking, and selling garden produce. Some purchase fish which they salt and take to Puerto Barrios or even Guatemala City to sell at a profit. Cash obtained by women through any of these means is theirs to spend as they see fit.

Women also influence community policy, largely through their women's organizations, many of which are sponsored by the Catholic church. These groups serve as channels through which news of general interest is transmitted, and when an individual or group wishes to introduce a new idea, voice a complaint about existing circumstances, or simply plan a community excursion to another town (a common form of recreation and also a business), it is the better part of valor to broach it first to the women at their meetings. They will discuss the issue at length, hear pros and cons from outsiders (men) invited for this purpose, and either condemn it or offer their support. These women's groups cultivate plots of land and sell the produce to raise money for church festivals, needy members, and burial expenses.

Entry Problems and Initial Copings

My first visit to Livingston took place at the end of the summer of 1955 when I had lived in Santa Maria. I was returning to the United States by ship from Puerto Barrios, and I decided to go to the nearby Carib village for a three-day visit before sailing. There are no roads leading to Livingston; one can reach it only by sea. In 1955, and still, to my knowledge, there was only one public launch to Livingston each day. It left Livingston at 4 A.M. for Barrios and left Barrios again at about 10:30 A.M., arriving in Livingston at noon. On my first visit, I missed the 10:30 boat, but managed to talk some young Carib men into taking me in a smaller craft, much against the advice of all observers. Halfway to Livingston our motor failed, and my two companions and I were stranded in a fairly heavy sea. We strung up a white shirt on a fishing pole as a signal and were fortuitously rescued by a government yacht carrying a team of malaria researchers to Lake Izabal, via Livingston and the Rio Dulce. My arrival among the Caribs was therefore accompanied by some fanfare, and I never afterward lived down the story of my brave, but foolhardy expedition. The escapade favorably impressed the people among whom I would later live for thirteen months.

When I returned in June, 1956, to make arrangements to live in Livingston, I was no stranger, even to those whom I had not met the year previously. I first asked about housing at the Ladino-owned hotel where I was temporarily quartered, but when I indicated I was interested in living in one of the Carib districts, the manager was shocked and said he could do nothing to help me. I next asked a Carib man who had served as cook on the yacht that rescued me the year before, and he quickly found an ideal spot for me. I rented a small (12' × 15') house situated among several others in a compound occupied by several siblings and some of their descendants. The eldest daughter of the eldest sister in this sibling group took me under her wing, washing my clothes, seeing that I was fed, guiding me about town, and serving ultimately as one of my most trusted friends and informants. From my back door I could look out into the common patio of the compound, and from my front door I could watch the activity on one of the most important routes to the beach and to a well. A public water faucet was located just outside my door, which was not only a personal convenience, but a favorite gossiping place as people waited their turn for water.

After making these arrangements, which the Caribs did not seem to think were strange, I went to Guatemala City for four days to buy equipment and re-establish contacts made the year before. On my return to Livingston, many persons volunteered their services to carry my baggage the half-mile or so (partly uphill) to my new abode and help me get settled. They refused any monetary compensation. Contrary to the situation in Santa Maria, where I might never have met an Indian had I not made an effort, in Livingston the people came in droves to my house to see and meet the oddball *gringa*. Rapport was then easy to establish, and in a very short time I was able to probe any area of the culture in which I was interested.

Active Research

Although the Caribs are certainly less reticent with and less suspicious of strangers than are the highland Indians of Guatemala, their attitudes and behavior toward me were not typical of their treatment of most other Caucasians—either Latin Americans or North Americans—with whom they came in contact. The Caribs are not above exploiting Caucasians by charging outrageous prices for goods and services, or even by robbing them when the opportunity arises. They enjoy making tourists and local Ladinos both in Livingston and in Puerto Barrios the butt of their jokes, although in the presence of tourists their demeanor is polite unless they feel offended. I am certain that my rapid and successful establishment of rapport was greatly facilitated by the circumstances of my initial visit to the village. I had proved my "fearlessness"—both of the sea (which was based more on ignorance than bravery) and of the Carib—and I had indicated that I lacked concern for the physical comforts usually demanded by Caucasian visitors and had a sincere interest in visiting their village at any cost. My later behavior was consistent with their interpretation of our first encounter, so I came to be treated almost as an equal. I too became the butt of jokes, but at least some of them were to my face.

The Carib did not hesitate to offer me their foods, which I never refused, even though some were not really acceptable to my palate, and they were delighted to find that I appreciated the local rum as much as they did. When I visited other villages in the company of some of my informants, I slept in a hammock, on the floor, or sandwiched in between the members of the family in a common bed. I was willing to make long-distance, sometimes overnight, journeys by dugout canoe, and I was not above smuggling soap, cigarettes, and other small items back into Guatemala just as they did. In their dances, I was never able to overcome a certain amount of built-in Western inhibition, but they recognized and appreciated my efforts. (On a return visit in 1962, I was able to teach *them* the twist!)

Fortunately for my field work's success, the exuberance and extroverted behavior of my Carib hosts helped me to overcome my own hesitancy to ask the personal questions required in my research. When they felt no qualms about asking me about my personal life, it was easy to retaliate, but this is not to say that there were no codes of etiquette or areas about which they were somewhat reluctant to speak. Personal quarrels were matters of some privacy, and witchcraft was more difficult to explore than most other subjects, but researching even these became possible with selected informants. Most importantly, there were no closed doors or fences. People simply appeared in each others' doorways, and I too was permitted this freedom. The only area in which I was unable to participate was fishing, which is almost exclusively a male activity. On one occasion, when I insisted upon taking out a small dugout canoe alone, an activity in which women do not typically indulge, I amused a crowd of on-lookers by rolling it over several times before I managed to keep my balance. I heard of this escapade for months afterward, and I was good-naturedly joshed for having assumed such an unfeminine role.

During my thirteen-month stay in Livingston I collected data through a variety of techniques. I accompanied various women of the compound during their daily rounds of activities. I attended social gatherings of all sorts, including dances, wakes, mass at the local Catholic church, rituals in honor of dead ancestors, women's meetings, cooperative rice-harvesting sessions, and cassava-making. I spent time just sitting about in the compound watching the activities there and questioning my hosts about things I did not understand. In time, I queried selected informants on special subjects, often in prearranged interviews either in their homes or, more often, in my house. I usually was able to take notes in their presence, since these were all people with whom I had previously built up rapport. With the assistance of three young men whom I trained for the job, I took a census of the entire Carib population in the town to determine family and household composition, age distribution, migratory patterns, and sources of income.

In the company of my primary woman informant, and sometimes alone, I made trips to nearby Puerto Barrios where I interviewed Caribs and non-Caribs and learned something of the history and operation of the United Fruit Company in that area. I also made a six-week trip to Honduras and visited many Carib villages and towns, always seeking relatives of my friends in Livingston, who never failed to give me a warm welcome. I made a similar trip to British Honduras, where I traveled along the seacoast in a small cabin cruiser of the Public Health Department visiting Carib villages otherwise inaccessible. During this trip I stayed in Belice for a week perusing the archives of that colony and learning something of the Creole culture and the interrelationships between Caribs and their non-Carib Negro neighbors in that colony.

With borrowed equipment I recorded music of different types, both traditional and modern, and I made a collection of items of material culture and took pictures of the methods of manufacturing them. At the local municipal offices I went through the birth, death, and court registries, and I collected information from schoolteachers on school attendance, curriculum, dropout rates, and so on. In short, I tried to immerse myself as completely as possible in the life of the people of the village. Each evening, unless some late activity deterred me, I typed notes that I had recorded during the day in small $3'' \times 5''$ notebooks. I filed paper slips ($5'' \times 7''$) containing typed data in a metal filing box. I tried to go back and review all my notes at least once a month, so that I might discover unrecognized relationships or inconsistencies to be checked further.

Obviously, one never gets all the data about everything in a community, and the problem becomes one of defining an area of research and then covering this as completely as possible, checking and cross-checking data with different informants to improve their reliability. One of the difficulties with the so-called community study is that the researcher often has no specific problem or hypothesis to investigate and simply tries to learn everything about the community as a whole, which is a self-defeating project. On the other hand, it is often impossible to construct a meaningful hypothesis before one's entry into a new field situation. In such cases, description must precede theorizing, but often the problem can be outlined after the research has been in progress for some time. After I had been in the field for five or six months I found myself increasingly intrigued by the kinship and family systems. I noted that non-Caribs, especially of the upper classes, spoke of the immorality of the Caribs and their high rates of illegitimacy and family disorganization. They also claimed that the Carib woman did all the work while the man simply sat around in his hammock or disappeared entirely from the domestic scene, presumably because he was too lazy or too irresponsible to maintain his wife and children.

The Carib communities I observed, however, did not seem to be either vice-ridden or lascivious. I also learned to admire the Carib man's efforts to find work in a difficult employment market. I became interested in trying to understand the structure by means of which these communities were able to maintain a measure of stability in what was clearly a changing world for them. There were some areas I did not research for lack of time or experience, for impracticality, and/or because I felt they were irrelevant to my central theme. For instance, I left virtually untouched the culture of the non-Carib elements of the local population, the Ladinos and the Hindu "Coolies." I got to know well one Ladino family—the most important one in town—and I knew a few Coolies slightly, but I never delved into their culture patterns. In part this was because the Caribs were clearly a group apart. They despised the Coolies and were looked down upon in return by the Ladinos, and I did not wish to endanger my position with the Caribs by spending too much time with either of these groups. For this same reason, I was unable to obtain quantitative information from the stores and small businesses concerning volume of trade, buying habits of their clients, credit arrangements, and so forth, as the stores were all owned by non-Caribs.

Another deficiency in my study was that I never found a satisfactory method of collecting household budgets systematically because of the nature of the culture itself. Although some women were literate, they were only barely so, and most could not keep records for me. Furthermore, the sources of income were so diverse and so irregular that most people could not give me any exact accounting. Male relatives would contribute sums of money when they were working, women earned varying amounts from small enterprises such as selling cassava or candy or bread, and children sometimes contributed money earned by running errands or doing odd jobs. Besides, much of the domestic economy depended on fish, which were either caught by members of the household itself, donated by relatives, bartered for other goods, or purchased, and on such home-grown products as rice, platanos, and root crops. It was clear that those households lucky enough to have attached *employed* males lived better than those with none, but I never got exact quantitative information from a large sample of households. Instead, I relied on qualitative data from case studies and personal observation to understand how the economic system operated.

Leaving the village after having lived there for thirteen months was a fairly casual matter. From the beginning everyone knew that I was to be there for approximately a year, so it was no surprise to them when I finally fixed a departure date, which soon became known throughout the town. Many persons brought presents of sea-shells, pretty seeds, hand-embroidered pillowcases, and lithographs of saints "to remember them by."

Most, however, when they saw me in the streets would simply say, *"Te vas, entonces? Bueno, que te vaya bien!"* (So you're leaving? Well, goodbye and good luck.) In a culture such as this, where people come and go with frequency, mine was just another departure. We all assumed, correctly so, that someday we would meet again. I have made two trips back to the town since, and I have been in contact with Carib migrants from Livingston in Guatemala City. Even now some of them write to me, usually for "loans" or for help in finding jobs.

Research in 1962

I returned to Livingston twice for about a week each time during 1962 while I was employed by INCAP to do research on diet and child-rearing practices in the country as a whole. On these visits, I spent a full day visiting special friends and acquaintances, and then settled down to straight interviewing with a few selected informants. Because I already knew the basic culture outlines, including patterns of child-rearing, it was possible for me in a very short time to fill in the blank or spotty areas, check one informant against another, and check all material against former data and observations. I already knew the people personally, so I was able to control my samples' characteristics by choosing persons known to be voluble and open, yet not prone to constructing tall stories simply to impress me. The latter tendency was one I constantly had to guard against, particularly since, when I checked *some* of these seeming fictions, they turned out to be true! I learned that some informants were more likely to be forthright and honest with me than others, and for the short-term investigation of selected topics such as diet and child-rearing I chose such people.

Another project, undertaken in collaboration with a Guatemalan pathologist also employed by INCAP, was collecting blood samples to determine certain factor frequencies and to assess nutritional status. After discussing the matter before the two women's clubs and obtaining the assistance of a young Carib man, I selected eighty unrelated adults with no known non-Carib ancestry as our sample population. Each was contacted personally before the technicians' arrival, informed of the nature of the study, and asked to participate. Each was promised a report indicating whether his blood was "healthy" or not. These reports were later mailed to the individuals, and if signs of anemia or venereal disease were present, they were advised to consult a physician. This ploy was so successful that when the technicians arrived in Livington, the sampling went smoothly and with no serious complaint on the Caribs' part. Contrary to what is often presumed, these people had few qualms about allowing samples of their blood to be taken. Their major fear (apart from a fear of the discomfort involved) was that the agency we represented would profit by selling the blood. Their relative sophistication in regard to Western medical practices and their knowledge that blood for medical purposes *is* often bought and sold lay behind their objections. The Caribs have a well-developed set of native beliefs and practices in regard to curing, but they also make extensive use of Western medical facilities available in Puerto Barrios and other cities.[4] Once we explained the situation, we had more subjects than we could actually handle.

In addition to these two short return visits to Livingston, I also completed a small research project concerning Caribs who had migrated to Guatemala City. In 1957, when I conducted my census of Livingston, 12 persons out of 211 "absentees" were said to be in the capital. But in the early 1960s, when I was living in Guatemala City, I was repeatedly contacted by Caribs whom I had known during my original field work in Livingston. All maintained that by this time there was a fairly large number of Black Caribs who had come to the city to "make their futures." In 1964 I worked out a one-page short-answer schedule, and with the help of two men who had previously acted as informants, I administred it to eighty-two Carib adults living in Guatemala City. Here, as in the research carried out on a regular but intermittent basis in Santa Maria, I found that as an anthropologist I had to adapt my field techniques considerably. Participant observation, in the usual sense of the word, was impossible. My observations were limited by the fact that I did not actually live in the type of neighborhood frequented by the Caribs, and the social structure of the city itself, of which I was a part, recast the entire nature of my rapport with them. Although I was working with the same people, many of whom I had known quite well in Livingston, their attitudes toward me were altered by the new environment of the city. They now perceived me as a member of the local upper-middle class—a status assignment over which I had no control. They remained friendly and readily invited me into their homes, but it was unthinkable that I remain overnight or accompany them about the city in their various domestic and recreational activities. One of the interesting findings of the research was that the Black Caribs in Guatemala City did not restrict their social contacts to the Carib group itself, but actively sought and participated

---

[4] The results of our analysis of the sickle-cell trait and the Diego factor are reported in Tejada, González, and Sanchez, 1965.

in relationships with other ethnic groups—especially with Ladinos. Many of the men were living in marital relationships with Ladino women, and in their work situations the Caribs constantly interacted with the Ladinos. They tended to live not in a cluster, but spread out through the lower-class neighborhoods of the city. The results of this study have been presented in González (1965).

Although I was welcomed into the Carib households, it was as a temporary visitor. Thus it would have been awkward and embarrassing had I tried to push my participant observation into nondomestic spheres. As part of my newly assigned role, I was requested to make small loans, help find jobs, donate old or outgrown clothes from my household to theirs, and even help them get out of jail. In many ways, this was my role in Santa Maria, a role also defined for me by the sociocultural system itself. In my opinion, this is the single most important distinction between resident and intermittent field work.

Summary and Evaluation

Anthropologists, missionaries, Peace Corps volunteers, or others who attempt to immerse themselves in a community in a foreign culture should realize that they must always occupy a special position within the social system. No matter how friendly the "natives"—no matter how great the rapport—one is never actually a native himself. Most, if not all, societies in the world today have been visited by people from beyond the immediate culture, and they have identified these visitors as *aliens*. These aliens may or may not be citizens of the same nation, may or may not be representatives of the same racial stock, may or may not share the same language. Wherever they come from, whoever they are, the important point is that the native culture itself will have certain defined statuses into which it may cast them, thus limiting their behavior patterns in certain ways.

The resident anthropologist, even though he may initially fall into one or another of the standard "foreign" categories of persons, is usually able to create for himself a special niche—alien still—but different from all the others. In short, he hopes to be placed in a class by himself, which from the point of view of the community being studied, may never again be filled by another foreigner. As such, his behavior may vary from the behavior expected of persons in the other established statuses. As long as the anthropologist continues to occupy this, *and only this*, status, he may be permitted a great deal of freedom in establishing behavior patterns considered "proper" for this new role.

On the other hand, the anthropologist involved in intermittent field work is, in a very real sense, living a double life. It is manifestly clear to the natives that when he is not with them he is somewhere else and probably living a very different sort of life. Even this knowledge may not seriously change the situation, unless the natives chance to observe him in his "other life." If the anthropologist's "off-hours" behavior fits into a category already known to the people he is studying, they may cast him in this other role while he is in their community. Depending upon the circumstances, he may then be regarded as and treated as a tourist, an administrator, a member of the local upper or middle class, a foreign imperialist, or anything else familiar to them. Any attempt on his part to act *outside* of the expected behavior patterns for this assigned role may be met with suspicion, uneasiness, or even contempt.[5] I do not wish to imply that field work under the latter circumstances is impossible, fruitless, or necessarily lacking in rigor. There is much that can still be done, but the investigator must recognize the limitations imposed by his role in the broader culture and learn to act within them.

Other limitations are necessarily imposed by the fact that one is not continually present in the community in the physical sense. There are disadvantages, as well as advantages, of working under intermittent conditions. First, the anthropologist misses much of the minutiae of the daily round of activities, as well as some of the rhythm of the yearly cycle. Even when he is there, his presence may alter otherwise normal behavior. He is thus forced to rely more heavily on interviews with selected key informants, and he has to develop a communication network through which he is informed of future special events of importance to him in his work. These include life-crisis rites, holiday or holy-day observances, special games, elections, or other communal activities such as hunts, a cooperative house-building or planting project, and so forth. Since the anthropologist is probably not viewed as a member of the community and since the people may not be aware of his special interests, he may not be informed of these events in advance unless he takes it upon himself to see that he is. He also has to learn to look

---

[5] Even when the anthropologist lives permanently among the people while doing field work, it will be recognized that his "real life" takes place elsewhere under different circumstances, of course. But in this case, his home identity will be totally foreign to their conceptual system, and as such, will not be likely to impinge upon his relationship with them. Similarly, if he leaves for brief periods for survey work or for mental and physical relaxation, this too can be interpreted *within* the context of the role he has established.

for clues that a special event is under preparation, so that he can inquire about it and make plans to attend.

Another disadvantage is that the field worker may have no home base within the community, no place to *go* when he is not physically with his informants. If he wishes to write notes in private, bathe, change clothes after a particularly messy activity, repair an item of equipment, or simply rest for a brief period, he may find it awkward to do so without actually leaving the community. Under some circumstances he may find it possible to rent or have built for him a small house or room that he may use for such purposes or for an occasional overnight stay. Some vehicles, such as panel trucks, may also be useful as combination offices and temporary quarters.

Transportation may also be a limiting factor in field work. Having one's own vehicle—preferably one equipped with sleeping bag, canned emergency food and water, a typewriter, change of clothes, and any other measuring or recording devices one may need—is not a necessity, but it will increase the ethnographer's efficiency and comfort. Lacking this, the investigator must depend on public transportation, restricting himself to studying only those communities on direct routes. Moreover, he may have to pass up good observational or interviewing situations in order to conform to departure schedules. The amount of equipment he can carry back and forth under such circumstances is also limited.

The ethnographer who uses an intermittent method of research will find some topics that are not amenable to his method. The first of these is political organization. In most societies, power and authority reside largely in the men, and since the men may frequently be absent from their homes during the day when the researcher is present, this subject is difficult to probe. If the investigator also happens to be a female, the magnitude of the difficulty is increased. The structure of specific political institutions and their functions may be determined by questioning selected informants, but this technique is less useful for imbedded or implicit functions. The gathering of case studies to illustrate how a system actually operates may be hampered by discontinuity in direct observation, and relying on key informants may prove risky, since the latter may tend to abstract from the actual situation, thus slanting the data. Moreover, for any subject highly charged with emotion, or for those that the people themselves are unaccustomed to dealing with verbally, the lack of continuous observation may be detrimental.

If research is largely carried out during the daytime, the investigator will miss entirely those activities usually conducted in the evening. Most experienced anthropologists will attest to the value of sharing recreational activities with the natives. This sharing not only increases rapport, but offers many opportunities to observe interaction among the members of the society for the purpose of sorting out statuses and patterns of visiting and analyzing values based on topics of conversation chosen by the natives themselves. Participation in social drinking, smoking, or other activities, listening in on story-telling or planning sessions, or simply sitting around chatting with the entire family, sodality, or any other formal or informal grouping of people is often one of the most rewarding of all field-work experiences.

The disadvantages of intermittent research are somewhat balanced by a few definite advantages. Indeed, the field worker forced to carry out intermittent research may turn the situation into a very favorable one. First of all, because he is in a position to return favors offered him, he can actively promote a reciprocal relationship between himself and his informants. Most resident anthropologists are usually unskilled in the activities required for maintaining the system within which they are living. They can, of course, return favors by giving the natives gifts and money, by helping them to write letters, by interpreting the actions of administrators or other foreigners, and by advising them on dealings with the outside world. The intermittent researcher, however, can endear himself to the natives by offering transportation to those wishing to travel for some purpose of their own, by making purchases, and by carrying letters or packages to absent friends or relatives. In any community accessible enough to be visited daily, chances are that the people will be involved in a number of extracommunity relationships and will welcome assistance of this kind.

Another advantage of the intermittent investigator is that he can more easily focus on one particular topic or problem. By continually working over his notes, and by referring to library resources (assuming that these exist at the "home" base) for comparison, the chances of missing large blocks of important information on a particular topic are lessened. Also, he can schedule his visits to coincide with important events (if the precautions noted above are taken) or with certain seasons of the year. Since intermittent work is likely to be extended over a period longer than one year, observations and impressions can be rechecked at the same point in the succeeding year or years.

Informants who feel socially obligated to the investigator for services rendered and who know of his special interests and limited time may be less likely to put him off a second time. Special sessions on particular subjects may be arranged with one or several informants together, and by recording the interview, information may be secured in a relatively efficient way. I found that such sessions were always more difficult while I was actually residing in the village, because my informants, knowing that I would be there at a later hour, or the next day, or the next week, tended to treat appointments casually. Attempts to tape group sessions during my year's residence in Livingston often broke down due to the natives' embarrassment, overeagerness, or desire to play. On the other hand, during my later brief visits, sessions that I arranged specifically for the purpose of gathering information on specific topics, say, traditional songs, mythology, or health and medicine were treated more seriously because the natives knew that my time was limited. These sessions were regarded as being something of an "occasion" and were well attended. I never attempted to hold group sessions among the Cakchiquel-speaking Indians, so I cannot compare them with the Caribs in this regard.

Certain topics, especially those ordinarily researched through selected key informants, lend themselves particularly well to investigation on an intermittent basis. The technological and social patterns involved in specialist occupations, such as those of midwife, curandero or shaman, potter, and weaver, are noteworthy in this respect. Repeated visits to a particular specialist to watch him work, to talk with him, and to record his work by camera or tape recorder can build up good rapport, and this type of study suffers in no way from the fact that the researcher does not actually live in town.

Personal topics such as genealogies, case studies involving witchcraft, and sexual behavior are best handled through intensive sessions with particularly well-known informants. The Youngs (1961) have shown in data from Mexico, however, that information from key informants is *not* reliable in respect to such topics as community dietary habits and public opinion on political matters. The researcher should check information given by key informants on these subjects against other sources of data when possible, and he should remember that the danger of obtaining only one person's impression is no different in intermittent field work than in resident work. Indeed, household budgets, dietary intakes, timed recordings of work patterns, and any recorded or archival materials present in the community may be even easier to obtain if an individual works on an intermittent basis—assuming that he is seen as representing some acceptable interest or agency from the larger society.

In summary, a comparison of these two techniques of field work indicates that important and reliable information may be gathered under either set of circumstances. The resident anthropologist's status and behavior will be different from the intermittent anthropologist's, however, and this may in part determine the type of problems he can most successfully pursue. Each method has distinct advantages and disadvantages of its own, and research problems should be conceptualized and attacked within the framework of the total situation.

The field-work situations described above may be contrasted in terms of the differences between the two ethnic groups involved. In using my own research for this purpose, the nature of my residence in each should be held constant. This is somewhat difficult to do, for the bulk of my work among the Black Carib was carried out on a long-term residential basis, with only a few brief visits some years later and some work among them in Guatemala City. On the other hand, I remained in residence in the highland Indian village for only two months, and I did most of my work over a two-year period of visiting. Clearly, these differences affected the way in which I was received by the two different communities and also possibly influenced my view of the situations.

In both cases I found the people as curious about me and the culture I represented as I was about them. The Caribs were more outgoing and direct in their relations with me, even from the beginning. The probability that this stemmed more from their culture than from the nature of my presence among them is reflected in numerous ways. Unlike Santa Maria, the houses and yards in Livingston are not walled or fenced in, and there is much more openness in the everyday comings and goings of the Caribs. Family arguments are frequently conducted out-of-doors, and neighbors and passersby observe and even participate in the dispute. Gossip is frequent and opinions are openly and loudly expressed. The Caribs are not reticent about sexual relationships. Not only is there public joking about sexual behavior, accompanied by appropriate gestures, but their dancing is uninhibited in the extreme in this regard.

In Santa Maria, gossip is also frequent, but it tends to take place in whispers behind closed doors. On the surface, and in the streets and other public places, one gets the impression that the community is happily homogeneous and almost completely without personal strife. Only after rapport with individuals is established does it become clear that it is ridden with factionalism, personal enmity, and maliciousness. Witchcraft is a feature in both cultures, but it takes different forms in each. Among the Caribs, personal misfortune is frequently interpreted as the result of not properly placating a wrathful dead ancestor. Although living individuals may also cause harm to their enemies through the use of *obeah*, or witchcraft, the Carib is usually well aware of his enemies and believes he can pin down the evildoer with the aid of a shaman. Witches with innate powers of doing harm are not a conceptual entity in this culture. (See González, n.d., for a further discussion and analysis of witchcraft.)

The villagers of Santa Maria believe that certain persons may be witches, but their identity is not always known. It is widely assumed that most witches operate in secret and take pains to preserve their anonymity. This again reflects the attitudes toward personal privacy and the restricted patterns of behavior in relation to one's fellows observed in this culture.

This same restraint continues to be seen in Santa Maria when one tries to obtain information concerning land ownership, other private property, or even dietary intake. Foster (1965) has discussed this lack of communication in relation to what he calls the "image of limited good," by which he means the idea that there is only so much of a given "good" to go around in a community, and if one individual accumulates a large amount of it, he does so at the expense of his fellows and is therefore to be criticized. In Santa Maria I was told by one informant that she was afraid to give information to the nutritionists conducting dietary surveys because she didn't want her fellow townsmen to know just how much food her family consumed, for fear they would "envy" her. She also feared that the government might take away food from those who had more than others and give it to the less fortunate. There is a similar reluctance to give accurate information concerning other possessions.

This attitude of restraint is unknown in Livingston. Horticultural lands are not privately owned, although house sites and gardens in town are. Most households depend on some kind of wage labor for their livelihood, and levels of income vary with the type of job held and the number of household members working. As the prevailing wage scales for different types of jobs are well known, secrecy in such matters would be pointless. Furthermore, a great deal of pride is taken in personal property—a visible mark of success. The informant is therefore more likely to overstate his material possessions and financial status.

Finally, I found that the relationship of both groups to other sectors of the larger society differed somewhat, and this also seems to have influenced the context in which I was accepted within each community. The social and cultural gulf between the Guatemalan Indian and the Ladino has been described by many investigators (especially Tumin, 1952). To this day there has been preserved in Guatemala a culturally defined complex of behavior patterns involving obsequiousness on the part of the Indian toward Ladinos and a patronizing and paternal attitude of the Ladinos toward the Indians. This is symbolized by the Indian ritual of giving small gifts of food to those Ladinos who visit or otherwise take notice of him, and seeking Ladinos as sponsors for his children in the *compadrazgo* system.[6] These actions confer upon the Indian the right to ask small favors of the Ladinos—loans, intercession with authorities on personal or community matters, help in finding a job, and so on.

The Black Carib, on the other hand, even though they occupy a low position in the social hierarchy of the Central American coastline, are notoriously nonobsequious in their relations with non-Caribs. They are aware of their social position, and they are conscious of the fact that non-Caribs (and nonblacks) control the government and the national economy, and thus Carib chances for obtaining work and increasing their standard of living. They react to this situation not with servility, but with a braggadocio for which they have achieved a reputation throughout the area. The Caribs—especially the men—exude self-confidence, both as individuals and in terms of their ethnic group, and for good reason, for they are often better educated than most Indians and many lower-class Ladinos in the area. In the colony of British Honduras, they are highly regarded because of this, and they are widely employed as elementary schoolteachers throughout that region. The Caribs are also considered to be good dock workers, sailors, and fishermen. In their dress they have a tendency toward the flamboyant, wearing bright colors and fashionable styles when they appear in non-Carib company or on special occasions in their own town. Unlike the Indian, they do not hesitate to "tell off" a Ladino when they feel they have been crossed. Many Ladinos and non-Carib blacks express a general fear and awe of Caribs, whom they believe to be particularly adept at "black magic." This reputation undoubtedly protects them somewhat in their personal relations with others, and at the same time helps maintain their position as a distinct social group.

These differences in personality structure, themselves reflections of the total social and cultural configurations, certainly affected the manner in which I was received in the two communities. My status and role were in part determined for me by the people I was studying, and I was successful to the extent that I was able to govern my behavior within this framework so as to maintain their respect. Among the Santa Maria Indians, themselves reserved in their behavior, I too had to maintain a certain reserve and observance of traditional formalities. I overstepped this in my first encounter with them when I bypassed the local

---

[6] *Compadrazgo* refers to the network of social relationships created by the custom of naming sponsors or godparents for various life-crisis rites such as baptism or marriage; a godparent and a real parent call each other "*compadre*," hence anthropologists name the entire system *compadrazgo*.

Indian authorities in arranging to live at the school. I also was out of line in asking questions about childbirth, questions deemed inappropriate for an unmarried woman and a foreigner. I eventually compensated for these errors by my subsequent behavior, but only because I reacted immediately to their disapproval and withdrawal.

On the other hand, the Caribs do not respect a reserved manner, and in a foreigner they interpret reserve as evidence of snobbery, prejudice, and distaste for them and their customs. As I pointed out, the fortuitous accident that preceded my first visit to Livingston helped me to establish a favorable image among the Caribs. Later, rather than shocking the Caribs with my questions, they often shocked me, and there were times when I was uncomfortable, yet forced to hide my discomfort in order to retain their respect. They thought nothing of asking me "personal" questions about my finances, sex life, religious beliefs, and politics. In a sense, the Indians of Santa Maria and the Black Caribs presented opposite extremes in terms of personality patterns, and my own personality fell somewhere in between.

Within the limitations imposed by the general cultural situation, the field worker can, indeed must, create a special niche for himself. There is always a tendency for the natives to classify the anthropologist with other foreigners they have known. The anthropologist must alter their perception of him, so that he may work outside of the narrow boundaries imposed by their expectations. The Caribs, because of their own respect for education and their broader experience with members of other cultures, were able to understand and accept as legitimate the idea of my conducting pure research. When they asked what I was doing among them, I simply told them that I wanted to find out as much as possible about their way of life. Among the Indians such an explanation did not make sense. For them, knowledge must be for *some purpose.* In Santa Maria, I identified myself as a schoolteacher, and although I am not sure they ever really understood why I might wish to teach others about their way of life, at least this was a familiar role and one they apparently accepted. I was also viewed in Santa Maria as a representative of a nutritional-research organization whose research activities and personnel were accepted because the Indians received medical attention in return. The Indians recognized that for some illnesses Western medicine was superior to their own, and in time they answered almost any question from representatives of the agency, *provided* these representatives behaved according to the Indians' expectations and customs. Eventually, I established rapport on an individual basis with my informants, and this made it possible to probe even more sensitive areas, such as how they felt about the research activities to which they were subjected. When informants began to tell me how and why they had on occasion deceived the clinic personnel on certain subjects, I felt that I had at last carved out my own special niche.

This analysis points up a well-known and accepted principle of field-work technique—know, as well as is possible ahead of time, the culture to be studied. This includes not only the culture itself, but the social context within which that culture exists and the patterns of behavior expected of persons foreign to that culture. Within this general framework, the field worker must always be sensitive to cues given by the natives, and he must learn to adapt his behavior as rapidly as possible so as not to offend them. In this, the anthropologist must recognize that his own personality is an important factor and that some personal stress is to be expected in the process of adjustment. Furthermore, the nature of the contact itself—whether long-term residence or repeated daily visits—will also alter the entire situation, and it must be taken into account if the investigator wishes to be successful in the ultimate goal of obtaining accurate and useful data for scientific purposes.

MOHAWK HEROES AND TRINIDADIAN PEASANTS

Morris Freilich

PART I: MOHAWK HEROES IN STRUCTURAL STEEL

Problem, Theory, and Research Design

New Yorkers sometimes read in their newspapers about a unique phenomenon in their midst: the Mohawk Indians who work on the steel structures of various buildings in and around their city. Articles, at times accompanied by pictures of smiling Indians, discuss these "brave" and "sure-footed" Mohawks. The question of why so many Mohawks work in structural steel is one that is often researched by students enrolled in colleges located in and around New York. In 1956, this problem was, in fact, my first professional research assignment. I used A. F. C. Wallace's paper "Some Psychological Determinants of Culture Change in an Iroquoian Community" as the foil in my proposal for research support. Wallace's paper suggested that Mohawks lack a fear of heights, and that this lack of fear explains their involvement with the steel industry. I argued that a negative trait (lack of fear) cannot have specific positive consequences (lead a tribe into steel work). I argued further that there is no functional value in a lack of fear of heights for steel work, and that in actuality the opposite is true: a normal fear of high places leads to caution that saves lives. A more plausible argument seemed to be that Mohawks frequently act *as if* they have no fear of heights. In presenting a subsidiary problem, "Why these acts of daredevilry?" I put forth my theoretical belief that sociocultural factors explain social and cultural phenomena better than do psychological factors. I had a vague notion that Mohawks in steel work represented some kind of cultural continuity. Thus, the questions I posed were (1) Why is it good, culturally, for a Mohawk male to be a structural steel worker? and (2) How does such a cultural "goodness" relate to Mohawk cultural history?

I had no research design, although questions which colleagues and friends asked about my work could have led to one. For example, they asked me about Mohawks who did not work in structural steel and about structural steel workers who were not Mohawks. I found questions such as these interesting but irrelevant to my project. Even the question "How will I know when I have successfully completed my project?" held little interest for me, probably because of my poor training in science and methodology and because of a dominant theme in the culture of many anthropology students that one's commitment is primarily to anthropology rather than to science.

I had had some interviewing experience prior to the Mohawk project, but I had received little training in this area. During my years as a graduate student at Columbia University, science and research methods were greatly underplayed. To become a "real" anthropologist, we learned, one finds a group that can be referred to as "mine." To work with several groups simultaneously, to be concerned with controls, to worry about the kinds of proofs one is presenting for an argument were not part of anthropology, as we learned it. Good anthropologists, those staunch and wily enough to survive the rigors of "primitive" living, returned with stories that demonstrated their popularity with the "natives" and their knowledge of the social structure and culture of "their" tribe. Research designs had no role in this work.

Passive or Adaptational Research

Adaptational research begins when one attempts to get a "passport" permitting free entry, unhampered travel, and communication privileges in the community, tribe, or group being researched. It ends when the researcher can say to himself, "I will probably be able to see this project through to some kind of (more or less) successful conclusion."

The environment of the group being researched. The reservation of the Mohawks I studied, Caughnawaga, is located about ten miles south of Montreal and is regarded as "home" by the Indians. To facilitate their finding work in structural steel, the Caughnawaga Mohawks have formed several small communities in eastern Canada and in the United States. The community I studied in Brooklyn, New York, began to develop about forty years ago. It is located in an area that has a variety of advantages for Mohawks. First, it is close to the headquarters of their union: Local 361 of the Iron Workers Union. Second, the Mohawks can here be less visibly "different," for here being different is the norm. At one time or another the area has attracted Germans, Norwegians, Italians, Irish, Syrians, Greeks, Negroes, Jews, and Puerto Ricans. Third, in this working-class area with easy access to buses and subways the Mohawks can live as they wish.

Entry and initial copings. The Brooklyn community with its multi-ethnic population and its lack of formal boundaries provided no entry problems for me. Nor were there any particular problems to entering the reservation at Caughnawaga. My first real problem was knowing how and where to start work. Three related questions needed immediate answers. First, *where* should I start working? At places where the Mohawks work? In their homes? In some of their recreational centers? Should I begin in Brooklyn? Should I start interviewing the women and then get to the steel workers, or should I do the reverse? Third, *how* should I begin researching? Should I have some formal questions to pose, or might it be better initially to "play" the interested observer? I decided to start work by contacting Dr. David Corey, the spiritual head of the Cuyler Presbyterian Church (on Pacific Street), who had helped me in an earlier project with Mohawks.[1] Dr. Corey was much involved with the Brooklyn

---

[1] I had previously contacted Dr. Corey for aid, when as an undergraduate at Brooklyn College, I wrote a short paper on Mohawks in Brooklyn.

Mohawks, many of whom were members of his congregation. To make his church services more attractive to the Mohawks, Dr. Corey conducted a monthly Sunday evening service in Mohawk. However, as I discovered after several visits to the church, only a small portion of the older Mohawks were interested in Dr. Corey's innovation. The younger Mohawks could hardly talk to their grandparents in Mohawk, let alone follow a church service in the language.

Dr. Corey believed that Mohawks work in high steel because they like to travel ("they have itchy feet"), and because they want to make good wages without going through a long training period, but Dr. Corey's ideas did not explain why occupations such as salesman, which also include much travel and few training requirements, do not attract Mohawks. His explanation also raised an additional question: Why does a group that supposedly is attracted to an occupation because of its monetary rewards have so little interest in money per se?

Dr. Corey gave me the names of several Mohawks on whom I could call. He also suggested that I visit his church and meet some of the Mohawks who were regular worshipers. Although I contacted a number of Dr. Corey's friends, these Mohawks either would not see me or allowed me but a brief noninformative interview.

I decided to start looking for Mohawks at their work sites. After many hours of wandering around construction sites in Manhattan and failing to locate any Mohawks, I decided to talk to some *non*-Indian steel workers about Mohawks in structural steel. Discussions with non-Indian steel workers provided almost no new information. My informants were convinced that Mohawks and other Indians were "sure-footed" and worked in steel because of the high wages. Further questioning clearly indicated that much of what the non-Indian construction workers "saw" was influenced by what they had read in newspapers and periodicals. This is not surprising, since the Mohawks themselves had completely accepted the "white man's" stereotype of the "sure-footed" and "fearless" Indian. Somewhat disheartened, I ended my search for Mohawks in construction sites and returned to the Brooklyn community.

In Brooklyn I again interviewed several of the people to whom Dr. Corey had referred me, none of whom worked in structural steel. I met elderly women, mainly mothers of young steel workers and wives of the older "pushers" (foremen). I explained my project as "a great interest in Mohawk history" and "an attempt to discover how things have changed." These women appeared interested in my work, but claimed to know little about structural steel and its magnetic fascination for Mohawk males. Finally, I met a Mohawk male while I was visiting his mother. This young steel worker showed no interest in talking to me. After several attempts at conversation, I received a half-serious invitation to meet him in the Wigwam bar the next day. However, when I arrived at the appointed time, the young man acted as if he did not know me. I was instantly depressed.

I sat at the bar of the Wigwam, drank beer, and developed a strong doubt as to my ability to complete my project. I dawdled over my drink and began to survey the bar's clientele and resources. The bartender, an Italian, suddenly showed a special interest in me and began to tell me of a recent "big fight" in the Wigwam. Several Puerto Rican males had come in one night and had overstayed their welcome. A few Indians politely asked them to leave, but the Puerto Ricans kept ordering more drinks. As a result, the Puerto Ricans were physically attacked and badly beaten in a brawl. In the words of the bartender:

> The Puerto Ricans ran outside and got into a big car. Four Mohawks went to the corners of the car, and they picked it off the ground like it was a toy. The Puerto Ricans couldn't leave. One Mohawk yelled: "Next time you come in here we'll throw you in the car, and then throw the car." The Puerto Ricans never came back!

Whether or not this story was true is irrelevant. Essentially the bartender's message was: "Stranger, this is a Mohawk hangout; if you stay here for very long you're likely to get beaten up and thrown out." I finished my beer and left. I decided, however, that if my project was to be successful, I had to make the Wigwam my headquarters. What better place to work with Mohawks than in what appeared to be (and was) their major recreational center? My problem now was how to get accepted as a member of Wigwam society.

The fact that the Italian bartender seemed quite at home in the Wigwam indicated that one need not be an Indian to be a Wigwam member. My research strategy was to frequent the Wigwam often but for very short periods of time and to create some doubts in the minds of club members as to whether I belonged or not. My morning visits to the Wigwam aroused no apparent antagonism from the Indians. A Mohawk would periodically decide that he did not feel like going to work that day, due to ill health, to bad weather, or just because he felt like loafing. Such individuals seemed to welcome the chance to talk. Few Mohawks were present during these morning hours, and no competition existed for the various resources of the bar: chairs, tables, men, and (sometimes) women to talk to. My presence was very obvious, yet there was never a suggestion that I was not welcome to sit, drink, and talk. At night when the Wigwam was full of Indians, there were always some Indians who eyed me suspiciously and (it seemed to me) threateningly. My initial night visits to the Wigwam were frequent but brief. I would buy a beer, sit at the bar, sip slowly, and look around for Indians I had met before. If I did not see anyone I knew, I left as soon as I had finished my drink. If I saw someone I knew, I tried to get into a conversation with him. Whether or not my informant seemed friendly, I left shortly thereafter, went to a nearby coffee shop, and jotted down what I had heard and seen.

I returned to the bar about an hour later, repeating the whole process several times each night. I soon discovered that a number of non-Indians appeared to have membership privileges. These Mohawkphiles drank here, dated Mohawk girls, wore moccasins, and traveled regularly to the reservation. In short, they strongly identified with, and were accepted by, the Mohawks. This indicated that I too could become a Wigwam member.

About a week after these regular, short-duration visits to the Wigwam, I became overconfident and stayed one night for a few hours without a break. Just when I thought I was really "in," a Mohawk who could have passed easily for a professional wrestler, suggested in menacing tones that I finish my beer and leave. I agreed that his idea was sound and left. The next evening I returned to my cautious strategy. As the days passed it became more and more probable that I would meet someone I knew at any particular visit to the Wigwam. As I sat and talked to Mohawks who did not seem to treat me as a stranger, I was observed by an audience whose cumulative size grew daily. Soon I began to recognize Mohawks with whom I had never spoken, but who had been around while I was conversing with others. It became relatively easy to strike up a conversation with these men. At times I heard Indians ask each other, "Who is he?" A typical answer was, "I don't know, but he seems to know a lot of people around here."

Within a few weeks, a young Indian (I will call him Joe) began to show signs of friendship. Joe was invariably broke, and after we ran out of my limited funds he began "bumming" drinks for the two of us. He invited me to his apartment, and I met (what I later found out to be) his commonlaw wife, his sister, and her commonlaw husband. To Joe, I was a nice kid, although I was white and a Jew. My admiration for Mohawks was in his eyes a sign of great maturity. The fact that I would listen attentively while he endlessly recounted his exploits in structural-steel gangs, his travels all over the country, his drinking bouts, his sexual exploits, and his beating up of men twice his size made my company desirable. However, he quickly indicated that my work at the university was of no interest to him. To Joe and to the large majority of the young steel workers whom I got to know, the university world was quite unimportant. More accurately, for them it did not exist. I learned to avoid any topic that dealt with my professional career, and I slowly developed the role of Joe's sidekick.

My acceptance in Mohawk Wigwam society was now steadily growing through a daily improvement in my friendship with Joe and a daily increase in numbers of Mohawks spoken to and in numbers who observed me speaking to Indians. Complete acceptance occurred once I had traveled to the reservation and lived in a Mohawk house as Joe's guest.

The prelude to this trip was as follows. While sitting in the Wigwam one Friday afternoon Joe asked me whether I had ever been to Caughnawaga. I said "No," and he then told me that he was going there within the next hour or so and asked me to come along. Although I knew that this trip would be important for the project, I had made some other plans for part of the weekend that I was not eager to break. I also thought that, since I had received this kind of an invitation once, I could get it again at some later date. Indeed, I had several rationalizations for not going to Caughnawaga that day. These reasons were all connected to the fact that middle-class Americans rarely leave the country at an hour's notice. My initial reaction to his offer was then not of the anthropologist expressing his glee that he had finally been successful in getting an invitation to spend a weekend with a good informant and his Indian friends, but rather that of a typical middle-class American, uneasy at the prospect of having to change his plans at the last minute and travel a great distance with minimal funds.

I told Joe that it really was a pity that he had not mentioned this trip earlier, but that I couldn't go because of lack of money and previous plans. Joe, who was accustomed to traveling all over the country with very little money and to changing major plans at a moment's notice, expressed disdain for my excuses. He said that a number of cars would be going to Canada that afternoon and evening, so that transportation would not be a problem. As to my financial situation, Joe indicated that when a group of Indians collectively had enough money to get to Caughnawaga almost anything one threw in the pot to help would be acceptable. He also mentioned that I could eat and sleep at his mother's house and that, if necessary, he would help me to borrow some money. I offered no further arguments and instead expressed my gratitude for all his help.

As the Mohawks discovered that I was off to Caughnawaga that day to stay with Joe, my position in Wigwam society began to change. Within the hour I heard someone refer to me as "Joe's friend." Although I was not aware of it at the time, an interesting process was beginning. Joe's early friendly come-ons had been the prelude to a sort of adoption process that other "whites" had gone through. His offer to "take" me to the reservation symbolized a certain stage in this process; he was broadcasting to his group that I was the type of non-Indian that one can accept. Whether or not they would accept me depended partly on Joe's status in the group and partly on how I continued to behave as my interactions with group members became more frequent and more intimate. As it turned out, my adoption by Joe was very fortunate, due to the status Joe held in Wigwam society and due to the role of Joe's mother in Caughnawaga. Although Joe was one of the smallest of the Mohawk steel workers, he was held in high esteem by the group due both to his "wild" fighting habits and to the role his mother assumed.

Ma Joe, a woman in her late forties, enjoyed having Joe's friends in her home. Her house was almost a structural parallel of the Wigwam bar in Brooklyn. At any time between 9 A.M. and midnight or after, one might find a young group of Mohawks sitting in Ma Joe's house, drinking, joking, swearing, and storytelling. Ma Joe was treated as one of the gang, and she loved it. During my first weekend at Caughnawaga I met about thirty young Mohawks and my living in Ma Joe's house itself almost assured me of membership in Wigwam society.

After my return from the reservation I was no longer a stranger; my new name, "Joe's friend," had stuck. People referred to me thus both directly and indirectly. It was clear that I now had acceptance by the group as a white man who was almost good enough to be an Indian.[2]

Once I had a legitimate right to be around Mohawks at almost any reasonable time and had achieved adequate rapport to talk to them as a nonstranger, I began to wonder how I could best work actively toward a successful completion of my project.

Active Research

The kind of active research activity that appears feasible in a given project is directly related to the kind of rapport achieved during the adaptational period of passive research. It is neces-

---

[2] It is interesting that historically Mohawk warriors used to capture men of non-Iroquoian tribes and frequently adopt them into their society. Thus, I, together with a number of other non-Indians, filled a legitimate role with a long history. Although I had told my name to dozens of Indians, as far as I can recall only four Mohawks ever used my real name or acted as if they knew it: Joe, Joe's mother, and two other young Mohawk males, the latter being rather marginal members of Mohawk society.

sary to consider *what* one has rapport to do, *with whom, when,* and under *what specific conditions.*

The rapport achieved and problems of rapport maintenance. A rule of thumb generally given to graduate students in anthropology is, "Be honest, present what you are doing in simple language, but present it as close to the truth as practically possible." I attempted to present myself as a graduate student in anthropology, very interested in Indians, particularly in Mohawks and their "glorious" history. Although I repeated my story to a considerable number of Mohawks, no information seemed to be passing from me to them. They either did not know who and what I was, or claimed not to *until* I became "Joe's friend." In their eyes, I had no social existence until I was adopted; before adoption I had no rapport. After adoption I had *adequate* rapport (for my project goals), but I never really achieved more than this, except in a few cases.

Once I had become an accepted member of Wigwam and Mohawks-in-Brooklyn society I tried to revert to the role of anthropologist. This attempt was generally fruitless. It was soon clear that any anthropological symbol was tabu to this project. I could use no pencils, notebooks, or questionnaires. I even failed in attempts to play the semianthropologist. For example, I tried saying, "Now that is really interesting; let me write that down so that I don't forget it." Suddenly my audience became hostile, and the few words I jotted down cost me much in rapport for the next few days. To continue doing research with the steel workers I had to keep a small notebook in my hip pocket and periodically go to the men's room in the bar or the outhouse at Caughnawaga and write notes to myself. As frequently as possible, I would go to a coffee shop to write down longer statements that could turn out to be important.

In short, during the active research stage I could play only the role of the "adopted Mohawk" if I wanted to maintain membership in the young Mohawk clique—the group that did structural steel work. To play this role, I had to fulfill certain obvious requirements: (1) I had to identify completely with Mohawks, including making frequent "broadcasts" of Indian superiority over all other groups and wearing some Indian clothing; (2) I had to make periodic trips to the reservation in the company of Mohawks; and (3) I had to have a high frequency interaction with Mohawks.

The data-getting strategy that paid off was simply being around Mohawks, watching, listening, and slipping away to write down any information collected. I did not adopt this strategy immediately for obvious reasons. Emotionally, I did not enjoy playing the equivalent of the undercover agent. Ethically, I had my doubts as to my right to work this way. And professionally, I had been taught that it was wise to remain "above board." Furthermore, I wanted "my tribe" to know that they had an anthropologist in their midst. Such knowledge would have legitimized the work of my first anthropological research project and would have been supportive during the *rite de passage* into the profession.

Data-collection techniques. After my fruitless attempts to write down information in the presence of Mohawks, I used another fruitless, but less harmful, approach. I began asking Mohawks direct questions concerning their fear of being up so high on narrow ledges. "Don't you ever see the newspapers? Haven't you heard about us before coming here? Indians are afraid of nothing. Steel work is in their blood. Indians are surefooted." This was the typical response to this line of questioning. In short, in terms of direct questions concerning fear of heights, the Indians presented the same statements that appear in the press about them. They were brave, surefooted daredevils, who were afraid of nothing and who had steel work in their blood. They had accepted the stereotype given them by the white man; they almost had me believing that the Mohawk was a fearless daredevil.

I next decided simply to stay around the Mohawks and talk about steel work whenever possible. Good ways of "staying around" Mohawks included (1) getting a job in structural steel work; (2) spending long periods of time daily in the Wigwam; and (3) riding up to the reservation with Mohawk steel workers. Getting a job in structural steel involved two problems. First, it is very difficult to get membership in the appropriate union, and, second, the more time one spends at a specific job site working with a relatively small number of Mohawks, the less time there is for staying around the Wigwam. I decided against trying to get a job in structural steel and concentrated my work activities in the Wigwam with periodic trips to the reservation.

As my task became more clearly defined in the Wigwam, to be a human camera and tape recorder, I began to observe some interesting phenomena I had previously overlooked. Prominently displayed around the room were drawings of Iroquois warriors and war scenes. Intermingled among these drawings, which included one of Custer's Last Stand, were helmets of structural steel workers who had fallen to their deaths. In one corner stood a large juke box filled with popular American records, and in another part of the barroom there was a small mechanical "bowling" game.

Although the Mohawks who frequented the Wigwam spent

most of their time just sitting, drinking, and talking, periodically there was some roughhousing. I observed that the younger Mohawks would frequently go out of their way to annoy a given individual and that after a few verbal bouts, the annoyer and the annoyed became antagonists in a physical battle, generally of short duration. After some fighting, with rare attention to Queensbury rules, the antagonists were separated by some of the audience, furniture was put back in place, and the group got back into the drinking-talking pattern. I was initially surprised at the lack of ill feeling that existed between the "fighters" after any given bout, particularly since there was much body-hurt involved. Joe, my adopter, described one of his fights as follows:

> After a lot of arguing, Angus hit me on the nose, then when I fell he gave me the boot in my face. I got up and knocked the —— out of him. . . . He came at me again. I hit him with a large beer bottle, right in the head. [Joe laughed heartily.]

As far as I knew, Joe and Angus remained as friendly after their bout as they had been before. Nor did the fights between other Mohawks lead to any permanent hostilities between either individual Indians or cliques. Further observations led me to conclude that these short fights almost invariably occurred between Mohawks who were roughly equal in size and weight. In fact, the only small Mohawk I ever saw attack a large Mohawk was Joe. Joe weighed about 150 pounds, stood about 5 feet 5 inches, and was quite muscular. It was not unusual to see him throw himself at a much larger man, get in a few blows, receive several blows in return, and then kid his way out of the "fight." Because of this behavioral pattern, Joe was known as "wild," or "crazy," but he was very much respected for his courage and fighting ability. The Mohawks found Joe somewhat unpredictable, and he enjoyed "being different" and the prestige it provided.

It seemed clear to me after observing a number of such fights that the younger Mohawks were playing a pecking-order game. As a young Indian began "feeling his oats," he believed he could take on someone who had beaten him previously and would engineer a bout. This kind of "fight" need not be long or drawn out. As soon as it was obvious who was superior, the group separated the combatants, so that the "game" could not disrupt the group by generating ill feelings between the antagonists. Joe, with his unorthodox involvement with men who greatly outsized and thus outranked him in the Wigwam, seemed to bypass the pecking-order game completely. Mohawks who were roughly equal to Joe in size and strength avoided "quarrels" with him, since he was known to attack the toughest Indians in the group. The big and very strong Indians seemed to respect Joe's ability to get in a few fast blows. However, no prestige was attached to fighting with a person who was so much smaller and thus lower in rank than they. Joe's unusual situation in the Wigwam gave him considerable notoriety and gave anyone closely associated with him—like myself—considerable publicity.

It should have been obvious to me that if a pecking-order game was really a part of Wigwam society, and if I was accepted as a legitimate member of this society, then I must expect to be asked to "play" by Mohawks who were roughly of my size and weight. It wasn't, and therefore, my first encounter with a gauntlet-throwing Mohawk was both distasteful and confusing. Bill, a muscular youth of about twenty, slightly taller but obviously much stronger than I, had been talking to me on and off for about fifteen minutes. He seemed to be angry about something. Finally he made the critical "play."

> BILL: How old did you say you were?
> MF: I'm twenty-eight. (I had not mentioned my age previously.)
> BILL: I can't believe you're that old. No, you're
>   no more than twenty.
> MF: Why do you think I'm not twenty-eight?
> BILL: A guy of twenty-eight would not talk stupid like you do!

I was obviously being challenged to fight. I pretended to misunderstand the challenge and continued receiving insult after insult. I parried verbally with statements such as "What gives you the idea that I'm stupid?" and "In what ways do I act silly?" Bill finally decided that he had "won" without showing his physical prowess. He announced it was a waste of time talking to me and walked off.

Bill was the first of several young Mohawks who in various ways made it clear that they were eager to fight me. Only a considerable amount of pride-swallowing prevented me from being badly beaten. The young Mohawks who were goading me to fight not only had much experience in this type of encounter, but they were also in excellent physical condition.

It soon became clear to all the Mohawks who frequented the Wigwam that I was no threat to the status of any Indian, large or small. I had placed myself on the lowest rung of the group's status system. My low rank was valuable because any higher rank would have required me to fight periodically with those just below me in order to maintain my rank. My loss of status in playing the cowardly "I will not fight" role was partly compensated for by being "Joe's friend" and partly balanced by the fact that I was not really Indian; if I were, it would have been almost impossible for me to attain the low-rank position without at least one fight.

The pecking-order game seemed to serve two major functions for social life in the Wigwam. First, it set up a ranking system: when a given Mohawk was throwing his weight around the bar, those who outranked him could easily get him back in line; those lower in rank had to put up with his abuses. Second, it permitted a Mohawk to play the role of "tough guy," a role that appeared to give them great personal satisfaction. Playing the tough-guy role was not limited to the situations involving the pecking-order game. Mohawks frequently went out of their way to annoy non-Indians in situations where such abuses were *almost* appropriate: police officers who stopped them would be treated with considerable hostility; young men who were trying to get served in stores or restaurants ahead of them would be abused and so forth. Whenever Mohawks felt that abuses and annoyances could be escalated into fights that they could win, they did so. Such fights were not the "friendly" bouts of Mohawk versus Mohawk; they were fights in which the combatants could be critically injured.

For example, Jack, an Indian in his early twenties, proudly related how he and his friend had "beaten up a couple of guys" in Canada. During the fight Jack pulled a knife and stabbed his antagonist. He was completely unconcerned that the man was in the hospital on the critical list. He said: "I like to fight. . . . That's how I have fun." His real concern was expressed as follows: "I can't go back to Canada, because the cops are looking for me." He was particularly upset because a Mohawk friend was getting married shortly, and he was unwilling to attend the wedding and risk getting arrested.

In the "tough-guy" role the Mohawks communicated to their associates the degree to which "the Hero" could be physically destructive. Their stories of wrecked cars and of breaking up "joints" in various cities showed a complete disregard for personal safety. At times a Mohawk would "act out" in a manner like the following to show he was tough:

> Late one evening, Jack, an Indian in his early twenties came into the Wigwam looking angry and drunk. He asked the barman for a bottle of beer. The barman, not wishing to serve him, did not reply. Jack jumped over the counter, took a bottle, drank half of it and then started toward the bathroom. The jukebox was playing as he passed it. He pulled back his arm and threw a long right-handed punch at the glass. The glass cracked and his hand bled profusely. When the barman yelled at him in anger he tried to fight the barman. Several onlookers (including myself) tried to get Jack to a nearby hospital. Jack, who was losing blood at a fast

rate, refused to go. The barman gave him a towel to wrap around his hand, and Jack yelled "I don't want your pity." (A few Indians made him wrap it around his wrist and hand.) Two Indians then grabbed Jack and told him they were going to take him to the Catholic clinic nearby. On the way, we (the group now included four Mohawks and myself) ran into several girls Jack knew. He waved the bloody towel at them and said he would not have his hand fixed unless they came along. When the now large group arrived at the clinic, Jack swore and cursed as the nuns were fixing his hand. He received an injection, four stitches, and was bandaged up. As we were leaving, Jack kept trying to indicate his disdain for everything that happened with respect to taking care of his hand. His final act of "disdain" was to urinate on the front door of the clinic. Later I asked Jack, "Why did you break the glass?" He replied: "I did not like the record that was playing."

Wigwam society included, besides the pecking-order system, a he-man role and an *esprit de corps* based on the notion that Mohawks were the greatest people in the world. My own membership in this system was tenuous, as exemplified by the following event:

I entered the Wigwam at about 10 o'clock one morning and found the place full of Mohawks. The weather was fine for structural steel work. It was dry, clear and warm; and it seemed strange that so many Mohawks should feel like staying away from work all at the same time. I asked a Mohawk sitting next to me why so many of the men were not working today. Suddenly most of the conversation that was going on stopped, and everyone seemed to be looking at the Indian next to me to hear what he would say. The young Indian took "center stage," as if on cue, and began telling me a long historical tale. In serious tones he discussed the death of a famous chief many, many years ago. "Chief (a garbled name) was a great and fearless Mohawk warrior," I was told. "Today is the day he died!" The Indian went on to describe how solemn a day this was for all Mohawks, and how very disrespectful it would be to the memory of their great chief to work on this sacred day. He concluded by saying that it was customary for the Mohawks who happened to be in Brooklyn on this day to come to the Wigwam and quietly drink to his memory. As the Mohawk spoke I tried hard to remember every word he was saying. This appeared to be important data on cultural persistence. Fortunately, near the end of his monologue I noticed an Indian near me suppress a smile. I realized then that this was a group joke, and I was expected to make some foolish reaction. I replied in a manner that indicated my understanding of the "joke"; everyone laughed heartily, and the typical barroom conversational buzz resumed.

After this incident I became more on guard for possible future put ons, a few of which occurred. However, none of the latter were as dramatic as the event described. I did not realize at the time that my low-status position in the pecking order, actually almost an outcast role, made me highly susceptible to the role of group's goat.

Activities found valuable for data collection. My trips to the reservation were most valuable for getting data on how a group of young Mohawks behave when they remain together continuously for eight or ten hours. A typical trip to Caughnawaga began with a sort of planning stage. Everyone in the Wigwam knew that a number of cars would be leaving some time on Friday for Caughnawaga. The problem for any given Mohawk who wanted to go was to find out exactly who was planning on driving, how many people were traveling with him, and who these passengers were. Mohawks wishing to leave would thus try to get in with a group they enjoyed that was leaving at about the time they wanted to leave. Although, according to Joe, any amount of money one had could be thrown into the pot for car expenses, the Mohawks who arranged the car pools tried to get about $15 from each passenger for the round trip. As far as I know, Mohawks with less than $15 were not turned away, but Mohawks who paid the $15 and did not return in the same car did not receive refunds. There were not, then, the many bookkeeping transactions common in middle-class American society.

Drinking started before the 400-mile trip, carried on during the trip, and helped celebrate its conclusion. The possibility of being stopped by police for drinking while driving occurred to the Mohawks, but it did not deter them from drinking. This type of behavior was part of a pattern of indirect challenges to authority figures to "do something about it," coupled with the implicit announcement to other Mohawks present that "I'm afraid of nothing." During the ride to Caughnawaga, the Indians boasted of their great recklessness in driving. For example:

> Joe boasted that he and his buddy Ronnie had been in eleven accidents together. Each time they managed to almost completely wreck the car they were in: "At one time we tried to turn over a Buick which was supposed never to turn over. We turned it over!" Another time Joe dared Ronnie to hit a pole at high speed. He did. In a third "accident" they attempted to break the accelerator. "We did not manage that, although we drove 120 miles an hour." Indians were supposed to be great drivers. They only smashed up cars for the fun of it. There was also usually much

boasting about how fast a given Indian had made the trip from Brooklyn to Caughnawaga. One young Indian claimed to have done it in 7½ hours.

The talk also invariably touched on wild sex escapades and Indians who broke a law and went to prison and the smarter ones who did not get caught. One of the groups I rode with included three Mohawks who boasted that they had been stopped by a couple of Canadian Mounties a few years before and accused of drunken driving. "We beat up the Mounties, took their guns and their wallets, and got away."

The trip to Caughnawaga always included a stop at Hoff's Diner in the Albany area. Hoff was an Indian, and most of the Mohawks traveling to and from the reservation would stop there. In the friendly atmosphere of Hoff's Diner, it was easy for the young steel workers to play the hero. They wisecracked with the waitresses, made passes at girls, and generally acted as if the diner belonged to them.

The next major event was crossing the border. Here again the Indians would go out of their way to let me know that they did not expect to be detained or annoyed in any way. Just before we got to the Canadian border an Indian would tell me to say I was a Mohawk. "That will stop any other questioning." They were special people. Apparently, the officials at both the American and Canadian sides of the border had been frequently annoyed by the Mohawks, and the effect was a minimal delay.

Upon reaching the reservation, the Mohawks would in some manner signal their arrival. One time a Mohawk got out and fired a hunting rifle several times into the air; usually the driver would start to honk the horn of the car. A group from Brooklyn had arrived, and they wanted all to know it.

Keeping Field Data

While doing observation-participation field work, I carried a small notebook and pencil and whenever possible jotted down a few words in the notebook to serve as mnemonic devices. I would periodically go off to get a soda or coffee in a nearby café, write my notes to myself, and then go back to the bar. When I got home I would attempt to reconstruct the events of the day with the help of my notebook.

There are, of course, a number of problems with this kind of field work. For one thing, it is possible to get caught, and for another the researcher must rely heavily on his memory. Although a small notebook can easily be hidden in a back pocket, situations arise when a notebook can become visible to the informants. It is thus essential that nothing be put in the note-book pocket, since when taking out the other item the notebook may fall out, and that the notebook not be in one's pocket when one sleeps in the house of an informant. While half asleep on Joe's mother's couch in Caughnawaga, I noticed that someone was going through my clothes. It turned out that Joe's drunken step-father was looking for my wallet to get money for liquor. Because he was drunk, he paid no attention to my little notebook, but his perusal of it might have had serious repercussions on my future field work.

After a certain amount of experience with this work I found that my memory served me far better than I expected. I tried to have in my notebook (1) the names of people I spoke to, (2) the subjects discussed, (3) the time of day, (4) any unusual occurrence, (5) any statistical data that I might quickly forget, such as the wages of a given man, ages, frequency of going to the reservation, etc. After going through the notebook and re-constructing events by the name, subject matter, time sequence, and occurrences, I usually felt fairly certain that little of the information I had received on a given day was lost.

Bowing Out

I did intensive field work with Mohawks during the months of June, July, August, and September of 1956. By the end of September, I was spending perhaps ten hours a week in research, although my wife and I spent several days in September at the reservation. I told many of my informants that I was going to do more work in graduate school and that I would try to be around as often as possible. "Bowing out" was essentially a simple process with the Mohawks for several reasons. First my apartment was no more than a forty-minute subway ride from the Wigwam. Second, the Mohawks were well accustomed to having someone "disappear" for several months (such absence never entailed mail from the absentee). Mohawks would get steel jobs all over the country and in Canada. When their as-signments were completed they usually came back to Brooklyn. However, the absence might be as long as six months or even much longer. From October, 1956, until March, 1957, I spent very few hours a week at the Wigwam. Indeed, many weeks passed without my going there at all. During the spring of 1957 I periodically met with a few Mohawks either in their houses or in the Wigwam. I had developed a correspondence with a Mo-hawk who stayed in Caughnawaga, and I continued to write to him and receive mail from him through May, 1957.

Results: The Modern Mohawk Warrior

The social life of the Mohawks, be it in the reservation, traveling to and from the reservation, or in and around the Wigwam, seemed to center around a role in which Indians reveled: *fearless hero*. The "fearless hero" indicated at every opportunity that he didn't give a hoot for safety, law, authority, and the culturally accepted propriety rules of other groups. This became clear to me from observation of and participation in Mohawk social life and from many long discussions with Mohawks who were involved in structural steel work. My information concerning Mohawks at and around work came from more limited sources. Such information did not include observing Mohawks at work, but came from discussions with Mohawks about work and from discussions with several non-Mohawk officials of Local 361 of the Iron Workers Union. Indirect information also came from discussions with teachers of Mohawk children as to the work ambitions of Mohawk youth.

Discussions with Mohawks working in structural steel were frequently very unrewarding. That the work in steel was important to them quickly became evident, but the how's and why's of the work were difficult to establish, since the Mohawks would generally only talk about it in a highly idealized fashion. The mundane aspects of steel work were never brought up. What seemed to be always at the core of talk about steel were the possibilities of daring exploits and how such possibilities were at times translated into action. Thus one Mohawk discussed the famous exploits of a work-gang leader whom I will call "Pusher Bob." According to this Mohawk steel worker:

> Bob was a real man. He was a pusher and did not call up and say 'Do so and so.' He came up and showed you. He would often swing around just hanging by his feet and when he pushed a pin in, it went. He would push them in [steel pins] with his bare hands.

Stories such as those were told to "prove" what great and fearless steel workers the Mohawks were. They were usually accompanied by statements such as "Caughnawaga Indians are the best steel workers in the world. It's in their blood." Or, "Steel work is in our blood; that is why we do it. I did not tell my son to go into construction work, but that is what he is doing."

Questions concerning Indians who were not in steel work led to information about structural steel work that was more plausible. Again, direct questions about a given man not working in a construction gang led to general answers, such as "I don't know, he just doesn't like steel work. . . . He likes something else.

... That's his business." Indirect probing led to such statements as "Jack was *no good;* he was scared to be on the bars." And, "Some Indians are not in steel work; *they couldn't make it.*" It quickly became apparent that it was not Jack's *fear of heights* that made him no good. Rather, it was Jack's letting his fears keep him from doing real man's work—work appropriate to the Mohawk male. Therefore, the Indian *who made it,* who lived up to the group's definition of what a real Mohawk male was like, worked on high narrow steel ledges and, like Pusher Bob, died with his structural steel boots on. The Indians who *couldn't make it* were those in occupations other than structural steel.

Data collected in this project indicated clearly that *Mohawks have a normal fear of heights.* I was fortunate to be in the Wigwam when a few inebriated Indians were discussing this very subject. Russell said, "I pray every morning that I'll come back alive." The others agreed that when they are up there on the outside of a building, they are afraid. Joe Ringer said, "I've yet to meet the man who's not afraid up there. . . . If you were not afraid you would not be a good steel worker as you would not be careful."

Usually, it is impossible to get Mohawks to admit fear of height for two reasons. First, the Indian has completely accepted the white man's stereotype of him as the "surefooted, fearless Indian." Second, a warrior is not afraid! A frequent statement of the Mohawks is, "Indians are afraid of nothing." Their fear of heights is the normal one of men who know that work on the girders is dangerous; however, just as the possibility of death did not deter the warrior from the warpath, it does not deter his descendant from structural steel work. In both cases, participating in dangerous activities is the sign of being a man.

In terms of Mohawk culture, a *man* is daring, fearless, and frequently destructive. He seeks rather than flees from dangerous activities. He challenges authority figures. This behavior was evident around the Wigwam, in Brooklyn, traveling to and from Caughnawaga, and in and around the reservation. It came to me that a shorthand formula to describe this behavior was, *To be a Mohawk male = to be a warrior = to be a steel worker.* This formula made much historical and current ethnographic data understandable. Historically, the Mohawks were frequently involved in small group warfare, and the male role *warrior* had become both extremely prestigious and socially rewarding. "Playing warrior" in the 1950s was simply a case of social structural persistence. The formula *warrior = steel worker* stems from (1) the essential similarities of the two ways of life and (2) the impossibility of playing "real" warrior. To analogize this to today's context, steel workers, like their warrior ancestors of old, leave for dangerous assignments with their gang of young men and an older leader (the pusher). There is a chance that some of them will not return alive, for steel work is dangerous work requiring all the ingredients of the warrior role: courage, strength, firmness of limb, and a willingness to face death. Those who do not die after the successful completion of an assignment come home and receive the praises of the camp. This analogy helps explain why Mohawks will spend sixteen to twenty hours traveling to and from the reservation to be there for perhaps but forty hours. The reservation is their real home, and when possible they want to hear the home folks sing "see the conquering hero comes."

The juxtaposition in the Wigwam of the helmets of the dead steel workers and the pictures of fighting Indians began to make more sense when I thought of structural steel workers as the *modern Mohawk warriors*. The concept *modern Mohawk warrior* also helped me to understand the meaning of a number of similar bits of false information I had been given. A number of Mohawks in the Wigwam, all middle-aged, had told me that they were "Big Chiefs" in the tribe. Upon checking this information I discovered that *none* of these men held any special chiefly tribal position. However, I found out that *all* of them were in charge of small structural-steel gangs; they were all "pushers." If one translates "big chief" not as important tribal chief but rather as "warrior chief," then the information I had received from the older men was not false. That is, the equation *war chief = pusher* makes Mohawk cultural sense, given that *warrior = steel worker*. Both the war chief (leader of the war party) and the "pusher" lead a party of young Indians to an assignment where they can play "hero" and return with booty to the community to receive its applause.

If love of the warrior role was a major explanatory principle for Mohawks in structural steel work, then one would expect Mohawk youths to shun all other types of employment. This expectation is indeed justified. My discussion with Mohawk youths and with their teachers in Brooklyn indicated that the Mohawk male can rarely be interested in continuing his schooling after completing the minimal requirements. He has fixed a goal in mind: *to be a steel worker*.

Evaluation

This study of the Mohawks in structural steel represents the classical "sink-or-swim" approach in anthropological research.

Very little training in research had been forced on me, nor did I seek it. The project was successful despite this, for a number of reasons. First, I was not isolated from my own cultural environment or from my colleagues and teachers. After a certain amount of intensive field work, I was back at Columbia University talking incessantly about Mohawks to anyone who would listen. I lectured, argued, debated, and told stories about Mohawks. I was trying to put together a variety of data, collected in a disorganized, unplanned fashion.

Second, I believe my extroverted personality fitted in nicely with the extroverted, "I-can-take-on-the-world" Mohawk warriors who frequented the Wigwam. True, I wouldn't fight, but I would do almost anything else. I was an intense, energetic, and highly motivated graduate student, determined to "make it" in anthropology. And, if "making it" meant driving at high speeds in old cars with drunken Mohawks, that is what I did.

Although I was constantly discussing my field work—a most rewarding technique—I did not do something that might have been extremely helpful: I did not make periodic summaries of what I thought I knew at a given time. Such summaries are helpful in predicting that a given set of phenomena will occur and in using such predictions to validate given data. Further, such predictions facilitate future adaptations to the culture the researcher is learning. For example, had I made summary statements concerning the pecking-order game, I would have been able to argue as follows:

> I hypothesize that a pecking-order game is here in progress and that all members of the system are involved in it. Further, I hypothesize that, most frequently, it is the younger members who must fight it out to maintain or increase their rank. I also believe that I have been accepted as a member of Wigwam society. *Therefore*, I must assume that I will be brought into this game and challenged to fight. What will I do when such a challenge occurs?

Had I summarized in writing what I thought I knew and considered its logical implications, I would not have found a particular challenge confusing and would not have had to make an on-the-spot decision as to how to answer it. Perhaps I would have decided to get involved in a few "fights," after talking to Joe about the situation ahead of time, and persuaded him to stop a fight as soon as it looked like I was likely to be hurt. A few fights of this kind with some of the lowest ranking Mohawks would have given me all the advantages of non-fighting (being thought below everyone) and in addition given me a more secure position among the Mohawk "warriors."

I believe that I also should have reverted to the role of anthropologist after I had obtained as much data as I could in the role of "adopted Mohawk." Put differently, after a point in the field work, I really had nothing (or very little) to lose by assuming the role of anthropologist. I could have devised some schedules or questionnaires and tried giving them to a cross section of the Brooklyn community. At worst I would have lost my status of adopted Mohawk. At best I might have obtained a lot of good information on exactly how the role of structural steel worker is equated with the role of warrior.

Some of the older Mohawks had indicated to me that the younger Mohawks were disinterested in the Mohawk language and in many aspects of the "old ways" and were not respectful to the older people. It might have been interesting to look into this schism between the generations and perhaps find in it an historical relation to the young Mohawk warriors who would rather be on the warpath than help in the more mundane activities of the tribe.

In short, my research time in the last few months of work with the Mohawks was not efficiently used. When there were only a few Mohawks around the Wigwam or the nearby Spar Bar, I could have spent the time talking to the older people. I could also have tried to gather more statistical information through the use of schedules. I was afraid, however, to lose the position I had attained, although at a specific time in the research project I could have well afforded to take the risk.

Due to a number of favorable accidents, namely, my personality, my "adoption," and my remaining alive, the work with the Mohawks was completed with a certain amount of success. Such "luck" can be hoped for, but it can rarely replace the carefully designed and planned project used by a well-trained researcher.

PART II: TRINIDADIAN PEASANTS AND THE NATURAL EXPERIMENT

Problem, Theory, and Research Design

Does geography determine men's lives? This problem has intrigued scholars and laymen for centuries; in modern times it has been the subject of many heated exchanges among social scientists.[3] Anthropologists, although rarely answering the question with a simple Yes, have often turned to environmental deterministic theories for an answer. Indeed, some fundamental ideas in cultural anthropology are closely connected to environmentalism: culture area, the study of man in his "natural habitat," and cultural evolution.

The anthropological belief that culture is the prime determinant in human affairs has been neatly linked to environmentalism by the concept, cultural ecology. Cultural ecology —a theoretical orientation developed by Julian Steward—isolates technology as the major cultural determinant of change and problems of survival as the critical change factor within the environment. An environment is then seen as presenting a group with subsistence problems that must be solved. Solutions to these subsistence problems depend upon the level of the group's technology. Given a set of subsistence problems (S) and a set of technological accomplishments (T), certain cultural forms (C) must be developed. That is, according to cultural-ecological theory, adaptations to environments by use of specific technologies constitute "creative processes," or $S \times T \to C$.

Cultural ecology has made an important contribution to anthropological theory and methodology, because testable propositions can be derived from this framework. For this very reason I was attracted to cultural ecology. My Mohawk study, though satisfactory, did not leave me with the kind of surety—that I-knew-I-knew feeling—that I wanted from my research. With the Mohawk material I was a captive of my intuition and post facto logic. I wanted to stand on firmer ground in my second research assignment, and cultural ecology seemed to provide a more "scientific" framework for it. The argument basic to this research project is as follows: (1) Given two groups with extremely different cultural traditions, and (2) given that both these groups finally settle in the same community and make a living in the same way, (3) both these groups should develop similar cultural forms *caused by* the same problems they face in making a living, if the cultural-ecological approach is correct. Or, in cultural-ecological language, two groups that share both a subsistence problem and technology for solving it should also share many basic cultural forms.

In a recent paper (Freilich, 1968), I described the design for this study as *after-only multi-experimental*. In other words,

---

[3] For an historical summary of approaches to environmental determinism, see my paper "Ecology and Culture: Environmental Determinism and the Ecological Approach in Anthropology," *Anthropological Quarterly*, 40:26–43, 1967.

it is an example of a study where two experimental groups have
been subjected to similar causal factors and where data on the
two groups became available only after the causal factors entered.[4] Research that uses experimental designs under natural
conditions falls under the general category of "natural experiments."

Natural experimenters work in "man-found" rather than
"man-made" laboratories. Therefore, my first problem was to
locate a community with the characteristics described. I did not
solve this problem by taking a quick "look around the world."
At the time this study was being developed, I was a member of
a Caribbean Seminar jointly run by Columbia University and
the Research Institute for the Study of Man (RISM), which
was preparing graduate students for field work in the Caribbean
with special emphasis on research problems in Trinidad. I expected to receive a research training fellowship from RISM that
would get me to Trinidad for the summer of 1957. If this ma-
terialized, I planned to spend some of that summer searching
for the kind of community required to test my cultural-ecological
hypothesis.

My readings on Trinidad indicated that this island would
probably have several communities with the required characteristics, for Trinidad has a large population of East Indians whose
cultural tradition is significantly different from that of the
island's majority population, Creoles, or local Negroes. A number
of mixed Indian-Creole communities also exist in Trinidad. In
Trinidad, many Creoles and East Indians earn a living in the
same manner and have done so for several generations, and this
was just the special type of situation I required.

---

[4] The classical experimental design has a before and after *experimental
group* and a before and after *control group*. It is frequently symbolized
as follows:

	Time	
	t_1	t_2
Experimental group	x'_1	x'_2
Control group	x_1	x_2

x and x' are identical in all critical variables; x' but not x is subjected
to the independent variable.

In this study there is no adequate data for the "before" period (t_1).
Although there are no control groups as such, each experimental group
functions as a "control" for the other. The after-only multi-experimental
design can be symbolized as:

	Time	
	t_1	t_2
Experimental group 1		x_2
Experimental group 2		y_2

I received a fellowship from RISM as well as research funds from the Social Science Research Council (SSRC). Thus, by the beginning of June, 1957, I was financially prepared for a prolonged stay in Trinidad and had digested much of the published ethnographic materials on the Caribbean.[5]

Adaptational Research

An anthropologist preparing to do research in a tropical climate is well advised to spend considerable time planning for climatic adaptation. Early in the planning stage, time should be allowed for whatever series of injections are required for the area. He must also plan for special clothing needs—strong, light shoes for walking, light outer clothing, and some rainproof garments. There may be special sleeping problems requiring tents, sleeping bags, and mosquito netting. Transportation problems requiring the purchase of a jeep or a functionally equivalent item must be looked into also. Most anthropologists take a considerable number of pictures so a camera expert's advice should be sought on the type of camera and film most likely to do the best job in a given climate. It is also important to have a special container for camera and equipment to protect them from the elements. Today a variety of inexpensive but highly effective tape recorders are available, but these too must be chosen with care, keeping in mind the special climatic conditions of one's research. Matters of general notekeeping that provide no problem at home are at times overlooked by the inexperienced researcher, but it is possible to arrive in an area where pencils, ball-point pens, paper, and note cards are both extremely difficult to get and then most expensive. I did not plan as adequately as I might have for my tropical trip and ran into unnecessary problems. Perhaps the best rule of thumb is to spend some time with an anthropologist who has worked in the general geographical area of one's research.

I arrived in Trinidad in June, 1957, and made my initial headquarters in a rooming house in Port-of-Spain. A few days later, while looking through a local telephone directory, I discovered a third cousin on the island and was invited to stay at his house for a week until my summer research began. This was a most welcome piece of luck. The culture shock one generally receives in the adaptational period of research in a foreign land

---

[5] I am much indebted to both the Research Institute for the Study of Man for this fellowship and to the director of RISM—Vera Rubin—for many helpful and much-needed assistances at various stages of this project and to the Social Science Research Council for their grant permitting me to do this natural experiment.

was greatly reduced for me by being around my newly-found family. My cousin Jacob, a man of about fifty who had worked as an engineer and now ran a rooming house and a restaurant, was most knowledgeable about the island, its geography, its politics, and its economic problems. He was an avid reader of newspapers, journals, and books and knew many Trinidadian officials personally. I quickly became friendly with him and his immediate family and with a close relative of Jacob's who was a manufacturer and an importer and exporter. In long discussions with these people I came to see the island through the eyes of some of its middle-class, long-time residents. Jacob, an aristocrat at heart, generally took the upper-class white man's point of view on most topics. He had rare intuition, however, and understood many of his prejudices in favor of businessmen and the land-owners of large estates. He thus frequently spoke of matters from both the Creoles' and the Indians' points of view. His rooming house was integrated, and he had had many opportunities to learn how the middle and lower classes feel about island affairs.

The field-training fellowship from RISM required that I spend a few months of research in a lower-class sugar-estate community—let me call it Sugarville—not far from Port-of-Spain. Before settling in Sugarville, RISM's field director planned trips for the seminar members, so that the group could see the island as a whole before we settled into our respective work sites. These trips around Trinidad, parties at the field director's house where we met the local intelligentsia, and our study seminars were all useful adaptation mechanisms to a very non-Protestant-ethic society.

With my wife, who was interested in collecting culture and personality data in Trinidad, I settled in Sugarville two weeks after arriving on the island. The Sugarville community was useful for my later research, because it was a mixed community of Indians and Creoles. In Sugarville, I also had an opportunity to make "cultural mistakes" before moving to the place where my SSRC research would be conducted. Many of the mistakes researchers make are a function of the differences between their culture of orientation and the research culture, and since my research culture in Sugarville was similar to that of my natural-experiment community, I had the opportunity to make "mistakes" in Sugarville that I would know better than to repeat later in my experimental research.

I could plan few data-gathering events that included both Creoles and Indians, since these two groups had a strong mutual dislike for each other. It was also obvious that research approaches toward Indians and Creoles would have to be very different because of the fundamental differences in the two groups' cultural traditions. Exactly what strategies would pay off well I did not discover until I had left Sugarville, but my experiences there at least alerted me to the types of problems I would be facing later during my stay in Trinidad.

In Sugarville I spent much of my spare time collecting information about the locations of ethnically mixed communities. I wanted to study in a peasant farming community, and information and advice collected from taxi drivers, schoolteachers, newspaper reporters, government agricultural experts, and lecturers in the College of Tropical Agriculture indicated one direction: to go east to a highland area known as Tamana. In this eastern highland area I discovered several villages that might meet my requirements, but the village I selected—Anamat—seemed the best choice for several reasons. First, its head teacher was extremely interested in my work and even offered to do a rough population check of the Creole and Indian peasants and to obtain some economic data on these groups. Teacher Ram—an Indian of Presbyterian faith—seemed quite popular in his village, and his interest in my work appeared to be a favorable sign for a successful project. Second, Anamat was a relatively isolated community. It had no electricity, gas, telephone, or major highways nearby, so that extraneous variables would not have to be controlled. Except for voting in major elections and participating in Carnival celebrations, the Anamatians were minimally involved with island culture. Third, a vacant building (a former school) was available to house us. It was an ideal house for my purposes, because it was located approximately in the center of the village and adjacent to the new school building and post office. Much village life could be observed through the windows of this structure. Fourth, several Anamatian peasants to whom Teacher Ram introduced me appeared cooperative and pleased about my prospective stay in Anamat.

After giving Teacher Ram about ten days for his initial survey, I visited him again and received the following information. First, the "average" Indian peasant of the village owned about the same amount of land as the "average" Creole peasant. Second, the major cash crops for all the peasants were cocoa and coffee. Third, all the Anamatians seemed to have similar ideas about how to cultivate their land. I was overjoyed with this information, because, although I realized that Ram's findings would have to be carefully checked, Anamat seemed to be *the* community for my study. Ram added one fact that he thought might prevent me from going there. He had understood that I wanted to be in "one community," but he had doubts as to whether Anamat filled this requirement. Some peasants, he told me, lived far away from the schoolhouse and the village shops, and some were rarely seen at village functions. I replied that this did not worry me particularly, keeping to myself the information that anthropologists, together with other social scientists, do not really know what a community is and thus can never be sure they are in one.

I decided to move to Anamat and told Teacher Ram to spread the word that I was writing a book about life in Trinidad and would start my studies there. I began to make inquiries in Port-of-Spain as to how one obtains permission to use a piece of government property: namely, the ex-schoolhouse. I was told to contact a certain government cabinet minister. Although interviewing government officials is far simpler in Trinidad than it is in America, many precious field-work days were lost cutting the red tape involved in getting the use of the ex-schoolhouse. My persistence and unorthodox ways of approaching high-ranking government officials finally produced a favorable decision. The dilapidated building was useless to the government, and the minister and his staff must have been glad to get me out of Port-of-Spain.

The move into the ex-schoolhouse was in retrospect a mixed blessing. The government had passed an income-tax law shortly before my arrival in Anamat. When I, claiming to be an anthropologist, arrived in the village and moved into a government-owned house, most of the peasants quickly jumped to the conclusion that I was a government tax spy. Their suspicions grew as I went about trying to obtain data from them from which I could deduce their incomes. In terms of my natural experiment, I had to determine (1) if the size of the land holdings of the Creoles as a group roughly equaled the total land belonging to Indians, and (2) if the model size of each group's holdings was roughly equal. I therefore asked all the peasants how much land they worked, how much of it they owned, and how much (if any) they rented. I also inquired into crop yields and other related matters. My questions, which I regarded as impersonal, were, much to my amazement, met with great suspicion. I later realized I was a tax spy in the eyes of the peasants, but even so I should have realized that questions relating to income are personal and almost invariably "tricky," since few groups like to divulge their earnings.

The Indians generally avoided my economic questions. Instead, they talked at length about the wonders of the Hindu religion and of their good family life. The Creoles similarly avoided economic questions, speaking instead about fêtes and the joys of Carnival.

I decided, temporarily, to stop all questions pertaining to the ecological adaptations of Anamatian peasants. I also decided to stay in Anamat and do a traditional community study, should statistics later indicate that the experimental controls, which I assumed existed, were absent. I still did not quite understand why the ecological questions received such a poor response, but I accepted the fact as a temporary failure. I began to follow the more traditional anthropological approach, which favored not pursuing anything specific in the early period, getting to know people, time patterns, and interactional settings, and in general trying to gain enough rapport for the more specific aspects of the study. I had made the mistake of rushing things because of my concern with the availability of specific controls for my natural experiment, and because I wanted to make up the time I had wasted in Port-of-Spain getting permission to use the ex-schoolhouse.

The rate at which rapport can be established with a people is in part a function of how quickly the researcher becomes involved in public events. I was fortunate to have moved to Anamat just prior to the deaths of the grandmother of one neighbor and the mother of another. My wife and I were invited to partake in the rituals associated with the two deaths, and we were quickly placed "on stage" where we were clearly visible to many community members. The presence of an anthropologist and his wife in Anamat soon became public knowledge, and introductions to many community members quickly followed. Within a week of these events, Ma Mac—one of the most respected members of the Creole community—visited us, a sign I took (though wrongly) of acceptance by the Creoles of the community. We returned Ma Mac's visit in short order, and my visits to her house were frequent throughout the study.

I began capitalizing on my wife's presence in the community. While I went around introducing myself to the farmers of the village and to anyone else I happened to see, my wife made friends with farmers' wives and daughters. Several of the neighbors' wives then visited us at our house, and their visits were quickly reciprocated. We met several other women at our neighbors' homes, and Teacher Ram's wife, an intelligent and helpful woman, became a most valuable friend. Like her husband, she was well liked in the community, and introductions coming from her helped my wife establish rapport with the peasants.

The Rams not only directly helped my research but were of considerable indirect assistance. The teacher and his wife were culturally intermediate between the peasants and my previous associates from Columbia University, so this couple's friendship provided a cultural and psychological bridge to the community. The Rams had spent most of their lives in a much larger and more urban community close to Port-of-Spain, and they were able to empathize with our feelings of isolation. Our friendship with this couple made life much happier in rural Anamat.

Shortly after settling in Anamat, I developed a friendship with one of the richest Indian peasants there, Mr. Rapas. I expected this friendship to "open up" the Indian community for research, but this did not occur. It took about a month of collecting and decoding vague bits of information received from both Creole and Indian Anamatians to reach the conclusion that Mr. Rapas was one of the most disliked people in Anamat, particularly by the Indians. My friendship with Mr. Rapas made my work with the other Indians more difficult, but as my ties with him weakened (due to conscious efforts on my part), relationships with other Indian peasants seemed to improve.

My rapport-getting was much facilitated by my ability to play an adequate game of cricket. The British had introduced cricket to Trinidad, and the sport was popular with young and old. My knowledge of the game soon brought me into contact with Mr. Ed, a rich Creole who had started one of the local cricket clubs. Mr. Ed's house was a hang-out for many of the Creole peasants, particularly for those who were directly involved in playing cricket. I was soon practicing with this group and their sons on late afternoons and weekends. After cricket practice we would all stop at Ed's house and have a scotch or two, and I would invite those present to "drop in" at my house any time they were in the vicinity. When the talk veered toward my work, as it invariably did, I took the opportunity to explain my research aims. My "explanation" usually went as follows: It was important for world peace that people get to know about each other, and I had been sent to obtain information about how Trinidadians live, so that a book could be written telling the world about them. I explained that since many people in Trinidad are engaged in farming, it was necessary for me to spend some time studying farmers, and that the friendliness of Anamat and its head teacher had made me select it as the headquarters for my research.

I slowly developed rapport to the extent that I could return to sensitive topics, but the research included a structural problem that was never completely solved: the Indians and the Creoles disliked each other so intensely that the better my relations developed with one group, the more the suspicions of the other group grew. It took the Anamatians a long time to accept the fact that I could honestly like both Creoles and Indians. I later found out that the peasants had concluded that my "strange" behavior had something to do with my work. The behavior they found strange was not only my friendship for Creoles *and*

Indians, but my regular attendance at Catholic, Presbyterian, Baptist, and Hindu prayer meetings, my perpetual readiness to assist an Anamatian—from driving him into a nearby market town to helping him repair his house—and the fact that all and sundry were given friendly hospitality whenever they visited our house.

One of my adaptational problems was simply how to manage my time. During our first week in Anamat, I was overwhelmed with the idea that I had one year in which I could do anything I wanted to. This tremendous freedom was somewhat frightening, and I spent several days worrying about how best to use my time. This in itself was rather a ridiculous waste of time, since I did not have the information to make an effective decision until much of the field work was completed. I finally decided to use my evenings for writing up field notes, to try and meet farmers on their land holdings during the mornings and early afternoon hours, and after a while to make specific appointments for interviews in the late afternoons.

At first I roamed the village with a small notebook and pencil looking for farmers and frequently not finding them. However, in my wanderings I noticed that Anamatians regularly congregated at a variety of village sites, the post office, rum shops, Benny's Shed (where the Village Council meetings and Agricultural Society meetings were held), the schoolhouse, at one of the three local stores, at Salmadie corner (where the two major roads of the village crossed), at the Catholic Church, and at one or other of the two cricket fields. At one of these village centers one could, by careful choice of time and place, meet and gossip with the locals. I used the centers as "information stations" and tried to spend some time each day at one or more of them.

As my village contacts grew, and as more and more Anamatians seemed willing to cooperate with me, I became optimistic as to the study's final outcome. In terms of the concepts I used, I had successfully completed the adaptational stage of the study. However, in other terms my adaptational research in Anamat never really ended, for I never completely adapted to living, thinking, and feeling in three cultures: Creole, East Indian, and White American.

Active Research

During the adaptational period, the anthropologist talks to people on subjects they wish to discuss and in ways they select, and he terminates such conversations in accordance with cues they provide. Data collection at this time is thus accurately described as "passive," and the actual data collected are generally only indirectly related to the problem being investigated. The anthropologist is thus eager to arrive at the active research stage as quickly as possible. Since a premature entry can, however, adversely affect the whole research program, it is well to look carefully for signs indicating the informants' readiness for active research. When the anthropologist approaches a typical group of informants and notices that his presence does not seem to change the information flow—they continue talking in essentially the same manner as before—he has a good sign that the adaptational period can be concluded. Other signs include receiving house invitations from informants of diverse social status and being invited to restricted community functions. In Anamat everyone was considered welcome at a funeral, at a wake, at the house of a sick individual, at a cricket match, and at a meeting of the Village Council. "Sunday breakfasts" (parties after church early on Sunday afternoon), birthday parties, wedding receptions, and Indian *pujas* (family prayer meetings) were all restricted community functions, participation in which was by invitation only. Invitations to the restricted functions of well-to-do Anamatians were particularly good signs of having successfully passed through the adaptational period.

About six weeks after arriving in Anamat, I returned to an active role in the research setting. That is, I questioned some informants on specific topics, interviewed in a planned manner, and continued discussing a topic long enough to get a satisfactory closure on the subject. This meant ignoring informants' cues that indicated their desire to change the topic. During this early entry stage into active research my rapport was not equally good with all the Anamatian peasants. With some informants it was excellent. For example, according to my field diary, I spent four hours walking over Mr. Dowell's estate and questioning him on highly specific matters. Our discussions included such sensitive topics as how good a farmer he considered himself to be, how he ranked himself vis-à-vis other Anamatian farmers, his average income from various crops, his regular expenditures on his estate, and many other related questions. Our discussions were cordial, and Dowell in no way indicated that I should change my line of questioning. In fact, he seemed to enjoy our talk, and he invited me to visit him one evening the following week so that he could explain how his records were kept. He kept figures on all his expenditures and on various income-producing activities, and his records, which he permitted me to examine at length, were a gold mine of excellent data. I achieved maximum rapport with Dowell, and I could count on his aid and advice throughout my stay in Trinidad.

With most of the community the rapport achieved six weeks

after "entry" was nowhere near as good as that achieved with Dowell. With some Anamatians my rapport was good only when discussing a limited number of topics. It began to decline when I brought up sensitive subjects. With some other informants I achieved only a minimal amount of rapport, and these weak relationships permitted neither controlled interviews for long durations nor interviews on sensitive topics.

The "whys" of this differential rapport are hard to pinpoint. My best informants in Anamat, at all stages of my study, were atypical in one way or another. Dowell was proud of his achievements in agriculture and of his abilities to successfully plan ahead and meet the goals he set himself. His involvement in agricultural matters, which included serious attention to government pamphlets and government agricultural officers, made him happy to "teach" agriculture to me, his (high-status) pupil. From very poor beginnings, Dowell had acquired one of the largest land holdings in the community. He reminded me frequently of the American "self-made man." My good rapport with him was partly a function of his willingness to broadcast his successes to me and partly due to the fact that his drive and energy were channeled mainly into work, which other Creole Anamatians did not think was the way a good Creole should live. Dowell thus had very few close friends in the village, and I was able to fill an important slot in his life: I admired him for that which he believed merited admiration.

Another example of an excellent informant who was somewhat apart from the group was Ma Mac, who considered herself part of Anamat's "aristocracy," and whose husband had left her enough land to live well. Her family's long history of wealth (as locally defined), her kinship connections to other well-to-do Anamatians, her daughter's marriage to a schoolteacher, and her son's passing the exams for the Trinidadian police force all gave substance to her aristocratic air. Mr. Ramli, another excellent informant, was much involved in "scientific" agriculture, was self-educated in Hindu scriptures, practiced Hindu religion in a highly orthodox manner, and held himself aloof from Creole-Indian conflicts. Mr. Bool lived alone, rarely involved himself with community affairs, gave long lectures (when given a chance) on the hypocrisy of the Catholic Church and the futility of any kind of religious worship, and generally considered himself the "philosopher" of the village. Mr. Brown was a bachelor who did not care enough for his estate or show enough interest in women to meet the community's approval. His great passion was horse racing rather than woman chasing, and as a result he was thought of as a "sissy" by community members.

It is important to distinguish between the problems of rapport achievement and maintenance with Indians and those with Creoles. Throughout my study these problems were quite different. Among the Indians my general rapport, my acceptance by the group as a short-duration member of the community, was largely a function of the total time I spent in the community. My general rapport grew over time both in size and in quality. In terms of size, I received ever more privileges as a "local" or, as one peasant put it, "one of us." In terms of quality, the general rapport I achieved with the Indians grew ever more "solid": my position with this group became ever less vulnerable as time passed. Various incorrect, inappropriate, or unappreciated acts on my part were ever less likely to result in a significant loss of previously achieved rapport. Differently put, my rapport "investment" with the Indian community as a whole became "safer" as my stay in the community lengthened.

Although my general rapport with the Creole community grew in size as the time I spent in the community increased, qualitatively the rapport did not become ever more "solid." That is, the rapport achieved at a given time remained quite vulnerable. My rapport investment was less "safe," and it was subject to decline if my interactions with the public decreased. My non-attendance at a Village Council meeting, at a cricket match, or at a fête had much more serious consequences from the Creole community than from the Indian community.

The specific rapport I attained, i.e., that achieved with specific individual members of Anamat—was also different between Indians and Creoles. Good rapport, once attained with a given Indian family, was rarely lost for the total duration of the study. With many Indian families I was treated almost as a family member and, in several, addressed by the younger people with a kinship term: "father's brother." Once I had attained these close ties, they were minimally influenced by interaction rates, specific acts on my part, or my positions on Trinidadian political matters.

Although I had many close friends among the Creole peasants, too, these relationships were more fluid than my ties with the Indians. For example, if I had not visited a typical Creole peasant for a week or two, some of my rapport seemed to have evaporated and some rapport building was necessary before getting down to serious (active) data collecting.

Associated with the solid rapport achieved with the Indians and the fluid rapport achieved with the Creoles was what I called a *differential spreadability factor*. Solid rapport was functionally related to maximum spreadability. That is, a good relationship with one Indian family greatly increased the probability of developing good relationships with another Indian family. A good relationship with a Creole family helped in developing relationships with other Creole families, but minimally so. Thus, although Ma Mac was highly thought of among the Creoles of Anamat and although my relationships with her and her family were excellent, these relationships did not appear to help me in developing ties with other Creoles. However, my equally good relationships with Ramli and his family helped me considerably to establish rapport with other Indian peasants.

Regular attendance at a variety of village public functions was a most useful technique for maintaining general rapport and for building on the specific rapport attained with Anamatians who attended the functions. Perhaps the most important village organization was the Village Council. This pseudogovernmental advisory organization was considered a waste of time by many Anamatians, and only ten to fifteen adults attended Village Council meetings with any regularity. However, all the village adults were concerned with what the Village Council was doing, and most Anamatians made infrequent appearances at the meetings.

Who the regular attenders were depended largely on who was currently running the Village Council—that is, whether the individual was a Creole or an Indian, whether he supported the People's National Movement (PNM) or the People's Democratic Party (PDP), and whether he lived at one end of the village (called "Salmadie") or at the other end (called "the Village"). Although formal authority within the Village Council lay in the hands of an elected chairman, the actual person who "ran things" might be the secretary, the vice-president, or any one of several officers who talked well and convincingly and seemed to know how to run an organization. The regular attenders were mainly those with some kind of social link to the man who "ran things"—a neighbor, friend, relation, or co-party member.

As in most organizational participations in field work, the anthropologist's strong identification with a given group has both positive and negative consequences for the research. The benefits I received from my strong involvement with the Village Council were as follows: my regular attendance at meetings was, for most Anamatians, a sign of real interest in the community's problems and its developmental plans. Those who believed this believed (wrongly) that my work with the Village Council was purely altruistic and unrelated to the basic objectives of the research. I was thus frequently complimented for the interest I showed in village affairs. At various special meetings I was asked to take the chair. This meant that I was supposed to begin proceedings by saying a few words. My speeches invariably included a plug for anthropology and its importance to world affairs, a statement of thanks for the great help I was receiving from the people of Anamat, and a reaffirmation of my willingness to help the Council in all its goals. The Village Council thus gave me the opportunity to speak publicly about my work, to publicly praise community members for past assistance, and thus to indirectly ensure that such assistances would be forthcoming in the future. Even when I did not chair meetings, my presence was still somewhat of a "commercial" for the project.

To those who considered the current political élite of the village misguided and (according to some Anamatians) working for personal rather than village goals, I was foolishly spending time doing the wrong things with the wrong people. For these Anamatians, a "broadcast" through local informational channels of my activities with the Village Council adversely affected my general rapport. However, on balance, I believe (and this is hard to demonstrate) that my work with the Village Council added to the rapport I achieved at any given time and greatly helped in rapport maintenance.

Some of my problems that were directly related to my Village Council activities were perhaps more of my own making than necessary outcomes of the involvement. One such problem related to island politics. Most of the "regulars" of the Village Council belonged to the PNM. My own political leanings favored this party also, and I made known my feelings to all who asked me a direct political question. I thus developed a special social persona for the community members: I was an anthropologist, actively involved with the Village Council clique, and an admirer of the PNM. My political stance had the advantage of getting me involved in long political discussions with many members of the community and in long political arguments with many others. These discussions and arguments provided good data on island and local politics. However, I also created some ill-feelings between myself and a few of the local peasants. Perhaps more careful thought to the impressions Anamatians were getting of me and greater skill in impression management might have led me to be more guarded about my feelings, especially in the area of politics.

In this context it is well to remember that an anthropologist in a field setting spends much of his time "on stage." People are looking at him, talking to him, and watching him talk to others seven days a week for long hours each day. In such a work setting it may not be wise to attempt more than a minimal amount of impression management. Impression management includes a certain amount of deception, which if discovered may badly hurt the research program. Our informants in the field, though frequently lacking in formal education, are not lacking in sensitivity and insight. They are capable of making and do make exceedingly accurate judgments about the researcher and his activities. Therefore, it may be wise for the field anthropologist to be himself in terms of personality, likes, and interests, as much as he can. Since I generally enjoy actively participating in groups with which I work, it would have been most difficult for me to stay away from Village Council involvements, and it would have been false to present myself as only an objective observer of island politics.

Although I lost some rapport with a few Anamatians because of my involvements with the Village Council and with island politics, I believe I came across to the village as "honest." The statements of an honest anthropologist are more likely to be accepted by the community at large. Statements such as, "These data I am collecting are all confidential, and you will never be associated with anything you tell me," must be believed by one's informants in order to get valid data. Thus a policy of honesty in presentation of self is for the researcher pragmatically the best policy.

It is fortunate for this study that most of the Creoles favored the party I supported, the PNM, that most Anamatians, Creole or Indian, were not strongly involved with island politics, that those who were strongly in favor of the PDP were Indians, and that my strong political stance did not emerge till late in the field work. That is, by the time all the Indian peasants knew my political inclinations, I had developed fairly good ties with them. Given that "solid" rather than "fluid" rapport could be and was developed with Indians, my favoring the PNM did minimal damage to relationships in Anamat. Fortunately, I had *not* supported the PDP, which would have politically antagonized many of the Creoles.

I regularly attended Catholic Church services (every other Sunday morning), Presbyterian Church services every Sunday afternoon, meetings of the local Agricultural Credit Society, and meetings of the Friendly Society. These centers were all useful for maintaining and developing rapport and for gathering much valuable ethnographic data.

Although most informants improve with time, some Anamatian peasants remained difficult to work with for the duration of my study. In a traditional anthropological study an informant who proves difficult can be substituted, for one can argue that someone else of similar age and status will probably provide equivalent information. However, in natural-experimental research the anthropologist is much concerned with the controls that exist for his experiment. A specific group of people must be worked with—in my case *all* the peasants of Anamat—and specific sets of information must be obtained. In short, having defined this study as a natural experiment I could not "give up" on any peasant in the community, no matter what problems I had getting data from him.

The natural-experimental approach had an additional requirement: I had to spend the large majority of my time in the village *with the peasants* in order to maximize the possibility of getting all the information I wanted from all the peasants of Anamat. Thus, in situations necessitating a choice of activities, the peasants always had first call on my time. For example, if I was invited to two "Sunday breakfasts" on the same day, of which one was given by a peasant farmer and the other by a nonpeasant, I invariably went to the former. My decisions in favor of the peasants rarely caused problems. The peasants represented the "upper class" of the community, and the Anamatians found my behavior understandable. It was reasonable to them that a white man should spend most of his time with people closest to his own class. A problem that was not so easily solved was what to do when a function among a group of East Indian peasants conflicted in time with a function among a group of Creole peasants. I sometimes went to both functions, staying a short time with each group and satisfying neither. More often, however, I attempted to alternate visits to Indian and Creole functions.

Our Creole housekeeper proved so valuable for my research that I promoted her to research assistant. Tina had lived in the village all her life and was surprisingly well-informed on local history and culture and even on small details of the lives of the Indians. In her short life she had been a teacher's assistant and had lived with four husbands, each of whom had left her with at least one child. Her constant good humor made her liked, even by those Anamatians who attacked her morals. Through her husbands and their families, her father and his family, her stepfather and his relatives, and her mother's family, she was related to a large number of local Creoles. Thus, her being identified with my research was of considerable value for rapport maintenance and development.

My "upranking" of Tina from housekeeper to research assistant was well accepted by the community. It was generally felt that I had given Tina the opportunity to "make good," and both she and the community were proud of her as she walked around with her notebook, setting up appointments for herself and for me, and giving interviews. Had Tina not been so generally liked it would have been necessary to hire an Indian assistant also, so as not to appear to be favoring the Creole community.

The job vacancy of "housekeeper" was of interest to Tina's friend Lee, and I was interested in hiring her. Although an Indian woman seemed to be preferable for this position, no one from the Indian community was available. I began the hiring process by asking people of the village about Lee and what they thought of my plans to hire her. Most of them said she would be a good person for Tina's old job, but several Anamatians disagreed. After much prodding, I was told by some of the latter that I would not be happy with Lee, since she was too much of a gossip. This information made me more interested than ever in hiring Lee, for out of the mouths of local gossips come many rewarding leads for anthropological investigations. Lee was hired, and her presence in the house was generally advantageous for the research. Lee, like Tina, had a family in the village, several members of whom became good informants. Her interest in talking about goings on in the community did indeed prove useful, but I discovered that a gossip in one's house is a two-edged sword: many happenings within the house become well known in the community.

Having two Creole women working for me, rather than one Creole and one Indian, was determined by the unavailability of Indian help when I needed it. This situation, however, did have some advantages for the project. First, the two Creole women got along well with each other and gave me no labor problems. An Indian assistant working alongside a Creole might have created considerable tension within the house, given the general antagonism between Creoles and Indians. Second, given the differential problems of rapport maintenance for Creoles and Indians respectively, stronger ties with the Creole community were established via my labor force.

Data-Getting Techniques

How much control over critical variables is necessary before a study merits the designation "natural experiment"? This question perhaps has no categorical answer.[6] From its designation as a natural experiment the work derived several benefits, for the label forced me to "think experiment." Thus, I was constantly comparing my own efforts with work performed in the

---

[6] For a comprehensive treatment of this and related questions, see my paper "The Natural Experiment: A Strategy for Anthropological Research," Ms. (1968).

laboratories of physical and biological scientists. I forced myself to be aware constantly of the reliability, validity, and comparability of the data I was collecting. By thinking experiment I remained concerned throughout my research with programing my research activities in a scientific way.

The problems I identified at the beginning of the active research period were as follows: (1) to find out exactly who belonged in my sample; (2) to get to know these people well enough so that they would answer very specific and often quite personal questions; (3) to know what questions to ask and how to ask them. I was helped in all these matters both by special informants and by hired help.

With the help of Teacher Ram I developed a list of fifty-seven peasants. This list, which was later augmented because of additional information, represented all the peasants Ram knew. (A peasant was defined as a farmer who worked only for himself and who derived the large majority of his income from working the land.[7]) I prepared a large work sheet with columns headed name, land owned, land rented, house location, first interview, date, subject discussed, second interview, date, subject discussed, and so on, with a final column for problems. Throughout the study this master list helped me keep track of work accomplished, work yet to be done, and major problems of the research. As I developed formal questionnaires I added them to the work sheet by title, so that I could keep track of who had received and answered a given questionnaire.

Use of special informants and hired help. Ram was very friendly with eight of the peasants and offered to accompany me to their houses on my first visit. His presence helped me to establish rapport and permitted me to initiate a dialogue between him and the peasant on the subject with which I had previously had difficulties obtaining information: the agricultural practices of Anamatians.

I asked both Ram and Tina to introduce me to peasant farmers whenever the opportunity arose, even if I had met the individual before. Although I had seen and met many peasants by this time, I still had difficulty in matching names with faces.

In several long interviews with Ram I questioned him on what he knew about each peasant on my list. This information was useful both for achieving better rapport with the peasants

---

[7] Many of the Anamatian peasants had side lines that provided extra income. Examples of such side lines include buying oxen and renting such "bulls" to those who need them to pull lumber out of the forest, working the "bull," and hunting wild animals.

and for checking on information that they later provided. Ram took his job as Head Teacher of Anamat very seriously. His deep interest in the education of the village children was in sharp contrast to the attitude of the previous Head Teacher, and Ram was greatly respected for his many educational efforts on behalf of the villagers. In his frequent contacts with Anamatians he came to know a great deal about local affairs, including how well given farmers were doing economically, and how they felt about a variety of phenomena from the running of the Village Council to attempts to set up a second cricket club. Ram found it neither embarrassing nor unethical to provide me with considerable data pertaining to the life-styles of the peasants in my sample. In exchange—so to speak—I made it clear that his information would be treated with complete confidence and that I would be happy to help him and his family in any way I could. Throughout the study I presented Ram with questions, problems, and hypotheses relating to the research, and he was always willing and able to help me.

I developed similar close working and friendly relationships with several Anamatian peasants, who as a group could be referred to as "special informants." The special informants differed in terms of the subjects they were willing and able to discuss at any length. They had in common, however, a special interest in my work and a wish to assist me in it. Among the best of my special informants were Dowell, Ma Mac, Brown, Ramli, Bool, and Paluk.

Dowell was a most valuable source of agricultural data. Through him I learned much about the types of soil in Anamat and about the scientific method of farming particular types of land. Although Dowell's notions of scientific agriculture were not completely in accord with those of various members of Trinidad's College of Tropical Agriculture, he did know the standards used by the Anamatian peasants. Further, he discussed in great detail the many things the local peasants did wrong, from not providing enough drains for their land to not removing trees that rarely bear, and from overloading their holdings with too many subsidiary crops, to not harvesting in the proper manner.

With Ramli, one of the better Indian farmers in Anamat, I developed good rapport and was always welcome in his house. If I visited on an evening when he had made no plans to go out, he would spend considerable time discussing his favorite topic: Hindu religion. He was particularly concerned with the irreligiosity of many Indians in Anamat. They did not make regular *pujas,* they were unconcerned with getting proper mates for their children, and their relationships with members of their extended families left much to be desired. According to Ramli, the young people were forgetting the traditional Hindu precepts. The "old times" were much better, and to Ramli there seemed no way to reverse the trend.

Ma Mac too eulogized the days "when the old heads were alive," when the island in general and Anamat in particular had "better living." She described the good times she had had as a girl in her father's house and often mentioned the private parties and dances that the "old heads" used to give. In the old days, "girls of reputation" were closely supervised. They were not allowed to go anywhere alone, unlike the girls of today.

Bool, whose fifth wife was Ma Mac's sister, gave me a less idealized version of the old days. He spoke at length of the troubles with the Indians when the latter were still indentured servants, with the difficulties people had in making a living, and (his favorite subject) how the church helped the poor to remain downtrodden. He was antagonistic to me and my work even before meeting me, and this had made it quite difficult for me to get to speak with him alone. After several unsuccessful efforts to use Ma Mac as a go-between[8] and several other unsuccessful ploys, I hit on an approach that worked. I went to him and, remembering that he considered himself a philosopher, told him I would prove to his satisfaction that I (then thirty) was actually older than he (then seventy). He found this topic quite fascinating. Briefly put, I argued that age should not be calculated in terms of how frequently we had taken a "ride around the sun" but rather in terms of the number and diversity of our experiences. In terms of the number and diversity of my experiences, I argued that I was older than he.

Bool was interested enough in this topic to spend a whole afternoon telling me his experiences. He did not appear overly interested in mine, and we never really settled the matter of who was older. However, I told him that our discussions that day were of great value to me as an anthropologist and that, since he seemed to have enjoyed our talk, he would probably enjoy future discussions with me. Although I could rarely get Bool to visit my house, he was always happy to see me in his. Data received from Bool were particularly valuable in the areas of local history and attitudes and activities of Creoles with respect to religion and marriage.

The data from Ramli, Ma Mac, and Bool helped me to re-

---

[8] This is a good example of the minimal spreadability of rapport among Creoles. Bool was not only a relative of Ma Mac but a good friend as well, yet my good relationship with her did little for me with respect to developing ties with Bool.

construct village social life as it had been when these informants were children. These data were also valuable as the basis for developing *history* questions dispersed among several question-naires.

Paluk, Ramli's brother, was generally recognized as the vil-lage "healer." Paluk, a man accustomed to thinking deeply on subjects in which he had an interest, was initially quite skeptical about my explanation of what I was doing in Anamat. However, he indicated an interest in anthropology, and I spent consider-able time discussing both my research interests in Anamat and anthropology's general aims. In a short time Paluk's skepticism vanished, and he became an admirer and disciple ready to do anything in his power to help in my work. He provided data on local medicine and people's attitudes and activities with re-spect to sickness and helped me to meet many of the peasants of Anamat. Since he "treated" Creoles and Indians alike—taking in recompense only what each individual could afford, usually in the form of produce—Paluk was greatly admired in the com-munity, and his introductions and "certifications" of my role were extremely valuable to my study. In addition, Paluk was a talented mechanic who was able to repair my second-hand Morris Minor. His firm stand that payment for "just doing a little ting on the car" would represent a denial of our friendship forced me to reciprocate in other ways. I took him to the beaches in my car and transported him to Indian weddings and to vari-ous community functions to which we were invited. Paluk, like Teacher Ram, could discuss a variety of problems pertaining to my research, but unlike Ram, he was not happy discussing Creole activities and culture at any length, and our talks were generally restricted to matters that pertained only to the Indians of Anamat.

Brown frequently came to our house in the evenings. He lived alone and so particularly enjoyed our invitations for din-ner, followed, at times, by some three-handed poker. As a special informant, Brown was most valuable in providing data on the beliefs, goals, values, and typical activities of young adult Cre-oles—those in approximately the 18–30 age bracket. Many of the young bachelors of Anamat considered Brown's house their hangout; thus the data he provided had a strong factual basis.

I had decided to use Tina as a sort of "Girl Friday" research assistant. She was set up with a "desk"—made by attaching two long planks to a wall—some "filing cabinets"—made from boxes obtained in the local stores—and pencils and paper and in-structed to write essays on every peasant in the community. The essays were supposed to follow categories traditional in ethnog-raphies—history, work, family and kinship, religious activities

—and to include anything else she considered interesting. In essence, I was using Tina as a paid special informant and asking her to discuss a far larger range of topics than I discussed with any particular nonpaid special informant. In order to save time I had her write the data, rather than tell it to me.

Lee, too, was most valuable as a special informant. She was particularly useful in helping me to understand the sex and mating habits of my subjects. She had a common-law husband and many "friends" and willingly discussed her sex life, what she expected from a given relationship, and her marriage and family goals. We talked at great length on these matters. Unlike Tina, who would rather write me an essay on these questions than talk about them, Lee enjoyed the verbal give and take. She "took" each of several pilot questionnaires I developed on mating and marriage, and her work contributed greatly to a final (very productive) questionnaire on mating, marriage, and the family that I gave to all the peasants.

Long discussions with special informants and hired help not only helped me to isolate significant matters for my formal questionnaires but helped me overcome a linguistic problem. Specifically, this problem—perhaps describable under a category such as "Terminological Traps for Field Workers"—is the temptation to think one knows a language, when the language he knows and the one spoken by his informants are referred to by the same word, say English. In Anamat, the locals spoke English and my native tongue is English, so I initially assumed that I had no communication problems. When I had prolonged conversations with the locals on fairly specific topics, however, I found that many of the messages that went from me to them were not being decoded in the way I had intended. Further, some of the messages I received from them did not make sense: I too had decoding problems. For example, certain statements made by the Anamatians have the same tonal sequence Americans use for questions. However, for the Anamatians most of these statements are not questions. Thus, "Jones, a fête-man, yes?" simply means that Jones likes to spend a lot of time, money, and energy having a good time. No *question* is here implied. Another difficulty was that many words had meanings quite different from the one I gave them. For example, "Smith a socialist, yes?" means that Smith likes to do a lot of socializing and has nothing to do with his politics.

By the time I developed formal questionnaires I was able to communicate quite effectively with my informants. However, in order to get reliable and valid data in Anamat, I found that I needed to have more than good rapport and an understanding of communication patterns. I needed an awareness of social reality as seen through the eyes of Creoles and Indians themselves, for I found that answers to my questions were only as good as the questions themselves. I also found that, for any given topic, the more diversified were my data-collecting procedures, the more valid were the data on that topic. Take for example my data on divorce with respect to the Creole peasants. After collecting some data on legal marriage, I assumed that the reason most Creoles seemed to favor common-law marriage was that to leave a legal wife required a divorce, whereas to rid oneself of a common-law wife, the husband simply left her. Because I had discovered, after achieving considerable rapport with most of the Anamatian peasants, that *no peasant in Anamat had been divorced,* I believed that very few had been legally married. However, I subsequently discovered that my data were *not valid,* because what I meant by divorce was not the same as what the peasant meant by this term. I had not tapped Creole social reality on this subject. I was led toward the collection of valid data on legal marriage in the following manner. During a visit with a Creole peasant I had a long discussion with his wife while my host was talking with a neighbor. My host had previously informed me that he was legally married and that his wife was still living. I therefore assumed that my hostess was my host's legally married wife. The information I received from her, however, was that (1) she was legally married, (2) her "lawful husband" lived in another village, (3) my host and she had been living happily in common-law marriage for several years, and (4) neither she nor my host had gone through any kind of divorce proceedings. I followed up this discussion by reinterviewing a number of peasants on the subject of divorce, querying them on the difficulties and expense of getting a divorce in Trinidad and the risks of abandoning a legal spouse. These discussions occurred within a variety of frameworks: informal interviews, group discussions, focused interviews, and, finally, as part of a formal questionnaire. The data I collected indicated quite unequivocally that (1) approximately one-third of the Creole peasants of Anamat had been legally married at some time, (2) most of the peasants did not currently reside with their legal wives, (3) no Anamatian peasant had ever received a legal divorce, (4) it was common practice to live with a common-law wife after leaving a legal wife, and (5) a given peasant's common-law wife is often some other man's legal wife. In brief, good rapport and poor questions initially provided reliable but invalid data on legal marriage.

For data to be comparable it obviously has to be valid. The problems of comparability, however, go beyond validity, since they entail covering similar areas of social reality for all groups being compared. I soon came to the conclusion that, to get this kind of "coverage," I would have to use (among other data-collecting procedures) formal questionnaires capable of eliciting both *statistical* and *normative* data. Statistical data would answer questions such as: How many acres of land do you own? How many children do you have? How often do you go to a fête? How often do you go to a *puja?* These kinds of data, which varied with the opportunities, abilities, or knowledge of the respondents, had to be analyzed in terms of averages, percentages, and frequencies. Such data, therefore, had to be obtained from every member of the sample, for unless everyone reveals, say, how much land he owns, it is not possible to compare accurately the average Creole land holdings with the average Indian land holdings.

Normative data I wanted to obtain were the rules Creoles and Indians followed. These included (1) *definitional rules* (What is considered a good fête, a good *puja*, a good cricket match?), (2) *operational or procedural rules* (How does one go about getting a wife, getting membership in the Village Council?), and (3) *evaluational rules* (How do you rank given scarce resources in order to know their relative importance?). I planned to obtain the same *amount* and *kind* of normative data from each member of my sample. However, I was not worried about a few poor responses to normative questions. That is, if a rule is really a rule then one gets at it long before all the members of the sample have answered questions about it.

Developing formal research tools: focused interviews and formal questionnaires. My first questionnaire was "Use of Time." After administering it to several informants I realized that many of my questions were not well understood. I decided, therefore, to put these questions to a limited number of Anamatians in the form of a "focused interview" before continuing with the formal questionnaire. During the focused interview I asked the informant several related questions in a chit-chat conversational manner. To minimize the fears of my informants, or just their reticence to talk "for the record," I did not record their answers during the interview. As soon as the interview was over I found some private place and wrote down a shorthand version of it, which I later transcribed for my files.

The focused interviews were given in a variety of settings. The most successful ones were those that occurred while I visited farmers on their holdings. I was often able to lend a hand in the work being done, and while we worked I probed for information. In addition to questions on the "topic of the day," I also inquired about their various trees and crops and listened admiringly while they discussed the many improvements they had made. Periodically, we rested, sucked citrus fruits, and discussed village affairs.

The focused interviews were facilitated by the rapport I had previously achieved, since it was necessary to keep an informant focused on limited subject matter often involving highly personal information. This work continued, with some minor interruptions, throughout October, November, and December. Before discussing the next stage of my study, it is necessary to describe these minor interruptions, since they represented important aspects of "living in the field."

Early in October Ram spoke to me of his efforts to bring educators to the village as part of an adult-educational program he was developing. I told him I would be delighted to participate in his program, and we quickly made up several posters to hang in the post office, at the two rum shops, and at the two general stores. The posters informed the public that all were invited to a free lecture on anthropology to be given at the school house, at 7:30 on October 22, as part of a series of lectures sponsored by the Anamat Adult Education Program. My first lecture was essentially the first lecture most anthropologists give in an introductory course. The turn-out by the community was far beyond my expectations; all the seats in the hall were filled, and many people were standing. As I later discovered, there was considerable drinking going on in the back rows, and many who came thought something was going to be given away. The second lecture, given on November 5, had a much smaller audience and was concerned with the different ways of life found in human societies. The third lecture, on "Race," on November 19, was better attended than the second, but not as well as the first. I later discovered that the size of my audience was, in part, a function of lunar time: the well-attended lectures were given on bright moonlit nights when the villagers like to be out. In addition to presenting some of the basic concepts and theories of anthropology, I tried to impress the Anamatians with (1) why it is important to be a good informant, and (2) how to be a good informant. In other words, I preached the value of anthropology: its contributions to world understanding, to racial peace, to mental health, and to understanding crime and criminals. The Anamatians were left with the distinct impression that about the only thing that anthropology could not do was to get a rascal into heaven. I'm sure they also believed that mine was almost a priestly calling and that those who gave me assistance were involved with God's work.

The Christmas season provides another minor interruption. By the middle of November many Anamatians were talking and planning for Christmas and forming *parang* groups: small groups of musicians who serenade their friends and neighbors with Christmas carols. Any house is fair game for a parang group, which can visit at any time from early evening till four or five o'clock in the morning. The hosts are supposed to provide the musicians with food and liquor, and the entertainers stay as long as things are lively. For data-collection and rapport maintenance reasons (and because I enjoy singing) I joined a *parang* group that included a guitarist, a drummer, and a cuatro (a four-stringed instrument) player.

The celebrations of the Christmas season were by no means all related to work, but as a resident anthropologist one is forever on stage and a central subject for community gossip. One never ceases to remember the hugeness of one's project in relationship to the time and energy available for its completion, and one is always on guard against behavior that might adversely affect the project. The state of being constantly on guard is physically, mentally, and emotionally exhausting, and by the end of December my wife and I decided we had to get away from the village for a short vacation.

Our plans for a vacation were favorably viewed by the locals, who gave us much useful information as to enjoyable places to visit on Tobago. Some of our informants had kin in Tobago and we said we might drop in if we had the time. We planned not to have the time, since visits to relatives of informants are but an extension of regular field work. We left the village on January 8 and returned on January 15.

The Tobago vacation was valuable in at least three ways. First, it provided a most needed rest. Second, although we were away for but a week it was possible to recapture on our return some of the feelings of strangeness we had when we first arrived in Anamat. After a prolonged stay in a community, many things are taken for granted, and many important sociocultural phenomena once considered "strange" and thus noted carefully begin to appear "normal." Seeing the village as strange again is thus a valuable help for observational-participational research. Third, and perhaps of greatest importance, many Anamatians believed we had left for good. Our return to the community was thus a rapport-getting device in itself. It was now much more convincing when we said "We really like it here in Anamat." And now we could add "Yes, Tobago is really very pretty, but here we have friends and can do our work well."

Formal questionnaires and changing work times. After returning from Tobago I carefully reviewed the data obtained in the focused interviews, revised the questionnaire I had earlier developed, and constructed additional questionnaires that were then administered topic by topic in the following sequence: (1) Use of Time, (2) History and Agriculture, (3) Food and Budgets, (4) Mating, Marriage, and Family, (5) Religion and Magic, (6) Work, (7) Fêtes, and (8) Income. Most peasants were not willing to sit through more than one questionnaire per visit, so most peasants had to be visited at least eight separate times. The formal questionnaires represented but a minimal set of stimuli to which all the peasants responded, and our discussions on the "topic of the day" frequently went on to many other topics as well. The questionnaires are reproduced in the appendix.

To several of the more verbally skilled peasants I gave a "class" questionnaire and used the data obtained therefrom as a base for several "seminars" on the subject of class. I would invite three or four peasants to my house, ostensibly to "have a little drink and exchange a few ideas." After the rum had loosened their tongues, I would raise questions about the class situation in Anamat. I asked such questions as, "Who would you say is of a higher class, Teacher Ram or Mr. Eddy?" After they had reached some consensus, I raised questions about the *criteria* that they used for the ranking. "Why do you put Ram higher than Eddy when Eddy is obviously much richer than Ram?" "Because Ram is *known all over;* he is known by the government," I was told. Also, "When Ram is sick he still gets paid. He has a regular income and does not have to work for it under the cocoa." Although the peasants were initially reticent to discuss community members, they invariably warmed up to the "game" and came to enjoy the discovery process involved in a cultural analysis.

To the wives and daughters of the Anamatian peasants, my wife gave (1) a life-history questionnaire, (2) a child-rearing questionnaire, (3) a questionnaire on woman's roles, (4) Thematic Apperception Tests, and (5) Rorschach tests. In some of this work she was assisted by Tina. Tina also administered all my questionnaires to a representative group of Indians and Creoles who were *not* peasants. In addition to these data-collecting activities Tina was responsible for checking all of my kinship data on the Creole community, which I was convinced was overly simplistic and in some areas completely in error due to my use of reliable but nonvalid data. I spent long hours with Tina, Lee, and several special informants on subjects such as (1) the relative advantages of common-law as against legal marriages, (2) sexual behavior of the Creole males and females, and (3) the differential attachments of Creoles to their nuclear families and their matrifocal families, respectively.

Tina's checking of my kinship data indicated precisely what

I had suspected. The Creole peasants almost invariably understated the number of wives they had lived with and rarely mentioned "outside women" with whom they had been intimate during given marriages. In most cases Tina was able to provide the names of specific women with whom Anamatian Creole peasants had lived, the length of these unions, and the (general known) reasons for their dissolution. She also knew of most of the "love affairs" (involvement with outside women) of the local peasants. However, she provided the latter information with considerable hesitancy, and only after I had myself discovered the sexual musical-chair game that was going on in the village.

I gave considerable thought to the question of trusting Tina to check my kinship and mating material. A "blabber-mouth" assistant with access to my writings could easily ruin the project. However, in terms of Tina's reputation in the village, and in terms of the experiences my wife and I had with her while she worked for us as cook and housekeeper, we decided she was a "safe risk." We never trusted Lee with any ethnographic data, because her reputation as a gossip was justified. Although I received much ethnographic data from her, I had to be most careful as to what was said or done when she was nearby.

Tina had an agile mind, she strongly identified with the project, and she showed an amazing ability to grasp the fundamentals of the anthropological approach to research. To my knowledge she never passed on any information she obtained.

I discovered the sexual musical-chair game referred to above through a change of routine in field-work procedure. Except for days when a special community affair had been planned, or when I had a specific invitation to the house of an Anamatian, I used my after-dinner hours to relax, receive visitors in my house, and write up the day's field-work data. I found this routine quite valuable: it provided some cultural continuity with my life in America, coming home from work and relaxing with the family; it kept me up to date with my data write-ups; and it made it possible for me to tell Anamatians, "You're welcome to drop in to my house anytime; but the best time to find me in is after dinner." And, indeed, several of my better informants did drop in to the benefit of this research.

Early in April of 1958, Peasant Jones had been taken to the hospital, and I decided to visit his wife to ask how he was. I arrived at her house at about 8 P.M. and found Mrs. Jones sparsely clad, in intimate conversation with an Anamatian male. I stayed for only a few minutes, since I had the distinct impression that my presence was an embarrassment to both my hostess and her guest. I discussed this incident with Tina the next day, and her initial attempts to make nothing of this incident led me to question her at length with reference to Mrs. Jones and her "lover" and to similar affairs in the village. Tina's information–essentially that many men had "lovers" in the village and that most of the wives knew what was going on—led me to begin roaming around the village in the evenings. My own observations and discussions with Tina and several Creole informants led to the isolation of the following subsystem: A certain man leaves his house on an evening to visit a girl friend or to have a fête with the boys. His wife, now alone, can be visited by one of her admirers. The second male, by leaving his wife alone in his own house, provides a place for a third man, and so forth.

These data—which shed great light on Creole mating and marriage and which were "a secret" only to me—were collected due to a change in my work patterns. The lesson is clear: fieldwork routines must be changed during the research period, so that the anthropologist gets a maximal understanding of community time rhythms.

Summary and Conclusions

Two major types of data—ecological and cultural—were collected from both the East Indians and the Negroes. The ecological data were collected to verify that the adaptations of East Indian and Negro peasants were indeed similar. The cultural data were collected in order to observe to what extent similarities in ecological adaptations had led to similar cultural practices in areas of social life not directly connected with subsistence activities. The data collected showed that the East Indians and the Negroes had the same general environmental conditions and made specific ecological adaptations that were similar enough to be considered the same for the purpose of this natural experiment. In brief, both groups:

1. shared the same climatic conditions
2. worked land of similar acreage
3. worked with similar biotic and edaphic (soils, relief, and drainage) features
4. spent similar amounts of time working the land
5. used the same folk-science technology
6. used the same kind and number of personnel (head of the house) to do most of the farming
7. worked to produce the same cashcrops: cocoa and coffee
8. worked to produce the same crops for home consumption (root crops)
9. shared the same market and transportation facilities
10. obtained similar incomes from their subsistence activities

Cultural data were obtained from both groups on economic practices, marriage, the family, extended kinship ties, authority patterns, leisure activities, expressive symbols, religious practices, involvement in social and political community affairs, and the various roles in their respective systems. The cultural data collected showed that East Indians and Creoles respectively were members of very different cultural systems.

Money was spent differently by East Indians and Creoles. Although the average Creole household contained only one child and the average East Indian household had three or four, both groups spent similar amounts for food and clothing. Thus, per family member, the East Indians spent far less on food and clothing than the Creoles. The East Indians, however, spend more money on housing and on education than the Creole. At the time of this study, two sons of East Indian peasants were studying in universities in England, and one other East Indian youth was planning to go to England. None of the Creole peasants had sons studying in a university, nor did any of the Creole youths plan on going to a university.

The Creoles spent more money than the East Indians on "fêtes": events where at least two of the following elements, people, talk, rum, music, dance, and sexual play, were available. If all or most of these elements were present at a given party, the Creole would consider himself to be at a "big fête" or "fête-for-so" (Freilich, 1961). The East Indian spent more money than the Creoles on religious matters. These usually took the form of the *puja*, a family prayer meeting held in the house or the yard of the person "making" the *puja*.

In short, Indians spent more money on capital items that would affect their future (housing, education, religion), while Creoles spent more money on noncapital items that were fairly quickly consumed. Going along with a different use of money by East Indians and Negroes was a different use of time: the East Indians were future oriented, whereas the Creoles were much more concerned with the present. The East Indians lived in a joint family setting: a household of three generations, with patrilineal inheritance, patriarchial authority, and patrilocal residence rules. Although the joint family household frequently split into nuclear households, the latter were usually placed within close proximity of each other, and close contacts were maintained between the members of a joint family. Although a given Indian might be living in his own house and be relatively independent economically, the directives of a father or an elder brother were still orders and not suggestions.

The Negroes lived in nuclear households but had strong affectionate ties to a matrifocal family: a three-generation consanguineal unit with a minimal membership of a mother, her brother, her sons and daughters, and her daughters' children. Authority patterns were here equalitarian. Directives were given by elder members of the family in the form of advice rather than orders.

The marriages of the East Indians were arranged by their elders, and the father of a young Indian girl would attempt to find a husband for his daughter who was of "good family" (i.e., of a caste which was at least of equal status with his own) and who lived in another village. The marriage was supposed to last for life. The Negroes selected their own mates and understood that a given marriage was supposed to last only as long as man and wife "cooperated"; when one or both parties thought that the proper "cooperation" no longer existed, it was time for them to separate. As the Anamatian Negro put it, a marriage was a "now-for-now" affair.

In terms of associational patterns the East Indians maintained a sharp separation of the sexes in all social activities. Be it at a family *puja* with fifty or more people congregating in and around one house, or during a friendly visit of a man and his wife, Indian women rarely interact with any of the males present. The Indian women understand and accept the fact that their place is with the other women who are present. The Indian men would similarly consider it improper to have social intercourse with the women on these occasions. Social intercourse across sex lines was greatly limited in Indian culture and occurred mostly between a man and his wife when they were alone. For Creoles a get-together without members of the opposite sex represents a very dull party. The associational activities of the Creole peasants in Anamat thus usually included interactions between members of both sexes.

The sociocultural systems of these two groups can be summarized as follows: East Indians are future oriented in time, use village space for most of their interactions, but extend such space to include the villages of the members of their extended family, are members of a joint family, possess a hierarchical authority structure, exchange goods and services by using money as a medium of exchange, exchange women (indirectly) with joint families of other villages, exchange information by the use of the English language, have supernatural, polytheistic sanctions, and have "family improvements" as a major goal.

The Creoles are present oriented in time, use the village space for most of their interactions, but extend this space, mainly by traveling to fêtes in other communities where they interact with friends, are members of a matrifocal-consanguineal family, possess a loose, equalitarian authority system, exchange goods and services by using money and the sexual services of women as media of exchange, exchange women (indirectly) with other matrifocal families on a temporary basis, exchange information by the use of the English language, have social tabus and fatalism as major forms of sanctions, and regard "being in a big fête" a major goal in life.

Elements that are similar in the two systems, such as use of the village for most interactions, use of money as a medium of exchange, and use of English as a means of exchanging information, cannot be related to the shared mode of cultural ecological adaptation. The use of the village for the majority of interactions is very similar to village life in most cultures: it cannot therefore be related to the common adaptations of the East Indian and Negro peasants. The use of money as a medium of exchange and the use of the English language are also unrelated to cocoa and coffee farming. The money (British West Indian dollar) and language used in Anamat are used all over Trinidad and are directly related to the fact that till recently Trinidad was a British colony.

The hypothesis that two groups of peasants—East Indian and Creole, respectively—who share a common mode of cultural ecological adaptation will also show a significant number of cultural similarities outside of economic-adaptive life, had to be rejected.

Bowing Out

By May of 1958 the Anamatians began to ask me when I was planning to leave the island. I answered that I would probably be leaving the village about the middle of June, when I had finished my work. At these times I spoke of my interest in spending a few days in each of several other Caribbean islands in order to get some ideas on Caribbean society and culture, greatly praised the inhabitants of Anamat, stressing my sincere gratitude for their help, discussed my intentions to keep in touch with my friends in the community by mail, and indicated that I hoped to return to Anamat as soon as I had the opportunity to do so.

Several Anamatians became quite involved in various details concerning our departure. I was given advice on to how to sell my car and receive a fair price for it. (The Anamatians had long realized that I did not fit their stereotype of the white man as an individual with lots of money.) They helped me to obtain two large trunks for the goods that I was taking back to America —including an Indian drum, two cutlasses, and some deer skins, all made by Anamatians. I was also provided with a truck and many willing hands to load and get these goods to the docks in Port-of-Spain.

Several days before our departure the Village Council gave a large going-away party in our honor, and teacher Ram's wife had a small dinner party for a few close friends. The long intensive interactions that my wife and I had with many Anamatians made leaving the community a deeply emotional experience, and we still remember well the last greetings between us and a representative group who came to see us off at the airport.

Evaluation

Many of the shortcomings of this study can be attributed to the following set of factors: attempting a too-ambitious project (the comparative study of two *complete* systems); not allowing enough time to do it; not having more funds for the work; and not being more concerned with experimental methodology, particularly experimental design. These factors are obviously related. If, for example, I had limited my study to comparing family and kinship relationships among peasants in Anamat who made a common ecological adaptation, I would have had plenty of time. If I had been more concerned with experimental methodology, I would have realized the great difficulties inherent in scientific comparisons of total systems and might well have limited my study. Given these problems, it is understandable that I rushed things in the adaptational period. The large amount of work facing me and the relatively short period of time I had to do it were facts I was conscious of throughout the study. I was pushing hard all the time, and this produced a state of mind not conducive to excellence in data gathering, particularly in the early periods of field work.

I could have obtained superior data had I been able to spend more money for paid assistants. Several of my special informants would have made first-rate research assistants, and I believe I could have got some of them to do this work for me during their non-busy farming periods. With extra funds I could have hired students and/or faculty from the College of Tropical Agriculture in Trinidad to do part-time research on the agricultural aspects of my study. Ideally, I should have spent the September through Christmas period doing *adaptational research*. Starting in January, 1958, I then could have had a complete year for active research. This additional time would have permitted more relaxed thinking time that could have been used to work out a superior comparative framework. A longer adaptational period would have probably changed my approach to village politics. Although I have argued for honesty in presenting one's self to one's subjects, my honesty in local politics should have been more subtle and less verbal. There were many political discussions in which I could have played a far more passive role than I actually did. Further, I could have presented my position less strongly and in a more comparative framework. That is, I could have said something like, "In my country I generally vote for the party that is more liberal and more socialistic in its approach to social problems. If I were a Trinidadian I would perhaps do the same. Given my limited knowledge of Trinidadian politics I guess I would support the P.N.M. However, I may be wrong about the benefits for Trinidad of P.N.M. politics."

The many problems I encountered in this study—how to design anthropological experiments, how to collect data for such, how to develop "rulers" (models) for comparing total systems, —had an unforeseen positive consequence, for they have provided me with work goals for the past ten years. Indeed, these problems are still foremost in my mind and may well keep me busy for another decade.

PART III: COMPARISONS BETWEEN MOHAWK AND TRINIDADIAN RESEARCH

The research done with the Mohawks and that done with the Trinidadian peasants was quite clearly very different in style, scope, and purpose. The sink-or-swim, get-your-own-tribe, participate-and-observe approach with the Mohawks was a common one for the graduate-student researcher in anthropology. Its manifest function was clearly to get research experience and raw data. Its latent function was (and perhaps still is) to weed out the anthropology-for-kicks student from the serious would-be professional. As an unsure graduate student relying more on energy and perspiration than education and inspiration, I did what appeared necessary in the Mohawk research: I went native. For various reasons, the Mohawk accepted me and allowed me to pick up crumbs of information pertaining to my research problem. During the actual field work I had difficulties playing my assumed role, "adopted" Mohawk, and I must have cut a strange figure to the Mohawk "warriors": the "chicken warrior."

Fortunately, and good fortune did indeed play an important part in the project, I did not have to tackle many of the problems of traditional anthropological research. I did not have to set up residence in a strange country and in a strange community, temporarily stop interacting with previous associates, learn a new language, or work in a sociopolitical environment foreign to my experience. For these reasons I did not have to bear the burden of culture shock—that strange feeling of anxiety that frequently attacks researchers working in very unfamiliar environments.

The Trinidadian research had as its dominant purpose getting material for a doctoral dissertation. In style, it therefore had much in common with the work of other doctors without dissertations. The attempts to do an experiment, to find a "natural laboratory," to test the Stewardian framework, and to diversify data-collecting methods are all aspects of the anthropologist who occupies a status somewhere in between student and professional. My secondary purposes were then, to do the "great study," to help make anthropology scientific, and to please my high-status friends (the members of my doctoral committee). That I should select a goal—to do a natural experiment—that was somewhat beyond my educational and experiential abilities is understandable in terms of my marginal status in anthropology. A possible adaptive mode for marginal role players in a system is to go beyond accepted standards to prove their worth to the system.

The Mohawk and Trinidadian research are examples of "secretive" versus "above-board" research, respectively. My work with Mohawks became fruitful when I dropped the role of anthropologist and assumed the role of Joe's sidekick. This kind of unorthodox field work had all the disadvantages generally attributed to it: no formal interviewing was possible, none of the Mohawks could be used as a field-work assistant, I had to be constantly wary of my notebook being discovered, and I could only minimally plan my work. That is, I had to adapt my data-getting procedures to the exigencies of Mohawk interaction and activities. The Trinidad work was distinctly different, and partly because of its "openness" it was much more enjoyable. The presentation of myself as a research anthropologist permitted me not only to use formal research techniques but also to develop a quasi-research organization in the field. What with my wife, Tina, Lee, and several very helpful special informants I had a "staff" that regularly provided valuable data. My role as research anthropologist could (and was) easily extended to include teaching anthropologist, and teaching the members of one's sample how to be good informants is a most rewarding field-work activity. (When the anthropologist assumes the role of "teacher in the field" he will probably also have to assume the role of pupil. After teaching them how to provide good data, the brighter informants in Anamat gave me instructions on how to be a more effective researcher.)

The Trinidad study was far from the perfect experiment. Indeed, ten years later I am still working on ways to achieve maximum control in anthropological experiments. However, this research, unlike the work with Mohawks, did go beyond the pilot-study stage. That is, a problem was presented in a solvable way, and data were collected that (ideally) could answer the questions posed. That my answer is far from definitive (see, Freilich 1960, 1963) does not imply that mine was merely a pilot study. Unlike a pilot study, which becomes more definitive with additional data-collecting activities, my study does not suffer from a lack of data. Its shortcomings stem rather from a lack of theoretical sophistication on my part as to what data to collect and how to use what I collected. When I analyzed my data, I did not know how to compare total systems. I thus was not able to state categorically that Creole and Indian peasant cultures in Anamat represent systems so significantly different that no causal effects can possibly be attributed to their shared mode of exploiting a basically similar environment. Nor could I say that systems similar to those of Anamatian Creoles and Indians in adapting to an environment similar to Anamat's by methods described in my study *would not* experience culture change due to their cultural-ecological adaptations. I am still hopeful that "lawlike" generalizations are possible in anthropology, and I still believe that anthropologists will have to do experimental work to arrive at laws of sociocultural change.

APPENDIX: QUESTIONNAIRES ADMINISTERED

Use of Time

1. What time does each person in the family rise in the morning?

2. Who prepares the meals? Gets water? Cooks? Washes up?

3. What time does each one leave the house for work? How long does it take to reach work?

4. What are the household tasks of each person living there?

5. What time is each meal? Who eats with whom at each meal?

6. What is usually eaten for tea, lunch, supper?

7. Does the family like wild meat better than shop meat?

8. How often is meat eaten?

9. Does anyone go fishing? How often? How often is fresh fish eaten? Are eggs liked at home?

10. How many eggs are used each week?

11. What time do grown-ups go to bed at night?

12. What things are done on Monday, Tuesday, Wednesday, Thursday, Friday, Saturday, Sunday? By each family person?

13. What sports do members of the house do? How often do they do it?

14. What is the busiest day of the week? Why?

15. What is the slowest day of the week? Why?

16. What day do you enjoy most? Why?

17. What day do you enjoy least? Why?

18. What time of day is enjoyed most? Why?

19. What time least? Why?

20. What month of the year do you like most? Why?

21. What month of the year do you like least? Why?

22. List the months in the order of your preference for them.

23. To what family gathering would some people from the house always go? Sometimes go?

24. Who would go in each case? Give preference: Who always? Who sometimes?

25. To what district gatherings would some people always go? Sometimes go? Who would go?

26. Who in the house has attended an Indian dinner (prayer meeting)? At whose house?

27. Who is the closest relative you have? Second closest? Third? Fourth? Fifth? (List as many as possible.)

28. How often do you see these people? Where? When?

29. Who visits you frequently? When?

30. Who do you visit? When?

31. Who do you like to be with best? Second best? Third best?

History and Agriculture

1. How much land do you work?

2. How much do you own?

3. How much do you rent?

4. How did you come by the land you own? How much was inherited? How much was purchased? Date of Purchase? From whom? Price? How much was paid in cash? How and when was balance paid?

5. How much land is owned jointly with other family members? With whom?

6. How would you describe the soil on your land?

7. What work do you regularly do on your land?

8. What work do you do that is seasonal?

9. Does your land have good drainage?

10. If not, why not? (Why don't you dig good drains and maintain good drains?)

11. What trees, plants, and shrubs do you have on your land? How many of the following?

Cocoa _____	Pewa _____	Coconut _____
Robusta coffee _____	Bread fruit _____	Cush-Cush _____
Arabica coffee _____	Pommecy-there _____	Dasheen _____
Banana _____	Avocado _____	Mango _____
Citrus fruits _____	Cashew _____	Mangosteen _____
Tonka beans _____	Cassava _____	Mahogany _____
	Cedar _____	Shatain _____
		Tania _____
		Yam _____

12. Any others?

13. From where did you get your agricultural knowledge?

14. Do you hire people to help you with some of your agricultural work? If Yes, why? If No, why not?

15. Who would you say are the best farmers in Anamat? What makes these people so good in agriculture?

16. Who are really poor farmers? What makes them so bad in agriculture? [My dichotomy of good versus poor farmers had to be changed. The Anamatians distinguished between poor, good, and very good farmers.]

17. How do you like agricultural work? [Here I probed on why this work was satisfying. This question usually led to a long discussion on such matters as the relative advantages of agriculture over other kinds of labor, the attitude of the "young generation" toward agriculture, and what the government should do to help farmers.]

Food and Budgets

1. How often is food bought? How much is bought?

2. How much is spent for clothes in a year, for yourself? How much for your wife? How much for the children?

3. How much is spent in a year for traveling and for fêting?

4. How often do you pay the shop?

5. How often do you make a big Sunday breakfast for friends or family? (For Indians, how often do you make a *puja*?)

6. How much does it usually cost you?

7. What is the biggest amount of credit you ever took?

8. Who controls money in the house? Who keeps it until it is needed? Who decides what to spend it on? Who is mainly responsible for saving?

9. Who goes to sell in the provision market? How often? How much money do you think you make a year from the market?

10. Do you buy more clothes for your family than your father did? Why?

11. Who entertained people in the house more, you or your father? Why?

12. In times of trouble, who would help you?

13. What things have you bought for the house in the past three years? Cash or credit?

14. Is there anything you are planning to buy for the house in the next few years? How will you pay for it?

15. Is there anything you are planning to get outside the house (like land or a new house)? How will you pay for it?

16. Who do you think will mind you when you are too old to work?

17. How much salary each two weeks would a person have to give you to get you to work in town?

18. What is the most money you ever had in your name in a bank book?

19. Do you expect your children will be richer than you? Why?

Mating, Marriage and Family

1. (a) "Better a good living than a bad marriage." Explain. (b) At what age should a man first live with a woman?

2. At what age should a woman first live with a man?

3. Which is better: trial or marriage right off? Why?

4. What benefit is there of the other?

5. What are the bad things about trial marriage?

6. How many trials should one make?

7. (a) Why don't some men get legally married? (b) "Marriage is a society." Explain. (c) Forgetting about the religious side, what is marriage?

8. Why won't some women get legally married?

9. Do you want your sons to make trial first? Why not daughters?

10. Why do men wish to marry? Why do women wish to marry?

11. Some couples lived together but never fought until they got legally married. Is this true? If so, why?

12. What should a man have before asking a woman to marry him legally? Why? Should any changes be made in an old place?

13. Who is supposed to bend more to make things work out? Why?

14. Is there any preference for marrying a virgin?

15. Is it better to marry a woman (or man) who has had many husbands (wives) before?

16. Why did you leave former wives (husbands)?

17. In whose house were the children brought up?

18. Whom did you ever advise to marry? Why?

19. Who ever tried to influence you to get legally married? Why?

20. If you had brought home any outside children, what would your mother say and do? Your father?

21. Does legal marriage make a man more respected?

22. What about a woman?

23. The difference between a natural child and a bastard is _____.

24. How old were you when you got your first keeper?

25. What are the duties of a keeper? Of a common-law husband? Of a mistress? Of a legal husband?

26. If you have no house of your own, where is it best to live?

27. Why are parents more vex (angry) if a daughter brings home a child than if a son does so?

28. Is American dating system better or here where girls meet boys in secret when they are living at their mother's house? Why or why not? What are advantages of each way? Bad things about each?

Religion and Magic

1. How many of the following functions have you attended in the past twenty-four months?

   a. Wakes. Whose, and who else from your family did go?

   b. Weddings. Where and who else from your family did go?

   c. Christenings. Whose and who else from your family did go?

   d. Prayer meetings (*pujas*). Whose and who else from your family did go?

   e. Any other big function. Whose and who else from your family did go?

2. The Christmas festivities usually cost you how much? (Give big items: liquor, food, clothes, furniture.)

3. How do you usually spend Good Friday? Easter Sunday? Easter Monday? Queen's Birthday? Carnival? St. Joseph's Day? Discovery Day? All Saints Day?

4. How do you keep a. *Magh Nahaan?* b. *Phagwa?* c. *Pitra Paksh* (lent)? d. *Devalli* (or *Lakhmi Puja*)? e. *Kartig Nahaan?* f. Are there any other Hindu Festivals, that you keep? Which ones? How?

5. Has prayer ever helped you or your family in times of trouble? Give examples. How often do you pray? For what reason?

6. Have dreams ever given you warnings? Foretold the future? Given you any other information?

7. How do you guard against *maljo* (the evil eye)? What can cure *maljo?* Why do some people usually get *maljo?* Did you or your family get it? From whom?

8. I know people who have been cured of different ailments by bush medicine. What bush has helped your family or you? Who got it and prepared it for you? How did they learn about this?

9. People have showed me *sukreyant* marks and have told me they saw *Papa Bois* and other spirits. Have you ever had any experience with these? Do you believe these people are telling the truth or lying? Explain.

10. Would you sleep in a cemetery for a whole night for a bet? Why, or why not?

11. Did you ever hear of the "Bucks of B.G.?" Was anyone you know ever helped by them?

12. Some people try to trick you out of money. How can one tell that an *Obeah* man really knows his science?

13. Why do you think God permits evil to stay in the world?

14. How can you prevent people working *Obeah* on you? What cures *Obeah?* Why are some people attacked this way?

15. How many pilgrimages have you been to in the last twenty-four months? Where to?

16. How many pilgrimages were you invited to and did not go? Why not?

Work

1. At what age did you leave school?

2. At what age did you work for a salary? Who got the money?

3. At what age did you keep your own salary? Why at this time?

4. At what age did you leave the house where you were brought up?

5. Do you work more hours each day than your father did? Why?

6. Do you work more days a week than your father did? Why?

7. How many times do you work on a Saturday afternoon? Why?

8. How many Sundays do you work during crop time? At other times?

9. Some men are very rich yet they still work hard. Are they foolish? Why?

10. How often does your wife help bring some money into the house? How often do your children?

11. A man should never work more than —— hours per day. Why?

12. If you won $50,000 on a sweepstake, how would that change your life (how would you live differently)?

13. What kind of work would you like your son to do, daughter?

14. "We should shoot work; kill him dead." Comment.

15. "To work hard is to be a slave." Comment.

16. When did you work hardest in your life?

17. Does hard work weaken a man's body?

18. In about 100 years from now machines will do all our work for us. (a) Will that be a good time to live in and why? (b) If things were like that today how would you pass the time away?

19. Why don't you want your sons to do agricultural work?

20. Do you like job work or day work better? Why?

Fêtes

1. How old were you when you started going around to (a) dances, (b) wakes, (c) prayers?

2. How often did you go to these before you got a wife (husband)?

3. How often are you in a fête these days?

4. Were you in many more in your younger days?

5. Some people get bad tempered when they drink and some get more cheerful and entertaining. How does rum affect you?

6. Did your father (mother) do more fêting in his time than you? Why?

7. How about your grandfather? (grandmother?)

8. Some say that when they fête they like to have a good fête man (woman) with them. What is a good fête man (woman)?

9. If you saved all that you spend, fêting, how much more money would you have today?

10. People say "Trinidad is a paradise." Do you agree? Why?

11. If a man earns $200 a month and it cost him $100 a month to eat and maintain his family, how much can he afford to spend on fête? Why?

12. Some people have money but don't enjoy it. Why make money if you can't enjoy it?

13. How often do you go to the pictures?

14. How often do you go to Sangre Grande? To Port-of-Spain? To the beach? To St. Benedict?

15. How often do you see family who live a good way off?

16. At whose house in Anamat did you ever take Sunday breakfast?

17. Work has to do with serious business; *fête* has to do with ————? (Informant was asked to complete this sentence)

18. How many godchildren do you have?

Income

1. Discuss yields from various crops.

2. Discuss income for the past six years. [Questions on income representing "sensitive" topics, were differently put to each informant, depending on my relationship with him and his mood at the time of the interview. Some informants with whom I had excellent rapport *were asked* for their records. Some others, after a long and tiring interview, made a statement such as "I'm too tired to go on with this; if you come back next week I'll have it all down on paper for you."]

RESEARCH
IN INDIVIDUALISTIC
SOCIETIES

Pertti J. Pelto

PART I: RESEARCH AMONG THE
SKOLT LAPPS OF FINLAND

Problem, Theory, and Research Design

Many anthropologists who went out to do doctoral field work in the 1950s approached the task with a strong commitment to do a holistic description of a particular community or tribe, equipped with a "kit" of traditional techniques of participant observation and interviewing—field "tools" with which we had had little or no experience. We had a general commitment to some sort of "structural-functional analysis," great apprehension about rapport-maintenance and other technical problems of the field, and next to nothing in the way of a detailed structured research design—at least this was true in my own case.

I chose field work among the Lapps of Finland mainly because I would have no language problem (I grew up speaking Finnish), and because I wanted to associate with Finnish anthropologists—probably more for sentimental reasons than any theoretical concern. Also, I did not have a field-research grant, and I felt that my slim savings, plus some research support from the Department of Anthropology at Berkeley would last longer in what I thought to be the relatively inexpensive living conditions in Finnish Lapland.

Although this makes my approach to field work in Lapland look more like an exploring expedition than a scientific project with specific research goals, from talking with other anthropologists who have completed their doctoral field work, it is now my impression that the lack of a research design did not significantly handicap my work among the Lapps. It appears that in many cases a detailed research design turns out to have little relationship to the research that finally emerges from a field trip. If one goes into a field situation where little is known in detail about the community or tribe, well-laid plans will often be gently set aside when the realities of the field are fully grasped.

In situations in which a lack of knowledge about the complexities of the specific field setting makes a prepacked design impractical, the researcher must have clear ideas about general modes of converting raw behavioral observations into scientifically useful constructs. If he is equipped with a sense of the pragmatic operationalizing of variables, and if he attends to problems of the representativeness and reliability of data, he will be able to adapt the realities of the local situation to careful hypothesis-testing developed in the course of field work.

Passive or Adaptational Research

The Lapps of arctic Europe number between 20,000 and 30,000 and are widely known for their intensive reindeer herding. The Lappish language, with its several mutually unintelligible subdivisions, belongs to the Finno-Ugric linguistic family, together with Finnish, Esthonian, Magyar, and some less well-known representatives in the U.S.S.R. Archaeological evidence and early historical chronicles make it clear that the Lapps inhabited large areas of the Fenno-Scandian peninsula before Scandinavians, Finns, and Russians migrated into these northern regions. The gradual expansion of agricultural and other settlements on the part of these latter groups has pushed the

nomadic and seminomadic Lapps into ever-diminishing territories.

The areas in which Lapps predominate today extend in an
arc from the mountainous central regions of Norway and
Sweden, across the "top" of Fenno-Scandia, terminating in the
Kola Peninsula of the Soviet Union. These regions are poorly
suited to agriculture (though some small crops are grown in
sheltered valleys), but they provide grazing areas for large
herds of reindeer, as well as rugged seacoasts, rivers, and inland lakes for fishing. Some of the inland Lapps, particularly in
Norway and Sweden, rely to a very large extent on the reindeer herds for their subsistence, but the eastern and northern
Lappish groups have a dual herding-fishing economy. Lapps in
the northernmost fjords of Norway have given up reindeer
herding entirely and make their living from fishing and small-
scale agriculture.

The Lapps today are citizens of the several national states
in which they are located and almost all of them are bilingual.
In most areas of Lapland there have been schools for several
generations. Church influence, too, has been strong for several
centuries in all parts of Lapland. Most Lapps are Lutherans,
having been Christianized by the Scandinavians, but the 2,000
or 3,000 Skolt and Kola Lapps are Russian Orthodox.

Modernization of lifeways is occurring at a rapid pace in
most parts of Lapland, and the Lapps have been quick to accept
innovations. Wage work—in the forest service, road crews, and
hydroelectric projects—provides an important supplement to
the incomes of many families, and technological devices such
as radios, outboard motors, chain saws, and gasoline-driven
washing machines are found in many households. Since 1962
the advent of the snowmobile has brought about a virtual technological revolution. The wholesale adoption of snowmobiles for
reindeer herding as well as for a variety of other transportational uses is currently effecting widespread changes in their
social and cultural patterns.

When I arrived in Finland in the winter of 1957 to discuss
field-work prospects with ethnographers at the University of
Helsinki, I quickly found that even the most enthusiastic field
men could tell me relatively little about types of communities
and ecological settings in Lapland; they were more oriented to
describing abstract ethnographic data, unrelated to particular
places and populations. Very little Finnish anthropology has
been carried out in terms of community studies. One outstanding exception is Karl Nickul's description of Suenjelsijd, a Skolt
Lappish community. His monograph (Nickul, 1948) presents a

total household-by-household census, maps of family territories, and descriptions of the yearly round of activities of particular individuals in terms of the special characteristics of their individual territories.

Karl Nickul was, then, my best informant in Helsinki concerning at least one corner of Lapland. However, since the time of his study, the Suenjel Skolts had been moved en masse to a new territory as a result of Finland's loss of Petsamo to the Soviet Union during World War II. Nickul had visited the postwar community and strongly urged me to go there—to Sevettijarvi—to do my field work. Several ethnographers in Helsinki tried to dissuade me from undertaking such a study, as they were convinced that the Skolts had "lost all their culture" through the war and relocation. Nothing remained for the anthropologist to study.

Several other communities were suggested to me, but the information available about size, composition, and present economic conditions was quite vague. Thus, on my departure from Helsinki I had very little information about specific communities, but carried with me the names of one or two persons in each of three communities—trusted informants and friends of the Helsinki ethnographers.

Considering the paucity of specific information that I was able to pick up in Helsinki, it was fortunate that I had been in Lapland previously, though only for three days. In 1955 I had made a brief winter excursion up the main Arctic highway through Finnish Lapland to the Norwegian coast. On this occasion I had met the editor of the Lapp newspaper, who lived in Inari, not far from the suggested research communities. I hoped that he would be my main source of further information about prospective research sites.

At Inari, editor (and reindeer man) Juhani Nuorgam welcomed me to the warmth of his home and proceeded to tell me about the Skolt community of Sevettijarvi as well as about Nuorgam, the northernmost Finnish Lapp community. He mentioned one or two other, less attractive, possibilities and reminded me that time is wasted in idle talk, for a reindeer roundup was about to begin at a corral about fifty miles northeast of Inari. Juhani felt that I should waste no time in going to the roundup site, for there I would meet men from a number of different communities.

Reindeer roundups are held several times each winter in all of the several dozen reindeer "districts" into which Finnish Lapland is divided. These roundups are necessary because of the modern practice of allowing reindeer herds to graze without supervision during the summer season, which results in a complete intermixing of the herds of the several hundred reindeer owners in any given district. In the fall, herders hired by the reindeer associations gather the herds within their respective districts and drive them to roundup sites, where each owner must identify and capture his own animals for winter herding. Reindeer roundups are attended by herders from a wide area, and meat buyers, hawkers of merchandise, tourists, and other visitors add heterogeneity and color to the gathering. Some roundups may last only three or four days, but frequently the larger roundups of the winter season continue for two weeks or more.

Since calving occurs in May and June, the early winter roundups involve a "counting of the harvest," and each reindeer owner is very concerned about how many calves have been born in his herd. Calves must be identified (a difficult task in the milling herd) and marked with the earmark of the owners. In addition to gathering his reindeer for winter herding, each owner slaughters some animals for home consumption and for sale to meat buyers from the various private and cooperative grocery stores of the region. Many reindeer are sold directly to buyers who attend the roundups, but Lapps can usually get better prices for their reindeer if they deliver them in person to the stores.

Juhani helped me prepare for my trip to the roundup. First he took me to the general store, where I was outfitted with essential equipment. He recommended felt boots with leather trim (this type of boot has an upturned toe, designed to fit "slip-on" ski straps). I'm sure he took great delight in picking out for me a pair of long Finnish-style backland skis. Most of the rest of my clothing and equipment he judged to be minimally adequate, but he suggested that I make further purchases of arctic clothing from the Lapps.

Although I was not fully committed to that Skolt community as my research location, Juhani and I felt that it would be wise to send all my equipment—books, paper, notebooks, and clothing —by snowmobile to Sevettijarvi, since I would travel by that same snowmobile as far as the roundup site and thus would not have to pay freight charges for my belongings. If I decided not to do field work in Sevettijarvi, I would be able to retrieve my possessions and go to a different community.

From Inari I traveled by bus a few miles north to the point where the postal-department snowmobile picked up mail and passengers bound for Sevettijarvi, which is about sixty miles to the northeast (accessible only by snowmobile in the winter and motorboat in the summer). The snowmobile was very crowded that day, for several men from Inari were also headed for the reindeer roundup. In the early afternoon we arrived at the substantial house of Pekan Mikko (an Inari Lapp). This was our take-off point for the roundup site, six miles to the north. At Pekan Mikko's house, like some other "bus stop" houses on the road to Sevettijarvi, one could sit, visit, rest or sleep for a while, and repair equipment. One could also buy coffee and coffee bread from Pekan Mikko's wife. It was also possible to cook food on her stove and to sleep on the floor overnight at no charge. I later realized that many important patterns relating to arctic hospitality were enacted that afternoon and evening in the two-room weatherbeaten "lodge."

In this part of the arctic no one would think of charging money for a place to sleep in his house. Most families even provide enough reindeer hides or other materials so their overnight guests can sleep in comfort. On the other hand, no family can afford to give coffee, coffee bread, and other food to the dozens of travelers who may stop at their house because of its strategic location on a well-traveled route. Some households, therefore, have adopted the practice of selling coffee and food to their "guests."

I arrived at Pekan Mikko's house on January 19, 1958. The arctic sun had been hiding for nearly two months, but the "back of winter was bent," and it now made its appearance for a few minutes each day. Though it was only a little past noon, very little daylight remained, and since I had never skied before, I delayed my departure until the next morning. In the meantime I observed other reindeer men arriving, greeting old friends, looking after their reindeer, and joining the festive scene. As darkness began to fall in early afternoon, thirty or more people had gathered in the little house, most of them having arrived by reindeer sled. From time to time a party of two or three men would leave for the roundup site, but they were soon replaced by new arrivals.

A modest snowstorm had developed, and from time to time. I walked about the yard, squinting through the falling snow at the landscape around me. The area of northeastern Finnish Lapland is boreal forest in the more southerly parts, with pine and fir forest mixed with birches. Lakes and bogs lie between moderately high ridges, formed by the last glaciation. In the middle of the region is large, many-fingered Lake Inari, fabled in Lappish lore. A focus of fishing activities, it is a main Lappish "highway" both winter and summer. North from Lake Inari the forests thin out quickly, although scattered stands of pine are found here and there. As the pine forest diminishes, muskeg swamps and small lakes take over, and stands of twisted birches brave the winds on the low ridges. The roundup site of Tsiuttijoki is located in one of the last outliers of pine trees, beyond which stretches the treeless, inhospitable tundra.

I faced the prospect of skiing to the reindeer roundup with some trepidation, since I had had little experience on skis. To allay my fears, I convinced myself that it would be simply a matter of sliding along the mainly flat terrain, following the well-marked trail of the reindeermen. Fortunately, I was able to discuss the situation with a young Skolt Lapp who had arrived on the snowmobile with me. I was pleased to notice that he had the same kind of felt boots that Juhani had picked out for me, and my confidence was further bolstered when he admired my new skis. Ondrei Semenoff was a soft-spoken and modest young man, almost nattily dressed in store-bought clothing (thus contrasting with most of the men, who wore the traditional multicolored Lappish tunics). He suggested that we ski together the next day, and he immediately became my first important informant, identifying persons, commenting on the coming events of the roundup, and answering some of my questions about reindeer herding.

It is a fulfillment of a central prophecy of field-work lore that Ondrei turned out to be marginal to the Skolt Lapp community—a lone wolf who wandered on the peripheries of Sevettijarvi, never settling down in the community and never straying very far away.[1]

Ondrei was a most unusual marginal man, for he appeared to be highly respected by all who knew him, and to my knowledge he was not in conflict with anyone. As an orphan who had had some sort of "nervous breakdown" years before, he had toned down the usually quiet speech of Skolt Lapps to nearly a whisper, and when he thought he had had too much social interaction, he would go out by himself to hunt and fish or to work for wages among the Finns.

Evening was an exciting time at Pekan Mikko's house, for many more reindeer men arrived out of the darkness, greeted their friends, exchanged news, and drove on in the pitch black toward the roundup. Although many had left, the floor was covered with sleepers when the lights were turned out. (Pekan Mikko's wife had given each of us a reindeer hide to use as a mattress.)

The next morning Ondrei and I set out, at what must have

---

[1] Anthropologists have often noted that the first persons to become friendly and informative with the field worker are frequently individuals who are in one sense or another atypical members of the local community. They may be deviants, social outcasts, persons who are particularly critical of their own community, or they may simply be those who have had more than the usual amount of contact with outsiders.

been a painfully slow pace for him, since long hunting and fishing trips on skis with a heavy pack were his special pleasures. As I expected, I *was* able to slide forward at a reasonable pace on my skis, but my forty-pound pack was very difficult to balance, and the tiniest changes of terrain were crises for me. Many times during the trip we were overtaken by reindeer sleds, so we tramped off the path into the deep snow and waited until they were gone. Often the reindeermen stopped to exchange news with Ondrei, who, perceiving that I was panting like a steam engine, converted these events into excuses to stop and rest.

A few times I failed to negotiate small hills or turns, and fell into the snow by the side of the path. Ondrei, who had chosen to ski behind me, would on these occasions find himself fascinated by a bird, an animal track, or simply the fresh morning air, ignoring my complicated struggles to get back on my feet. By his standards (and mine) any direct aid or even verbal exchange in those moments would have caused acute embarrassment.

About midday we arrived at the Tsiuttijoki roundup, where genial chaos reigned. Dogs were barking, groups of Lapps, Finns, and Norwegians were arriving and making camp, and a large proportion of the population appeared to be fairly drunk. I was later to find that the first day of any roundup—before the work begins—is generally a day of celebration, and men go to great lengths to procure expensive (and often illegal) liquor for the occasion. (Liquor is legally available only to stores in the state alcohol monopoly, so the "middlemen" who bring most of the liquor to the roundup are technically bootleggers.)

At the center of the roundup camp there were several large log-and-clapboard buildings that served as coffee houses during the roundup. Coffee and rolls were available all day, and at mealtimes hearty reindeer stews or boiled cod were served. At night these coffee houses became the sleeping quarters of all who were not shareholders (or friends of shareholders) in the dozen or so sleeping cabins in the camp.

The reindeer roundup, particularly on opening day, proved to be an ideal time to make initial contact with a Lapp community. An air of friendship and camaraderie pervaded the scene, and visitors from the outside world are expected and welcomed. Under these circumstances I quickly became acquainted with a number of Skolt Lapps, including their village headman, Jaakko Sverloff. I carried greetings to him from Karl Nickul, who had suggested that perhaps Jaakko would be of some assistance to me. Jaakko agreed to help me if he could, and suggested that the school buildings at Sevettijarvi would be a suitable place for me to set up residence. A message was dispatched to the schoolteacher to inquire further into this possibility.

There is much time for idling and talk at a reindeer roundup, since the work can be carried out only in daylight, and in midwinter the working day is at most only six hours long. Moreover, even during working hours there are always dozens of people in the coffee houses, resting and getting warmed up for more work in the corral. I talked with many willing informants, particularly about reindeer herding—a topic of limitless interest to these people. They were also most helpful (and amused) with my initial attempts to learn the Skolt Lappish language. As we could converse in Finnish, the Skolts were very pleased that I showed interest in their "insignificant" language.

In the roundup corral I was permitted to try my hand at roping reindeer, and some of the young men (who were there mainly for a lark anyway) spent much time explaining the intricacies of roping and branding and demonstrating the difficulties of the work. Several of my younger informants—ranging in age from eighteen to twenty-five—were clumsy and ineffectual at roping reindeer, but I learned enough about the work from watching them to make myself useful to the more experienced men who were, I hoped, my more important informants.

I had by now met several of the older men whom I took to be leaders among the Skolt Lapps (including Jaakko, the headman), so I asked Ondrei if it would be proper to offer Jaakko and some of the others a bottle of liquor. Ondrei and I quickly worked up a brief guest list and adjourned with this small group of Skolts to one of the tiny cabins a few hundred yards from the main part of the camp. Believing that he owned the cabin we were occupying, I handed the bottle of liquor to Illep Fofanoff and asked if he would serve as host.

Skolts often drink liquor by adding it to coffee or tea. If the drinking is done in proper ritual fashion, a single cup is used. The host passes the cup to each person in turn, and ritual greetings are exchanged by the drinker and host, followed by a verbal greeting to each person assembled. What I had expected to be an occasion of the usual Skolt jollity and chatter turned into a somewhat solemn ritual occasion. Illep, Jaakko, and some of the others talked at length about the recent history of the Skolts, the loss of their homeland, their difficulties with the new situation, and their wishes and dreams for the future. It seemed as though they were delivering a sort of prolegomenon to field work, impressing on me the gravity of my task and the importance of the spiritual bonds between the field worker and the community. This might seem to be an exaggeration of one relatively insignificant field-work event but for the fact that the events and tone of that meeting are still vividly in my memory.

The roundup lasted for about a week, after which groups of men herded their reindeer back to their own territories. Jaakko had agreed to give me transportation by reindeer sled to Sevettijarvi. It took us two days to travel the approximately fifty miles to Sevettijarvi. We stopped at many houses on the way; drank tea, exchanged news, and discussed my field work. Part of our slowness was due to a blinding snowstorm during the last third of the journey. Thus, by the time I arrived at the school house at Sevettijarvi, I had met almost all of the adult men of the Skolt community, had talked at length with some of them, and had numerous invitations to visit in the months to come.

My entry into the community by way of the reindeer roundup was a much greater stroke of luck than I had originally believed. Although the schoolteacher (who willingly rented me a room) claimed to be a "man of the people," I immediately experienced alienation from the Skolts on moving into the school. They did not enjoy visiting at the school, and to a certain extent I was out of touch with the communication grapevine, simply because of my location at what first appeared to be the hub of this scattered arctic community. When I later moved into a Skolt house for the last nine months of my work, I found myself much more in contact with news and events.

An experienced anthropologist would quickly note that my initial moves at the reindeer roundup included behavior that could have gotten me into trouble. For example, I made assumptions about social patterns and about the identity of the "leaders" that could have seriously damaged rapport if my hunches were wrong. One might well inquire whether I was aware of the possibility of problems concerning factional cleavages, family and neighborhood loyalties, or other aspects of social alignments that can seriously affect field work. The fact is, I was simply a lucky innocent. My initial contacts and opening moves ran afoul of no problems of social cleavages or "in-group touchiness," because among the Skolts there are no significant factions. Besides, the remarkably open-minded Lapps are not easily offended, especially if the newcomer is moderately careful of their feelings.

Possibly all the advice one needs for beginning field work and building rapport with Skolt Lapps is (1) speak softly and keep listening and (2) take no overt notice of their relatively plain food, simple cabins, ragged clothing, and general paucity of material possessions. Skolts appear to think of these as signs that outsiders interpret as indicators of Skolt social inferiority.

My wife joined me at the Sevettijarvi school in February,

about a month after I began field work. She stayed in the field until August, and during that time my working habits were arranged around our one-room household in the schoolteacher's quarters. Since she spoke little Finnish she hesitated to interact very much with the Lapps, but after gaining more competence in the language she visited the nearby homes, carried on simple conversations, and occasionally accompanied me on excursions to more distant households.

To some extent, my wife's presence lent an additional note of respectability to my position. She also contributed in certain practical ways to the collection of data. She helped in mapping the community and took notes on child-training behavior and clothing patterns. On the other hand, an argument can be made that the presence of the anthropologist's wife in the field (if she is not a fully participating partner in the work) reduces his mobility and provides too easy a retreat from the continued confrontation with the general frustrations and difficulties of even the most benign field-work situation. The presence of a wife does tend to make one's own residence more private, which could be an advantage in many field-work situations, but in Sevettijarvi (it seems to me) this made it more difficult for Skolt individuals to just "drop in" to chat with me. These statements are not intended as generalizations about wives (or husbands) in field work, and they are inapplicable to those situations in which a couple operates as a cooperating field-work team.

Active Research: Getting on with the Field Work

Certain aspects of my initial contact with Sevettijarvi had lasting effects on the shape of my field work. I had quickly fallen into the quiet informality and passivity of conversational style that seems characteristic of the Skolts, so that persistent questioning on single topics over longer periods of time—as is required in much of field interviewing—was difficult to maintain and tended to break down rapport quickly. My financial state did not allow me to pay informants, so all conversations and interviews were in the form of a friendly exchange of information. I gradually realized that my field work would have to be based more on participant observation than on interviewing. For some time after my field work was completed I felt chagrined about having been able to obtain so few formal interviews, but when I later came to understand the general problems of reliability and validity of interview data, this lack seemed to me rather more of a virtue than a weakness.

Data from interviews frequently reveal a mixture of ideal

and actual behavior that is extremely difficult to disentangle. Furthermore, it seems to me that an anthropologist who trains his informants to produce clear, unambiguous descriptions of cultural practices may be eliciting statements of cultural patterns that give false impressions of uniformity because the informant believes that that is what the anthropologist wants. At least among the Skolt Lapps I found that most informants' verbal descriptions of cultural patterns failed to account for the range of variation in actual behavior among these people. Most people in most societies are polite, and they have no wish to burden the outsider (including the anthropologist) with the detailed intricacies of what actually goes on in their world.

In any case I was forced to confine my field work mainly to observing and participating in the activities of the Skolts and noting the patterns of actual behavior, rather than relying on their verbal reports. This style of field work has obvious limitations if the anthropologist is studying a large, complex society, but among the people of Sevettijarvi the settings for action are few, and the actions are quite public. There is very little "backstage" in Skolt life, possibly because the Skolts have traditionally lived "back in the woods" in single-family clusters, each in its own territory. Protected from the outside world, *all* of their patterns of living are in a sense "backstage," since visitors (especially in prewar days) were few and far between. But the visitor who does come, and stays to see what is going on, finds that most Lapp social action is open to public view.

To describe the general patterns of behavior among the Skolt Lapps and their neighbors required that I focus attention primarily on the seventy-odd households in the region, staying in some of them long enough to see the normal rounds and schedules of activity at various times of the year. I also had to attend as many reindeer roundups as possible, noting who was there, what they did, and any changes or variations from one roundup to another. Participating and observing at calving camps and the more distant herding operations involved some traveling and required that I give at least the impression of assisting in the work, for among the Lapps it is not easy to explain one's presence and to ask for favors (and information) unless one takes a hand in the herding activities. The same general situation applies to fishing.

Religious and other ceremonial occasions play only a minor role in Skolt life. Skolts flock to the church on those infrequent occasions four or five times a year when the priest arrives to conduct religious services, but they do not appear to be interested in elaborating on the basic rituals of their Russian Orthodox faith, and they seem to invoke few religious ideas in discussing or evaluating behavior. Weddings are, of course, important celebrations, which are difficult to cover thoroughly, since they occur so seldom and since one's own participation in the dancing and feasting makes it difficult to note "everything" that is going on. Drinking sessions at people's houses, as well as occasional dances sponsored by young people, constitute minor ritual occasions. The fairly secularized Easter celebration is the outstanding point in the celebrational calendar. But all this is thin ritual fare, and even a casual observer finds no difficulty in keeping up with what is going on, particularly since there are no secret rituals, no clandestine societies, no behind-the-scenes manipulators, and no substantial fears of outside intrusion into the ceremonial scene.

None of the behavior settings essential to a description of Sevettijarvi cultural patterns require difficult feats of interview-and-observation, but because the people are scattered widely over the land the field worker must, like the Skolts themselves, maintain a high degree of mobility. My good informant and friend Artto Sverloff sounded like a busy academician as he listed the different places and "conferences" to which he intended to go. "Now there is this roundup, then a trip to Norway to the merchant, then back to the herds for a bit, rest up a day, and off to the roundup at Vatsari." Just to keep up with Artto and his activities would have been a tiring task, but I also had to spend large segments of time in a number of different parts of the scattered stage of Skolt social action. Sometimes much could be accomplished by making a trip of several days' duration to a number of houses one after another, and asking in each one, "Well, what's the news and what have you been doing lately?"

One of the important conceptual elements of anthropological theory is the idea of the corporacy of social groups, with implications of cooperative action, decision-making, distribution of proceeds, and so on. During the early part of my field work I made little progress in identifying and describing corporate groups and their "functions," and I felt that my field work was therefore faulty. But it gradually dawned on me that the community I was investigating actually had very little communal ownership, did not engage in group decision-making, and evidenced few other actions of a corporate nature. I then realized that I was observing a society with a high degree of individualism and self-reliance, though with none of the overtones of aggressive competition and hostility often ascribed to individualistic societies.

Midway in my field work, then, the idea of "individualism" became a prominent construct around which I organized my thinking and my field work. I reviewed my previous field notes and other materials for actions and verbal statements that could be construed as concrete manifestations of individualism. For example, some of the reindeer meetings I had attended could be described as conversations of individuals, each speaking in his own interest and each apparently having veto power, with no clear leader or authority exercising much influence over the others.

I had looked for signs that Jaakko, the headman, was a leader and decision-maker for his people, but I could find little evidence indicating that his wishes and ideas had significant effect on people other than perhaps his close kin. (He exercised very little authority over his nephew and heir, who was a member of his household.) From time to time at the roundup and other places I heard comments that could be construed as general indicators of values reflecting individualism. For example, several times I heard people use the expression *"Jish Tiedak,"* which can be translated as "You yourself know (best)," and which is sometimes stated after asking or suggesting that a person do something.

Action in the reindeer roundup, and in other herding activities, always seemed to be organized in terms of individual reindeer owners looking after their self-interests, with only nominal cooperation among even kinsmen or neighbors. Winter herds were most often made up of the reindeer of several owners, frequently groups of brothers or other related individuals, but the joint winter herds involved only minimal cooperation. There was no organization for deciding on work patterns, there was little division of labor, and each owner went out to the herd (to mark a calf, castrate a bull, or kill a reindeer for food) whenever he felt like it, without consulting the other owners. Also, individuals frequently went alone on market trips, fishing expeditions, or to reindeer roundups, although they appeared to enjoy the companionship of other persons if their individual interests happened to coincide to such an extent that they found it convenient to travel together. In all such activities, the Skolt Lapps appeared to prefer companionship if it was available, but group activities were seldom carried out in such form that companionship implied the dependence of one man on another.

In thinking over all the incidents and anecdotes that suggested individualism, I recalled Ondrei's behavior during my awkward skiing entree to that first reindeer roundup. It seemed to me that Ondrei, in those actions and, more importantly, in his entire life-style, exemplified the Skolt emphasis on self-reliance.

In some ways, I found it hard to find positive evidence of

"individualism," since the concept often implies simply a *lack* of definite communality of property and procedures. Had I the chance to do the field work over, I think I would now have some better ways to operationalize the concept of individualism. The behavioral material that I amassed about Skolt Lapp individualism still seems to me convincing as a body of data, but I wish that I had been able to make systematic observations that would permit precise comparisons with other less individualistic societies. For example, I wish I had sampled the amounts of time Skolt Lapps spent in solitary activity as compared with group tasks and recorded more carefully the details of decision-making, for both are potentially significant types of information on individualism.

My personal inclinations have always been to include personality data about individuals as a key part of research, but I had no specific plans for collecting projective tests or other such materials among the Skolts. Toward the latter part of field work, particularly after I had left the school building and moved in with Jaakko's family, I found it easy to get individual Skolts to go into some detail about their life histories. I collected a number of such narratives, from both males and females, and frequently secured recollections and reports of dreams from these same people. Also, on numerous occasions when I was with groups of reindeer herders I was able to get them to recall their dreams, sometimes with additional commentary about the dreams and their meanings. When there was time at breakfast I often asked the men what they had dreamed the night before, and, in turn, told my own dreams to them. I collected these dreams because I felt that they would provide data on the personality characteristics that underlay the overt behavior that I observed.

Once, while we were hunting reindeer calves on a beautiful crisp autumn day, I reported to my companions that I had dreamed of a dead reindeer lying on the side of a hill. About two hours later, we encountered a dead reindeer in a situation somewhat approximating that which I had described. From that time, some of the men seemed to regard my dreams as having special significance.

Recording and Storing of Data

In many field-work situations I had my notebook handy and jotted down notes from time to time as the roundup, fishing, or other activity progressed. Often though, when temperatures were well below freezing, I could write for only a few minutes before I had to put my mittens back on. In these cases (and in some other situations) I had to record the data several hours after the events had taken place. In the interim significant details often escaped me, and it was, of course, very difficult to make up the deficiency.

My plan was to type up the day's field notes each evening, or, at the latest, the next morning. However, I was frequently at a roundup or other activity for as long as two weeks at a time, which meant that on returning to home base I would have to schedule lengthy typing sessions to catch up on back notes. While typing up my notes, I often recalled significant events that I had not jotted down in my notebook. I wrote up these additional notes in the same manner as the information from my notebook, although the nature of the materials often made it clear which data had been written on the spot and which were later recollections. These addenda to my field notes often pertained to routes, chronologies, and other details of travel from one activity area to another.

Often during field work the anthropologist gets hunches about patterns either not mentioned in his notes or mentioned only in passing. I occasionally wrote short essays on such materials (sometimes in the form of letters from the field), including in them observations of behavior that I had not previously recorded. In my opinion, these field "essays" are valuable because they show up the gaps in one's data and often suggest new lines of inquiry. Since the data in them often depend on incidents recalled from the past weeks and months of field work, it is better to regard them as hunches for further investigation rather than as established data.

Much of my field work was aimed at recording *action*, and I took numerous color photographs to illustrate observed behavior. (It is, of course, a rare field worker who does not carry a camera among his equipment.) Since my processed slides were delivered to me in the field, I passed many enjoyable hours showing them to the interested Skolts. This worked wonders for rapport, and it is hard for me to imagine that there would be people anywhere who would not appreciate the chance to be photographed if they can see the results. Sometimes I gave copies of the photographs to my subjects. Taking pictures, then, served both as a means of recording data and building rapport.

However, I did not use my photographs as primary research tools. Even though I noted that the Lapps' reactions and comments to the pictures were interesting and informative, I never showed a selected set of photographs as a "projective technique." I now believe that a selected set of pictures, for example, of different instrumental activities (something like the Spindlers' Instrumental Activities Inventory), would have yielded much data about the Lapps perceptions of various tasks and occupations.

Bowing Out

In April, 1959, I had been in the field over a year and had just spent several days with a cluster of Skolt families at the northeastern tip of the Sevettijarvi community. I told these families that I was now planning to return to the United States, but that I hoped to see them again before too many years. After a few more days of work around the central settlement (mostly spent in packing and mailing my books, notes, and papers), I set out on skis, intending to stop at nearly every house on the snowmobile road to "civilization." It was a beautifully clear late winter day and, skiing somewhat more effectively than on that first day fifteen months before, I made good time between houses. The visits in the houses became progressively longer, however, so that before I reached the last house I was overtaken by the snowmobile, on which I completed my departure from the community.

During the first years after the initial field work I corresponded fairly regularly with Artto Sverloff and occasionally with several others in the community, but this correspondence slackened considerably, and I received only one or two letters in the past year. It is somewhat difficult to obtain precise and useful data by correspondence, but I did occasionally ask specific questions of my Skolt Lapp friends, and their replies were often sufficiently detailed to be quite useful as supplemental field information.

Summary and Evaluation of the Field Project

If we accept the proposition that my main task in the field work was to produce a well-rounded description of a Skolt Lapp community, my venture was successful. My monograph, *Individualism in Skolt Lapp Society,* was published in a Finnish ethnographic series, and has served as the descriptive foundation on which I have constructed the beginnings of a theoretical structure dealing with types of societies (Pelto, 1962a, 1963a).

In my description of the Sevettijarvi Skolt community as an "individualistic society," I pointed out some of the ways in which Skolt individuals learn patterns of self-reliance and autonomy from a very early age. The genesis of this individual self-reliance appears to be in the nurturant, permissive atmosphere of the nuclear family, which is the most important unit of social organization, as it is the only type of group among the Skolts that displays a significant degree of corporate property and action.

Children among the Skolt Lapps are not given many responsibilities for work or ritual activity. Although they gradually become exposed to the general content of adult roles, they are not pushed to learn rapidly, to "get ahead," or to perform an ever-growing share of the family workload. Also, no formal initiation rites or other ceremonies signal transitions toward adult life. When an individual has experienced a great amount of personal choice and flexibility throughout his childhood, it would appear likely that, as an adult, he will show self-reliance and autonomy of action.

There are curbs to this individuality of expression, however, particularly in the area of aggression toward other persons. The Skolt child, though generally treated permissively, is severely reprimanded or spanked for his aggressive acts. Apparently the lesson of nonaggression is effectively learned by most individuals, for fighting is very infrequent, even though events such as the reindeer roundups involve both economic conflict and alcohol—a combination that in some societies could easily generate serious hostile acts.

I have suggested that the characteristics of Skolt culture, society, and personality outlined above have important effects on the way in which the Skolts have adapted to the accelerated pace of culture change in Finnish Lapland. Some of the main features of their adaptation to cultural change can be outlined as follows:

1. Changes are accepted without overt resistance.
2. Individuals adjust by changes in role content and by adopting new roles.
3. Acceptance of changes by individuals has led to decreases in the formal integration of the community.
4. There has been no development of hostile attitudes toward outsiders.
5. No "nativistic reactions" have appeared.
6. There have been no significant signs of factionalism.

In analyzing the theoretical significance of these data from Lapland, I looked for comparable data about adaptations to culture change from other "loose" (individualistic) societies. From the available literature it appeared that there are important parallels in the culture-change patterns of the Lapps and those found in some other relatively individualistic societies, such as the Fort Nelson Slave and the Chippewa. These acculturation patterns appear to contrast sharply with modes of accommodation found in "tight" societies such as the Zuni and other Pueblo communities.

The formulations about "tight" and "loose" societies that grew out of my research among the Skolt Lapps are not intended as a simple two-part typology. Rather, these contrasting types of societal organization represent the polar extremes of a hypothetical continuum. I suggest that this tight-loose dimension of variation in human societies may be a predictor of a number of significant cultural characteristics (Pelto, 1968).

There are many gaps in my description of the Skolt Lapp community, as there generally are with any descriptive monograph. I would like to have had more complete and systematic descriptions of socialization practices and more complete data on individual psychological characteristics in the form of projective tests and other materials. Three years after completing my initial field work I returned to Sevettijarvi for a summer of field work, during which I collected a series of responses to a modified form of the Thematic Apperception Test.

I had postulated that the individualistic (or "loose") patterns of social interaction found among the Skolts would be related to a personality characteristic that I labeled "social uninvolvement." Since the active reindeer herders appeared to exemplify most fully the individualistic aspects of this cultural system, I expected that they would be the ones who exhibited the least "social involvement." From a quantified content analysis of the TAT responses I found statistically significant confirmation for this hypothesis. The more "reindeer-oriented" individuals gave TAT responses that indicated significantly less social interaction than did the responses of the persons who are committed to wage work and other "modern" roles (Pelto, 1962b).

I am not now content with the empirical underpinnings of my description of the Skolt Lapps. Like most of my anthropological contemporaries, I was not in 1958–1959 particularly concerned with representative sampling or other refinements. Consequently, it would be difficult for me to compare my Lappish data in a systematic, quantified way with data from other cultures. Furthermore, in any future restudy of the Skolt community I will be handicapped by my lack of numerical data in analyzing cultural changes within that community itself. In retrospect, the field research was naïve in theoretical orientation, and my lack of methodological sophistication (particularly the nonquantification of some of the observed behavior patterns) weakened the potential usefulness of this work.

PART II: RESEARCH IN NORTHERN MINNESOTA COMMUNITIES (THE UPPER MISSISSIPPI RESEARCH PROJECT)

Problem, Theory, and Research Design

Research projects often originate directly from investigators' theoretical interests. However, there are many projects that come into being because some agency, administrator, or other interested person approached the anthropologist with a specific question or set of problems. My research in northern Minnesota is an instance of the latter situation.

In the fall of 1963, Dr. Howard C. Reid, director of the Mental Health Center at North City, Minnesota, came to me to discuss the feasibility of developing an interdisciplinary research project on mental health and community structure in the area served by his Center. Financial support for the project was available from the George W. Nielson Foundation of Minnesota, and a three-year study was planned, involving collaboration between the psychiatric personnel of the Mental Health Center and anthropologists from the University of Minnesota. After a number of visits to North City and surrounding towns, I collaborated with Dr. Reid and his associates in drafting a research proposal that called for collecting psychiatric, psychological, and cultural data in a series of White and Indian communities in the five-county area served by the Mental Health Center. Research was begun early in 1964, although full-scale field work in the communities did not start until summer of that year. Most of the field work was confined to summer seasons, since this is the period when graduate students and faculty members are freed from their academic schedules.

Since my own involvement in this research project was only one facet of a many-sided cooperative effort, my description here does not cover the varied activities of the psychiatrist, psychologist, social workers, and other members of the research team. To facilitate comparisons with my solo research project among the Skolts, I will concentrate here on details of anthropological field work, most of which was carried out by graduate students from the University of Minnesota working under my direction.

Dr. Reid and his associates were interested in investigating the relationships between economic and psychiatric problems in the area around North City. For some years the region has been regarded as economically depressed. Incomes are low, jobs are uncertain, and there are high levels of seasonal unemployment. The economic poverty of the Indian population adds to the social ills of the area. The Mental Health Center personnel felt that the population showed high rates of mental disturbance, and that the economic depression of the area was associated with a high incidence of psychiatric depression. These observations provided the basis for a series of hypotheses around which the research operations were built.

The following general objectives of the project were stated in our research proposal:

1. to obtain information about the individual personality structures of the people of the Upper Mississippi Research Project area
2. to gain a better understanding of the cultural, social, and economic characteristics of the study area as a particular type of society
3. to develop better understanding of the relationships of individual psychological attributes to cultural and socioeconomic factors
4. to gain a better understanding of Indian-White interrelations in the study area
5. to gain better understanding of the roles and functions of special groups (e.g., the summer residents and tourists) in the area

The details of the research operation were further specified and outlined in a series of hypotheses that we planned to test. They included statements of the interrelationships of psychological (and psychiatric) characteristics and the following sociocultural variables:

1. relative economic deprivation
2. degrees of social organization (and disorganization) of households and communities
3. religious preferences and activities
4. ethnic background
5. patterns of child rearing
6. education and occupation
7. degrees of articulation to the state and national social system

We planned to operationalize these variables in terms of psychological tests (including the Thematic Apperception Test and the Minnesota Multiphase Personality Inventory), psychiatric interviews, a lengthy questionnaire about individual households and their members, and participant observation and interviewing of informants in the selected research communities. A series of four White communities, three Indian communities, a mixed Indian-White communuity, and two neighborhoods in North City were selected as areas for intensive research.

As frequently happens with research projects, we somewhat overestimated the amount of research that could be accomplished in the course of three years with our available resources ($30,000 per year). However, a series of fortunate circumstances made it possible to accomplish a large portion of the original research design, as well as to add significant studies to it that were not originally projected in our proposal. First, our field crew was enlarged because of the participation of graduate students from the University of Minnesota who were supported by fellowships administered by the Department of Anthropology, and, second, we were able to hire badly needed additional typists and clerical assistants from North City College at very small expense to the project through the Work-Study Program of the Office of Economic Opportunity's "War on Poverty."

The research project was structured in terms of the hypotheses we wanted to test, using the research tools that had been specifically indicated in the original research proposal. The work of individual researchers was therefore shaped (and constrained) by the necessity of collecting comparable data by standardized techniques in the different communities. On the other hand, we wanted to obtain general ethnographic descriptions in each of the communities, in order to provide a context for evaluating and explaining the questionnaire and test data. For the anthropologist working in a given community, the research situation had the following characteristics:

1. Much of the data-gathering had to be carried out in accord with the dictates of the project directors, but each researcher was also free to innovate and to pursue personal interests in field work.

2. The need for comparing data across communities required strict attention to the representativeness of the data. A system of random sampling was used to select the households for questionnaire interviews and other quantified data-gathering.

3. Field workers in each community were not autonomous researchers. They were not free to change the directions of the research, particularly the standardized questionnaire and the psychological test data, to meet local conditions.

4. Weekly research meetings and the recreational activities that followed in the evening helped to maintain the flow of information and ideas among project personnel and also had important effects on field workers' morale.

5. Since the research populations were all participants in the same general cultural system as that of the anthropologists, there were no serious problems of language or marked dis-

crepancies in culture, though both the White and the Indian cultures of northern Minnesota differed in some important respects from the cultural backgrounds of the anthropologists. The differences were particularly evident in the northern Minnesotans' habituation to an outdoor life. Their experiences and interests run in the direction of hunting, fishing, logging, and farming. While many of these people showed evident respect for higher education and "book knowledge," they were not familiar with the intellectual interests and modes of theoretical discourse that are the daily fare of anthropological field workers. These statements apply to Indians as well as to Whites in the area; in addition, differences in the life-style of Indians, their participation in pow wows, their family relationships, and their relatively severe economic deprivation contributed to the cultural contrasts between field workers and the local population.

Passive or Adaptational Research

The environment and the people. North central Minnesota is cut-over land, marginal for agriculture, marginal for lumbering, and too far from population centers to have attracted much manufacturing. Sixty or seventy years ago loggers flocked into the area to harvest the rich stands of pine, spruce, and fir, leaving the present scrub forests of jackpine, birch, "popple," and second-growth spruce. There are hundreds of lakes in the region, with plentiful "northerns," "walleyes," bass, trout, "muskies," and other fish. Fishermen from all over the nation pour into the area in the summertime, and many tourists pass through—stopping to admire the twenty-five-foot statue of Paul Bunyan that symbolizes North City's former pre-eminence in big-timber production. Occasionally tourists take a side trip to the Deer Lake Reservation to see modern Chippewa Indians, though usually they are content to buy Indian souvenirs (many of them made in Japan) at the shops and stands in North City and in nearby towns.

There are still many farms (mainly mixed dairy-cattle-and-pigs) in the area, though they dwindle in number each year. Farmsteads far from North City are served by towns with general stores, movie houses, and other small business establishments. Both townsmen and farm people augment their slim incomes by cutting pulp, taking summer construction jobs in North Dakota, in Minneapolis and St. Paul, or on the Iron Range (a hundred miles to the east), or by means of a variety of other part-time or seasonal occupations.

The population (approximately 63,000 people in the five counties) is of Scandinavian, German, British, and Slavic origin.

There are very few Negroes, Asiatics, or Southern Europeans. The area's original inhabitants, the Chippewa Indians, are in evidence everywhere (there are three reservations within sixty miles of North City).

Since many inhabitants are descendants of loggers and homesteaders (as well as hunting-and-trapping Indians), the people hold strong individualistic values, which are given visible expression in the spacing of their homes far from each other, their considerable occupational mobility, and their stated dislike of city life.

Because of the economic handicaps of the region, out-migration rates are high, most of the young people leaving the area after finishing high school, if not before. The population has been declining since World War II, and many formerly prosperous logging towns have been reduced to near ghost-town status.

The general socioeconomic situation of the area arouses a marked ambivalence in the remaining inhabitants. The natural beauty of northern Minnesota, the relative freedom of action, the uncrowdedness, and the rich recreational opportunities are highly prized, but at the same time people view the economic marginality of the area as chronic and admit that young people do well to leave for greener pastures.

Steps in research. During the first summer of field work we developed the questionnaire that was to be the main instrument for collecting sociocultural data in the sample households. Field workers had at least a month to observe and interview informally in their communities before the questionnaire was ready to use. It is highly likely, of course, that the relative cultural similarities of the field workers and the research populations made a longer period of passive research and rapport-building relatively unnecessary, but it should also be mentioned that we found the population of north central Minnesota singularly open and friendly, and amenable to being the objects of a social-scientific study. Most of the inhabitants of the area are heavily dependent on the summer tourist and resort trade, and their frequent interaction with outsiders may have accounted for their ready acceptance of the researchers.

The Research Coordinator, J. Anthony Paredes, and I made the initial contacts in the research communities, so that the graduate students could on their arrival be introduced to community leaders. Introductions were usually arranged between field workers and mayors, heads of local civic organizations, high-school principals, or other local leaders. The field workers made further contacts with ministers, policemen, editors, and other important persons in the early stages of their field work.

News items about the project had been circulated to the local papers, and in some cases field workers were able to describe the nature of their research objectives to civic clubs, garden clubs, church groups, and other local associations. Many other persons who were not reached by these modes of information were nevertheless agreeable to interviews and other research contacts. A few people, less than 15 percent of the sample population, refused to answer the questionnaire. In almost all cases field workers found themselves fairly quickly drawn into friendly interaction with many social townspeople. For example, in the village of Asheville, our field worker, Steve Schensul, found himself quickly fitting into the social life of the younger segment of the population. Steve's cultural background (New York, Jewish) contrasted markedly with the lifeways of the local people, and the novelty of his speech and mannerisms may have been a positive attraction to the townspeople.

Active Research

Anthropologists rarely enjoy administering questionnaires, and our field staff was no exception, especially when they learned we had created an interview schedule some thirty-five pages long that required at least two hours to administer, containing queries on education, occupation, migration history, work history, recreational patterns, religious activities, locations and situations of kinsmen, and a great range of other information. Merely leafing through this questionnaire to familiarize themselves with it struck fear into the hearts of our researchers.

The graduate students' unhappy feelings about the questionnaire were aggravated by the fact that the interviews were to be conducted among unknown people of a randomly selected sample, rather than among the field workers' new friends and key informants. Therefore, much of the general rapport and familiarization that they had developed in their first month of field work was of no practical importance to them when they approached the homes of their sample respondents, questionnaire in hand.

We were moderately suprised to find that people were willing to answer the questions in our interview schedule, even personal items about incomes, debts, and best friends. A few respondents said later that they thought some of the questions were "pretty personal," but they seemed to be reassured by our claim that the data would be used anonymously, mainly in the form of statistical tabulations and other highly impersonalized analyses. Others clearly enjoyed the two to four hours of intensive questioning, and some respondents commented on the emotional satisfaction gained in reviewing one's entire life situation—an intellectual exercise most people rarely have occasion to attempt.

It is possible that our questionnaire procedure was readily accepted by the northern Minnesotans because they were accustomed to census interviewers, agricultural surveys, and other government-sponsored information-gathering procedures. Also, during the period of our research project a number of Community Action Programs and Area Redevelopment Projects came into being and were widely publicized in the research area. The pace of cultural change all over the United States appears to have produced a growing awareness among rural people of the importance of "scientific" information.

People so frequently asked "Why pick me?" that we found it useful to explain to them the concept of random sampling—"like picking names out of a hat." We pointed out to them that many city people and government officials have opinions and ideas about life in these communities without ever having talked directly with the people out on the farms and in the little towns. We asked the respondents if they agreed with us that it would be a good idea to find out from the people themselves what life is like in northern Minnesota, rather than relying on the opinions of the newspaper editors, politicians, casual travelers, and the handful of wealthy people in North City. This question frequently evoked a very positive response.

Since the Indians of the area have a reputation for taciturnity, and since they generally are less educated than the White inhabitants, we expected to encounter difficulties in administering the questionnaire in the Chippewa communities. We were pleasantly surprised to find that the Chippewa, too, answered the details of the questionnaire with no great hesitation.

There were, of course, moments of tension and difficulty with a few respondents. On one occasion I approached a farm family in the rural outlier of Asheville and was encouraged by a warm show of friendliness. As I began to interview the housewife (with her husband observing), she asked me to prove my identity. I produced the identification card signed by Dr. Reid of the Mental Health Center that all the field workers carried. After some comments about the ease with which such cards could be forged, she hesitantly agreed to proceed with the interview. We proceeded only as far as the section in which I asked her about the location of her siblings. "That's just the kind of stuff the Commies would want to know about," she said, and then accused me of being an undercover worker for the "conspiracy." I urged her to call Dr. Reid to verify my identity, but she demurred, saying that I probably had him "wrapped around my little finger." When I suggested that she contact the University to check on my credentials she said that that place was so full of Communists that she wouldn't trust any information she received from there.

It was clear that I would get no further with the questionnaire, so I put it away and continued our conversation. She became fairly amiable as she described her teaching activities in the local grade school and her suggestions for civic betterment. She seemed to harbor no grudge against me and discussed a number of topics in a calm, rational manner. But she would not answer my questionnaire, since she was afraid that it was part of what she believed to be an already widely developed Communist plot to take over the United States.

On numerous occasions we found that when the questionnaire was finished, the respondent wished to continue telling us his opinions and ideas about life and the state of the world. Some respondents felt (and rightly) that there were many important questions we had failed to include in our questionnaire and that the omissions needed to be corrected before the interviewer left.

Although it is hard to establish objective evidence for this, we occasionally had the feeling that the very act of getting so much personal information about individuals put us on a special footing with them, generated a sudden intimacy. We were no longer "strangers," even though we had never met before.

Rural respondents frequently served food or coffee to the field worker in the course of, or immediately following, the interview. On one occasion I walked into the yard of a farm family near Solberg, announced my mission, and was informed that the woman of the house would not be home for a couple of hours, as she had gone to town to shop. The farmer and his son invited me into the house and served me coffee and ice cream and cake while we talked and waited for the wife to return. When my respondent returned, the interview (which involved the whole family), required another three and a half hours. Preparations for supper, milking the cows, and other chores were delayed as we laboriously made our way through the thirty-five pages of questions.

The lengthy questionnaire interview was emotionally very taxing for our field workers, so that few of us cared to administer more than seven or eight in the course of a week. Tension and embarrassment during the interview appeared to be generated mainly by the field worker's own notions about privacy, rather than sensitivity on the part of respondents. Beginning field workers repeatedly spoke of the agonies of anxiety they experienced when approaching a prospective respondent. They also reported great feelings of relief at the end of a successful questionnaire, together with a surge of rapport with their respondents.

As contrasted with formal questionnaire interviewing, participant observation and informal interviewing are extremely variable modes of field work. Our field workers engaged in a wide variety of activities, such as attending town-council meetings, harvesting wild rice with Indian companions, fishing, playing softball with the town team, and socializing at the local tavern.

A particularly important aspect of participant observation developed around local community celebrations. The people of Asheville celebrated their community's existence and solidarity on the Fourth of July, while Draketon held a three-day town fair in the middle of August. Each of our eight research communities held some sort of community celebration during the course of each summer.

Invoking standard anthropological ideas about the meaning of ritual, we felt that full coverage of these special events would give us a great deal of insight into the social structure and special interests of the local communities. We hypothesized that the summer celebrations would serve some of the same kinds of functions as have been attributed to village ceremonials in non-Western societies. Preparations for the Draketon Fair involved an organizational structure that illuminated some of the main social alignments of the town. Also, the ceremonial tug-o'-war between the townsmen and the farmers dramatized a social division that appeared to be important in many aspects of the community's social life. At James Lake the annual Water Carnival was attended by only a handful of Indians, clearly reflecting an important social fact in that sharply divided community.

In both Indian and White communities the annual summer celebrations were important occasions for "homecoming" and reaffirming kinship and neighborhood ties. The emotional significance of long-established social ties can be activated on these ritual occasions, even though the ties are becoming increasingly weak as northern Minnesotans scatter to urban areas and elsewhere in search of better standards of living.

Whenever possible, we arranged to have one or two additional field workers on hand in a community during the local festival. It was the task of the resident field worker to find out as much as possible about the organization, scheduling, and leadership of the festival, so that the extra field workers would have maximum possibilities for effectively covering the various events.

Since the resident field worker was usually fairly well known in the town by the time of the celebration, he was often asked by the townspeople to help with a variety of chores and errands. The new field workers also frequently found themselves lending a hand to the celebration committee. At the Draketon Fair, two of us were judges at the children's races and the "baseball scramble," and the field worker's wife helped judge the queen contestants. At the tug-o'-war between townsmen and countrymen we could have found ourselves in serious trouble in our complicated judging responsibilities had the countrymen not won a quick and decisive victory. At the James Lake Water Carnival two of our field workers entered the canoe jousting and log-rolling events, but experienced quick and wet defeats at the hands of the local boys.

At an Indian pow wow, one of our field workers was deputized to help maintain law and order, but he resigned when he realized that a man with a badge pinned to his shirt causes unrest among the celebrants if he walks around busily taking notes. Our dancing at the pow wows was far from expert, but our performances appear at least to have had favorable consequences for rapport maintenance.

Wherever anthropologists carry out research, they participate in such local activities as these. It is important to note, however, that many of the activities described above were engaged in by field workers who had little or no previous introduction to the community. We often relied on "instant rapport," rapport generated on the spot. These tactics appear to have been successfully mainly because of the following three factors. First, the people we studied were remarkably open and friendly (or at least tolerant) toward outsiders. This was partly, I feel, a reflection of their individualistic social orientation. Second, the importance of tourism in the area makes access into the public affairs of these communities extremely easy for the outsider. Summer is a special time when the region is full of outsiders with money for local pockets. In fact, many of the local celebrations are intended at least in part as tourist attractions. And, third, it can be suggested that secular celebrations, in an area that is rapidly losing personnel to the outside world, are especially open to the attentions of outsiders, particularly if the outsiders are willing to "help out" in activities in which local organizations may be lacking in sufficient manpower.

Anthropological field workers have often found that after an absence from the research community they experience increased rapport and social warmth on return to the field. Even if he has been gone for only a short time, the anthropologist is welcomed back like a missing relative. Some anthropologists feel that their return to the community after a brief absence is interpreted by the people as final proof that he is sincerely interested in them. Our returns to the field situation in northern Minnesota for the second and third summers appear to have had some of these rapport-building consequences. We occasionally made weekend trips to the field during the winter, and these expressions of hardiness in the face of winter's storms and subzero temperatures seem to have had favorable effects on our relationships with the local people. Perhaps this was because in winter they feel themselves to be out of contact with the outside world. Tourists and warm-weather friends are all far to the south, the economy stagnates, and unemployment lists are long. Even very brief visits during the dead of winter surprised our informants and disposed them favorably toward our continued field work.

Field-work operations did not always go smoothly, however. In every community there were a few individuals who refused to answer the questionnaire and who avoided interviews with the anthropologists. Some respondents answered the questionnaire, but declined to participate in the psychological tests. As expected, a large proportion of our research sample failed to fill out and return the lengthy Minnesota Multiphasic Personality Inventory (MMPI). The wonder is that so many *did* cooperate in this tedious chore.

Participant observation among some drunken citizens of James Lake got one first-year graduate student into deep waters, for on at least two different occasions individuals threatened to beat him up. Steady nerves, quick thinking, a reputation for complete honesty, and the calculated advertisement of the fact that he habitually carried little money were probably factors in his finishing the summer's field work without physical harm. Luck is an important element in field work.

Not all would-be anthropologists are equally competent in the intricacies of questionnaire interviewing, participant observation, and other elements of field work. Also, there are great variations in personal style among field workers. Some of our researchers were successful in maintaining a very out-going and sociable style of field work. Others were more retiring and shy, without apparently hampering effective data-collection.

One of our field workers was heartily disliked by many of his fellow researchers for a wide variety of subtle but significant violations of tact and sensitivity. We later discovered that he had offended the people in his research community too. Intensive field work the next summer by a researcher who is a paragon of tact smoothed over the ruffled feelings in the village of Balsamville.

Bowing Out

Although we had informed the newspapers, local officials, and other persons in the research area that our project would last for three years, we frequently mentioned to our respondents that our interests in the area and its people would not terminate abruptly at the end of the project. We anticipated that some anthropologists would continue to do research in these communities,, and the continued presence of the Mental Health Center at North City gave an impression of continuity to the research project. In addition, the Research Coordinator of the project was offered a position at North State College (in North City) at the termination of the project. It was understood that he would continue to be active in certain action projects in the area, particularly in some community-leadership seminars sponsored by the University Extension Service. Some graduate students in anthropology at the University will probably carry out research projects in the area and avail themselves of the great amounts of data already collected on the research communities.

The end of the three-year project was marked by a diminution of activity rather than an abrupt termination. During the three years, the rhythm of field work had quickened during the summer and slackened during the winter, and at the end of each summer we left the area, bidding farewell to the local people with whom we were most closely associated, promising to return occasionally in the winter, and talking hopefully of the activities of the summer to come. In some communities the field workers came and went so often that the people may have come to feel that some sort of permanent tie had developed between anthropologists and the local community.

Integration of the Research Team

The lone anthropologist in his field-work station is continuously faced with the problem of maintaining and improving social relationships with the people he is studying. In a larger project, particularly if it is multidisciplinary, maintaining effective social relationships *within* the research group itself is often the most pressing problem.

The largest responsibility for maintaining interdisciplinary communication in our project was put in the hands of our Research Coordinator, J. Anthony Paredes, who remained in the research area throughout the project. His office was set up in the Mental Health Center, and he maintained daily contact with the psychiatrist, psychologist, and social worker. Ideas and attitudes of the Center staff members were forwarded by him to the anthropologists at the University (particularly during the winter months), and he was responsible for organizing conferences or other activities involving the research team.

In the summer, weekly research meetings were held at the Mental Health Center, with the senior research team and all the field workers participating. These meetings usually began with reports from individual field workers, followed by general discussion of their research data. One important function of these meetings was to inform the Mental Health Center personnel of the activities of the field workers, since the staff had fewer opportunities to visit the research communities than did the Coordinator and the senior anthropologist. At the same time, the presentation of field reports made it possible for the MHC staff members to comment on the psychological and psychiatric relevance of the anthropological data. Often the MHC members were able to relate information about their individual patients to the discussions of community and household organization.

As seems to be true in practically all interdisciplinary research projects, important communications problems developed. The MHC staff and the anthropologists differed significantly in theoretical orientation and practical concerns. The differences between an "in-the-clinic" perspective and the perspective of the field worker are great, regardless of similar interests in case materials as data. It should be noted also that the clinic personnel were occupied with managing a great many psychiatric patients and had little time to devote to the project; on the other hand, the anthropologists were free to devote their time almost wholly to research.

During the winter months I occasionally was able to travel to North City for research conferences, but these meetings were not frequent enough to maintain effective communications between MHC staff and the anthropological segment of the research team. Had it not been for the efforts of Research-coordinator Paredes in the Mental Health Center, serious problems in maintaining the integration of the project would have developed.

The research design appears to have provided significant integrating features also. A product of joint deliberations between the Mental Health Center staff and myself, the research design incorporated ideas and attitudes of both "sides" of the research team and was regarded as a kind of charter to which differences of opinion could be referred. I feel that the specificity of *some* of the elements in the research proposal, including the listing of general aims, hypotheses to be tested, and the description of research instruments, provided a basis for settling differences of opinion and also served as a standard of measurement against which actual research operations could be evaluated and discussed. Had our original research design been as amorphous as is sometimes the case in projects of this sort, we might have had much greater difficulties in maintaining even minimally effective communications.

Concrete Results of the Project

As the fruits of three years of research, the project produced the following data:

1. a large compilation of economic and social statistics for the entire five-county area
2. general descriptive materials, household questionnaire data, and psychological test materials on three White communities and one mixed Indian-White community, as well as substantial data on two other White communities and two neighborhoods in North City
3. general descriptive materials, household questionnaire data, some life-history materials, and other miscellaneous data on three Indian communities
4. a substantial body of ethnographic data on community celebrations in both Indian and White communities
5. a collection of data on performances in verbal and nonverbal achievement tasks in a mixed Indian-White school that makes possible a controlled comparison of Indian and White pupils in a single research setting
6. collections of short essays from pupils in several schools in the area
7. a set of psychological test materials (MMPI and TAT) on a random sample of Mental Health Center patients
8. a collection of responses to the Family Interaction Apprehension Test in two North City samples and one sample of Mental Health Center patients
9. a collection of questionnaire responses and general ethnographic data on wild-rice harvesting in the Broken Reed Reservation area
10. other miscellaneous collections of primary data

As the bibliography on pp. 605-608 indicates, six M.A. theses based on these materials have already been completed. Two doctoral theses will be based entirely on materials from the research area, and another thesis will involve comparisons of northern Minnesota data with similar data from East Africa. One paper presenting materials from the research project has been published (Schensul, Paredes, and Pelto), and others have been submitted to publishers. One senior honors thesis on wild-rice harvesting has also been completed.

An important secondary result of the research project was the opportunity it gave for substantial field-work experience for eighteen graduate students in anthropology.

Summary and Evaluation

While we were unable to collect all the data specified in our research proposal, we did gather materials on a number of topics that were not specified in the original design. These "extra" studies included an analysis of celebrations in White communities, data on Chippewa pow wows, descriptions of wild-rice harvesting, and a study of achievement orientation among pupils in a mixed Indian-White school. The general structure of the project made it possible to allocate research attention into areas of culture and general community structure whose importance could not be foreseen at the beginning of the project. Our study of community celebrations, for example, provides possibilities not only for comparing ritual activities within the research area itself, but also for comparing these community celebrations with those in non-Western cultures.

At this time we are only in the early stages of data analysis, so we are only partially able to perceive and enumerate the strengths and weaknesses of our project. Some of the weaknesses that have become apparent to us so far are as follows.

1. Our plans were too elaborate given the time and financial support available to us. In most cases reduction in the scope of quantifiable data was offset by "bonus" data not originally specified in our research proposal; nonetheless, we sometimes experienced a sense of frustration at not being able to carry out all the details of the research design. For example, we were able to collect psychological data from only one of the Indian communities.

2. The questionnaire should have been precoded, to make it easier to transfer the information to IBM cards. Even though important segments of the questionnaire were relatively open-ended (and would have to be coded *after* administration), earlier attention to the problems of content coding would have greatly speeded up our analysis of data.

3. More data-analysis should have been carried out during the project, instead of waiting until nearly all the data had been gathered. Certain aspects of our materials, particularly those based on the questionnaire, were examined during the first and second years of the research project. However, if more data had been analyzed in the course of the research, it would have been

possible to achieve greater flexibility, including some reformulation of data-gathering techniques.

4. Most of our research was carried out in the summer. Although we did have one full-time anthropologist in the research area throughout the year, it seems that we know more about the summer situations of those communities than we do about the winter. Thus we have little control over seasonal variations that may be of significance.

5. The research project was designed to study the characteristics of people in their home communities, and only a small portion of the research was directed to the data and activities of the Mental Health Center itself. The involvement of the Mental Health Center personnel could have been more effective if a larger portion of the project had been designed around the on-going activities of the Center.

6. During the first summer greater care should have gone into maintaining communication with the field workers. Too often during the early part of the project inexperienced field workers had to cope with a multiplicity of decisions and problems without adequate direction.

7. Instructions and procedures for mapping and census-taking should have been more clearly specified, so that the relatively inexperienced field workers would have had more definite tasks in the beginning phases of work.

Although we will have a much clearer perception of the project when data analysis has proceeded further, some of the strengths of this research include the following.

1. The decision to pay careful attention to problems of sampling and to the production of quantifiable data created an attitude of empiricism and precision of observation that markedly affected the quality of all field work. Researchers came to be highly sensitive to the empirically observable bases of their "qualitative" generalizations. Any statement about "usual" or "typical" behavior in the communities was likely to be examined in terms of the key question: "Would this statement (about a culture pattern) hold true if I observed an adequate sample of people in a variety of circumstances, and at different times?"

2. The "hard data" from the questionnaires provided us with clear evidence for *variations* in behavior (e.g., religious activity, patterns of social interaction, etc.), and forced us to seek ways to describe intragroup differences, rather than concentrating solely on "normal," "average," or other unimodal conceptualizations of culture patterns.

3. The combination of quantifiable data-gathering with less structured field-work techniques appeared to be satisfying to field workers and seemed to produce community portraits that were rich in descriptive detail, yet firmly supported by replicable,

"operationalized" foundations. Statements about average incomes or average unemployment for particular communities have made sense only when we can think of these statistics in relation to the situations of particular individuals and families. On the other hand, data from particular observation and interviewing of key informants have frequently been more interpretable and useful when viewed in the perspective of quantified information.

4. Including graduate students at practically all phases of research planning and theoretical discussion greatly increased the effectiveness of the field workers and substantially improved the design and direction of the project. Even inexperienced field workers quickly notice potentially productive avenues of research, as well as gaps in project planning, if they are given an opportunity to express their views in research meetings.

5. The "multi-instrument–multi-community" approach to research appeared to be highly productive. For example, in the assessment of psychological characteristics there are serious weaknesses and handicaps in all currently available research tools. Our decision to use the MMPI, Thematic Apperception Tests, *and* psychiatric interviews (as well as some secondary psychological research instruments), gave us some control over the weaknesses inherent in any one mode of data collection. Also, the collection of similar data in several different communities permitted us to examine certain hypotheses in a series of parallel tests with independently collected bodies of comparable information.

One of the most significant findings of our northern Minnesota research was that living conditions among rural low-income groups are very different from the portrait of poverty we encounter in descriptions of urban slums. Many of the families in our research sample, who are by technical definition "poverty-stricken," own their own homes, have ample supplies of high-protein foods (many have food freezers), and in a number of other ways are unlike families of comparable income levels in the cities. On the other hand, these people realize that they are marginal to the general American affluence that they learn about through newspapers, magazines, and television. As the younger people of northern Minnesota flock to the cities in search of steady jobs and the supposedly more exciting entertainments of metropolitan life, the people who remain in the home towns experience an increasingly poignant "relative deprivation."

The rural residents still idealize the independence and neighborliness of rural life. However, they also tend to seek the material advantages and "sophistication" associated with America's centers of population. Their low incomes (average annual income is $3,100 per family) do not permit the attainment of these goals.

In comparing White and Indian standards of living in northern Minnesota, we found that the Indians generally have lower paid jobs and higher unemployment levels than the Whites of the area. However, one community of Chippewa Indians had a *higher* average annual income than almost all of the neighboring white towns, and most of the able-bodied males of the community are fully employed. This unusually successful Indian community has been able to take advantage of economic opportunities in the nearby Iron Range of northeastern Minnesota, partly because of the efforts of one of the local Indian leaders.

From my experience with the Skolt Lapps I had become interested in the personality characteristic of "social involvement" as it relates to economic and social adaptations. This personality characteristic is also important in northern Minnesota, for we find that the people who have the lowest incomes and standard of living in the area are the persons who are the *least* socially involved. They are also the persons with the fewest ties (through newspapers, television, club memberships, travel) to the broader social system. We believe that in northern Minnesota, as in Lapland, successful economic adaptations in earlier decades were characterized by concentration on the struggle with nature, through hard work. Social *un*involvement was adaptive. Now things have changed. Economic success requires more education, more interpersonal skills, and more knowledge about the outside social system. The people who are adapting successfully are those whose personalities tend toward high social involvement.

Our personality data also indicate that, as one might expect, the economically unsuccessful people in northern Minnesota show more psychological depression than their wealthier neighbors. Aside from the effects of different standards of living, we find that life in this marginal rural area seems more frustrating to women than to men. The positive advantages of rural life—the hunting, fishing, and other outdoor activities—appear to be more satisfying to the men than to their wives, as indicated by the frustration scores on psychological tests.

PART III: COMPARISONS OF THE TWO RESEARCH PROJECTS

At first glance it might appear that the two research experiences described above are so dissimilar that comparisons would not be fruitful. However, examination of the two projects suggests some important observations about anthropological research methods.

Basic Similarities

The projects in northern Finland and northern Minnesota had generally similar theoretical frames of reference that involved interrelated elements of culture, social structure, and personality. In both cases the community was the focus of research, though in the second project the scene of study was broadened to include a series of communities, rather than just one.

A major effort in both cases was expended in participant observation and interviewing of informants, in the belief that these methods of general scanning and accumulation of data about the lifeways of a community are essential for understanding and contextualizing more quantified or abstracted kinds of information.

Data on individual households and the individual members of households are of central importance in both cases, perhaps because of the individualized nature of both cultures. This "individualistic" tendency of both the Lapps and the northern Minnesotans appears to account for the generally open reception accorded the field workers and for the field workers' relative lack of concentration on the structure of organizations in those communities. In both cases the political states in which the research populations are located are completely open to research, and no political problems were encountered in obtaining permission to carry out our studies. Both research populations are located in northern areas with severe winters. Marked seasonal variations in behavior patterns (and field-work patterns) resulted, and winter-time transportation problems were serious in both instances. Serious language problems were not encountered in either study. Translators were not necessary, although fluency with Lappish would certainly enhance research in Lapland, as would fluency in Chippewa improve aspects of the northern Minnesota research situation.

Some Important Differences

Three important differences that are immediately obvious are (1) in Lapland I worked alone, and in Minnesota I was part of an interdisciplinary team, (2) more psychological data were collected in Minnesota, partly because of the interests of the Mental Health Center, and (3) representative quantifiable data were a strong feature of the second project as compared with the Lapp study.

The size and interdisciplinary nature of the northern Minnesota project had an important effect on the style of our research, but it should be kept in mind that much of the general design of the project could have been carried out in miniature by one anthropologist working in a single community. The interdisciplinary project adds special problems of organization and communication, but it does not account for the major differences in research design and emphasis that distinguish the two projects. Similarly, the gathering of psychological (and even psychiatric) data is of secondary importance in contrasting the two research efforts. I was interested in the psychological characteristics of individuals during my first project among the Lapps, even though my use of psychological data was far from systematic.

The really major difference between these two projects is that in Minnesota I was much concerned with the representativeness of information, and made an attempt to collect materials that could be evaluated at least in part by statistical analysis. This difference stems from my dissatisfaction with my Lapland data.

The problems with the Lapland data are illustrated by a type of statement that recurs repeatedly in the pages of my monograph *Individualism in Skolt Lapp Society*. For example, I mention that fictive kinship is frequently a facilitating factor in economic transactions and cite the case of Lari Sverloff undertaking to sell a crippled reindeer for his godfather. I also cite an instance in which Jaakko Killanen and Jaakko Gauriloff mentioned that it would be all right to shoot a reindeer calf belonging to one's godfather because compensation could be easily arranged. In that statement, which is a secondary comment related to a generalized discussion about ritual or fictive kinship patterns among the Skolt Lapps, I give little additional evidence for my generalization concerning economic aspects of the relationship. Yet the generalization might be an important one that could be used in cross-cultural comparisons if one trusted the data. It is easy to see how a researcher carrying out cross-cultural tests of fictive kinship might extract just that piece of information and assign the Skolt Lapps to a category such as "economic transactions significantly related to fictive kinship relations."

In looking back over my field notes from Lapland, I believe that my information was not significantly inaccurate. On the other hand, I would have some difficulty in claiming that I have further evidence for it. The credibility of my statement that fictive kinship is frequently a facilitating factor in economic transactions (and many other statements in the monograph) rests on my general credibility as a reporter of information about the Skolt Lapps, but a careful reader may well ask, "What about the relationship of economic transactions to fictive kinship among all the rest of the Skolt Lapps?" Some data in my monograph are based on quantified and tabulated data (e.g., a census of households and an official list of reindeer owned by individuals in the community). This is the type of data that nearly everyone quantifies, or gives some semblance of quantifying, almost as a matter of course. Statements concerning "typical" cultural patterns (of ritual kinship or almost anything else of this sort) involve data that many anthropologists assume to be regularly patterned—therefore raising no problems of sampling or representativeness. My monograph contains many assumptions that certain types of statements require only anecdotal or illustrative evidence.

In retrospect, I feel that some of my assumptions about patterning were unjustified and that, in fact, every pattern of behavior is likely to show a range of variation within even the smallest communities. If I repeated the project, I would base a much larger number of my generalizations about Skolt Lapp cultural behavior on systematically collected data—questionnaires, or observations of a randomly selected sample of persons. If I carried out such a research procedure, it would be important to describe the operations clearly, giving the reader a better chance to assess the credibility of my generalizations.

Some anthropologists count instances of specific behaviors, use questionnaires, and employ standardized methods of collecting evidence. It is my feeling that quantifiable methods of data collection, and careful description of the operations involved, should become the standard practice of all ethnographers. It would, of course, be a tremendously large and cumbersome task (probably impossible in practice) to get satisfactory quantifiable, representative information on every single culture pattern that one wishes to report for a particular community.

Among social scientists there is often a tendency to assume that the computerized synthesizing of data provides a solution to our methodological problems. Although I believe that there are numbers of ways in which computers are useful for analyzing and synthesizing data, the aim of the Upper Mississippi Research Project was not so much to organize all data-gathering in terms of eventual synthesis by computers as it was to make sure that the field worker as a research instrument would be relatively reliable. When confronted with reliable information about ranges of variation within even the simplest groups, the anthropologist can be sensitized to the need for making representative observations. Without such sensitizing, anthropologists may be sidetracked by the prejudices and distortions of a few key informants or by their own unrepresentative sampling of favorite research locations and situations.

A closely related problem is that our intention to test specific hypotheses in Minnesota forced us to define *how* to observe the variables involved in these hypotheses. Rules of observation can always be changed in the field; in fact, rules of observation pertaining to particular variables should probably always be based on preliminary field work in or prior knowledge of the specific research communities. Without a conscious "field operationalizing" of research methods, the anthropologist is always tempted to fill in blanks in his descriptive data with his own hunches, impressionistic observations, or illustrative anecdotes.

Increased concern with the credibility of ethnographic data accounts for many of the major differences between the Lapland research project and the research in northern Minnesota. Problems of credibility were not really solved in northern Minnesota, but some progress was made. I believe that the northern Minnesota data include a quantified base of information that can be used for comparisons with other communities. In future studies of these same communities researchers will be able to make fairly specific assessments of changes in cultural patterns, if they use similar methods of collecting data.

Among the Skolt Lapps I found differences in commitment to reindeer herding, differences in involvement with fishing activities, major differences in orientation toward new wage-work opportunities, differences in child-rearing practices, and even interesting differences in language use within this very small community. In northern Minnesota our questionnaire data and other information document intracommunity variations in behavior in practically every significant dimension we have examined.[2]

My experience in these two research projects persuades me that intracommunity variations in behavior constitute one of the major keys to theoretical advances in anthropology. However, as long as anthropological theory continues to be based on modal cultural patterns in particular communities and societies (which are then compared cross-culturally in statistical and other analyses), research literature will be hampered by confusing contradictions in data. Some of these contradictions come to light when two different anthropologists study the same com-

---

[2] Conceivably, such variations in behavior within small communities are much more noticeable and important in "individualistic" societies than in more corporately organized communities. That question, of course, could be an interesting topic for future research.

munity and report differences in behavioral patterning that would require incompatible coding or reporting of the data. These problems in the anthropological data become more tractable if attention is paid to ranges of variations in behavior.

From my experience in both Lapland and northern Minnesota, I feel that many significant theoretical propositions in anthropology can be examined by means of intracommunity or intrasocietal studies. Although much hypothesis-testing in sociology and psychology has been carried out in the form of intracultural and intrasocietal comparison, anthropologists have questioned some of these studies because of the possibility that the results are peculiar to Western culture or to American middle-class culture. Future research models in all of the social sciences, it seems to me, will require intracommunity examinations of propositions, but this research will have to be carried out in parallel series in different cultural settings if cross-cultural applicability is claimed for the generalizations.

INTENSIVE FIELD WORK AND SCOPE SAMPLING: METHODS FOR STUDYING THE SAME PROBLEM AT DIFFERENT LEVELS

Melvin L. Perlman

PART I: TORO

Problem, Theory, and Research Design

Early in 1959 I was offered a position as Junior Research Fellow of the East African Institute of Social Research (EAISR), Makerere University College, in Kampala, Uganda.[1] The Insti-

[1] I am grateful to the Social Science Research •Council for a Research Training Fellowship that supported the latter stages of the field research described in this chapter. Grateful acknowledgment is also made to the Institute of International Studies, University of California, Berkeley, for a Comparative/International Grant. I also wish to thank Aidan Southall, Morris Freilich, and Jonathan Kelley for helpful comments on an earlier draft of this chapter.

tute had advertised for a social anthropologist to do a study of marriage and family life in contemporary Uganda, so when I accepted the two-and-a-half-year contract I knew the topic of my research. Although I had had no previous field-work experience and had not done library research specifically on that topic, I was at the time working on a general bibliography of African women (1960a).

I was to work under the supervision of the Director of the Institute, who at that time was Professor Aidan W. Southall, and to work out the details of the research in consultation with him. As it turned out, Professor Southall had to leave Kampala for a field trip within a few days after my arrival in mid-April of 1959. Consequently, we had very little time to discuss the research at that particular time. We did decide, however, to divide the research into two parts: first, intensive field work in one district of Uganda to study the problems in depth and to establish the main patterns, and second, less intensive comparative work elsewhere to test the validity of these patterns for other parts of Uganda.

We also decided at this time that I would do the intensive field work in Toro District in western Uganda. One of the important reasons for choosing Toro was the large-scale migration of men, and some women, from Toro to Kampala, some 200 miles to the east, in search of work. We assumed that migration was one of the significant factors affecting family life in the rural areas of Uganda, and Toro provided an opportunity to investigate this assumption in depth. Moreover, the Uganda Government was supporting my research, and district officers were anxious to have some information on labor migration, which was also having an important effect on the Toro economy. Furthermore, Toro was one of the few remaining districts in Uganda for which a basic ethnography had not yet been published.

Professor Southall suggested that in Toro I settle down in Mwenge County, which is one of the two most important and populous counties in the district. It is also located on the main road to Kampala, the capital of Uganda, and we assumed that a signifiant portion of the Toro labor migrants were coming from this county. Moreover, one of my main objectives for the first few months was to learn the language and familiarize myself with traditional customs, and Mwenge County was known as one of the most traditional in the district. It had often produced and trained Toro kings, it had relatively few foreigners, and the purest language of the Toro, Rutoro, was spoken there.

Within ten days of my arrival in Uganda I set out with my wife and twenty-month-old daughter for the field. During those ten days most of my time had to be spent in making practical arrangements for the trip, and there was relatively little time to discuss the substantive aspects of the research with Professor Southall, who in any case was engaged in making final preparations for his own trip. Two months later we were to meet again. In the meantime the plan was for me to settle down in a Toro village, learn the language, start making contacts, and pick up as much information as possible in an on-the-spot investigation from which I could afterwards work out more specific research objectives and a feasible research design.

After two months in the field I returned to Kampala for the semiannual EAISR Conference for which I wrote a paper outlining the major objectives of my intensive study of Toro. I stated that one of the most important aspects of the study would be an attempt to establish the main types of marriage, with an analysis of spouses in terms of such categories as occupation, income, and religion. I wanted to know whether certain categories of people were attracted to certain types of marriages, and in particular I wanted to study the extent to which an existing or emerging élite used ring marriage (sometimes called Christian or statutory marriage) as one of its badges of respectability. In addition to ring marriage there was also the traditional customary marriage, and I suggested there might be some other distinctions to be made as well. With regard to these different types of marital unions, I intended to investigate the importance and incidence of polygyny and the payment of bridewealth and the incidence of divorce and separation, as well as to search for indexes of and factors affecting the stability of marriage.

The legal aspect of the study was also very important in my outline, as I knew that more than one system of law governed marriage and family institutions. I had to find out, for example, what constituted a marriage and a divorce according to customary law, the marriage law of the Uganda Protectorate, and the law of the Christian missions. Were these systems of law very different from case law and contemporary court decisions? How did they relate to the actual practices of various groups, including the élite?

My outline called for an investigation of the position of women, domestic relationships, and the breakdown of kinship obligations. These were to include study of the guardianship of children, tensions in the position of adolescents, and patterns of family authority and discipline.

Finally, I planned to analyze the social structure of the local group as the context within which the above factors operated, and to trace the causes of changes in that structure.

Although my objectives were now on paper, they were by no means rigidly set. I was already familiar with the field situation, and I anticipated that some changes would be necessary. I could not predict, however, that a major reorientation of the study would occur as a result of the data that I later collected.

The usual custom in Toro, and in Africa generally, is for the bridegroom and/or his father to make a bridewealth payment (traditionally in livestock but increasingly in cash in recent years) to the father of the bride. My investigations in Toro revealed, however, that many people were living together as man and wife and were socially accepted as a married couple, even though no bridewealth had been paid. This led me to inquire not only why, but also how this new practice got started. Before long, I found myself engaged in historical research, for I realized that I could not properly understand the present without first understanding the past. This course ultimately led to an analysis of social change, especially the processes of change. Studying changes in marriage and family life led in turn to a further broadening of the scope of my inquiry, for I finally realized that such changes were part of a more general change in the role relationships of men and women, both within and outside of the family, especially the degree of equality in those relationships.

During my first two months in the field I had only the frailest of research designs. My aims were simply to make contacts, learn the language, and collect enough information to make further more detailed plans. I had to play it by ear, and make as much headway as possible without antagonizing people and jeopardizing my chances of remaining in the area chosen.

During these first two months I managed to obtain enough information to formulate the more specific and—I hoped—feasible research design that I discussed in my conference paper in Kampala. I stated that my chief problem was how to achieve the correct balance between statistically valid material on the one hand, and sufficiently detailed material on the other hand. It was clearly important to make very intensive observations of families, even very small numbers of them, and to take personal histories, especially of old people, to find out what was happening to their children. Yet, at the same time, I wanted to know just how representative the detailed material would be, and this meant some kind of sample. The kind of sample I was considering would have consisted of all homesteads in a given geographical area, preferably the village in which I was living, because I knew I could obtain more reliable data on all the people in that village than I could on a similar number of people spread out over a larger area. It would be so time consuming to get such detailed qualitative information, however, that I questioned whether it was worthwhile to spend the necessary time to visit all 180 homesteads in the village.

Though I did not have a clear-cut answer to the problem of how to obtain data that would be both sufficiently detailed and statistically valid, I did have a flexible working plan. I did not know which factors were most significant and which others could eventually be ignored for purposes of a sample, so I decided to postpone the sample, settle down in one place, and start making intensive observations of small numbers of families in an attempt to gain a more or less complete picture of family life with as much detailed information as possible, none of it in isolation. Then, if the information was readily forthcoming, I planned to continue in this way to cover the smallest residentially definable unit, which, in Toro, was a ridge or hillside or a named sub-village containing between ten and twenty homesteads.

After returning to Toro from the Kampala conference I followed this general plan for the first few months. I managed to do a detailed study of the marital histories of all thirty-one adult women living on the two ridges closest to my house. I started with the women because there happened to be several women householders living near me, but in the final sample I included the marital histories of both men and women. I also collected a considerable amount of data on all 180-odd homesteads in the village.

My plan called for me to stop at this point and take stock of the nature and amount of data I had obtained. If the information seemed relevant to the inquiry at hand, and if, relatively speaking, there was a considerable amount of it, I planned to continue in the same village. But if I was not finding the answers to my questions, and if the data were scant and difficult to obtain, I was going to fold up my tent and try elsewhere. I figured that even if I decided to move at this point, at a later date I could still compare the data from this subvillage with those of other similar subvillages.

The next EAISR Conference was coming up in December, and the paper I wrote for it (1959) was a useful way of taking stock of what I had learned so far. I had hoped by that time to have some indication of what the most significant variables were going to be, and I even hoped to develop some hypotheses. My paper showed that I had enough data to demonstrate that very important changes were taking place in the social structure of Toro generally and in the family in particular. Although I produced no explanatory hypotheses at this stage, I had a good idea of what the significant factors would be, and in general the results encouraged me to stay on in the same village and extend the sample.

Colleagues at the conference were very helpful in pointing out gaps in the data and new lines of inquiry that had not occurred to me. Although writing a conference paper every six months was quite a chore at the time, in the long run these periodic breaks contributed a great deal to my research. I was forced to stop and see how much I did or did not know about various aspects of the research. This helped me to recognize at regular intervals that I did not know as much as I thought I did, and also to specify the kinds of data that were lacking. Critical comments from professional colleagues gave me new ideas and helped me put my research into comparative perspective. I also gained stimulation from participating in the discussions on other papers. These breaks in the field work were thus invaluable aids in the progress of the research and provided a much needed change of pace and respite from the daily tensions of life in the field.

I spent an additional four months in the first village, extending the sample to include all households in the geographical area within approximately a one-mile radius of my house, in which there were 90 homesteads or about half of the village. This was sufficient for statistical purposes (detailed marital histories for 100 men and 127 women).

My plan now called for moving to another village to get comparative data. The choice of a second village was determined by a number of factors. Most important, I wanted a village near the town of Fort Portal, district headquarters of Toro, because of my interest in investigating the direction of change. I wanted to see how family life was being affected by the proximity of the town, with its opportunities for wage employment and its major missionary centers and other sources of new ideas. I also wanted a village populated mainly by Toro, and one having a land situation comparable to that in the first village, i.e., containing owners of freehold land, their tenants, and those having customary rights of occupation in Crown Land, now called African Trust Land. With the help of the county chief of Burahya, the other important and populous county in Toro, a suitable village was located about four miles south of Fort Portal. The first village is about 25 miles east of Fort Portal on the Kampala road.

Having studied 90 homesteads in the first village in Mwenge County, I decided to choose an equal number in this second village to have two samples of comparable size. But here it was not possible simply to concentrate on the geographical area around my house, because the sample would then have been too heavily weighted in favor of the wealthy landowners and would have excluded most of the poor workers. I had taken a census that showed a total of 265 homesteads in this second periurban village and considerable geographical variation, which was not true of the first village. Consequently I selected a stratified ran-

dom sample of 90 homesteads, keeping it balanced for householders in regard to age, religion, land situation, sex, occupation
for men, and settlement area, this last referring to the location
of a named area within the total area of four square miles. This
stratified random sample also provided some sort of check on
my first sample of a geographical area.

I was confident of getting sufficiently reliable data from a
random sample in the second village, because I now spoke the
language fluently and knew exactly what data to collect. Moreover, the density of population in the second village (303 per
square mile) was more than twice that in the first village. This
permitted me to get around more quickly and to check my information, because the villagers lived close enough to one another to be well informed of each other's social life.

I completed the second sample in six months (whereas the
first one had taken about eight months), collecting a great deal
of additional data as well. It would have been very difficult to
complete it in less time, because it was only through a prolonged
stay that I was able to gain the support of a sufficient number
of reliable informants to ensure the accuracy of the data. Sufficient time was also necessary for the continued close observation
of family life in the vicinity of my house.

Thus, I eventually solved the problem of getting both statistically adequate and sufficiently detailed data by first observing
closely a small number of families to determine what the significant variables would be, and then extending the sample for
these variables to include 465 persons (married and unmarried)
and their 625 marriages in two villages, all the while continuing
intensive observations of families in my immediate vicinity.

This was the central problem of my research design, and its
solution emerged slowly over time from a general and flexible
plan that allowed for later reassessments and new decisions as
I learned more and more about the people, their customs, and the
conditions under which I had to work. Anthropologists often
have to plan research for areas about which little is known, and
here a flexible research design seems most suitable as it permits
the researcher to develop a plan based on sufficient knowledge of
the conditions.

Passive or Adaptational Research

Environment. Access to Toro is easy by automobile, as one of
the main roads connects it directly with Kampala. Toro District
consists largely of a plateau, most of which is more than 4,000
feet above sea level. This altitude ensures a mild climate—an
average annual temperature of about 70° with very little varia-

tion—even though the equator passes through the southern part
of the district. The plateau is densely covered with bush, and in
some of the valleys overgrown forest conditions are found. Large
papyrus swamps and rocky granite outcrops are common. In the
central area in which I did research there are rolling grasslands
and occasional lines of grass-covered hills.

The most characteristic feature of the countryside of central
Toro is its ridges or hillsides, separated by the branches of a
river. The Toro live in scattered settlements on these ridges,
several of which make up what I have called a village. There
were ten such ridges in the first village I studied, covering an
area of over six square miles. There may be two or three such
villages in the smallest political unit, the parish, which has a
chief and a council. A village may be the responsibility of a
subchief, as was true of the second village I studied.

The people live scattered over the hillsides in rectangular
mud-and-wattle houses, usually within shouting distance of one
another. Most of the houses are grassroofed, though some of the
more affluent householders now have tin roofs, and a few even
have cement houses. Typically a house is surrounded by a banana
plantation and gardens consisting mainly of subsistence crops,
though a few cash crops are also grown. Water is obtained from
wells, or in the rainy season by catching rainwater from a tin
roof. Shops (selling matches, cigarettes, a few commercial drugs,
paraffin, candy, yard goods, a few canned goods, sugar, salt, tea,
and the like), markets for many kinds of food, including freshly
slaughtered meat, bars selling native beer, a medical dispensary,
schools, and the Christian missions are all within walking (or
cycling) distance.

Entry problems and initial copings. Professor Southall had written to the district commissioner of Toro to request permission
for me to carry out my study there. Accordingly, when I arrived in Toro I went directly to see the commissioner, who gave
me a letter of introduction to the county chief of Mwenge, the
area in which I wanted to begin my investigations. The next
day I drove out to Mwenge with my family to see the county
chief, who said he had no objections to my presence in the area,
although he wanted me to speak to his council.

With one of the subcounty chiefs serving as my interpreter,
I explained to the council that I was from EAISR, affiliated with
Makerere University College, that I was not from the government, though I had its permission to do my work, and that I
came as a friend and wanted to learn their language and their
customs so that I could write a book in which their customs and
their history would be preserved. Council members wanted me

to obtain permission from the native government as well as from the protectorate government, and expressed the hope that my book would also be published in their language (Rutoro) so that they and their children could benefit from it. They wanted to know if we would eat with them at the same table, and I assured them that we would; this was important as they felt that only friends would eat at the same table. Fortunately, I had already learned a well-known Rutoro proverb, which I now repeated for them; they enjoyed it and immediately taught us a new one. All in all everything went very well, and we were granted permission to do the study. We were made to feel welcome, and the whole thing went off much better than I had expected. But as I was to find out later, difficulties lay ahead.

Permission to do the study was granted quickly by the prime minister of Toro, but I did not think to get his permission in writing. I also made a courtesy visit to the Toro king. I made contact with local missionaries who were more than willing to help. One elderly Catholic priest who had been in the country for more than fifty years had some written documents, to which he gave me access.

It had been my intention to remain in government rest houses during the two months of introductory field work before returning to Kampala for the EAISR Conference in July, 1959. However, an assistant district commissioner with considerable experience in the area advised me to live in a tent to be closer to the people and to dissociate myself from the government whose officers lived in these rest houses while on tour in the rural areas. I took this advice and started making plans, the major question being where to pitch my tent.

I made arrangements to visit each of Mwenge's five sub-counties. The major factors in my choice of a subcounty were three. First, I wanted an area sufficiently close to the main road to Kampala that its inhabitants could be expected to show the effects of contact with the capital. Proximity to the road also meant that a medical dispensary would be located within a few miles, and this was important because, in addition to my wife, I also had with me our baby daughter. The second factor was whether the response I received when I visited the five subcounty headquarters was positive or negative. This included not only the response of the chiefs (all of whom were very cooperative), but also of the council members and the ordinary people who attended the discussions. The third factor was proximity to the county headquarters where I was later to attend various meetings and court sessions. I wanted to be far enough away to study rural life not dominated by the headquarters, and yet not be so far away that it would severely restrict the frequency with which I could get to headquarters for important meetings and court sessions. On the basis of these criteria, I decided to settle in the subcounty of Musale in which the county headquarters itself is located; it is right on the main road to Kampala, and I had received a favorable response from the people in this area.

The next problem was the choice of the exact area in which to pitch my tent. Again, a favorable response from the local people was a crucial factor, indeed, the decisive one. I knew that good rapport would be essential to obtain reliable data. In addition, however, I also wanted to settle in an area that had a combination of the different types of land tenure in Toro, so as to be able to investigate the differential effects of these upon marriage and family life. This ultimately proved to be very important, because, as I later discovered, approximately 85 percent of Toro's livestock was wiped out in rinderpest epidemics in the decade from 1910 to 1920, and ever since buying land in freehold tenure has been the major means of investing wealth.

We visited three sites, all fairly near the main road and all suggested by the chiefs. In two of the three, conditions for obtaining water were not good, nor were we made to feel welcome. The third site was the village we eventually chose, mainly because we were made to feel welcome and because the water conditions were better. We found out later, however, that our welcome was not shared by everyone, including the landowner on whose land the parish chief had suggested we pitch our tent. This landowner wanted me to get a letter of authorization from the prime minister, and he wanted to discuss the matter in the highest council of Toro and in other councils down through the hierarchy. I obtained the letter, which I had by then learned would also be useful in other situations, but the county chief and others advised me not to settle on the land in question as the owner was a trouble maker. Instead, they suggested I settle on crown land, which belongs to all the people, and on which I would not have to pay any rent. We agreed with this idea, and the parish chief allotted us an area near the council house on the main road. It was not the best place from which to observe family life, but it was the best I could do for the time being. I figured that I would be staying there for less than two months and hoped to move off the road and further into the village on my return from Kampala. In the meantime this rather neutral site allowed me to get some information about all areas of the parish on the basis of which I later selected the specific village in which I wanted to settle.

After almost a month in my tent on the road I suggested to the parish chief that, upon my return from Kampala, I would like to move into the village north of the main road. The matter was discussed at the next meeting of the parish council to which I presented my request. Some were for it and some against it, and I was informed that a final decision would be taken at the next council meeting. I was later told privately that the people liked me, but they were also afraid of me. Some of them thought that I was a government spy and had the intention of increasing their taxes and/or taking away their land. Again I discovered that those who had welcomed me warmly at the beginning did not represent the whole village.

I did my best to counteract these fears, mainly by learning to speak their language and by showing a genuine and friendly interest in their customs. I knew they especially liked the idea that I would write a book that would benefit their children by preserving their customs. Finally after a long discussion at the next council meeting I was granted permission to move into the village north of the road. Obtaining this permission was one of the most important tests of my entire field work experience. Until that time I was very unsure of myself and of how the field work would progress. Also thereafter I felt uncertain about the field work, especially as long as the research topic remained vaguely defined. As I got more data and was thus able to define the problem more specifically, I became more sure of myself. I wanted the people to like me and trust me—as this was the basis for good rapport—but I was never sure whether they did or not, because they were always very polite to Westerners. They were more afraid of me than anything else, and it was difficult to make headway at the beginning.

Housekeeping problems. With recommendations from the missionaries and chiefs we hired a houseboy to help with the cooking and laundering and a porter to fetch water and firewood. On the whole our relationships with them were good, though at the beginning there were some problems of communication and misunderstanding. For example, I once asked the houseboy to wash the car, and shortly thereafter we noticed that he was in bad spirits. He soon reported that he had never washed anyone's car before, and he felt that such work was beneath his dignity as a houseboy. I apologized, saying that customs in my country were different. From this experience I learned something of the strength of their ideas about status positions. On another occasion I asked the houseboy to clean my shoes. Eager to do a thorough job of it, he submerged my leather shoes in water. But these were minor problems. The main things to which one had to adjust were the lack of efficiency and the much slower pace of life. We did not really experience much culture shock. Both my wife and I had previously lived in a number of other foreign countries, and so we were fairly used to making the kind of adjustments that it was necessary for us to make in Uganda.

When we returned from the conference in Kampala, we decided to build a house because it was so crowded in the tent for a family of three, and also because a house would be more secure against the weather. We had to live in our tent for more than six weeks, however, for that was how long it took the men we hired to build two very small houses and dig a latrine. This was an exasperating example of the aforementioned slow pace of life. The houses were mud-and-wattle like the others in the village, and though I did not do an expert job of it I eventually put the tin roofs on myself to save both time and money. Tin roofs were important to us so that we could catch rainwater. The two small houses were connected by a porch on which we put a bench for visitors. We lived outside most of the time, and the porch was a nice place to interview informants. The smaller house $(10' \times 10')$ was a combination kitchen and storehouse, and the larger $(12' \times 12')$ served as office and bedroom.

Our daily life started very early in the morning when we were awakened by the roosters. We kept chickens for eating and bought milk from our neighbors. With the help of a houseboy-shambaboy we also grew some vegetables not available in the local markets and shops. We had no refrigerator, but that was no problem, for we ate meat as soon as we bought it and learned that bad eggs float in water. All drinking water had to be boiled and filtered for which we had the usual camp filter. Once we found a frog inside the filter, but that was an exception. We had no bathtub for ourselves, but we did have a plastic inflatable one for the baby.

On the whole, our health problems were not serious. We took precautions against taeniasis by cooking our meat in a pressure cooker, and we avoided eating meat at other people's homes. As all meat had to be thoroughly cooked, its variety was limited to stew, tongue, liver, and chicken. The pressure cooker was one of the most valuable items we took to the field. Although we all took prophylactic pills every day, this did not completely prevent us from contracting malaria, a mild case of which each of us (including the child) had once or twice. In the late afternoon we arranged the mosquito nets over the beds in preparation for the evening, and in the evening we read or worked by the light of a pressure lamp.

Having a small child in the field was not as much of a problem as one might assume. She was old enough to eat the same food as we did, and the climate was healthy—plenty of sunshine and fresh air. We did have to watch her, of course, as, for example, we once found a snake in the tent. We also had to make sure that she kept on her socks and shoes to prevent her from getting jiggers on her feet. We all had jiggers until we learned from the missionaries to spread insecticide powder inside our shoes.

We also had other provoking but minor troubles. For example, we had mice in our house that ate our shoes and made noise at night. We tried all kinds of poisons and traps with little success. Finally, our houseboy found the larger mice and killed them with a broom, and put the baby mice out in the sunshine where they died. Termites ate a few of our books. One day we spilled some milk on the dirt floor, and the next day we had an army of red ants going through the kitchen.

Rapport gaining: problems and solutions. Many people were suspicious of me from the beginning, and I attempted to gain their confidence and establish good rapport in several ways. I spoke to the county, subcounty, and parish councils as already described. Parish chiefs in whose councils I had not spoken stopped me in the market and asked if I would speak to the crowd, which I readily agreed to do. From the very beginning I exchanged gifts and invitations to lunch with chiefs and other notables, and then gradually with other informants as I met and began to develop relationships with them. A feast with several chiefs was the first occasion on which we had to eat with our hands; we were rather clumsy at the beginning, but with practice became as adept as others.

My wife joined the women's community-development club and eventually developed a very good relationship with the club leader, who became one of our best informants. She taught the women knitting and English, and I gave some English lessons to the men. In return the women taught her how to make bead necklaces. My wife also developed a friendly relationship with a pot maker who, as we found out later, wanted a ride to Kampala! In the meantime, however, she was a useful informant.

Like most relationships, the researcher-informant relationship is often based ultimately on some kind of exchange, either clearly present or hoped for in the future. We wanted reliable information, and we offered something in return. In the beginning we had a beer party for a large number of people, and later we offered beer in our home to our best informants. I gave rides into town to fellow villagers, brought back their goats from the market and their children from school, and took emergency cases to the medical dispensary. We were careful to give out no medicine stronger than aspirin, for if someone to whom we had given some stronger medicine had fallen seriously ill or died, we would almost certainly have been blamed. In fact, I eventually learned so much about most people in the village that some thought I had powers of witchcraft.

Another way in which I established rapport was through the presence of my family. The villagers had all seen white men before: British Government officers and European and American missionaries. Although there were some women missionaries, teachers, and nurses in the area, no white family had ever lived among them in their village, and few had ever even seen a white child, much less one who played happily with their own children. This attracted visitors and neighbors and helped to break down barriers of communication, alleviate suspicion, and gain rapport. My daughter occasionally served as my visiting card; when she wandered into someone's house or backyard, I was not far behind.

I made myself visible at the shops and bars and encouraged informants to talk by offering them cigarettes and buying them beer. I attended the council meetings every week and regularly showed up at public ceremonies and functions, both to demonstrate my genuine interest in their affairs and to observe what was happening. We participated in their lives in every way we could. We even caught, cooked, and ate grasshoppers, considered a delicacy in Uganda. Like my neighbors I worked in my garden, and many people appreciated that and "thanked me for working," a common expression. My wife and I were each accepted into a prominent clan (i.e., two different clans), and we were called by Rutoro nicknames, like everyone else.

My object was to carve a niche and a role for myself as a man genuinely interested in the people and in their customs, a role that would be clearly different and distinct from that of the district officers. I had been suspected of being a government spy, so I did everything possible to repudiate my similarity to, and my association with, these officers.

Active Research

Rapport achieved and problems of rapport maintenance. Given the rapport I achieved, I had no difficulty in attending all public ceremonies, meetings, and other functions. It was more difficult to gain admittance to ostensibly private meetings, as I was rarely invited to these except by close neighbors. After I had been there for a few months, however, I was tipped off by close informants of the time and place of certain meetings, marriage negotiations, for example, in which I was particularly interested. When I heard that a prospective bridegroom was going to request a man's daughter in marriage, I just showed up at the appropriate time and place. As guests must be shown proper hospitality and respect in this culture, I was never thrown out, and was usually given a position of honor.

I could not conduct formal interviews with most people or take notes in front of them; this was possible only with the relatively few educated people who understood my work. Others became suspicious when I started asking questions about their personal marital histories. Christians did not like to admit, for example, that they had at one time (or even still had) two or more wives. But in those cases where I had learned the truth from friends, neighbors, or relatives of the interviewee, I would confront him with the fact, although always in a joking manner, by mentioning, for instance, the first name of a former wife. At that point the interviewee—realizing that I knew too much already—usually told me everything for fear that his enemies would tell me even worse things about him. Although he might insist that he had lived with this woman for only six months and that he had hardly counted her as a real wife, he had at least confirmed my information. Later, I checked his story on the length of time, coming back to confront him again and again if necessary. Although I visited most people only once or twice—after first learning as much as possible about them from others—I had to go back to see some of them as many as five times until I was satisfied that all the data were accurate.

If I was getting a great deal of information all at once and was having difficulty remembering the details, I simply went out to the latrine and recorded the data. I also employed an elderly and very respected former parish chief as my assistant, and after each visit he helped me to remember and record the information accurately, as well as to assess its reliability. Although he said very little and asked no questions, his very presence helped to provide an atmosphere in which people felt more at ease and in which the interviewee was more likely to tell the truth. My assistant knew the villagers well and had previously told me all he knew about them. He also informed me, of course, whenever he thought someone was lying. I always had three or four sources of information for each person's marital history, but whenever I had reason to question the accuracy of the data, I got additional sources, sometimes as many as eight for a single person. One time the villagers found out that a man was secretly giving me information and threatened to burn his house down. He stopped giving me information for a while, and nothing ever happened to his house.

Although I did most of the interviewing myself, my wife helped interview the women in the first village. Fortunately, I was also able to interview women with no difficulty, usually even if the husband was not at home; it was only the older women who told me to come back later when the man of the house would be at home. It should be remembered that I did not conduct regular formal interviews as such; from the point of view of the informants, I was merely paying a friendly visit as a neighbor, although of course they knew I was interested in their customs. I used these visits to elicit information not only about the interviewee's particular marital history, but also about his attitudes towards bridewealth, polygyny, the birth of children out of wedlock, and Christian marriage.

I also collected data outside the villages. I obtained data on migration by informally interviewing labor migrants from Toro while they were in Kampala, as well as by obtaining information in Toro District itself. Having established a good relationship with the prime minister, I requested and was granted special permission to attend the meetings of the Toro District Council in Fort Portal. Historical documentation was obtained from the missions, the county and subcounty headquarters, and the government files in both Fort Portal and Kampala.

Data-getting techniques. One of the settings I found most useful for data collection was an inheritance ceremony. It provided an opportunity to observe the decision-making process for important family matters. I noted for example that a subchief from a distant village, who was not a member of the clan of the deceased (though he was a half-brother, having the same mother), had a very important influence on the division of property. I was able to check verbal reports concerning the proportion of property inherited by women. I saw how the widow herself managed to determine her own future, sometimes refusing to be inherited by a brother of the deceased. I saw how outstanding debts and old conflicts were brought to light and resolved so that the next generation could live in peace.

Another important setting for my study was, of course, a marriage. First, through a series of negotiations I observed how affinal relations were established, and how the amount of bridewealth was set. Later at the wedding itself I saw, among other things, how important distinctions were made between the bride's people and the groom's people, and a series of rituals that provided important clues to the meaning of marriage for the Toro. I also attended a number of other kinds of ceremonies, including funerals, twin ceremonies, and a seance of a spirit-possession cult, but these were less directly related to the main purpose of my study.

Parish council meetings were combined with court sessions, and these provided another useful setting for the collection of data. I noted, for example, the kinds of problems with which the community was concerned, judicial procedure, sanctions available to the chief, and the degree of his authority over others. Although not many family cases came to court at this level, those that did revealed such underlying conflicts as jealousy between co-wives. Such conflicts did not always come to light in the more formal higher courts, where I heard a larger number of family cases. Occasionally I was lucky enough to witness the settlement of a dispute in the very informal setting of a group of neighbors and old men specifically called together for that purpose.

The village bars were frequented mainly by men, as they were not considered respectable meeting places for women. Nevertheless a few women were always there, and it was important for me to know who they were and to listen to the men's comments about them. The bar was also a good place for making informal contacts that were later followed up by home visits and invitations to my home. In this sense my front porch was also a useful setting for data collection. When I was living on the main road, the local shop there was a useful place to pick up the news of the day, but I later found specific informants who provided better information.

There were also a number of places outside the village where I collected data on occasion. These included medical dispensaries, a debating club, an exhibition sponsored by the Community Development Women's Clubs, the Toro District Council, and an annual county conference at which problems of marriage and family life were discussed. I also visited the schools from which I eventually obtained a series of essays by senior secondary students concerning their attitudes toward family customs, new and old.

Once I decided to do the sample of marital histories, it became a basic and regular activity. Indeed, it was good to have the commitment to finish the sample as it forced me to go out and visit people every day. To complement and check the data I was getting from these personal histories, I also collected data—with the help of an assistant—from the records of the parish chief (especially the amount of poll tax paid, which was based on an inventory of property plus a salary statement), the subcounty chief (registers of births, marriages, and deaths), and the missionaries (Christian marriages and number of adherents). At the same time I visited and interviewed these and other notables.

At almost all times an assistant and/or my wife was copying, and if necessary translating, some sort of documentation. These included those already mentioned above plus records of the debating society, district and county conferences, various files in the office of the district commissioner, and very importantly, judgments and other essential facts from the records of evidence of over 1,200 native court cases dealing with various aspects of marriage and family life. In order to help me interpret all the court data, I followed a few cases from their inception at the local level up through the appeal courts.

My participation in ceremonies and meetings, both public and private, was never so deep that I lost my perspective as an observer. The first time I drank native beer it went to my head rather quickly, and thereafter I was more careful. To obtain additional data I had my assistant record his own activities as a participant observer, including sufficiently important activities that occurred when he was off duty. For a period of a few weeks he also recorded the activities by the hour of each member of a few families living in my immediate vicinity. Among other things this was directed toward getting data on the differential economic contributions of men and women.

My various activities brought me in contact with a series of different kinds of informants. At the very beginning I had to rely on government officers, missionaries, and educated Toro. Later my employees also served as informants. Little by little I developed a series of reliable informants in the village who represented various status positions in the society: men and women, young and old, chiefs and commoners, educated and illiterate, religious and pagan, landowners, tenants, and those on crown land, teachers, shopkeepers, cultivators, cattle owners, porters, labor migrants, and others.

The five or six families of neighbors in my immediate vicinity also constituted a special category of informants. These were the people I visited most often, and to whom I regularly brought gifts. Eventually I could drop in on them informally at any time; they took little notice of me, continuing to go about their regular affairs. I also showed up if I heard any arguments or trouble! Very late one night I heard the eleven-year-old daughter of a neighbor screaming and showed up in time to find her receiving a severe beating from her stepmother, an event about which I would not otherwise have heard anything. I proceeded of course to inquire into the incident. These were the neighbors who also invited me and my wife to witness such family affairs as a birth, a child-naming ceremony, and a marriage, and who invited me to join an ad hoc group of men to settle a dispute between a daughter and her husband.

In contrast to these neighbors, I also had a number of

casual visitors, the reliability of whose information was difficult to judge. The entire village was another category of informants when I took a census. After several months I found a few special informants who were willing to provide information secretly about the marital histories of their friends, relatives, and neighbors. Establishing such a relationship was risky. As already mentioned, one of them was threatened with arson. One of them could have betrayed me, which could have led to my being ejected from the village, but they proved essential to my gaining reliable data about all those in the sample, which also constituted a separate category of informants. The labor migrants I visited and interviewed informally in Kampala made up yet another group of informants.

Techniques for recording and storing data. I kept a daily journal in which I recorded most of the data, especially at the beginning. Daily entries ranged anywhere from a paragraph to several pages. I typed an original and two carbons, sending one carbon to Kampala to keep Professor Southall informed of my progress and also for safekeeping. On the second carbon my wife copied the subject categories into which I had classified the data—paragraph by paragraph—on the original. Then she cut the second carbon into paragraphs and classified the clippings in a subject notebook, making appropriate cross-references. The system worked well for a while, but ultimately it became too time consuming for both of us. I continued to record all the data but did not have time to classify them.

What one needs, I think, is a technique of recording data that is sufficiently systematic so that it is possible to know and to find relatively easily the kinds of data already collected (e.g., so as to determine what is still needed), and yet not be overly time consuming. We eventually worked out a better system for recording data from the marital-history sample. With the aid of the chiefs I drew a map and put every house in the village on it, numbering each homestead. Then I started a loose-leaf file with several sheets of paper for each homestead. All data on the sample were typed directly on the sheets for the appropriate household by number and then cross-referenced in the daily journal. In that way all information about people in the same household was kept together, and I still had a record of what happened on each day. Before visiting a household I gathered as much information as possible from several sources about all members of the household in question. The different sources were compared, and the essential facts plus missing data and discrepancies were noted in a small pocket-sized notebook, so that I could easily refresh my memory just before walking into the house for a visit. Right after the visit I typed the data on its appropriate sheet in the file.

I also used a series of blue notebooks in which for each of a hundred pages there was also an extra sheet for a carbon copy. Again the carbons were sent to Kampala for safekeeping. These notebooks were mainly used in public conferences, debates, the courts, and in interviews with educated people when I could take notes in front of them. I noted in my daily journal the topic, persons interviewed, and page numbers in the blue notebook.

Essays, court cases, and other kinds of documentation were recorded on regular lined paper. I usually had no choice in the case of the essays, but it would have been better to record the court data (and the essays where possible) on the so-called McBee cards, which have a series of holes on all four sides. This would have permitted a relatively rapid content analysis of the data using a punch and needle, and the data would have been recorded in a more permanent form.

I used two still cameras (one for black and white and one for color) plus an 8 mm. movie camera small enough to fit into my pocket. During the first few months I used the cameras very little so as not to arouse suspicion. After I had established myself in the village, however, I usually took them to the various ceremonies and meetings I attended. If it was a private affair I obtained permission, rarely denied, to use them. I used my movie camera, for example, to film my neighbors making banana beer. I stored all films, as well as notes and extra supplies, in a metal box.

I did not have a tape recorder, but given the few occasions on which I could have used it and the necessity of transcription, it would not have been very useful.

Bowing Out

I made it known several weeks in advance that I would soon be leaving. Several people wanted to buy parts of my house, e.g., the tin roof and the roof poles, and the wooden doors and windows. I immediately agreed, which made it clear to them that I had no intention of attempting to establish myself permanently in the area and that I was making no attempt to claim any land. Before leaving I paid a visit to the parish chief to thank him and say good-by. My attempt to conduct myself properly throughout my entire stay—rather than anything I did in the final few days—will make it possible, I believe, for me or for another researcher to return to this area and be welcome.

Summary and Evaluation

After twenty months in Uganda (sixteen months actually in Toro) I had collected enough data to answer most of the questions posed in my first conference paper, as well as the questions of broader scope that emerged later. Limited space makes it impossible to provide here the answers to all these questions, but I can briefly summarize the main trends.[2]

In the nineteenth century Toro had strong social institutions backed by sanctions that ensured a high degree of conformity to norms. Marriage was closely related to the social system in a number of ways, including the fact that it established political and other relations between groups. Conjugal institutions expressed status inequalities, especially in the relationship of a woman with her father and with her husband. The pattern was one in which a woman was transferred at an early age from the control of her father to that of her husband, and polygyny ensured that there was always a sufficient supply of husbands. Though they remained subordinate to their husbands, women could and did receive a considerable measure of respect, especially as they grew older and their children married.

By 1935 the ordered existence of the previous century was being disturbed in several ways. British rule had been established, facilitating freedom of movement, eventually as far as Kampala for some, and Christian missions had been set up in various parts of the country. In the face of these new circumstances, traditional sanctions weakened, and the breach of norms increased. This led to conflict in many institutions, including conjugal ones.

The essence of the old pattern in which a woman remained subordinate first to her father and then to her husband remained unchanged. It was only in the degree of her subordination—now less complete—that there was any alteration. Slight though this change was at first, it was a significant first step toward the greater equality between spouses already being encouraged by the church. Upper- and lower-class women were following different paths toward that goal, but eventually all women were to achieve new relationships with men.

By 1950 far-reaching changes fostered a growing individualism. Particularly significant were the alternatives open to daughters and wives to escape from those fathers and husbands who attempted to subordinate them to an intolerable degree.

---

[2] A more detailed analysis is contained in an earlier article (1966), and a full account appears in my forthcoming book, *Toro Marriage* (n.d.).

Though conflicts between spouses produced individual suffering and hardship, including divorces, they also led over a period of time to greater equality in the husband-wife relationship in Toro society as a whole. Indeed, in view of the strength of male opinion, that goal could be achieved only through considerable conflict, which was sometimes a more effective means than higher education.

Young women were beginning to hope for and expect a new kind of relationship with their husbands, and a few were attaining it. Although the older generation changed very little, the majority had moved forward along the arduous path toward greater equality.

At the present time, education in Toro, including that for girls, is increasing. Women's clubs are very active and play an important educational role. About half the population profess Christianity, but relatively few are deeply convinced.

The majority in central Toro are subsistence farmers. Near the town of Fort Portal, the district headquarters of Toro, increasing numbers are going into wage employment, and this has led to a strong emphasis on individualism. Both men and women, especially from central Toro, are migrating in increasing numbers to the large urban center of Kampala. This migration is related to the decrease in male authority in the family, and more generally to the conflict of goals between the men and their families.

Democratic concepts have been slow to gain a foothold in Toro. Hierarchical ideas still remain important, though they are not as pervasive as in the past. The extended family and the neighborhood have become more important in the social organization than the lineage. Class distinctions are more evident now than they were a decade ago, though they are more apparent near Fort Portal than in the outlying areas. Today the distinction between social classes—partly a heritage from the past—is based largely on wealth and higher education.

The old conjugal institutions of customary marriage and bridewealth may disappear in Toro. If this happens, it will be of little functional significance, as there are now other conjugal institutions to replace them. The decrease in the importance of bridewealth is a reflection of a major and very significant change in the father-daughter relationship as regards marriage: to an increasing extent, a girl, not her father, transfers rights in herself to her husband.

Polygyny remains about as common as it was in the previous period, especially in the rural areas, and this appears to be associated with its continued functional importance. If there is any decrease in the institution, it is near the town, where women are somewhat more highly educated, have greater opportunities to become financially independent, and therefore more often refuse to become second wives.

The number and percentage of children born out of wedlock has considerably increased over the past half-century, a trend clearly associated with the increasing independence of women. Women have considerable power to name the father of their child, and this enhances their status vis-à-vis men.

At the present time concubinage is by far the most frequent type of union being contracted. Its high frequency is associated with the desire for it by young people and with the inability or unwillingness of the woman's father to stop it. What young people really want (women at an earlier age than men) is a permanent and harmonious conjugal relationship. The institution of concubinage allows them to strive with a minimum of conflict to achieve this aim, because they can easily continue searching for the most suitable mate. This aim is often very difficult to achieve in view of the rapidly changing relationship between husband and wife. Concubinage also allows that relationship to continue to change with a minimum of strain, even though there has often been considerable conflict.

Only a small minority of people, mainly of the upper class, now contract ring marriages. A major conflict has arisen between the desire, on the one hand, to follow the rules of Christianity and also to gain the prestige of a ring marriage, and the reluctance, on the other hand, to commit oneself to a permanent union without sufficient confidence that the relationship with the first spouse chosen will be harmonious and successful. This conflict is associated with the rapidly changing role expectations of husband and wife. Ring marriage is ill adapted to the present needs of young people striving to achieve a permanent relationship with someone whose expectations of the husband-wife relationship are fairly similar to their own. This largely accounts for the small number of people now contracting this type of union. Even some of those who do so find it necessary to modify ring marriage to suit their own needs better.

The enhancing of the status of women in Toro has important implications for marriage. Married women need no longer view the status of divorcée as unattractive, and girls who have never been married may not be very anxious to get married. Unmarried women can still produce children outside marriage; indeed, that they can do so is related to their rising status. Most women prefer marriage, but as the unmarried state can be so attractive, a conflict arises for women who desire the advantages of both.

The man is still the dominant partner in the husband-wife relationship; it is the degree of subordination that is at issue. On the whole, men are successful in their attempt to assert their dominance, because if one woman will not accept it, another one usually will. The vast majority of women do not demand absolute equality with men, but rather a sufficient measure of it to ensure that they obtain their fair share of whatever life has to offer, including greater freedom and responsibility to participate in decisions that affect them and their families. These demands often involve considerable conflict and strain, but conflict is an inevitable part of the process that has been going on now for half a century or more—that of redefining the roles of the sexes in relation to one another.

My study of Toro fills a major gap in the ethnography and history of the Interlacustrine Bantu area of East Africa and presents an analysis of changes in marriage and family life in Toro. The data are now available on punch cards and are thus in a form that can easily be used by other researchers for comparative purposes. Also, they are sufficiently rich to form the basis of at least one more book (now in preparation), this one on occupational mobility in Toro.

If I were to do the same project today, I would place greater emphasis on language study so that I could speak the language fluently just as soon as possible. No other factor is more important for gaining and maintaining rapport and for obtaining reliable data. Also, the language is an essential type of data in itself. I would try also to make time to add to the sample a third village, relatively remote and far from the towns and main roads, to serve as a check on the rapidity of change in Toro conjugal institutions. Finally, I would add a psychologist or psychological anthropologist to the team (or obtain appropriate training myself) because of the ultimate importance of psychological data to a comprehensive understanding of the processes of social change.

PART II: UGANDA

Problem, Theory, and Research Design

The major aims of the second part of my study were to find out how widespread the Toro customs were in the rest of the country, and what new customs, attitudes, and values would be discovered elsewhere in Uganda. By this time I had a clear idea of the specific problems involved, and I had answers to most of my questions for one society. Thus, it was possible to devise a much more explicit research design for the country as a whole. (Even so, I later made an important change in my plans.) My major problem was how to cover a whole country in a short time (about eight months from September, 1961, to April, 1962) and still get sufficient and reliable data that would be both representative and theoretically relevant.

It seemed obvious that in the short time remaining I could not possibly do research in all fifteen or so districts of Uganda, which contain peoples of more than twenty numerically important societies. Thus some selection and concentration of effort was necessary, but what were the criteria of choice to be? The diversity was so great that I could not pick a representative sample in the strict sense, but I wanted to include societies that would at least exemplify that diversity.

Although Uganda is a small country, it contains societies of three important language and ethnic groupings—Bantu, Nilotic, and Nilo-Hamitic—and I included at least one of each of these in my sample. There are four major political and geographical divisions (provinces) in Uganda, and again I included one society from each. I also selected societies from among the most populous districts, with the ultimate result that the populations of the four districts chosen plus Toro constituted more than 40 percent of the total population of Uganda. This included Buganda—an entire province in itself and by far the most populous society in the country.

In addition to the above criteria I also took into consideration the existing ethnographic and historical literature on Uganda. I had come to realize the importance of the past for understanding the present, including the direction and rate of social change, and thus I tried to avoid selecting societies for which there were little reliable historical data. A number of good ethnographies by professional anthropologists had already been published for several contemporary Uganda societies, and others were in preparation. It was my intention to contact these anthropologists later to obtain, if possible, additional unpublished data. But there were a few populous districts in Uganda in which no anthropologist had worked recently, and this was one factor in my choice of two societies—Teso and Lango.

A factor in the choice of another district, Kigezi, was that I already had some knowledge of the people from a previous project in applied anthropology (carried out between the intensive study of Toro and the beginning of the comparative research on the rest of Uganda). Their language was sufficiently close to Rutoro that I could understand them and make myself understood.

But more important than the above mentioned criteria was the theoretical relevance of the societies chosen. The strategic selection of cases because of their theoretical relevance has recently been referred to as "scope sampling" (Willer, 1967: 114), and this is what I did in Uganda. Professor Southall had distinguished two main traditional family systems in Uganda, which he referred to as Nilotic and Interlacustrine, Toro being classified as the latter (1960:209–210). The Nilotic system is characterized by a fairly high bridewealth, complete transfer of the wife's procreative capacity to the husband and his lineage, close identification of the wife with her husband's group, rare divorce, virtually no property owned by the wife, and localized descent groups. In the Interlacustrine system, bridewealth is much lower, the husband does not completely own the reproductive powers of his wife, who also maintains strong links to her own descent group, divorce is more frequent, some women own property, and descent groups are not localized to any large degree.

It was clear, therefore, that I had to include a Nilotic society in my study to constitute a contrast to the Toro. I chose Lango because it was an excellent example of this type of society, and because no anthropologist had worked there recently, although we do have an excellent early ethnography (Driberg, 1923). Moreover, Lango is one of the more populous districts, it is in Northern Province, and the people speak a Nilotic language.

With Toro and Lango as clear examples of the two main types of family system, I needed a society to constitute the intermediate spot on the continuum for future hypothesis-testing. Also, my research in Toro had convinced me that—at least for the problems I was studying—the status of women was a crucial variable, and it could more easily be put onto a continuum than a general family type made up of several different factors. A paper I had written on property rights of Uganda women (1960b), plus my applied research among the Kigezi peoples, led me to assume that the status of women in Kigezi was intermediate to that of women in Toro (where it was high) and Lango (where it was low). I have now analyzed some court data (1969) that provide further support for this assumption. I chose Kigezi also partly because it is a populous Bantu society in Western Province about which I already had some knowledge and language facility.

I included two more societies, one from each of the two main types of family system, to increase the size of my sample and to provide a check on data obtained in Toro and Lango. These two additions, Teso and Buganda, also provided an opportunity for a controlled comparison within each main type. That is, by holding type of family system constant, I could vary other important variables. From the literature I knew that Teso had a Nilotic family type, and—also like Lango—it was at the lower end of the status-of-women continuum. However, both the British Administration and the Christian missions had established themselves at an earlier date in Teso than in Lango, which was theoretically important because of the emphasis in my study on factors of change. I chose Teso also partly because it is a populous, Nilo-Hamitic-speaking society in Eastern Province in which no professional anthropologist has done intensive research.

Both Buganda and Toro are clear examples of the Interlacustrine family type, and the women in both are also at the higher end of the status continuum. But again the agents of change, especially the Christian missions, had penetrated and established themselves sooner in Buganda than in Toro. Furthermore, the economy has developed at a much faster rate in Buganda than in Toro (and indeed faster than in the rest of the country in general). I discuss the effect of these and other factors in my recent comparative analysis of the status of women in Buganda and Toro (1969). Buganda is a Bantu society and, as already mentioned, constitutes an entire province in itself and is by far the most populous society in the country. I selected Buganda even though I realized that because of political disturbances at the time I would probably not be able to get into the rural areas to collect data. For the rural data I assumed that I could rely on the work of a number of anthropologists who have done research there, and thus in Buganda I concentrated my efforts in and around the city of Kampala. Furthermore, there are good historical data and an excellent early ethnography (Roscoe, 1911) for Buganda.

Having selected four societies in which to do comparative research, my next problems were what kinds of data to collect, and how to ensure that the data would be both sufficient and reliable, given the time and resources available. To obtain enough data for my purposes in the short time available, I had to use as many assistants as I could afford. But what kinds of important data could assistants collect that I would consider sufficiently reliable?

The study of social change had become a very important part of the whole project, and thus it was essential to obtain historical data. In Africa, there are precious few historical documents from which one can obtain primary data. Among the most important of these are the court records, which are rich in information about attitudes, actions, values, and norms. Moreover, this fascinating record of culture has been written by Africans themselves, which is true for very few—if any—other historical documents, certainly no others that are so rich in the data of daily living and so abundant and continuous over the years. In short, court records constitute a gold mine of primary data.

In view of their great importance, I decided to collect as much court data as possible. I could easily train assistants to do this in very little time, as long as they could write legibly and translate well into English. To obtain sufficiently qualified assistants I had to pay them well, but the result fully justified the expense. I was so convinced of the importance of these data that I spent everything I could to obtain them, and this was a drain on the budget, because at one point I had seven assistants to pay. To further ensure the reliability of the data, I supervised the assistants very carefully until I was sure they were working properly.

I collected a second major type of data through a series of interviews with reliable and knowledgeable people, who were sufficiently educated to understand my work and usually very willing to provide information. For this purpose I devised an open-ended questionnaire, which is reproduced in the appendix.

With the cooperation of senior-secondary and teacher-training-college teachers I collected student essays on selected aspects of marriage and family customs, new and old, including their own attitudes and aspirations. This was aimed at getting data on the trend of contemporary change and the ideas of the coming generation. I collected more than 200 essays.

The plan also called for me to obtain any additional historical documents that I could find. These included copies of by-laws passed by the various district councils, letters, and other memoranda that could indicate the influence or lack of it of the native governments on marriage and family life.

Finally, it was my intention to live for several weeks in a rural village in each of the societies (excluding Buganda) as a participant observer. I hoped to attend weddings and participate in various other marriage and family affairs. I wanted to observe and question people in all walks of life in order to try to get a feeling for what marriage and the family meant to various segments of each population. I planned to attend as many court sessions as possible, particularly those dealing with marriage and family cases, both to obtain current data and to provide a background with which to interpret and evaluate the existing court records.

The execution of the research design outlined above called for a considerable amount of careful organization. In making arrangements I was very fortunate to have the willing cooperation of the district officers of the British Government. No matter where I went in Uganda, I found them to be extremely helpful. I had written to them in advance, requesting permission to do the study and outlining my needs. Permission was granted without delay, and they not only took care of necessary preparations in terms of housing or permits to pitch my tent, but also helped me to find useful contacts and arrange interviews.

Thus the research had been fairly carefully planned in advance. This did not prevent me, however, from making the following important change: While in Lango I made arrangements to travel around to various regions of the district, and I noted that at one point my travels would take me very close to the border of the neighboring district, Acholi. I decided to make a short three-day trip to the Acholi capital just to pick up copies of by-laws and any other available relevant documents, arrange to have students write essays, and then interview as many people as time permitted. As Acholi is also a Nilotic society, my basic intention was to try to check quickly the assumption that Lango could serve as a fairly typical example of the Nilotic type of family system.

I wrote to the District Commissioner of Acholi to make arrangements, mentioning the sort of people I would like to interview. With admirable efficiency he saw to it that the little time I had would be well spent. When I arrived I was handed an agenda of appointments that made it possible in less than three days to complete eleven interviews of about two hours each with some of the most important personalities in the district, as well as others with special competence in the area of my study. Furthermore, I discovered some surprising and very significant facts that convinced me that I could not easily accept the assumption that Lango marriage and family customs were typical of Nilotic societies in Uganda. For example, all informants, including senior judges, agreed that a court will only rarely grant a divorce, and that marriage cannot be terminated outside of court. In other parts of Uganda the divorce issue is almost always settled outside of court, and such cases as appear in court are in effect debts for the return of the bridewealth.

Having learned so much of importance in so little time, I decided to add a new dimension to the research design, namely a quick trip of three to four days to each of the remaining districts of Uganda to do what I had done in Acholi. I wanted to make sure that I would not miss anything else of such major significance. Also, a short visit to each district would provide me with a little background to evaluate the existing literature on these districts. Given the kind of cooperation that I had received from the district officers, I figured that I could do the remaining ten or so districts in about six weeks. In the end, therefore, my entire study of Uganda comprised three levels: an intensive study of Toro, major comparisons in four other strategically selected districts, and finally a quick survey in all remaining districts of the country. Thus, even with a more explicit research design I still made an important change of plans. This suggests that in doing research in relatively unknown areas anthropologists need to remain flexible while working within the framework of a general plan.

Adaptational Research

Environment. Environmental conditions in Uganda generally, at least insofar as they could significantly affect an anthropologist's research, are not very different from those in Toro. It is relatively easy to obtain access to any of the towns by automobile, and essential supplies are available in all these towns. The British Government had established a fairly uniform political hierarchy (including counties and subcounties) in each district. This meant that I was able easily to collect court data that were clearly comparable from one district to another. It also meant that there were recognized spokesmen in each district from whom it was possible to get information as well as access to any existing documents.

The majority of the people live in the rural areas, though there is at least one town in each district that serves as the government headquarters and as the center for missionary activities, schools, commerce, social clubs if any, and the like. In practice this meant that I could organize my survey research around the country in terms of short visits to these towns, where I was then able to interview most of the people from whom I would be likely to get reliable information. Occasionally, an old chief had retired to his rural home and I went to interview him there. In the four districts in which I did major comparisons and in which I lived in the rural areas, the people were not so scattered that it was difficult to contact them.

Entry problems and initial copings. While in Kampala I wrote to the district commissioner of Lango, explained who I was and briefly what I wanted to do, and requested his permission. I also asked for his help in obtaining assistants and in arranging accommodation in a local rest house, though I indicated that I would also bring my tent. I received an encouraging reply and made preparations for the trip.

When I arrived in the Lango capital, Lira, one of the assistant district commissioners had already screened a number of applicants for positions as my assistants. I interviewed the two best ones and hired them both, one to work on the court records and the other to serve as my interpreter. It did not take me more than a day to inspect the court records, decide what I wanted translated, and train my first assistant to do the job.

The next problem was to find a nearby rural village in which I could settle for a few weeks. I wanted to participate in village life and yet not be so far from Lira that it would be difficult to get into the town to interview important personalities and to supervise the work of my assistant.

There were several temporary rest houses in villages within fifteen miles of Lira. The crucial consideration in selecting one of these would be to find some relatively influential person in the local community who could understand my work, help to overcome suspicion among the villagers, and introduce me to important people in the area. The district commissioner recommended a man who lived some thirteen miles from Lira. I met the man the next day, and he agreed to help me.

A few days after my arrival in his village, I learned that customs varied in different parts of the district. I checked this information and found that there seemed to be a distinction between eastern and western Lango. Consequently, I decided to visit and attend court sessions in a village in each region. I also arranged to have my assistants translate court records from the subcounty courts in both of the villages. I had not originally intended to spend much time on the lower courts, but the possibility of discovering important differences between the two regions convinced me that I should spend more time. Fortunately, one of my assistants was from eastern Lango, and he helped me to gain entry into and information about this distant and very rural area of the district. In western Lango I had no choice but to go through official channels; I was received politely, but not as warmly as in the eastern part of the district.

I used special contacts wherever possible to gain entry and establish rapport, because it would have been extremely difficult and time consuming to attempt to establish good rapport on my own, given the very limited time at my disposal and my lack (outside of Toro and Kigezi) of language facility. In the three to five weeks I had in each of the major comparison districts, I spent most of my time either interviewing people who would be likely to provide reliable information because they understood my work, or I personally witnessed relevant interaction (e.g., in court or at weddings) and thus obtained primary data directly.

In Teso and Kigezi I used the general approach described above for gaining entry and rapport in Lango. I made no attempt to settle in a village in Buganda, because political upheavals at that time would have made research hazardous and information highly unreliable. In Teso, although I obtained plenty of reliable data in interviews and collected some excellent data from the court records, I was less successful on the level of participant observation, because I was unable to establish a special contact. The district commissioner had warned me from the beginning that he could be of little assistance in helping me to gain the confidence of the Teso people, and although the secretary general and the chairman of the district council in Teso promised to find someone to help me, in fact they never did. I think this may have had something to do with certain political problems in Teso at the time.

In Kigezi I hardly needed a "friend," nor did I need an interpreter because I had already done some research among these people and had sufficient language facility to communicate with them directly. I have already emphasized the importance of knowing the language, and in this case it clearly made a significant difference in the ease with which I was able to establish rapport.

Housekeeping problems. I had to be very mobile, as I traveled relatively rapidly from one society to the next, especially in the final survey when I spent only three to four days in each district. At the same time I had to be prepared for the contingency that I would find no available accommodation, and thus I was forced to carry a considerable amount of camping equipment, including a tent, cooking utensils, lamps, and beds, to accommodate both myself and my loyal houseboy-cook.[3] Often we were able to stay at a government rest house, though on other occasions we had to pitch our tent.

As there were few mechanics available, and then only in the main towns, I had to learn something of the trade myself, and carried all necessary tools and spare parts with me. I had a secondhand, seven-year-old van, which I had to keep in very good running condition, considering the long distances that we traveled over rough roads.

---

[3] During the comparative study of the rest of Uganda, my family remained in Kampala, where our second and third children were born.

As I traveled across the country I was able to buy essential food in shops and markets, though the diet was not very varied. I brought some canned goods with me from Kampala as they were cheaper there and sometimes not available in small shops in the countryside. Water was not usually a problem as we always tried to pitch our tent near a good source of water.

The temporary rest houses in Lango had no doors, which made it difficult to keep out the mosquitoes at night. We draped the doorways with sacks and sheets, but this did not help much, so I sometimes finished typing out my notes on a camp bed underneath a mosquito net.

Active Research

Rapport gaining: problems and solutions. With so limited a time in each district I could not hope to establish contact with a large number of informants. Yet I had to try to get reliable information from different segments of each population. My plan was to interview a series of people of different statuses in the hope that they would bring forth the views of all major elements in each population.

The problem of maintaining rapport did not really arise, because I knew in advance that I would see most informants only one time. Therefore I concentrated my interviews on people who would be likely to understand my research and be willing to help. I hoped thereby to obtain the most reliable data possible under the circumstances. In most cases I believe I received truthful answers to my questions, though my informants did not always know the answers to all of them.

By the time I did the final survey in the remaining districts of Uganda, I was already in an advanced stage of my research on marriage and family life. This meant that I knew exactly what I was looking for and did not have to lose precious time on questions that I already knew were of little theoretical significance. I had had sufficient experience in dealing with people in Uganda on these questions to have learned the appropriate techniques for eliciting the kind of information required, and I knew in advance what most of the possible answers to my questions were, as well as how the various answers fitted into a number of different patterns, each one being internally consistent. To the extent that the replies did not form a consistent pattern, I was able to confront my interviewee immediately with the inconsistency and either learn something new about the situation, or make some assessment about the reliability of that particular informant's information. My general knowledge, by that time, of the problems of marriage and family life gave

me the insight to probe more deeply so as to find really significant similarities and differences. Also, the topic of family life
was not politically explosive, which was surely a factor in my
being able to get reliable data.

Data-getting techniques. In each of the four major comparison
districts I wanted to get information from the court records to
compare with that which I already had from Toro. My assistants
worked in three levels of courts in each district (outside Buganda) : the highest native court, at least one county court
(sometimes as many as six), and at least one subcounty court
(sometimes as many as four). In Buganda I confined my researches to the highest native court only, because inspection of
the court records revealed that the lower courts contained very
few marriage and family cases.

For each court investigated, I collected two major types
of information. First of all, we made a simple listing of the
number of cases per year per type, with a separate list for
civil original, criminal original, civil appeal, and criminal appeal cases. This information was obtained for every year as
far as the records went back, which in some cases was to 1912.
I have comparable records back to 1904 for Toro. I obtained
translations into English of the judgments of all cases dealing
with marriage and family life in a selected sample number of
years. Where the volume of litigation was low I was able to
get translations for every year; where it was high I got them
for every second or third year. I concentrated on the judgments
because in them, fortunately, the judges typically sum up the
positions of both sides, and give their specific reasons for their
verdict. Thus the judgment contains a capsulated version of the
whole case, including a statement of any relevant customary
laws and a specification of how they apply to the dispute in
question.

The major types of cases that were translated were adultery
(with and without pregnancy), fornication (with and without
pregnancy), abduction of a married woman, abduction of a
young girl, divorce, failure to pay bridewealth, failure to return
bridewealth, custody of a child, disputed paternity, inheritance,
rape, and witchcraft (which sometimes conceals family disputes). I collected over 4,000 cases, including those from Toro.
In addition I also obtained information concerning the population and number of tax payers for each court investigated. In
those areas where they were available and deemed to be relatively reliable, I collected data from the birth, death, and marriage registers.

I attended as many court sessions as possible in the major

comparison districts. With the help of my interpreter I took verbatim notes on marriage and family cases. I also took notes on procedure and the degree and type of formality of the court. This not only provided additional data per se, but also a background for interpreting the many cases collected from the court records. The court sessions and the historical data collected from the five different societies gave me some grasp of the meanings of justice to these various peoples.

In the major comparison societies most of my time was spent in court sessions (already discussed), interviewing, and participant observation. In the survey of the remaining districts of Uganda interviewing took up almost all of my time. In choosing people to interview I tried to select those most knowledgeable and likely to provide reliable information. In the survey districts, appointments were usually arranged for me in advance, but I myself specified in a letter to the district commissioner the kinds of people I wanted to see. These usually included the chief judge and one or two of his senior magistrates, plus an old chief or other notable who was well versed in the laws and customs of the people, one or two influential women—perhaps the Women's Community Development Officer and the Chairman of the local branch of the Uganda Council of Women, one or two missionaries who had been in the district for many years, a subcounty chief together with his parish chiefs, as they were very close to the people, and the district commissioner himself and any of his district officers who were acquainted with the customs of the people.

In the major comparison societies I interviewed a larger number of the same kinds of people, plus teachers, mothers' union workers, district council members (including women), and others. Sometimes I interviewed a whole group of people. For example, my "friend" in Lango once took me to see one of the important clan heads in the village. When I arrived I found a gathering of some twenty-five men, five women, and a group of ten young men, and a few children. I asked all kinds of questions for a period of two hours, and they were all answered patiently by one or another of the main leaders. A whole series of questions about women was answered by one of the women, and then another agreed that all she had said was correct, and so did all the men. My "friend" also told me afterward that he thought that all that had been said during the session was accurate.

All interviews were fairly formal in the sense that I took notes in front of informants. However, I did not always ask questions in the same sequence or use exactly the same wording. Rather I usually had something of a conversation with informants in which I responded to what they had said in such a way as to encourage them to provide new information, to draw them out further, point out inconsistencies in what they had already said, and probe more deeply. It was for this reason that I used an open-ended questionnaire (see the appendix) to which I occasionally added new questions where relevant when I had learned something new. These new questions were incorporated in later interviews, including of course those in the final survey of remaining Uganda districts, by which time the questionnaire had become more standardized. Even then I kept probing for new information and could not always anticipate the next question I was going to ask. Also in this final period I did not usually need an interpreter because most of my informants spoke English. In some other cases the interviewee was a sufficiently important personage to have his own interpreter.

I tried to get answers to as many questions as possible from all informants, but did not always succeed in doing so. Some informants answered "I don't know" more often than others. Some informants were experts (e.g., judges), and it was therefore important to obtain detailed information from them not obtainable from other regular informants. Some of these experts were very busy and unable to talk to me for more than about an hour, whereas I interviewed most informants for an hour and a half to two hours. This meant, of course, a further limitation on the number of general questions that could be answered by the experts.

I did not attempt to obtain comparable data sufficient for statistical analysis, although with over 200 interviews I can do some statistical analysis for some of the questions, especially those that usually elicited a clear-cut answer. My major aim, given the short period of time available for the survey, was to try to gain data as reliable as possible from a few key informants in each society.

The three marriage ceremonies I attended gave me an opportunity to make direct comparisons with the various marriages that I had seen in Toro. For instance, I saw a feast for a church wedding in Kigezi, and I noted that the Christian aspect of it was much more prominent—even in a small village—than in any that I had seen in Toro, where the Christian aspect of the marriage was often over as soon as the couple had left the church. In Kigezi the local catechist read from the Bible at the wedding feast and made a short speech emphasizing the importance of giving gifts to the newlyweds. (A pot was later put on the table, and more than fifty people put some money into it.)

This general observation about the importance of Christian marriage for people in Kigezi was later confirmed in interviews. My presence at the wedding gave me an opportunity to inquire in detail about the various things that were taking place, as well as others both preceding and following this event. While at the wedding I made useful contacts that I followed up later and that provided information on a variety of topics. In general, these and other events gave me the chance to observe and talk to ordinary people and to compare their views and behavior with what I had heard in interviews with important personalities.

A considerable amount of data came from the aforementioned essays (over 200 actual essays plus notes on about 50 others) by senior-secondary and teacher-training-college students. I let the teachers decide whether to tell their students that the essays were for me, and in almost all cases students were not given this information in the hope that their essays would then constitute a more accurate reflection of their real attitudes and aspirations.

These students were of an age (ranging from about fifteen to twenty) to have thought seriously about questions of marriage and family life. Indeed, it was a topic of considerable interest to them, and most were very articulate about it. Some of their topics were "Has the Bridewealth Any Useful Purpose?," "Men Should Have Many Wives," "Women Have the Same Rights as Men," and "How Far Should Customs of the Past in Regard to Marriage Be Kept?"

By-laws on marriage and family life and related correspondence provided further information. Occasionally an old chief or other notable wrote a text for me on marriage customs in the past, which I then had translated. While in Kampala I maintained a file of newspaper clippings of articles on marriage, family, and the status of women. I read some of the pertinent literature for background knowledge, and I used this literature as a guide in devising points to check in the field, looking especially for any changes that may have taken place. I also spent a little time consulting materials that are available only in the libraries and government files in Kampala.

The activities of this project are not yet complete. With the help of a research assistant I am analyzing all the relevant literature I can find. Furthermore, I still intend to contact the anthropologists who did intensive field work in the various societies of Uganda to find out what relevant data—in addition to their published works—they may have.

Techniques for recording and storing data. I used the same techniques for recording and storing data as I had used in my study of Toro. As I conducted many interviews in which I took notes in front of people, I used the blue duplicate books most often and correspondingly typed fewer notes based on participant observation. Court data and essays were recorded on regular lined paper, though again it would have been better to use McBee cards wherever possible. All over Uganda I took many photographs, including ones of court sessions and weddings, wherever possible. All notes, films, and supplies were stored in a metal box.

Bowing Out

Bowing out was really not a problem because I had not been in any district—including those in which I did major comparisons—long enough for my coming and going to make much difference to anyone. Again the important thing was that I attempted to conduct myself properly throughout my stay.

Summary and Evaluation

As I have not finished the analysis, it is not yet possible to specify the answers to the various questions posed in the comparative study of marriage and family life in Uganda. However, I do have the data with which to produce answers, and I have written one aspect of the study—that concerning law and the status of women. In a paper (1969) containing the first analysis of court data from all five societies (Toro plus the four major comparison districts), I delineated basic dimensions of the concept of the status of women, so as to develop it into a theoretically useful concept for cross-cultural purposes. I assessed the significance of my Uganda data for relevant hypotheses on factors affecting the degree of inequality in husband-wife relationships that have been advanced on the basis of research in Western countries. I proposed additional factors and explanatory hypotheses not only on this particular point, but on a wide spectrum of behavior related to the status of women. I pointed out the importance of a modern systems approach (Buckley, 1967) for handling so many hypotheses on a complex problem. Finally, I demonstrated that court data could be used to arrive at a fairly reliable index of the status of women.

A comparative book on Uganda will be the culmination of this project. Essentially it is a study to explain the process of change in male-female relationships both within and outside the family, especially as these are affected by legal institutions (the courts in particular), and to explain how and why such changes occur differently in different types of family systems that are correlated with different stratification systems. The five Uganda societies in which I collected substantial amounts of data were strategically chosen to cover a very broad spectrum from the most egalitarian segmentary society (Lango) to one of the strongest and most hierarchically organized kingdoms in all Africa (Buganda). Moreover, the two basic problems (1) the nature and extent of changing male-female relationships, as well as other relationships relevant to an understanding of social stratification, and (2) the processes of social change involved, are very general and have broad comparative implications. Theories about them are not peculiar to Uganda, but can be tested in other parts of Africa as well as elsewhere in the world.

A major aspect of my study of the processes of social change is my attempt to understand mechanisms of social control. Traditional approaches to this problem have often been simplistic, assuming either that it was sufficient to enact a law in order to change a prevailing social pattern, or that laws running counter to mores could not prove effective means of social control. A more sophisticated approach seeks the conditions under which a change in the law results in a change of mores. In contrast to both of these, my own approach is that of studying and seeking to establish the nature of the underlying *process* involved. I believe a very complex feedback process is going on, and therefore that it is much more fruitful to use a dynamic model than a static model that attempts to hold constant certain variables and artificially isolate others in an attempt to specify conditions. I view the problem as extremely complex, requiring a modern systems theory approach (Buckley, 1967). This framework is based on modern systems research, especially general systems research, cybernetics, and information and communication theory. It views the sociocultural system as a complex, adaptive system which, by its very nature, continually generates, elaborates, and restructures patterns of meanings, actions, and interactions. Thus it is a model within which we can actually analyze the processes of social change.

In summary, my comparative research in Uganda contained a program for collecting as much reliable data as possible in a short time, data that would be both representative and theoretically relevant (for which I used scope sampling). To achieve these purposes I made a strategic selection of four societies in which to do major comparisons, and I later did a quick survey in each of the other districts of Uganda. Other main elements of the research design were these:

1. Selection of relevant data (e.g., from court records) with an emphasis on existing documentation that could be collected by qualified—though easily trained—assistants.
2. Selection of key informants likely to be most knowledgeable and reliable for extended, open-ended interviews.
3. Asking informants to provide additional written documentation (e.g., essays, texts).
4. Participant observation based on some language facility where possible, and/or through friendly contacts; such participant observation was very useful in interpreting and evaluating the other kinds of data I collected.
5. Collection of existing relevant documentation (e.g., by-laws, correspondence).

The formulation and execution of the second part of my research program were heavily dependent upon my prior knowledge of the problems under investigation. My intensive field work in Toro enabled me to know which factors were most important and therefore what kinds of data to collect, which questions to emphasize, which to omit, and how to assess the significance and the reliability of the answers.

My final survey of the rest of Uganda provided me with a basis on which to interpret and assess the writings of other field workers who have done intensive work there. Also, it gave me the chance to note the latest trends in each district, and to see to what extent changes have taken place since their work was done some years ago. The comparative data obtained in my final survey helped immensely to broaden my scope, especially in regard to the theoretical problems involved in the study of marriage and family life. This survey was not a part of the original research design, which suggests again the importance of remaining flexible within the framework of a general plan.

An evaluation of the project must also take into consideration the ease with which others can use the data. All court cases have been coded, and the data have been punched onto more than 13,000 cards, a set of which (plus a set of the 4,000-odd cards on Toro individuals and marriages) will be made available in machine-readable form to other researchers. These data are rich and will form the basis of additional future publications of my own.

If I were to do this study over again, I would turn it into a small team project to include two graduate students or colleagues, plus a specialist in psychology or social psychology (assuming that I could get suitable personnel and sufficient funds). Each of the three anthropologists would be responsible for doing intensive studies in two societies speaking similar languages (e.g., Toro and Kigezi), and the psychologist (essential for studying the role of the individual in the processes of social change) would travel between the six strategically selected societies doing appropriate tests and observations on individuals and interpersonal relations (cf. Goldschmidt, 1965).

When I first did this study I had no choice but to do it alone. In a restudy, however, it would be a distinct advantage to have a small team so as to be able to gain better and more intensive knowledge about each of the major comparison societies in the study. After all, there is a limit to the number of languages that one man can learn well, and I am convinced that a knowledge of the language is the key to a proper understanding of a culture.

COMPARISON OF TORO AND UGANDA

In studying Toro and Uganda I was, of course, investigating the same set of substantive problems. Starting originally from a study of marriage and family life with an emphasis on the effect of legal institutions, I later broadened the inquiry in an attempt to explain the processes of change in male-female relationships both within and outside the family. Ultimately my concern is to explain how and why such changes occur differently in different types of family systems that are correlated with differing stratification systems.

The research design in studying these two groups was broadly similar in that I attempted to remain flexible while working within the framework of a general plan. The environments were relatively similar, at least insofar as they could significantly affect my work. Two of the important settings for data collection were the same: court sessions and marriages. Finally, I used the same techniques for recording and storing the data.

The differences in the two groups far exceeded these similarities. The most important difference was that in the rest of Uganda I investigated the problems in a vastly more extended and heterogeneous area, and yet I had to accomplish it in much less time than I had spent in Toro. Many of the specific differences in methods flowed from this basic difference. For example, in Toro I spent a great deal of time learning the language and establishing and maintaining personal rapport. In the rest of Uganda I had to rely on the language facility already acquired wherever possible (Kigezi), and elsewhere gain entry and rapport through friendly contacts; the problem of maintaining rapport did not really arise because I saw almost all informants only once.

In Toro I spent much time checking the reliability of the most minute details of individual marital histories, whereas in the rest of Uganda I tried to select informants who would be likely to provide reliable data in more formal interviews. In Toro also I had much more time for participant observation and was thus able to gain additional data in other settings, such as inheritance ceremonies and ostensibly private marriage negotiations. Another difference, of course, was that in Toro I lived in only two villages, whereas in the rest of Uganda I had to remain extremely mobile. Moreover, I had to devote a considerable amount of my already limited time writing letters to make advance arrangements and maintaining contact with my various assistants who were working in widely separated parts of the country.

Some changes in methods were due to the simple fact that by the time I did the investigation of the larger area I had a better grasp of the problems and also more experience as a field worker. My greater understanding of the problems permitted the formulation of a more explicit research design, and my greater experience and confidence helped me to execute the plan more effectively. The final survey was carried out at the end of my third year in Uganda, and I had a good idea of what I was looking for, as well as how to go about finding it.

Three years of field work is a long time, and at the end of it I was looking forward to our return to Europe. I had not been homesick, as I had my family with me, and wherever we lived we regarded as our home. I was still a graduate student, and we had not yet settled down anywhere. Although we got tired of asking the same questions all the time, our life in Uganda provided a rich experience and some variety. During the latter part of our stay we lived near Fort Portal, where we had some European friends. We also got back to Kampala every six months for a conference, at which time we made contact with colleagues. In spite of our long stay, we really had no strong urge to get away from Africa. As the research progressed, I felt that I was on the right track, and I wanted to collect as much data as possible while I had the chance. Sixteen months in the Toro villages were quite enough for my wife, however, and she was very happy to return to Kampala when she was expecting our second child. Thereafter, I carried on the second part of my research on my own.

The general political environment did not much affect my investigations in a negative sense, although it did prevent me from collecting data in a Buganda village and was at least partly responsible for my less successful participant observation in Teso. These were minor obstacles, however, in comparison to the positive value of an essentially stable political environment in the rest of the country and the presence of colonial government officers able and willing to render important services.

Methodological adaptation to the sociocultural situation was not for the most part a difficult problem, because in the rest of Uganda I collected limited kinds of data (e.g., court records, essays) that were available in comparable form in all societies. The major kind of adaptation necessary took place in the interviews during which I had to think quickly in response to the sometimes new information that I was receiving, and then pose unanticipated questions so as to probe more deeply and to check the reliability of the data.

There were no changes in methods as a result of accidents per se, though I sometimes stumbled by chance upon some information that then led me to make changes in research design. But this was simply part of my general policy of remaining sufficiently flexible to make such changes whenever I considered them necessary.

The two investigations were originally conceived as two complementary parts of what was really a single study of Uganda. This is particularly significant from the point of view of obtaining comparable data for testing theories and hypotheses. In the social sciences there has been a justifiable demand for testable and tested theories (e.g., Willer, 1967:xix), but to date this call has gone largely unanswered. We lack theories to explain complex social phenomena (including, for example, social inequality and the processes of social change) involving different units of analysis, many variables, many relationships between these variables, and nonlinear as well as linear relationships. The use of a modern systems theory approach will go a long way toward providing an appropriate theoretical framework. But the difficulty has been not only the lack of theory, but also a lack of comparable data. Having myself collected comparable data in various Uganda societies, I am now in a position to make a contribution toward satisfying this demand.

It is seldom that one individual is in a position to collect and apply himself to different sets of data, an approach that is very illuminating for the whole study (Perlman: in press). A key element in this approach is the intensive study of one area to discover theoretically significant variables, followed by the collection of comparative data elsewhere on these variables. The result has been a combination of considerably greater depth and breadth of both qualitative and quantitative data—strategically collected for both theoretical and representational factors—than is usual in such country-wide studies. Moreover, this broad comparative study of a whole country covers a time span of more than fifty years.

My comparative research in the rest of Uganda also made me aware of theoretical problems not encountered in Toro. Quite naturally, this led to a re-examination of my Toro data in the light of what I had learned in other parts of Uganda. The comparative research across the country thus put me in a position to formulate a wider theoretical approach to the study that could have been attained only with difficulty, if at all, from reading alone.

In this chapter I have compared the methods used for an intensive study of one society with other methods used to study the same set of problems in a whole country. But the two investigations are really complementary parts of a single broad study of Uganda, and I would like to emphasize the usefulness of using a combination of methods. In this way it is possible to profit from the advantages of each, and yet not be hampered by their differing limitations (cf. Riley, 1963:69–75). Any single method will have important limitations, but a combination of methods can largely overcome this disadvantage.

APPENDIX

Marriage and Family Life Questionnaire

1. What percentage of the sexual unions these days start without the payment of a bridewealth? In what percentage of those does the boy eventually pay something to the girl's father? What are the attitudes of the people toward unions in which no bridewealth has been paid? To what extent is the boy ridiculed for not paying anything to the girl's father? What opportunities have boys and girls to meet one another, or does frequent "trial marriage" result from lack of such opportunity?

2. Is the bridewealth usually paid in installments or all at once? If in installments what percentage of it must be paid before the boy can get the girl to live in his house? Once he gets the girl, does he usually finish paying the remainder?

3. What percentage of the marriages are Christian or Moslem (i.e., under protectorate government law), as opposed to customary native marriage? What are the attitudes toward Christian

or Moslem marriage—i.e., do the people like it or not, and why? To what extent is such a marriage considered to be a symbol of prestige?

4. What percentage of the men have more than one wife? Is polygyny considered to be economically profitable? That is, can a man actually make money (or does he lose money) by taking a second wife? What is the attitude of (a) the men and (b) the women toward polygyny? Are there any men who dislike it, or any women who are refusing to become second wives? Do co-wives have separate houses? Around one compound or completely separate? What happens when the man decides to build one big house with a tin roof?

5. How frequent is divorce (or separation for Christian marriage)? Percentage? What are the most important causes for divorce? That is, for what reasons will the woman run away from her husband? And for what reasons will he send her away? Is it necessary to go to court to get a divorce?

6. What percentage of the unmarried girls are producing illegitimate children, i.e., at the home of their fathers? Does the boy who impregnated the girl usually claim the child? If so, does he have to pay any compensation to her father? How much? At what age can he take the child? For those children who are not claimed by their fathers (genitors), do they have any disabilities while growing up in the home of their mother's father or mother's brother? That is, can they easily (or with difficulty) get clothes, school fees, bridewealth, inherited property? After a girl has produced an illegitimate child or two, can she easily get married to another man, or will other men not want to marry her, saying that she is "second hand"? If they do marry her, will the amount of the bridewealth be the same or not? Lower or higher? And how does the amount of the bridewealth for an educated girl compare with that for an uneducated girl?

7. How frequent is adultery? Does the case usually go to court, or is it usually settled out of court, or is it settled by fighting, or not at all? Or are most people clever enough not to be caught? If it goes to court, how much is the fine? What part goes to the husband? If settled out of court, how much compensation does the husband get? To what extent is he likely to just forgive the adulterer, accepting only beer? What are the most important causes of adultery? For example, if the husbands were to give their wives more money for the things they want, would the wives then be less willing to commit adultery?

8. What chance does a woman have now of becoming financially independent? To what extent are women taking advantage of

that opportunity, by building their own houses, refusing to re-marry, or to marry at all in the first place, and maintaining themselves, taking a man into their house for only so long as they want him there? Can a woman take a case to court by herself? Are there many cases in which women take cases to court against their husbands for beating and injuring them? Are there any, or many women who repay their own bridewealth by working or by finding another husband? On the basis of what evidence are cases of disputed paternity settled? Are there many such cases or not? To what extent do women participate in political councils—parish, subcounty, county, district levels? Are there many girls who leave their studies in the middle to get married, or do they prefer to get their certificates first (teacher or nurse)? If a girl has some education, is she then less willing to cultivate in the garden?

9. To what extent is family authority decreasing? Are children still as respectful and obedient to their parents as they used to be in the past? What effect does education have upon this? If it is decreasing, what are the most important causes for it?

NETWORK ANALYSIS AND PROCESSES OF ADAPTATION AMONG ECUADORIAN AND NOVA SCOTIAN NEGROES[1]

Norman E. Whitten, Jr.

PART I: ECUADOR

Problem, Theory, and Research Design

While working on my master's degree in 1959–1960, I decided to undertake long-range field work with Negroes living in a tropical region of Central or South America. I had been working

[1] The Ecuadorian study was made possible by Public Health Fellowship MH 14,333 and by supplements M-54447 SSS and MH 06978-01 SSS R04 from the National Institute of Mental Health. Nova Scotian field research was carried out by the support of two NIMH small grants (MH 12809-01 and MH 13750-01) and by a faculty research grant from Washington University. I deeply appreciate the academic and scientific freedom permitted under the aegis of NIMH sponsorship. Dorothea S. Whitten worked continuously with me in the field in Nova Scotia and contributed consider-

on a diffusion study of occultism among North Carolina Negroes, and I had come to the conclusion that the casting and removing of spells, together with attendant problems of a mystic and profane nature, stemmed fundamentally from a pre-eighteenth-century European complex brought to the Piedmont and other areas of the American South by early settlers concerned with routing the devil from Whites, Indians, and Negroes alike. I decided that the elements of magical thought usually regarded as African were those common to magical thought anywhere, and that the particular stylistic traits characteristic of lower-class Negroes in central North Carolina were far more similar to their European counterparts than to anything African. The traits that seemed most African were also described in the handbooks of the Spanish Inquisition and well-codified in fifteenth- and sixteenth-century Spain (Whitten, 1961, 1962). During the period when I was intrigued with the process of untangling traits and themes through history, I read Richard Adams' paper "Cultural Components of Central America" (1956) and George Foster's book *Culture and Conquest: America's Spanish Heritage* (1960). Both of these works strongly influenced my decision to undertake field work with Latin American Negroes.

I was convinced by my work in North Carolina that even sophisticated scholars confuse breeding populations and the mechanisms of gene flow with processes whereby culture spreads, changes, and endures by responding to natural and sociocultural settings, and so I aimed my work toward "Afro-Americans" and their concomitant cultural complexes. My initial research problem was to determine the cultural traits and themes that tend to characterize Negroes living in intimate contact with tribal Indians and national mestizos (people of mixed descent), and then trace the historical derivations of these traits. I hypothesized that both Negroes and mestizos would be characterized by their heritage of Hispanic culture, and that in a setting of ethnic plurality, particular adaptations would lead to different configurations that could be interpreted as Indian-Hispanic for the mestizo and African-Hispanic for the Negro. I soon dropped the "hyphenated approach," which relates by association phenotype and culture, and began to ask questions about the ethnohistory of Negroes and mestizos in specific regions—questions about the slave trade and early boss-worker relationships, missions, devil searches, witch-hunting, and racism, within various New World institutions. In other words, I wanted to attempt to interpret

ably to the preparation of this manuscript. Portions of this chapter appear in *Afro-American Anthropology*, eds. N. E. Whitten and J. F. Szwed, New York, Free Press, 1969.

the concept "conquest culture" (Foster, 1960) by studying a segment of an ethnically plural region in Central or South America.

When I suggested this to one of my doctoral advisers, I was told that these ideas were "old hat" and that Herskovits and his students had already overworked the Afro-American field in terms of cultural complexes and trait diffusion.[2] I did not accept the "old hat" argument, but I did succumb to another: "There are so many things going on in Latin America (and everywhere else today), why bury your head in a morass of traits, complexes themes, ethnohistoric tendencies, and abstractions of plurality? Why not focus on the immediate processes so disturbing the neo-colonial world in the kind of ethnic setting that intrigues you the most, leaving the questions of provenience aside until you fully understand the processes whereby people survive, improve their lot, deal with the economic, political, and cultural factors of an expanding world, while at the same time maintaining an ethnic identity within a plural framework?" After accepting this argument, I busily worked through literature on development, social change, class structure, economic anthropology, and community-level politics.

There were any number of possible sites for the study I envisaged, and I mapped out areas in Peru, Ecuador, Nicaragua, and Honduras that seemed suitable for investigation. My final decision, to work in Ecuador, was made on the basis of the immediate first-hand knowledge of my doctoral adviser, who had visited western Ecuador, knew something of the situation existing between Negroes, Indians, and mestizos, and had written provocatively on the relationship of reciprocal labor groups to economic opportunity (Erasmus, 1957). During the fall of 1960, I applied for field funds to the National Institute of Mental Health, proposing an exploratory study of the relationship of socioeconomic class to family organization and to the process whereby value orientations emerge from primary socialization. My long-range goals, as stated in 1960, included the development of methodological perspectives that would enable an investigator to view change as an ongoing process of social life.

I received funds allowing me to visit western Ecuador for the summer of 1961, during which time my research entered what is herein called the "passive" or "adaptational" phase. My only design at this time was to visit the northern highlands and

---

[2] Professor Melville J. Herskovits is the author of *The Myth of the Negro Past* and *The New World Negro*. For many years he and his students at Northwestern University engaged in historical and ethnographic work on problems of Afro-American studies.

the northwest rain forest on the coast, to get some idea of the situation existing as highlands and coastal systems conjoined economically and politically, and to decide on an area for subsequent investigation. I remember one piece of advice given by my adviser, near the eve of my departure: "For Christ's sake, find out what they do!" I have never forgotten this, and I did indeed intend to learn as much as possible about how people survived with little or no money in a cash economy.

Passive or Adaptational Research

Money and research go hand in hand, and I have yet to go into the field with secure funds. The NIMH approved my fellowship award during its March review, but could not notify me of supplemental field funds for the summer of 1961 until June of that year. As June dragged on I decided to borrow money on the assumption that the grant would be forthcoming. On the day of my departure, word came that money would be available, and off I went. Although I had passed Spanish language examinations for advanced degrees, I had never had formal training in conversational Spanish. My idea was to learn as much as possible in the field, rather than to use the summer studying conversational Spanish. Although I do not regret this decision, I do not necessarily recommend it to others.

I flew to Quito on Aviación Ecuatoriana, got a taxi to a hotel, dumped my duffle bag, took a bath, put on trousers, shirt, and canvas shoes, and went for a walk. Within half an hour, I realized why so many people thought I must be either a *gringo* or crazy: Having come from a North Carolina summer, I had become quite informal in attire and had not put on any socks. In Quito, only Indians go without socks on the streets of town.

After walking continuously for about five hours, I returned to the hotel to eat and to make some phone calls. I contacted the Servicio Cooperativo Interamericano de Salud Pública (SCISP) and began to search for an Ecuadorian friend of a friend of mine. I do not need to go into the details of my initial experiences in Quito to indicate the first stages of "passive research." Suffice it to say that finding people without addresses involved networks that familiarized me with a number of officials and their offices, that I met many people who helped in one way or another, and that, within a few days, I had received a free pass to ride the Quito-San Lorenzo railroad and free use of a section of a railroad house for the summer. By arising early (around 6:00 or 7:00 A.M.), and walking, riding buses and cabs, visiting people in offices whether or not I had an introduction, and eating and drinking in small bars and saloons, rather than the larger hotel restaurants, I had literally dozens of interesting experiences with young, middle-aged, and elderly Ecuadorians from various walks of life. Even with a poor knowledge of Spanish, I felt that I knew enough about the country in a few days to seriously doubt all information given to me by North Americans, save one, Herbert Hunter, formerly of the SCISP, and the only American I found in 1961 who was not completely full of unfounded rumors and weird notions of Ecuador and its people.

Only alone or with a single companion can one appreciate the friendliness of the people in Quito. Only by eating in small establishments can one realize the ease with which "contacts" are made and expanded. People whom I casually met took me to a nearby resort, to various bars and night spots, on tours of the city, and all were more than willing to try to make me understand their view of what was happening in their country. My "day" usually ended sometime after midnight.

Within six days I was ready to leave. I had decided to travel first to San Lorenzo, near the Colombian border, rather than to the large town of Esmeraldas, capital of the province of Esmeraldas. A friend of a friend met me at my hotel at 4:00 A.M. and drove me to the railroad station. There I secured a ticket and began a sixteen-hour journey through the Ecuadorian highlands, turning at Ibarra and beginning a descent from 9,000 feet to the sea-level port town of San Lorenzo.

There are two ways to reach the Ecuadorian sector of the Pacific rain forest, which extends north from Muisne to the Río Mira in Ecuador and continues northward through Darien Province of southern Panama: one can travel by road (since 1962), plane, or boat to Esmeraldas and take a banana or cargo boat north, or one can travel by rail. The railroad reached the coast in 1957, linking economically and politically the tropical northern Pacific littoral with both the arid and the rainy Sierran slopes of the western cordillera of the north Ecuadorian Andes. Plunging through a mosaic of ecological zones from arid to semitropical to tropical, the "Autocarril" (a delapitated Ford bus of 1940 vintage outfitted for service on narrow-gauge rails) lends a special thrill to field entrée. Stop by stop, mile by tortuous mile the various peoples of the Sierra and then the coast come and go with their fruit, animals, and dried fish, pushing, shoving, cursing, and bemoaning the fate of those destined to ride third class on a bus with scarcely room for first-class passengers. (First-class passengers sit in marked seats, two or three on a two-seat bench; second-class passengers stand; and third-class hang on as best they can.) My first trip was unusually crowded and boisterous, for I had unwittingly embarked on a day during which various military, legal, and semiofficial personnel of highland bureaucracies were paying a visit to San Lorenzo and the "new town" of the coast. After a lunch stop in Ibarra, on we went, drinking scotch, arguadiente, "fresca" (ground oatmeal and water), and eating *maíz tostados* (parched and toasted corn), boiled potatoes, cow's skin, and fruit, spitting, cursing, laughing, sleeping, and with a half dozen visitors vomiting out the windows.

I did not like the Sierra during my first sojourn in it, and I liked the arid slopes even less, a dislike I no longer have. We entered the coastal plain at dark, coming into San Lorenzo in a driving rainstorm to the mutters of the highlanders about the inherent dangers of Negro *costeños*. Following the highlanders to the "Imperial Hotel" (the remnants of the nineteenth-century British exploitation of the province), I dumped my duffle bag in a room with a friend from the train, ate a meal with the highlanders, and then, to their horror, immediately left to see San Lorenzo. Somehow, I liked San Lorenzo from the start, apparently an unusual feeling. The rain let up by 11:00 P.M., the three saloons blared forth their music, the air was invigorating with the salt smell from the incoming tide, and the townspeople began to gather, laughing, yelling, drinking, and dancing. It was Saturday and the saloons were open until 3:00 A.M., running under their own electric power (electricity supplied to the town by the Junta Autónoma is shut off at 10:00 P.M., so the saloons have their own kerosene generators). I received nothing short of a mild shock when, promptly at 3:00 A.M., the lights went out. Never again will I wonder what is meant by the total darkness of the tropical night! I found my way back to the hotel only to discover that the door was locked and bolted, an unusual precaution, but one apparently used when the hotel is full of strangers. Not wanting to cause a commotion I made myself comfortable near the doorway, slept a bit, and went quietly in to find my room when the "Guatchiman" (watchman) opened the door at 4:30 A.M. to allow departing guests to get on the Autocarril. It seemed that far more than twenty-four hours had passed when I finally crawled under a mosquito net in San Lorenzo.

The highlanders disapproved of, and were embarrassed by, my entrée ("The *gringo* didn't know anything at all; he didn't even find the proper officials the first night to arrange for his accommodations"), but nothing could have pleased the people of San Lorenzo more ("The *gringo* came out on Saturday night to see the people, and the highlanders locked him out of the hotel"). I did not learn of these attitudes, of course, until long after.

Early the next day an official from the Junta Autónoma showed me a room in a railroad shack that I could use for the summer, and I began familiarizing myself with the ethnically plural community of San Lorenzo, preparing myself for more reconnaissance on the northern coast. Let me quote from my later study (1965) to give an idea of what San Lorenzo is like:

> San Lorenzo is a hot, rainy setting for life; it is reached from the highlands by a train trip resembling a roller-coaster ride down the western slopes of the Andes. Landslides make the trip particularly treacherous between December and June. From the coast the only means of transportation are the small, rugged banana and cargo boats that ply between Guayaquil and Limones and occasionally put in at San Lorenzo. Otherwise the interior can be reached only by dugout canoe or "launch." The only scheduled ferry service is a near-daily Limones-San Lorenzo launch service, the launch being a dugout canoe with balsa floats and built-up sides, powered by an outboard motor.
>
> In spite of such difficulties in traveling to and from this Ecuadorian frontier, growth and development are continuous. The expanding population and growing commerce are bringing a measure of prosperity to San Lorenzo, but they are also taking their toll in health. There is virtually no sanitation; rats and flies seem to be everywhere; infant mortality is very high, venereal disease rampant, and tetanus infections increasing. At the same time, malaria and yaws have been nearly eradicated by government programs. The people are poor, but far from miserable. People in San Lorenzo generally believe that something good is going to happen; on the whole they are outwardly oriented, open to changes that promise a tangible benefit, and inquisitive about the ways of others. (1965:2)

Two important factors facilitated my work in San Lorenzo and in other parts of the northwest sector of Esmeraldas province. First, I became very close to a highland physician, Dr. Aurelio Fuentes Contreras, who was working on the coast without his family, because he did not want to take his children out of school in Quito and did not have enough capital to begin a practice in the highlands. Dr. Fuentes had been in San Lorenzo since before the railroad sections were linked together, and he was intrigued by my interest in the port and his country. I treasure his friendship, and I credit Dr. Fuentes with facilitating my work with the highlanders and with some of the Negroes of the community. Second, against all advice from the highlanders, I continuously interacted with the Negroes of the town. I asked permission to go with them when they fished, walked with them to their plots of land, visited them in their homes, took their pictures, danced, drank, and ate with them, and did my best to imitate their speech.

I alienated most highlanders by this behavior, as well as some of the coastal rural police, one of whom arrested me one day for lack of sufficient papers. Fortunately, Dr. Fuentes was able to mediate some of these interethnic clashes and keep his ethnic group from employing effective informal sanctions on my "unseemly" behavior. I also became quite close to a couple of visiting engineering students from the highlands, both of whom followed me around town and, by the end of summer, took deliberate steps to make friends with the Negroes closest to me. They were both somewhat surprised by the positive response with which their overtures were met.

I never found a steady male informant in San Lorenzo or elsewhere on the rain-forest coast. The general problem was that the closer I got to a Negro from the lower class, the more he felt obliged to give me whatever information I seemed to want. I learned, however, to talk to groups of people whose kinship, family, and social situation I knew, asking questions that would start an argument and then listening to the drift of the argument. I also learned to change the context and line of questioning often enough to avoid indicating "exactly" what I was after. I shall have more to say about this in the section on "active" research.

Housekeeping was no problem in 1961. In the small four-room railroad building in which I had been given a room lived as many as fifteen people at various times. I slept on a bed with a thin mattress and without a mosquito net, and I wrote field notes there on a small table. Otherwise, I avoided my room as much as possible. I simply kept my notes in a box designed to hold 5″ × 8″ cards, and kept the box in a polyethylene bag. Because of the crowded conditions, people from the community would not visit me. but in that setting I was able to perceive the attitude of highlanders toward the coastal people. For the most part, their attitude was one of disgust and fear.

In 1961, San Lorenzo was booming, and the ambience of a boom town seemed to help rapport along. Three saloons were open nightly, and hundreds of people from the Sierra passed through the town to see what was happening and to weigh the advantages of investing in coastal land. I moved on to Limones and Borbón by launch, and then returned to San Lorenzo, rented a canoe and a motor, and with Dr. Fuentes, and Gonzalo, a Negro who could speak a little Cayapa, embarked on a five-day trip to the Río Cayapas. Here we visited with the Cayapa Indians, and traveled as far up the river as we could by canoe and motor to San Miguel de los Cayapas.

Upon returning to San Lorenzo in early August, I participated in my first marimba dance. I was completely struck by the

African rhythms and by the seeming incongruity of the exotic marimba dance in relation to the rest of "frontier" San Lorenzo life. I decided to learn as much as possible about the social significance of the dance on my return.

Finally, for no particular reason, I decided to give a "Draw a Picture Test" to the school children.[3] Dr. Fuentes and I worked out a formula, talked to the teachers, and got them all to practice giving *exactly* the same instructions: "Make a picture of a person," and when all the children had finished, "Now turn the picture over and draw a picture of a person of the opposite sex." The people thought it was wonderful that the *gringo* was doing an experiment in San Lorenzo. In fact, the secret about the test was well kept, and the 200 or so children thought that it was an art exam. The teachers had never heard the school so quiet as during the exam, and people throughout the town expressed friendly surprise when I went to collect the pictures. In broadcasting my presence as something unique, the DAP test worked wonders, but in other ways it probably failed. More about this anon.

I left San Lorenzo in early August, soon after the marimba dance, an event that occurs sporadically in San Lorenzo (see Whitten, 1967a, 1967b, 1968; Whitten and Fuentes, 1966). A couple of highlanders and several Negroes saw me off. After a few days in Quito, I flew to Esmeraldas for a week that started well, but ended with a series of light fevers, between which I did manage to travel up the Río Esmeraldas, and both north and south for a few miles along the coasts. After a final week in Quito, I left for home to prepare for the active phase of research. I had lost about thirty pounds and had intestinal problems, but otherwise I wished to return to study San Lorenzo.

Active Research

By January, 1963, I had completed all work for the Ph.D. degree in anthropology except the thesis. I returned to San Lorenzo in mid-January, 1963, leaving my wife of five months in Chapel Hill to complete her work for a doctoral degree in sociology, and to earn sufficient money to maintain our apartment and join me by the summer. I would be working on slim funds, and my wife would be doing yeoman service to complete her work and prepare to join me in the field.

Although I had traveled with only bare necessities on my

---

[3] The "DAP" test is a very easy-to-give projective test predicated on the assumption that drawings represent stylized conceptions of the subjects' ideas about their bodies and environment. See Freeman (1955:570–571).

first trip, I chose my equipment more carefully for the active stage of my research. In a steamer trunk I had a small tape recorder, camera and accessories, tapes, film, typewriter, books, and minor miscellany (flashlight, hunting knife, twenty-five packages of Fizzies [tablets that fizz into various flavors of carbonated soft drinks when dropped into water], for children, etc.). A duffle bag containing field clothes, a suitcase with a pair of trousers, sport coat, and sweater for use in Quito, and a brief case with immediate essentials completed what I considered at that time to be rather heavy equipment.

Two attempts to reach San Lorenzo by rail were futile because landslides had destroyed sections of the railroad, so I flew to Esmeraldas, took a banana boat north to Limones, and the launch to San Lorenzo. While in Esmeraldas, I met a cousin of a woman who was in charge of the mail in San Lorenzo and carried a note to her. Although such note carrying was common, my offer was apparently deeply appreciated and facilitated my re-entry into San Lorenzo. The recipient, as post-mistress, was central to the passage of information to and from the outside world, and therefore she was quite respected. She spread word that I had done her an important favor, and she said nice things about me whenever she had the opportunity.

My return to San Lorenzo was very gratifying. The Negroes whom I had known before made a considerable effort to let me know how much they appreciated my return, and some of the highlanders indicated great interest in my study of their community. Others, however, were not so helpful. They wanted to know the results of the earlier study, particularly the results of the DAP test, their expressed reason being a desire to know whether the Negroes "were as smart as the highlanders." A couple of people insisted that I comment on the I.Q. of the schoolchildren, and several teachers let me know that they did not appreciate my returning without some interesting results. I had asked a favor of them; what had I done in return?

The Junta Autónoma again granted me a place to live. During that winter, when the rains were heavy on the Sierran slopes and no trains could move because of landslides, I used an entire section of a long residential building. I had a small living room and a small bedroom. The living room contained two tables and space for books; the bedroom contained a bed to which I immediately added a mosquito net. With the privacy of my own quarters a number of townspeople began to visit me. They were perfectly willing to spend time talking to me and, a bit later, to serve as paid informants. Once the highlanders knew that Negroes were visiting me, however, interaction with them nearly ceased, except for specified occasions. The two exceptions to my ostracism by the highlanders were Dr. Aurelio Fuentes Contreras and Sr. José Oñate, a lumberman, who remained courteous and close to me throughout my work. I probably would not have retained my residence without the periodic mediation of Aurelio Fuentes with other officials.

Rapport grew steadily, with no more than ordinary interpersonal squabbles, disappointments, or accusations of exploitation. People in San Lorenzo, particularly the Negroes, are interested in the outside world, and their willingness to share information and to interact in their own context assures the investigator of good rapport. Getting reliable information through good rapport, however, is another matter. Rather than discuss actual data-gathering techniques in anecdotal form, I prefer to discuss them one by one. It must be understood that many techniques, sometimes all, would be used in the course of a day.

Data-Gathering Techniques

Presentation of self. I presented myself as a graduate student trying to get a Ph.D. degree in anthropology and told everyone that the purpose of my study was to get enough information to write a thesis. I never succumbed to the title "Doctor," nor would I let people call me "Don" or refer to me in this way. Although I accepted and used the title *Señor* reciprocally with most highlanders, I worked hard to stay on a first-name basis with the Negroes. I called men by their first name, or simply "hombre," although I used the standard "Señorita" and "Señora" for the women, unless I knew them quite well. Many of my friends called me, simply, "Norman" as time went by, and those of the middle class in San Lorenzo adopted the term "Mr. Norman" for me. The "Mr. Norman" title, however, came to be one used publicly, in address, while "Norman" was used by the majority in private. To break down the use of "Mr." I used to return it to my friends—shouting across the street, "Oh, Mr. Frasco," or ""Yyyaa, Mr. Chilicano." This technique facilitated their acceptance of me as a normal human being. After a month in San Lorenzo, I heard a rumor from some highlanders that a number of lower-class people had been referring to me as "El hombre Norman"; the rumor was substantiated, and, of all the things in San Lorenzo that happened to me, this pleased me the most. Somehow, I managed to be regarded as simply a "man" in the eyes of those with whom I had come to work.

I presented my interests as holistic by showing equal interest in everything people told me, recording on the spot the names of things, people, places, and ideas. For a while I could see people imitating me: one person would squat and pretend to write, while another would point to a canoe, or to himself, and explain something that was (to the speaker) terribly obvious, but that the man pretending to write found terribly difficult. This game subsided after a month, at about the time I became known as a "man," and my notebook and pen came to be regarded as a part of my being, just as a machete becomes part of the being of one who works in the forest.

Many things had happened to my friends since 1961, and I used such events as a starting point to demonstrate my holistic interests. Gonzalo had formed a band. I began to ask about the music, his background, the background of the members, the names of the songs, and to ask for instruction in the rhythms and melodies. I asked where he played, and why he played there. Before I knew it, I was on sensitive ground, because Gonzalo was providing the live music at a recruitment center for the developing Communist party in San Lorenzo. I continued with questions of when the band played, what else went on in the "Club Deportivo" (sporting club), why the president and vice-president would not let me attend meetings, what he thought about politics, and what his father and other relatives thought. I liked to switch topics in our conversations to see what would happen. Gonzalo had visited the Río Cayapas with me, so I asked for Chibchan names of instruments, and then what the Cayapa thought of Communism. Since the latter question was greeted with hilarity, "What do the Cayapa know of politics?," I could inquire into the subject more deeply than I could into the Communist club in San Lorenzo. "Don't the Cayapa have politics? Why do you have Communism and the Cayapa no politics?" By discussing the hypothetical case of whether or not the Cayapa could be interested in Communist politics, Gonzalo and his friends would get into ideological discussions that I, at least in the early phases of research, could not generate by direct questioning.

Humberto had a new girl friend and was also suffering from a very painful venereal infection of the lymph glands (probably lymphogranuloma venereum). I asked about his *hembra* (female), her looks, background, where he kept her, how he managed to have two girl friends and still go out with prostitutes on Saturday night. I asked where his money came from, who his girl friends lived with, and whether or not they knew of each other. Before long, he was talking freely about prostitutes and dancing, and I began to ask him questions about music similar to those that I had asked Gonzalo, including the relationship of the Club Deportivo to the saloons and the saloons to the marimba house.

Almost any conversation could then lead to an intertwining of information on subjects as varied as sex, household composition, music, dancing, politics, and affairs outside the community. Wherever possible I tried to proceed from the basis of the personal involvement of an informant outward in as many directions as possible. It was not long before I got the reputation of being interested in "everything." My problem was then to make sure that the "everything" did not simply revolve around the things that I could think of to ask about. Participant observation kept my field of knowledge expanding, and kept me from getting too "programmed" on set courses of discussion.

Mechanical techniques of recording information. I transferred all information from conversation recorded in my note pads to $5'' \times 8''$ slips, to which a carbon was attached. This technique is described by Honigmann (1954:91,92). In general, the date went in the upper left-hand corner, a note as to subject in the middle, and the informant and context in the upper right-hand corner. I tried to keep one ethnographic item on one slip, but found this impossible. What I did do was to add extra slips cross-referencing long descriptions that could be filed in a variety of ways. Every couple of weeks I took an hour or two to thumb through the slips, making notes on obvious gaps in my knowledge and on subjects that seemed worth pursuing.

In a daily log I recorded information about the weather, major events of the day, my own state of physical and mental health, and remarks on interpersonal relationships. It is of great value to me now, when I read notes about, say, the hostility of a given informant, to check my own situation in the log. More often than not, I note that hostility in an informant occurred on a dismal rainy day when I had severe intestinal cramps, and when I wanted to find out about something that no one knew anything about!

I taped music and some conversations, but I simply did not have enough tapes, or strong enough batteries, to use my small tape recorder for interview work. I drew kinship diagrams and a map on shelf paper, and recorded a house-to-house survey and a diagram of household composition on $11'' \times 18''$ paper, not on the $5'' \times 8''$ slips. I typed all my notes except those involving diagrams. Once a month I mailed a copy of my field notes to my wife in the United States.

I stored tapes and film in polyethylene bags containing silica gel until they could be mailed. Periodically, I placed the silica gel on rocks in the sun to dry it out. I also periodically fumigated my notes, clothes, and papers. From railroad, nautical, church, and military maps I prepared a map of the community and the surrounding area. I then altered this map to take into account my own observations and the concepts of *barrio* (ward) boundaries given to me by various people in the community (see Whitten, 1965, appendix).

Participant observation. During my 1963 field work I stated my goal as a study "of an entire ethnically plural community, although my main interest is the place of the Negroes in the community, their economic, social, and political means of coping with change, and their capacity for controlling their own fate in a world of changing systems." (Whitten, 1965:4) It now seems a bit odd to me, in the light of this goal, that my only discussion of participation was subsumed by the statement, "In general, I lived the life of the people" (Whitten, 1965:1), for this means living a "plural life."

I tried to allow myself five hours or more each day for activities other than working with informants, conducting interviews, or systematically collecting data. For at least five hours a day, I did one of two things. Sometimes I walked around the town, allowing myself to be detained by anyone for as long as he wished, and stopping to watch, and help if possible, anyone doing anything of interest to me or to the actor (e.g., making a canoe, fixing a sail, planting a garden, killing a pig, beating a child). At other times, I worked, either in San Lorenzo or in the hinterland, visited with relatives of my informants and friends, fished, stripped mangrove bark, and cut timber. During such participation I learned as a child would learn, and people taught me much as they would teach a child—by thrusting something upon me and then correcting my stance and actions. I gradually learned to handle a large dugout canoe, a heavy axe, machete, hand line, and harpoon. As I learned to perform such mundane tasks as to broadcast corn seeds and plant seedlings, I became painfully aware of all the minor and major hindrances to life on the fringe of mangrove swamp and tropical forest.

I relaxed with the people, too, visiting homes, saloons, cantinas, and taking part in every group activity that I could, always being careful, however, to participate as much as possible as a Negro of my approximate age would, not as a "community leader" such as a priest or political official. I learned to dance folk and national dances in the *costeño* style, and I learned the rudiments of drumming and marimba playing.[4]

When traveling with Negroes I ate with them, and occa-

---

[4] *Costeño* refers to a person who manifests coastal ways in speech, dress, and presentation of self.

sionally when visiting various parts of the community I took snacks with people who were eating. In 1961 I had endeavored to eat all of my meals with the Negroes, but in 1963 I completely routinized my meal schedule in the highland fashion by eating with the highlanders in the Salón Ibarra. I did this for two reasons. First, it seemed to satisfy most of the townspeople to know that, at least at mealtime, I was taken care of and could be found if needed. Second, mealtime became my time for associating with the people responsible for public and private capital expenditures in San Lorenzo.

My two means of interaction resulted in constant strain. The better I learned the lifeways of the Negro *costeños,* the more alienated I became from most, but not all, of the highlanders. There were a couple of people in particular who delighted in badgering me during mealtime. Imagine, if you will, a long hot morning and afternoon trying to learn to move a canoe through mangrove roots, while people whom you respect a great deal make no bones about your being inept and taking their time from the really valuable job of getting fish to eat. You return to a small building in the evening for supper, missing lunch because of the nature of the Negroes' working day, to a barrage of questions and criticisms. "Where were you at noon? The Negroes do not bring you back at noon because they do not like you. Have you seen *El Comercio* [the Quito newspaper]; Americans are beating their Negroes again. You Americans are too prejudiced; you study Negroes but do not help them. Here we let the infra-humans vote." By this time I would be in an emotional bind, wishing to debate with the serranos but also feeling compelled to listen to them to understand just what they were saying and what it reflected about their attitudes.

Brushing the flies (sometimes hundreds of them) from a plate of food, I would listen to conversations about money, business, the Junta Autónoma, and national and local politics and attempt to take part as though I were an interested Ecuadorian, hoping that no one would again try to sanction my daily behavior and associations.

Participant observation is not simply an exciting means whereby one learns the lifeways of a people better and better as every day goes by. Although I did learn them better, it was frequently my own actions that provided the catalyst for discussion. In retrospect, such catalytic action is intellectually rewarding, but it is also emotionally trying. I never had trouble at the end of a day falling exhausted into a deep sleep.

One final aspect of my participation in the lifeways of the San Lorenzeños deserves mention. Since the routines of the townspeople involved two different concepts of time, I had to endeavor to get at least a rough idea as to what went on through various twenty-four-hour periods. The sawmills, Junta Autónoma offices, and one public restaurant (the Salón Ibarra) were on national time, as was the normal work day for dock crews and the Junta Autónoma workmen. But those who fished, farmed, and traded, and otherwise lived by means necessitating an awareness of the tidal flows worked on a time schedule determined by the lunar day. People leaving or entering San Lorenzo usually tried to adjust their day to the rise and fall of the 12-foot tides, which occurred once every 24 hours and 51 minutes. Before I knew enough about the rhythms of men and women in different occupations, I found it necessary to adjust my "days" in various ways, too, so as to get some sense of who was doing what, when. Accordingly, I would sometimes retire in the afternoon, getting up as the lights went out and wander around town until dawn. At other times I would get up before dawn, or begin my participation in the afternoon. There was no time in a 24-hour period when something was not going on in San Lorenzo. I did what I could to sample the different routines and rhythms, always trying, however, to satisfy the national time system for meals and thereby thwart accusations of not liking highlanders by not showing up for breakfast, dinner, and supper at the Salón Ibarra. "Participation" in the life of a dynamic, class-stratified town of nearly 3,000 inhabitants, ethnically divided between highlands and coast and Negro and non-Negro and working on two time systems, is a worthwhile goal, but never a complete reality for all sectors.

Daily informant work. Within two weeks of my return to San Lorenzo in 1963, I began to work intensively with several Negro informants from different walks of life and with two highlanders. Two of the Negroes could be described as "proletarian," by which I mean that they preferred short-run cash gains to the time investment necessary for peasant life. One was unusually intelligent. Within a few days he was able to draw genealogies rapidly and could read my notes upside down. In two months, by fooling with my typewriter as he talked to me, he had learned to peck out sentences on my typewriter and wrote a letter to my wife, which I mailed to her, telling her about my activities in San Lorenzo. He was also an inveterate prevaricator, but always with a discernable motive: to place himself in the most advantageous position according to his perception of social relationships at any particular time. The other was unintelligent, illiterate, and somewhat alcoholic, a condition uncommon in San Lorenzo. He was a man known to "do anything" for money, but of all the people in San Lorenzo, he turned out to be the most reliable in terms of his actual knowledge of community life. As long as I would pay him for his time, directly or indirectly, he gave me factual information. The Negro *teniente político* in San Lorenzo also became an informant, but I shall describe my relationship with him later.[5] Several middle-class Negroes gave me information from time to time. I would work with these men in their shops, usually but not always with my lower-class informants as go-betweens. I also worked with several farmers and fishermen, men who could be called peasants.

My two highland informants were in positions of respect and could be regarded as members of the local élite. I worked with them constantly to understand the gossip and the invidious comparisons taking place during social events, and to understand the background, financial position, and general goals of the other highlanders. Both highland informants allotted exactly one hour a day to me, no more and no less. When in the role of informant, they worked over whatever data I suggested, often recommending people who could give me more detail. Since both men were involved with politicians, bureaucrats, and local entrepreneurs and labor organizers, and since both intended to learn, while in San Lorenzo, as much as possible about the economics and politics of the region, both were valuable informants and both became my friends. I feel that I gave little to the two highlanders who helped me so much. They paved the way for me and gave me several hundred hours of their time, and I could repay them only a mere pittance.

Informant work with the Negro *costeños* was an entirely different experience. I noted earlier that I never found a steady informant on the coast. By this I meant I never found one who could sit and talk about genealogical relations, or folktales, or relate texts from songs for any length of time. Rather, my daily paid informants tended to direct my attention to various economic, status, and political concerns, regardless of the immediate topic of our discussion. If I had money to pay for information, they reasoned, then I must be important, and as an important person it was necessary to direct my attention to the center of strategy playing, as the informants perceived advantageous strategic networks at any time.

I shall illustrate this by discussing genealogical work with one informant, since it was through genealogical method that my above generalizations were originally formulated. Not long after my return to San Lorenzo in 1963, I asked Humberto if

---

[5] A *teniente político*, "political lieutenant," is an appointed civil administrator at the parish level of government. For a full analysis of administration, politics, and graft in western Ecuador, see Whitten, 1965, 1969.

he would like to earn money on a day-to-day basis. It was apparent that he had been eagerly awaiting my return, and that he wanted to give me information and to receive some cash gain for his information. It was also apparent that he could not afford to sit around different parts of the community waiting for me to become interested in something and then attach himself to me, later hinting that he had lost a day of dock work because he was helping me. He agreed to come to my house daily at a particular time, and to talk to me for two or three hours, for which time I would pay the equivalent of a half-day's pay unloading a boat, or working for the Junta Autónoma.

I began to work with him by making a triangle and saying, "This is you, do you have a woman?" (I knew that he was not married.) I drew double lines leading to the circle representing his woman, and then asked if he had children. He said yes, and I drew a single line from the double line indicating his two children. I asked if he had a brother or a sister and marked his three brothers and two sisters on the paper, using standard genealogical notation. I asked for their names and got no answer. Humberto began to giggle a bit and said, "Norman, look, what is this again?" He went through the simple rudiments of kinship notation, from man to sex link with a woman, to the children and he said, "The children were by another woman." It then appeared that each child was by a different woman. Immediately, he wanted to tell me who the fathers of other children by these women were and who they were related to. As we worked with names, sexual relationships, and genealogical ties, his knowledge grew, so that, at the end of three hours, he could work with genealogical charts as well as most graduate students at the end of the first two weeks in a course in kinship!

Humberto began showing up with friends and relatives whom he felt could fill in our growing genealogical chart (which I expanded on shelf paper). Altogether, more than thirty ancillary informants were involved in my conversations with Humberto. Informally, in other contexts, these informants continued their interaction with me, always supplying data of one kind or another. As we worked, Humberto became increasingly resistant to my using *his* triangle as an Ego reference point. This puzzled me, because the kinship system was obviously "bilateral" and because Ego-oriented aggregates of relatives functioned in economic contexts and in times of crisis. Why then didn't Humberto stress himself as central to his network of meaningful relatives? I began to discover that Humberto was primarily interested in any series of links that would connect him to a man or group of relatives on the rise socioeconomically in San Lorenzo. Important people as defined by Humberto were the culturally *significant* Egos, since they could provide security to those who helped them in their economic and social strategies (Whitten, 1965:148–194; 1968; 1969). Humberto, then, sought *his* meaningful Ego locus in a "more important" kinsman. In working with the genealogies of people *on the rise,* I found no such difficulties in identifying Ego reference points: those moving upward socioeconomically traced their relatives outward, just as their relatives traced their ties "inward" toward the economic, social, or political locus at any one time.

What became intriguing to me was that I was becoming an economic locus. Humberto and his friends and relatives (and the friends and relatives of my other informants) wanted me to have close ties with those of their relatives with the most economic, social, and political power. Humberto and the others kept telling me, for example, what a friend I had in José Calzada, whom I had never even met. It turned out that people close to me would talk as though I were very close to someone on whom they normally depended in order to make a quasi-genealogical connection between me, on whom they were temporarily dependent, and the locus of their strategic network of kinsmen, on whom they were dependent in terms of long-range strategies.

These tactics became apparent even when we worked on such simple things as the names of fruits, vegetables, or fish. Informants would be dissatisfied with my questions and begin telling me who would give me fruit or fish, or who would tell me the "real" names of various fruits or fish. Invariably, this person would be someone whom the informants regarded as a locus for determining their meaningful kinsmen.

Informant work thus became a game in which I sought fillers for traditional ethnographic categories while trying to figure out just what the immediate frame of reference of an informant might be. I learned a great deal about the strategies of kinship shuffling in the context of community socioeconomic mobility and power structure from the informants' tactics. Yet, I still find it difficult to say that this story, or that song, is "normally" a part of the folklore of the Pacific littoral. Only by changing contexts, and by keeping an informant off balance, could I double-check texts, stories, songs, and other aspects of the expressive life of the San Lorenzeños. Fortunately, of course, I was participating in daily life and thereby continuously checking my informant work.

Although informant work in San Lorenzo drew me inexorably toward loci of power and influence, I overtly avoided contact with the immediately powerful except at formal occasions or during relatively structured interviews. Only toward the end of my stay did I begin to interact informally with the "leaders," preferring always to keep my primary identity with the mass of Negro lower-class *costeños.*

Musical contexts. The music of the Pacific lowlands intrigues me. Like the Negro *costeños,* I am drawn by the drums and the yodeling falsettos of men and women to inquire what has happened. Inquiries about the music eventually led me to a deeper understanding of the mechanisms by which kinsmen reckon their ties to one another and by which apparent contradictions are ritually resolved.

Music is the dominant expressive mode in the *currulao,* or marimba dance, the *arrullos* and *chiqualos,* or wakes for dead children, the *alabados* and *novenarios* (wakes for dead adults), the *arrullos,* or spirituals for saints, and in the contexts of saloon dancing and fiestas. I took a strong interest in the various events, trying to behave as the Negro *costeños* behaved. I might note here that most highlanders treat the *currulao* and saloon music the same in terms of behavior, but they are regarded as very different by the Negro *costeños.* I rapidly learned how to behave in different contexts, including how much to drink, how much to give to others, when to ask a woman to dance, and when to wait to be asked, but it took a long time for me to associate the behavior in these different contexts to the meaning and significance of the behavior.

Many puzzling aspects of behavior in musical contexts arose. For example, it became obvious that the texts that men and women actually sang did not seem to be the same as those they *said* they sang. Also, at times people claimed ignorance of their folk music, while at other times they could be immediately stimulated to play and sing complicated and obscure songs with strikingly African rhythms that were quite unlike the national music and the coastal variants of the national music.

Most important for my continuing rapport in the community was the fact that I behaved differently in different musical contexts. Because of this people whom I knew fairly well behaved differently toward me during the *currulao* than they did, for example, in a saloon. Even more interesting was that some people tried to assume the role of "expert" during a *currulao* or wake or when I tried to learn a previously unfamiliar national dance. Frequently, someone who knew me well would tell the self-styled "instructor" that his behavior was out of place, and by listening and taking careful notes on such controversies over "proper" behavior, my file of information on musical contexts grew steadily.

Although I could behave properly during musical events, and

could even stimulate an event through indirect requests, I did not feel that I really understood the significance of music until I had spent over a year analyzing data and another year checking my generalizations in the Pacific lowlands of Colombia during 1964 and 1965. I recently summed up the significance of music in the Pacific lowlands as follows:

> We can regard the *currulao* and saloon musical contexts as being in symbolic opposition, and regard the other three musical contexts as supporting social relationships which form the basis for symbolic strategies portrayed in the *currulao* and saloon contexts. The *currulao* provides an expressive context which allows for realignments of household and marital structure when necessity demands it, but also provides stability for the particular structure at the time of the *currulao*. The saloon, on the other hand, provides the instrumental context of actual facile fission in domestic units, and at the same time establishes an expressive context in which economically feasible reciprocity can be established, or portrayed, through the exchange of acceptable tokens. (Whitten, 1968:60)

Most important here, I suppose, are the following functions of my intensive interest in music and its significance. First, my interest eventually led me to draw together data from many areas of life, and to study the remarkable cultural continuity as represented by African musical forms and the readjustments and adaptations of the social system to the fluctuating economic situation. Second, my interest was appreciated by the majority of Negro *costeños* for whom music meant a great deal. Third, my interest in music could be "activated" in times of political unrest. When accused of being a spy, or a CIA agent, or something similar, I could "fall back" on my interests in music and challenge the person making inquiries in terms of *his* interests; or I could ask him to help me with a confusing musical text. Fourth, musical events allowed me to see my best friends behaving in different roles and gave them the opportunity to redefine my role. Fifth, the music gave me a reason to carry a tape-recorder around and an opportunity to double-check texts with important people; during such double-checks we would range into a number of subjects, including sensitive areas of politics during a time of national upheaval. Finally, Dr. Fuentes also became interested in Negro folk music and began to work with me, gathering data on his own and gathering texts as I recorded. This collaboration intensified the bond between us, and in 1966 we published an article together.

Survey and census. From the beginning of my work I wanted to make a survey of every household in San Lorenzo, noting its composition and getting some idea of the ramifying kinship ties (and ties through affinal and attenuated affinal bonds) to other townsmen and to dispersed relatives. I also wanted information on income and ownership. During this survey I intended to use a short questionnaire and to probe in directions of political interest and concepts of meaningful kinsmen and friends. Because of the touchy nature of census material, I waited until I had been in San Lorenzo for more than three months in 1963 before attempting a survey. After designing the questionnaire, I discussed all the questions with Dr. Fuentes, the local priest (an Italian missionary), and the *teniente político*, who was at the time a Negro *costeño* attached to most of the important families through affinal bonds and regarded as "safe" by most of the townspeople. I carefully avoided telling the police or the Comisario what I was doing, letting them question me in front of the townspeople, but always being properly evasive, trying to turn their questions around to get them to answer my questions. I have formally summed up my aims during this survey as follows:

> . . . I administered a systematic house-to-house survey, designed and developed in the field, to check data gained from work with informants, more general interviewing, and participation in community and hinterland life. In conducting this survey, I was accompanied by the *teniente político* . . . a highly respected Negro who had lived in San Lorenzo for 17 years. The responses that his presence evoked, together with his intimate knowledge of all the old families (he had married a daughter of one of the most prominent Negroes in town), and most of the recent marriages and births, provided me with a wealth of detail I should never have been able to gather on my own. I paid the *teniente político* three *sucres* (about 15 cents) for each household; everyone knew that I was paying him, and for the most part members of the community took great pride in a local Negro's being paid to help the North American anthropologist. All data from the survey were again checked with several other Negroes, who were persuaded to give me more detail on families suspected of having been reticent—or inaccurate. Information on marriage was checked against official records in San Lorenzo and Limones and the archives of the Catholic missionaries. Finally, I returned to many households without the *teniente político*, to check seemingly contradictory or unusual information. (Whitten, 1965:6–7)

It took nearly three months to complete the census. On the back of each questionnaire, I drew a chart of the household composition and then made notes as to the location of as many relatives and friends as I could. I was particularly concerned with the kinship and affinal bonds existing between contiguous households, the definition of "household head," and the concept of "household" itself. One problem that had to be dealt with was the discrepancy between official census definitions of household and the folk concepts of household and household composition. The national census might define as one household what the San Lorenzeños regarded as three or four separate households (*casas*). Then again, San Lorenzeños would occasionally refer to one household as extending between two spatially distinct edifices, defined by the national census as two or more households. When I made it clear that I had no connection with the national census, people began to explain their household, family, and kindred relationships, even complaining occasionally about local officials who refused to listen to their concepts of household organization.

The *teniente político* insisted from the outset that he would ask the questions on the questionnaire and do all of the writing. The three-sided dialogues between *teniente político*, respondent or respondents, and myself were very valuable. I tried to take notes on the context and as much as possible of the discussions that developed. I discussed these conversations and attendant problems with the *teniente político* in the evenings, showing him my diagrams and asking him about information that seemed to me to be odd or contradictory. He soon began making diagrams of his own and comparing them with mine, occasionally filling in additional data gathered during his fairly frequent visits to other communities.

The census of San Lorenzo did far more than merely enumerate individuals and household composition. In fact, we frequently experimented, changing the contexts of the discussion to see what different answers we would get. In this sense we used an objective questionnaire as a projective test; instead of scrambling pictures or words, we used objective questions and scrambled the context as much as possible. The census served another, personal end. By April, 1963, during the most intensive period of census activities, I became terribly sick with worm infection and amoebic dysentery, complicated by paratyphoid that produced fevers and rapid fatigue. Although I could still move from house to house on census activities, fishing or woods work had become impossible, so I was able to devote all my time and all the energy I had to the census. The census served as a means to get inside every house and to meet most of the people in the community at least once. I took as many notes as I could on household furnishings, and wherever possible I asked questions about politics and the economics of community life.

Rumor and gossip. As time went by, my work and questions naturally led to a situation whereby I could easily be central to a network of gossip. Information came to me from many sources. People who did not like my informants told me stories about them, and my informants were always telling me a bit of gossip or scandal about their friends, neighbors, and enemies. I tried to provoke and stimulate gossipy discussions in order to see where discussions would lead, but I tried not to participate in invidious gossip unless it seemed necessary to do so in order to ensure a firmer position in the community.

Usually, gossip in San Lorenzo revolved around the expansion of real, ritual, or fictive kinship relationships to important or potentially important individuals. Such gossip also revolved around concepts of economic, social, and political importance. I never repeated information gained from the *teniente político,* from my survey, or from paid informant work. I did, however, talk about experiences and individuals in the context of my participation. Such gossip was expected; in fact, it became clear that some things would be casually told to me with full knowledge that I would likely repeat them at dinner or to one of my informants and friends. In this way, through communication networks interlaced with rumors about political and economic events, and through gossip about important and not-so-important individuals, I came to learn how the lattice of intersecting ties could be rearranged in the face of change in economic and political spheres. By making diagrams (sociometric analyses) of events and personal gossip at different times, I was able to see a bit more clearly just how people defined action sets oriented toward short-run gains. Many of the results of such analyses have been published (Whitten, 1965).

I resisted gossip and a clear presentation of self when traveling with informants and friends until I had spent enough time in a strange community to know what the immediate events shaping information flow might be. I answered direct questions pertaining to what many called my "mission" by nonsense replies. *"Pa' fume cachimba, y baile marimba"* ("I will smoke your clay pipe and dance your *currulao"*) was one of my favorite answers. This invariably provoked hilarity because smoking the *cachimbo* is a strictly Negro *costeño* pastime in this area, as is dancing the *currulao* (marimba). By changing the ending on *"cachimbo"* from *"o"* to *"a"* to make it rhyme with *marimba,* I did what most *costeños* do when they want to tease highlanders. By giving this response, I could define myself as a marginal insider and force questioners to joke with me in the coastal manner, not question me in the highland manner.

A notion of "layers of meaning" is necessary to understand the full thrust of such mild joking. For example, highlanders did not understand why my use of *"cachimba"* was humorous, for *"cachimba"* is the "correct" term for pipe. So it is, *but* the Negroes regard their clay pipe as very strong and of low quality, and so change the *"-a"* ending to *"-o,"* implying that their pipe is more of a "smokestack," or representative of the smoke rising from the firing of a cane field, or of a little *trapiche* or home-run sugar mill.

Special events. My work in northwest Ecuador was facilitated by a number of special events. While I was there, the Junta Autónoma workers struck against the Junta Autónoma officials, the Province of Esmeraldas struck against the nation, a *teniente político* was ousted from office, and a military junta overthrew the government of President Carlos Arosemena. Every time something happened at the national or regional level, reorganizations had to take place in San Lorenzo, and with each reorganization I built up case material on the sociopolitical process. Also, during my stay in San Lorenzo, the northwest sector of Esmeraldas province saw the beginning of a lumber boom and an expansion of tourism stimulated by the increased number of ships coming to San Lorenzo and by the possibilities of development in the area.

I tried to keep case histories of individuals central to local events during times of national and regional upheaval, noting their gains and losses, and trying to understand how alliances shifted in the face of changing advantages and new alternatives.

Archival work. Fortunately for my interests in special events, I was working in a community with a small-scale literate tradition. Every time a club or organization was founded, membership lists were made, officers selected, and copies of the minutes kept. I collected every list of every organization I could discover for a ten-year period from the towns of Limones (the center of the *cantón*) and San Lorenzo (the center of the *municipio*). I also utilized the files of the *teniente político,* the *jefe político,*[6] the *comisario nacional de policía,* the naval base, Catholic missionaries, malaria-campaign workers, local files of the only physician in the region, some of the records of the lumber dealers, and whatever information I could get from ship captains, officers, and crew on taxes, fees, graft, and so forth. I kept a file of clippings from *El Comercio* and some other papers and magazines and collected and used periodicals and short monographs on the northwest coast. Through my friend the post-mistress, I

---

[6] The *jefe político* is the civil administrative officer at the *Cantón* level, while the Comisario is representative of the supreme court of justice at either parish or cantón level.

obtained some duplicates of foreign propaganda sent to labor-union leaders and to officials in San Lorenzo. The local Italian priest also supplied me with pamphlets that gave me some idea of the material available to and possibly influencing some of the San Lorenzeños.

Bowing Out

Everyone knew that in June my wife would come from the United States and that she and I would spend some time seeing other parts of Ecuador and then would return together to San Lorenzo for a while. Our time together in San Lorenzo was, however, shortened by two factors. First, a military coup delayed us for a short time in the highlands, and second, our personal situation became complicated by several unexpected financial difficulties that by mid-July left us with scarcely any money to spend. Nevertheless, we returned to San Lorenzo to work as hard as possible to find out what had happened since the military coup of July 11. We arrived in San Lorenzo on July 22 and immediately began to make it clear that our time would be far more limited than we had hoped and expected.

Everyone was delighted that we had returned. Many apparently felt that, due to the coup and some problems with the railroad, we might not come back as I had promised. Our return was most welcome, and we immediately began getting to know people as a couple; at the same time, we began the process of bowing out.

When I introduced my wife to my informants and friends, I told them that we would soon be leaving. We began to give some gifts and to regard special events, e.g., a marimba dance and a saloon party, as our "last." People saw us packing notes and equipment and began, perhaps for the first time, to realize that all of the information I had gathered was going with me to the United States. Since northwest Ecuador is an area of mobile people, no stigma was attached to our leaving, and no one told us that we should stay in San Lorenzo and help with its problems. Many people asked us to come back, and women were particularly nice to my wife, asking her to come for a longer stay.

Early in the pre-dawn of August 2 we left; no highlanders accompanied us this time to the Autocarril, but a Negro *costeño* and his two children (of whom I had become extremely fond) were there to bid us adieu.

In 1964 during field work in Tumaco, Colombia (north of San Lorenzo, Ecuador), I found the family who said good-bye at our last morning in town and, during a brief revisit to San

Lorenzo in 1965, I was delighted to find that a great many people turned out to greet me and treat me like a returning relative. In 1968 I spent a month in San Lorenzo, again delighting in renewed friendships. Sadly, however, others have not had my experience. Although Peace Corps volunteers have lived in San Lorenzo since 1963, they seemed to have antagonized nearly everyone, highlanders and *costeños* alike. Why, I don't know, and I do not wish to guess.

Summary and Evaluation

The problem that emerged from my preliminary work in 1961 and to which I addressed myself in 1963 was to understand the processes of ongoing change resulting from the opening of northwest Ecuador by a railroad linking a port town to the capital city. With a sketchy base line from a visit by Ferdon (1950) in the 1940s, and with comparisons made to political and social processes during two governmental overthrows in 1961 and 1963, I felt that a technical description of the manipulative processes of people within the framework of their social organization would give a microevolutionary view of change.

By focusing on networks of interpersonal relationships radiating from successful individuals, instead of seeking dysfunctions in institutional "groups," I was able (in northwest Ecuador as well as in southwest Colombia during 1964–1965) to develop a model of social structure. This model demonstrates that work-group heads, politicians, and economically successful individuals invest heavily in social capital. They rely, that is, on interpersonal ties as mechanisms of redistribution in times of need. People in northwest Ecuador use their social capital to gain indirect control over the distribution of inputs from the cash economy, which is externally generated. They do this, I found, by directing inputs into, and through, a network of cooperating kinsmen. Although definable groups are ephemeral, loosely knit networks tend to endure, some transferring membership through three generations. The most important feature of social structure in northwest Ecuador, I found, was that individuals could rise within their own communities by investing in social capital and by using social-capital resources to advance during economic booms and maintaining a relatively dormant but potentially valuable network during depression periods.

The interpersonal ties that cluster around striving individuals may be viewed as adaptable to fluctuations in the externally generated money economy. Individuals can mobilize such "fluid" social capital to influence carriers of the economy—absentee élites and managerial "whites"—so the system functions, regardless of the particular type of input. For example, tagua booms, banana booms, and lumber booms have all produced rapid adjustments, reinforced symbolically from within the community.

I found that in western Ecuador cultural values reflect the structure of upward mobility. Economic and political success within the community have a positive value, even to the unsuccessful. It is expected that individuals will strive to exploit newcomers, and that the successful exploiters will rise in status and wealth. The expectation allows for rapid restructuring of interpersonal networks and justifies the use of the term *adaptable* to describe the Pacific littoral social system. Obviously, by the time I finished my work I had reintensified my interest in theories of change, theories that allow for the characterization of capacities and on-going processes of social and cultural change. I published, first, a monograph on San Lorenzo (Whitten, 1965), followed by several more technical analyses on the cultural features contributing to opportunistic adaptation to a fluctuating money economy (Whitten, 1966, 1967a, 1967b, 1968, 1969). In the 1969 paper I developed a model of social organization built on a sequence of "successful strategies," which I think is predictive of the meanings and organizational functions of social activities of individuals in the Pacific littoral of Ecuador and Colombia. A note on methods in my conclusion states that:

> In order to apply my model of successful strategies, however, it is necessary to know what the economic possibilities are, and also to discern the available social and political capital. One should know, to use a model of developmental sequence of strategies, not only what people are doing and trying to do, but also what their *possibilities of success will be*. Methodologically, this involves, at some point, the development of a model which attempts to see daily activities as part of emergent organizations, and organizations as phases of a developmental cycle, the developmental cycle being a dynamic representation of a dominant aspect of social structure. The data for such a model are the qualitative data gained through genealogical method and the life history approach. No "new anthropology" is required, only a more creative, generalizing approach to data gained from proven methods.

Ideas such as this began to influence my field work as I moved, first to Colombia, and then to the study of relatively isolated Negro communities in Anglo-America. I became less interested in new and innovative field methods and increasingly interested in just how far one could generalize from field data.

Were I to redo my work in Ecuador, I would try to develop a generative, predictive model earlier in my field work and then devise a scheme for testing it in another community. I have already begun to test and expand the model developed for the Pacific lowlands, and I will soon begin testing its applicability intraculturally and interculturally.

PART II: NOVA SCOTIA[7]

Problem, Theory, and Research Design

While continuing field work in Colombia during 1964–1965, I read about a relocation project for Negroes in Halifax, Nova Scotia. The article mentioned other communities of Negroes in Nova Scotia that whetted my interest. I wrote to a sociologist and to an anthropologist at Dalhousie University in Halifax, who passed my letter on to others, and I learned a bit about the history and contemporary situation of Negro Nova Scotians. It seemed to me, after working with materials from western Colombia and Ecuador for nearly five years, that I needed a change of ecological zone, but a continuation of general interest. Also, I had been wondering what general model to use in understanding the social system of Negroes in the Pacific littoral. Should I consider them as peasants? Should I emphasize the results of slavery? Perhaps I had not considered as fully as I should cultural continuities from Africa.

It seemed that Nova Scotian Negroes living in ethnically identifiable communities within a depressed part of Canada should be in a structural position comparable to that of the Negroes of the Pacific littoral who live on the fringe of larger systems. As a secondary interest, I wanted to expand the literature on New World Negroes a bit. Accordingly, I proposed to the NIMH that I spend the summer in exploratory field research in Nova Scotia. The following quotation will give my concept of research and theoretical design prior to a visit to Nova Scotia:

> The basic notion guiding this research is that uprooted people tend to adapt first to their ecological setting using their most

---

[7] Deliberate attempts have been made in this section of the chapter to disguise people and places. In some instances data have been deliberately scrambled to ensure many of my friends among Negro and white Nova Scotians the anonymity they requested. Some idiosyncratic characteristics of particular communities have not been mentioned to divert attention from the community in which we resided. Also, characteristic features of Negro communities throughout the Canadian Maritimes are included as though they existed in Norfolk.

accessible social capital—kinship. In a changing system one expects kinship to provide instrumentalities for coping with the larger society while at the same time providing an acceptable basis for community social solidarity. Reflections and projections of people's awareness of their own system are transmitted generation by generation through what is usually called oral literature, or folklore. Ecology itself is part of a larger social field defined by the changing economic, social, and political orders of the larger society. . . .

The proposed study is the outgrowth of my research with Negroes in similar social situations in Ecuador and Colombia. The Ecuadorian and Colombian work sensitized me to the adaptive mechanisms developed by the Negroes in coping with economic and social marginality. The socioeconomic situation of the Nova Scotian Negroes is structurally similar to that of the Ecuadorian and Colombian Negroes. But the environment is, of course, different. Nova Scotia has been chosen to continue investigation of Negro groups in marginal relations to the larger society precisely because of the environmental difference. It is suggested that in comparing Nova Scotian and west Ecuadorian and Colombian Negro social organization certain regularities will be found that can be related to socioeconomic marginality, regardless of natural environment and specific historical circumstance. At the same time, other patterned differences will emerge due to the different ecological adaptations and due to different sociocultural adaptations arising as a result of specific historical factors.

I stated at this preliminary stage of formulating research, that:

By demonstrating the adaptive mechanisms functioning to maintain a marginal, uprooted people who make up a part-society in a changing social system, it is hoped to redefine the problem of the dynamics of social organization, cultural change, and coping mechanisms frequently characteristic of New World Negroes.

Finally, in terms of methods, I proposed the following:

The approach to research will combine a general area survey with intensive participant ethnography. About one month will be spent in traveling to every Negro community in Nova Scotia. This will be followed by at least one month of residence in a Negro settlement (to be chosen on the basis of the preliminary survey), where daily work with informants will be combined with a survey of household composition and economic patterns. Informant work will begin with the taking of genealogies and will proceed toward a systematic survey of household and community economic, social, and political modes of adaptation to the larger sociocultural system. Very careful attention will be given to the Negroes' own conceptualization of their lifeways and patterns of adaptation, both in interview situations and by collecting and analyzing folktales, folksongs, and other manifestations of common traditions of folk explanation. Careful note will be made of the content transmitted to, and accepted by, children. Children's games, sayings, songs, and other patterned behavioral characteristics will be analyzed as learning devices and as projections of parental adaptive patterns.

In other words, my work in Nova Scotia was designed as a first step toward developing formulations relevant to the study of adaptive strategies of marginal people. I was also specifically concerned with the cultural mechanisms whereby people transmit reliable concepts from generation to generation. It was planned that my wife and I would work together, first surveying the various communities that seemed relevant to our research, and then working together within a particular community with people from all walks of life.

Passive or Adaptational Research

Washington University granted us sufficient funds to buy basic supplies and to subsist for about a month in Nova Scotia. An NIMH small grant for exploratory research provided the funds for the second two months of the summer of 1966. We drove to Nova Scotia in a Volkswagen squareback sedan with camping equipment, books, two typewriters, a cocker spaniel, and a variety of office aids. Having contacted various officials and academicians in advance and having read quite a bit about Negroes living in the Canadian Maritime Provinces, we arrived prepared for conferences and discussions with "experts" prior to beginning our survey. Since we intended to work out of Halifax during the first month, we took a couple of rooms near Dalhousie University, and began rapidly to orient ourselves to Nova Scotia, to officials responsible for research, and to applied programs that might impinge on Negroes living in ethnically identifiable communities. We also began to meet some Nova Scotian Negroes.

The Institute of Public Affairs, part of Dalhousie University, appointed me as temporary research associate for the summer and aided in establishing key contacts with heads of welfare organizations, civil rights groups, and institute heads. Everyone welcomed the initiation of my research and seemed to look forward to continued investigations by my wife and me. Very good advice was given to us in and around Halifax, and within a day we thought we knew the proper people to call in the Negro communities, and the proper way to enter. Little did we understand at this point the formal and informal systems operating in Nova Scotia! People told us what the "proper" thing to do was, without telling us that, in terms of practical entry, the "proper" system was not likely to work.

The largest concentration of Negroes in Nova Scotia is on the Dartmouth side of the Halifax-Dartmouth twin cities. Here, within a fifteen-mile radius there are three Negro communities, collectively containing an ethnically distinct population of approximately 4,000 to 5,000 Negroes, officially separated into three rural communities and an urban sector of Dartmouth. About the same number of Negroes live on the Halifax side in two distinctive urban zones (one of which is in the process of relocation) and in scattered, outlying rural communities. There are Negro communities south of Halifax, scattered from Yarmouth to the Windsor Plains area along the Bay of Fundy, and on the eastern side of the province. North of Halifax there are communities ranging from Guysborough east to Antigonish, with some scattered communities just south of the isthmus connecting Nova Scotia to New Brunswick (cf. Winks, 1964). On Cape Breton Island there are Negro communities in Glace Bay and Sidney. We intended to visit, for at least a brief period, every community ethnically identified as "colored" in Nova Scotia, and if possible, in Prince Edward Island and New Brunswick.

Since we had a car, and were working in an English-speaking area, we anticipated gaining considerable knowledge fairly rapidly. Our initial introductions brought us into contact with the college-educated and technically trained strata of Negroes— among them civil-rights activists, community administrators, and educators. They were all favorably disposed to our work, and they encouraged us to try to work on the Dartmouth side of the twin cities. Since the greatest amount of ethnohistorical data (cf. Fergusson, 1948) and folk history of Nova Scotian Negroes pertains to the Dartmouth region, and since the people of this area do seem to represent a crystallization of cultural content at greatest manifest variance with Nova Scotian "white" society, we were eager to make friends there and find a place to live in one of the three communities.

Following what we regarded as good advice from knowledgeable people responsible for various aspects of welfare for Negroes in the Dartmouth area, we phoned a number of responsible people, among them the councilor for the largest Negro settlement. We were told that phoning prior to direct encounter was the proper thing to do, and that to try to meet a community official without first phoning would be rude. We were also strongly advised that contact with community members prior to contact with the "leaders" was improper and would cause serious problems. My phone conversation with ministers went well, and I was encouraged to call the councilor, which I did with disastrous results. I introduced myself as an anthropologist from the United States, interested in problems encountered by people in rural communities in different parts of the Americas. Following procedures common in the United States and supported by educated Nova Scotians, I said that I was particularly interested in Negro communities kept somewhat outside of the larger social and economic system. I was told, politely, but firmly, that the people of the rural Dartmouth region had had enough of outsiders who insulted and hurt them under the guise of research, that the people of the region were as human as I, and that I might turn my attention to other communities in the province. I was asked why I chose "Negroes" and when I explained that Negroes, more than others, had been excluded from full participation, I was again told that the people of rural Nova Scotia were all alike, and that the colored people were tired of being regarded as somehow different, because there was no difference.

This encounter came as something of a blow to us. Within the first week of research we had blundered in such a manner as to alienate the person with whom we presumably had to make friends if we were to work in the area of our choice. We later found that we made two basic errors. First, when Nova Scotians tell one to first call the official responsible for a community, they are paying due respect to the official, but they do not expect the investigator to take this advice. They expect that the investigator will establish an enduring contact with someone who can introduce him to the official. Crucial to this procedure is that the investigator be first known to the person who will make the introduction, for the middleman may be held responsible for the investigator's mistakes. The recommendation to call relieves anyone from responsibility for the call, and hence it is not expected that a person will follow this advice. Second, it is not expected that one will use the term *Negro* in referring to Nova Scotians ethnically identified as colored. The use of ethnic terminology (including the term *colored*) is reserved for those who are already a part of the system. It is strongly felt that outsiders should not recognize differences until they have lived in the province long enough to become familiar with all of the connotations of ethnic terms. The most effective way to approach an official, we found, is to recognize no ethnic distinctions whatsoever, thereby forcing the official to make the preliminary distinction (e.g., between colored community and white community). By so doing the investigator is in a position to immediately inquire as to the significance of ethnicity. Had we acted a bit more slowly, and ignored ethnic differences, we might have succeeded in gaining early entrée, but we erred by assuming that we knew the best way to do things in Anglo-America. By talking too much, and not reflecting carefully on the possible connotations attached to our "instructions," our work bogged down for a time.

One other factor hindered our entry. Whites and Negroes responsible for various aspects of Negro welfare assumed that we would not and could not live in the Negro community. Because their assumptions were firmly grounded, they would talk to us as though we were preparing for residence in one community or another, assuming that there was a mutual understanding that we were talking about living "close to" the Negro community. They assumed that our stated goal was an expression of an ideal, while we regarded our statements as declaring a manifest intention. In fact, there are probably Nova Scotians whom we got to know who are still not fully aware that we eventually did take up residence in a Negro community. They accept our statement as to residence as evidence that we achieved satisfactory rapport in another area of the province.

It should be noted here that in the 1950s a journalist published an article about Negroes in a Nova Scotian community that did inestimable damage, in my opinion, to continuing ethnic relations and to the possibilities of research among Negro Nova Scotians. Posing as a social-science investigator, the reporter apparently attempted a crash analysis of a community, publishing the results in a sensationalized article in a prominent magazine. The people mentioned in the article knew nothing of the pending publication until it appeared on the newsstands. To this day a person claiming to be doing "research" with Negroes is mistrusted in most of Nova Scotia, and with good reason. Research, particularly in the Halifax-Dartmouth area, has thus far meant one of two things: sensationalized reporting with racist overtones, or a survey preparatory to relocation or some other welfare move, which many people understandably fear will work to their detriment.

From the third week in June to the middle of July, my wife and I engaged in three principal activities: informal contacts with Negroes in the Halifax-Dartmouth area and attendance at their prominent events, a survey of the Negro communities in southern Nova Scotia, and archival work, which itself became a sort of field setting, as we shall see.

From our base in Halifax we tried to attend all significant events in the rural and urban Negro communities, as well as civil-rights meetings and other functions to which Negroes were invited. The best place to establish rapport was at Baptisms. The

Baptisms in the Negro communities take place in the summer months, and there is a Baptism nearly every Sunday in July and a few in August in one community or another. People visit one another's communities and expect interested outsiders to attend. The Baptism is held at a lake or stream near the community church, where services are held before and after the ceremony. "Lunch" or "tea" (a good-sized dinner) is served in people's homes, after which there is an evening service. At the evening service there is usually a visiting choir from another Negro community. It is expected that everyone in the community attending the Baptism will be invited to someone's home for lunch.

During the first Baptism of the summer, the minister of the community invited us to join him for lunch. He also invited a number of community members not only from the town in which the Baptism was being held that week, but also from other settlements that would be having Baptisms in subsequent weeks. Through these contacts, and by attending all Baptisms, we received invitations for lunch. We were treated cordially and accepted as people who wanted to get acquainted, not just write something and leave. Although no one in the largest community ever invited us to his home, several people did tell us that they "would have invited us" if they "could have found us," or that they "told X to invite us and he must have forgot," or that "we thought you would be eating at Y's house." Outside of their home communities, Negroes we became acquainted with were very friendly, open, and interested in us and our work. But inside the community, closure asserted itself, and we could find no one willing to let us live with them. "After all," one person told us, "I have to live in this community. I like you fellers and trust you, but other snoopers will think I'm up to no good." We began to internalize the attitude that people asking questions are "snoopers" and that, as whites living in a Negro community in Nova Scotia, we would be functioning as "spies" by trying to dig into the structure of Negro Nova Scotian life. By mid-July, 1966, we had, with regret, abandoned the idea of living in a community on the Dartmouth side of the Halifax-Dartmouth twin cities. We continued our contacts, however, in hopes of moving in during the next year.

Our contacts in and around Halifax expanded as we attended services of various sorts, the most interesting being the more fundamental Protestant services. I remember one where we were treated very well, because we were accompanied by a prominent song leader and two prominent deaconesses. After listening to the public confessions, I was a bit startled to hear my hostess mumble to me, "Don't you have anything to say?"

Being asked to speak did not bother me, but being asked to con-
fess was something else. Since I did not respond, she stood up
and explained that our presence was due to the workings of
God: "I wanted to attend the service, but did not know how I
would get here. I wanted to hear brother Rigsby sing, but had
no way of arranging a church 'singsong.' I prayed for help.
Then along came these fellers from the States and talked to me,
and along came the singer and talked to me, and God directed
all of us to the same car and the car brought us all to the
church for the lovely service by the movement of God's hand."
She said she guessed God had sent us to her. Then she jabbed
me in the ribs and said loud enough for everyone to hear, "Don't
you have a few words to say, brother?" I stood up and told
people how glad I was to be there, that I taught at a college
in the United States, and that whenever possible my wife and
I spent summers and sometimes longer periods with people living in other parts of the Americas, because we wanted to know
more people in our part of the world. I said that we especially
liked the beautiful music in the Halifax area and that I hoped
the people would let us come into their church again to worship
with them, get to know them better, and listen to their music.

Important here was presenting ourselves in such a way
that we had a right to be in church services, but were not expected to be missionaries or ministers. Most whites who frequent Negro churches in Nova Scotia are carriers of the Word,
and we certainly did not want to give that impression, but
church attendance is essential in Nova Scotia if an investigator
is to be privy to the symbolic and power structure of a Negro
or white community. I stressed an interest in music because I
did like it, and because the ceremony was so dominated by
singing. If we were asked why we were interested in this particular community, our answer was: "We can read about Cape
Breton Island, the eastern shore, the cities and large towns;
we can read all about the Scotch, the Irish, the Germans, and
the English; but no one seems to talk about you people, who
are also a part of Nova Scotian history." In our interest in
music and history we found a common meeting ground with
most community members in Negro Nova Scotia. People thought
that their music was the best in the province, and they were
curious about their history. They could tell us about their music
and their ideas of their history, and I perused archival sources
for concrete information to give them about their history. As
long as we stayed out of the communities near Dartmouth,
except for special events, our relationships steadily impro

In the stage of adaptational research around the H
area, we found our tape recorder to be an especially he

search device. I had been reluctant to use it at first, because people objected so strongly to even the appearance of a camera and because I thought they might regard a tape recorder as a sinister device for recording their conversations. This was not the case. Tape recording is associated with music, and to record music is desirable. I found that a number of people had access to tape recorders and were delighted to find that I could copy tapes for them for their own use. In fact, after the church service mentioned above, the lead singer asked me to record his singing, which I did. We became quite friendly, and I spent a good many hours talking to him. In this way I began to collect some genealogies and some information about his life history. By this time we had begun our survey of other communities, so I could ask him about places we had visited. He would usually begin by telling me about his relatives in the various communities. When we later moved to a community in southwestern Nova Scotia, several people enjoyed listening to the tapes we had made and then volunteered to let us tape them.

In general, we proceeded slowly in the Halifax-Dartmouth area, and we succeeded in convincing people that we would not harm them and that we were genuinely interested in their lifeways. But because of their association of "research" with applied surveys or sensational reporting, we were effectively blocked from taking up residence in one of the communities. Perhaps we could have wielded some power through Dalhousie University and the welfare services to get a residence in a public building, but we felt that this would violate the principle of open, scientific research. We felt our moving into a community where our neighbors would be afraid of what their neighbors would think was to assume the role of intruder.

Our survey of Nova Scotian Negro communities consisted of driving to various places, mapping the Negro area, talking to some officials about the Negroes in order to get their impressions and concepts of segregation and interethnic relations, and visiting with relatives of people with whom we had already achieved some degree of rapport in the Halifax-Dartmouth area. We were interested in getting a sense of the basic economic mode of people in ethnically identifiable communities and in finding a community in which we would be allowed to live for the remainder of the summer. We also wanted information on the basic economic mode of surrounding areas and in finding an area in which we could work without the whites getting unnecessarily concerned.

In general, we found that Canadian Maritime Negro communities are characteristically removed from both the coastal fishing and commercial centers and the inland lumber centers.

We regard them as "grafted" onto both; there is scarcely a store in any Negro community in Nova Scotia, except for small rooms in a home where cokes, bread, and a few bare necessities are sold. Although the Negroes' residential base is ethnically segregated from the white community (except in Halifax), they are nevertheless *dependent* for goods and services on the neighboring white communities. White Nova Scotians may described the Negroes' lifeways as based on "agriculture" and "woodlot," but the basis is spurious. For the most part, the majority of Negroes live by foraging off the adjacent white communities. Our problem in understanding the economics of these communities became the problem of understanding the strategies people adopt to live on charity and welfare, while keeping a modicum of self-respect and self-esteem in a larger society that stresses the virtues of work and measures the worth of the individual by his economic success.

Our survey could not be extended, as we had hoped, to all of Nova Scotia due to red tape involved in receiving our funds. Travel costs more money than does work within a community, and by mid-June we did not have the funds to extend our survey north. We limited ourselves to working from Halifax south, leaving a survey of the north for a later time.

Archival work in and around the Halifax area became an extension of the field situation. Since people expressed an interest in their history, I volunteered to search for anything they would like to know about. Many people wanted to know more about the old land grants. Were the Negroes given land? If so, how much? Many people mentioned the Ripton Report, which presumably established Negroes in the area now known as Africville on Bedford Basin in Halifax. This was particularly important, because people in that area were now being relocated. Many felt, and still feel, that the city should have provided water and sewerage facilities to the community, rather than uprooting them after more than a century of occupation.

When I asked for specific information at the Public Archives of Nova Scotia I was presented with secondary reports. When I asked to see primary sources, red tape began to ensnarl my search. To see primary sources I needed special permission and letters of recommendation. I was told that a number of lawyers had already worked on the "colored people's claims" and found them unsupported. I explained that I was equally interested in folk history, legend, myth, and written scholarly history and explained that I was not there to challenge the establishment's view of history, but my explanations were to no avail. Time ran out, and I had to content myself with secondary sources.

We had a very different experience in the Provincial House

in downtown Halifax, where we explained our situation and asked first for information about communities on the Bay of Fundy and then gradually moved back to the more sensitive subject of land distribution in the Halifax-Dartmouth area. Had we begun our search in the Provincial House instead of at the Public Archives, our progress would undoubtedly have been much more rapid. We collected many interesting scholarly tracts, public statistics, and popular materials, and discussed our findings with our friends in the Negro communities, even lending them some of the materials we had Xeroxed.

An adequate history of the Negro Nova Scotians is yet to be written, but materials are available in Nova Scotia that refute the prevalent folk belief, fostered by white Nova Scotians, that most of the contemporary Negroes of Nova Scotia are the descendants of free people who entered the province during and after the War of 1812 (cf. Fergusson, 1948).

The small high-school and college-educated Negro sector became somewhat upset by evidence of slavery in Nova Scotia, as did many white Nova Scotians. However, many members of the rural communities accepted the findings, and the few civil-rights militants found in the information a new argument. As one young man put it, "Here they [the whites] have been telling us that our ancestors came as free as anyone but too ignorant to take advantage of this land; but if they came as slaves then they [the whites] are wrong—we didn't have the same chance. No wonder we don't have as much today." In 1899 the Nova Scotian Historical Society published a monograph entitled *The Slave in Canada* (Smith, 1899). "Why isn't this monograph ever mentioned in high schools or colleges when the question of our history arises?" asked one civil-rights leader.

By mid-July we were ready to move into a community of Negroes in southwestern Nova Scotia. I will call the community Norfolk, since I know no community by that name in Nova Scotia. I will not identify it other than to say that it is in the county that the Leightons and their associates (Leighton, 1959; Leighton, 1963; Hughes, 1960) call "Stirling County," and that it is grafted onto a community included in the Stirling County Study.

We had visited Norfolk during our reconnaissance travels in June, 1966, and we were impressed by the possibility of later residing there. Excellent relations have been established with the people of southwestern Nova Scotia by the Leighton researchers, for their work is not identified with either applied social welfare or sensational journalism. In fact, two members of the Leighton team, one a Canadian, the other an African, have lived briefly in Norfolk. After meeting various people and following two or three leads for a residence, several people hit on the idea of our renting a house owned by a West Indian woman who spent a good deal of time outside of the community. We contacted the woman, made arrangements by early July, and moved to the community in mid-July.

I immediately found a scythe, began mowing the tall mid-summer grass, removed some boulders from her driveway, and in other ways began to assume the role of a man fixing up his house (or as the people of the area say, "frigging around the house"). During our initial entry, our landlady visited the house to "open it" and hired a neighbor to help iron and clean up. When the landlady returned to her job, the neighbor and her eight children stayed around, asking questions, and telling us about people and things in the community. Thus began the most intense relationship we have ever had with an informant. Our conversations expanded from our first moment of entry to the extent that, by the time I got my typewriter unpacked, I already had many notes to write, and information was still flowing. This experience is rather rare, I suspect, in field work. We literally had trouble slowing our new neighbor down enough to get oriented.

In our first two weeks in Norfolk we had found a house across the street from a woman who was trying to find out how to fit into community life; we had found a marginal person in a marginal community. This was our first important breakthrough. This person was unusually intelligent, perceptive, and remarkably verbal. She could not resist telling us everything she could think of about any person whom we happened to mention or to whom we were introduced. She was a known gossipmonger and she was known—and perhaps feared—for her strikingly accurate memory and for her unwillingness to take note of the "proper time and place" for spreading information. People knew that we were hearing the community gossip from our first moment of residence.

Second, we were personally introduced to responsible individuals in the community by a man known to them through both research and political channels. Although we were formally "placed" in Norfolk by the officials, we used their resources only to gain the name of our landlady.

Third, we were actually taking up residence in Norfolk, not traveling from house to house asking for information. People could observe us in our daily (and nightly) rounds and could discuss and evaluate us on this basis.

Fourth, the timing of our move to Norfolk was propitious, because in the late summer many people visit the community from Canadian and United States cities. It is a time for renewing friendships and for intensifying kinship bonds. There were many community "singsongs" during the month, and there was also some church politicking in which we unwittingly played a minor role. At church we were surprised to be well received by the head song-leader of Norfolk, because church officials are usually somewhat reticent. We learned that this person, who was physically ill and in need of welfare from outside the community, looked on any outsider as a possible source of assistance. Since the majority of white people visiting the community are either welfare personnel, medical personnel, or religious people, who are believed to have healing and political powers, he could scarcely be blamed for making friends with us. Through him we gained access to the more "respectable" contingent of the Norfolk prestige hierarchy.

Finally, during our first two weeks of residence in Norfolk, a visit was made to the town by deacons from the Halifax-Dartmouth region. All of them knew us from the Baptisms, and we had dined after a Baptism in one of their homes. They were frankly surprised that we were actually living in the community, and they carried back word to the Halifax-Dartmouth area that we were serious when we said that we would like to live in one of the communities labeled as "colored."

We immediately began intensive informant work with our neighbor, whom I shall call Gloria. After a couple of days, I told Gloria that I wanted to know everything that she wanted to tell me, but that it would be much easier for us if we could ask questions and work at specified times. We said that we would pay her an hourly wage for talking to us, provided that she would allow us to interrupt, to ask questions, and to probe various areas. In other words, we began almost immediately to systematically elicit information and to train an informant. We spent over a hundred hours during August in *formal* work with Gloria. Frequently, she would return soon after a formal session to pay a social call, during which she would tell us things she felt she could not mention during "working hours."

For example, during her informal social calls Gloria would tell us about ourselves in the context of Norfolk life. We owe to her, for instance, the information that a number of people thought that we were members of the Protestant sect known as Jehovah's Witnesses probably because of the similarity between *Witness* and *Whitten*. Gloria not only suggested the relationship, but pointed out to us that advocates of the Sect thought we were ignoring them, whereas non-Jehovah's Witnesses were avoiding us. We were advised by Gloria to manifest an interest in drinking in order to break the stereotype. (Jehovah's Witnesses shun all alcoholic beverages.) She suggested the "proper way": that I drink with one of the men on Sunday, who would quietly spread the word that we were indeed "normal." On Sunday a young man showed up, and I gave him a beer; we talked a little while and he left. Later his father, a deacon in the church, came by; we talked of religious matters and he left. In this way we were introduced to the Nova Scotian conceptions of proper behavior: drink in one context, get religion in another; don't mix contexts, and you won't have any trouble. What was so striking was the manner in which Gloria sensed that which we needed to know in the community and went about engineering social relationships that she thought would benefit our work. Gloria was unique among our Nova Scotian friends, though her behavior would have been characteristic of normal relationships with informants in western Ecuador.

Although Gloria moved us into networks of interaction, she continuously cut herself out of them, a fact that never ceased to distress her. Somehow, although she could verbalize the proper model of social relationships, her manifest activities indicated that some underlying strategy necessary for success escaped her. We began to wonder what it was that Gloria did wrong and why her obvious knowledge of people and their behavior in Norfolk and elsewhere worked so often to her personal disadvantage. In solving this problem we developed, at least partially, a model of adaptation appropriate to the networks of interaction into which we were drawn by Gloria and others.

Our relationship with a second informant, Deacon Johnston, a leader in the African Baptist Church, was of another nature. He wanted to teach us about the larger area, not just about the community. We traveled with him and his wife and their children to see fishing, farming, and logging activities, and we talked at length with them about their experiences in the southern region of Nova Scotia and eastern New Brunswick. Through them we met relatives and friends, but we gained little data about their relatives. It was Gloria who filled in the details and helped us to draw genealogies. (Curiously, it was through the Johnstons that we first learned of Gloria's closest relatives and details of her immediate life history.) Travel with the Johnstons also led us into a complex of faith healing in the region and sensitized us to some of the mutually exploitive Negro-white relationships that take place in the economics of faith healing.

We attended all formal meetings and events during the month of August, contributing to them and working to help set them up. We also endeavored to interact with people who did not attend such events and to participate in aspects of sacred and secular life that were mutually contradictory, but that occurred in different contexts. By so doing, we reinforced our continuous statements that we were interested in everything.

We left Norfolk around the first of September, a time when relatives and friends of our informants who had been visiting Norfolk for the summer were also leaving. During the week just before our departure, we invited a friend from a nearby town to visit the community and to show movies of Nova Scotia, an event that was well attended, and that people seemed to appreciate and to accept as our token of thanks to them for a rewarding six weeks. Just before we left, the song leader of the church had to enter a Halifax hospital. We drove him to Halifax and helped his family with the remnants of our NIMH grant. Although this was intended as an act of friendship, not a research strategy, it solidified our position in the community, but it also exposed us to a source of exploitation upon our return. We let people know that we would be returning during the summer of 1967 to visit for three months with them and to learn more about that area of Nova Scotia.

Active Research

The results of our active research during the summer of 1966 led to a reformulation of our research proposal. In spite of good rapport, two excellent informants, and children continuously around the house, we could get very little material on folk tales, legends, or myths that indicated a heritage of adaptation to a marginal existence. In other words, a part of our original idea had to be abandoned. The children's poems and sayings were characteristic of the northeast, and the country in general, and "Old Miss Brown went to town, got to the corner and her britches fell down" told us little about symbolic adaptation. Immediately upon our return to the United States, we applied to the NIMH for a second small grant to work on a new problem, "a problem which arose from our participant observation in Norfolk, and from intensive, daily informant work with two key informants." We stated the problem this way:

> The problem is to understand the cognitive and conceptual systems underlying the classificatory scheme of mental illness which ranges from classes of people regarded as "mental" through "foolish" to "kind of funny." This classificatory model, intrinsic to the postulates of mental illness employed by Negroes (and others) in southwestern Nova Scotia, helps to establish a system of *invidious sanctions within interpersonal networks* whereby individuals seem to be able to prevent their relatives and friends from moving up within a community by making constant reference to mental illness in respective networks of kinsmen.
>
> This problem became apparent only during the last two weeks in Norfolk, after a great deal of confidence of informants had been

gained. While collecting genealogies, it began to become apparent that people remembered one another's genealogies, but tended to "forget" their own. Our best informant finally cleared up the problem by suggesting that if we would only mark all of the "mentals" and "foolish" people in X's family tree, we would know considerably more about the kind of person we were dealing with (X was our other principal informant). It also became apparent that those who cooperated with one another seemed to be concerned with deriding one another, or making invidious comparisons when not cooperating. At this point [fall, 1966] it seemed to us that those who cooperate in one context must deride one another in another context. A favorite way of deriding one another is to refer to mental illness in one's genealogy. Because of the invidious aspect of concepts of mental illness, we find people being classified differently according to the *immediate position* of the classifier in intra-community and inter-community associational networks.

I returned to Nova Scotia by car near the first of June, 1967, and my wife followed by plane in early July. I was met at the ferry by Deacon Johnston, the song leader, one of the two really good informants with whom we had established close contact in 1966. I returned with him to the house we had rented the summer before, and he and I began to clean up a bit. He invited me for supper at his house, and I began to pick up the threads of the previous summer as though there had been no break at all.

Data-Gathering Techniques

Presentation of self. I presented myself as a college teacher interested in living with people to understand their lives better. I explained that I taught anthropology, and that I needed to live with people in order to really understand anthropology. To those who wanted more information, we explained that we were on a government grant that provided us with equipment and living expenses. We showed people our manner of writing and filing notes, our genealogies, maps, and mechanical aids (typewriter), and we allowed children to watch us work, knowing that they constantly reported exactly what we did. A couple of people asked if I were working on a dissertation and when I replied in the negative they then asked if I were a "doctor." I said that I was a "doctor of philosophy in anthropology." One person decided that I must be similar to a psychiatrist, and a couple of visitors from Boston decided that I was like the professors in that city and, like some of them, interested in retreating into a wooded area for the summer.

The majority of people simply decided that they would regard us as people who liked the province and were "trying to fit in." I avoided "explaining my mission" in church, and in fact, I persuaded a couple of deacons to help me engineer situations so that the minister would not call on me for a full explanation during a prayer meeting. My reluctance was based on the tendency for ministers to ask: "Why do you choose a Negro community to study?" I did not mind answering this sort of question privately, but I knew that any public discussion of segregation in Nova Scotia would offend the congregation.

People generally regarded us as belonging to an older age group, particularly when we were together. In general, all of the people over sixty, and many between forty and sixty called us by our first names. But some of the people our age and a little older insisted on calling us "Mr. and Mrs. Whitten," although these titles were dropped when we interacted with them singly.

We also presented ourselves as people who could help in emergencies and we were frequently called upon to take someone to the hospital. We made quite a few trips to ferries to pick up summer visitors and to return departing guests. Following the death of the mother of one of our close friends we made our car available to convey flowers and to pick up people at a ferry.

Mechanical techniques of recording information. We used the same techniques in Nova Scotia as we had in Ecuador, but with better equipment. The 5″ × 8″ slip system was continued, as was the keeping of a daily log. During 1967 two informants agreed to talk with a tape recorder running, and we recorded approximately 75 hours of trained informant work. This material is particularly valuable in eliciting conceptual categories. For example, the subtle descriptions of what makes a person "foolish" can be completely preserved for future analysis.

Whenever music was being played or sung, I recorded it, which pleased everyone. We made copies of tapes for those who wanted them and even recorded an entire funeral for members of a family upon their request. We made kinship diagrams and a map on shelf paper. We did not conduct a house-to-house survey. Our work was facilitated by an electric typewriter, and, in Halifax, a Xerox machine in the Provincial House, which enabled us to copy manuscript material pertaining to history and ethnohistory.

Film was mailed immediately to Kodak Laboratories, and no particular methods for storing tapes were necessary.

Participant observation. In and around Norfolk we visited the homes of friends and opened our home to visits by people from different walks of life. We traveled with people, attended their church services, their parties, and shared with some of them moments of grief as well as happiness. We were invited to dinner and to visit relatives and friends in different communities. Many of the church services we attended were in other communities. Our participation was the fullest in the symbolic and recreational spheres of life; we were involved only tangentially in the economic and political spheres.

During church services many of the tensions of daily life are symbolically expressed. Such tensions pertain to the results of poverty and to interpersonal conflicts resulting from divisive claims to prestige in a basically egalitarian system. Confessions and even the singing of spirituals are oriented not only to propitiating supernatural realms, but also to the subtle sanctioning of members. By attending all services, in the community and outside of the community, our awareness of the tensions, interpersonal conflicts, and cooperation considerably increased. The underlying meanings of dozens of spirituals became apparent as we began to build associations between personalities, events, and the use of favorite songs. It also became apparent that church as a meaningful context of symbolic expression is restricted to about 20 percent or less of the adult population, except when the explicit purpose of a church meeting is a "singsong" at which time the attendance rises to sometimes 60 percent or even more. However, events occurring in the context of church are discussed, reinterpreted, and spread through the community, so that individuals are aware of implied sanctions and reinforced norms, even if they are not present.

Fortunately, in Norfolk, the song leader realized that we preferred to observe and to record singing, and he avoided calling on us for a testimony or confession. Perhaps I should note here that although I found it fascinating to learn to dance the *currulao* and to learn to act properly in what to me is an "exotic" setting in Ecuador, I shrank from giving testimony in a fundamentalist protestant manner.

We were frequently invited to dinner or to spend an evening in someone's home. Such occasions were ideal for the informal gathering of data pertaining to cooperation and competition. We found that the conversation rapidly turned, at such events, to the negative qualities of a dozen or so persons. At first we thought that the people who were being discussed must be enemies of our hosts, but we soon learned that they were the individuals most closely involved in strategic networks of relationships—networks that could and would be tapped in case of actual financial need. Such invidious gossip about close friends seems to have several functions in Nova Scotia. Basically, it hinders entry through one friend to another. If I am close to

Henry and he is close to John, but Henry insists to me that John is "no good," then it is difficult for me to approach John through Henry. It seems to me that invidious gossip about one's closest friends protects a given Ego's investment in his "social capital." Such investment is one tactic of a more general strategy of survival in a system stressing the worth of individuals, but not providing the economic base necessary to individual worth, except through welfare, which is, itself, testimony to the individual's inability to earn his way in life. Unfortunately, invidious gossip as a complementary tactic of protection also serves to deprecate the very person making the comparisons. If a man's friends are untrustworthy and he must interact with them, what is the worth of a man?

Attitudes such as those abstracted above are expressed to outsiders during meals. Sometimes, the host even cries as he thinks about his life, his friends, and his chances for success. Crying, or near-crying among close associates is a socially standardized way of expressing the extreme pressures of a marginal existence in a land that is reputedly rich.

The ethnographer in this system finds that he may not be trusted unless he, too, engages in invidious gossip. We found that we could avoid hurting our neighbors by gossiping mainly about our colleagues back at Washington University. But, on the local scene we also had to admit that John, or Alexander, or Mary had faults, making sure that we enumerated faults that would also reflect on ourselves. For example, by speaking of a Norfolk community member's love of drink, we could scarcely know about a person's habits without sharing them ourselves. To be a "healthy sinner" but to keep sin a secret is the proper way to present one's self where we worked in Nova Scotia; such proper presentation is reinforced through mealtime conversations.

Stuttering, like crying, is a mechanism for lowering one's self-esteem while gossiping about others. By stuttering and by confusing oneself, some of the "sting" is removed from invidious comparisons. I found, on my return to Washington University, that I had developed a stylized stutter, which asserted itself at embarrassing moments.

Taking people places in a car, or occasionally riding with them in a truck, proved valuable. During travel people talked nearly continuously about their friends and relatives in other communities, explaining relationships and describing the faults of their relatives. By making it clear that we would take people wherever they would like to go, we could gain access to information on networks of interaction ramifying throughout central and southern Nova Scotia. In fact, it is probably accurate to say that we were doing an ethnography of intersecting networks, not a community study. This is because most of the individuals crucial to the livelihood of relatives are found scattered in different communities. Many networks included individuals in the Halifax-Dartmouth area.

Intrahousehold analysis leads to different intercommunity linkages, we found. By traveling separately with husband and wife we were introduced to different routes and different people. Such travel afforded us a much clearer picture of the dynamics of social organization and the adaptive capacity of the marginal Negroes of Nova Scotia and carried us into dozens of homes to which we might not have gained entry had we been living in the community instead of passing through. We found that a strategic role was that of stranger to a community, loosely connected by tenuous relationship to a relative close in genealogical ties but living far from the community itself.

Travel of any sort also provoked discussion of interethnic relationships, something that is difficult to get people to talk about within their own community. Once on the road, our friends would explain to us the nature of segregation, including the subtle ways in which it affected them. We learned of problems in restaurants and theaters, on the streets and in various people's homes. In general, a patterned statement continually arose from the stories and illustrations: segregation is strongest closest to home. While Norfolk Negroes might be excluded from restaurants, theater, and school in the adjacent white community, they would be admitted to those in a more distant community. They would sometimes explain, when asked about some form of discrimination in a more distant community, that the Negroes there had "brought it on themselves." Finally, traveling to people's homes meant reciprocity when other people were traveling through Norfolk, and by traveling with informants we were able to keep abreast of gossip and news from about 18 communities. In 1967 we drove 12,000 miles within Nova Scotia.

The concept of "travel" among Negro Nova Scotians includes the idea of spreading news or gossip. While this is positively valued outside of the community, it is negatively valued within the community. Since a vehicle (i.e., a car) is a proper mode of travel outside of the community, one is less suspect if he also uses a car to visit friends in the community. One is not expected to do much "traveling" within the community unless one travels by vehicle. People are not supposed to walk through a settlement, going from door to door, chatting briefly with numbers of people along the way. It is expected that those with cars will drive from place to place (even though the distance may be negligible) and chat and gossip from the vantage point of a car. One of the major criticisms of outsiders is that they do too much "traveling" (i.e., walking) in the settlement. Fortunately, we learned this early, for our inclination would otherwise have been to walk from house to house, visiting and talking. We learned to use our car as much as possible, sometimes parking it at one end of the community and then visiting several people there before moving it to another area. As long as the car was traveling, we were relatively safe, but for us to travel without the car was to imply that we were spreading gossip.

Unlike my field work in Ecuador, information flow in Nova Scotia was severely limited in work contexts. When asked about some aspect of his activity the individual standing in a group of men would generally answer, "Yup" or "Nope" or "Mm." If he responded at all to a question while working, it would be to say, "Stay around long enough and you'll find out." Only by getting an individual alone, and in my own house, could I really elicit information pertaining to the work day in woods or field. I worked with the men, cutting some wood, helping them move furniture, bargaining for fish, cleaning around houses, but I could not do too much with those whose primary reliance for economic security was on welfare contacts, formal and informal. I tried to loiter in Norfolk Center, the white community, but found I was hurting the chances of the Negro loiterers for part-time work, so I gave this up, substituting instead observations made from a distance and later informant work to find out who had hired whom for what purpose.

People liked to have me work with them, and they spoke well of me, but they simply gave no information when they were working. The experience of my wife was different. She could talk to women while they were working (i.e., cooking, washing, cleaning) and could get considerable information, provided that she did not try to "travel" within the community. It was expected that she would make one visit to someone's home, help them, and in return be treated to gossip. It was not expected that she would visit different people on successive days, for to do so would be to provoke too much gossip and thereby be placed in the category of one who "travels" within the community.

In general, then, participation in the lifeways of Nova Scotian Negroes was most valuable when we were in sociosymbolic (religious) contexts, or when we were traveling outside of the community. Work contexts were not, for me at least, particularly profitable, although I did, of course, learn quite a bit through them. The most valuable context was daily informant work.

Daily informant work. Gloria was fascinated by us, by our motives, and by our stated interests in the community. She was also desperately trying to understand the dynamics of the community that was excluding her from her notion of full participation. Her life seemed to confuse her. She had grown up in the area, then moved to Halifax, returning later with broadened knowledge and a hope of "fitting in," only to be repulsed. Gloria was ready to explain what she could to strangers in the hope of better understanding the situation herself.[8]

Deacon Johnston was a man well respected in the settlement, and he, too, had a problem. He had injured himself in such a way as to be unable to work in the woods, the only kind of work his financial means allowed, but he was not sufficiently disabled to receive a disability pension. He needed capital to begin a small business peddling fish, but he could get the capital only through his pension fund, and a man on a pension was officially prohibited from working. He wanted us to understand his position and help him figure out a way to begin working again, without the pressing pain involved in strenuous labor.

Both of these people became superb informants; both were destitute. Both contributed enormously to our work, and received in return money as well as such side benefits as free travel as long as we were in Nova Scotia. The compensation they received, however, was terribly small compared to their contribution. They are still destitute in a system where the likelihood of their increasing their opportunities is extraordinarily slim.

Informant work with Gloria began with a subject dear to her: the taking of genealogies. I began with Gloria in much the same way as I had in northwest Ecuador. I showed her the symbols for male and female and for consanguineal and affinal bonds. She immediately grasped the signifiance of the kinship diagram and began asking questions about where to begin, whether we should begin with the old folks or the young, whether we should indicate all children by different unions, and so forth. She actually demanded information about symbols to use for legal marriage, consensual union, and children by men other than the husband while husband and wife were cohabiting. In other words, she anticipated many of the sources of confusion common to graduate students in anthropology. I showed her the mechanics of representing kinship structure, and I helped her place relatives when she wanted me to, but I always encouraged her to describe relatives, marriages, and her concept of relationships in any way she chose. She watched me make charts as we talked, and she would frequently correct my statements or questions by pointing out a position on the chart.

While my diagrams of relatives and affinal relationships ex-

---

[8] Very limited and somewhat scrambled personal data are given on Gloria in order to assure maximum protection of anonymity.

panded, my wife kept detailed notes on other features of our discussion. For example, Gloria was fond of discussing the ailments of the people she mentioned. My wife endeavored to record in Gloria's own words the various afflictions of various people, both within the community and outside of it.

As we worked with Gloria in 1966, it became increasingly apparent that her memory of other people's relatives was far more reliable than her memory of her own relatives. By mid-August, 1966, we had placed nearly 2,000 people on intersecting genealogical diagrams. The residence of the people we placed ranged from Los Angeles to Boston and from Calgary to Toronto and Montreal. We double-checked this information with other people, both formally and informally, and found Gloria's knowledge to be remarkably accurate, including her knowledge of disputes and breaks in family ties of people living thousands of miles away. Sometime around mid-August while we were discussing the genealogy of Deacon Johnston, Gloria made a suggestion. We had colored pens on the table and had used various colors to help sort out the charts and to indicate interrelationships. Gloria suggested that we color yellow all of the personalities who had what she regarded as some inheritable disorder.

She suggested, specifically, that if we would mark all of the "mentals," "foolish," and the people "slow to learn" and "kind of funny" in Deacon Johnston's family tree and the family tree of his wife, Martha, we would know considerably more about the kind of people we were dealing with. Not until 1967, when we continued our work with a full set of genealogies covering over 2,000 people and including local descriptions of the illness, real and reputed, of several hundred people, did we begin to realize that Deacon Johnston, Martha, one of Martha's daughters by another man, and Gloria could all be regarded as making up a network of relationships in which vital economic and communication exchanges took place.

Martha's and Deacon Johnston's genealogical ties to their dispersed kindred were crucial to their survival in Norfolk. Gloria, who was unrelated to the Johnstons, could readily provide information about the Johnston's genealogies, but she insisted on presenting these data in terms of inheritable or potentially inheritable mental illness. At the same time, Gloria was one of several critical community links connecting the intrahousehold exchanges of Martha and Deacon Johnston to relatives dispersed through other communities. This she did by her invidious gossip with visiting relatives of the Johnstons, the most prominent gossip partner being Martha's daughter, a person never mentioned by Martha until Gloria described her to us.

It would take an entire paper to illustrate the exchanges in this Johnston-Gloria ramifying network, and such a paper is planned. Suffice it here to say that Gloria would work without pay for Martha when Martha had a number of guests. The guests Martha entertained gave gifts of money to her in return for her hospitality. This money was frequently allocated in terms of need, and need was determined by reference to gossip with Gloria. Money from visiting relatives was used to run the household when Deacon Johnston was without income. Deacon Johnston would provide Gloria with fish and firewood when she had none, doing so without the approval of Martha, who opposed such charity. By invidious gossip aimed at Martha, Gloria supplied Martha's daughter with information about Martha's needs, and Martha's daughter sent money home when she heard about such needs and also supplied Gloria with clothes and other household items from time to time.

Had we not observed such economic exchanges (of which the above is merely a brief sketch), we would have inferred that the four people mentioned were very unlikely to ever help one another out. Even within readily discernible family lines it seemed as if those who cooperated to maintain one another at a marginal economic level derided one another on a social level.

We began to find that the "structural amnesia" when it came to remembering one's own genealogies was functionally related to the invidious gossip used among people cooperating in networks of economic exchange. When we discovered that a favorite way of deriding a person with whom one is cooperating is to list infirmities in that person's genealogy and to suggest that infirmities, or their proclivities, are transmitted from generation to generation, we understood the working of structural amnesia. People forget their genealogies, or refuse to discuss them with close associates, because they are afraid of transmitting any knowledge about possible inheritable mental illness. The more a person derides his friends (most of whom are related to him in some way) and the more he employs concepts of inheritance, the more his own mental stability can be questioned on genealogical grounds. In other words, the concept of inheritable mental illness seems to function as a brake to invidious gossip.

By the time we had worked for several weeks with Gloria, people in the community knew that we had a sense of genealogical connections, and intensive informant work was not necessary to elicit information on other people's friends and relatives. By training Gloria in genealogical method, but by not training other friends and informants, we were able to maintain a check on our introducing pattern and structure into trained informant work. On the whole, we found that Gloria learned techniques with extraordinary rapidity and used the techniques to communicate to us more effectively her conceptions of the significance of relationships.

Because of Gloria's remarkable memory and flare for genealogical skills, we developed a map of households with her. We first worked through households in our community and then in an adjacent community. She suggested in mid-summer, 1967, that she take paper and pencils when she visited relatives in other communities and work out household compositions and genealogical connections between the households. In this way she added to our files notes on about 1,000 *more* Negro Nova Scotians. As nearly as we could determine, she was as accurate as any professional investigator in this work. After working through the genealogies Gloria spent hours reworking them with us, discussing each individual and the significance of her own comments. During 1967 most of these sessions were recorded on tapes, which, together with my notes and charts on genealogy and my wife's notes on mental illness and other features of our discussions of illness and personality, represent a full record of our transactions with Gloria.

We also worked on Gloria's own life history and on event analysis of community activities. We found that discussion about her children was quite valuable. She had moved around a great deal and had had eight children by the time she was twenty-six, so each child had come along within a context of changing social, economic, and personal patterns. When we asked her about, say, William's birth, she immediately recalled relationships with her husband, where they were getting money at that time, the state of health of the other children, who took care of them when she was having William, what she later owed relatives and friends in return for help, and so forth.

There were two problems involved with informant work with Gloria. First, she always brought her eight children with her, and they, naturally, wanted attention and rapidly became bored. My wife tried to keep them and the two dogs (Gloria usually brought a dog with her also) relatively quiet while taking notes with me. She fed the children and played games with them. At the same time, my wife was also working with the children, for she kept careful notes on their concepts and choices of foods and about patterns emerging in their play. Similar work was done with many other children, but not to the same degree of intensity.

Second, we sometimes had difficulty in finding time to do our other work in the settlement. We had to try to avoid accusations that the only person we listened to was Gloria. There was no single solution to this problem, but, fortunately, Gloria too wanted to avoid accusations of monopolizing our time.

Work with Deacon Johnston involved discussions of the entire area. He was endeavoring to understand an ethnically plural region that he regarded as having the capacity to alleviate his poverty. He was searching for a source of income that did not involve physical labor, which was obviously quite painful to him because of an injury three years before. Deacon Johnston could also give what he considered to be encapsulated information about folk medicine, local politics, church financing, and dozens of other topics. This information was of primary value in stimulating informal discussions with other people. By finding key issues and phrases, and by seeking points of dispute or moderate sensitivity in church and community affairs with Deacon Johnston, my sensitivity to subtleties in daily gossip increased.

The most important material gained in this informant work involved Johnston's attempts to "do the impossible"—to engineer a full army-disability pension for himself and to use this pension to set up an active fish-peddling trade. As his attempts failed one after another, I moved, physically and mentally, with him toward an agonizing understanding of the ramifying interpersonal networks that involve white and Negro Nova Scotians with local politics, local welfare, and informal exchanges of capital and goods and that usually lead to a dead end as far as economic advance is concerned. I experienced quite deeply the despair of upward socioeconomic orientation and the continuous leveling of potential capital resources. I felt, as did Deacon Johnston, that he was on a tread mill. In a sense we learned together the nature of mobility in Negro Nova Scotia.

In summary, informant work in Nova Scotia turned out to be intensive and continuous, and it involved my wife and me not only in the collection of a wealth of data, but also in frustrating and at times emotionally trying situations. We absorbed some of the pain of the failure of our informants and friends, only to realize the even deeper pain of the never-ending search for livelihood and for acceptance in which the usual adjustment to economic marginality results in the cultural perpetuation of marginality itself by the mechanisms of invidious sanctions imposed on those who do try to move upward in power over economic resources.

Open-ended and structured interviews. In addition to our participant observation, travel, and intensive informant work, we conducted a number of open-ended and structured interviews in the community. For example, my wife interviewed two of the best-known midwives about specific techniques and several women about their relatives. I interviewed many people known as church authorities in the community, always requesting any records that might be available. In general, direct access to records about the community and the role of various individuals in the community was not difficult. We tried to introduce informal queries about on-going events and about relationships between persons with whom we were particularly familiar as we did structured interviewing. Actually, we gained more information about the respondents' personal situation and life history than about the subject of the interview. Life was so trying in this setting that people could not seem to focus for long on history or the organization of the church or any other matter without bringing the subject back to themselves and their relatives and neighbors. The best setting for interviewing women seemed to be in their own kitchen, while the best setting for men was in my house, when my wife was not at home. We found role segregation essential to eliciting data during structured interviews. Only with Gloria could both of us work in an interview context, though, as I have said, we did travel with, and thereby informally gain a great deal of information from, the Johnstons and from other couples.

Because of the stigma on "traveling" in the community, we decided against a door-to-door survey. We also felt that, since a number of welfare workers were preparing to do a survey in the province, we might become associated with them if we began asking direct questions about household composition and economic circumstance.

Bowing Out

Whenever my wife and I drove off alone or talked about leaving, people wondered if we were "sneaking out" earlier than anticipated. Our actual departure was facilitated by the convention of the African Baptist Association held toward the end of August, 1967, in Dartmouth. We had some work to do in Dartmouth and Halifax, and so we left a few days before the convention with the understanding that we would see people from Norfolk at the convention. This we did, while using our residence at Norfolk to gain entrée into the Dartmouth communities before and during the African Baptist Convention. We renewed friendships in Dartmouth and traded information with some Dartmouth-area Negroes about their Norfolk relatives and acquaintances. We also recorded music during the African Baptist Association Convention.

After the meeting, we said good-bye to those returning to

Norfolk and started back to St. Louis. We have kept in touch
wth some of our friends in Norfolk and elsewhere since our
departure, and we plan to continue these contacts.

Summary and Evaluation

In a sense, the Nova Scotia work was not designed as a full
ethnography. We were interested in problems of adaptive response to larger environments, and we regarded the Nova
Scotian field work as an opportunity to examine processes of
adaptation to economic, social, and political marginality in a
cultural setting quite different from South America. Since the
work took place only in the summer, we were not able to gain
an adequate picture of the yearly round of activities in this
northern temperate zone. We saw only the best of the Negro
Nova Scotian lifeways, for summer is when relatives visit, when
there are a number of public festivities, and when the struggle
for warmth and food is not an overriding consideration. In a
preliminary fashion, we began the work that we proposed: to
gain a preliminary understanding of some of the dimensions of
adaptive response to marginality.

In the Canadian Maritimes we found segmental, interpene-
trating personal networks with local and dispersed segments that
gave individuals a social-capital insurance within their communities by providing information channels for exploiting formal
and informal welfare agencies. We also found that cultural
sanctions on individuals striving upward invoked references to
the network of cooperating, or potentially cooperating, kinsmen.
The innovation of such sanctions was particularly evident among
cooperating kinsmen themselves. In other words, upward striving invoked an automatic devaluation, in quality, of social-capital
resources. Social capital seemed "frozen," not "fluid."

To understand the cultural mechanism of invidious sanctions that devaluates social capital, we had to work with the
rudiments of Maritime ethnopsychology, together with the tacti-
cal use of the ethnopsychological framework in Negro communities. For our analysis it is important to note that the classificatory
model (including "mentals," "foolish people," etc.) supports a
system of invidious sanctions within interpersonal networks
wherein individuals are usually able to prevent their relatives
and friends from moving up within a community. This is accomplished by reference to mental illness in respective networks
of kinsmen, and by reminding strivers, including one's own
reference points for relatively successful coping, of transferable
and potentially inheritable illness and handicaps in their net-

work of relatives. Illness fear in Canadian Maritime communities seems to us, at this stage of our analysis, to be structurally similar to witchfear in other parts of the world (cf. Honigmann, 1959; Middleton and Winter, 1963).

Our data from 1966 and our attempts to examine our ideas through our travel and network analysis during the summer of 1967 have led us to tentatively conclude that people can seldom rise in their own communities except by moving through a series of networks and by giving conspicuously to the African Baptist Association. Such conspicuous giving usually eventuates in a lonesome adult, with attenuated economic resources, and with very tenuous social-capital insurance. Such individuals are frequently leaders in church affairs and serve in religious contexts as symbols of misery. They portray their burdens through song, prayer, and testimony, distributing their misery through the community and contributing to the game of invidious sanctions, for if the best in the community are so unhappy, then surely there is something wrong with any happy strivers.

The alternative to the leveling effect of intracommunity striving is outward migration together with the maintenance of network ties providing strategic mechanisms for later reincorporation, presumably at an improved economic level. Outward movement is accompanied by economic aid to relatives who remain in the community, and this aid, together with annual or biannual visits, provides an old-age insurance policy that is cashed in when the migrant returns, in his declining years, to the intracommunity game of invidious sanctions. The more material wealth the migrant has accumulated during his life, the more he owes his network of cooperating relatives upon his return, the theory being that if he returns solvent, it must be because he did not provide sufficiently for resident relatives during his absence. Economic success within a community is negatively valued, because it is seen as curtailing adaptive advantage of other persons vis-à-vis the economy imposed from the outside.

It is expected that individuals *will* strive to exploit newcomers, but that they *should not* so strive. People within the personal network of strivers work to keep successful exploiters from rising in status and wealth. Such endeavors may take the form of derision of the striver vis-à-vis other outsiders, denouncement to welfare personnel, and the spreading of damaging gossip through adjacent white communities. The sanctions imposed on the structuring of interpersonal networks justifies the concept of *specific adaptation* for the Canadian maritime Negroes' social system. The system is characterized by specialized exploitation of marginal resources, to the point where marginality itself is culturally perpetuated not through disorganization but through cultural emphasis on leveling within strategic networks for adaptation.

To date, in Nova Scotia, we feel that we have made a beginning toward understanding microevolutionary change. Future work must involve a full study of the more closed communities near Dartmouth, and the study must be at least a year in duration. Also, the situation developing in Halifax-Dartmouth urban areas that might be characterized as "incipient black power" needs careful attention. It seems to us that a radical change in the adaptive capacity of Negro Nova Scotians is the only way to break the barriers of overt and covert discrimination on the one hand, and specific adaptation to economic marginality within the rural communities on the other hand.

PART III: COMPARISONS BETWEEN FIELD WORK IN ECUADOR AND NOVA SCOTIA

The differences between research with Ecuadorian and Nova Scotian Negroes within their respective plural systems are many, and any one specific difference could provoke considerable discussion in terms of the ways in which methods were adapted to specific settings. For example, in Ecuador I worked alone most of the time, in Spanish, in a nucleated community of nominal Catholics undergoing social and cultural change in the context of a fluctuating cash economy. I became terribly ill for a period of time, and I suffered considerable weakness from dysentery and fever. Transportation was exclusively by local means.

In Nova Scotia, on the other hand, I worked most of the time with my wife, in English, and remained in good health. The settlement in which we resided could be described as a "linear" community strung out for nearly two miles along a dirt road. Although they are subjected to television and radio and living in a broad north American framework of radical change, the fundamentalist Protestant Nova Scotian Negroes seemed to be intensifying their adaptation to economic marginality. We provided a major source of transportation to our friends and informants, and our car freed us from dependence upon local transportation (whether this is good or bad is another matter). In Ecuador the idea of being studied seemed positively valued, whereas in Nova Scotia it was negatively valued. Obviously, each variable had its effect on our field methods.

I should like to focus on network analysis in the two settings and to indicate how the same general modified genealogical method in Ecuador and Nova Scotia led to different pathways of social acceptance and opened our eyes to different modalities of adaptation in the two areas.

There seem to be tendencies today to assume that networks themselves can be analyzed and classified without reference to the cultural significance attached to people's own explicit or implicit notions of their "social capital." The papers presented at a Conference on "New Approaches in Social Anthropology" (Banton, 1966, Vol. 4) appear to reinforce a position taken by Leach (1954:17), who suggests that "it is the underlying structural pattern that has real significance. . . . Particular structures can assume a variety of cultural interpretations . . . and different structures can be represented by the same set of cultural symbols." I agree, in the broadest sense, with Leach, but I cannot accept the part of his argument that asserts that it is the underlying structure that has "real" significance. My own underlying model of social structure is that of continuing organizational readjustment, implying change, while that of Leach is continuing organizational adjustment, implying equilibrium. My reluctance in accepting the argument of Leach also stems from attempts to compare similar underlying structures. I shall try to justify these statements below.

In both Nova Scotia and Ecuador the underlying structure of social relationships that is expressed through various cultural mechanisms can be regarded as a "personal network," defined by Mitchell (1966:55) as "a series a relationships which an individual builds up around himself on a personal basis." Making such a statement, however, is only to begin to understand the nature of personal networks in a context of social change. Raymond T. Smith (1962:33) has called attention to the overemphasis that scholars have placed on the study of the social organization of "New World Negroes" by their close attention to family and household structure. He tells us that such a focus "has tended to divert attention from the networks of relationship linking households to each other." Because of his programmatic statement, some comments on our attempts during the past seven years to use techniques of network analysis are doubly important.

It seems to me that a study of the adaptive capacity of aggregates of people in marginal socioeconomic circumstances must consider the overt cultural pattern within which strings of social capital may advance or retard individuals' capacity to strive toward economic success in various systems. Without a cultural mechanism to support a drive toward success, the tendency to maximize opportunities to exploit improved economic circumstances would decline, thereby necessitating the disruptive effects of radical social change with concomitant processes of cultural revitalization.

The methodological significance of these remarks must now be discussed. I would argue that, marginal though he may be to the cultural orientations of a given people, and peripheral though he may be to their social, economic, and political system, a competent ethnographer becomes central to a data-gathering, rumor-distributing network that usurps power from other systems. Because the anthropologist must learn as much as possible in a short time, he is bound to make close friends and through them to work outward in ever-ramifying networks of interpersonal relationships. Networks are discernible lines of linkages in an exchange system, and communication mechanisms are linkages in such a system. Inasmuch as the ethnographer's focus is the continual quest for knowledge about a given people's lifeways, he inevitably presses close friends and informants for insights into their covert and overt knowledge.

I suggest that people whom the ethnographer comes to know best in a given system perceive, in one way or another, some strategic advantage to continued association with an outsider. I further suggest that their perceptions and their tactics to involve the anthropologist more firmly in their network of relationships can generate data valuable to the analysis of cultural mechanisms of network formation and maintenance. Seen from this perspective, then, part of the anthropologist's problem is to understand the methods and mechanisms by which people are placing him in a lattice of ramifying ties.

Let us now compare the cultural patterning of Ecuadorian and Nova Scotian Negroes' manipulation of the ethnographer. In northwest Ecuador I found that I was inevitably drawn to the various loci that my principal informants and friends regarded as central to their adjustive tactics. Their idea was to move my economic potential closer to the social and political center (an important social or political figure) from which they were reckoning relationships at any given time. Centricity became apparent once I understood that the general adjustive tactics of my friends was to bolster the center of their network with economic capital that they could then borrow if necessary through the channels established by kinship bonds and bonds of attenuated affinity (Whitten, 1968).

To the extent that attention had to focus on me in order to move me, I was central to a network of individuals that could be regarded as usurping economic power from legitimate, traditional, loci—the perceived centers of dispersion, the sibling-

ships of local stem kindreds (Whitten, 1965). To the extent
that I moved toward the center of dispersal, I became a component
of exchange in ramifying networks of individuals radiating,
at any given time, from various important individuals
vying for power in a fluctuating economic and political system.
To ignore my role in the daily machinations of San Lorenzeños
would have been to close my eyes to the significance of the
adaptive capacity of the system. It is logical that a system in
which individuals have the capacity for incorporating newcomers
is a system in which the economic capital of the newcomers
is potentially open to exploitive redistribution by co-actors in
adjustive encounters with a social organization.

I would characterize the system of network formation and
centricity in the networks of northwest Ecuador as *associational*.
Knowledge involves one in the actual activities of persons about
whom one is learning. As informants explained the nature of
their family, kinship, and friendship bonds, they worked to involve
me with those same friends and relatives. Knowledge itself
was directly associated with cooperative activities with
other persons. If A told me about B and B's relatives, he usually
tried to involve me with B and through B to B's relatives,
frequently completing the string of linkages by indicating both
the *central person* in the network and *his own position* at various
points in networks of association. Associational networks
were always potential avenues of distribution that functioned
when short-run economic gain was possible.

In Nova Scotia *distributional networks* were apparent, but,
with the notable exception of Gloria, we did not learn of them
by having our informant involve us in his distributional system
through direct information. Informant work in Norfolk, although
valuable in giving us knowledge about over 3,000 people,
also served to close in boundaries of association. The more we
learned about distributional networks, the more informants and
friends sought to block our access to the links in a distributional
chain. Gloria, who acted so much like an Ecuadorian by trying
to involve us, was the most effectively blocked of all Norfolk's
residents. Deacon Johnston, who would have involved us in
associations bringing him economic gain, sadly learned that
the sort of association that he was seeking did not exist.

The actual distributional networks that we regarded as tapping
the meager capital resources of an actor in adjustive encounters
within the Nova Scotian system continuously forced
the actor to make his own associational linkages. If A told me
about B and B's relatives, he would strive to keep me from
knowing B personally, preferring, instead, to either tap my
capital and increase his competitive exchange advantage with

B by including C and D through new prestations to them, or by forcing me to make my own dyadic contract with B. By making my own arrangement with A and another separate one with B, I would become central to some aspect of the livelihood of both A and B, and in the context of that aspect, A and B would be competitors for my resources. A side effect of this competition between A and B might be the leveling of my own resources, so that equitable dyadic exchange could take place through all three of us. The sort of centricity I have been describing could be termed *distributional*.

In both systems of distributional and associational centricity, the investigator can plot and discuss networks of economic exchange, political favors, social prestige, and communication. But, in associational centricity, interaction networks draw the investigator into the system he is analyzing, whereas in distributional centricity the investigator tends to be repelled from interaction networks by the very tactics used to involve his resources (including information). Returning now to Leach's point (1954:17), we can say that, *although the personal networks are structurally similar in northwest Ecuador and Nova Scotia, the stylized cultural game of exchange through them is quite different*. The effect of this overt cultural difference on the adaptive capacity of the two systems will be apparent shortly.

Obviously, from Gloria's perception of the distributional game, it is clear that one cannot contrast associational centricity with distributional centricity for all individuals. However, from one culture to another we can say that the relative emphasis placed on the alternative strategies can vary.

Where the investigator is working in a system with relative emphasis on distributional centricity, he is forced into active involvement with a number of significant Egos who will be placed in competition with each other. Alternatively, and less desirably in terms of data gathering, he is forced to rely on a single informant. I would argue that the strategy characterized under the rubric "distributional centricity" serves to fragment the adaptive advantage of aggregates of people who consider it personally advantageous to exclude their partner and thereby hinder exploitation of new resources at the very time when rapid mobilization becomes necessary.

Because I analyzed my own changing role set as it became increasingly central to a network of exchange and power radiating from informants and friends, I have come to characterize the Ecuadorian situation as generally adaptable, and the Nova Scotian situation as specifically adapted. Each functions equally well in its specific ecological niche. The Ecuadorian system allows for rapid exploitation of short-run economic inputs within a fluctuating cash economy, whereas the Nova Scotian system allows for distribution of gains through welfare agencies that perpetuate life in a poor area. In terms of potential for change, however, I would think that the generally adaptable system would have greater potential to change than the specifically adapted system.

These statements on "network analysis," the role of the investigator, tactics, strategies, and evaluations of the adaptive capacity of social systems are designed to convey a polemic. Data gathering through modified genealogical method inevitably involves the investigator in activities of strategy and power within the arena in which he is working. The investigator cannot disregard his strategic significance in a system and insist that he is "merely gathering data" if he is to understand the dynamics of adaptation of a given people. Having understood his role in a system, there is no reason why the field investigator should not characterize the capacity of the system to exploit opportunities. Only by daring a characterization are we likely to gain the opportunity to later test our ideas.

Of course, there is a danger inherent in characterization. The investigator's generalization can be taken as normative and programmatic. Phrases such as "specific adaptation to marginality" or "culture of poverty" can be taken as end products and can be used invidiously or pejoratively as excuses to not help the economically depressed. Biological determinism reflecting standard racism of past generations can (and probably is) evolving into cultural determinism that justifies varieties of modern racism.

Proceeding from methods to generalization about whole systems, I would argue, at this point in my research among Negroes living in ethnically identifiable rural communities in the New World, that in the process of adaptation to economic marginality at least two courses are available to progressive harnessing of the energy of the larger system. On the one hand, tendencies toward increased adaptability are manifest in the Pacific littoral system; on the other hand, tendencies toward specific adaptation, toward increasing the consistency within the extant structure of marginality, are apparent in eastern Maritime Canada. The two processes may not be mutually exclusive in different parts of the New World, but they may be contrasted, from an evolutionary perspective, when comparing northwest Ecuador with eastern Maritime Canada. Regardless of underlying structural similarity, the former appears to have the cultural capacity for systematic social-structural transformation, whereas the latter seems to represent a cultural capacity for cyclical repetition of marginality itself. Having based many of my statements on the results of network analyses that involve the investigator's own role in the system, I should add that, if the investigator wishes to take an applied role in speeding up change in the two systems, the role would have to be very different.

In Ecuador the investigator would need to help people find more stable (i.e., *consistent*) sources of capital that they would have no problem utilizing to bolster a firm social-structural basis in change. In the Canadian Maritimes the investigator would have to help people find *and accept* a political mechanism to radical change: a mechanism to unsnare the mesh of invidious sanctions pertaining to inheritable mental illness while emphasizing the exploitation of the resources of the larger system. One hundred and fifty years or more of racism, poverty, and formal and informal welfare have taken their toll in the avenues of adaptation. The present system is not desirable, and to imply that "specifically adapted" connotes in any way cultural satisfaction is to distort the meaning inherent in this argument. Such a conclusion is frustrating. In Ecuador it demands access to mechanisms of international commerce, while in Nova Scotia it demands access to the resources of international radical politics.

What have these statements to do with a comparison of methods used in Ecuador and Nova Scotia? The answer is that the ethnographic gathering of data itself involves a process that has strategic significance for actors in changing situations. Since the anthropologist is thereby *ipso facto* an agent of change, he may use his role and his effect to generalize to areas of interest that include the capacity of systems to change. This comparative statement is offered as a modest attempt to illustrate the string of associations that have emerged from the nomothetic perspective of my own field work.

OPEN NETWORKS AND NATIVE FORMALISM: THE MANDAYA AND PITJANDJARA CASES

Aram A. Yengoyan

The Mandaya of the Philippines and the Pitjandjara of western Australia have radically different cultural elements and social institutions and radically different ways of conceptualizing environmental and social phenomena. Among the Pitjandjara of the western desert of Australia, for instance, linguistic designations for marriage groupings and arrangements, tribal "segments," moieties, and semimoieties are widespread and clearly definable. Ideological conceptions of the Pitjandjara's social world are mental constructs that are verbally expressible.

The Mandaya of southeastern Mindanao, Philippines, however, present a different case, for they have no linguistic categories for territorial and social groupings. Yet, individuals and families combine for social action, form groups that are of a temporary nature, and get jobs done in a context in which permanent formal groupings for joint action are absent. Groups form to achieve certain ends and disband upon completion of the goals. In this situation, the ethnographer must analyze territorial groups and social activity in laymen's terms, not in Mandaya or social anthropological terms.

My research design, techniques, methods, and analysis differed in both cases, yet I did attempt to maintain a certain amount of standardization in them. There are types of data that are basic to social anthropology, and ideally the categorization and analysis of this information may lead to general propositions. I hope that in this comparison of two societies whose adaptational, ideological, and sociological modes of existence are markedly different I can make clear both the differences and the similarities in design, approaches, and analysis that characterize them.

PART I: THE MANDAYA

Problem, Theory, and Research Design

The Mandaya are a non-Islamic, non-Christian population inhabiting the eastern cordillera and coastal areas of the provinces of Davao, Agusan, and Surigao del Sur in Mindanao in the Philippines. Earlier accounts of the Mandaya indicate that they once numbered between 25,000 and 35,000 and represented one of the most powerful warring groups in eastern Mindanao. The only definitive account of the Mandaya is by Fay-Cooper Cole (1913), who spent seven months in the Davao Gulf area in 1910. Other early sources are Garvan (1931), the *cartas* of the early Jesuit missionaries, and various travel accounts.

My own work among the Mandaya took place from 1960 to 1962 and again in the summer of 1965.[1] By the early 1960s I knew something of the general features of Mandaya sociocultural organization, so my research did not start from scratch. My original problem was to enumerate and evaluate those spatial environmental variables such as rainfall, topography, soils, leaching processes, erosion, and vegetation that, as the popula-

[1] Financial support for the first field work (1960–1962) came from the Ford Foundation Foreign Area Training Fellowship Program. The Agricultural Development Council, New York, supported the 1965 field work.

tion adapts to them, effect observed variations in social organization. In other words, mine was an ecological study of shifting cultivation, and my problem was to qualify and quantify the major environmental and demographic factors that structure Mandaya social organization.

The Mandaya are shifting (i.e., swidden) cultivators of upland rice, root crops, vegetables, and fruits, and I hoped that my study would provide information applicable to Southeast Asian shifting cultivation, as well as a means of testing some general propositions on shifting cultivation set forth by Conklin (1957), Leach (1950), and Pelzer (1945). I also planned to make a detailed analysis of environmental factors as they relate to demographic composition, subsistence activities, and social units of exploitation.

I chose this particular problem and area for a number of reasons. First, traditional ecological approaches in anthropology have assumed that the presence of cultivation turns environment from a "limiting" into a "creative" factor in cultural development. It has been said that environmental influences on hunting-gathering societies mold a population's subsistence and social activity, but that with cultivation, even of a neolithic type, environment helps to develop new and varied cultural responses to different situations. Although this may be true in the over-all evolutionary perspectives of cultural growth, there are a number of shifting cultivation populations whose structures and responses are still regulated, directly or indirectly, by environmental factors. Furthermore, the socioeconomic unit of exploitation among shifting cultivators may be smaller and more flexible than the role of the band or horde in hunting and gathering societies. In comparing them, one finds a number of parallels between food-collecting peoples and simple food-producing economies that can be traced to environmental variables.

I chose eastern Mindanao and the Mandaya partly because of the lack of contemporary anthropological work in the area, and partly because Cole's and Garvan's earlier accounts suggested that the tribal peoples of eastern Mindanao are somewhat different from the tribal populations of western Mindanao (e.g., Subanun) in having an active warfare pattern and a political system based on organized warfare. Although warfare ended in the 1920s, I collected sufficient information from older informants to present in my doctoral dissertation (1964) a general description of warfare patterns and their relationship to man-land ratios.

One of the first tasks I undertook upon arriving in Mindanao was to survey the upland Mandaya areas on the Pacific coast cordillera from Mati, Davao, to Bislig, Surigao. I also surveyed

Mandaya areas near the upper Agusan River communities of Compostela and Monkayo. I collected survey information by hiking for six to eight weeks through the upland and coastal foothill areas of the eastern Davao municipalities of Mati, Manay, Caraga, Baganga, and Cateel, as well as Lingig and Bislig in Surigao, recording data as I went on cropping patterns, areas of cultivation, settlement size, routes of trade and exchange, and various traditional practices.

It soon became apparent to me that the Mandaya were no longer an economically homogeneous population. Along the eastern Mindanao coast and foothills, they were involved in the cultivation of abaca (Manila hemp) as a cash crop. The commercial commitment to abaca production varied with specific areas and within the same regional population. In most cases, they still cultivated rice and/or corn, though in a limited way, and they planted garden crops for subsistence.

My next problem was to decide which of the two modes of environmental and economic adaptation—the subsistence-based rice-cultivating upland area or the cash-oriented abaca-cultivating foothill area—to choose as my research site. My surveys indicated that I should study both areas if I wished to demarcate, analyze, and explain the organizational responses to varying ecological factors and external pressures. I chose, in 1960–1962, to analyze traditional Mandaya cultivation in the upland rice areas, and I returned in 1965 to study the foothill abaca areas.

Although on my first field trip I dealt primarily with the upland areas, I also collected comparative data on the foothill populations. I devoted the summer of 1965 to studying marketing networks and other economic processes among the abaca cultivators.

The eastern Mindanao coast is a high-rainfall zone where the basic contrast between wet and dry seasons is not marked. As one moves from the coast to the upland interiors, any wet-dry contrast becomes even less obvious. The upland groups around Pagpawan and Toacanga (upper Manay and Caraga) practice shifting cultivation, but, because of the extensive rainfall, they are unable to burn or "fire" the cut growth effectively.

The mean annual rainfall in the uplands for the period from January, 1961, to January, 1962, was 168 inches in 224 days of rain. The longest period without rain was five days, but this "dry spell" occurred only once in that twelve-month period. In the absence of "firing," there is, of course, a limited amount of ash return, and what ash there is has to be highly leached to extract the alkaline elements that are essential for rice cultivation. Thus, I realized that I must alter my original research design to account for these variations in terms of man-hour/

yield ratios, man-hours per swidden cycle, labor outputs, and total yields per swidden.

With my surveys completed and my original problem and research design reanalyzed, I had to choose a specific locality for study. The typical situation was represented by the eastern cordillera population, who had not had intensive contact with the lowland Bisayans. Most of the Mandaya in the upper Agusan River drainage were involved in a lowland social network. With the exception of Mati municipality, none of the other four east-coast municipalities are connected to one another by roads. The only means of transportation between east-coast settlements are outrigger powerized *bancas* or launches carrying copra, hemp, food supplies, and commercial items among the settlements.

Environment of the Group

I selected the upland areas of Manay and Caraga municipalities for study. The uplands (generally called Pagpawan) could be reached from the coast in a two- or three-day hike. Furthermore, the upland rice-cultivation systems were operative, and the Mandaya were not yet fully involved in the lowland Philippine social system that characterizes many of the coastal towns and villages. Also access to Mati and the other east-coast municipalities was still possible.

In eastern Mindanao cocoanuts are farmed on the coastal lowlands and in the mangrove swamps; grasslands and secondary forest rise to an elevation of 1,500 feet in the foothill areas; and the interior uplands are of mixed primary and secondary forest growth. With the exception of the Baganga and Cateel areas, the flat coastal lowlands are not very extensive, since the foothills at times approach the Pacific Ocean. A number of rivers and streams originating in the uplands dissect the foothills, and communication in the foothills is generally difficult for this reason. In the foothills are small-scale dispersed abaca cultivators who also grow rice, corn, root crops, and vegetables. Upland areas are mountainous, thickly forested, and marked by swift flowing streams and rivers that empty into the Pacific Ocean. The high rainfall in the uplands creates exceedingly muddy and damp conditions.

The settlement pattern of the upland Mandaya rice cultivators makes it difficult for the ethnographer to move from one family to another, since nuclear families occupy a single dwelling that is adjacent to their swidden (rice field). Swiddens are occupied for only one cultivation cycle, thus each family changes its residence every year. I found that the combination one-family one-household one-field one-year occurred 96.4 percent of the time during the 1960–1962 period. Because the population is scattered, highly distributed, and mobile, I spent a vast amount of time hiking from one household to another. (Households are anywhere from a half-kilometer to two kilometers apart.) Compact population clusters with fields radiating from them are emerging in some of the foothill populations, where sedentarization is increasing due to the intensive cultivation of abaca, but in the uplands I often felt frustrated when I tallied up the time I spent in just getting from household to household.

When town officials asked me what the reasons were for my prolonged stay in the area, I explained to them, as well as to the uplanders, that I was interested in investigating the problems and methods of shifting cultivation (*kaingin*) in terms of crop productivity, labor, exchanges, and related matters. They assumed from this that I was concerned with such practical ends as how to increase rice production and control *mosaic* (a virus that seriously debilitates abaca plants). I was never squarely confronted with specific questions on these practical matters, and in most cases I attempted to avoid such discussions. Since national and provincial officials have shown no interest in the east-coast Davao populations, my presence and investigations were assumed to be of some benefit. Furthermore, most lowland people in the Philippines were friendly toward Americans in 1960–1962, when the CIA scare had not permeated to these rural areas. In 1965 one of the village teachers asked me if I had any connection with the CIA. Friendliness toward Americans has markedly decreased in the past few years.

Active Research

After I stated my general and vague field aims, the town officials agreed to provide assistance, and through them and Catholic missionaries in the towns of Manay and Caraga I had an entrée to householders in the uplands. Although uplanders have little permanent contact with coastal populations, most of them acquire certain material goods such as kerosene and clothing from foothill and coastal merchants.

I settled in Capasnan, because, first, it was on the main trail to Toacanga and Lemento-og and had access to foothill abaca-cultivating communities. Also, Capasnan provided environmental and economic variation in terms of differential forest cover, varying field sizes, and cropping patterns.

An abandoned dwelling in Capasnan was loaned to me by one of the older and better known household heads. Although the owner continuously rejected any form of payment or service for the dwelling, I gave him a number of small gifts such as kerosene lamps, liquor, Chinese medicinal wine, and canned goods.

My house, like all houses in Mandaya, was perched atop a dozen or so posts about six feet above the ground. The walls and roofs were constructed of native grasses and palms woven and matted together. The walls and roofs usually last about a year, since they decay quite rapidly in that humid climate. When the householder moves to a new swidden site, he takes with him the pilings and the roof beams.

One of my major problems was obtaining food. Since the uplanders are on a subsistence economy, staples cannot be purchased for long-term use. Rice accounts for less than half of the yearly family diet, with root crops providing the bulk of family subsistence needs. I bought rice, canned goods, and catsup in Manay town and transported them to Capasnan by horseback or human carriers. (Catsup was an important part of my diet, if for nothing more than to make the food palatable.) For nearly six months I obtained most of my subsistence needs from Manay, except for root crops, fruits, and vegetables. As time went on, this method of obtaining food became so time consuming that I abandoned it, except for two necessities, catsup and liquor.

Conversing in Mandaya took longer than I expected, and initially I used an interpreter. When my proficiency increased, the interpreter's function became less important, but I was never able to dispense with him entirely. Mandaya is fairly close grammatically to Cebuano, the *lingua franca* of eastern Mindanao, and learning Cebuano in the field facilitated communication and allowed me to "plug in" Mandaya vocabulary when needed.

I usually had two assistants in the field. One was an Illongo speaker from Cotabato, who had accompanied me on my early surveys and whose reliability I had already assessed, and the other was a Mandaya in his mid-twenties, who was well known to both the uplanders and the foothill populations. I first met Gerardo, my Illongo field assistant, in Compostela, a logging town in Northern Davao Province, when I was visiting personal friends there. Since my salaries for field assistants were better than labor wages, the young man agreed to assist me during my field work, provided I would use my contacts in Davao City to guarantee him a job after the work was fully completed. Malang, my Mandaya assistant, was recommended to me by the elders in Pagpawan as one who was reliable and perceptive, though somewhat restless. I paid equal salaries to both assistants. As time went on, Gerardo and Malang were anxious for me to discuss my observations and ideas with them, which I readily did. I found this type of discourse most fruitful in checking my "ethno-bias."

I had almost no trouble with either assistant, for they had different roles to play in terms of the Pagpawan uplanders and so there was no conflict or competition between them. The assistance provided by each differed depending on what types of problems were being investigated. Malang, who lived with his parents and spent most nights in my house or out courting young girls, provided information on gossip, gambling coalitions during the post-harvest period, and marital problems and feuds among the uplanders. I rechecked most of his observations to assess their reliability. Gerardo helped me to obtain quantified data on yields, acreage, and labor exchange.

Establishing Rapport

Problems of rapport are difficult to enumerate and discuss. For one thing, rapport is always being "gained" and "lost," so one never feels that rapport problems have been surmounted. In the initial stages of the work, people knew that I was interested in methods and problems of cultivation and other sociocultural factors affecting the modes of subsistence. At the time, rats were plaguing the uplands of Manay and Caraga and significantly reducing rice yields, and many felt that my interest in cultivation might alleviate the condition. Because many welcomed me on this account, rapport was easily established. The quality of the uplanders' responses was "restricted," by which I mean that their replies, comments, and statements were only in terms of precisely what I asked—nothing more or less. The general attitude of the Mandaya, as I perceived it, was that the sooner I obtained the information I required, the sooner I would have a "solution" to their problem.

At first, I established rapport primarily through the male elders in Pagpawan, who introduced me to different household members and explained why I was there. These introductions became unnecessary after a while, for my presence and purpose were soon widely known. When interviewing a respondent for the first time, I always inquired about crops, cropping activities, and techniques utilized, for I found these topics provided the best means to start my work. In all conversations throughout the entire project I inquired first about particular events or acts and gradually moved into abstract realms. The Mandaya are very detail conscious and always asked me if I had recorded all details correctly. On the level of generalizations where rules are not always rigidly applied, the Mandaya often throw out statements for debate. In group interviewing, the discussions and disputes that resulted from such general statements were most fruitful in revealing how various individuals perceived the social alignments of which they were a part. I participated in these general discussions by reviewing past cases and observing how interpretations of what had happened changed, depending on the flow of the conversation.

One of the best examples of this process is litigation. There are few hard and fast rules or legal norms that cover many cases, but the particulars of how cases are settled are important, and the various contestants in litigation will bring up those cases that are relevant to the point they are making, using them to support their position. I had recorded a number of cases and could use these to argue against the Mandaya to understand how they would respond. The details in each particular case are spelled out very clearly, and the focus is on those cases from which a general settlement emerges. In future cases pertaining to similar problems, the principle of settlement is not utilized, but the particular cases are cited again.

After three or four months, most uplanders felt that I was saturated with information and would depart. But problems and questions led to new inquiries. Furthermore, during this period, I had participated in a series of the drinking bouts that accompany most rituals. My participation in these sessions markedly increased my rapport with the Mandaya, and my fame spread far beyond the confines of the area of investigation.

By expressing an interest in and striking up a conversation about such "neutral" subjects as cultivation techniques, flora, fauna, and cropping patterns, I eventually led the Mandaya into more subjective and personal aspects of their social life. The only major concern of my informants was that I would turn over my data on field sizes and yields to the tax officials. This doubt did not fade during the entire 1960–1962 period. On my second trip to Manay in 1965, however, the doubt had been assuaged, since no increase in taxation had occurred during my three years' absence.

Once my general purpose was known to the Mandaya males, I was able to proceed with my investigation of shifting cultivation and its social concomitants. With the assistance of my field associates, I collected information on interaction networks, exchanges, and "neighborhoods." Most Mandaya could not conceptualize why I wanted to know who talks with whom about what, or whom one asks for services and loans. In general, the more abstract my inquiries became, the slower were the responses. To maintain what rapport I had achieved and to expand my inquiries to new topics, I unconsciously and consciously changed the directions of my probings, switching from abstract topics to more concrete ones, such as the number of rice varieties planted, what a "good" harvest means, types of wild foods collected, medicinal plants and their uses, and forecasts on rain. Inquiries of this type evoked wide enthusiasm; young boys even began to collect wild foods and medicinal herbs for me. Once their interest was partially restored, I moved again into more abstract realms. My respondents would discuss and argue over most of my questions, and a few with whom I became very close gave me deep insight into these matters.

With Mandaya women, rapport was very poor. Female *ballyan* (part-time medical practitioners and mediums) either limited their conversations with me or totally avoided me. Even in questioning them about "neutral" subjects such as the time spent in planting, husking rice, and so forth, their replies were short and uninformative. Furthermore, females systematically kept me from observing the rituals surrounding the planting and harvesting of rice. In most cases, these rituals were held in areas inaccessible to me, or I was told about them after they were over. This secretiveness among the females was most effective in excluding me from these areas of Mandaya culture.

During no time in the field did I so much as consider obtaining a female field assistant. Since I was unmarried at the time, hiring a female assistant would have implied that I wanted her services for purposes beyond my basic field interests. To avoid gossip on such matters, I seldom dealt directly with females and interviewed them only in the presence of their husbands, male siblings, or fathers. My behavior was interpreted as a sign that I was a homosexual, since in the eyes of the locals all men at my age (twenty-five) should have access to an occasional female companion. I had none, and this bothered some people.

The rapport I gradually gained with the females of Mandaya was severely damaged in July, 1961, when a *hadji* (Muslim religious teacher) came to the eastern Davao coast.[2] Although the Mandaya are in general a non-Islamic population, in Davao some Mandaya communities around Mayo Bay were converted to Islam during the late nineteenth century, but this conversion did not entail that the converts completely deny their original tradition. Islamic and Mandaya supernatural categories are basically the same, but the former's are more embracing and more powerful. The female *ballyan* asked me to tell the *hadji* to go away because his activities would disrupt the existing cultural life, but I refused to do so, for I believed that his presence

---

[2] The Mandaya use the term *hadji* to mean a proselytizer for Islam. Among Muslim populations, *hadji* refers to the pilgrimage to Mecca.

would have little impact on the Mandaya culture. Nevertheless, I was tagged by the females as not being concerned about Mandaya modes of life. For six or eight months after this event, I was continuously kept from observing rituals and other major religious activities, except for the ceremonial sacrifices that accompany the planting and harvesting of each swidden. The males recognized what was occurring, joked about it to me, and told me not to worry for all would soon be healed. The breach was, however, never completely healed.

I refused the *ballyan,* because I felt that it was not my concern to force the situation. In the past, other *hadji* had come to Pagpawan, and their impact had always been short-lived and superficial. My involvement would have disrupted a previous pattern and might have generated the *hadji's* antagonisms toward the Pagpawan population and me with the possible long-range effects of more rigorous proselytization. Although I was thereafter ostracized from religious activities, I still think that my course of action was the only choice I had.

On my second trip in 1965, the females were somewhat more open, but they were still uncertain about my intentions. Needless to say, my information on women's activities, except in regard to rice cultivation and economic activities, is poor or nil.

Data-Gathering Techniques

I used various techniques to obtain and record data. I employed a standard questionnaire for collecting information on each rice field (swidden) occupied or recently occupied. This questionnaire contained mainly inquiries that could be quantified or answered with a simple Yes or No. Information on rice yields, crops grown, and varieties per crop was gleaned from the questionnaire. Besides providing a useful as well as simple means for collecting and combining vast amounts of quantified data, the questionnaire allowed me to go through my data periodically to recheck certain features and to determine how these features were related to other phenomena. Although the questionnaires were most useful in gathering data amenable to quantification, they took a good deal of time to administer. In most cases, they could not be fully completed in a single encounter with an informant. Usually informants became restless after an hour of interviewing, and most questionnaires took three or four meetings with an individual before they were fully worked out. The ideal is a fully completed and perfected questionnaire, but only seldom did I obtain a significant number of completed schedules.

I also took a genealogical census covering every family in

the district. This census permitted me to infer changes in mobility and interaction among kinsmen and nonkinsmen. The aim of a genealogical census is to obtain data on a particular individual and to note his relationships with kin and nonkin, but the real strength of this approach depends on the extensiveness of the information collected. Primarily, one collects information on a respondent and all his kinsmen, fictive and nonfictive, in terms of birthplace, age, sex, occupation, marriage (wife's name, family, when married, where married and circumstances of marriage, number of offspring per wife, and living offspring), source and amount of income and what the respondent thinks is the source and amount of income of his kin, expectations of services, inheritance, support, and friendship from others and vice versa, the property held by others, and the kind, amount, location, disposition, and possible inheritance of the property by the respondent.

Within this approach, the respondent not only lists his relationships to others, but relates how he views each of these individuals in terms of the categories listed above. I attempted in this broad collection of data to get away from the relatively static approach that usually plagues the collection and interpretation of genealogies. As the respondent places himself within the larger context of kin, fictive kin, and nonkin, he defines his own social position and enumerates his expectations of and demands on others and of others on him. Since the Mandaya population is highly mobile, this genealogical data allowed me to evaluate the importance of kin relations vis-à-vis spatial distribution in determining how each respondent manipulates the surrounding human resources.

I conducted most open-ended interviewing during the evenings, since the natives worked in their fields during the day. My house in Capasnan became a nightly meeting place for most males. Nearly every night anywhere from two to ten men would come over and spend a few hours talking, smoking, and drinking. My kerosene lamp, flickering in the darkness until 10 or 11 P.M., as well as a good supply of tobacco and liquor, induced them to stop by to talk about their activities and my work. I also did most of my intensive interviewing in this setting. With the pressures of daily activity at a minimum, the men could relax and talk.

In most cases, two or three men would listen in as I administered the questionnaire or conducted interviews on points of mutual interest. Most questions were not discussed by the bystanders, but some inspired great interest in all concerned. Long discussions resulted from questions on bride price, bride service, amounts paid in various cases, and, most important, divorce and its social consequences. Divorce is rare among the upland Mandaya, and the men usually had little or no precedent in arguing from and for different positions.

Other occasions also permitted interviewing and group discussion. During rice rituals many distant families gathered for collective activity, accompanied by the drinking of rum, Chinese medicinal wine, and *tuba* (fermented cocoanut sap). In fact, these settings were most important for obtaining primary information and for observing the responses of others to my questioning and the arguments that certain points sometimes provoked. These discussions and arguments never resulted in a consensus, which is indicative of how the Mandaya view the decision-making process. As the Mandaya conceptualize it, a consensus does not occur naturally; thus they see no reason for striving for it. Each person states and holds a position to the bitter end.

Other forms of activity permitted observation. After the final rice harvest and prior to the selection of a new swidden site, Mandayas from various neighborhoods meet in a central location within the *bagani* domain for feasting, dancing, courting, and gambling. Gambling is a favorite pastime, but it is only during the postharvest period that the intensity of betting reaches its peak. Betting on cock fights is widespread in the uplands, as is betting on painted bones or match sticks and their various possible combinations. Nearly all male household heads within a domain participate to varying degrees in these gambling bouts, which may last for five or six days.

Gambling often determines coalition formations and differential support of individuals. Nearly all men who have harvested rice or who own extra pigs or chickens utilize these food items for gambling. Initially, the process of sorting out the early losers is swift. As the players gradually lose segments of their harvest, they shift their bets and resources to another player who is known to be an astute gambler. This pooling of resources occurs after the first day. After the first three days, only six or eight players out of perhaps as many as eighty survive. It is at this point that the real drama starts, since the surviving participants become more cautious and continuously re-evaluate their resources and strategy. The Mandaya claim that the ideal gambling bout ends when one man, or at most two, controls the full range of goods that were bet from the initial play. If this end is realized, all those who backed the winner at various stages claim what they contributed and what their capital acquired in the winning process. In actuality, most of the earnings of the winners are redistributed so that each player regains his original investment. Gambling may thus be interpreted as a means not of financial gain, but of demonstrating male skill and prowess.

I did not directly participate in gambling for a number of reasons. First, the rules of play were unknown to me, and I did not wish to hold up the activity while someone explained them to me. But more important, I think that my active participation would have made the other players self-conscious about what they did and who they backed in varying circumstances. Through observation I was able to capture the picture and process of gambling and its socioeconomic structure. One of my assistants participated in the gambling with two sacks of *humay* (unhusked rice), which I contributed. He was eliminated within the early rounds, but was told by the elders that if I would contribute more rice he would be readmitted. I was regarded as an unending source of food items, which was not the case.

Observing the gambling permitted me to evaluate the differential importance of kinship relations, space, and skill in the process of temporary coalition formations. Everyone knows who the most skilled gamblers are, but the shifting of resources to various parties does not take place until at least half of the original contestants are eliminated. The first coalitions among individuals are based on spatial factors, with individuals residing within the same neighborhoods pooling resources as each individual thinks his end is in sight. As players are gradually eliminated, the bonds of kin and space give way, and the onlookers support men who are the most skilled and whose resources are not in jeopardy of dwindling.

Techniques for recording and storing data. I did not record questionnaire data in duplicate, and this was a mistake, for had I lost the data I would not have been able to reconstruct it from memory. All field notes should always be recorded in duplicate or even triplicate. Extra copies should be mailed to someone who can store your notes until your return from the field. The duplicating of questionnaire information is a tedious job, but it should be done.

I recorded interviews by hand, then wrote them up in a legal-size ledger. I cross-listed all cases so I would have a check on how information collected in one interview fitted with other interview information. I made carbon copies of all recorded interviews. I did not use a tape recorder in the field, but recorded observation in a small notebook for transcription at a more convenient time.

I recorded most data on punch cards (Unisort Analysis Card, Burroughs, Form Y-9). These 5″ × 8″ punch cards are easily stored in metal or cardboard file boxes. Each card contains information for a particular culture category. The information is typed directly on the card and the attached carbon. After the data are typed in, each card is punched with a hand-punch. Form Y-9 has ninety-one single categories; thus an almost infinite variety of possible combinations can be punched. The establishing of categories and their numerical designations requires one to maintain category uniformity throughout the study. I originally started out with forty to fifty categories, but as my work progressed, I abandoned some of the original categories as unnecessary and subdivided other categories into finer units. For example, I found the category "native flora" much too broad; more precise designations were needed. After four or five months of field work, I had established categories that I maintained throughout the study. In most cases, a particular card was punched for three or four categories, but in other cases the full range of a social event might require up to ten particular categories.

The great advantage of hand-punch cards is that the data are not particularized or atomized into smaller meaningless units. Each event, observation, or fact is typed directly onto the cards as it occurs, and thus the unity of the event is maintained. Yet the categorization allows the researcher to determine how certain phenomena, such as household economic output, are related to, say, interaction with various kinsmen. If these data are recorded in a regular notebook, then a number of cross-listings with other items is necessary. The punch-card method avoids excessive cross-numbering in numerous notebooks, yet allows one to analyze the notes easily when needed. With a hand sorter, one can go through his notes quickly in attempting to get at what information he has on a particular phenomenon and how it relates to other events. The cost of cards, punch, and hand sorter amounted to $30 in 1960.

All typed cards should be punched immediately and filed in the appropriate category. One thus has access to his notes at all times, whereas the recording of information in more sophisticated ways requires expensive, nonportable, and highly technical machinery.

I recorded genealogies on wrapping paper, listing precise information on each individual on separate sheets under a numerical designation. Most of my genealogies are woefully incomplete. With the high rate of population mobility, most families moved out of neighborhoods before I could recheck particulars. Also, by mistake, I took several genealogies twice.

I found it profitable to take one or two breaks during my field stay. This permitted me to reassess my original problem and to reread my notes in order to discern common features and patterns. By staying too close to the data at all times, the field worker may miss the larger setting until it is too late to recheck important events and facts. During the 1960–1962 trip, I took a number of short breaks down to Manay town or to Davao City. These short trips are also beneficial for maintenance of sanity. They permitted me to get in touch with the outside by reading newspapers, writing letters, drinking cold beer, and talking to the inhabitants of Manay about recent national and international political events. I found myself reading novels of various types in the field and would suggest that each field worker take a number of cheap paperback volumes with him. The reading of nonanthropological materials may provide a balance to one's becoming emotionally and intellectually overextended.

If possible, copies of notes should be sent to someone who knows about your work and topic, and who will read them and return comments and constructive criticism. The perceptions of another worker are unique and useful in posing new problems for investigation.

Departing from the field in 1962 was not traumatic. When I made preparations to leave, a number of men hinted that they would like any items that I was abandoning. I announced that I would dispose of my possessions but only when a number of people were present. I distributed these items a few days before my departure, taking no payment for them, since their value was practically nil. Yet, my turning over of the commodities to the males was in a way a token payment for their assistance in my field work. I had paid none of my informants in cash or goods, though I had distributed tobacco and occasionally liquor generously. A few women sought my kerosene lamps, which I gave to them.

I knew that the men with whom I was on very friendly terms were discussing the matter of my return among themselves. During my last week, they asked me if I would return. I told them that I would like to come back in three or four years, but that I would spend most of my time investigating abaca cultivation in the foothill areas. Most of them could not accept my plans for returning and laughed at my answer.

On the day of my departure a number of men and boys accompanied me to Manay town. They stayed in Manay for a few days until my plans were finalized. I gave my United States address to a few town merchants and a Catholic priest in Manay in case someone wanted to contact me. In April, 1962, I left Manay for Davao City.

During the interim period from 1962 to 1965, I occasionally received letters from coastal people relating recent events among the upland Mandaya. I also received requests for shoes, with tracings of feet enclosed, during my three-year absence. A number of these requests were filled.

In 1965 I returned to upper Manay, much to the surprise of the Mandaya. Acquaintances were renewed with little difficulty. The uplanders gave me running accounts of the past years' happenings. Field work during the second trip was much easier, since I knew how to avoid preliminary problems and mistakes. Since my departure in 1965 I have received letters on recent events and still maintain contact with a few coastal families.

Summary

As noted earlier, my original intention was to make an ecological study of upland rice cultivation with emphasis on how environmental variables influence social organization and spatial mobility. After surveying the eastern Davao coast, I selected the Mandaya of Upper Caraga and Manay for study. I found, however, that upland Mandaya shifting cultivation is not typical of this part of Mindanao due to the wet climate, which precludes the normal burning process in the agricultural cycle. My interest focused, therefore, on a descriptive analysis of the cultivation system and its relationships to labor, production, and environmental factors. I found that variations in cultivation patterns and microenvironmental factors were related to socioeconomic units and neighborhood networks. Great population mobility and the absence of permanent social units and cognized spatial groupings reflect the demands of the cultivation system. Upland rice-cultivating may thus be regarded as an adaptation to environmental factors that combine to produce an intricate and infinite number of microenvironmental niches.

The upland rice systems are a segment of a larger complex. Shifting cultivation exists in the densely forested uplands, but the foothill Mandaya have adapted to the grasslands and secondary forest growth by cultivating abaca. Abaca production requires a new and different set of capital inputs along with increasing involvement in a semipeasant market economy. Participation in a cash economy in turn generates new demands on the household economy. In 1965, I began my work among the abaca cultivators to determine the full range of change in Mandaya social structure resulting from the economic readaptation to a new productive base. I also investigated abaca-marketing networks and other economic processes, such as the ability of household units to withhold goods and activity or interaction from the market and how price or market knowledge was obtained by household units who are not in direct daily contact with the markets in Manay, Santiago, or Caraga. Partial results of this work on rice and abaca cultivation have been published (Yengoyan, 1964, 1965, 1966a, 1966b, 1966c, and in press).

One of the major problems in working with cognatic societies like the Mandaya is determining group structure. The only Mandaya verbal category pertaining to social groups is the term for *family*. Beyond the family, there are no formal cognized social units that are capable of being linguistically blocked and verbally expressed. Domains are demarcated by natural features. The term for kindred *(kalumonan)* is verbally expressed, but it is the widest recognized kin category and is not a group. In situations like this, one must *induce* group structure by investigating interaction patterns—finding out who interacts with whom, when, why, and how often. Social networks and interaction rates must be abstracted from the detailed collecting and analyzing of sociograms.

How are these data, which cannot be attached to a formally cognized social structure, expressed? What kinds of units or groupings are utilized? In the Mandaya case, I have had to use terminology from layman's English rather than from the language of anthropology to express these relationships. I have used the terms *neighborhood* and *community* by defining them with reference to my analysis of the data. Formal anthropological categories are primarily social categories pertaining to groups based on kinship, descent, and marriage principles. For the most part, the vocabulary of social anthropology has few terms for groups based only on spatial principles.

If I were to redo my field work among the Mandaya, I think I would investigate a number of different problems and approach others in a different way. I would put more emphasis on learning the language, and on determining how individuals cognize their social and natural environments and how their cognition influences their realm of choice. In tackling this problem, I would investigate economic activities and environmental factors, articulation with neighboring social units, and the perception of rituals and their importance in noneconomic activities. In most cases, the Mandaya formally express ideal relationships with little allowance for variation. In actuality, the organizational level of activity is flexible enough to permit a wide range of choice as a means of achieving certain ends. How the Mandaya view this discrepancy and reconcile it—verbally and socially—is a major problem that needs investigation. A detailed knowledge of the language and of how linguistic categories influence verbal permutations, perceptions, and behavior is crucial and of the utmost interest.

PART II: THE PITJANDJARA

Problem, Theory, and Research Design

The Pitjandjara are an aboriginal people living in the western desert of central Australia. At present the Pitjandjara are scattered throughout the southern half of the western desert from Jigalong to Warburton Mission (West Australia), to the northwest areas of the state of South Australia, and north to Areyonga native settlement in the Northern Territory. My own work among the Pitjandjara was in South Australia from the Tomkinson Ranges east to Ernabella Mission and north to the Petermann Ranges. The native groups in this area are not unknown in anthropological literature. The early works of Basedow (1914, 1925) were followed with more definitive studies into various aspects of social anthropology. Elkin (1931, 1938–1940) has worked on kinship and social structure, Tindale (1935, 1936, 1959, 1963, 1965) on material culture, mythology, and initiation, and Mountford (1950, 1965) on legends and art.

I worked among the Pitjandjara from May, 1966, to June, 1967.[3] The Pitjandjara are fairly well known among the Australian aborigines, so I undertook a detailed study of certain social phenomena. My project goals were as follows:

1. To reconstruct and ascertain the nature of precontact local organization and more inclusive sociogeographic units. Since local organization represents a key relationship between social structure and environmental exploitation, this segment of the project would provide data on how local units adapted to varying environmental factors, both spatially and seasonally.

2. To investigate the demographic structure of various groups and how these factors are related to variations in certain aspects of social organization, such as marital arrangements and section systems. Factors such as sex ratios, age structure, marriage rates, marriage ages, fertility and mortality rates, number of eligible females per male at any one time, etc., are crucial in assessing such questions as the number of required females for optimal operation of certain marital arrangements, the nature and functioning of connubiums, the spatial distribution of eligible mates

---

[3] The Australian Institute of Aboriginal Studies supported the field work during this period. Transportation to and from Australia was provided by the Australian-American Educational Foundation (Fulbright).

and variations in prescriptive marriage patterns, and changes in social organization due to population fluctuation.

I wanted to investigate the first problem described above because local organization is the articulating unit between social organization and environmental factors. The typical and ideal description of aboriginal Australian local organization was originally set forth by Radcliffe-Brown (1913, 1918, 1930) and emphasized in a general context by Steward (1936, 1955) and Service (1962). Radcliffe-Brown's description of the patrilineal, exogamous, territorially based horde has recently been reviewed by Meggitt (1962) and Hiatt (1965), who claim that aboriginal local organization was not as structured as Radcliffe-Brown claimed and in fact that its composition and structure varied over time and space.

Although local organization in the western desert is no longer operative, this change has occurred only within the past twenty years. It is still possible to reconstruct ethnographically local group areas with the assistance of tribal elders who have recently come in from the bush. Important water sources and totemic sites can be mapped with a degree of assurance, but the evaluation of group composition and changes have to be recorded with great care. This problem will be discussed later. The focus on local organization was primarily designed to contribute additional data on this topic and the ongoing discourse on aboriginal local groupings (Stanner, 1965; Hiatt, 1966).

I chose my second problem because I have had a long-term interest in demographic analysis. Although most demographic measures and indexes cannot be utilized in small societies due to limited samples and poor data, the determination of basic population characteristics is critical to an understanding of social phenomena. This approach is not new; many scholars have discussed the relevance of demographic interconnections, but detailed descriptions are generally not available. Furthermore, Rose (1960) has provided an excellent ethnographic description of Wanindiljaugwa marriage categories, age classification, and sex distribution. His account is probably one of the first sources that demonstrate how demographic factors influence the operation of marriage rules. My own goal was to investigate similar factors in a population living in geographic and climatic surroundings different from the semitropical, densely populated Wanindiljaugwa, who live on Groote Eylandt in the Gulf of Carpentaria. In 1968, I published a preliminary investigation of the interrelationships between population size and the statistical confirmation of marriage rules, but this work was not based on my 1966–1967 field data.

In the field I followed my original research design with only minor modifications, although collecting population data was difficult for a number of reasons, the major one being that the Pitjandjara were not interested and/or did not know what I was getting at. In most cases, direct questioning on this subject was nearly impossible. A fuller discussion of the methods I used in my demographic analysis will be given later.

Analyzing local organization also proved difficult. I could transmit to the aborigines some notion of spatial entities and geographic units, and in general the tribal elders showed interest in mapping out various areas. The composition of residential groups was difficult to determine, but I tested my reconstructions to my satisfaction in a case involving the mining of chrysoprase (Australian jade) in the Mt. Davis area.

The Mandaya had had a general interest in my work since it overlapped with their own interests, but my field interest in demographic analysis and the determination of social categories was not shared by the Pitjandjara. The tribal elders were concerned, almost imbued, with the past in terms of mythology, legends, rituals, the dreamtime, and a complex symbolism.

The Environment of the Group

In the Musgrave-Tomkinson-Petermann Ranges, the average rainfall is six to ten inches per year, and thus the area is classified as a desert, though it is very different from the deserts of North Africa. In only a few localities (e.g., the Simpson desert) does one find sand-swept dunes with a complete absence of vegetation. Average rainfall figures mean little in terms of the floral and faunal composition, but drought is the rule and rain the exception. When I started field work in 1966, the center's desert flowers, grasses, scrub, and trees were responding to rainfall after a severe drought of six or eight years. Even in a wet cycle, however, vegetation is sparse. Low-lying scrub and grasses are most typical of the Musgrave area. Vast stretches of spinifix grass (*Triodia aristata*) and mulga trees (*Acacia aneura*) are common, and desert oaks (*Casuarina decaisneana*) and gum trees (*Eucalyptus rostrata, Eucalyptus papuanus*) are interspersed in sand hills and creek beds, respectively.

Faunal composition and density vary with the vegetation cover. Fauna native to the area—kangaroos, emus, euros, dingoes, rabbits, wild camels, and lizards—is in short supply, but the aborigines are able to detect species of nearly all genera by tracking dung droppings. The exploitation of fauna for subsistence is regarded as man's work, although the importance of game in the daily precontact diet was not as significant as vegetable foods, which were and still are gathered by women. However, fauna is of utmost importance in myth, ritual, and daily conversation.

The Musgrave Ranges, like most of the ranges in the western desert, are not very high, but in a land where salt pans, flat terrain, and gently rolling hills provide a routine uniformity, almost any unsual peak is named and stressed for purposes of direction. Most of the ranges contain water in the form of creeks, rock pools, and natural dams. Creeks are normally dry, but, in general, surface waters are obtainable by digging a six-to-eight-foot well. An excellent description of the environment of the Musgrave-Mann-Petermann Ranges is provided by Finlayson (1936).

Most of the states in Australia maintain reserves for their aboriginal populations; aborigines are, however, free to leave any reserve at any time. To work on a reserve, one must first obtain a permit from the organization that handles aboriginal affairs. Prior to arriving in Australia, I had obtained the necessary permits for my wife, my daughter, and myself from the Department of Aboriginal Affairs in Adelaide. These permits were checked on our arrival in Adelaide before we were allowed to proceed to the native settlement at Amáta (Musgrave Park), the major settlement on the 27,000-square-mile Northwest Aboriginal Reserve. Later, we obtained permits from the Welfare Department in Alice Springs to gain entrance to Northern Territory reserves such as Aneyonga and the future settlement site at Docker Creek in the Petermanns.

Active Research

My choice of the Amáta-Ernabella area was based on a number of factors. First, I had reports that the Pitjandjara population in this vicinity was large enough to supply good data on marriage rates and demographic composition. Second, the tribal orientation of the population still exists, though the economic structure of traditional aboriginal life has changed. Third, Amáta is about 350 miles southwest of Alice Springs, which could be my base of operation. Furthermore, permission to work at Amáta and assistance from the Ernabella Mission made some problems of introduction much easier.

In Adelaide, I obtained a Land Rover and a 6′ × 13′ house trailer or caravan that was to be the residence for my wife, our two-year-old daughter, and myself. This equipment was acquired from the Bureau of Supply, Commonwealth of Australia, and financed by the Australian Institute of Aboriginal Studies. In May, 1966, we left Adelaide for Alice Springs on the "Ghan," a narrow-gauge train that makes this run twice a week. The Land Rover and caravan were also loaded on the train. After a week in Alice Springs, where we bought food supplies and camping gear, we drove south to Kulgera Station and then due west to Victory Downs homestead, Mulga Park homestead, and Amáta. The initial trip took two days with the caravan, but normally the trip can be made in a long day's travel.

Amáta (Musgrave Park) is the government settlement for the Northwest Reserve. The settlement staff consists of a superintendent, nurse, building overseer, stockman, mechanic, welfare officer, and a patrol officer. The settlement was established in 1961, and in 1966 the population was not more than 350. A number of native men and women work for wages in construction and fence building. A settlement store sells basic staples to the locals, and fresh beef is sold three times a week. A herd of 300 to 400 cows is kept in neighboring paddocks.

We parked our caravan alongside a bough shelter for the duration of the field work. The hospital provided bathing facilities, and we had access to a tap of bore water. My family stayed with me until the height of the summer when I took them to Alice Springs. We bought most of our canned food from the local store; fresh vegetables and fruits were flown in on the Saturday mail plane from Alice Springs.

Establishing Rapport

Establishing rapport at the initial stages of the work was not very difficult. Most Pitjandjara are accustomed to inquiries of all kinds, and I think they have probably gone through the full range of investigation. Their interests revolve around the past as manifested in myth, ritual, totemism, and the dreamtime. Totemism, mythological beings, and creation legends are discussed almost daily by the male elders. The young men have their dreamtime, but they are not as concerned with it as the elders.

Although I did not specifically collect stories of legends and myths, any field worker must show marked interest in them if he hopes to move on to an investigation of other aspects of social organization. Once the elders recognized my patience in listening to their discussions and jotting down copious notes, they permitted me to ask them questions on other subjects, provided these were also related to the past. The natives were very cooperative in helping me to work out a formal description of group structure and marriage systems, since they view "skin groups" (sections) as possessing a mythological basis for their existence. I had great difficulty, however, in eking out suitable responses to my demographic questions on age and number of offspring, because the Pitjandjara cannot answer these types of inquiries in a formal manner. They disagree over the order of births in their families and even over the number of spouses they have had. The range of disagreement would commonly result in one or at most two points of view, so I could recheck the discrepancies in my own quantitative data.

Inquiries on local organization and territorial units were of more interest to the Pitjandjara but for different reasons. Since I had a vehicle, I could take a number of men with me to map totemic sites, water sources, and important environmental features. Nearly all Pitjandjara thoroughly enjoy going on trips, and thus my interest in local groupings and territory was matched by their interests. Their willingness and cooperation resulted in my acquiring much information on many aspects of local organization, but I had to recheck most of this data thoroughly for its factual basis.

The see-saw pattern of rapport gaining and rapport maintaining depended on how formal my questions were and how far removed they were from mythology and dreamtime. Replies to formal inquiries seldom resulted in an argument or debate, and most participating individuals simply would nod in agreement. When my probings moved into more nebulous areas, however, the group discussion increased markedly. For example, exactly how and why certain social categories are linked with other categories in terms of descent and marriage are conceptualized in a very formal manner following established and undebatable rules. However, variations of the rule are also recognized and accepted, up to a point. Certain "optional" marriages are allowed within limits, and how, when, and why these kinds of marriages occur are up for debate. I sought this kind of information to determine how far the Pitjandjara could conceptualize from the ideal cognized system.

Data-Gathering Techniques

In general, I used the same techniques for the Pitjandjara as for the Mandaya, but with more emphasis on genealogical materials, since most Pitjandjara social relationships are established within genealogical contexts. I recorded Pitjandjara genealogies with more concern for details, and so the completion of one genealogy took two to three times longer than those I recorded among the Mandaya. This time differential is due to the greater emphasis on lineality among the Pitjandjara, where actual descent may be traced back for three or four generations. Among the Mandaya, lineal emphasis is almost absent, and only those descended from a former *bagani* chief can trace their descent as far as to the grandparental generations. Determining relationships within a genealogical framework was a difficult task accomplished through a number of means, but determining all possible connections between individuals was even more difficult, since the Pitjandjara consciously obscure kinship terminology and relationships that have occurred as a result of prohibited or optional unions.

I used questionnaires only to record demographic data. Since most demographic data were also recorded in a genealogical framework, there were overlapping data depending on the strategy employed.

I conducted interviews with adults of both sexes and occasionally with children, but these were always highly unsatisfactory. In most cases, a group of elders would cluster around my trailer, and the interview would consist of a joint discussion of my inquiries. This procedure worked well on "neutral" subjects, but when I desired specific personal information I generally sought to interview the particular individual alone. I interviewed young men during the evenings after they finished their work. My wife and the nurses at Amáta and Ernabella Mission provided me with certain demographic data on the females. Male field workers are viewed with suspicion by Pitjandjara females, especially when they inquire about personal matters.

Most of the data on birth rates, deaths, infant mortality, and demographic matters pertaining to females was collected by my wife, who is a professional dietician. Her assistance in the field was very important not only in information processing, but in maintaining rapport with the females. When an ethnographer has his wife and children with him in the field, females and young children are likely to cluster around his quarters, as they did around our trailer, for conversation, tea, tobacco, and flour. I obtained much vital information in these informal gatherings. Our daughter was at first shy toward the native children but soon she was part of a play group. On other occasions my wife and she accompanied the females when they went out hunting for rabbits.

Another major source of demographic data was the birth and death records at Ernabella Mission and at Amáta. At Ernabella these records go back to 1941, while at Amáta they start in 1961. Information from these records provided me with a fairly good means of determining ages of individuals under twenty, the ages at death, recent births per female at the Mission or on the government reserve, and emigration and immigration rates from the settlement and its environs.

I did most of my interviewing in the aboriginal camp, which is about half a mile from the settlement. Males who are not working usually are in the camp until noon. In the early afternoon they walk to the settlement and would often gather at my trailer, which they viewed as a fairly good source of tea, sugar, and tobacco. In the late afternoon, Tommie Dodd's house became a focal point for discussions.[4] Nearly once a day, every male would make his way to Tommie's house to obtain information on the European staff. I often interviewed at Tommie's house and checked previously collected information there.

If I desired to interview selectively, either on an individual basis or with two or three men, I would drive them out into the "bush" for a few hours. They greatly appreciated these short trips as a means of getting away from the camp routine and hunting with their .22-caliber rifles. After a few hours of hunting, I would boil a billy can (a half-gallon tin bucket) of water and make tea before starting my questioning. Most of my "personalized" interviewing was done in this manner. In general this method was excellent, since it took us away from the camp surroundings, which permit no privacy whatsoever. Sometimes at nights a few men would visit my trailer for tobacco, and further questioning would then take place.

Techniques for recording and storing data. My techniques for recording and storing data were similar to those I used among the Mandaya. I recorded much of my ethnographic data on punch cards. I made carbon copies of all notes and sent them to a colleague in the United States. The preservation of notes and film was much easier in Australia than in the Philippines, where the humid climate quickly deteriorates them. My wife and child left in April of 1967 and I left in June. My wife's departure from the field was not easy, since she had made a number of close friends, both among the aborigines and the European staff. On my final move from Amáta to Alice Springs via Ernabella, I gave almost all my possessions to a number of men who had been of assistance during the field work. Earlier, my wife had given clothing to the women who had worked with her. Although most aborigines are illiterate, I am in communication with them through correspondence with various staff members at the Mission and at Amáta settlement. Bowing out of the field was not a problem, since most of my close informants realized that I was planning to return for further work in the near future. Also it is

---

[4] Tommie Dodd is a half-caste in his late eighties who has lived in the Musgrave area for at least thirty years. Tom's house has always been a center of activity for the old men who know that Tom is the only one who is in touch with the European staff and who knows their ways. He is thus an intermediary of information. Initially Tom was one of my interpreters, but he became much more than that. His invaluable knowledge of the environment and historic events was of immense importance to the project.

my impression that the people know that I am concerned about their activities. Recently one of the females who worked closely with my wife named her latest daughter after our daughter. This information was communicated to us through the missionary at Ernabella.

Summary

The analysis of local organization, its ideology and its composition, as stated in my original research design was difficult to achieve. Local organization is no longer operative, and its ethnographic reconstruction is difficult and not fully reliable. I mapped out territorial domains or spheres, and in general I could demarcate the Pitjandjara's notion of "country." As the Pitjandjara move away from their ancestral areas, their knowledge of minute geographic and subsistence details declines. In his ancestral area, for example, a Pitjandjara knows with a high degree of refinement where certain foods occur, in what abundance, and at what times. He also knows all sources of water and can estimate very precisely how long a given population can stay in a particular locality without exhausting the water supply, but this fineness of qualitative and quantitative information decreases as he moves into adjacent and extra-adjacent areas. The degree of the precision of their knowledge helped me in mapping out territorial units and determining their coexistence with totemic and sacred sites.

It is very difficult to establish the composition of pre-contact local groups. Residence group composition must have been flexible, since nearly all males have a wider geographic knowledge than one would assume if a strict patrilocality rule was actually adhered to. It appears that young men moved among different residence groups after they completed the basic rites of passage, such as tooth evulsion, circumcision, and subincision. Subincision usually took place when they were in their late teens or early twenties, and residential changes took place after subincision and prior to marriage, which for males is in their late twenties or early thirties. Since multiple relationships existed among all local units, it was easy to shift residence. With marriage and the birth of his first child, the male would commonly return to his ancestral residence units.

Establishing actual group composition is virtually impossible, because the pre-European economic structure is no longer operative. Yet the Pitjandjara still maintain the ideology of their area, as was made clear in 1966–1967 over the mining of chrysoprase (Australian jade) at Mt. Davis. The Mt. Davis male elders are ambivalent about the mining, one reason being that the Mt.

Davis country belongs only to those individuals who were born in the area, have *malupiti* (kangaroo) dreamtime, or have kinship relations with one who is from the area.

The third factor and its interpretation is most interesting. Many of those who claim kinship ties base their case on matrilineal or affinal linkages. Some of these claims are valid; others are slim to say the least. Distant consanguines or affines from the area are "discovered," and a case for kinship is made. The Mt. Davis elders view matrilineal and affinal ties as quasi-acceptable, but they regard some of the more distant "creations" as dubious at best. The flexibility with which kin ties are arranged with the Mt. Davis group is not a new phenomenon. In general, there is a set of varied means by which one gains access to the area. Even kinship relations in the dreamtime may serve as an entrée to the mines. In one case, a man from the Deering Hills area south of Mt. Davis with a *tjurki* (owl) dreamtime gained access to the chrysoprase mines on the grounds that the *tjurki* is related to the *malupiti*. Many people, however, were not clear on what the relationship was, if one did indeed exist.

I do not think that I could have accomplished much more than I did in my analysis of local organization. With the gradual shift into a money economy, the aborigines will not return to their pre-European economic activities, except in a sporadic and random manner. With the gradual shift from a subsistence to a "hand-out" and/or wage economy, the economic role of females, which was most important in the hunting and gathering economy, is now virtually nil. Rose (1965) discusses the present economic role of aboriginal women and its sociological consequences.

My demographic analysis was more successful. Although the population is no longer in strict equilibrium, I could ascertain the rate of population increase, despite the fact that I could not use most demographic approaches, methods, and techniques due to the small samples, lack of census materials, and incomplete data. Estimating ages is most difficult and has always been a problem in working with aborigines. Genealogical recording of surviving children among females past menopause reveals gaps that may have been caused by infanticide, death in infancy, or death in childhood. If females have a full bearing period of twenty to twenty-five years, one is then able to determine with some degree of assurance the missing offspring and thus the birth rate. By determining the rank order of births among surviving offspring, one is able to place individuals at five-year intervals and then note the gaps between siblings. In estimating ages, my errors continuously reoccurred, but the error was standardized in the same direction and roughly in the same range of years.

For males in their thirties, estimates were always lower, and for males in their forties and fifties my estimates were commonly greater. Data on death rates are even more difficult to obtain, since deceased kinsmen are quickly forgotten and their names are not mentioned. At present I am analyzing my data, but the gaps in the materials are ever-increasing, and more detailed information is unavailable.

If I were starting the project now, I would make a more detailed study of ideology and its interconnection with population dispersal and mobility. Pitjandjara mythology reflects population movements, since the spatial element of myth is stressed more than the legendary details in a given locality. The Aranda and Walbiri have a richness in the quality and quantity of their mythology in given localities, but the western desert population appears to lack this feature. Instead, myth is traced over vast tracts of land, emerges with no regularity, and the myth or dreamtime story is concerned with events as the particular fauna moved from place to place. My data on this interrelationship were collected during the latter half of my stay among the Pitjandjara and are not complete, but I think the motifs have been worked out, and a contrast with other central Australian groups may be noted.

I am not sure that more formal training in demographic analysis would have helped. The data are really not amenable to more sophisticated demographic indexes, so I think one should not force a formal analysis on them.

The Pitjandjara, like most aboriginal populations in Australia, possess a highly formalized conception of society and ideology. This extreme formalism is not only a mental exercise, but it is also verbally expressed in a number of contexts. In explaining sections systems ("skins," as they are called), a Pitjandjara sketches the ideal system on the ground in a formal graphic design and then discusses the ramifications of the system in terms of the rules of operation. At times, graphic representations and ensuing discussions approximate the formalism of Radcliffe-Brown or Lévi-Strauss in their approaches to Australian social structure. Furthermore, the Pitjandjara are able to conceptualize and to account for variations in the manifestation of rules. When optional or wrong marriages occur, kinship relationships and terminology are consciously altered to make things "straight again." Sections also reflect these changes. The only way a field worker can trace these "tamperings" is to take complete genealogies to the most ascending generation and then work back to the present. In other cases, the field worker can create fictitious situations of wrong unions, variations in group composition, sitting arrangements at rituals, etc., and observe how the people account for these differences in terms of the cognized system.

In a population like the Pitjandjara, where social units are formally cognized, linguistically blocked, and verbally expressed, an analysis of ideal social structure is not difficult. Since the arrangement of social groups and marriage relationships is expressed by specific terminologies, the field worker can describe the structure by utilizing formal Pitjandjara categories that practically cover the full range of possible groupings. Anthropological accounts of aboriginal Australian social systems are not due exclusively to our formalistic approaches, because the natives themselves are equally formalistic in their conception of how the system ideally works.

Native structural categories provide the initial basis for the investigation of group activities and relationships. *De facto* group composition, rates of interaction, the statistical confirmation of stated rules; and so forth must be analyzed quantitatively. The charter of a social system must be viewed in terms of what occurs "on the ground," and marked discrepancies between the two levels of analysis must be noted and explained in terms of ecological and demographic factors. Among the Pitjandjara, the major problem is not to *induce* group structure, which is obtained through the verbal expression of formal native categories, but to *deduce* it as it exists and operates in reality and determine to what extent reality mirrors the idealized cognized system.

PART III: COMPARISONS BETWEEN THE MANDAYA AND THE PITJANDJARA

In both cases, I used with varying degrees of emphasis such anthropological techniques as the recording of genealogies, questionnaires, and participant observation. In societies where descent is important and permanent groups are based on lineality, using genealogies to ascertain genealogical depth and alliances between social units is important. When descent is not a factor, as among the Mandaya, genealogy does not affect the formation of groups. In order to analyze the factors behind social activity and cohesion, the ethnographer must investigate the spatial arrangements of households and the cooperation among families seeking certain ends.

The particular problem of one's field work always dictates the methods and techniques employed and the varying emphasis on different ways of obtaining data. There is no single kit of anthropological tools that is utilizable in all field work, nor is there a finite number of approaches that will render "answers" in all cases. Once a set of problems for investigation has been established, the investigator must demarcate the variables that are crucial to an analysis of the problem or problems. Each variable must be analyzed in terms of the kind of data required, the units of measurement for such data, and the interrelationships of particular events. Ideally, the next step is to determine how each of the variables varies with the others. The interconnections among variables can be viewed both in a quantitative and qualitative manner. In a quantitative sense, a change in the value of one variable will influence other variables and their operation. Thus, among the Pitjandjara, verbalized marriage rules can be statistically confirmed only by observing the 600–800 individuals interacting in the system. If population size was very much smaller, these rules could not be operationalized.

Which of the various anthropological techniques and methods the researcher uses depends on the problem, the critical variables that constitute the problem, and the required data. The field worker should be familiar with different techniques, both anthropological and nonanthropological, and use those techniques that are the most meaningful in terms of his research strategy.

Although I used most anthropological techniques with varying emphasis in both field experiences, the two projects were so radically different that I had to explore fully, before making any headway, the differences in the two problems, the data I needed, and my interpretations of the data, as well as the differences in the two cultures themselves. In my initial field trip to the Mandaya, I had many problems of adjustment, and in the first six months I made many mistakes, asked untimely questions, became impatient with my respondents, and so forth. Most of these problems were ironed out by the latter half of the work. This period of adjustment was totally absent when I returned to the Mandaya in 1965. I knew most of the people and did not repeat my earlier errors. In a four-month period I accomplished what it would have taken me six months to do during the first trip.

My initial adjustments in working with the Pitjandjara were of a different order. I had learned a lesson from my past experiences and thus avoided many common errors. One of my major problems in both research areas was accepting and evaluating individuals' statements at face value. Field workers know that statements, especially general ones, cannot be accepted at face value and should be checked with other sources of information. Among the Mandaya, I had to check and recheck most initial statements. This process of sorting and resorting interview material not only reveals the basic patterns of certain activities, but also permits the researcher to determine the range of variation of socially acceptable and unacceptable behavior.

I called general statements made by the Pitjandjara "structural" statements—accounts of how a particular activity, be it social, ceremonial, or mythological, operates. On most occasions I checked these statements with other sources and found a very high degree of consensus. They expressed the "structure" of a particular activity to me in a clear, lucid manner. Furthermore, these verbalized structural statements are abstracted by the natives from the range of events and the various means by which selected ends may be achieved. For example, the sitting arrangement for a *corroboree* (a ritual gathering) is established by kinship linkages, which are summarized through section and kin terminology. There are rules for this arrangement, but there are also acceptable variations that may be employed in case the rule cannot be manifested. The *corroboree* must be performed regardless of the absence of certain individuals. When some are absent, modifications exist to maintain the performance.

As stated earlier, the researcher's methods and data differ from case to case, depending on the problem. Among the Mandaya, my interest in interaction networks and spatial influences required my collecting information on who interacts with whom, why, when, and so forth. I obtained interaction data not only by observation but also by interviewing individuals on who and why certain individuals are selected as task-group members to achieve certain ends. Organizational data of this type cannot be systematically compared to an ideal set of rules that dictates how activities should be manifest. Variations are expected in acquiring certain ends. My interpretation of interaction data was based on how groups are formed for certain jobs, on what principles, how groups persist, and how groups change composition to meet new demands. Verbalized structural models are absent among the Mandaya; thus the observer must induce structural patterns from the data. Consequently, the abstracted structure might have no basis on how the Mandaya conceptualize their modes of activity.

To ascertain population characteristics among the Pitjandjara, I collected detailed information on sex and age distributions, fertility rates, death rates by age and sex, and so forth. Due to the paucity of the demographic data, my interpretation of it was not based on stochastic demographic models. Population features were related to the optimal operation of connubiums, prescriptive marriage patterns, and other sociological features. I interpreted organizational features—the working arrangements of a society that processes activity in terms of social

ends through the manifestation of choice to meet new adjustments (Firth, 1964:45)—in terms of demographic requirements
that influence the frequency with which stated rules actually
occur. Thus I viewed the organization of social activity in two
ways. One based on demographic and ecological features, which
are prerequisites to the statistical confirmation of ideally stated
rules. The other was to ascertain the gap between the structural
system, which is a formal verbalized model of how cultural events
should be manifested, and the ways in which social requirements
are actually fulfilled.

The ethnographer is fully expected to vary his methods as
his problems and interpretations vary, but in comparing the
two field experiences, I believe that the differences in the cultures
themselves were most important in establishing the framework
of my analysis. Social structure as traditionally utilized in
anthropology is concerned with analyzing formal social properties (groups and rules) based on permanency and continuity.
Some cultures possess verbal categories to denote permanent social context. The Pitjandjara categorize almost all conceivable
groupings for social, ceremonial, and economic purposes, but the
importance of these groups is markedly different. For example,
it was only during the last few weeks of my field work in
Australia that I obtained the moiety designations. Moieties are
functionally not important for the organization of activity; thus
the terms are seldom employed. Groups are cognized, linguistically demarcated, and verbalized, and the rules for social discourse are openly stated, so the major problem for the field
worker is to investigate what actually takes place and how. In
such cases, one's analysis moves from the general statements and
ideal system, which are expressed and moderately easy to obtain,
to the particulars of how the system works, given population
fluctuations or the absence of certain group members.

As stated earlier, the analysis of Mandaya social organization was quite different from the Pitjandjara, both in terms of
the data collected and the analysis. Among the Mandaya, organizational activity emerges to meet specific goals, and on-going
associations are absent, except in the case of warrior groups.
An analysis of individual and group interaction among the Mandaya must be viewed in terms of fulfilling certain jobs and not as
permanent structural entities that persist regardless of the
presence or absence of tasks and goals. The absence of enduring
groups—both on the ground and as cognized mental constructs—
attests to the utilization of a framework based on group emer-
gence and dispersal based on specific aims.

My personal reactions while doing field work among the
Mandaya and Pitjandjara also varied. The Mandaya appeared

to be more withdrawn and less demonstrative than the Pitjand-jara, not only toward me but toward each other. Most of them were neutral toward me, responding only in terms of my inquiries, yet I had a number of Mandaya friends who accepted me and were very open with me. It was most gratifying to be able to communicate with at least a few individuals on personal matters.

My initial desire to be accepted by the Mandaya evaporated soon after the debacle with the females and the Muslim proselytizer. It was at this point that I realized that the ideal of being completely accepted by a particular group is a romantic myth. In most cases one ends up with a handful of warm friends with whom communication is easy. Like most populations, the Mandaya had a segment of people who did not like me and who made no attempt to hide their contempt. They felt that I was acquiring information about them for future use by the government.

Although the Mandaya recognize themselves as being different from the lowland Filipinos, they are aware of and make little attempt to resist the changes that are slowly drawing them into the orbit of a market economy and an agricultural-based peasant population. The Pitjandjara are also aware of the impact of European ways on their society, but they possess a great deal of pride in their mythological and ceremonial existence, and this gives real meaning to their lifeways. This religious structure is something that the "black fella" has and the whites do not have. They are proud of this and, when an outsider shows interest in learning their myths and rituals, the Pitjandjara male knows that he must take the initiative and show the novice the true way. Thus I felt that the Pitjandjara viewed me as an equal from another social system, not as a member of a superior and dominant society. I was eager to learn their patterns of life, and they were patient in showing me the Pitjandjara way.

The ethnographer who feels he is a special personality who must be accepted and "liked" by all the members of the group he is working with is fairly naïve. No one is liked and accepted by everyone, even in his own culture, so there is no reason why he should be completely accepted in an alien society. In both Mandaya and Australia, many people did not accept me, and I could not have cared less. Nor did this type of mutual negativism depress me, since I suspect that there are certain personality types with whom I could not interact, regardless of their culture and background. I see no reason to modify my behavior, channel my thoughts, or be continuously "up tight" in the hope of acquiring universal acceptance.

This raises the question of going "native." I felt at home in both fields, but never more at home than in my own culture.

The Mandaya and Pitjandjara recognized that I was racially and culturally different, and their expectations of my behavior were well established. They know that whites wear trousers and shirts, are not subincised, do not have totems, and do not believe in *asuwang* spirits. It is practically impossible to immerse yourself fully in another culture, especially when the host culture has a stereotype of what you think and do. The Pitjandjara are very ethnocentric about their way of life and maintain stereotypes both of other aboriginal populations and of Europeans. I was placed in a role, and certain behavioral responses were expected of me. However, it should not be assumed that one must not deviate from his recognized cultural patterns. A cultural "straight jacket" is not the answer. One should be himself, while taking into account the norms of behavior he is studying and operating within.

Homesickness was seldom a major problem, although we became a little concerned when news from the outside was slow in arriving. Both my wife and I occasionally missed things that we were accustomed to in the States, but these were not critical. I always desired information on college football results, and eventually one of my colleagues at the university sent me clippings of game results. Most of the time I was too busy with my work to feel lonely, and my wife was too busy taking care of our daughter. If loneliness did set in, we went to Alice Springs to see friends and relax.

Living conditions in the two field areas were markedly different. My wife did not accompany me to Mandayaland, because of the limited facilities available to me. The tropical environment of Mindanao, with its great frequency of sickness, malaria, and generally hot and humid conditions, proved worse than the hot deserts of Australia, but both of us had adjustments to make in the desert. Our trailer proved much too small for the three of us, but we had no alternative. The major adjustment was keeping warm during the winter. Winter nights in the desert are very cold, and our caravan had no heating unit. Thus the winter nights proved utterly miserable, whereas heat in the summer was so intense as to virtually rule out a good night's sleep.

In Australia and the Philippines, the local and national political situation did not hinder my activities, nor did any revolutions or drastic political changes that might have altered my plans take place. Australian government agencies dealing with aboriginal affairs asked me for short interim reports that contained abstracts of my field-work progress. In the Philippines, the upland populations are not subject to formal governmental agencies, though a national integration committee exists with limited effective power.

The upland rice-cultivating Mandaya, who are not taxed by municipal officials, were initially hesitant in revealing information on crop yields, acreage planted, and other aspects of economic activity that might be used against them. The foothill, cash-crop abaca cultivators were more aware of their activities and the possibilities of being taxed. In every case, the Mandaya males underestimate their holdings and yields when questioned on this subject. Eventually, the differences between their statements and my measurements of yields and land became standardized. My data on economic activities were never seen by local officials, nor was I asked about them. On my second trip to Mandayaland, I obtained more precise information, because the people had lost their fear of my using the data against them for taxation purposes.

Before leaving for the Philippines, I had been warned that studying shifting cultivation populations is difficult because of the scattered settlement pattern and the high population mobility. This is quite true. With each Mandaya family/household separated from the others by a half to two kilometers, the amount of time spent in walking up and down hillsides and across creeks is significant. When one arrives at a household clearing, only the one family residing in the household can be interviewed. After completing the necessary inquiries, I would move to another household clearing. My hiking time between households varied from twenty minutes to an hour, depending on the distance and terrain. The people cluster only during post-harvest rituals and gambling, labor exchanges during agricultural phases, and *rites de passage*.

The Pitjandjara are now settled in clusters varying from 30 to 50 people around homesteads and between 300 to 400 live at Ernabella Mission and at the Amáta government settlement. Large semistable populations are conducive to the collecting of long-run statistical data as well as to maximum interviewing and checking and rechecking. In general, these population conditions yield more return for the time spent in the field. Also in Australia I had access to a vehicle that allowed me to "go bush" with the elders when I was working on local group areas of exploitation. In Manay municipality and the uplands of the Philippines, my legs provided the only means of transportation, since roads, trails, and vehicles were not available.

In summary, although there are marked environmental, demographic, economic, and social contrasts between these two populations, I used similar methods in both cases, but with varying emphases. A commonly recognized block of inquiries is the substance of social anthropology, and these questions are pursued in all field work. To explain the how's and why's of a particular social organization requires an investigation of cultural and noncultural phenomena that may relate to social institutions. If the investigation of these relationships is of prime concern, then one must equip himself with the necessary techniques and methods to understand the interconnections both on an empirical and a theoretical level. Ultimately, there should be no limit on the techniques and methods used by the social anthropologist. The particular set of problems for investigation will determine where he will acquire his "tools," and he should not limit himself in using methods from other disciplines when they are necessary. Nor should he be fearful about transgressing traditional anthropological domains or spheres of activity that might prove more of a burden than an asset.

A COMPARISON OF FIELD RESEARCH IN CANADA AND POLYNESIA

Robert J. Maxwell

PART I: A MARITIME PROVINCE

In view of the increasing number of large-scale research projects, it is becoming unrealistic to assume that the anthropologist
will conduct his initial field work as a lone, pioneering, more or
less rugged cartographer of human culture. Rather, the chances
are that he will participate in field research as a low-level, but not
necessarily unimportant cog in some greater research machine.

In 1963, as a second-year graduate student in anthropology
at Cornell, I faced the problem of summer employment. Late in
the spring, I had received a telephone call from the U.S. Army,
tentatively confirming my appointment for the summer as a

cultural anthropologist at the Aberdeen Proving Grounds, a position for which I had applied some months earlier.

But at the same time, I. Thomas Stone called me unexpectedly and invited me to work for the Cornell Program in Social Psychiatry, also known as the Stirling County Study, a large and well-financed project operating in one of the Canadian Maritime Provinces. I was at the time nearly completely ignorant of the activities of the project, but I accepted immediately because the Cornell Program offered field work—as opposed to the office work at Aberdeen—and because many of my friends and fellow students were to spend the summer with the program.

Tom Stone asked me to attend a brief meeting of the summer team at Rand Hall on the Cornell campus. There, he and Alice Nangeroni, who were to guide the summer's effort, provided the research assistants with background information on the project and informed us of what ground was to be covered and what information collected between July and September.

In short, the summer would be spent in collecting ethnographic materials and psychiatric questionnaires from five communities. Each community would have its own resident ethnographer who would, at the end of the summer, write up his notes in a community study. In addition, there would be two "roving psychiatric reporters," who were to travel from town to town as conditions necessitated and administer questionnaires to a random sample of household heads. Thomas Revak, a student at Cornell Medical College, was designated as one of the interviewers, and I was to be the other.

We then discussed personal requirements for field work in rural Canada. These were nothing extraordinary. We needed to bring no special clothing, but we were encouraged to maintain a neat and fairly conservative public image. It would not be necessary for me to shave off my beard, but the girls were discouraged from wearing shorts around the research area. Housing, we were told, was readily available, but each research assistant was urged to find a car for summer use, particularly Thomas Revak and myself, who would be more mobile than the resident ethnographers.

The tone of this first meeting was relaxed. Alice Nangeroni and Tom Stone referred to consultants whom we were to meet later, but most of the summer field workers had been drawn from the sociology and anthropology departments of Cornell, and we all knew each other.

Problem, Theory, and Research Design

The background information, which Alice filled in for us, can be briefly stated here. In 1949, Alexander Leighton and his colleagues began an investigation that was later to become the Stirling County Study. Their primary purpose was to find out if there was any correlation between the living conditions in several communities in a Maritime Province and the prevalence of psychiatric disorder among the residents. Using a combination of techniques and theory derived from anthropology, sociology, psychology, and psychiatry, they did in fact find a number of correspondences between the two phenomena. The conditions of life that seemed most conducive to poor mental health were organized under the generic concept of sociocultural disintegration, and ten criteria were isolated by which communities could be judged in these terms. These criteria were (1) economic inadequacy, (2) cultural confusion, meaning essentially a lack of clear-cut ethnic identity, (3) widespread secularization, (4) high frequency of broken homes, (5) few and weak associations such as visiting patterns and organizational memberships, (6) few and weak leaders, (7) few patterns of recreation, (8) high frequency of interpersonal hostility, (9) high frequency of crime and delinquency, and (10) a weak and fragmented network of communications. The psychological concomitants of these community conditions were suspicion, anxiety, depression, and an unrealistic view of human affairs.

Over time, the program evolved into the most broadly based descriptive and analytical investigation, and when Tom and I joined it we knew only that our job was to administer questionnaires to people in order to determine, among other things, their degree of manifest psychopathology. That was our restricted objective. I have, even today, only a general grasp of the motivations and impulses of this corporate project. The data files at Rand Hall are so huge, so overwhelming in their quantity of detail, that one must either be in a highly responsible position within the program or else have an electronic brain at his disposal to reduce the mass of material to comprehensible proportions. As one who worked for the program at a humble level and for a single summer, I could not. But in the end I found that unfamiliarity with the program did not work to my disadvantage as an interviewer, because my responsibilities were limited and pretty clearly defined, and I needed to make few autonomous decisions.

Passive or Adaptational Research

Stirling County is rural, with a population of somewhat more than 20,000. This population is scattered through the region in small towns and villages, connected with each other primarily by dirt roads. Settlements stretch along the coastline and extend only about ten miles into the rougher inland country.

I worked in three separate communities with an urban center (the term "urban" being a relative one) called Bristol, a fishing and resort town with about 3,000 people.[1] The communities I worked in—Wolf River, Weavers, and Sibley—were ranged along the coast south of Bristol, and none had more than 1,000 inhabitants.

The countryside is quite beautiful, with rolling hills of buff dried grass ("honey-brown" in the travel folders) and stands of evergreens. In the backwoods are scattered forests of larger trees, spruce and pine, with a thick carpet of needles over the ground. In spring and summer, the open meadows are filled with berries and wild flowers. The sky is usually clear and bright, the atmosphere always crisp. It is a pretty place to do field work.

Aside from the scenic appeal of the area, the natural environment of the area exerted a considerable ecological influence on its residents. The great expanse of the bay that fronted this coast provided catch for fishermen; the cleared meadows allowed some not too productive farming (often managed with horse instead of tractor) ; and the timber yielded cordwood for loggers, logging as a large-scale operation having died many years before. The proximity of Bristol gave residents of these three communities an opportunity to commute to work at various commercial and service enterprises. Finally, the area was peaceful and attractive enough to draw a considerable number of tourists and summer residents, some of them fairly wealthy.

The three most noticeable factions in the community consisted of English Baptists, French Roman Catholics, and Negro Protestants of various denominations. There was little hostility among the three groups—the English and French having lived side by side for hundreds of years—but the social distinctions were real enough. They are listed above in their order of dominance.

Our entry into the site was eased by the fact that the project was such an old and established one that many of the residents already knew of it, either because they had been interviewed before or had heard of it (usually favorably) from someone else. We were also extremely fortunate in having a director and immediate supervisor (Leighton and Nangeroni) who both possessed an unusual capacity for managing social situations, however critical.

There were, of course, immediate problems to solve. It was suggested at the first Bristol meeting that Tom Revak and I, who were to form a team, might room together, and I accepted

---

[1] All people and places have been given code names.

the suggestion. Tom was at the time living in the house of an important political personage in Bristol, where I joined him. The tone of our interaction was and still is jocular and friendly, and our hosts were genial and hospitable. Because we were to work in Wolf River, Sibley, and Weavers, all to the south, however, we decided to move the twenty miles or so into that area. Moreover, the wind, which seemed to have an uncanny sense of direction, had been wafting the awful stench of the Bristol fish-meal processing plant in our direction, and mostly at night. This was no joke. We were losing sleep.

While we coped with housing problems, the organization and implementation of the program progressed. Phil Silverman, Doug Calkins, Tom, and I, who had no previous experience in interviewing, went north to a different county for a test run with the questionnaires. The purpose of the test interview was to familiarize us with the general procedure of administration. The questionnaire was the same one we would use in Stirling County, but this northern county was "safe" for test runs: it was out of the sample area, and none of the people taking the questionnaire would ever become a real informant. No matter how irretrievably we might alienate these respondents, the project would not suffer. On my first attempt, I drew the wife of a physics professor. This may have seemed like poor preparation for the original purpose of the program: investigating economically disadvantaged towns. But it was valuable experience. First of all, it gave me a chance to overcome my own initial anxiety. I have never enjoyed either giving public performances or imposing on people, and giving questionnaires seemed to me to involve both. However, after the first few minutes of the test run, I settled down and found that it wasn't so bad. The woman seemed actually flattered that someone would take the trouble to ask her all these questions about herself and her life style. Then, too, I learned during the interview, at least to some limited extent, how to guide the informant's monologue into relevant channels. The problem of containing the scope of the informant's answers would be more acute with less sophisticated informants, who had even less conception of the purpose of the interview.

At about the time these test interviews were being run, Phil and Ingrid Silverman moved out of a small two-story white cottage, and Tom and I moved into it. It was centrally located in the research area, in the coastal town of Alley Brook (two general stores, a dozen or so scattered houses, and a dilapidated boat dock), and it was set back off a side road in an acre of cleared ground grown over with wild roses. Our landlady lived about three hundred yards down the road. We could see her trim house from our lawn. She was kind, approachable, and considerably interested in the project, but we had little time to spend with her.

Once a week, the staff met at the Bristol Mental Health Center. Each week one member would give a progress report or read a paper, and a general discussion would follow. These informal seminars were of some value not only because they gave a more complete picture of the over-all research set-up and its workings, but because they gave the members of the team a chance to get together and know each other better. It was important to know not only what was going on, but whom you were working with.

Active Research

Having gotten settled, we were now ready to begin producing. We had three specific responsibilities. In the order of their importance to the project they were: (1) to collect questionnaires from a sample of male and female household heads in Wolf River, Weavers, and Sibley; (2) to keep field notes bearing on problems of rapport and on whatever community gossip we happened to pick up; and (3) to keep a brief informal journal of ideas and experiences that might be brought up at the seminars or might in some other way possibly be of value.

The questionnaire itself was a long one, covering a variety of topics from subsistence to physical health and religion. On an average day, Tom and I would get up at about 8:30, pack a few questionnaires into our briefcases, and drive off in our separate cars to hit one or more of the targets on our list of sample households. Usually we tried one or two houses where the selected household head was not available, but sooner or later we would find an informant and administer the questionnaire to him, a procedure that took about two hours. The informant might grow bored after the first thirty minutes, and one could be sure the interviewer was even more bored. Tom and I would meet at the general store at around noon and eat lunch. Then in the afternoon we repeated the same process. If the household head was never at home during the week (if, for example, he worked in Bristol), we were generally successful in arranging for an appointment during the evenings or on the weekends. There were days when we were able to collect only one questionnaire, but often we collected more; we averaged about twelve successful interviews a week.

The number of questionnaires completed during a week may sound like a trivial or meaningless index of one's own progress in field work, but it was the only index we had. Without it we would have lacked immediate feedback and never known how well or how poorly we were doing. When Tom and I realized that a norm of twelve questionnaires per week was crystallizing, we had something to strive for, and some means of assessing our progress. We came to feel guilty if we collected only ten, and we felt pleasantly virtuous if we collected fifteen.

The resident field workers, whose primary duty was developing an ethnography of their community, were also collecting questionnaires, but it was expected that they would come up with fewer than Tom and I, who were devoting all of our time to the job. About midway through the summer, however, one of the field workers began collecting far more than his "share" of questionnaires. At first, there was admiration for him, then, as he continued at his furious tempo, generalized puzzlement. Finally, when he showed no signs of letting up, a kind of pique spread through the research community. All those questionnaires, how could he do it? The answer turned out to be a fairly simple one. This field worker was taking one fifteen-milligram spansule of Dexedrine every work-day morning. Nevertheless, he was doing a fine job on his questionnaires: they were complete and were not lacking in marginal notes. It was instructive that these extra questionnaires, which benefited the project itself, were less important to the majority of the field workers than their own sense of self-adequacy. Nobody likes a rate-buster.

Tom and I were keeping a record of our visits to the sample houses, and whether or not the visits were productive, on a master sheet. This was the only record, aside from the completed questionnaires themselves, of what we had done during the summer. Alas, I lost this record toward the end. I am not sure how important the master sheet was, but I consider its loss the greatest technical error of the summer.

None of the research assistants, whether community residents or roving interviewers, was equipped with a tape recorder, but all of us took field notes anyway. Tom and I took fewer than the others, and ours seemed to consist mainly of somewhat bizarre incidents that one experiences outside of his cultural cocoon. One afternoon, for example, he and I drove together to a northern town to informally cover and personally enjoy the Cherry Festival. On the outskirts of town we passed a pair of legs stretched out on the highway. There seemed to have been some sort of accident, so we backed the car into the traffic and Tom, a medical student, got out to ask the woman kneeling next to this prostrate Indian what the trouble was. "Too much Cherry Festival." We then manuevered Joe, who was a Micmac and completely drunk, into the car. His wife sat in the back seat with him, urging him not to vomit on Tom's upholstery, and we drove the two to the reservation, a few miles away, where we engaged Joe's wife in a genuinely informative and refreshing interview on Indian life.

Problems of rapport with our respondents were almost independent of our own behavior. Our interviews were for the most part one-shot affairs. We knocked on the door, were accepted or not accepted. If accepted, we spent two hours reading questions aloud and marking down answers. We were friendly and innocuous, and we never saw most of our respondents twice.

We sustained a refusal rate that was within reasonable limits. We encountered few people who were truly hostile, either to us or to the group we represented. There were occasions, however, when respondents reacted with suspicion. A Negro woman in Sibley was standing in the middle of a field, surrounded by her six children, when I approached her. I gave her the usual speech, which went something like this: "Hi, there! My name is Bob Maxwell and I'm with the Cornell Program. You might have heard of the program. We're interested in learning about the people who live in Stirling County and how they make their living. Now you might wonder just *why* we are interested in this. First of all, we think it is good to know these things. Just like some scientists study plants, we like to study the way people live. Second, some day the government might like to make some improvements in your town, and we would like to know what kinds of improvements are most needed."

This robust woman folded her arms across her chest, glowered at me, and demanded to know why we had chosen *her*. I repeated that part of the speech dealing with the aims of the project, elaborating it somewhat, and concluded with a brief discourse on the theory of probability. At this point she exploded, and suggested that I was, in fact, an agent of the Canadian Government in the process of locating Negroes in order that they later be rounded up and shipped to Africa. I flipped open my questionnaire and read her an item dealing with any scars that she or her children might have, then asked her of what possible use that might be to a secret agent. "That would just help them identify us," she said (correctly, I guess). I showed her my student's ID card, my official-looking ID card from the program, my driver's license, and my stack pass from Cornell, and finally managed to convince her that I was not an agent of the Canadian Government. She then speculated that I might be, instead, a *Russian* agent, "trying to figure out the best place to drop the bomb." I could restrain my appreciation of this ludicrous situation no longer, so I started laughing and told her she was accusing me of being a Communist simply because my hair was red. She began chuckling herself and, after punching me heartily and painfully in the arm, asked me into her cabin, where I was able to interview her without further trouble. She was friendly and frank when she opened up.

Occurrences like these were far from typical. Ordinarily we were ushered politely into the kitchen, which is the room where business is conducted. (We found that approaching the back door instead of the front elicited a less formal and perhaps warmer response and helped to disperse the impression that we were strangers to the area.) We sat at the kitchen table, sometimes with a cup of coffee, and often surrounded by curious children, pencilling in our respondents' answers to our questions. We always noted in our summary of the interview whether other members of the family were present, although if they were this seemed to make little difference in the answers we received. Respondents were remarkably free in discussing, for example, their psychiatric problems in front of us and in front of their own families. This is probably a function of psycholinguistics as much as of sociology. There are different conotata, associations, and secondary benefits when one describes himself as having had a "nervous breakdown" or as having "weak nerves," as opposed to identifying himself as psychotic or neurotic. The emphasis in the latter two terms is on the formal characteristics of the disorder. They are in effect dirty names, no matter how clinical they sound. "Nervous breakdown" and "weak nerves," on the other hand, may imply conditions for which the respondent himself is not responsible. That is, one may have weak nerves in the same way as he may have a weak heart.

Some informants played games with us. Not very often, but a few times, we were taken into a kitchen full of house guests and there we tried to interview the household head in an ethos of curious amusement. We might ask: "Do your hands shake?— always, often, sometimes, seldom, or never?" The audience would find the question funny, and the informant, glancing slyly at his guests, would string the interviewer along: "Well, the morning I was supposed to marry Jenny . . ." This wouldn't have been so bad, but after the informant and his guests were sufficiently entertained, the informant would break off the interview and ask us to come back some other time, and thereafter he would consistently refuse to be interviewed. Half-completed interviews did not help either the project or our egos.

At least one of the interviews was eerie more than anything else. An old woman in Wolf River sat in the parlor with her cadaverous and trembling son, while I ran through the questionnaire. Her weatherbeaten house was located in an orchard of withering apple trees that looked as if they might have been planted in pre-contact days. The sky was gloomy and the wind high. As I entered the psychiatric section of the questionnaire, I began to sense that there was something out of the ordinary about her responses, and I gradually realized that she was psychotic. When I reached an item dealing with hallucinations, she began running down the list: she saw blue lights at night floating up to her window, she heard voices in the sky, and so on. Her son offered somewhat realistic but still highly implausible interpretations for her experiences. And then the wind rose, moaning and whistling in the barren apple trees, the old house creaked, and the interviewer experienced a gross pilomotor response.

Tom and I kept journals of the informal sort. Anything that seemed interesting or in any way valuable to us was written up in our field notes. We wrote in concert, for example, a partially ordered scale of informant cooperativeness, because the scale included in our questionnaire seemed to us inadequate to cover the range and character of reactions we elicited. We took photographs only for personal purposes: photos of the research area could not be published by the project, because such publication would have destroyed confidentiality.

Because of the nature of our interaction with questionnaire respondents, our relationships with fellow field workers and with fellow residents at Alley Brook became subjectively more important to us. Our fellow field workers were without exception admirable people, and we took great pleasure in them. There were no important conflicts. The research machine worked smoothly and with relative efficiency. The differences in field techniques that did exist were the effects of stylistic tendencies and differential responsibility rather than of character. One resident field worker found himself gradually tending to identify with the lesser-statused but lively Acadian French members of his community, rather than with the community leaders themselves, who were English Baptists. Another adapted with great facility to the monotonous kind of existence led by the local housewives: rocking for innumerable hours, through innumerable quiet afternoons, contemplating the summer's crop of vegetables and wondering whose car that was stirring up all the dust down the road. This was unbearable for me.

Tom and I had taken early to visiting our friends and co-workers in the evening and discussing the occupational events of the day or the week over Canadian beer. We found working with each other was intellectually rewarding and great fun besides. There was a Saturday night, moonlit and exciting, when Tom and I returned home from one of these visits and passed the crumbling dock on the bay near our house in Alley Brook. We noticed two boats moored there: one, a rowboat, the other a sailboat of considerable size and value. We decided that the rowboat would be an excellent vessel to take into the center of the bay, so we cast off and rowed out, and having exhausted the potential of this environmental resource, returned to the dock to take the large sailboat out for a short cruise. In the end, we were unable to, because neither of us could untie hawser knots. Perhaps it was a good thing, because neither of us knew how to sail either.

After about a month, we were told our cottage was no longer available for rent, and Tom and I, unable to find another place on such short notice, moved into the boathouse of Dr. Leighton's residence, near Bristol. There was a gap between the roof and the walls of the boathouse (which actually contained boats) and squadrons of moths flew into our room every evening, coating everything, including our food, with a thin film of iridescent moth-wing powder. Some of them were huge and kept us awake at night, battering themselves against the screens. At four o'clock in the morning they began to sound like owls.

We finally located a neat white house on an acre near Alley Brook and moved into that. Other than the table and chair we had been able to borrow, we had no furniture, so we lounged and slept on the floor. We paid the landlord $20 a month in rent, and we could have bought the house and its land for $1,500 Canadian. This time we had amiable neighbors. Too amiable in some ways: the landlord's children were in our hair day and night. Our next-door neighbor brought us a loaf of home-made bread and asked us what he should do about his occasionally overwhelming feelings of nervousness and tension. We could only tell him that a great many other people experienced the same sort of thing.

Bowing Out

When our psychiatric interviewing was at an end, Tom returned to New York. But since I was to stay in Alley Brook until mid-September, I was asked to cover very briefly the town of Weavers, which had had no resident ethnographer during the summer. We needed more information on certain subjects, such as seasonal patterns of visiting, which were not covered by the questionnaire. I covered Weavers at some cost to my psyche. My conception of an adequate community description differed vastly from the kind of report it was possible for me to prepare in only two weeks. My anxiety level was so high that I functioned poorly, although I still managed to collect the necessary materials.

When I had to leave it was with real regret. The cohesiveness and camaraderie of the research staff had been truly pleasurable, and the residents of the area had been warm and receptive, particularly some of the French families, whom we invited to a final staff party. The natural setting was pastoral and peaceful. For a while, I even entertained the possibility of staying on as a clinician at the Bristol Mental Health Clinic. I didn't know anything about psychiatry, but I knew what I liked.

Summary and Evaluation

It is difficult to summarize or evaluate the research done during that summer in Stirling County. No major problems were solved. The program was to be activated again the following summer. We were not able to draw up any tables of findings, or any lists of conclusions. What data we had gathered would be added to a larger pool, and part of it would be processed during the school year. What we had done was to make some progress toward a long-range goal. Even if the group had been able to synthesize the summer's work and present this synthesis as a "finding," I myself would have had little share in it, because of the specificity of my role. All of the field assistants assumed that their work had been satisfactory because our rapport with community members and informants had been generally good, our interview rate was kept at a high enough level to make us feel comfortable with it, and there was a recurrent filtering down of positive feedback from our superiors. I myself discovered little of a general nature that had not been already published, or soon would be. I had no clear image of the structure or relative status of any of the communities that I worked in, although my experience suggested that the people living in these towns included a great majority of respectable persons, a few leaders, and a few deviants, and that almost all of them felt a general sense of satisfaction with their rural, monotonous, unharried existence. But this is only my impression.

PART II: WEST OF PANGO PANGO[2]

Problem, Theory, and Research Design

Field work in a nonindustrialized society was one of the prerequisites for the Ph.D. program in anthropology at Cornell, so in 1964, after my work in Canada, I applied for a research

---

[2] Traditional Samoan orthography is misleading. "Pango Pango," for example, is usually written "Pago Pago." I have modified the spellings here, so that they more closely approximate English pronunciation.

grant from the National Institute of Mental Health, whose operations are happily predicated on a broad definition of mental-health research.

In trying to decide what problem to investigate, and where to investigate it, I had previously assumed that I would exploit my areas of specialization, psychology and China, and research some problem in psychological anthropology on Taiwan or in Hong Kong. However, the more I thought about it, the less the idea of living with the Chinese appealed to me. I enjoyed Chinese food, but not certain aspects of Oriental culture, specifically filial piety and wariness toward outsiders. Furthermore, I had had enough contact with the written language to know how agonizing it could be.

It occurred to me that, as an anthropologist, I was perfectly free to go anywhere my passport would permit, and study any problem I liked, and so, one night, I took out a globe and spun it around a few times, picking out exotic and exciting-sounding places. I thought briefly of studying sex in Sweden, but dismissed the area as having too harsh a winter. Tahiti, on the other hand, impressed me as a kind of Sweden, from the point of view of sexual behavior, with a pleasant climate.

The question I finally decided to research was, assuming that sex is a recurring positive drive, what is the nature of the sex-anxiety determinants that create a balance in males between complete promiscuity and complete celibacy?

Why this problem? I justified my choice of a problem, sexual behavior and its hypothetical negative, sex anxiety, in a number of ways. First, it seemed remarkable to me that so little quantitative work had been done in such an important area of human behavior. There were impressionistic case studies, one or two cross-cultural surveys—Malinowski, Ford, and Beach—and not much else! Second, I was genuinely curious about what sort of social forces might inhibit sexual freedom. Third, being rather cynical, I found it difficult to accept the image of Tahitian sexual behavior that is fostered by the mass media. One reads of all those lovely *vahines* and strapping lads and their freedom from *Angst,* and one thinks, "Fine, except that it can't be so." There are deterrents to promiscuity. There is jealousy. There is the church. There is the extended family. There is—if nothing else—the incest taboo. Finally, I settled on this problem in this area because nothing else suggested itself. I was not committed to any particular problem, any theoretical point of view, any level of analysis, or any geographic area. But I was, on the whole, more interested in sex in Tahiti than, say, subsistence patterns in Peoria. Also, Papeete contained a flourishing colony of Hakka-speaking Chinese. I never seriously thought my knowledge of the rudiments of Mandarin would do me very much good with Hakka speakers, but my general knowledge of the Far East and China might help me in a comparative study of sexual behavior among the permissive Polynesians and the restrictive Chinese.

My research problem had to be clearly defined and my methodology had to be structured, because NIMH grants are not awarded to those with only a loose idea of what they will be investigating. My research design, as I described it in my application, was comparative. I proposed that various independent variables (strong conceptions of private property, authoritarian households, the virginity mystique, and birth order and heirhood) affected certain mediating variables (consistently harsh training in self-discipline) and led to such manifestations of sex anxiety as impotence and interest in model sex, such as pornography. I would take observations from both the Chinese and the Tahitians.

My proposed strategy was to give all informants questionnaires and then try to assess (1) the extent to which they had been exposed to and had internalized the anxiety determinants, and (2) the extent to which they showed evidence of sex anxiety. These two groups of variables would be expected to vary with each other. The twist in my research proposal was that I would try to generate anxiety in the subjects by showing them nude photographs and then measuring the amount of perspiration on their fingertips. In theory, the Chinese should have sweated more than the Tahitians. Of course, not having specialized in Polynesia, I could not specify questionnaire items or structure interviews until I had gotten there and assessed the situation. But I did expect to use translations of the F scale as an index of authoritarianism.

With my application in the mail, I enlisted the aid of a girl from Barbados to help me draft a letter to the governor of French Polynesia. Her letter, in rolling and poetic French, begged the governor's permission to allow me to conduct my research project in his territory. After the letter was mailed, I spent a few weeks reading about Tahiti and watching "Adventures in Paradise" on television, until, almost simultaneously, I received notices that I had been awarded the research grant and denied permission to do field work in Tahiti.

The essence of the terse note that I received from the governor's secretary was that the government felt there was already enough research going on in Tahiti. That may have been the real reason, but at the same time the French were preparing for a series of nuclear tests in that area, and one wonders whether or not the possibility occurred to them that in addition to being an anthropologist I might be an agent for the CIA. Whatever it was, the governor was adamant; even the help of Margaret Mead was unavailing. Where should I go? I needed a place where two populations lived side by side, one high in sex anxiety, the other low. Most modern Micronesia was *terra incognita*, but the Marquesans were reputed to be surly, the Marshallese missionized to the point where it was scandalous for a man to remove his T-shirt. The Fijians lived in a society where conservative Methodism overlay traditional British reserve. In the end, I gambled on Samoa. *Coming of Age in Samoa* suggested a pretty playful atmosphere, and a call to Melvin Ember at Antioch College assured me that there were a number of Orientals living on fishing boats in Pango Pango harbor, so that a comparative design was still suitable.

I collected my gear, which consisted of a small traveling bag, a large black steamer trunk (full of papers and pencils, cameras, sleeping bag, tape recorder, 7,000 8″ × 5″ field-note cards, and other odds and ends), and a cumbersome two-room tent, which was hell to carry and which I was never to use.

The same day I was to leave, I received a telegram from the governor of American Samoa, granting me permission to land. I showed up at the dock in time to see my gear loaded aboard the ship, spent the evening in a Greek café on the waterfront, and next morning found myself at sea, nursing the muscles I had strained doing all those Greek dances. My preparations and departure were chaotic, but I naïvely expected the field work itself to be different.

Passive Research

Environment of the group. Samoa lies south-southwest of Hawaii, about twelve degrees south of the equator. Surrounding it are the island groups of Tonga, Fiji, and Ellice. This is not to say that the area is crowded. Those island dots on maps are actually separated by vast expanses of utterly empty Pacific Ocean.

Beginning about 4,000 years ago, canoe-loads of Indonesians filtered down into Melanesia and continued sailing eastward, against the trade winds, to New Zealand, then across to Easter Island (a barren windswept place), and north to Hawaii, forming a gigantic Polynesian triangle. No one knows how long ago Samoa was discovered and populated by these resourceful folk, but in years subsequent to the initial landings a strong and viable body of custom was built up, based on subsistence patterns involving fishing, gathering, and the cultivation of domestic plants and animals. Religion and sheer material wealth were relatively unimportant, but kinship ties, descent patterns, community service, and political activities received considerable emphasis. Attention was given to personal and collective dignity, politeness and ceremony, the correct observance of fairly reasonable social rules (for example: don't be pompous; don't kill your neighbors without good reason; act your age), and, within this framework of hortative propositions, the enjoyment of the good things of life.

What might have been a rather boring existence was enlivened by feasting and license on some ceremonial occasions and by brief, irregular, but lethal wars between villages and, externally, with the Tongans. (The Samoan heroes of these wars appear even today in popular mythology. They may or may not have been real, as Achilles or Nimrod may or may not have been real, but the entertainment value of the stories is not lessened.)

In 1722, when the islands were discovered by Jacob Roggeveen, a Dutchman, the Samoans were increasingly bombarded by Euroamerican values and materials, and the tempo of social change picked up rapidly.

Today the islands of the Samoan group are divided politically into two units. Western Samoa, composed of the two largest islands, received its independence in 1962. American Samoa consists of one large island, Tutila, and three smaller ones to the east: Ofu, Olosenga, and Ta'u, called the Manu'an group. Together the four American islands make up a land area of seventy-five square miles or so, about the size of Rhode Island. All the islands are quite rugged and mountainous. Most of the settlements are found along the relatively narrow strip of flat coastal land. In many parts of the island this strip is barely wide enough for a footpath. Beaches are not a noticeable feature of the coastline; the sea pounds directly against sharp lava cliffs.

Samoa was ceded to America in 1900. The principal reason for Samoa's importance to America lay in its strategic location and its fine, deep harbor, Pango Pango Bay. The Navy ruled American Samoa and used Pango Pango as a coaling station early in the century. Gradually, as coal-burning ships were phased out, the island lost some of its military importance. The naval administration was dissolved in 1951, and the territory was transferred to the Department of the Interior.

Political life is presently structured into something resembling a pyramid. At the village level, a council of chiefs sits together irregularly to elect a mayor to deal with minor interfamily disputes, such as arguments over land ownership, and to organize communal labor. There are also fourteen appointed county chiefs, who rule the traditional precontact subdistricts of the islands, handle intervillage disputes, and appoint their own police force. The next most inclusive administrative unit is the district, of which there are three, each represented at the meetings of the central legislature by a district governor. The district governor is appointed by the governor of American Samoa and is ordinarily the chief title-holder in his district.

The central government consists of three groups: (1) an executive council of a dozen or so chiefs, whose function it is to advise the governor of American Samoa; (2) a senate of about the same size, designed to represent the three districts; and (3) a house of representatives, made up of about twenty men, popularly elected by secret ballot. Presiding over all of these administrative and legislative groups is the governor and his assistants. The governor, an official appointed from the ranks of the Department of the Interior, has the power of veto over any legislation passed by the two houses, but relations between him and the popular representatives are such that he may use other subtle means of control.

The hub of the central government is in an area referred to as Pango Pango, although it is technically part of the village of Fangatongo. Here live about 5,000 of the approximately 30,000 American Samoans, and virtually all of the 300 or 400 resident Americans and Europeans. The docks and warehouses are here, as are the post office, the Bank of American Samoa, most of the governmental offices, the police station, the jail, the rather run-down hospital, and the five taverns. Buses, trucks, motorbikes, and small Japanese cars grind noisily up and down the narrow streets; the steep green hills are crowded with flimsy tin-roofed houses; the sidewalks are busy with Samoans during the day, and here and there among the gaily dressed dark people a pale Caucasian, in white shirt and tie, may be seen hurrying someplace or other. In Pango Pango one can almost feel he is downtown in any small American community on a busy afternoon.

Out in the villages, life seems more tranquil. After the morning buses have taken the children off to school and the working men off to their labor (most of them make the standard wage of about 45¢ an hour), the remaining adults and preschool children gather together their tools and stroll off into the bush to work on their small gardens. As the villagers go about their business, one senses a general spirit of cheerfulness. The workingmen on the morning bus often break into group song as it departs. The prevailing mood is one of optimism and enthusiasm. ("One good thing about Samoa," a workman told me later, "everything here is free. Not like in the states." He was doing manual labor under a blazing tropical sun eight hours per day, six days per week, for 42¢ an hour.) Nobody seems particularly harassed or hurried, and there may be good ecological reasons for this. There are, after all, few places like Samoa, where you

and I, Reader, might be stripped of all the accouterments of
civilization, set down alone in the middle of a forest, and be almost as certain of year-round survival as we are in our class-
rooms.

Entry Problem and Initial Copings

When I left the states I knew nothing about Polynesia except
what I had read. The jumble of ethnographic facts in my head
made little sense. My impression of Polynesia from watching
"Adventures in Paradise" was of a fragmented Miami Beach
without the hotels. I looked forward to the experience of field
work with only two reservations. (1) The Samoans raised pigs
and killed them for feasts: how would I react when a pig had his
brains beaten out in my presence? And (2) In Ithaca I rose at
noon and turned in at about four in the morning. Could I possibly adapt myself to a schedule in which people got up at *dawn?*
(Both of these turned out to be needless worries. I easily
adapted.)

When the Matson freighter I traveled on put into Pango
Pango in the late morning of April Fool's Day, 1965, I stood on
the flying bridge and watched the Samoan line handlers. They
wore only long skirt-like loincloths and rubber thongs, and
walked with a sort of swooping stride. One of the men had a
flower behind his ear. My over-all and completely erroneous impression was that they were all a bit effeminate.

Ashore, I went directly to the office of the governor, armed
with $700 worth of traveler's checks, a passport, a copy of my
research-grant award, and the landing permit I had received
just before leaving the states. I was asked to wait outside the
lieutenant governor's office. As I sat there I looked over my
credentials again and could see no gaps. Whatever policy dominated the government of French Polynesia, I couldn't imagine
any reason why I might be denied permission to conduct my
research in American Samoa: I was well-funded, and my status
and purposes were legitimate.

This assessment turned out to be accurate, and the lieutenant
governor, after I had introduced myself, seemed regretful that
it was. I had expected to be greeted with some interest, if not
eager enthusiasm, but his comments were terse and discourag-
ing. "You can't just walk into a village and set up a tent, you
know." Although he couldn't very easily prevent me from living
and working in American Samoa, he ran through a list of reasons
why it might be advantageous for everyone concerned if I went
elsewhere—"maybe Fiji." The lieutenant governor then told me
that I would be expected to stay in the Rainmaker Hotel, the

only hotel on the island, but that this hotel might be filled up. "If you don't have a place to stay the night," he added "you might as well not unload your luggage because you'll be on the ship when it leaves tomorrow morning." I was then ordered to report to the attorney general's office and check in with him.

The attorney general informed me that the government was wary of long-term visitors, because "we get a lot of kooks who think all they need to do is come down here and drink coconut milk and grow beards." (I shaved off my own beard the same day.) He seemed completely unimpressed by the copy of my award notice, by my status at Cornell, or by the fact that Margaret Mead had suggested Samoa to me as a research site. He asked me to return to his office that afternoon with $200 in *cash* —he didn't care where I got it—to post as a bond, and to arrange for a letter to be sent to him from the chairman of my department, Allan Holmberg, stating that I was a student in good standing and not a subversive on the lam. Finally, I was told that I had permission to remain in American Samoa for thirty days, providing I could find lodging for the night. At the end of that period I would have to apply for permission to stay longer, and this application would involve my being called up before a board of examiners in the Immigration Office. I could not understand the hostility of these decision-makers at the time, but I later concluded that the Caucasian population of the island could be organized neatly into a system, every Caucasian having his slot ("teacher," "merchant," and so on), but that I, newly arrived and with a purpose that could only be vaguely conceived of, increased entropy in the system.

The Rainmaker Hotel had sufficient room (at $8 per day, including meals), but before I had an opportunity to register I had fallen into conversation with a sixty-year-old Samoan man in the Pango Bar who insisted I spend the night at his place. His house, on the outskirts of town, was small, a single room with a single bed. He insisted too that I use the bed and that he sleep on the floor beside it. I objected, but he would have nothing else. I thought at the time that he was an exceptionally kind Samoan, but he wasn't. He was typically kind. The old man's real name is Sam Fouolo.

We awoke at dawn to the clucking of several dozen chickens that had just flapped down from their roosts in the branches of the breadfruit trees. We ate fried eggs and biscuits. The muggy morning air smelled of dead things, urine, rotting wood, and the sweet waxy flowers Sam called *bua*.

I could have lived with Sam, but Pango Pango seemed too Westernized an area. I had a mental model, a fairly accurate one as it turned out, in which Pango Pango and Manu'a represented the urban and folk ends of a continuum along which other communities were normally distributed. I wanted something near the mode, so that whatever village I finally chose to work in would be more nearly representative.

Downtown again, I asked pedestrians at random if there were any boarding houses in the outer villages. I was relieved to find that most of the Samoans I spoke to knew English, and one man, cunningly attired in shirt and tie, sports jacket, and loincloth, directed me to the house of a woman living in a medium-sized village about six miles west of Pango Pango. Her name was Susan Allen, and she was said to be building a boarding house which might now be ready to receive guests.

The road to Susan's village, Laovele, meanders for several miles along the coastline, turns gradually inland, skirting the airport, and then abruptly south to the sea. Susan's long house, built in the traditional style, was open to the breeze of the ocean, the rollers of which broke into a tiny lagoon a hundred feet away. The ceiling was high and wide, the coral floor covered with clean woven mats, and the interior furnished with simple chairs and couches covered with bright prints. The fronds of the potted palms scattered around inside rustled slightly in the breeze. This is where Susan catered to parties and where she entertained business executives, bankers, and admirals. I did not see a finer house while I was in the field.

Susan herself lived in a smaller Western house immediately behind the long dwelling house. She made it clear that she was not running a boarding house, but that I was welcome to use one of the two luxurious beds until I was settled somewhere else. The only stipulation was that I must pay nothing, for otherwise she would feel obligated to constantly look out for my welfare.

A week after I moved in I bought a motorbike and used this to travel from one end of Tutuila to the other, checking the villages to see if the remoter settlements were in any ways more traditional than the ones closer to Pango Pango. They did not seem especially so. The villages that I could reach by bike all had their share of local vehicles, were supplied with electricity and television, served as home for commuting wage workers, and were part of an organized school system. I learned also that even the villages on the north shore of Tutuila, where no roads reached, supplied wage workers for the downtown area, although commuting meant a twice-daily hike over a thousand-foot mountain pass.

I also made a five-day trip to the islands of the Manu'a group, spending most of that time in the village of Fitiuta on Ta'u Island as the guest of a family who had kinship ties with Laovele. There were some noticeable differences. The people spoke what they referred to as "pure Samoan," corresponding perhaps to BBC English, while people from Tutuila and Western Samoa spoke a kind of slang most of the time, only activating their "pure Samoan" during on-stage performances. Then, too, in Fitiuta, opportunities for wage work were strictly limited, there was no electricity, few canned goods were available and no alcohol, and little English was spoken.

After my return from Manu'a, I felt I had a fairly good estimate of the range of Westernization in American Samoa. A month after my arrival, then, I felt it was time to choose the village I would be living in for the next two years. I sat in front of Susan's house in the shade of one of her dwarf palms, sipping milk from a freshly opened coconut, and looking out over Laovele. The thatched huts of the village were sprinkled about the town square, and the fresh trade winds sent curlers booming up against the lava outcroppings. It was very pleasant. I decided that Laovele village was as good as any to work in, because it seemed about average, because the trades dispersed mosquitoes and kept the effective temperature reasonably low, and because it was accessible to the downtown area.

That evening I asked Susan what she thought of the idea. She was quite a bright woman, part-Samoan, with a foot in both cultures, so to speak. Her suggestion was that I ask the permission of Chief Tangaloa, who lived at the other end of the village. I did so the same evening, but with some hesitation: how does one approach a Samoan chief and a county chief at that? I was admitted into the living room of the big blue house by Tangaloa's grandson, Petelu. The chief, seated comfortably in an armchair, greeted me in Samoan and gestured for me to sit down on the couch. I smiled, thanked him in Samoan, and sat down, but before I could present my request, the old chief instructed one of the children to turn on the television set.

For the next hour and a half everyone in the room watched Henry Fonda cavort on the screen. Tangaloa rested with his bare feet propped up on a low table. He was a massive man, not tall or heavily muscled so much as fat. He was about sixty-five years old and tatooed with bluish-black geometric designs around his hips and from navel to knee. His whole manner was relaxed and easy-going. He chuckled during the combat scenes and apparently was interested in the story, although he could not understand the English dialogue. (His wife thought the story, as it unfolded on the television screen, was really happening to real people!) Occasionally, Tangaloa would look over at me and smile, and I sensed that he had no better idea of how to handle me than I did of how to handle him.

After the show, Tangaloa indicated to me, through one of

his talking chiefs, that I had his permission to stay and work in the village. He assured me that it would not be necessary for me to set up my tent. He and his family would provide a house. I should be ready at 7:30 the next morning. As I walked home through the darkened village, my impression of Tangaloa was that he was a nice old fellow. Because of the many differences between us—age, status, language—I could not anticipate how close he and I were to become, but within a year he was to ask if he could adopt me into his family and give me a title.

The next morning I was awakened by Tangaloa: "Greetings, White Man, not up yet?" I pulled on my shirt as Tangaloa opened Susan's refrigerator and extracted two beers for us. A group of men and women were waiting respectfully outside to prepare my new house. Still groggy, I followed the group down the road. What was to be my house was a far cry from the opulence of Susan's: a small thatch-roofed hut with a smaller tin-roofed shed built into one side of it. The shed had wooden walls, the hut section was open. The Samoans chased the current occupants—pigs, horses, and chickens—outside and began sweeping the dirt floor clear of their droppings. Tangaloa ordered the hut to be furnished with materials from other households of the family. And, with alacrity, the young men stocked the hut with a small frame bed, floor mats, table and small bench, and mosquito netting. The following day, the men and I painted the interior of the shed green. This color, in combination with the yellow insect-repellent light bulb overhead, made for a bilious effect, but I was at least living Samoan-style. I stayed in this hut from May through September.

Rapport Gaining

Laovele, like all other villages, was organized into several extended families, each headed by a chief or a talking chief. (The difference between the two kinds of chiefs is largely a ceremonial one; for everyday purposes, they are the same.) Most of the extended families are subdivided into smaller branches within the village. The subdivisions are headed by relatively minor chiefs. The hut I was living in belonged to a branch of Tangaloa's family. Since the chief in charge of this branch was crippled, authority was handed down informally to one of his sons, Ioane, a 32-year-old English-speaking man who was friendly and generous, as indeed most Samoans are, but emotionally intense. His concern for my well-being, his solicitousness, in time became oppressive. For example, he informed me that the dirt road running past my hut was a favorite haunt of ghosts. Although ghosts did not bother anyone unless they are provoked, it seems that they were provoked by the fact that my light burned after the other villagers had retired for the night. I kept it lit until I finished typing up my notes of the day's events—about midnight. Therefore, Ioane wanted to know, would I kindly respect the wishes of his household and extinguish the light by 10:30? I did, of course. But this cut off two irreplaceable hours of my writing time.

It was not Ioane, however, who was the cause of my moving from his hut in September, but rather two of his five children. These children stole from me, in five months, an indeterminable amount of money (usually in five- and ten-dollar units) from my dwindling supply, postage stamps (which turned up later as colorful decorations on the faces of the kids), matches, a butane lighter, pencils, pens, snapshots, and my winter overcoat. One expects this sort of thing from Samoan children, and I quickly learned that if something is stolen, one does not take measures to find out who did it, as that can only cause trouble. Instead, one tries to prevent its happening again by buying stronger locks for the doors and windows, finding safer hiding places, and so on.

The usual procedures may have eventually proved effective for my personal things, but the children were making inroads into my research equipment. I would return from a trip to the other end of the village to find my Unisort cards being used as drawing pads. Some of the photographs and slides that formed part of the ethnographic record disappeared. Toward September, I discovered that some filed notes had been folded into paper airplanes and were being sailed around outside. I mentioned to Ioane that I could live without the personal items but that the success of my research depended on my being able to maintain a record of what had happened in the village, and that if this material were tampered with or stolen I would suffer later. Ioane's advice was to keep everything locked up and not worry so much about material goods. Not long after this, Ioane and I came back to my hut from a Labor Day celebration. Two reels of already exposed 8-millimeter movie film had been unrolled and chopped up with a knife. This was an irreplaceable loss.

I lost my temper and shouted at the boy who had confessed to "finding" my film, then contacted Tangaloa and asked him if I might live with him in his house. He had made me a standing invitation, and he welcomed me now. That taken care of, I had to inform Ioane of my decision to move. The poor man had warned me over and over that if I ever left his house he would be ashamed before the whole village. They would all gossip about him and say that he was incapable of taking care of his guest. Upon receiving the bad news, Ioane did not do much to avoid the attention of the villagers. He moaned with increasing volume and finally began punching holes through the wooden walls of the shed. As a crowd gathered to watch his performance, I was dragged to safety by the ladies, but he continued sobbing and screaming and beating the earth until one of the larger women of the village pushed him to the floor and sat on his chest to quiet him down. I was filled with anger and guilt. Thrust into life with a Samoan family, I had lasted only six months.

But the move turned out to be an excellent development in some ways. At Tangaloa's house I was given a small room to myself. My frame bed was brought up, and locks were provided for the door. The atmosphere was entirely different: much more pleasant for me personally and much more conducive to work. There had been an almost constant tension at Ioane's and a certain lack of warmth. For example, one of the dogs at Ioane's had broken its leg, and the children of the house had gone out of their way to torment it. I finally adopted the scrawny beast so that I could protect it and not have to listen to its distracting howling. Here at Tangaloa's the children were respectfully distant. Nothing was stolen, the household animals were merely ignored, and I had much greater freedom: nobody warned me about gossip or ghosts, and I could come and go as I pleased.

Active Research

Shortly after I had settled in at Tangaloa's, I began to understand how to deal with the varous groups on the island. There were, first of all, the group of American administrators and merchants in the downtown area. After my confrontation with the governor's aides and several subsequent encounters with the *palangi* (white and Western) élite, I realized there was little hope of establishing rapport with this group. I had deliberately sought out representatives of the government at Susan's parties, because I was beginning to feel the need to get out of my small hut and discuss such things as entropy and civil rights with knowledgeable people in comfortable English. Things did not turn out as well as they might have, however. I had forgotten—if I had ever known—how to manage myself in the presence of solidly middle-class American citizens, and I presented myself, although unwittingly, as an eccentric churl. For example, at one of Susan's parties I assembled my fingertip-sweat-measuring materials and gave all of the guests a test. There was no way they could get out of it with any grace, and so they allowed me to go about happily measuring their anxiety levels while they cast mystified glances at one another. In the two years I was in the field, I became friends with only five *palangis*.

I did not do much better with the part-Samoan élite. In a

way, I represented that part of Samoa they seemed eager to forget: I was poor; I was living with a poor family in a leaking hut with a dirt floor; and I had no important downtown friends. As the months went by I grew increasingly uncomfortable in the presence of both the *palangi* and the part-Samoan élite. One reason for this was financial. My graduate-fellowship checks were supposed to be routed through the international teller of a New York bank, then to my account in the Bank of American Samoa. But somebody, whether through accident or intention, had intercepted the checks for half of the annual stipend, opened an account in my name in a bank in Jackson Heights, Long Island, and begun cashing checks on the account, spending my money. After I had discovered this, it took several more months to straighten the affair out. Thus, for the period from January to September, 1966, I received only $650 from my graduate fellowship, and at one point I was down to about $5 in liquid assets. Another reason was my appearance. I had to use the same razor blades for about a month, and my hair, cut by Ioane, was not that of a male model out of *Playboy*. Infected mosquito bites had healed and left my body flecked with white spots, and for two months I had an eye infection that kept my lids swollen and inflamed. Two sores on my chin were ulcerating. I was sunburned, and I had lost weight, and once, catching a glimpse of myself in the rear-view mirror of my Honda, I was somewhat startled at what I saw. The élite were so clean-cut and they placed so much stock in appearance that I found it embarrassing to present myself to them.

As much as I felt the need to communicate with the élite, I gave up trying to associate with them and settled down into the life of the village, having by this time begun to appreciate the fact that it was easier in many ways to get along with the relatively tolerant and mostly indifferent Samoans than with the Americans.

My rapport with the Laovele villagers was as good as it was bad with the élite. At first, of course, the untitled men and their families were nervous when I talked to them. Some of the villagers—and the majority of young children—had had no contact with white Westerners. I was a stranger and could not readily be fitted into their model of a structured society. The preschool children cried with fright if I came near them. I took three measures to define my role in the village. (Although these measures may sound deceptively deliberate here, they were not well thought out at the time.)

First, I visited, in the presence of Tangaloa's adolescent grandson, Petelu, all eighty houses in the village and personally met most of the 460 inhabitants. During these initial visits, each lasting about half an hour, I explained that I was a teacher from America and that my purpose was to learn about the Samoan way of life so that I could instruct American schoolchildren. In addition to giving the villagers a chance to get to know me, these visits were valuable because I used them to get basic background data on the composition and characteristics of the household such as age, sex, birth order, place of birth, and so on. The untitled villagers seemed to go through three phases in their attitude toward me: from deference, to curiosity, to friendly tolerance.

The second measure I took was to associate myself openly with the villagers, particularly with the family of Tangaloa. Often in the mornings I accompanied Tangaloa on his bus trips to town. If he paid an informal visit to another village chief, I tagged along. I learned to play cricket with the young men of the village and, on payday evenings, chipped in for beer and played poker. This was not only good experience—most of the things I learned went into field notes—but it was often enjoyable.

Finally, one of my informants showed me around the high school where he taught. I noticed a Ditto machine and asked if I might have the privilege of using it. The first thing I did was type up a stencil in basic English, explaining who I was and why I was there. I then distributed copies of this paper to many of the villagers.

On the whole, these methods, combined with the fact of my sheer physical presence over a long period of time, were effective in defining my role, although there were a few qualifications. Two of the village ladies began spreading rumors that I was a spy. One of them later became friendly with me. The other remained antagonistic and hostile throughout my stay, but she abused everyone else in the village too.

It also became clear that my participation in the chiefly mode of life was to be limited. I was too young to look like a chief, my command of Samoan was deficient, I too often engaged in activities pursued by the younger untitled men, and I was temperamentally unsuited to the chiefly life. This did not interfere with my relationships with the village chiefs, but it did set certain limits on my ability to identify with them.

On only one occasion did I notice any wariness toward me and my purposes on the part of the chiefs. Three of them visited Tangaloa's one evening to watch television. Afterwards, they told me they wanted to talk to me for a moment and give me advice about the book I intended to write. In essence, this advice was that many years ago a *palangi* woman had come to Laovele to live and had later written a book about her experiences. This book was full of bad stories about Laovele and about Samoa in general. I should not follow her example and shame the Samoan people. The *palangi* woman was Margaret Mead and the book was *Coming of Age in Samoa,* which had been read by many of the educated Samoans and part-Samoans. I did not try to correct their misunderstanding, but I told them I would be extremely careful not to write stories that would make anyone ashamed.

In all unfamiliar situations, I tried to handle the Samoans by being quiet, appreciative, and observant. When the situation permitted, as at mealtimes and parties, I tried to be helpful by washing dishes, acting as bartender, and sometimes trying to translate English remarks into Samoan for Tangaloa's benefit. Inevitably, there were times when I broke etiquette. I once walked into a council meeting to serve food to the chiefs while I was dressed in shorts instead of a loincloth, and a few times while cleaning up after dinner I was ridiculed by the children for stepping over Tangaloa's body as he lay on the floor. I should have walked around in back of him, but I had a hard time remembering this rule.

Tangaloa was only of limited value to me in my research, as we could carry on only a rudimentary conversation without a translator. Besides, Tangaloa did not know a great deal about the details of Samoan social structure. At one time a debate was being carried on in the pages of the *American Anthropologist* over the meanings of certain terms referring to kinship groups in Samoa. Whole pages were devoted to arguments about what sort of group was indicated by the term *aingasa.* I thought I might solve the problem simply by asking Tangaloa, the senior title-holder of Laovele and the chief of the county, but neither he nor anyone else I asked was sure what the term meant.

Four people did prove of considerable value. Toni, a Samoan of my own age, was a teacher. He lived in Laovele with his *palangi* wife, whom he had married in the states while attending college. He was an extremely sensitive man, who suffered from great ontological anxiety generated by his orientation toward Western life. He was the only person in the village I could always trust to tell me the truth. He periodically drank too much and became muddled and aggressive, but he willingly translated materials for me and frequently acted as my assistant when I went about the village. When he left for Honolulu some months before the end of my stay in the field, he was careful to transfer the responsibility he had assumed to two other young men in the village, neither of whom, unfortunately, had his persistence and interest.

Toni and I had become friends immediately, but another valuable informant was at first reluctant to associate with me.

This was Tafua, a thirty-year-old part-Samoan who had spent two years in the U.S. Marine Corps and another year in a California business college. He headed a branch of Tangaloa's family. I sometimes addressed him as Tafua, his chief's title, and sometimes used his *palangi* name (Dan Young). After I knew him better, I simply called him "Chief" or even "Big Chief."

At our first meeting, Tafua was reserved and formal. Later, he told me that his initial behavior had been prompted by his family's suspicions of me. They could not understand why I was hanging around the village, and they thought I was just another beach bum in my loincloth and unshaven face. When they had a clearer idea of my status, and when my appearance had improved, their attitudes changed and I began spending a lot of time with him. All together, Tafua and I must have made our way through several thousand bottles of beer while we sat around his house in the evenings, slapping mosquitos and gossiping about the village and about Samoan culture. He was not the best of informants, but his conversational style was comfortably American. One of the items on my general questionnaire was: "Who is your best friend in the village?" Tafau's response was: "Well, I guess that's a guy named Maxwell."

Tangaloa's grandson, Petelu, a teenager, was a great help as a translator. Through him I was able to tap the adolescent subculture of the village. Our relationship had its ups and downs (I punched him; he chased me with a bush knife: this is called "maintaining rapport"), but even the downs were instructive. Petelu's liking and respect for me were such that he was able to force himself to divulge the most embarrassing and humiliating facts about himself, something very few people were able to do. I did not realize the extent to which I acted as a role model for him until one afternoon when he told me that he always prayed to God for help when he was called upon to recite in class. In a mood more iconoclastic than usual, I dismissed the idea of belief in God as nonsensical, equivalent to belief in ghosts and spirits. The following day Petelu told me: "You know, Meki, I used to bow my head and pray before I got up to talk; now I put my head down and say bad words to God." Petelu was a troubled and unstable boy. My notes are filled with his transgressions and, once in a while, his statements to me as he struggled for some kind of insight.

Finally, there was Roy Wescott, also known as Tui Atua. Our first meeting was a strange one. I was at a general store downtown and noticed a bearded *palangi* playing the juke box. He wore no shirt, and was dressed only in a velvet loincloth. A chief's necklace of pandanus seeds hung around his neck, and he carried a fly whisk in one hand and a barbed spear in the other. He was an extraordinary presence in downtown Pango Pango. I approached him with queries and discovered, to our mutual delight, that he was an anthropologist with a Ph.D. from Stanford, and that he lived in Salatoa, a village near Laovele. What a bonanza. I visited him weekly, and found him perceptive, articulate, and full of Samoan lore. We had some jolly moments developing concepts like "instant culture," instant culture being the result of questioning Samoans about why they follow some seemingly purposeless custom. Why, for example, is it tabu for Samoans to watch a mare foal? Nobody consciously knows the answer to this question. An ordinary informant, however, will not admit ignorance but will invent a reason. The mare will be ashamed if anyone watches her, or the colt will die of fright. An informant's answer may go into one's notes as "culture," and yet, being an unshared *post hoc* improvisation, the statement has nothing to do with "culture."

We also developed a typology of lies. A unilateral lie, for example, is told to delude the listener for the benefit of the teller. A reciprocal lie is a long-drawn-out fantasy engaged in by two or more people for the purposes of mutual flattery and entertainment. Liar A might tell Liar B that he is deeply appreciative of B's friendship, that B's status is exalted, and that he plans to shower B with gifts next payday; B then makes a similar speech. All the statements are recognized as false, but in the context of the reciprocal lie are accepted as true. In addition to providing me with a source of *palangi* humor and filling me in about some less salient aspects of Samoan life, Tui Atua encouraged me when my work went badly and I felt numb with frustration. He had done considerable field work himself in the Amazon basin, and he was understanding and compassionate when I needed to blow off steam.

Data-Getting Techniques

Long before I left Ioane's family, it was clear that the neatly constructed scheme I had contrived to collect material on sexual behavior was not going to work. First, the range of subjects covered in conversation with a chief is necessarily limited. One does not casually visit a chief in his home and inquire about his attitude toward masturbation, for example. It would be an outrageous breach of etiquette. Second, the untitled men may talk about sex under intimate circumstances, such as all-male parties, but it is difficult to guide this sort of banter into productive channels. Furthermore, the sexual experience disclosed by the speaker has to be carefully edited beforehand, particularly if the girls involved in the story have brothers present at the gathering, for even speaking about flirting with someone's sister can provoke an argument. Finally, it was in conversation about sex that the reciprocal lie seemed to acquire epic qualities. The relative utilities of entertainment and truth were so disproportionate that it was safest to believe nothing that was said in these contexts. I regularly listened to tales of personal conquests, superhuman masculine endurance, and incredible female responsiveness that were later revealed to be entirely untrue.

If it was difficult to believe the sexual material that was going into my field notes, it was impossible to administer the objective test I had devised to measure sexual anxiety. A solution of ferrous chloride was essential for my fingerprint test for anxiety, but the anhydrous crystals, procured through the hospital, became hydrous within a few days. The test had worked well enough in Ithaca (and on later occasions after my return from the field) but under unprotected tropical conditions it was useless. I tested a man whose girl friend was bearing his illegitimate child in the hut next door. When he showed no measurable arousal I dropped the idea of an experiment in sex anxiety.

It took about five months for me to acclimate myself to Samoa, to become familiar with the island as a whole and with Laovele in particular, to gain some rudimentary understanding of the language, and to collect census-type data on the village residents. By the end of those first five months I had also discovered that my research design was completely inappropriate.

I needed *some* workable plan. I wanted to do more than another descriptive study on political structure or kinship, and yet I was isolated and without funds in a small village, with no access to an academic library, let alone any collection of relevant theoretical literature. There was a small bookstore in Pango Pango, however, which stocked mostly paperbacks, including a variety of Penguins. One of the books I ran across happened to be Hans Eysenck's *Fact and Fiction in Psychology*, a popular exposition of personality structure, focusing on the dimension of introversion-extroversion. On Monday afternoons, after I had picked up my mail, I used to retreat to a remote corner of the Seaside Club in Pango Pango and read for a few hours. On one of these Mondays I read Eysenck's description of an extrovert:

> The typical extrovert is sociable, likes parties, has many friends, needs to have people to talk to, and does not like reading or studying by himself. He craves excitment, takes chances, often sticks his neck out, acts on the spur of the moment, and is generally an impulsive individual. He is fond of practical jokes, always has a ready answer, likes to "laugh and be merry." He prefers to keep moving and doing things, tends to be aggressive, and loses his temper quickly. Altogether, his feelings are not kept under tight control, and he is not always a reliable person.

I had something like an intellectual mystic experience when I read this. If we disregard the highly structured ceremonies and the hyperdignified public behavior of the chiefs, most of the Samoan people seemed to fit Eysenck's description. The playfulness, the gregariousness, the expressiveness, the optimism: it all began falling into place. I had read Eysenck before, but I now began going over the literature with renewed interest. I asked friends in Ithaca to go through my library and pick out some relevant books and articles to send to me, and in the meantime I began devising tests and questionnaires that might be factor-saturated, as they say, and pretested them on some Samoan friends.

The strategy I adopted had to be a simple one. The only test materials I could use were ones I had with me, and I had no knowledgeable professionals to confer with. Nor any time to waste. I tried out a number of perceptual and motor tests and disregarded all but three. One test that I retained used a rotating spiral to generate a visual aftereffect. I spun the spiral for one minute, then shut it off and asked the subject to tell me when the aftereffect disappeared. Each subject had eight trials. I had to improvise the materials for this test, so I cut out a cardboard circle and drew a spiral on it with a ballpoint pen, attaching this to the take-up reel of a tape recorder. Ideally, the spiral should have rotated at 100 revolutions per minute. My spiral rotated at 118, which meant that at close distances one felt his eyeballs would fall out of his head. I had all of the subjects sit far enough away to preclude their having this sensation. For various theoretical reasons, extroverts were expected to experience shorter aftereffects than introverts, and this is apparently what happened.

The motor test was similarly rough. I had brought the Kasanin-Hanfmann Concept Formation Test with me. This consists of twenty-two small wooden blocks of different shapes, sizes, and colors. The subject is instructed to sort the blocks into piles, according to which characteristics of the blocks he chooses as the basis for his categorization. The "correct" concept is the shape of the block. This is trickier than it sounds, and the subject does not usually get it until he is given a series of hints. The number of hints he needs presumably reflects his difficulty in concept formation. It was immediately clear that the test was useless for Samoans. The accompanying instructions told me that the test was suitable for any population, even small children, schizophrenics, and mental defectives. But some of the Samoans were so test-naïve that they could not understand what I wanted from them, even after I had explicitly given them the *answer*, in both English and Samoan. Nevertheless, I improvised a task in which subjects sorted the Kasanin-

Hanfmann blocks into four piles as quickly as possible. They had twenty trials of ten seconds apiece. I thought that their performances would yield a number of parameters, such as number of errors, which might be affected by extroversion.

Another test required concentration. I recorded forty digits in Samoan, chosen from a table of random numbers, and asked the subject to tell me whenever he heard three odd or even numbers in a row. Extraverts, presumed to be more readily distracted and somewhat more careless, were expected to perform more poorly.

I also used three questionnaires. One, from the Minnesota Multiphasic Personality Inventory, was designed to measure "ego strength." I hoped that this would give me some idea of the emotional stability of my subjects. In addition, I developed a questionnaire that was supposed to reveal ethnocentrism, which is assumed to be associated with right-wing extroversion. This contained such items as: "There are getting to be too many *palangis* in Samoa." I also developed a larger questionnaire of some hundred items, which I hoped covered the rest of the kinds of behaviors and attitudes that might differentiate extroverts from introverts in Samoan culture, including self-descriptive adjective checklists. Toni helped me to translate the items so there were Samoan and English versions of each questionnaire, but because of the high probability of falsification, I always remained doubtful about the ultimate value of questionnaire data.

Finally, I collected data on the nonreactive behavior of subjects at beer parties, gambling sessions, and fist fights. The outcome of such public activities, even when I did not participate in them, tended to become common knowledge in the village rather quickly.

Before I administered any of the tests I drew a sample of fifty adult men, representing about eighty percent of the adult male population. Picking the sample was a simple enough process. I merely wrote the name of each adult man on a $3'' \times 5''$ filing card, shuffled the deck, and chose the first fifty, with a reserve of five to cover refusals.

Immediately after taking the sample, I asked three of the more informed and reliable men of the village to serve as judges to rank the sample men on extroversion, which I defined for them in simple and culturally appropriate terms. The amount of agreement among these three judges, operating independently of each other, was astounding. I then took the mean extroversion rank of all of the sample men and administered as many objective tests and questionnaires to them as I could, at the same time continuing to collect life-record data, with the intention of correlating everything after my return to the United States. To the extent that a man was extroverted according to the judges' rank, he should show up as extroverted in the objective tests, in his replies to questionnaire items, and in his public behavior. I intended later to repeat certain of these operations for some of the Oriental fishermen downtown in order to preserve my original comparative design.

Theoretically and methodologically, the project was obtrusively sloppy. Was this only a broad study of temperament? What could the results tell us about culture? How could I be sure the results meant what I said they meant unless I could control for such variables as the amount of illumination in the test room, the presence of others, and the respondents' motivation and intelligence? In fact, I did not expect outstanding results, but I felt that the study had a certain appeal, and I felt it was an improvement over an orthodox ethnographic study designed to support the proposition that Samoans were extroverts, with the evidence cast in anecdotal form. At least my study seemed original, since neither psychologists nor anthropologists had seriously considered doing anything with the theory of introversion-extroversion outside of Euroamerican cultural settings.[3] And at least it would be replicable. I was playing a maximin game, high in risk, but with great potential pay-off.

Throughout the sixteen months that I administered the tests, I also collected other information, less relevant to introversion-extroversion. With the aid of Toni and the other assistants, I gathered dreams, Thematic-Apperception Test protocols, notes on ghosts and ghost possession, Samoan medicine, and some village gossip and random material on Samoan culture, on the assumption that one might as well get as much information as he can while in the field.

On the wall of my room I kept a small chart. Across the top, I had the names of the several tests I planned to administer to the sample. Down the left side were listed the names of the sample men. When I finished testing a sample man, I drew an X in the appropriate cell of the matrix. This chart was good to have around, not only because it formed a record of who had taken what tests, but because it provided me with visible feedback on the progress of the research. As the weeks passed, I gleefully watched the X's march across the chart.

Progress was good for the first few months, but then a deep slump, lasting more than half a year, occurred. This was followed by a partial recovery, though my progress never did regain the momentum it had lost. There were four major reasons for the slump.

First, I had been associated with a girl in Ithaca for three

---

[3] C. A. Valentine of Washington University is an exception, but I was unaware of his interests at the time.

years who had abruptly stopped writing to me shortly after I arrived in the field, although I had kept up my part of the correspondence. I continued writing to her, and three months after I began the testing, I received a note from her. The rhetoric was thoroughly ambiguous, but the message was clear enough. I was profoundly depressed. At the time, I could imagine nothing more painful than this happening to me while I was in the field. And nothing did. My first impulse, after gulping down a tranquilizer, was to "lose myself in my work." However, I quickly found that I was too preoccupied with the exquisite grief I was experiencing to deal with my Samoan informants. I decided that losing one's self in one's work was not an infallible method of dealing with internal distress, so I returned to my room, closed the door, and sat on the bed, drinking beer and reading escapist fiction for three days and nights, after which I returned shakily to the world. The effects of this experience were detrimental to my field work for about a year. I became argumentative, I drank too much beer, I was more easily bored and distracted, and, on the whole, I was less interested in informal concourse with the Samoans, who neither understood nor cared what was happening.

In addition to this idiosyncratic problem, there was the more general one of progressive boredom. This was probably inevitable. After the first thirty administrations I grew to hate the tests. The partial results, which I kept a rough tally of, seemed equivocal. I was tired of the same gossip and the same daily routine. My interest in the project did not revive until I began working with the Orientals. I managed in the end to fill in most of the cells on the progress chart, but I performed at a much lower level of efficiency than I might have. Two years was too long, for me anyway.

The third major reason for the slump in my progress was that the villagers themselves were losing interest. When the novelty of my presence wore off, I found it increasingly difficult to corner my subjects for testing. I had contacted the "easy" members of the sample early in the game, and the men I had not yet been able to test were the ones who were hardly ever available or who were unwilling to cooperate but too polite to say so. Tangaloa's wife, for example, supplied me with detailed accounts of her dreams at first, but in later months, when I casually asked her about her dreams, she would shake her head, smiling, and remark to the other ladies, "Meki is still at it."

Another reason I didn't get more done was that I was sick during much of this period. I had already gone through the usual problems with pinworms, fungus, and digestive disorders. But a few months after the testing began I contracted a relatively severe virus infection that stayed with me for more than a month. I had hardly recovered from it when I found my ear was infected as a complication of the virus. Not long after that cleared up I caught some sort of skin disease that involved both my neck and my ears. It smelled bad and looked worse, and I was too embarrassed to work in public. I had the skin disorder diagnosed at the hospital, but because of the misrouting of my fellowship checks I couldn't buy the prescribed medicine.

For these reasons and others, the research abruptly slowed down and remained relatively slow until the last few months.

During most of the testing period I generally rose at about 7:30, just as the children were leaving for school. I spent perhaps two hours drinking coffee and writing personal letters. The house was empty in the morning: Tangaloa was downtown drinking beer with one of the other chiefs, and his wife and the other ladies were out working in their taro patches. Toward noon, I spent a few hours typing up my notes. Then Tangaloa came back and delivered to me a bottle of cold beer with great mock ceremony. When he had gone to bed to sleep it off, I ate lunch, usually a can of tuna fish and a chunk of boiled taro, which is something like a gray turnip. I spent the afternoons wandering around the village, tape recorder in one hand, woven basket full of test materials in the other, trying to contact one of my sample men. After dinner I sat around chatting with the young men of the household, then spent the evening either visiting some of the wage workers or chatting with Tafua.

I generally stayed awake for an hour or two after the village had gone to sleep, during which time I either wrote more letters, finished up my notes, or lay in bed reading. (During my field work I read everything Conan Doyle ever wrote about Sherlock Holmes: I seemed to need exposure to that solitary and introverted theoretician as a functional corrective to my Samoan companions.)

Some of the settings for data collection, in rough order of their importance, might include: (1) Tangaloa's house; (2) the lawn of Tangaloa's house; (3) the houses of the subjects; (4) Tafua's house; (5) the Pango Bar; (6) the bush surrounding Laovele; and (7) the village of Salatoa, where Tui Atua and some other informants lived. I often simply visited the villagers in the evening, when the wage workers were home, and listened to their conversation. It was easier to do this with the younger men. In addition, I sometimes worked in the bush with both the men and the women, learning how to plant, cultivate, and harvest crops. A patch of giant taro I had planted for Tangaloa was always referred to by the old chief as belonging to me. He was pretty proud of it as a manifestation of my family spirit.

Sports and other forms of recreation were also profitable. I was awful at cricket, but playing it gave me a chance to pick up gossip when our side was at bat. The activity I enjoyed most was fishing, but it was dangerous. The sharp rocks were slippery and treacherous. During my stay, one man was killed and several injured trying to get lines into the water. I dutifully attended parties and dances, I drank with the men at Tafua's general store and in the downtown pubs, and I occasionally gambled with them. I lost consistently and so was eagerly welcomed as a participant in poker games. The parties and celebrations afforded me quantitative data on some behaviors that were directly relevant to the thesis: I might watch a sample man work his way through a case of beer or jot down the names of the participants in a fist fight.

In addition to visiting, working, and recreating, I courted a girl in Salatoa. Lili stole quarters from my pockets, but she was a delightful creature, childlike and full of meaningless promises. Sometimes I fantasied marrying her and taking her back to New York, but I realized fully how impractical that would be.

In a few months we were pretty close, and I was staying at her hut until quite late, her parents and her half-dozen siblings scattered around us, dozing or asleep. After a while I realized what a dangerous situation this was. An untimely awakening by her father or mother could be catastrophic. It could not go on. I decided finally that the most effective way to end the relationship was to stop seeing Lili. So by the end of five months my visits to her were rare, and she had found another boyfriend. So much for love in the South Seas.

Most of the informants and assistants would not accept cash payment for their help, except as a ceremonial gift on a special occasion. On the other hand, they were all quite willing to accept presents. I distributed, not recklessly, beer and whiskey to some of the men, yard goods and towels to the ladies, and other more expensive items to special assistants. I bought Petelu an English racing bicycle, which somebody stole from him a month later. These were all legitimate field expenses under my NIMH grant. One item of payment, however, was so unusual that I decided not to charge it to NIMH. Tafua had some data that I sorely needed: a list of villagers owing money to his general store and the specific amounts involved. He refused to allow me access to his records until the day I was to leave the island. When the day arrived, Tafua was still reluctant to let me copy the figures, but he finally yielded after I promised to send him one hundred lurid novels from the states.

Techniques for recording and storing data. I carried a notebook and pen whenever possible, because they were exceptionally reliable, cheap, convenient, and relatively inconspicuous when in use. If conditions seemed right, or if they demanded it, I took along a tape recorder, still camera, and/or a movie camera. One of the tape recorders proved invaluable, a Japanese model somewhat larger than a transistor radio, carried on a shoulder strap. Its most useful features were the external controls and the microphone, which was fitted, diaphragm-side out, into a hole in the leather case. This made it possible to surreptitiously turn the recorder on and orient it toward a speaker without his knowing that he was being recorded. In more sophisticated societies, it might be less necessary to keep a speaker in ignorance, but in Samoa it was essential if conversations were not to be subject to extensive internal editing.

The climate was a poor one for hard equipment. The $350 Uher recorder lasted only four months. The expensive movie camera—complete with fast-motion and lap dissolves—lasted about six months, and the still camera about the same. It was not possible to get replacement parts for any equipment. My new typewriter, which began rusting within a week of my arrival, actually worked until the end of my stay, though by that time some parts of it were held together with elastic bands. In all I went through four tape recorders and two still cameras. The last recorder and camera could not be referred to NIMH for payment because I had exhausted my funds for equipment.

My characteristic technique for recording and storing test data was to administer the test, immediately write the subject's responses in a notebook, take the notebook back to my room, rewrite the information into a second notebook, and finally type it into my formal field notes, so that I had the test data recorded in three files, each file stored in a different place. More general information, such as village gossip, I wrote in a notebook or recorded on tape, then typed directly into my field notes. The note cards were of tough Dennison paper. I hid them under the bed in my room, where, except for occasional wettings during heavy rains, they remained undisturbed. Hidden in the same place were the manilla envelopes in which I kept spontaneous productions of the villagers—such as letters or drawings—as well as government, school, and religious publications, and a collection of leaves from medicinal plants. I sent all films and movies to the states in order to protect them from fungus and thieves.

Bowing Out

As the end of my stay approached, I began associating more and more with the Korean fishermen. The problems involved in dealing with them were somewhat different and need not be gone into here. The important thing is that the new phase of the study kept me away from Laovele for large parts of the day. I came to know more intimately some of the members of Tangaloa's extended family who lived in Pango Pango. In particular I struck up a friendship with a part-Chinese merchant who had been Tangaloa's son-in-law. Ah Fat was a hard-working but generous man, and he often invited me to move in with him.

Meantime, rapport with Petelu was declining. His behavior, which had been so good, was deteriorating. I still functioned as his friend and confidante, but he was violating my acquired system of Samoan ethics, forcefully attacking his younger sister with a beer bottle and then struggling with our mutual socio-logical mother when she tried to restrain him. She once gave me permission to discipline him, but whenever he aggressed I re-treated for fear I would lose control if I got angry. Eventually, he came into conflict with the law and spent a few weeks in jail. After his release, his performance again began deteriorating. Then, one night, he stealthily wheeled my Honda off into the bush. He brought it back the next day but it was too late. The limits of my tolerance were breached. I dressed the fellow down in mighty tones and threatened to have him sent back to jail, but I had to give up the intention when our mother begged me, tears in her eyes, to forgive Petelu. However, within the week, Tangaloa's house was visited by the Samoan judge whom the court had designated as Petelu's guardian. Somehow, the judge had heard of the incident involving my Honda. As he remon-strated with Petelu, I noticed Tangaloa and his wife watching me coolly, and I sensed that they thought I was the informer. Actually, the judge and Tangaloa were old drinking partners, so that Petelu was in no danger of going back to jail, but the role of informer is a dangerous role to assume. Family trouble is supposed to be handled within the family. Going outside the household with information or complaints short circuits the whole established power structure. Neither Tangaloa nor his wife spoke to me for the rest of the day.

So, following local tradition, I packed my belongings, left Tangaloa's house, and moved in with his ex-son-in-law in Pango Pango. I spent the rest of my stay working with the Koreans and gambling with Ah Fat and his guests in the evenings. The prospect of returning to the states would have seemed a happy one, but I continued to feel bad about the trouble with Tangaloa and his family. My spirits were not improved by an article in the *Samoan Times*, accompanied by a photo of me looking par-ticularly gloomy and untidy, and referring to me as "Dr. Robert Max," who was studying "land distribution." The editor of the *Times* was one of my few élite friends, and I viewed this faulty information as a symbol of my faulty communications with the *palangis* in general.

Summary and Evaluation

My research problem had two aspects: (1) In what ways do extroverts behave differently from introverts in Samoa? And (2) how extroverted are the Samoans compared to other groups, such as Koreans? I found persuasive evidence that there are differences between Samoan extroverts and Samoan introverts in the predicted directions, but my sample of Koreans—all young, hard-working fishermen away from home—was too small and biased to provide adequate grounds for comparing the two cultural groups.

I divided my attack on the problem into four phases: (1) the collecting of sociological background data on the sample men; (2) the collecting of objective test data; (3) the collecting of questionnaires; and (4) the continuous recording of the stream of relevant gossip and overt behavior. I completed all four phases for the Samoans, and I had intended to work with equal intensity among the Koreans during the second half of my stay, but Laovele kept me occupied longer than I had anticipated, and I was not able to get past the second phase for the fishermen.

Early in the course of my research I found that the rotating-spiral that I had devised was correlating extremely well with the judges' extroversion rankings of the sample men. I decided to use the perceptual test as a definition of extroversion, rather than the rankings, because I felt it was more valid, it yielded cardinal data, and I could later give the perceptual test to any other group I worked with and thus would be able to do comparisons.

The results are not yet all in, but it is clear that duration of aftereffect reflects Samoan attitudes and behavior. A shorter aftereffect (i.e., extroversion) is associated with frequency of sexual activity, travel out of the village for noneducational reasons, card-playing, fist-fighting, money owed to others, drinking, smoking, and errors on jobs requiring vigilance and care. It is negatively associated with travel for educational reasons and with educational attainment.

These results, which are only partial, tend to support Eysenck's theory. One finding—that introversion increases with age—is the opposite of what the theory might predict. There were several other distributions that seemed random when they should have been positive, but because of the lack of control over the conditions of test administration, it is impossible to say whether there was really no association or whether an association was masked by the effects of varying conditions.

In terms of the research proposal first sent to NIMH, the field work was a total loss. I accomplished nothing that I had originally intended to do. But having almost accidentally hit upon a suitable and interesting theory, I was able to develop a series of tests and systematic observations that provided me with enough data for a dissertation.

The evidence was such that, if the study had been written by someone else and I were reading it, I would probably believe that Samoan extroverts and introverts behave in the suggested ways. I would probably not be unshakably convinced of the validity of any particular finding; rather, my belief would rest on the over-all impact of a series of relatively weak correlations, instead of on one or two strong ones.

In addition to the thesis-relevant information, I have material on the sociological characteristics of the village, the dreams of the inhabitants, a series of their drawings (the "House-Tree-Person Test"), some 200 modified Thematic Apperception Test protocols, a possible scale of Westernization in housing, and general information on the way people in Laovele pattern their lives. Some of this is soft data which I will not make any attempt to quantify, but descriptive studies can in themselves be valuable. For example, I probably know more about Petelu's psychodynamics than anyone else in his family. I recorded his rapid change from a conscientious boy to an errant adolescent. I knew he had been impotent, that he was shocked by the *palangi* girls downtown in their bikinis, that he was jealous of the men he saw talking to his mother. I watched the pattern of his friendships change, and I saw him grow increasingly free of his family's control. I either knew or could guess some of the things behind this change. This is the stuff of which enlightening case histories are made.

I have similar, though less complete information on a "witch doctor," as the Samoans call them. Lili's mother practiced Samoan medicine and communicated with the ghosts who sometimes possessed her neighbors.

All of these data are recorded on about 1,500 note cards and have not yet been analyzed, although the information is of potential value.

It is possible to imagine ways in which the research could have been improved. I overestimated the amount of work I could get done. The cross-cultural effort was largely a waste of time. I should have devoted more time to studying the language. I am poor at languages and could follow only simple conversations in Samoan (usually they are interspersed with English words). Occasionally, I understood well enough to inject a comment in Samoan. This happened so rarely that once, when it happened, a discussant turned sharply to me and said, full of surprise and suspicion, "You know everything we say!" Oddly enough, when I visited Toni in Honolulu, my Samoan was infuriatingly good, almost as good as my English.

If I were to do the study again, I would select a battery of suitable tests in collaboration with a psychologist and supply myself with proper equipment. I doubt, however, that, given the same research problem, I would change the design significantly. There are certain limitations built into the environment. Most questionnaire data would still be questionable, for instance, and elaborate machines are worthless in a partly electrified village in the tropics.

I would try to maintain closer contact with the élite groups. The governor and his aides could have been of enormous help. And some of the *palangi* religious leaders had been in the islands for thirty years or more. I would also try to court the part-Samoan élite, too, for they seemed to take particular pride in their mythology and were not as likely to lie as the ordinary villagers were.

If I were doing the field work alone or in an isolated area, I would take it in smaller chunks if possible, because of the diminishing marginal utility of each month in the field after the first few. Sensitivities are soon dulled, and periodic interruptions would presumably restore perspicacity and zest.

If I did field work somewhere other than Samoa, I would like it to be in a place where I had previously spent some time, even as little as one day. And I suppose, if possible, I would arrange to work with one or two other compatible behavioral scientists. The limitations built into the environment are hardly more important than the ones built into the researcher himself.

Finally, I am not very business-minded, but I thought I had kept a fairly accurate record of my expenses for NIMH. Next time, however, I would emphasize the importance of expense accounting, having discovered after the termination of the grant that I owed $1,000 to the administrators because of a misunderstanding over the allocation of funds.

PART III: COMPARISONS OF RESEARCH BETWEEN GROUPS

Both studies were concerned with the collection of psychological and ethnographic materials in a community setting. A large part of the information was gathered through the administration of questionnaires, and there was also some amount of participant observation in both settings, though this was much more limited in Canada than in Samoa.

Both research population were fairly cooperative, compared to other groups that might be imagined, such as professional criminals, active acid heads, or members of ghettos. The settings in each case were rural, with all that this implies in the way of kinship bonds, gossip, solidarity, and so on. Most, but not all of the people involved in the studies were English-speaking. The research designs were at least minimally organized, and the object of the research was not only general description but hypothesis-testing as well.

Though the common language in both settings was English, language was, nevertheless, a problem in Samoa, but not in Canada. And field experience in the northeastern woodlands, even in summer, was no preparation for a tropical rain forest, even one cooled by the trade winds. In the brisk atmosphere of Maritime Canada, it is possible to plunge immediately into one's work, so that much can be accomplished in a single summer. Acclimation in Samoa, on the other hand, requires about a month, during which any physical labor, even walking, is exhausting.

The Stirling County Study covered several communities, whereas my research in Samoa was conducted chiefly in a single village. This represents in part a difference in emphasis, the unit of analysis in Canada being the community, in Samoa the individual. In other words, the Stirling County Study was more interested in comparing towns in varying stages of disorganization, whereas I was more interested in comparing people.

In the Stirling County project, I, as a psychiatric interviewer, assumed a specific role: namely, that of hired interviewer. In Samoa, my role was a general one. I went from door to door interviewing the residents, but I also lived with my subjects, worked and played with them. This general role is by far the trickier to manage. Sooner or later, the field worker does something stupid and, as a member of the community he is studying, his behavior is bound to affect his rapport with the other community members. "Rapport" here is not meant to indicate some abstract goal, but rather the very real state of open communication channels. When your rapport is poor in a place like Samoa, you are not likely to come up with the kind of information you need.

One of the most salient contrasts between research in the two sites was that of personal responsibility for the outcome. Giving interviews to strangers is a rather mechanical task requiring a minimum of thought. It is quite another thing to live with the knowledge that upon the results of your research rest not only your immediate professional future but the responsibility for having fruitfully used (or, alternatively, wasted) a year or two of your life, about 3 percent of your earthly existence. It is this knowledge that moves the field worker to question continually the adequacy of his plans and operations, so that in a way the research design becomes organic. This sense of total responsibility is a burden at times, but without it field work would be jejune indeed, and the results (even if they were very good) would not be a source of much satisfaction.

A long, uninterrupted stay in the field—say, six months or more—is a far cry from a brief summer expedition. On the one hand, the longer the field worker stays, the more he adapts to his new environment, adopts its standards or behavior, and comes to act in terms of its background expectancies. On the other hand, the longer he stays, the less sensitive he becomes to what is going on around him and the more likely he is to take the new culture for granted. The dulling process is the same one we find in learning a new language. At first we are exceedingly aware of the rules of grammar, syntax, and pronunciation; but as we become fluent, these linguistic habits become routine, and we are no longer aware of them. Involvement with another culture can take us only so far. Beyond a certain point we lose perspective and become merely another member of that culture. If this were not true, all American anthropologists would be experts in American culture, whereas, we are sometimes told, we are really "too close" to our own culture to be objective about it. Furthermore, long stays in strange settings can cause the field worker to become isolated, both personally and in terms of his discipline; this was true in my own case, though others may find themselves more adaptable or dedicated than I.

My physical visibility was much greater in Samoa than in Canada. This could have been a problem if I had spent a shorter time in Samoa than I actually did, or if the Samoans were more prejudiced against Caucasians.

What about the similarity of the research setting to the field worker's culture of orientation? In general, of course, the more similar the setting, the more easily one is able to pass for a native. But passing too becomes less problematic the longer one lives in the community. Interestingly enough, I found that —boring as Samoa sometimes was—I was often more comfortable with the Laovele villagers than I was with the somewhat taciturn English Canadians. I was not able to take up the emotionally evanescent life style of the villagers, but I was touched by their expressions of warmth, and I was able to learn that social blunders, or professional blunders, or anything else, do not matter all that much in the long run. For all the discord I caused in Tangaloa's household, I now write and exchange gifts with him and with Petelu. I could fly to Laovele tomorrow and be welcomed back into the family. In Samoa, *gaffes* are quickly forgiven or forgotten, because, I think, of the Samoan's recognition of what the Gestaltists used to call common fate. "We all go into the same hole in the ground," was the way Lili's father once put it, crudely but effectively.

TOWARD
A FORMALIZATION
OF FIELD WORK

Morris Freilich

PART I: THE NATURAL HISTORY
OF A FIELD PROJECT

How and when does a field project start? What determines the choice of a field site? What problems regularly face the anthropological researcher? These and similar questions receive various answers in the ten chapters in this book. My own utilization of these diverse "data" will attempt to describe the natural history of an anthropological research project in a manner that facilitates the development of a formal model of field work.[1]

---

[1] The term *data* will be used here to refer to information provided by the contributors.

Moments of critical decision making will be isolated, labeled as problems, and discussed. Where relevant, the solutions of the ten contributors will be used to illustrate possible and (at times) maximal adaptations to such problem situations. In the final portion of this chapter, I will present the critical variables that have to be considered in a formal treatment of field work. In brief, this essay is pragmatic. Its goal is to help the would-be anthropologist get into the field and, once there, to complete his mission successfully. Hopefully it will also be of some value to full-fledged anthropologists and to others interested in studying man in his natural environments.[2]

Two types of field-work problems are discussed in this chapter: pragmatic-sequential and theoretical. Most experienced anthropologists would probably solve the pragmatic-sequential problems (1–8) in similar ways. These problems follow each other in a rather obvious and logical progression; it is only after a prior problem is solved that the one following it occurs. The eight problems the would-be anthropologist faces are as follows:

1. Selecting a graduate program
2. Developing a specialization
3. Working up a good research proposal
4. Getting funds for research
5. Making plans for leaving the country
6. Developing a strategy for entry into the community or communities to be researched
7. Ensuring one's physical and psychological survival in the field
8. Combatting rumors that one is a spy

The theoretical problems (9–14) are not so clear-cut, nor do their solutions necessarily find considerable consensus. Most of these problems relate to theories of human behavior; the balance relate to theories of methodology. These theoretical problems do not follow any logical sequence. I present them in the following somewhat arbitrary order:

9. Self-socialization
10. Framework specification
11. Participant-observing
12. Rapport and exchange
13. Active research
14. Ethics and sanity maintenance

---

[2] The views presented in this essay—ideas, constructs, generalizations, etc. —are not necessarily those with which the contributors agree or find useful. Responsibility for this essay is thus completely mine. I wish to thank the contributors for their comments on an earlier draft. Their ideas and opinions, while not always accepted, considerably improved the final presentation by forcing me to think through my own approach more rigorously.

PART II: PRAGMATIC-SEQUENTIAL FIELD PROBLEMS

Problem 1: Selecting a Graduate Program

An anthropological field study, particularly the first one done by the researcher, has no obvious starting point. It is hard to tell exactly when William Schwab and Melvin Perlman first got involved deeply enough in Africa to want to spend years doing research there. John Gulick developed an interest in the Middle East when he visited that area during World War II, but the idea of doing a community study in the Middle East did not crystalize until he entered graduate school. Pertti Pelto's work in Finland was largely due to an emotional attachment to that country, developed prior to his interest in anthropology. In the case of every contributor in the book it is difficult to pinpoint the start of the causal chain of events that finally took him to a specific field site. Somewhat arbitrarily, then, I will consider the selection of a university for graduate studies in anthropology as the starting point of the first field study.

The selection of a place for doctoral studies will have important influences on the future field-work career of the anthropologist.[3] Most graduate departments of anthropology have a limited number of focuses regarding where research should be done, with whom, within what theoretical frameworks, and with how much emphasis on systematic data-collecting and -recording procedures. The influence of departmental focuses is clear in the cases of Schwab and Perlman (who worked in African programs), of Aram Yengoyan and myself (who worked in departments with an ecological approach to culture), and of Robert Maxwell (who worked in a department strongly emphasizing cross-discipline research).

Problem 2: Developing a Specialization

Like most professionals in modern social systems, anthropologists find it impossible to be well versed in all aspects of their

---

[3] "Fellow Newsletters" and "Guide to Graduate Departments in Anthropology" contain information on the structure, goals, and membership of graduate departments of anthropology and make it possible for a would-be anthropologist to plan more rationally for his professional future.

discipline. The modern social or cultural anthropologist has accepted not only that his knowledge of archaeology and linguistics will be limited, but also that he will be unable to keep up with the literature in all areas of cultural anthropology. His knowledge of ethnographic writings will progressively become more and more limited as his own work becomes concentrated in a given area of the world. In brief, the anthropologist generally becomes a specialist in a culture area, and within that area a specialist in a topic that has received special attention. For example, in an area where considerable trading takes place, it is important for the anthropologist to become acquainted with the literature of economics. An important subspecialization today is economic anthropology. For Africanists, political anthropology becomes a highly important subdiscipline, since it is rarely possible to understand an African cultural setting without a good knowledge of special types of political organization and of political theory in general. In India, where social stratification is an all-important phenomenon, the anthropologist must understand the meaning of caste and the ways in which given castes move up and down the social hierarchy in the part of India he is studying.

In some parts of the world, and for given types of studies, the relative importance of research methodology differs. Africanists, for example, are rarely satisfied with a one-year field study, and they often spend more time preparing for a given study than do those researching other parts of the world. Schwab, for example, spent a year in London doing intensive preparation for his field work in Nigeria. Further, it should be noted that some studies, such as those done by Schwab and Perlman, cannot follow traditional methods of cultural anthropology; the researcher must become familiar with survey techniques, developing questionnaires, statistics, and computer programming.

The problems the anthropologist selects for study further distinguish him and make him an expert in a given subarea in anthropology. Thus culture change may be an important subject for some researchers, and work on such problems may necessitate reading about theories of change. An interest in "individualistic societies" caused Pelto to give up a geographic emphasis and do research anywhere in the world with groups that appear to live in "loose" rather than "tight" societies. Similarly, Norman Whitten's interest in adaptive strategies and my own in natural experiments will lead us anywhere in the world that our topics can be well researched.

In sum, the would-be anthropologist will enter a graduate department that, although limited in focuses, will include anthropologists with some diversity in specializations. To become a modern professional—contrasted with a professional such as Franz Boas, who mastered much of what was known in most branches of anthropology—the graduate student will have to specialize. His problem is how to do this rationally.

Most graduate departments will force a great variety of knowledge on the entering student. Depending on the charismatic qualities of the instructors, the student might think of himself as a linguist one month, an Africanist the second, and a Caribbeanist the third. However as time passes, the question, "What kind of field work should I do for my dissertation?," looms ever larger. Sooner or later the fateful step must be taken to leave the nest of the graduate department for the reality of the professional world of research.

The student who carefully studies "A Guide to Planning Field Research" (Appendix, p. 585) should receive considerable assistance in planning for his flight from the nest, particularly if he keeps a "problems notebook" and regards C. Wright Mills' *The Sociological Imagination* as his bible. Here I will deal only with the essence of the specialization problem: *forming a strong attachment to at least one professor in the graduate department and attempting to draw him into the role of high-status friend.* The wise student (as a low-status subordinate) attempts to develop with at least one professor a relationship that has the structural characteristics of the relationship of boy to mother's brother (see Freilich, 1964). As anyone familiar with exchange theory might predict, a one-way attachment (i.e., student to professor or boy to mother's brother) is a rare phenomenon in social life. Within the university system some professors send "signals" to some students, indicating their availability as high-status friends. Whether the student initiates signals requesting a professor to step into this role or whether the professor makes the first overture is irrelevant here. For our purposes it is noteworthy that, once a high-status-friend (HSF) to low-status-subordinate (LSS) relationship has developed, the HSF thereafter becomes a major determinant in the specialities the student develops, and thus in the kind of research he will be doing. Under the influence of Cornelius Osgood, John Honigmann has spent considerable time doing research in northern North America. Stimulated by Hans Wieschhoff's intense interest in Africa as a "scientific enigma," William Schwab began an African research career that already has lasted for twenty years and may well continue for his complete professional life. Carleton Coon's interest and enthusiasm in modern Middle Eastern cultures helped John Gulick decide on the Middle East as his area specialty. Charles Erasmus influenced Norman

Whitten to work in the country where he had done research, and Charles Wagley and Conrad Arensberg developed and nurtured my interest in the Caribbean and in community studies, respectively.[4]

Problem 3: Developing a Specific Research Proposal

The problem of developing a specific research proposal is to some extent solved before it arises. Once a student is working in a graduate department and once the high-status—low-status relationship has been firmly established, many important decisions have already been made concerning where the first field project will take place and what kinds of problems it will deal with. However, the "data" clearly indicate the existence of two additional factors that are influential here; anthropology's strong attachment to field work and the highly pragmatic, indeed opportunistic, orientation of many anthropologists. Examining all these factors, we find a decision-making structure that appears to function as follows: Within a department with limited focuses for place and type of research, a student develops an interest in a given part of the world in terms of a specific set of theoretical problems. Somehow, the high-status–low-status relationship develops, and through it and other departmental influences, the student learns that in the last analysis it is the ability to do good field work, and to think of field work as a joyful and pleasurable experience, that is the mark of a "real" anthropologist.

Having become oriented to the idea of working in a particular part of the world, the student also learns that it is wise to grasp research opportunities when they arise, even though such research may not be in the precise area of his specialization or interest. Three contributors, Nancie González, Robert Maxwell, and myself, guided more by the "cult of field work" than by an attachment to a particular group whose culture we found fascinating, worked first in areas where we had no deep interest.

---

[4] The high-status professor to low-status student relationship has some similarities to the relationhip that exists between a mother's brother and sister's son in societies such as Tikopia. In both situations (the university and Tikopia) a superior in status "plays down" his rank while relating to a specific status inferior. The high-status friend is thus able to influence the behavior of a status inferior without creating additional tension, and to reduce already existing tension. It might be interesting to speculate further about why some status holders—like some professors—add the responsibilities of high-status friend to an already heavy work load. My analysis of this puzzle includes, as part of the seductive appeal of the role, its information-collection potential and its tension-reducing functions. (See Freilich, 1969.)

We had learned an important lesson in grantsmanship: second projects are easier to finance than first ones.

Given the general sparsity of funds for anthropological research, the lack of certainty that a particular project will be funded, and the anthropologist's dedication to field work, opportunism becomes a useful, even necessary, strategy for field work. The essence of opportunism is flexibility; a slight attachment to highly specific research problems and a minimal involvement with systematic theory.

Problem 4: Funding Field Work

Finding funds to cover the expenses of a field trip is very much a part of the natural history of an anthropological study. The "data" on this problem and on the exit problem are understandably sparse, since both are marginal to the general focus of this book: the problems of living and working in the field. However, the importance of the funding problem makes it reasonable to go beyond the "data" here in order to present several facts worthy of considerable thought. Funding an anthropological project is a time-consuming procedure; the time between the germ of an idea for field work and the point when a grant-giving agency has promised to provide a specific sum of money may be years. Grant-giving agencies will rarely allot funds to a researcher unless considerable library research has been done by others on the problem and unless the applicant appears qualified to do research in a foreign country. These agencies have to be convinced that money invested in a study is money well spent. They require good answers to the following questions: Is the anthropologist a good researcher? Does he understand field work well? Has he had enough research experience to handle a project alone? Does he understand the dimensions of his problems? Has he demonstrated to a reasonable degree that the project can be accomplished in the time specified in the application and with the funds applied for? Is his problem well defined and nicely linked to theoretical questions currently considered important or "hot"? Has he operationalized his critical variables? Does he know what data will "answer" his problem? Does he have a well-developed data-collection strategy? Has he mapped out his data-analysis procedures well? When can a final report reasonably be expected? How will he support himself while doing his data analysis and write-ups?

How well does the anthropologist know the part of the world he plans to do research in? More specifically, how well does he know the specific area within which he expects to live while doing his research? Is he fluent in the language of the natives? If not, how does he expect to communicate with them and develop good rapport? Does he know the history and current political situation of the area? Does he understand, and has he planned for, the various problems that will exist while doing his research? Has he taken the time and trouble to go through the various "chains of command" to get permission to enter the country and to enter the specific area within which research will be done? Has he made arrangements for housing?

How sophisticated an individual is this researcher? Does he understand that successful research requires the building up of many contacts? Has he contacted many scholars familiar with this type of research? Has he made it his business to get to know people in the country of his research? Has he previously traveled? In short, is this type of person a "good bet" for the investment of research funds?

The researcher should consider the question "How will I support myself while analyzing my data?" very seriously before mailing his application for funds. The anthropologist generally returns from field trips heavily laden with ethnographic data. He has an obligation to share his data and his conclusions with the total scientific community as soon as he can. This obligation can best be met if he attempts to obtain funds for analysis and write-ups *before* leaving for the field. A rather curious aspect of grantsmanship is that it is extremely difficult to obtain funds for *data already collected*.

Once a project is funded, there are numerous details to handle before the anthropologist is ready to leave the country. These details, which are discussed below under exit problems, are extremely time consuming. It is necessary, therefore, to apply for funds early enough to allow time for all the details of leaving the country. Some funding agencies inform applicants of the success of their applications only once a year, and these letters may not come until the very time when the anthropologist had planned to leave for the field (see Whitten, p. 339). In such cases the anthropologist may have to decide to gamble on the success of his research proposal (as Whitten did) and make preparations for his trip before knowing exactly where the money for it will come from. In short, much long-term planning and hard work is required to solve the funding problem successfully.

Problem 5: Planning for Leaving: Exit Problems

Prior to his exit from his culture of orientation the anthropologist must make plans

1. To obtain his immunization shots
2. To obtain passports, visas, and other types of entry permits
3. To program travel and layovers
4. To purchase equipment for use in the field or to plan to make such purchases overseas
5. To obtain letters of recommendation and identification for use overseas
6. To make arrangements for processing films taken during field work
7. To arrange for someone to keep a copy of field notes sent home to ensure against loss, fire, theft, or capture

These and related practical matters pertaining to field work are often poorly handled by the inexperienced researcher, and understandably so, for the period during which exit problems must be handled is also the period when the anthropologist is completely caught up in the excitement of the forthcoming field trip. His mind is full of the anticipated joys of life in the field, rather than on such mundane concerns as injections and permits. The temptation exists, therefore, to devote all his energies to the more intellectual aspects of the forthcoming trip: reading about the area of research, talking to people who know the culture to be researched, and so forth.

One important field-work problem that merits considerable thought during the exit period is adapting to isolation. The anthropologist should expect to experience three related forms of isolation while doing field work: *psychological,* characterized by a feeling of loneliness; *sociological,* characterized by a lack of identification with things going on in the community of research and with its members; and *cultural,* characterized by a feeling of separation from the social situations and customs of one's culture of orientation. The anthropologist must expect this feeling of psychological and socio-cultural isolation and must anticipate the "normal" response: depression. Depression or related psychic states occur not necessarily because the anthropologist is neurotic or because he suffers from some psychological disability. They occur because the anthropologist *is* different from the natives among whom he lives: his professional goals, his personal habits, his tastes in food, clothing, and entertainment, and his cultural background all function to separate and isolate him from the natives and their culture. When the anthropologist feels isolated, when he suffers from psychological, social, or cultural deprivation, it is a sure sign that he has used up his reservoir of psychic energy; his psyche requires either a "recharge" or a rest. The solution to the isolation problem is a planned strategy for psychic escape, and such plans can and should start during the exit period. That is, by including in his field kitbag such items as novels, a transistor radio (and a spare one or two in case of mechanical difficulties), a good supply of liquor, and the names of people to visit in towns near his field-work site, the anthropologist can, albeit only for short periods, build in an escape from his environment. The pains of psycho-socio-cultural isolation come through very clearly in Bronislaw Malinowski's diaries. Had he possessed greater understanding of the isolation problems faced by *all* field workers, Malinowski would undoubtedly not have felt so guilty about his own strategies for coping with those problems. Hortense Powdermaker considered the question of escape important enough to devote a whole chapter to it in *Stranger and Friend*.

The field worker who takes his family with him has gone a long way toward solving many of the isolation problems. John Gulick suffered less when his family was with him in Lebanon than when he had left them at home. Similarly, those of us who had our families with us in the field suffered less from the isolation problem than did Robert Maxwell, a bachelor, in Samoa.

Some anthropologists are fortunate in developing deep friendships in the field, and these relationships help to reduce isolation problems. In describing his congenial relationship with Old Man and Nitla, John Honigmann states that it was a "piece of good fortune that I have rarely since had in field work." William Schwab describes his close relationship with the King in Oshogbo as follows: "I had learned not only to respect and admire the king but had developed a warm camaraderie with him that one rarely achieves with another individual. I was his 'Oyinbo' or 'white man' while he was my 'chief clerk.' " Norman Whitten writes of a treasured friendship with Dr. Fuentes and close ties to a couple of visiting engineering students. In Trinidad I was fortunate to discover long-lost relatives who were always ready to provide me with friendship and hospitality.

It is tempting for the anthropologist, off on his first field trip, to dream of an idyllic existence. The perfect life in a "primitive" culture, full of *gemeinschaftlich* intimacies and exotic experiences, is often contrasted with the superficialities of urban living in modern societies. It is better to maintain a more realistic picture of field work: there are many pleasures, exotic experiences, and happy occasions, but these are combined with harder work than ever before experienced, periodic minor difficulties, and personal problems such as the feelings of isolation.

Problem 6: Entry Problems

In discussing the entry problem, Gans has written, "The participant-observer's first problem is that of entry. He gets his data on the basis of being admitted to the situations he wants to study and, once there, to persuade people to let him stay." (1968:309.)

As a sociologist, Gans generally discusses research as something done in the country in which the researcher resides as a citizen; for him, therefore, the first problem is being admitted to *situations*. For the anthropologist, however, who more often than not thinks of research as something to do in a culture other than his own, the entry problem is, first, to get permission to spend considerable time working in some foreign land, second, to be allowed to settle in a given community, and, finally, to gain admittance to given situations. Thus for the anthropologist, the entry problem has many different levels and its difficulty will depend on the following matters:

1. The distance of the field site from the culture of orientation
2. The type of research site selected and whether it is "normal" or special, i.e., a reservation, a hospital, a jail
3. The type of country in which the research will be done
4. The political situation of the country in which research is being planned

The field worker's problems will vary, depending on whether he is in an Iron Curtain country with consular relationships with the culture of orientation (Russia, for instance) or an Iron Curtain country without consular relationships with the culture of orientation (Cuba), whether in a country closely allied to his culture of orientation, or a country that is part of the neutral block. A country beset by "palace revolutions," one in political upheaval, or one involved in armed conflict will present the field worker with problems peculiar to those situations. The wise researcher will make it his business to be well informed about the political situation of the country in which he plans to work, so that, along with a better understanding of his research project, he can be prepared for a variety of probable contingencies. I will deal only briefly here with problems of country entry. The novice is advised to read the Appendix for additional information pertaining to this problem.

The data that facilitate a successful solution to the entry problem are, by and large, available to the researcher during and before the exit period; thus most anthropologists will have completely solved their country-entry problems before leaving for the field. However, because of the need to grasp available possibilities when pursuing field work, quick changes are sometimes necessary at the very beginning of a field trip. Such changes may make some previously accomplished work ineffective. For example, on John Honigmann's first field trip, transportation problems led him to undertake a study not previously planned. Given the fast-changing political situations of the modern world, country-entry problems will continue to plague the field worker, even though he attempts to solve them before leaving home. Revolutions, civil wars, border conflicts, political assassinations, riots, mass strikes, and similar events may keep the anthropologist from completely solving his country-entry problems until he actually lands and receives formal permission, in person, to stay and do his work. Even if the country of research is free of political "upheavals" at the time of research, the formal rituals of entry into a foreign land may cause some temporary inconveniences. Robert Maxwell's description of his arrival in Samoa indicates the bothersome nature of governmental red tape.

In essence, country-entry problems are relatively easy to handle; that is, either one receives permission to reside and do research in a given country, or one does not receive it. If the anthropologist is denied entry into the country in which he planned his research, he can either appeal the verdict or accept it. The alternatives are not generally so simple with community-entry problems. The community in which the anthropologist does research may lack a formalized chain of command through which he can work. Or, given the presence of a formal authority structure, it may be that permission to live in the community should be obtained from an informal authority structure, the latter being the real power in that area. Permission to enter the community selected for research is often difficult to obtain, because it is often difficult to discover whose permission is required. Very frequently, it is not until passive research is almost over that the anthropologist discovers who really runs the village.

A useful strategy to facilitate community entry is to develop a number of general contacts: individuals who know something about the group that the anthropologist wishes to study. The experienced anthropologist will attempt to make such contacts while he is solving his exit problems: He will spend considerable time getting to know people who have colleagues, friends, or relatives in the country of research. Thus, soon after he has settled in his country of research, the anthropologist can approach his general contacts with some statement such as: "I'm a colleague of your friend Jack Jones. He asked me to look you up because he thought you would be interested in my research."

Some contacts are developed easily because of the researcher's affiliation with a particular organization. For example, John Gulick, as a university professor, was immediately able to develop general contacts at the American University in Beirut. Pertti Pelto could contact ethnographers at the University of Helsinki. Melvin Perlman, whose research was supported by the East African Institute of Social Research, had contacts built into his work. Making use of her background in nutrition, Nancie González was able to establish contacts with the directors of INCAP, and with the aid of INCAP she was able to meet a woman who was helpful in facilitating community entry.

Contacts established with local officials are sometimes good enough to secure smooth entry into the community. Perlman's contact with the District Commissioner of Toro (made through Professor Southall) led to a letter of introduction to the County Chief of Mwenge, who in turn presented Perlman to his Council. Contacts with local officials, together with those established with Catholic missionaries, helped Aram Yengoyan arrive at his Mandayan research site. My own use of a church contact, Dr. Cory, helped me to introduce myself to a number of Mohawks.

With luck, the anthropologist's general contacts will be able to help him develop good relationships with the local officialdom. Irrespective of how he enters the community, the experienced researcher will probably have difficulties with some important community members. For example, although John Gulick's first study had the support of an important status-holder in the community (the priest), this did not solve all of his community-entry problems. Indeed, it helped to create some difficulties, for the priest and the mayor belonged to different factions, and the strong support of the priest created problems for Gulick in relating to the mayor. Norman Whitten bypassed local officials in his first project, with mixed results. On the one hand, he suffered ridicule from the *mestizos* and on one occasion had to spend some time in jail; on the other hand, he thereby attained status vis-à-vis the Negro *costeños*. Robert Maxwell, too, might have bypassed the local power hierarchy and thereby increased his field problems had not an informant suggested that he seek Chief Tangaloa's permission to reside in Laovele.

Difficulties related to community-entry problems increase according to how much a project is based on a very specific research design that is connected to a very specific theoretical problem. For example, in selecting a village for his first study, Melvin Perlman was limited by the fact that he needed to situate himself in Mwenge County. The choice for his second village was even more restrictive: he needed a village that was situated near the town of Fort Portal (to investigate the direction of sociocultural change) and that had characteristics comparable to the first village. In Trinidad, I was restricted to studying a community where peasant farming was being done by East Indians and local Negroes, where the number of Indian and Negro peasants was approximately the same, and where both groups made a similar adaptation to the land. By the time I had discovered Anamat, I had found only two other villages that could meet the requirements of my research design.

A *local sponsor,* an individual who personally takes the anthropologist into the research community and introduces him to many community members, is a very useful contact to develop before settling into a community. Under optimal conditions the local sponsor is respected by the élite of the community and is well known by many community members. An effective local sponsor can help the anthropologist meet community members who will support his research and aid him in field work. Good local sponsors help the anthropologist develop *native sponsors:* people who live in the community being researched, who understand what the researcher is doing, who are ready to support this kind of work, and who will communicate these positive feelings to other community members. Through the help of a local sponsor, a priest's son, Gulick was introduced to a native sponsor, a priest, who was an important individual in the community. Through a general contact in Esmeraldas, Whitten met a native sponsor, the post mistress of San Lorenzo, who thereafter was some help in gaining Whitten rapport with the other natives. Through general contacts in Helsinki, Pelto obtained the names of a number of trusted informants who lived in three communities that were interesting for Pelto's research. Here, general contacts led directly to a number of possible native sponsors. Another general contact got Pelto out into the field just when a reindeer roundup was to begin and helped him get outfitted with essential equipment.

Entry–re-entry techniques. A useful technique for rapport development is what may be called "entry–re-entry." When an anthropologist leaves a community and then returns, the inhabitants generally treat him like a long-lost friend. On returning to Santa Maria after an absence of seven years, González discovered that her old informants remembered her well—even many whose names she had forgotten. Whitten, too, found that after returning to San Lorenzo his rapport with his informants greatly increased. The entry–re-entry technique appears to communicate trustworthiness, for the researcher often indicates on leaving that he plans to return. Actually returning indicates that his word can be relied on, and that he has an *interest* in the local population. Why else had he returned?

Problem 7: Survival Problems

Once he has entered the community, the anthropologist requires some kind of dwelling unit to provide shelter from the elements,

to give him a place to eat, work, sleep, keep his valuables, and to provide him with some kind of privacy. Often one of a very few possible "homes" available is a structure that either belongs to the government or is in some way intimately connected with the "government" by the natives. For example, my "home" in Trinidad was a government-owned former schoolhouse. This kind of housing unit, while often centrally located, has serious disadvantages for the anthropologist: in the minds of community members, the researcher becomes a "government man," and this association makes the spy problem far more difficult to handle.

A possible alternative to settling in a structure that is neither owned by nor closely connected with the government is to move in with a native family. Depending on the researcher's personality and living and working habits and those of the members of the selected family, this may be either a highly successful adaptation to one part of the survival problem or it may prove catastrophic for the whole research project. In a winter location among the Kaska, John and Irma Honigmann happily integrated themselves into something between a completely separate abode and a room in someone's house: they had their own one-room cabin in the winter settlement of a matrifocally extended family.

Maxwell's experience in a Samoan household illustrates the kind of difficulties a researcher may have to face if he lives in close contact with a local family. Since he was disturbing the "ghosts" that passed by the house at night, Maxwell had to stop work by 10:30 P.M. "Hoarding material goods" was frowned upon, so he had few sanctions to use against the local children who continually stole his money, personal items, and research supplies, and spoiled his films.

It is generally agreed that the best adaptation to the survival problem is to reside in a separate structure, and one that has no connection to any governmental body. The situations of the Whittens in Nova Scotia, of Yengoyan among the Mandaya, and of the Honigmanns in Frobisher Bay indicate that it is often possible for the anthropologist to obtain a dwelling that permits some degree of physical and psychological comfort. Should several independent dwellings be available to the investigator, it is generally wise to select the one most centrally located. It is then possible to travel quickly to the various parts of one's community and to "stay in touch" with daily events.

Perlman and Yengoyan were able to take their dwelling places with them. The use of a tent or a house trailer provides the anthropologist with considerable freedom as to where to do his study, allows him to avoid the mistake of moving into government-owned property, and often permits a "center-of-com-munity" location.

The value of a separate dwelling for the psychological com-fort of the researcher is, to my mind, inestimable. Over and above the cultural, social, and psychological isolation of the researcher is the strain of playing a "center stage" role for long hours, seven days a week. Further, as Whitten points out, the researcher is often the catalyst for many of the discussions that take place around him, and while "such catalytic action is intellectually rewarding . . . [it is also] to say the least emo-tionally trying." A separate dwelling can function (at times, at least) as a retreat from the pressures of observation, par-ticipation, and catalytic action. It is also a temporary escape from the emotionally difficult role of "nice guy," a role that is often considered linked to anthropological research. In his own dwelling the anthropologist can periodically lock the door, pull down the shades, and relax. He can invite in individuals whose company is desired more because they are fun than because they are good informants. I had the good fortune to find several such individuals in Trinidad. One in particular was a regular visitor to my house. We played poker, drank, and (on my part) attempted to keep away from subjects directly connected with my research.

The physical strains of life in the field are discussed at length in Chapter 1. Here I will add only that proper planning begun long before leaving for the field can minimize the diffi-culties that will surely arise. The anthropologist who has kept himself physically fit, trained his palate and stomach to accept strange foods, outfitted himself with clothing suitable for the weather conditions in his research community, "roughed it" in basic training or scouting, and learned to meet frequent chal-lenges with equanimity not only will conquer the problems of physical survival, but also will have considerable fun doing so.

Problem 8: The Spy Problem

In anthropological field studies, particularly during the passive-research period, it is highly probable that many natives will be convinced that the anthropologist is a spy. As indicated above the inexperienced researcher often presents the natives with "facts" that appear to substantiate their suspicions. By arriving at the "wrong" time (just after a tax law has been passed), by moving into the "wrong" type of house (a government-owned house), by entering the community without the proper introduc-tions, or by being introduced by the "wrong" type of person, the anthropologist can strengthen local beliefs that he is a spy and can create a situation in which it is difficult to develop rapport with the natives.

The anthropologist's best defense against the spy problem is to completely disassociate himself from the government. Accomplishing this is no simple matter, for the anthropologist is faced with a dilemma: he needs governmental suport for his study, yet he must appear not to be associated with the government. To get governmental support he must visit governmental offices and make a good impression on local officials. If such visits are successful, the anthropologist obtains letters giving him permission to enter given areas and to stay and work. He also obtains letters of introduction to local officeholders. In brief, solving the community-entry problem requires that he develop good relationships with governmental officers, but solving the spy problem requires him to disassociate himself from the government. How can the anthropologist do both? The natives who get to know about the support the researcher has received from governmental officers must surely ask themselves, "Why has this stranger been given permission to come here and ask questions?" In terms of this analysis, Schwab's early field-work problems can be better understood:

> I had come to Oshogbo with the active support of the colonial administration, but I assured them that I was not part of the government . . . Despite my self-definition as a research worker only [my initial image was] . . . closely associated with the government. I believe the people looked on me as a strange and deviant colonial administrator.

The anthropologist could more convincingly deny governmental connections if he entered the community without going through regular governmental channels. If he did this, however, he would lose the positive benefits of having governmental support. Again to quote Schwab:

> With the support of the Ataoja, the king of Oshogbo, and the Assistant District Officer, the colonial administrator in the area, I was able to hold a number of open meetings attended by the chiefs, educated members of the community and other influential people. . . . These meetings culminated in a reception in my honor where the chiefs and other influential people publicly promised their support and cooperation in the study.

Further, the researcher who does not get proper clearance for his work may have serious problems with local authorities. Even minor oversights in this area can lead to problems. Whitten, for example, could have saved himself some difficulties if he had made sure that the local police were informed of his presence and of the nature of his work. As it was, he was arrested one day for lack of sufficient identification. My own work with the Caughnawaga Mohawks often involved some infraction of the law (both in America and in Canada). Although I had a few documents with which to identify myself, I had notified no government officers of my work. The cars I drove in with Mohawks invariably traveled at speeds far above those posted and the Mohawks regularly made themselves obnoxious to all authority figures they encountered, but no group with which I traveled was ever arrested. In this case my luck was better than my judgment.

In most situations it is wise for the anthropologist to go through the proper governmental channels and then to tell his informants about the contacts he has developed with the government and just why these contacts are necessary. Having made such declarations, the anthropologist must assiduously avoid doing anything that will strengthen the belief that he is a spy.

How is it possible for the researcher to know the places, people, and interactions to avoid so as not to reinforce his spy image? How does he get enough information so that phenomena that might "prove" that he has a close connection with the government are regularly avoided? One answer to this problem seems to be to ask one's local sponsor a series of critical questions. What is the relationship between the government and the villagers of my community? Does the government have the strong support of most of the natives? If not, why not? If it has such support, what kinds of things is the government doing and planning that are least liked by the natives? Under what kinds of official sponsorship can I come into the village without being dubbed a government man or a spy? Should some people continue to consider me a spy, what do you think they would have in mind? Matters such as land tax? Income tax? Some kind of illegal business dealings? What kinds of behavior on my part would be most easily misinterpreted as "things a spy would do" or "things a government man would do"? Where do government people stay when they come to these parts? What places do government people often frequent? What places do government officers never frequent?

In addition to using the information received from these and related questions as a guide to acceptable behavior, the anthropologist can greatly benefit from a special kind of assistance from the local sponsor: an introduction to a few natives who live in the community and who are likely to support his project and might be willing to speak well on his behalf. If used well by the anthropologist, such native sponsors can be of inestimable value in solving the spy problem. If the native sponsor is himself very highly regarded in the community, his very presence in the anthropologist's house may be enough to allay the fears of many natives. If, in addition, the native sponsor is used as an assistant, the benefits derived from his help can be increased. That is, an intelligent native sponsor can be told the problem and asked to suggest solutions. The anthropologist might say something like, "Researchers all over the world are often thought of as spying on the natives. What do you think I can do so that people here do not think of me this way?" Solutions may be suggested that the anthropologist had hardly considered. In my study of rural communities in Missouri, an individual well versed in local culture helped me to develop a series of strategies that were effective in dealing with the spy problem for myself and my research assistants. In addition, these strategies provided us with what I call *precontact rapport*. Local radio stations, editors of local newspapers, ministers of local churches, and local agricultural officers were contacted, the project was described to them, and their assistance was requested. They were asked to communicate to the natives that we were all *bona fide* researchers, working for the good of everyone. In most cases such help was forthcoming, and through these kinds of communications, which included pictures of some researchers in local newspapers, we all met with far less resistance than we had anticipated.

Schwab's relationship with the king, a native sponsor of very high status, must have helped greatly in solving his spy problem among the Oshogbo. Similarly my "adopter" among the Mohawks not only indicated that I was above suspicion because I was "his boy," but in actuality assumed some responsibility for my behavior by making me a quasi-member of his mother's household in Caughnawaga. The natives now had two people to hold accountable for anything that might go wrong due to my presence.

In her study of American Negroes in "Indanola," Hortense Powdermaker was fortunate enough to have two native sponsors: William Percy, an aristocratic white man, and Mrs. Annie Wilson, a leader of the Negro community. These two individuals did much to assure the success of the project, particularly in the early months of field work. In Lebanon, John Gulick's major native sponsor, the local priest, greatly facilitated his research.

In brief, it is possible to use local sponsors and native sponsors to good advantage, once it is clearly understood that a field project almost invariably includes the spy problem. Such sponsors can "broadcast" information to the natives concerning the trustworthiness of the anthropologist. Their very readiness to be seen with him, to be defined as a "friend" of the anthropologist is of great value to the study. The "data" along with research experiences not discussed in this book indicate that the following phenomena will also help alleviate the difficulties caused by the spy problem: bringing one's wife and children into the field; dressing in local styles; learning to converse well in the native language, and in particular using local "magical words" whenever such are appropriate; eating and drinking with the natives as often as possible; and participating in minor illicit activities.

PART III: THEORETICAL FIELD PROBLEMS

Problem 9: The Socialization Problem

To do participant-observation research an anthropologist must be able to participate in a variety of collective enterprises, but in order to participate meaningfully he must be familiar with conventional meanings and related common experiences that are acquired only through participant-observation. The anthropologist is thus caught in a vicious cycle from which he seldom escapes until the passive-research period is over. In the pre-entry period, as the field worker delves into the literature on his group's history, economy, political organization, and religion, he is beginning the process of self-socialization in the native culture that will stand him in good stead once he reaches his community. Self-socialization continues as he works on his exit problem and as he concerns himself with developing strategies to solve the spy problem.

Once the anthropologist enters the community and sets up residence, the socialization problem has entered its critical stage: he must now translate all his information into correct behavior. He must, somehow, become a minimally socialized native. This is a difficult task, for at this time the anthropologist is in a situation somewhat analogous to that of the very young child. He has only a minimal mastery of the local language. He has little knowledge of basic social rituals for beginning or closing an encounter with an acquaintance, friend, superior, or inferior. He does not know the topics that are properly discussed in given social settings—at meal times, at ceremonial occasions, in settings where males and females are present—nor is he aware of how to act toward particular élite members of the community. These and similar matters that the young child must learn must also be learned by the anthropologist or he will not be able to practice his major field method: observation and participation.

Although the child has a set of role players—father, mother, siblings, peers—whose duty it is to teach him the basics of local culture, the anthropologist must first find such teachers and then convince them he is no spy! The child has no additional culture to stand in the way of learning what his socializers teach. The anthropologist has at least two additional sets of rules that regularly interfere with his becoming socialized in the native culture: his culture of orientation and his field-work culture. The socialization problems of the anthropologist thus appear to have similarities to the problems faced by a hardened criminal attempting to rehabilitate himself in society. Like the anthropologist, the criminal has at least one other set of rules for behavior (the criminal subculture) that interferes with his attempts to learn the local culture.

Thus far, two types of informants or sponsors have been identified who assist the anthropologist in solving his spy problem. The local sponsor does not live in the community about to be researched, but knows much about the local culture, trusts the anthropologist, and is willing to help him become accepted by community members. The native sponsor is a member of the community to be researched, trusts the anthropologist, and is willing to help him achieve his goals. Both types of informant can be used in the socialization problem, for both can help the anthropologist learn the rudiments of local culture, particularly phenomena about which the anthropologist knows enough to be able to ask meaningful questions. With respect to many phenomena, however, the anthropologist's ignorance will be so great that he does not even know the right questions to ask. In these areas he will have to socialize himself by watching what the natives do and listening to what they say. He can then, at appropriate times, conduct experiments in which he mimics behavior previously observed. If negative sanctions do not follow his public experiments, he can feel reasonably sure that he has properly learned a given bit of local culture.

The anthropologist who has entered a community for a prolonged stay is well advised to use observation and participation to help solve the basic field-work problem of his own socialization. Information from observation and participation can be linked to the socialization lessons received from local and native sponsors. When observed phenomena are minimally understood by the anthropologist, he can then question his sponsors about these matters. With a little luck he may find at least one sponsor who can be trained to play the socializer role extremely well:

to anticipate the kinds of situations the anthropologist is likely to encounter and to coach him in the proper behavior. The training of such a sponsor requires considerable thought by the researcher to determine what questions to ask the "socialization" sponsor and how to ask those questions. The "data" clearly show that many of the contributors had difficulties in the field that could have been avoided if some of their informants had been used as socializing sponsors. Any informant is only as useful as the questions that are put to him, and "good" questions are those that are intimately related to an adequate theory of human behavior, a theory that is both predictive and translatable into operational terminology.

Problem 10: Framework Specification

The anthropologist requires an adequate theory of sociocultural life in order to handle the serious business of field work. Such a theory functions as a guide for almost every move the anthropologist makes in the field. It lies behind his decisions to tackle one subject before some other; it directs the researcher to certain places and events ahead of others; it aids in the selection of informants and the use of other research techniques; in brief, it makes systematic field work possible. It will be argued here that an adequate theory for field work currently does not exist, and that the inadequate theoretical ideas that are generally taken into the field hamper rather than help field work. Moreover, these inadequate theoretical notions tend to stay with the field worker for much of his research career because it is more comfortable to push them down toward the subconscious level than it is to lift them into the forefront of one's thinking and to examine them critically. This generalization is well illustrated by an exception to it. After many years of field work in a variety of environments, John Honigmann evaluated at least one part of his theoretical framework: "My experience in Frobisher Bay, along with study based on reading, shook the theory of culture with which I had hitherto operated. . . . I suspect that the organization of a culture at any moment is fundamentally the product of accident or contingency." Honigmann, himself the author of a popular textbook on culture (1963), finds his own theory inadequate for field work, yet has not found any other theory adequate to replace it.

An adequate theory of sociocultural life must, I maintain, deal with two constructs of critical importance in field work: culture and community. To be adequate for field-work purposes such a theory needs a minimal number of elements that are translatable into operations. Minimal elements are required because the anthropologist in the field cannot be expected to refer constantly to a text on the subject. He needs a simple theory with a few basic constructs that can be memorized and used as guides to action. He needs a theory that can be simply operationalized. Such a simple, operationally meaningful theory can then be adapted to the specialized needs of each field worker.

A *theory* of culture and community that is adequate for field work cannot be presented here for the simple reason that I do not know how to do it at this time. Such a theory would have to take an adequate theory of culture and systematically link it to an adequate theory of community. The final system would then have to be demonstratively predictive. However, it is possible to present here the next best thing: two models, one for culture and one for community. These models are an attempt to map what I consider the critical elements of culture and community. As models they do not have to be demonstratively predictive, but only intuitively predictive. A model, as a skeleton of a theory, predicts only that it can be followed usefully. The model indicates to its users what is important, and if it is used for much research, it will grow into a theory. To describe the maps or models of culture and community presented in Figures 1–5 and to show that they have utility requires a somewhat lengthy exposition.

Culture. As the essays in this volume are perused, it becomes obvious that field workers often fail to make effective decisions because they are burdened by the knowledge of a concept: *culture*. Although culture has been defined by almost every famous anthropologist who ever lived, and although it has been subjected to considerable analytical treatment, most anthropologists are still rather vague about its meaning. This is particularly true when the meaning of culture is put to the acid test: when attempts are made to use the concept in field work. In the field the anthropologist needs a rather low-level, operational definition of culture, a definition that assists him in his daily research and that is simple enough to carry around in his head. Such a definition does not currently exist, so the anthropologist is generally forced to revert to a definition used by the intelligent natives of his own society. Culture thus becomes a "way of life." Considered as a "way of life" culture is simple enough to carry around in one's head, and the phrase has certain pleasant qualities. For example, it can seduce its user into thinking he understands culture. But "a way" of life implies "one way," and that one way is generally designated by a variety of additional terms: tradition, ideal culture, basic values and beliefs, idealized norms, and so forth. If one way of life exists (a basic postulate underlying this general meaning of culture) and if many people do not follow various aspects of this "way" (an empirical conclusion proved by many studies), then many people must be "deviants."

The observant reader will have noted, however, that many situations exist in his own culture of orientation in which *the* way is almost invariably *not followed.* For example, many people frequently misrepresent their income and expenses on their income-tax forms; budget-makers almost invariably pad their budgets with either fictitious expenses or exaggerated amounts for a given item; and salesmen almost invariably present their products as being far more superior than they are. All these are examples of how ideal cultural rules, rules for honesty, integrity, and fair dealings with one's government and one's fellow citizens, are broken. It hardly seems reasonable to refer to all the many rule-breakers in a given population as deviants, particularly since this type of "deviation" is by and large expected. The padded budget, for example, is an expected strategy, commonly used as part of normal operational procedures. So expected is it that a counterstrategy has been developed by those who are responsible for providing the funds: they regularly lop off a certain percentage of all proposed budgets on the assumption that the reduced amount better mirrors the needs of the budget-maker than his original statement. This example, it should be noted, illustrates a rather important principle: when "deviations" are frequently made by large percentages of a population, they somehow become transformed into normal aspects of the system. When many people often do the wrong thing (culturally speaking), this thing becomes defined as "right" (socially speaking). Moreover, in such a situation, the individual who keeps doing the culturally right thing (the proper) rather than the socially right thing (the smart) is thought of as a *schlemiel.*[5] The budget-maker who presents a budget that accurately mirrors the needs of his organization is a *schlemiel:* his activities do harm to the organization for which he works and in the long run create considerable havoc in the total system. The *schlemiel's* budget—like those of other budget-makers—gets cut by the regular percentage, with the result that his organization is not able to function in its regular way.

The concept of culture, then, while an important contribu-

---

[5] A *schlemiel* in Eastern European *shtetl* culture is an actor who is constantly in trouble not because he has bad luck but because he constantly acts in foolish ways. My analysis indicates that the *schlemiel* is always in trouble because he lives in terms of a basic misundertanding of sociocultural reality: he believes that cultural rules must always be followed.

tion to the philosophy of knowledge, barely scratches the surface of the socio-cultural reality the field worker is attempting to uncover. For all its general value in distinguishing various aspects of human life from those of animal societies, and for all its value in highly theoretical discussions, the anthropologist going on a field trip is often wise to leave "culture" at home.

Culture, as traditionally defined, has caused field workers problems everywhere. The contributors to this book had troubles directly related to this concept's inadequacies. For example, in preparing for field work in the Middle East, John Gulick consulted sources on Maronite culture in that region. His library research provided him with a confusing and almost worthless base on which to build his own field research. After attempting to piece together a composite picture of Maronite family life, kinship, and village structure, Gulick was left with several sets of inconsistent data. In his own words,

> How, I wondered, could patrilineage endogamy be reconciled with a rule forbidding *bilateral* first-cousin marriage? How, in reality, could household, lineage, and village be cohesive in-groups *simultaneously* for the same individual? How could *all* households consist of extended families at the same time? And how could a system of strong unilineal kin groups be functionally consistent with a system of kinship terms which G. P. Murdock had just christened "Sudanese"? I began to suspect that, aside from possible inaccuracies, the various sources expressed idealized norms more than they did generally observable realities.

Gulick concludes that observable realities are clearly distinguishable from idealized norms (or culture), and that such idealized norms themselves provide a minimally useful description of the socio-cultural scene they supposedly depict.

In Nova Scotia, the Whittens were told that the proper way (i.e., the culturally correct way) to obtain permission to enter Negro communities was to go directly to the man in charge and to present him with papers of identification, recommendations, and a statement of the purpose of the research. By following this proper line of conduct the Whittens immediately alienated a key power figure in the system, and their research received a serious setback. Norman Whitten's explanation for the error provides interesting insight into the problem an anthropologist faces when he uses the concept of culture in the field of research.

> First, when Nova Scotians tell one to first call the official responsible for a community they are paying due respect to the official, but, they do not expect the investigator to take this advice. [Further . . . the white and Negro Nova Scotians responsible for various aspects of Negro welfare] assumed that our stated goal

[of living in a Negro community] was an expression of an ideal, while we regarded our statements as declaring a manifest intention.

In anthropological language, the informants provided the Whittens with a cultural ideal for entering the community. They probably assumed that the researcher understood the foolishness of following this ideal. In turn, they assumed that the Whittens were providing them with a cultural ideal for field work: to live in the community being researched. From their own experiences they considered this cultural ideal also one which the wise white man does not follow.

These two examples indicate that, at the very least, two sets of rules seem to govern the behavior of natives: *cultural rules* —traditional guides to action, which in some cases it is pure foolishness to follow—and *operational rules*—guides to action that non-*schlemiels* are often expected to follow in lieu of cultural rules. A more sophisticated approach to the concept of culture can, I believe, be made by introducing the concept of operational rules. To explain this concept meaningfully, it is necessary to present the processes through which operational rules develop.

The anthropological activity called participant-observation is a successful research strategy largely because it makes use of a basic aspect of life anywhere as lived by anyone considered "normal": participating in what is going on and observing activities considered interesting, important, and fun. The average native in the street is a participant-observer: I will call him a "human participant observer" to distinguish him from the anthropologist who is a "research participant-observer." Although the human participant-observer is generally not well trained in observational methods and techniques and although he is neither participating nor observing for the purpose of collecting systematic data on the nature of his social system, he is doing participant-observation in order to get data. For purposes of work, play, malice, mischief, or helpful action, the native wants to know "what's happening" (a phrase often used as a greeting in Anamat, Trinidad). The human participant-observer wants to know what kind of cocoa crop his neighbor has obtained after spending much time redigging ditches to improve drainage, when Ma Jones is due to give birth, and when sick Jack is likely to die.

Although much of the information collected by a human participant-observer is not formally recorded, that which is considered most important does get "recorded" in the memory banks of many community members. Role players exist who find it useful—for business or pleasure—to develop skills for "recording," "storing," and "retrieving" information. Bartenders

Figure 1 Guides to Action

TYPES OF GUIDES		CONSENSUS	
		Absent	*Present*
TRADITIONAL *("The Proper")*		*Cultural guides*	*Cultural rules*
EMPIRICAL *(The "Smart")*	*Rational*	*Private guides*	*Operational rules*
	Speculative	*Suspicions*	*Rumors*

(Left axis: INSTITUTIONALIZATION — TOTAL to NONE. Top axis: CONSENSUS — NONE to 100%)

and barbers "store" community information primarily for instrumental ends: it's good for business. The community gossip stores it mainly for expressive purposes: he enjoys telling people things. As information locally collected grows, it is analyzed and reanalyzed during encounters between community members and their families and friends outside the community. In some cases these analytical discussions are very pleasant affairs, since most of the discussants develop consensus respecting a given informational summary; in other cases conflict and anger develop as discussants disagree about the meaning or validity of certain bits of information.

Some of the information summarized by community members is highly speculative; indeed, it is often difficult to demonstrate that the "summary" is accurate. These information summaries, referred to hereafter as "speculative guides," are made, discussed for a while, then modified. They rarely "remain" in any given form long enough to develop into meaningful guides for action for many community members.

Other information that community members possess guides behavior for long periods. This durable or solid information is usefully divided into *rational guides,* informational summaries that reflect the everyday experiences of natives and *traditional guides,* informational summaries that are handed down from an older generation to a younger one. In brief, human participant-observers collect information and summarize such data in three categories: speculative, rational, and traditional guides, and thereafter differentially use their own analyses as guides for behavior. Taken as a whole, these three sets of guides represent a human guidance system (see Figure 1).

Figure 2   Truth Tests of Scientists and Quasi-Scientists

	Scientists	*Quasi-Scientists (Natives)*
	Reliability	
	1. Accuracy or precision of a measuring instrument	1. Consensus = Reliability
	2. Error variance	2. No consensus = No reliability
	Validity	
	1. *Content* Measures judged for presumed relevance via specific directions	1. *Traditional* Authority of tradition
	2. *Predictive* Prediction to an outside source	2. *Rational* A reasoning or rational analysis based on past experience and predictions of future outcomes
	3. *Construct* (Theory)	3. *Speculative*

As previously indicated, some of these data summaries are agreed-upon generalizations; that is, they have developed considerable consensus. Others do not enjoy widespread support. Although the degree of consensus is most realistically viewed as a continuum, for the sake of simplicity a dichotomous distinction will be maintained in the model: without consensus, with consensus. Figure 1 thus represents a three-set human guidance system, where culture is one set: traditional guides that include cultural rules and cultural guides.

Basic to this analysis is the notion that man, wherever we find him, is a quasi-social scientist.

If the native in the street is really a quasi-scientist, then one must assume that he struggles for truth in ways not unlike those of real scientists. That this is so is demonstrable. The native as a quasi-scientist seeks truth to achieve better control over his environment. The real scientist has essentially the same goal, but he does not like "mushy" words like truth, preferring such "tough" words as "reliability" and "validity." The real scientist has developed sophisticated ways to test for truth, while the quasi-scientist has only several rule-of-thumb tests. Strangely enough, these rule-of-thumb truth tests bear more than a slight resemblance to the truth tests of real scientists. But, on closer examination, is this really strange? No, because the real scientist of today searching for "hard data" was the quasi-scientist of yesterday absorbing whatever data came along, hard or soft. Since the native and the scientist both share a common humanity, they both want essentially the same thing: control through prediction abilities. The chief difference between the scientist and the native is that the former has developed an insatiable passion for predictions, whereas the native pursues prediction less ardently, yet regularly and constantly.

To predict, one needs correct and reliable information. When a scientist wants to know whether a certain piece of information is reliable, he questions the precision of the instrument used to collect the information. If the instrument is precise, the scientist assumes that the information is reliable, since he assumes that the same information would be obtained again and again by anyone using the same instrument under similar environmental conditions. When a native wants to know whether a piece of information is correct, he is not very concerned with the precise instrument used (generally the eyes and ears of other natives) but rather with how well the instrument was used and how accurately the results of using it are being reported.

What of validity? Do natives everywhere really do validity testing? I believe so, and here they face the same tough problems scientists do when they attempt to answer the question: "Are we really measuring what we think we are measuring?" For the man in the street, the native or quasi-scientist, the question goes something like: "Is x (the phenomena I am concerned with) really what I think it is?" Following Fred Kerlinger, it is useful to distinguish between three major types of validity: content, predictive, and construct. It is interesting and instructive to find that natives everywhere appear to make essentially the same distinctions.

Content validation is essentially a matter of *judgment*. The statement "this (x) has content validity" is a declaration that x is "true" because one or more *authoritative judges* say so. They "know" because they have carefully examined the content of x in terms of specific directions for making judgments. For natives everywhere "the authoritative statements of judges" can be translated as "the authority of tradition."

Predictive validity is characterized by prediction to *an outside source*. The "outside source" natives use, I suggest, is information that can be described as "experience." That is, given a new piece of information (i), the native asks himself "Is (i) true?" The truth test the native often uses—predictive validity testing—is simply the question "Is (i) reasonable in terms of my previous experience?" Deductive reasoning on the basis of "an outside source" (i.e., past experience) is for the native what predictive validity is for the scientist.

Construct validity asks the question "Why does x have the properties it seems to have?" The answer to this type of question is obviously a theoretical statement. Thus construct validity is an attempt to explain a phenomena by developing theories. The real scientist, who uses construct validity, creates theory and systematically tests it; the quasi-scientist who uses construct validity just "creates theory": he speculates. Speculative reasoning by natives is thus equatable with construct validity. The similarities and differences between the scientific approach to truth (reliability and validity) and the native's approach to truth are shown in Figure 2. Natives can now be presented realistically as actors who use their experiences and other information from the past to guide actions in the present and the future.

Precisely how they use this information is probably unknowable at present, given current theories of human behavior and currently available research methodology. I suggest, however, that a good approximation of what occurs would be the following. As information flows in, natives code it for reliability and validity. Depending on the nature of the information, different validity tests are used, but all information gets the same reliability test: consensus. After the coding procedure, information is differentially labeled so it can be used as a guide. Each society will have its own labels, but they can be referred to here as cultural guides and cultural rules (traditional guides), private guides and operational rules (rational guides), and suspicions and rumors (speculative guides). This analysis is summarized in Figure 3. The two axes of the graph are *validity*, V and *reliability*, R. The V axis is subdivided by two arbitrarily placed lines that distinguish the various validity criteria used to code data: traditional, rational, and speculative. The R axis is cut by a line (r_0) separating guides that have consensus ($r+$) from those lacking consensus ($r-$).

How does this six-box model help the anthropologist in the field? Specific answers will be provided in other sections of this essay with reference to such matters as participant-observation, rapport, and active research. Here, however, I will provide a general answer and a set of rules to make the model operational.

**Figure 3   Native Truth-Tests and Informational Types:
The V-R Guidance System**

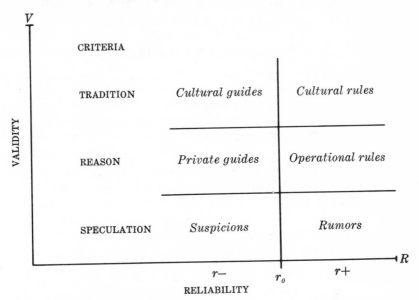

Key: V=validity axis; R=reliability axis;
    $r-$, lacks reliability (lacks consensus);
    $r+$, has reliability (has consensus);
    r_0, "boundary" between the reliable and
        the unreliable

The natives, it is assumed, divide their world into what is proper (traditional) and what is smart (rational and speculative). What is smart is then subdivided into what is probably smart (rational), and what is possibly smart (speculative). What is smart and what is proper are then dichotomized into what is popular (has consensus), and what is not popular (lacks consensus).[6]

What is proper is information that comes from the past. This accumulated knowledge of past generations is a guidance subsystem with a long history; it therefore has qualities other guidance subsystems (rational, speculative) do not have. It has been institutionalized. It has been clearly labeled as "informa-

---

[6] This activity of dichotomizing reality is, according to many scholars, a basic aspect of human thinking. Kelly, for example, presents it as a corollary in his theory of personality as follows: "Dichotomy Corollary: A person's construction system is composed of a finite number of dichotomous constructs." George A. Kelly, *A Theory of Personality*, New York: W. W. Norton, 1963, p. 103.

tion that guides." Parts of it have been translated into the various "community languages" of the system.[7] It is channeled through all the major socialization or indoctrination structures of the system. It is provided with the halo of "goodness" and given the support of formal sanctions.

Traditional guides are identified by three types of questions:

1. Properness questions: "What is the proper way to _____?
   Is it proper to _____?"
2. Socialization questions: "What are children taught concerning _____?"
3. Sanctioning questions: "If _____ is not done, what will happen?"

Information concerning what is smart has not been around long and is therefore not yet institutionalized. However, the "in" natives know the smart ways to do things from how to get a new house for less money in North America to how to get a new wife for fewer cows in East Africa.

Rational guides are identified by three types of questions:

1. Smartness questions: "What is the smart way to _____?
   Is it smart to _____?"
2. Transmission of information questions: "Having found out that S is the smart way, how does one learn S around here?"
3. Sanctioning questions: "If S is not done, what will happen?"

The smart with consensus must be distinguished from the smart without consensus. Further, it is necessary to distinguish what is probably smart (rational guides) from what is possibly smart (speculative guides). To isolate speculative guides, the researcher can do the following: Once he has discovered information that is S (or smart), he can develop questions like, "If S_1 (a given smart thing) is done, how likely is it that the doer will have reached his goals in the best way?" I leave the researcher to do his own experimenting here, for discovering the theory created by native theoreticians and estimating its effectiveness is just as tricky as discovering and testing theories in the social sciences.

A lengthy support of this framework is outside the scope of this essay, but a model of it will be presented in "Manufacturing Culture: Man the Scientist" (M.S.).[8] Central to this model is

---

[7] A distinction is made here between a dialect, or regional variation of a language, and a "community language." The latter as envisioned here, includes the special words, phrases, sentences, and meanings used while communicating with a particular subgroup, say infants.

[8] A brief review of this work follows: The model presented is, in its essence, a theory of how culture (cultural rules and guides) is "manufactured" and the nature of the "manufacturer," *Homo sapiens*. As new cul-

Figure 4   Informational Movements and the V-R Guidance System

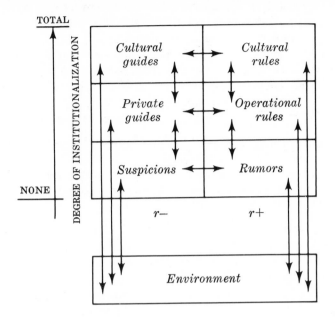

Key: *Informational flows* ⟶

the distinction between cultural rules and operational rules, and to a large degree the model stands or falls on the value of this distinction. I believe this distinction has considerable validity, and it fits in with my experiences as both a research participant-observer and a human participant-observer. The distinction between the proper and the smart has considerable utility for field work as described above; in addition, it helps to isolate the process whereby certain guides become culture. In terms of this model the smart (operational rules) becomes institutionalized and transformed into the proper (cultural rules) too late. By the time smart decisions become proper decisions, they are no

---

ture is produced, old culture "dies"; thus this model presents a theory of change. Speculative guides either meet rationality tests and develop into rational guides or they stay in their box or they die. Private guides develop consensus and attain the status of operational rules, or they stay as private guides, or they lose status and become suspicions that soon die. What happens to this rule system depends on how adaptive it is within its environment. Operational rules similarly stay in their box or become institutionalized and raised in status to cultural rules, or lose status and become rumors that die. What happens again depends on how well the operational rules function in their environment. What happens to cultural rules and how quickly they become cultural guides is again a function of the degree to which these sets of rules are adaptive for their environments. This process keeps going on "in circles" with some cultural guides going "downhill" into private guides, suspicion, and death (see Figure 4).

longer smart, for two reasons: First, by then everyone knows about them, and thus they have lost their competitive advantage; and, second, the general environment has changed, and what was smart before may be smart no longer.

From Charles Valentine's field experiences in Negro ghettoes and elsewhere I get very direct proof of the utility of distinguishing between cultural rules and operational rules. In concluding that it is foolish to expect to be able to derive all values from everyday behavior, Valentine writes

> What is prized and endorsed in a cultural system is not always manifest or practically available in the exigencies of on-going existence. Anthropologists therefore do not expect to find all the values that lend inner coherence to a way of life directly or overtly expressed in everyday life. (1968:7)

In my terminology, Valentine is saying that some cultural rules (values) cannot be translated into action because they are not adaptive to their environment. Such rules, however, function on a deeper psychological level and lend meaning to life. But given that everyday life continues, some guides other than cultural rules must be influencing behavior. What are they? My model calls them operational rules.

With respect to culture itself, Laura Thompson, who in two excellent books has carefully reviewed a large range of writings related to this concept (1963; 1969), has just come to the conclusion that "Whatever else a culture may be, it is primarily a group problem-solving device instituted by a human community to cope with its basic problems." (1969:6.) The model as presented treats culture as but *one* problem-solving device, one of many "programs" that guide action. Such a treatment of culture provides a framework within which we can solve a key problem that Dr. Thompson isolates: "to understand culture as a process and to understand also how cultures may be used to create and organize healthy viable communities." (1969:343.) As here envisioned, culture is information. To understand culture as a process thus requires an understanding of how information "moves"; what conditions lead to exchanges of information; how information gets stored, coded, interpreted; and the nature of local retrieval systems.

John M. Roberts in *The Self-Management of Culture* has demonstrated the value of regarding "all culture as information and to view any single culture as an 'information economy' in which information is received or created, stored, retrieved, transmitted, utilized and even lost." (1964:438.) My model, the *V-R* Guidance System (Figure 3) has but minor quibbles with Roberts' framework. I would reword his statement as follows: It is valuable to view culture as information which guides behavior and to attempt to isolate other informational systems which also guide human action.

This informational approach to culture fits in with such treatises as *Communication and Culture* (Smith, 1966), where language and culture are closely integrated, and it is becoming ever more useful for understanding sociocultural change (Rogers, 1969, for example).

If it is postulated that culture is a type of information dealing with the proper, and that this information is "old" and has become "proper" partly due to its age, the question remains: How has this information managed to live so long? My answer is, because it has been of adaptive value. Culture, as a type of information, has managed to compete successfully with other informational systems that have attempted to take over as master guides for the human computer known as *Homo sapiens*. Built into this model, however, is the notion that the old must die; cultural information, that is, gets replaced in time by operational rules, because the latter have become adaptively superior. In brief, operational rules continually replace cultural rules, get relabeled, and then get replaced by new operational rules.

This model of culture postulates that an understanding of process on the cultural level requires an understanding of process on a noncultural level. This sounds obvious, but some anthropologists will continue to resist coming down from the heights of the superorganic into the marketplace of informational exchanges.

Just as linguists sometimes find it useful to leave the cultural level and study animal communication to better understand human communication, so I predict that anthropologists will find it increasingly valuable to leave the cultural level and study informational systems that do not have the status of culture. The community is the obvious place to begin such a research program, but for successful work we need an operational framework for community studies that uses information as its base.

Community. The traditional anthropological field study involves a group of natives living in a locality and practicing some variant of traditional culture mixed with operational rules and personal generalizations. In attempting to achieve the role of marginal native the anthropologist, traditionally, has moved into the locality in which the natives live and has resided there for a year or more. Anthropological studies take the researcher out of his community and put him into the community (or communities) of his informants. A basic knowledge of the meaning of community appears to be a prerequisite for good field work; yet this information is not easily acquired.

Definitions of community are usually vague and of great variety and number. A study by George Hillery lists ninety-four such definitions and still does not claim to exhaust the conceptions provided by scholars who have studied the community. After summarizing much of the available literature on the community and commenting on the great variety of definitions in current usage for this concept, Nels Anderson concludes: "In other words, the nature and extent of one's community is largely a matter of individual definition." Harold Kaufman, who also discusses the available studies on the community, goes even further when he suggests that none of the available definitions is of any use in isolating this unit for study. He writes: "How, especially in this complex world, does one find the community? Making explicit the criteria of community action which sets off community from non-community activities is a crucial problem in interactional theory."

Is it possible to isolate a unity called the "community"? I believe so. Hillery, in an attempt to get a definition utilizing areas of agreement, concludes that most students are in basic agreement that a community consists of persons in social interaction within a geographic area and having one or more additional ties. For greater utility the definition should be operational.[9] To operationally define the community we need then to delimit a geographic area where interaction occurs and where such interaction is considered community living. How is this to be done? I have developed a model for community (Freilich, 1963) that can now be restated in a manner useful for linking "community" to "culture."

A community is a communication system with a name or identification tag, and a definable membership who share information with each other and thereby develop both a common set of operational rules and strongly shared sentiments. Communities are of two types: primary, where members regularly and frequently meet, face to face, at predetermined places called *centers;* and secondary, where informational exchanges are not necessarily face to face nor frequent, and where centers as such are not *the* places where information is necessarily exchanged and stored. The major focus of anthropological research has been on primary communities, and, unless otherwise specified, "community" will refer to "primary community."

---

[9] An operational definition is a rule that states that the term applies to a given case if specified operations performed in that case yield a characteristic result. For a comprehensive discussion of operationalism see, Carl G. Hempel, "Operationalism, Observation and Scientific Terms," *Philosophy of Science*, Arthur Danto and Sidney Morgenbesser (eds.), New York: Meridian Books, 1960, pp. 101–120.

Since communities involve people and people have traditions, a community is more than a human communication system with operational rules. In addition a community must have at least a set of cultural rules and a set of cultural guides. Since some people are also guided by personal guides, a community now becomes an interactional group that shares at least one total guidance system (cultural rules, cultural guides, operational rules, and personal guides). That is, a community becomes a group with a unique *V-R* Guidance System. Since community information is shared at centers and since an important effect of exchanges at centers is to process information and (in time) raise or lower the status of respective guidance systems, the centers themselves can be described as information banks. Information is brought to these information banks and stored by making deposits in the minds of other users of these centers.

The precise nature of this storing process can only be discovered through empirical research. However, it can be postulated on the basis of common experience that all the natives that frequent a given center at the same time do not all communicate with everyone else present. The natives form little interactional units and divide those present into what I call associational groups. A given individual probably interacts with his associational group and gives perhaps little more than a nod of recognition to the members of another associational group. If a given individual is a member of two associational groups, both of which are represented at a given center at a given time, he would have to select his preferred group and interact wi+h it. At times such as these, an individual with plural group membership might spend part of his time with each group.

As informational banks, some centers are clearly "richer" than others; more people come more regularly to these popular banks.

For each center, by using f for the frequency of meetings per year of an associational group, d for the average duration of such meetings, n for the number of personnel within such a group, and a for the number of different associational groups which meet there, the following equation of popularity of a center (and its information-gathering abilities) can be set up:

$$PC_1 = \sum_1^a (fdn)$$

That is, the popularity of center 1 equals the sum of $(f \times d \times n)$ for all the associational groups using that center. By using this formula, an index of popularity can be arrived at for the various centers of a community. Centers could also be distinguished by the type of information that is generally brought there. In some centers it is primarily cultural rules that are discussed. Here cultural information has almost a monopoly and, should noncultural data be brought in, such discussions will quickly be sanctioned by a high-status individual, bringing information exchanges (i.e., conversations) back to the cultural, the proper. In these centers (and conceptually) cultural rules always "win," should some competition arise with another informational set. In other centers the reverse may be true. Figure 5 indicates the possibilities when cultural rules (as information) compete as topics of conversation with operational rules as information.

Centers where traditional information almost invariably "wins" over rational information will be referred to as "square" centers. Predictably, the older natives will both control and frequent these centers. The young, fast-climbing natives will also interact here as well as a few "spies" for the rest of the community. Centers where rational information is usually able to shut out much talk on the traditional-information level will be referred to as "swinging" centers. The younger natives will come there regularly as will older natives who are slumming. Centers where traditional information and rational information both get a good hearing will be referred to as "political" centers, and these, predictably, will get a cross section of the native population. They will have considerable conflict, at times, for it is there that "cultural manufacture" and "culture death" occur. Finally, centers where rational information and traditional information both lose out to speculative data will be called "arty" centers. These centers will attract the marginals of the community from the schizophrenic to the genius.

Some communities, like the one John Honigmann lived in among the Kaska, are clearly "swinging." Others, like the patient community of my research in a mental hospital (1960), are "arty." "Square" communities are often described in papers

Figure 5   Centers Typed by Kind of Information Generally "Banked"

RATIONAL INFORMATION	TRADITIONAL INFORMATION	
	"WINS"	"LOSES"
"WINS"	*Political*	*Swinging*
"LOSES"	*Square*	*Arty*

entitled something like "Cultural Persistence Among _____,"
while "political" communities are those where rule change is
imminent. In "Political Systems of Highland Burma," Leach
(1954) appears to be discussing "political" communities which
he caught in the process of change. Thus cultural rules and
operational rules both "win." In Leach's analysis *gum*sa takes
over from *gum*la, and is itself replaced by *gum*sa, in a continuous cycle.

The framework for community can be summarized as follows: geographically, the primary community is a set of centers
related to each other by their regular use by a unique set of
associational groups. Socially, it is a number of associational
groups and their households who use a given set of interrelated
centers more often than they use any other set of interrelated
centers. Further, it is that group of people that shares at least
three unique informational sets—traditional guides, rational
guides, and speculative guides. These three sets of guides are
"stored" at centers differentiated as "square," "swinging," "political," and "arty."

To the extent the guide-to-action model presented above has
utility for field work, this framework, too, has value. That is,
within this framework for community it is possible to study
cultural process as previously discussed. More directly, referring
to the main focus of this book, this framework guides the anthropologist in deciding where to do participant-observation research. Clearly it would appear wise to hang out at popular
centers as much as possible, for this is where the information is.
However, not all popular centers are equally useful for the researcher at all periods of field work. For example, during the
passive-research period, when rapport development is an important task, the anthropologist must be very concerned with his
image. Centers defined as arty and swinging may not be places
that the anthropologist should frequent. The safest places for
the early periods of research are the square centers; the most
exciting and yet still appropriate places are the political centers.
The researcher with this model in mind can ask native sponsors
to lead him to square and political centers that are popular, and
to take him there at times when such centers are most crowded.
Participant-observation research and cultural theory both gain
from using this framework. Having discussed the latter at
length, let me go on to the former.

Problem 11: How To Be a Participant-Observer

The anthropologist preparing for his first field trip is generally
told to go into the community, to be a participant-observer, and

to do very little formal work during the early days of his stay. Many difficulties are inherent in this advice. How can one participate if one has little knowledge of the system? Where does one go to observe? What does one observe? What does one record? When is the recording to be done, while participating and observing, or after? The two activities encompassed by the phrase *participant-observer* are best analyzed separately.

Implicit in instructions to go into the community and observe is the word "everything," for without a well-defined problem it is hard to know what data may prove to be of immense value to the study and what data are irrelevant. Clearly, one cannot observe everything in a community. The researcher cannot be everywhere and thus many things will be happening that he does not observe at all. Also, any given situation contains too much information for one observer to absorb completely, so some phenomena will completely escape him. Hence from the moment of entry, the anthropologist faces the problem of selecting which sites to observe, and on which phenomena to focus his attention.

With all the situations which can be observed with profit, it might be assumed that the researcher is constantly in a state of anxiety, worrying whether he is where he should be. Generally, as indicated by the "data," this is not so. The factors that influence an anthropologist's presence at a given site and at a given time are many; they include the location of his house, the major roles he has assumed for field work, the rapport he has developed, the major goal(s) for that period of field work, and the local culture.

Around the dwelling of the anthropologist lies an area of "instant information," social space within which whatever goes on immediately impinges on the senses of the anthropologist. A neighbor quarrels with his wife, chastizes his son, fights with a tradesman, or has trouble getting his bull to a good grazing area; these and similar phenomena catch the interest of the anthropologist not because they are meaningful to his project, but because they are there. Proximity influences observation.

Role and rapport also directly influence what the anthropologist observes. A dwelling site provides shelter and privacy; it also provides the researcher with neighbors and the role of neighbor. Neighbors are expected to do things for each other, and the wise anthropologist has inquired of his socializing sponsor precisely what his duties will be in this role. Being a neighbor may necessitate his presence at parties, marriages, and funerals, and the researcher may have to absent himself from situations more pertinent to his study in order to fulfill these obligations.

The rapport achieved in the community during the early days of passive research is small, for the anthropologist is at this time playing the role of privileged stranger: he is minimally accepted as a researcher, who will reside temporarily in the area; he has the support of a few native informants, but he has few or no really close relationships with the natives. The privileged stranger, unlike the marginal native (a role developed later in field work), cannot barge into a native house uninvited. Unlike Honigmann among the Kaska, he cannot easily crash parties, for once inside he would lack the rapport to justify the fact of his presence with the ease necessary for a continued favorable image in the community. The sites to which a privileged stranger can easily go for observational work without anyone's permission are the community's *public centers:* interactional sites that are open to the public.

Public centers can usefully be distinguished from *private centers,* or interactional sites that are not open to the public. Both public and private centers are distinguishable from *special centers,* closed interactional sites whose membership is less restricted than that of private centers, but still requires membership privileges for use. Private centers are generally exemplified by households, but do not always refer to such. Among the Caribs, for example, González found that there were no closed doors and fences. In this community people's doorways took on the function of public centers. Among the Cakchiquel Indians, the houses themselves were very much private centers: "Most houses are screened from the street by high adobe walls. . . . Each household is thus assured of its privacy, and one does not casually intrude without advance warning." Special centers represent a midpoint between private and public centers. The native, socializing sponsor can again be useful in helping the anthropologist to find public, special, and private centers in which to do his observational work.

Opportunities to observe are also frequently a function of climate and cultural practices. During the cold winters of the North, movement in and out of centers of whatever type becomes difficult, and public centers "well stocked" with people in less inclement weather are no longer so useful for observational activities. Thus Honigmann tells us: "The onset of winter along the Upper Laird considerably limited my opportunities to observe people. As a result, I began to depend much more exclusively on talking to informants in my home or theirs and data came to consist primarily of verbal statements."

Moving to a winter settlement, another cultural practice, again influenced observational behavior for Honigmann: "Our winter location, with its eight related adults and six children, provided a good opportunity to get to know people closely and to observe interaction in much less distracting circumstances than in Lower Post." Honigmann also discusses the problems of the researcher who becomes a member of a private center and thus worries whether the information he is collecting is typical of the total community. These comments are worthy of amplification particularly regarding situations in which the researcher is not cut off from the rest of the community. By becoming a meals-boarder with the priest's family, Gulick became a member of a private center and, as such, privy to information of an intimate and valuable nature. However, his close attachment with the priest and his family made it more difficult to get information from some other members of the community. In general terms, the more closely the anthropologist attaches himself to *one* private center, the more difficult it is to gain entry into *all* private centers of the community.

A definite advantage can be achieved by transforming a particular private center (the researcher's own dwelling) into a *special center,* a place where a particular type of native (one who receives membership rights) is so welcome and so well rewarded for coming that he regularly attends. Somehow Yengoyan managed to do just that in Capasnan:

> My house in Capasnan became a nightly meeting place for most males. Nearly every night anywhere from two to ten men would come over and spend a few hours talking, smoking, and drinking. My kerosene lamp, flickering in the darkness until 10 or 11 P.M., as well as a good supply of tobacco and liquor, induced them to stop by to talk about their activities and my work.

As a member of an audience, say at some ritual, the researcher need not dissipate his energies and time by active participation; he can simply watch and listen. In such situations he might be tempted to stay as long as he is allowed, and this research strategy is viable under the condition that he can take notes while observing. If note-taking is not possible or practical, we need to concern ourselves with Gulick's statements on attention span and memory capacity: "I discovered [he writes] that my own attention span was limited to about one hour, and that in longer encounters much was lost as far as my notes were concerned."

In considering attention span and memory capacity, we have gone from where and under what conditions observation is done to what is observed and how well it is recorded. It is useful here to introduce the distinction between *molar* and *molecular observation* (Kerlinger, 1964:510). The molar approach "takes large behavioral wholes as units of observation. Complete inter-

Figure 6 Types of Observational Strategies in Terms of Degree of Inference and Size of Unit Observed

INFERENCES MADE	SIZE OF UNIT OBSERVED	
	SMALL	LARGE
FEW OR NONE	*Molecular*	*Large unit*
MANY	*Inferential*	*Molar*

action units may be specified as observational targets. Verbal behavior may be broken down into complete interchanges between two or more individuals, or into whole paragraphs or sentences." The observer using the molar approach starts with a general, broadly defined variable and considers and records a variety of behavior under one rubric. "He depends on his experience and interpretation of the meaning of the actions he is observing." The molecular approach, however, "takes small segments of behavior as units of observation." The observer using this approach "seeks to push his own experience and interpretation out of the observational picture. He records what he sees and no more."

Kerlinger has linked together two variables which are usefully separated: size of unit observed and degree of inference used. By putting these variables "against" each other, as in Figure 6, we get four types of observational techniques which may be useful at different times in field work and at different sites: molecular (where the unit observed is small, and few or no inferences are made), large unit (where the unit observed is large, and few or no inferences are made), inferential (where the unit observed is small, and many inferences are made), and molar (where the unit observed is large, and where many inferences are made).

In any given situation, at any particular period of research, the anthropologist can usefully ask himself: What kind of data have I come here to get? The answer to this question may suggest one of the four styles of observation mentioned above. Early in field work, when everything is very strange, small-unit observation may not be the best strategy, since the anthropologist is trying to take in a lot of things at once. Also, inferences made at this time are likely to be wrong; thus large-unit observation would be the best method in the early stages of field work. As the researcher gets to know the basic rituals of everyday encounters and wishes to test his understanding of this subsystem, he might want to try molar observation and check his inferences with a good informant. As a problem develops out of passive research and is refined so that specific data is needed to test given hypotheses, a molecular approach seems called for. In brief, with a set of labels to identify types of possible observational modes, the anthropologist can plan more rationally his observational strategies within particular types of sites where his own role is predictable.

Buford Junker has developed a typology based on the notion that four kinds of data exist in any given socio-cultural situation: *public*—"what everyone knows and can talk about," *confidential*—information that is "told in confidence," *secret*—"what is known to members of an in-group who avoid letting it be known to an outsider, since its exclusive possession is important to the in-group's solidarity and continued existence," and *private*—"what is personal to an individual." (Junker, 1960:34–35.) Junker identifies four modes (he calls them "roles") used by researchers in the field for presenting themselves to the community. Each mode is useful for getting a particular kind of information. The four modes are: complete participant, participant as observer, observer as participant, and complete observer (1960:35–37):

> I. Complete Participant—In this role, the observer's activities as such are wholly concealed. The field worker is or becomes a complete member of an in-group, thus sharing secret information guarded from outsiders. . . .
> II. Participant as Observer—In this role, the field-workers observer activities are not wholly concealed, but are "kept under wraps" as it were, or subordinated to activities as participant, activities which give the people in the situation the main bases for evaluating the field-worker in his role. This role may limit access to some kinds of information, perhaps especially at the secret level. . . .
> III. Observer as Participant—This is the role in which the observer activities as such are made publicly known at the outset, are more or less publicly sponsored by people in the situation studied, and are intentionally *not* "kept under wraps." The role may provide access to a wide range of information: and even secrets may be given to the field-worker when he becomes known for keeping them, as well as for guarding confidential information. . . .
> IV. Complete Observer—This describes a range of roles in which at one extreme, the observer hides behind a one-way mirror, perhaps equipped with sound film facilities, and at the other extreme, his activities are completely public in a special type of theoretical group where there are, by consensus, "no secrets" and "nothing sacred."

Junker's analysis isolates a number of critical variables that are part of field work: participation, observation, types of information collectable, openness of researcher (his relative aboveboardness or misrepresentation of self), and sponsorship of the research (degree of public acceptance of the project and the researcher). However, in pulling together these critical variables, he develops a typology that has limited utility for anthropological research, as he himself would probably agree. For instance, his typology "assumes" that participation is an activity subservient to the real business of field work, observation. It is clear from the "data" and from generally accepted understandings of field work that participation is, in and of itself, an important research technique.

The contributors got more or less involved in in-depth participation not because they differentially valued participation as a research technique, but because age, sex, roles available for the researcher, and his general image in the community influenced the frequency and intensity of participation research. At the age of thirty, for example, Honigmann found intense pleasure in active participation in Kaska Indian culture, but years later when he returned to the Far North his age made it difficult for him to be as freely involved in native culture. Among the Frobisher Bay Eskimo he was an older, more reserved anthropologist with higher status, and he considered it desirable to maintain more social distance between himself and the natives.

While revolt against one's culture of orientation and an attachment to notions of cultural relativity will tend to push the researcher into intense involvement with the native culture, some aspects of the researcher's culture of orientation are likely to restrict the amount of his participation. Irrespective of how the anthropologist participates, however, participation itself is viewed as a valuable data-collecting technique. Participation, as Junker indicates, often involves deception, the nature of which is quite complex. The researcher participates for ulterior purposes, many of which cannot be discussed regularly without embarrassment to all concerned. The researcher practicing some degree of deception on the natives must act as a human participant-observer while actually being a research participant-observer. In situations where the researcher presents himself as a human participant-observer, he appears almost like a real native. Such situations occur on every field trip, for certain situations are not conducive to clear visibility of the anthropological role. During rituals and celebrations, the presence of someone in the obvious role of research participant-observer can spoil a mood that the natives have gone to great lengths to create. If the anthropologist often acts like a human participant-observer or like a real native, is it possible for him always to remain a real anthropologist? Is there not a strong temptation, indeed a magnetic pull, in these situations for the anthropologist to "go native"? A person may drink (participate in native culture), drink heavily (participate fully, in depth, but still know who he is, and what he is supposed to be doing), get drunk (temporarily go native), or become a drunk (go native and stay in that condition).

Going-going-gone native. Honigmann tells us that among the Kaska he attended practically every dance given in the Lower Post, joined home-brew parties whether invited or not, contributed to potlatches, helped to set fishnets and repair houses, visited extensively, exchanged gifts with the Indians at Christmas, and got deeply involved with local problems. González speaks of eating all foods that were offered her, showing an active appreciation of local rum, sleeping in the manner of the natives (on a hammock, on the floor, or sandwiched in between other members of the family in a common bed), making long-distance journeys by dugout canoe, and joining her informants in their small-scale smuggling activities. Perlman and his wife kept chickens, ate with their hands, joined local clubs, regularly showed up at public ceremonies and functions, and participated in Toro life in every possible way. Yengoyan's participation in drinking bouts made him famous among the Mandaya. Whitten summarized his activities among Ecuadorians as "In general, I lived the life of the people." Maxwell's field-work life was intimately involved with many people around him. Schwab speaks of developing intimate friendships with some individuals and families among the Oshogbo and in general "sharing in their day-to-day activities." Gulick lived in a native house and became intimately involved with his field-work "family." I was a very involved participator both with Mohawks and with Trinidadian peasants. From at least one point of view—living in terms of the native culture—all these examples are aspects of going native, yet in each case the anthropologist did not think he had gone native. Why not? First, we may not have realized that at times we really did go native. Second, living the life of the native in itself does not necessarily mean going native.

E. E. Evans-Pritchard has said the following about field work (1964:77–79):

> The anthropologist must spend sufficient time on the study, he must throughout be in close contact with the people among whom he is working, he must communicate with them solely through their own language, and he must study their entire culture and social life. . . . [He must] put himself in a position which enables

him to establish ties of intimacy with them. . . . [H]e learns
through action as well as by ear and eye what goes on around
him. . . . By living among the natives as far as he can like one
of themselves the anthropologist puts himself on a level with
them. . . . It is evident that he can only establish this intimacy if
he makes himself in some degree a member of their society and
lives, thinks, and feels in their culture since only he, and not they,
can make the necessary transference.

Through extensive and intensive participation in native life,
the anthropologist can finally reach that point of cultural understanding whereby he is able to live, think, and feel like the
natives. A goal in anthropological field work, then, is to become a native *culturally*. In order to do this, the anthropologist
also must become "in some degree a member of their society."
Evans-Pritchard has here made a subtle, but critically important distinction between culture, which includes rules for
living, thinking, and acting, and society, which is a collectivity
whose "capital" includes the assignment of membership rights.
In terms of culture, he tells us to go native as far as you can,
live like they do, make a total cultural transference, for only
through such a transference can you fully communicate with
the natives and understand their cultural reality. In terms of
society, however, he tells us that the anthropologist must make
himself a member of their society but only "in some degree."
Here the anthropologist is told not to leap out of membership
of his own society and into complete membership in theirs.
However, this technique leaves the anthropologist somewhere
between his own society and the native society. He is really
being told to become a marginal native in terms of sociological
membership, but in terms of cultural know-how he is advised
to become a real native. The anthropologist who attempts to
pass as a real native has gone beyond the boundaries of field-
work methodology. Going native socially is therefore "bad" for
several reasons. The researcher who goes native socially and
stays "a native" is no longer an anthropologist, for he has
lost his original perspective and is no longer primarily involved
with the goals which brought him into the community. His
major goal now is to be socially accepted as a real native by
other real natives, but the researcher does not have the option
of being both an anthropologist (going native culturally) and a
native (going native socially and culturally) for the following
reasons.

The researcher who goes native culturally and stays an
anthropologist socially can and will take the information he
has obtained out of the native categories and put them into
anthropological categories. Such transformations are always

time consuming and often extremely difficult. Above and beyond the long, tedious hours of doing content analysis on one's data, there is the need to make frequent leaps, back and forth, from native culture to systemic anthropology. The point is essentially simple, although difficult to communicate to those inexperienced in anthropological research: No obvious way currently exists to translate ethnographic data collected in one cultural system into a description which will be meaningful to all who are interested in cultural anthropology. It is only the anthropologist who is still in the field socially and who has gone native culturally who will be able and willing to spend long, tedious hours playing cultural hopscotch: jumping in and out of different cultural systems in order to present his data as meaningfully as possible.

The distinction between going native culturally and going native socially appears useful since it permits a fuller understanding of the "data" as well as of the field-work experiences of other anthropologists. For example, it helps to explain the following interesting statement made by Hortense Powdermaker (1966:115):

> *Although I enjoyed those brief moments of feeling at one* with the woman dancers at the initiation rites and although I was fairly involved in this Stone-Age society, I never fooled myself that I had "gone-native." I participated rather freely, but remained an anthropologist.

At first glance it would seem that a contradiction exists in the sentence "I participated rather freely, but remained an anthropologist." Surely, one might ask, the anthropologist is supposed to participate rather freely, so why the "but" before the ending? In terms of my analysis, Professor Powdermaker's statement very much requires the "but" because she is really saying: "Although I participated rather freely and went native culturally, I avoided the temptation to go native socially. I continued to remember who I was, and what I was there for; that is, I remained an anthropologist."

The temptation to go native socially cannot be overcome. All anthropologists who get intensely involved with a culture and its people go native both socially and culturally, albeit for relatively short periods of time. Good anthropologists shift back to the role of field worker so quickly that they hardly realize they left it. We might say that the field worker who is both strongly attached to anthropology and intensely involved with field work gets "drunk" from constant and heavy intakes of native cultural information. During such periodic states of "drunkenness," he climbs over the social-membership fence and, in addition to going native culturally, also goes native socially. The "drink" soon wears off, however. As he reaches home and sees his tool kit (field notebook, questionnaires, camera, etc.), it and other symbols and signals related to the role of anthropologist call him back to sobriety. He then climbs over the fence in the reverse direction, back into the anthropological community. Such periodic states of "drunkenness" have a few rather interesting "hangover" effects. First, important cultural data obtained while "drunk" are remembered and are available for ethnographic analysis. Second, important emotional ties have been developed with one's "drinking" partners. As the anthropologist slips out of the role of field worker and into one of several roles available to him (friend, neighbor, blood brother, or whatever) a closeness develops with some natives which cannot be achieved while in the role of field worker. Unless we accept the assumption that the anthropologist periodically climbs over the fence and becomes a real native, it is hard to explain the intense feelings mutually developed between field workers and some of their informants. Further, without the role of temporary native, we must assume a sharp distinction between the world of emotions (feelings, sentiments, identifications) and the world of the intellect (learning, knowing, understanding). It is more consistent with modern psychology to assume that basic links exist between emotion and intellect. Therefore, it is necessary to postulate that *a complete understanding (on an intellectual level) is only possible if there was also (at least temporarily) complete identification*. This postulate gains considerable credence when analysis is made of a type of encounter often found in field work: the work-break game.

The work-break game. At certain times, and in certain types of situations, the anthropologist and some natives find it mutually advantageous to make believe that the anthropologist is not working, that he is indeed taking a break. While participating in this game, all players make believe that the anthropologist is a human participant-observer rather than a research participant-observer. The rules of the game are simple: good moves are those which make the deception more believable; average moves neither help nor harm the deception; and moves which are not permitted are those which uncover the reality of the situation. The latter bring to light, for all to see, that the anthropologist in reality *is working:* he is just covering his role of researcher with the role of human participant-observer. The anthropologist is a key player in the game, and his behavior is critical to its continuance. He must find a role which is consistent with the situation he is in and which is believable in terms of the relationships previously developed with the other players. Thus he might move into the role of neighbor, friend, guest, or blood brother to the host (another key player, usually the individual in charge of the place in which the game is played). Whatever role is assumed, however, symbols and signals related to anthropology must be well hidden. What is absent from this game are phenomena such as notebooks, pencils, questionnaires, and questions which other players would not normally ask. Once in a given role the anthropologist somehow provides cues to the other players, so that they can make appropriate moves. It may be that the choice of his role is not in the anthropologist's control. At such times, he watches carefully for cues from others present, particularly from the host. As soon as he has adequate information to determine what role has been given to him, the anthropologist steps into it and plays his part as well as he can.

The essential proof that this game exists and is played in the way described rests on five propositions: (1) Natives everywhere finally discover that the anthropologist is always at work. (2) It is often difficult for the natives to deal with this strange phenomenon: the constantly working researcher. (3) By the time they discover this strange piece of information, the community as a whole has developed considerable consensus about his presence: The anthropologist is considered a desirable addition to local life, and it is not likely that the community will force him to leave. (4) The anthropologist often finds himself in a dilemma: to achieve his research goals he constantly must be collecting data. However, in many situations it is extremely embarrassing to appear to be working. The anthropologist, like the natives, is ready to grasp opportunities to make such inherently embarrassing situations more pleasant. (5) The work-break game is a variant of many interactional forms practiced by most members of the human species. Hence, neither the anthropologist nor the natives have to learn very much which is essentially foreign to their experiences to play work-break. They simply adapt behavioral modes previously used in situations of embarrassment and ambivalence where continued interaction was considered desirable.

When it becomes clearly and generally known that encounters with the anthropologist are invariably for the serious purpose of work, a native *appears* to have two possible options when invited to help the anthropologist do field work. He can say Yes, or he can say No. In point of fact, the native has a third option: to change an obvious field-work encounter into the work-break game. Again, either subtly or unsubtly, the native can indicate to the anthropologist (and he often does) that at this particular time he does not want to work nor does he really want the anthropologist to leave. If the anthropologist accepts this countersuggestion by the native—namely, that the field worker is welcome to stay around as long as he does not force the native to play the role of informant—it generally implies that the work-break game is on. Knowing that the anthropologist is always "on the job" the native understands that the work-break game is truly a game: an encounter whose obvious or surface goals are pleasure for participants, but which may include more serious subsurface goals.

Clearly, work-break has great advantages for the anthropologist. Rapport is being built with all the other players in a situation where a work role would lead to a loss of rapport for the researcher and embarrassment for all present. At prayers, parties, marriages, and deaths a working anthropologist would stand out as an incongruity. The sensitive researcher at these times comes and "participates," but he leaves his notebook hidden. Ostensibly he is there out of neighborliness, respect for the deceased, friendship for the host, or whatever, but he really is working. He knows this, and so do the natives. The mood of these situations is left "culturally correct": this facilitates both the goals of the natives—to be allowed to live their lives in normal fashion—and the goals of the field worker—to see their sociocultural reality, relatively unbiased by the effects of his presence.

The work-break game is not only regularly played during field work, but when played well has interesting consequences. As the anthropologist and the native continue to play work-break, and as the game continues to be played well, the informant can temporarily forget that his guest is actually doing field work. That such "forgetting" really takes place is very clear from my own field-work data. After being in Anamat for several months, a number of informants, independently, made statements such as the following: "Since you like our country and our village so much, you really should get yourself some land and stay here." This type of message was generally followed with statements such as "You really one of us, yes?" Thus the informant can at times hide the make-believe aspect of the work-break game so well that he can truly enjoy the anthropologist as a person who (generally) is knowledgeable, well-traveled, ready to be of help in all kinds of projects, and (often) sympathetic and helpful with respect to the psychic needs of his informants. It is also clear that the informant is not alone in hiding the make-believe aspect of the game from his consciousness. The anthropologist too often gets far more involved in the work-break game than research-methods textbooks may consider wise. He too often temporarily forgets his field-worker role and acts fully and intensely in the role assumed for the work-break game. Such behavior makes it easier for the natives to take this game seriously. The anthropologist can more easily temporarily forget he is doing field work. That is, sometimes the work-break game ends not with the anthropologist leaving for home nor with his switching back into the role of field worker but rather with the anthropologist assuming one of several roles within the category of complete human participant-observer: colloquially, he has gone native. The game has ceased to be a game, and now two or more actors (anthropologist and native[s]) talk and act in ways they honestly think and feel. That many anthropologists go native temporarily during the work-break game is clear from the "data" and from other writings. An important clue here is the fact that many have written of their intense sorrow in leaving a particular field site. It is difficult to imagine how such deep sorrow at parting could be felt if the anthropologist had not, at times, completely disregarded his field-work role and assumed the universal human roles of friend and good neighbor.

In sum, going native, if for short periods of time, is not just to be understood as doing something which is "bad": leaving the anthropological fold, attempting to deceive oneself and the natives, making a fool of oneself, etc. Going native can also be thought of as getting back into the ranks of humanity, regenerating the psyche to withstand the pressures which constantly affect the field work. Further, such trips into complete involvement with native culture and society yield rich ethnographic fruits.

Developing a participant-observer Typology. The work-break game can be summarized as follows: a researcher enters a situation not conducive to work and, with the help of those present, slips into the role of make-believe native. While playing make-believe native, the anthropologist is subjected to pressures to completely abandon the researcher role and become a temporary native. The temporary native is a complete participant. It is a behavioral mode which, it can be postulated, has as its opposite the zero participant, an individual who is present in a given situation, but does not participate. To participate is to influence the environment. Once the anthropologist is observed by others, he necessarily influences the environment, even if he speaks to no one and just stands in a corner doing nothing. How then can the anthropologist be present and not participate? The key seems to lie in the word "observed"; that is, if the anthropologist is present, yet his presence is unobserved, he can be a zero

participant, or what Junker calls "a complete observer." Unlike
the sociological zero participant who can, at times, hide behind
one-way mirrors and observe without being observed, the anthropologist who desires to be a zero participant must find other
ways of "hiding." Following Marion Pearsall, such other ways
exist, particularly if research is conducted in urban settings,
where the researcher could slip into

> . . . a number of relatively invisible roles such as janitor, cleaning
> woman, elevator operator. . . . And personnel in large, busy or-
> ganizations such as modern hospitals are often so intent on their
> work that undetected observation of their activities is possible
> for brief even extended periods. (1965:37.)

Following Mrs. Pearsall's analysis, we can say that some roles
are relatively invisible in all environments, and in addition to
these "invisible roles" there are other roles which gain a degree
of invisibility in high n environments (colloquially, "where it's
crowded"), and where the n people present are all actively involved in their roles (colloquially, "where people are busy").

For the anthropologist to use this information in a field
study, he must know precisely what it is that gives a role such
as cleaning woman a low degree of visibility. I suggest that the
cleaning woman is relatively invisible because she is rarely
known as a person, but only as a sort of human thing which
does cleaning. Further, this human thing is relatively invisible
only to those whose work is unrelated to office cleaning. In the
language of Merton's role theory (1957), we tend "to see"
those people who are in the role set we are in, when we assume
a given status. While in the status bookkeeper, for example, I
would have no reason to see the cleaning woman, who for me is
a human thing rather than a person. The human thing takes on
characteristics of other things in my environment, such as typewriters, pencils, etc., all of which are "seen" if and when I need
to use them, but otherwise remain relatively invisible. There is
an important difference, however, between human things and
nonhuman things: typewriters become visible when needed for
use; cleaning women become visible when needed for use, and
also when someone wishes to be "friendly." "Friendliness" is
important for our discussion if it includes questions concerning
the feelings of the human thing as it acts (feelings immediately
distinguish human things from nonhuman things) and the
history of the human thing, how it got there, what it did before
it came here. In many high n environments it is frequently
possible to remain a human thing and escape "feeling" and
"historical" questions; it is possible to stay invisible.

The anthropologist who desires to play the role of zero

participant needs to overcome the following problems. First, morally this role is difficult to condone. As Pearsall put it:

> . . . true identity and purpose are hidden in a way difficult to defend morally and only dubiously defensible scientifically. . . . There is, moreover, the constant threat of exposure and the still greater possibility that the hoped-for anonymity of a later report will be unmasked, releasing all the righteous indignation reserved for spies and traitors. (1965:38.)

Second, it is extremely difficult to enter the type of community traditionally studied by anthropologists as a human thing. That is, systems studied by anthropologists are often of the *Gemeinschaft* type and such systems often do not include a phenomenon such as a human thing. Third, the anthropologist who successfully enters as a human thing will find it difficult to escape friendly questions, for two reasons: (1) as a stranger, the anthropologist's presence would arouse curiosity leading to friendly historical questions; and (2) the research environments of anthropologists are rarely high n environments.

Thus far an attempt has been made to isolate three roles which lie in different positions on a participation continuum. These roles are labeled zero participant, make-believe native, and temporary native. Between zero participant and make-believe native there are two roles which have previously been referred to and which now can be fitted into this developing typology: privileged stranger and marginal native. The privileged stranger, by definition, is a low-level participator whose acceptance by the natives is minimal; they put up with his presence as long as he does not interfere too much (i.e., participate too much) in their life. The marginal native is accepted almost as a member of the system, albeit a strange kind of member. The marginal native is "invited" to play the work-break game, during which he temporarily increases the degree of his participation. These ideas can be summarized as in Figure 7.

Figure 7   Levels of Participation in Anthropological Research

Z-P	P-S	$\boxed{\text{M-N}}$	MB-N	T-N
0	1	2	3	4

Participation Continuum

Key: *Z-P* "Zero" Participant
P-S Privileged Stranger
M-N The Strategic Role, MARGINAL NATIVE
MB-N Make-Believe Native
T-N Temporary Native

Figure 8   A Participant-Observer Typology

PARTICIPATION ROLE	OBSERVATION MODES			
	MOLECULAR (A)	LARGE UNIT (B)	INFERENTIAL (C)	MOLAR (D)
ZERO PARTICIPANT (0)	*OA*	*OB*	*OC*	*OD*
PRIVILEGED STRANGER (1)	*1A*	*1B*	*1C*	*1D*
KEY ROLE MARGINAL NATIVE (2)	*2A*	*2B*	*2C*	*2D*
MAKE-BELIEVE NATIVE (3)	*3A*	*3B*	*3C*	*3D*
TEMPORARY NATIVE (4)	*4A*	*4B*	*4C*	*4D*

When the participation types in Figure 7 are linked with the observational modes shown in Figure 6, we get the participant-observer typology shown in Figure 8. It will be clear in later discussion (see problem 13) that the logical possibilities shown in Figure 8 are not all useful strategies for participant- observation research.

Problem 12: Rapport and Exchange

During the passive-research period, the anthropologist is solving many research problems and trying to develop enough rapport to be permitted to stay and begin active research. Rapport development can be analyzed from at least two viewpoints: humanistic and engineering. The humanistic viewpoint sees rapport development in a "romantic" light: Chopin, candlelight, pressed duck, white wine, and "the girl" with whom one has rapport. The job of the anthropologist is interpreted as working toward "establishing ourselves as trustworthy, sympathetic, and interested." (Berreman, 1968.) According to the humanistic view, rapport can be achieved by anyone who is a good and humane human being. The humanistic view, although useful, misses an important difference between being a researcher and being a native, between being a human participant-observer and being a research participant-observer. The research participant-observer is always acting with the central purpose of collecting ethnographic data. That the native, too, is collecting ethnographic data is both undeniable and central to my model of culture. The native, however, is collecting data quite incidentally; his main goals are focused on other things—making a prayer meeting, playing cards, or being a host. The researcher, being human, is necessarily a human participant-observer; however, that role is incidental to his main role which focuses on collecting data on kinship, social organization, religion, economic life, etc. Differently stated, the researcher and the native are mirror images of each other; each has as central to his role what the other has as incidental to his.

Another view of rapport useful for field work is the engineering view which sees rapport in cold terms. The research participant-observer manipulates situations and people to get data, and he manipulates himself to gain rapport, so that more (quantitatively) and better (in terms of reliability and validity) data are collected. This view, although somewhat Machiavellian, is more helpful for training researchers in the strategies of rapport achievement and development. The *art* of becoming the kind of human being who can gain rapport is almost unteachable in the short time allotted for graduate studies. *Strategies* for engineering rapport development, however, can be taught simply and learned easily.

Achieving great rapport does not necessarily mean having *good* relationships. It does mean having relationships: regular interactions, involving all kinds of sentiments and the regular exchange of information. Rapport means an agreement to communicate: an agreement time-bound and linked to a number of additional conditions, such as what natives can expect to get for communicating, and what kinds of information the anthropologist can expect to receive. Therefore, rapport is *a conditional agreement to communicate*. To understand rapport well enough to develop ways to teach someone how to develop it requires an understanding of (1) the kinds of conditions which lead to agreements to communicate; (2) the relationships which exist between the different conditions natives require in order to communicate with the anthropologist and the different types of information they are willing to pass on; and (3) the relationship between types of communications systems which are set up between natives and anthropologists and the types of cultures and social structures anthropologists work in. Such understanding can be attained by considering three variables central to all forms of human communication: risk, time costs, and communication net profit (c.n.p.).

When an anthropologist asks a native for information he is usually asking him to assume the rational risks of communicating with a researcher. These risks, while superficially similar to those present in any communication situation, are actually rather special. The marginal native, unlike the other community members, is not expected to remain in the community for more than a year or two, thus he probably will not be around to be held accountable for problems which may develop because he was given certain kinds of information. Further, not being a real member of the community, he is not as much subject to community controls as are other community members; thus he has great freedom to do what he wishes with the information he collects. Being a constant collector of data, the anthropologist obtains an ever-expanding pool of information concerning local affairs. Each additional bit of information helps to identify a total system, the understanding of which represents a type of power. With respect to certain questions asked by the anthropologist, the native can usually evaluate the rational risks he is asked to assume. Hesitancies are not (as sometimes assumed by novices) the result of slow informational processing by dull-witted natives; rather they represent the working out of difficult decisions for the informant. The native asks himself, "Is it too risky to provide this information, given my knowledge of the researcher?" The rational risks are the ones a rational native generally assumes, since, irrespective of the rewards provided for the information being given, the consequences of being wrong are not terribly serious. It is worth taking the chance.

In some situations, however, when an informant is asked for information, the anthropologist wants the native to assume more than the normal risks that most rational natives would assume. The native is being asked to be a speculator and take the chance of being ruined, in local terms. In situations where the native must assume speculative risks, the anthropologist is viewed by the community as someone who cannot be trusted with information. Thus, anyone who communicates with the anthropologist takes the chance of, at worst, being executed by members of the community (or by the government), and at best, of being ostracized by other community members.

A primary condition for rapport is, therefore, the elimination of all speculative risks for the native. Objectively, the anthropologist is indeed a spy for an organization, but one which wishes the natives well, rather than harm. As a "spy" for social science, the anthropologist often acts in ways not unlike other spies; thus the natives somehow must quickly be taught the nature of social science, its general methodology, and the particular approaches used by anthropologists. In attempting to solve the spy problem, the anthropologist is also providing a primary condition for rapport development. The native's fears of community sanctions for communicating with this stranger are also quite realistic. To achieve a situation with minimal risk for the informant, the anthropologist must engage in image building from the moment he enters the community. His project should be well publicized with particular emphasis placed on the value of the research for the community. The anthropologist, entering the community at a favorable time, under the auspices of well-liked local and native sponsors, and with a good publicity campaign, can project an image of an individual acceptable to the total community. Communications with this type of researcher will carry no stigma and, therefore, will bring no negative sanctions from other community members. Destroying the harmful view of spy and creating a positive image of a useful, temporary addition to the community will jointly meet the primary conditions to communicate.

Once major communication risks are handled successfully the anthropologist will have achieved a collective stamp of approval which we might call image rapport. The community as a whole is now prepared to enter into agreements to communicate with the anthropologist, and any agreement between native and researcher is, in part, risk ensured by the community. It is possible to have rapport with certain natives without having image rapport. What this means is that the community, as a total system, believes it too risky to enter into a communications agreement with the anthropologist, even though a few natives are willing to take the risk. These are the speculators who "live in" the two bottom boxes of my cultural model (Figure 1). Predictably, in such situations the anthropologist must pay dearly for the information he is getting. It is wise in such situations for the researcher to ask himself: "Why is this informant taking such a chance?" "Under these conditions, how valid is the information being received?"

It is also possible to envisage a situation where image rapport exists but where direct rapport has not been achieved with many natives. This is the film-star situation, a situation where image rapport is very high and where, if necessary, communications agreements could be made with ease.

Secondary conditions pertaining to rapport achievement, maintenance, and development are, by and large, much more tied to specific research sites than are primary conditions. One highly general secondary condition is that image rapport will (at a minimum) remain at the level it was at, when a given agreement to communicate was made. Another general secondary condition is that the researcher will consider the time costs involved in communications with him, and structure such exchanges so that the native completes a given encounter under conditions of communication net profit (c.n.p.). That is, given the native's evaluation of his input, time which could be used for other purposes and rational risks for communicating with a stranger, and given the native's subjective output, his evaluations of what he receives out of interactions with the anthropologist, output minus input should produce some kind of subjectively defined profit. Testing for continued c.n.p. is thus intrinsically a part of rapport maintenance.

The anthropologist concerned with rapport development beyond the stage of image rapport must give considerable thought to his exchange-capital situation. That is, a fundamental principle upon which I base my analysis of rapport is that, purely on the level of information exchanges, where a native and an anthropologist are engaged in a business encounter, and where the anthropologist only gives the native general information (questions, comments, discursive statements) and the native reciprocates with information, it is the anthropologist, not the native, who ends the encounter with a c.n.p. However, from the viewpoint of rapport development, regardless of what the anthropologist receives from an encounter, the native should always leave it with a c.n.p. What do anthropologists have to offer natives so that research encounters can always terminate with a c.n.p. for the natives? Let us first look at the "data." For purposes of brevity I will discuss only the most obvious examples of rapport capital and its usage.

Aram Yengoyan's Mandayan informants believed that his research into their agricultural practices would help rid them of the rats that were plaguing the uplands of Manay and Caraga and significantly reducing rice yields. This kind of "hope capital" is often a part of the researcher's total exchange capital. Yengoyan was fortunate because a major focus of his study —enumerating and evaluating "spatial environmental variables such as rainfall, topography, soils, leaching processes . . . etc." —was also a cultural focus of the Mandayan cultivators he was researching. Yengoyan discovered that, "A general concern with faunal, floral and other environmental categories was of overriding interest to most men." After discussions about concrete environmental matters such as the number of rice varieties planted, the meaning of a "good harvest," and the types of wild foods collected, so much enthusiasm was generated that "young boys even began to collect wild foods and medicinal herbs for me."

Exchange capital can also be "created" by the anthropologist, and although this involves spending money, such "creations" are often superior to simply paying informants in cash. An excellent example of created exchange capital is Yengoyan's "men's club." Friendly informants could visit Yengoyan at his Capasnan residence, and invariably they would find a bright environment (a kerosene lamp burned until the late hours of the night), friendly faces, and a good supply of tobacco and liquor. The value of Yengoyan's "men's club" lay not only in the fact that reciprocity was built into encounters with the natives but also because the natives' time costs were low, while their "outputs" were high. In Yengoyan's words: "With the pressure of daily activity at a minimum, men could relax and talk." This analysis indicates that whether natives make a net profit and whether such a profit is high or low is partly a function of what kind of time the native is giving. Yengoyan had managed to take relatively free time from his informants and was paying with excellent currency. Liquor, tobacco, and good fellowship in return for their free time gave the natives an excellent bargain. Predictably, then, Yengoyan must have had excellent rapport with the members of his "men's club."

History was part of the cultural focus of the Oshogbo, and William Schwab could use his interest in their history as part of his exchange capital. Schwab's excellent relationship with the King further provided him with high image rapport, a kind of halo which could be transformed into exchange capital in a given encounter with an informant.

The anthropologist has, as part of his exchange capital, a variety of services to offer natives. Robert Maxwell tells us that in Samoa "When the situation permitted, as at mealtimes and parties, I tried to be helpful by washing dishes, acting as bartender, and sometimes trying to translate English remarks into Samoan for Tangaloa's benefit." In Trinidad, I wrote letters for illiterate older peasants, helped some peasants during the cocoa and coffee harvests, acted as chairman for special meetings of the Village Council and, like Maxwell, tried to make myself useful when I could.

Melvin Perlman and his wife taught English to Toro natives and Mrs. Perlman taught the women knitting. By bringing his wife and child into the field, Perlman increased his image rapport. In his words, "no white family had ever lived among them in their village, and few had ever seen a white child, much less one who played happily with their own children."

Money is an obvious and often very useful form of payment for services rendered to the anthropologist. Unfortunately the anthropologist has only a limited amount of cash, and it must be carefully hoarded to last through to the conclusion of his field work. With his limited budget the anthropologist must take great precautions to be sure that funds earmarked for food for himself and his family are not spent on paying an informant who will work only for money. Some additional problems exist regarding cash payments for information. It is not often clear whether an informant wants money and whether the anthropologist might not be insulting him by offering money for what the native considers a friendly exchange of ideas. One of my best informants in Trinidad not only provided me with excellent data on all levels but also was my car mechanic for the whole time. Day or night, as long as he had no fixed appointment somewhere else, he made himself available to take care of the many problems my little Morris Minor gave me. Not once would he accept a cash payment for any of his services to me (I did buy him an expensive book on automobiles and their repair), and I often felt quite embarrassed in my payments discussions with him. The anthropologist must, therefore, offer cash payments to informants as subtly as possible and be prepared to provide another kind of payment if the informant rejects the money.

It is not always very clear *how much* an informant should get after he has agreed to accept money payments. Norman Whitten used an approach that many other researchers might wish to emulate: he paid Humberto the equivalent of what his informant would have received had he spent the same amount of time doing his regular work. It should be noted that this approach is easily adapted to those informants who work for an employer but is not so easily handled for informants who work for themselves.

Finally, an informant who works for money might begin to consider this kind of work a "good deal" and, therefore, when topics come up about which he has little information, the paid informant might decide to manufacture information simply to keep his job as informant and its monetary rewards. Hence, the paid informant must be handled with special techniques; somehow built into this communication encounter there must be rewards for correct information and negative sanctions for incorrect information. Understandably, the whole matter must be handled with caution so that a good and honest informant is not lost and so that an unreliable informant who is sanctioned for false data does not take actions (spread rumors, etc.) that will hurt the researcher's image in the community. It has been my experience, however, that sanctions made against unreliable informants help rather than hurt the researcher's image; the anthropologist becomes known as a person who does not easily fall for what my Trinidadian informants called "low dodges."

Sentiments shared by the researcher and the natives are another important item of exchange capital. Being liked, trusted, and admired is often a function of the closeness of fit between the anthropologist's expressed beliefs, values, and sentiments and those of the natives. When such sharing occurs the researcher provides the informant with a valuable commodity which Craig Lundberg calls "confirmation." Confirmation can be defined usefully as "a person's desire to be *appreciated*." Appreciation can be shown in many ways, but surely its highest form is emulation. John Honigmann among the Kaska showed his informants maximal appreciation by honestly emulating their feelings concerning important phenomena in their environment. In his words:

> I came to share the Indians' opinions . . . I resented strongly as they did the missionarys' brash intrusion on a potlatch feast, and I deplored with them the deadness of the post in August. . . . I sympathetically viewed the Indians' alienation from the Eurocanadian power. . . . I shared their positive attitudes toward drinking and regarded as recreational some of its accompanying behaviors. I also accepted permissively the Kaska sexual behavior . . .

The anthropologist seems to have two different types of exchange capital to give to the natives: limited and inexhaustible. Limited-exchange capital provides for use as working capital or exchange currency valued objects such as tobacco, alcoholic beverages, cigarettes, medicines, first-aid equipment, gifts of various sorts, and money. These exchange items are limited, since they must be purchased with research funds, which themselves are limited. The value of dealing with limited-exchange currency is that bits of it can be offered to informants with whom the researcher has only a nodding acquaintance. That is, limited-exchange currency is good as "come-on" currency, leading natives to wonder, "if I get good things just by offering a few friendly remarks to the anthropologist, what might I receive from a deeper relationship?" Providing potential informants with limited-exchange currency serves two functions: positively, potential informants are transformed into actual informants; negatively, informants and the native population as a whole gain an incorrect view of the anthropologist's total resources and may regard him as an immensely wealthy person.

Informants who have been enticed with limited-exchange currency can later be told of the true state of the anthropologist's exchange capital. Such information need not be a sad blow for the informants, because they can also be told of the presence of various types of exchange capital that are inexhaustible. The anthropologist's inexhaustible capital includes the following:

1. Specialized knowledge, including proficiency in writing (in English, or some other valued language for the informant), first-aid techniques, techniques for dealing with governmental red tape, information relating to educational opportunities for natives, etc.

2. Offers of personal service, including working with the natives in private or communal projects, helping natives in various jobs

3. Use of the anthropologist's property, camera, rifle, car

4. Hope capital, providing hope for a better life, by research in agriculture or in cultural mixture situations

5. Cultural-focus capital, using the cultural focus as a discussion topic, in exchange, so to speak, for being allowed to go on into other informational spheres

6. Status-assignment capital

7. Confirmation capital, showing appreciation for the natives and their way of life by emulating their feelings and by other forms of emotional identification.

The anthropologist's input into relationships with natives has been spelled out quite specifically; the natives' inputs must be similarly analyzed. For purposes of the rapport model being developed, I will assume the following: First, image rapport can be treated as a constant, K. Second, speculative risks do not exist for the natives; that is, from the native's point of view in a given situation speculative risks are zero. Finally, rational risks vary in direct proportion to the quality of information they provide, the number of different topics the informant is willing to discuss with the researcher, and the amount of time (on the average) the informant is willing to give the anthropologist. These three aspects of rational risks: level of information, l, number of topics, t, and time spent with the anthropologist, T, are usefully discussed separately.

Four types of field-work encounters can be isolated with respect to the level of information provided by an informant:

W encounters, where public information is provided
X encounters, where confidential information is provided
Y encounters, where secret information is provided
Z encounters, where private information is provided

Junker's typology of informational types obtainable in field work (1960:34) already discussed is useful as a typology of field encounters. Each type of encounter can be associated with a level of risk-taking for the informant. An informant who only involves himself with the anthropologist in W encounters (i.e., a W informant) is assuming minimal risks in his dealings with the researcher. The public information this informant provides could have been obtained almost anywhere in the community, and therefore, should such information be misused by the anthropologist the finger of guilt cannot easily be pointed to any particular community member. An X informant, however, takes risks which can more easily get him into trouble. By providing confidential information the X informant gives data that are potentially more harmful to the community if misused (hence, its confidential nature), and he is more easily identified as the giver of such information. Similarly, Y informants and Z informants, respectively, take more risks than either W or X informants, and a Z informant takes more risks than a Y informant.

In brief, I am assuming that a native has some kind of risk gauge which shows his risks going up as he involves himself in W, X, Y, and Z encounters, and that an informant who is ready to take Z risks (i.e., who will involve himself in Z encounters) will also take W, X, and Y risks, that one who takes Y risks will take W and X risks, and that one who takes X risks will also take W risks—all in good Guttman-scale fashion (Kretch, *et al.*, 1962:154–7).

I also will assume the existence of a risk-taking unit u, which relates to W, X, Y, Z in the following ways:

$$W = 2u \qquad X = 10u \qquad Y = 40u \qquad Z = 100u$$

This imaginary risk scale assumes that X, or confidential information, is five times as risky to provide as W, or public information; that Y, or secret information, is four times as risky to provide as X; and finally, that Z, or private information, is two and a half times as risky to provide as Y. Each native will have his own subjective risk scale, which I assume not to be significantly different from this imaginary scale. Further, I assume that lacking good data in this area the scale presented is a useful starting point for later more sophisticated scales.

The second important variable in the natives' risk gauge is the number of topics which are discussed in a typical encounter or interview. The more topics discussed on any given level (W, X, Y, or Z), the greater the risk the informant is taking that such information will be used against him personally or against the community. For the sake of simplicity, an informant's behavior in a typical encounter could be described as involving few topics, coded as one (1) or involving many topics, coded as two (2). These codes are presented for

Figure 9   An "Imaginary" Risk Chart

INFORMATION LEVEL (*l*)	RISK UNITS (*u*)	NUMBER OF TOPICS (*t*)	RISKS PER HOUR
Z (PRIVATE)	*100*	*2*	*200u*
Z (PRIVATE)	*100*	*1*	*100u*
Y (SECRET)	*40*	*2*	*80u*
Y (SECRET)	*40*	*1*	*40u*
X (CONFIDENTIAL)	*10*	*2*	*20u*
X (CONFIDENTIAL)	*10*	*1*	*10u*
W (PUBLIC)	*2*	*2*	*4u*
W (PUBLIC)	*2*	*1*	*2u*

Key: "*u*" is here presented as a per hour risk unit.

1=few topics; *2*=many topics; is a "doubler" of risk units (a "2" multiplier).

use as *u* multipliers. Thus a 2X native is an informant willing to assume twenty (2 × 10) risk units. Such a man can be referred to as a 20*u* informant, and so on through the scale.

The time a native is willing to use for communication with an anthropologist is obviously related to risk-taking: the more time spent with the anthropologist (other things being equal), the more information is received by the researcher and the larger the risk assumed by the informant. What I am suggesting is that natives can be described in terms of their typical risk-taking behavior in an average encounter with the anthropologist by a code which first presents the level of information the informant provides (*W, X, Y,* or *Z*), then describes the number of topics the informant will discuss, code 1 or code 2, and then lists the average length of time the informant spends with the anthropologist in hours (1, 2, 3, etc.). For example, informant Jones can be described as a Y-2-2 or someone who will discuss secret information on many topics for an average of two hours at a time. Once coded in this manner, each informant can be described in terms of his average risk-taking behavior with the anthropologist; thus a Y-2-2 informant takes 160 (40 × 2 × 2) risk units with the anthropologist per interview. Such an informant is therefore a 160*u* informant, and the rapport an anthropologist has with a Y-2-2 informant can also be described as equal to 160*u*. That is, the rapport of any researcher with a given informant is equal to that informant's average risk-taking behavior with the researcher.

Natives are assumed to refer to a risk chart which might be pictured as in Figure 9 and to calculate their risks (inputs) in a given encounter against the rewards or payments from such an encounter (outputs). Irrespective of payments received, the anthropologist's rapport in a given encounter E is equal to the total risk $(l \times t \times T)u$ a native is prepared to assume.

Rapport can now be defined as a conditional agreement to communicate, such that given any two units (say) A and N in regular communication, A's rapport with N is equal to N's average risk investment with A. Conversely, N's rapport with A is equal to A's average risk investment with N. It is now possible to have a better understanding of why, at times, as the "data" indicate, rapport appears to go up and down within a relatively small time period. From within this model, there are three possible answers: (1) since the last encounter, the native has weighted the u's higher; thus what appears to be the same situation to the anthropologist appears to the native as a riskier situation; (2) the native may have felt "cheated" in the last encounter with the anthropologist, believing that the risks he assumed were not compensated for adequately; or (3) both (1) and (2) may occur together.

The definition of rapport developed here and the analyses that led up to it have a number of interesting aspects. It appears that in any relationship involving communication, rapport may be at times symmetrical (A's rapport with N is equal to N's rapport with A) or asymmetrical (A's rapport with N is greater or less than N's rapport with A). It also appears that in anthropological field work, where some rapport exists between an anthropologist A and a native N, A generally has higher rapport with N than N has with A. Since, by definition, the rapport of A is equal to the risk-taking behavior of N, this means that N takes more risks dealing with A than A takes in dealing with N. Therefore, it is only just that the native be compensated for the extra risks he takes. It is now quite clear why the marginals of a community rush to relate to the anthropologist, and why anthropologists are generally advised to be wary of this kind of informant. The marginal members of the community often have little status in their system; thus the risks they take in talking to the anthropologist are small when compared to those of persons with higher status. The anthropologist, on the other hand, takes greater risks by relating to the marginals than by talking to the "average" natives. By communicating with marginals, the anthropologist may cut off a future supply of "average" informants; therefore, he is advised to be cautious with these early informants.

In creating an imaginary risk chart (which I assume has some important links to the native's own risk chart), I have built into this model of rapport two strategies for increasing rapport: *the time-increase strategy* and *the communications net profit (c.n.p.) strategy.* The time-increase strategy can be explained as follows: Let us assume that an anthropologist has an X-2-1 informant (i.e., one who provides confidential information on many topics for an average interview of one hour) from whom he wants secret data (Y data). The anthropologist can reason to himself, "My X-2-1 informant is taking 20 risk units with me ($10 \times 2 \times 1$). I want him to go up to about $40u$. I can get him up to $40u$ by attempting to increase his average interview time." The first step in this strategy is to change this informant from an X-2-1 to an X-2-2. The native's risk has now doubled to $40u$, which, according to my risk gauge, puts him on the level of a Y-1-1. That is, by increasing the time involvement of an X informant, he can be made to assume the same amount of risk as a Y informant. Once this native has been engineered into assuming *more* risks, it should be simple to engineer him into assuming *higher-level* risks.

The communication-net-profit strategy for increasing the rapport of the anthropologist (i.e., increasing the risks of the natives) is (where such resources are available) to give the native a high net profit for risk assumption. It is assumed that the native who receives high profits for low-level risk can be engineered to hope for much higher profits for higher-level risk taking.

If the rapport the anthropologist has with a native N is equal to N's agreement to assume n risk units per average encounter, then different sociocultural systems can be distinguished in terms of how long such agreements will last, and what relationship exists between a contract or agreement *made* with native N_1 and a contract *about to be made* with native N_2 In my essay on Trinidadian peasants, I referred to "length of contract" by words such as "melting" and "solid" rapport. I said I had melting rapport with the Negro peasants and "solid" rapport with the Indian peasants. It is now clear what it was, precisely, that I had identified. The Negro peasants lived in a system where the dominant time value can be described as "now-for-now." In such a system no agreements are expected to last. One lives with a wife now-for-now, and one makes agreements with an anthropologist now-for-now. The fact that a peasant had taken n risk units with me yesterday meant that while he is likely to take the same number of risks today, he also reserves the right to change his mind. High-frequency interactions with Negro peasants helped remind them of the nature of the risks they had previously taken and helped to make up their minds in the direction I wanted. A spacing of a week or so between contacts almost meant that a totally new risk-taking agreement had to be made. The Indian peasants, however, lived in a future-oriented time system. Once a risk-taking agreement had been made by them, it was expected to last, just as agreements they made with each other were expected to last. Sociocultural systems are thus usefully examined for their time orientations, and such an examination will provide the anthropologist with data about how often he must interact with key informants to maintain a given level of rapport.

What I call the spreadability factor—how far rapport achieved with native N_1 spreads to other members of the system—can now be better analyzed as the *risk-underwriting factor*. Among the Negro peasants of Anamat, equality was considered a highly important theme: irrespective of a peasant's actual status in the system, all peasants were considered equal. One peasant thus did not have the power to underwrite risks for another. However, with the Indian peasants, a well-developed and time-honored stratification system placed some Indians above others. Those in higher-ranked positions could underwrite risks for those in lower statuses. Rapport, or willingness to assume given communication risks, thus spreads more easily in stratified sociocultural systems and spreads less easily in equalitarian systems.

Rapport identification. Thus far, rapport has been analyzed as if an explicit agreement or contract is made between an anthropologist and each of his native informants. It seems from the discussion above that such an agreement clearly spells out how many risk units a given native is likely to accept, and what payments he should receive. In actuality, *explicit* agreements are not usually made; yet *implicit* in the encounters which anthropologists have with natives is an agreement by the natives to assume given risk units and to receive given rewards from the anthropologist. After an anthropologist has been in a locality for a month or so, he will have developed agreements with given natives such that these informants could be identified as W-1-1, Y-1-2, or whatever. What is much more difficult to identify are the time conditions and the payment conditions of the agreement.

How is it that the anthropologist, without an explicit agreement, knows how to code his informants in terms of their risk-taking behavior with him (i.e., in terms of his rapport with them)? The anthropologist, by the very nature of his work, is information hungry. As soon as an anthropologist receives some information from a native, he keeps asking for more. The anthropologist is constantly probing for the upper limits of his informants' risk-taking behavior. By such constant probing, a threshold is reached with each informant beyond which it is not easy to go without causing the native some pain. However, when it comes to examining the time base of an agreement or the precise nature of the exchanges which have been set up between anthropologist and native, no such regular experimentation occurs. And it is here that the anthropologist frequently runs into problems. Not understanding the time factor in these agreements or a previous payment condition, or some other condition, he has difficulty in explaining the ups and downs of his rapport with given natives.

Within this model, rapport tests must be made often in the field. By using a risk chart such as the one provided in Figure 9 (it is probably wise to make a different risk chart for each sociocultural system studied), the risks informants assume in relating to the anthropologist can be estimated roughly. Payments can then be made suitable to the risks assumed and in terms of local values assigned to the different types of currencies within the anthropologist's exchange capital. Special informants can be used to identify the nature of risks taken by the average native and to help identify what types of payments are most suitable for given types of natives.

To conclude this discussion, I must make the point that this view of rapport better mirrors field situations and the actual behavior of field workers than does the humanistic model. If that is so, why do many well-respected and extremely able anthropologists cling tightly to the humanistic model? First, the humanistic viewpoint fits in closely with ideas many of us were taught in graduate school. Although we were given very little information concerning field work as an enterprise, somehow what was transmitted was a humanistic approach to the field and to everything related to it. Second, anthropologists can easily be deceived into taking seriously a general role they assume in the field: the role of "nice guy." The "nice guy" anthropologist, while in the field, appears ready to do favors for everyone; he is always interested in everything that is going on, concerned with everyone's welfare, and is rarely angry, upset, or hostile. He is almost goodness personified. The feedback information on playing the "nice guy" role can make it difficult for the anthropologist to accept himself for what he really is: quite a Machiavellian character. He has to be, because "nice guys" do not get data from hostile Rhodesians, tough Mohawks, or suspicious natives anywhere. It may be easier for us to accept the engineering character of our work in the field if we realize that the natives, by and large, are not deceived by our "nice guy" masks, as the following example clearly shows. A biologist from Harvard had spent several months in Anamat prior to my arrival. After I had been in the village for some time, I was told of an interesting debate that the villagers were having: they were arguing over who was "more friendly," the biologist or I. I was later told of the consensus which the Anamatians reached on this question. "Mr. Morris is friendlier, but it has to do with his work."

Third, the humanistic view of rapport is regularly reinforced by a false assumption that many of us take into the field: the *capital poverty assumption*. Those with the humanistic viewpoint believe that all the poor anthropologist has to give the natives in exchange for information is his friendship. This assumption, though clearly incorrect in terms of the above discussion, is an understandable error, for the anthropologist has relative poverty of capital resources rather than absolute poverty. That is, when the anthropologist runs a check on his capital and comes to the conclusion that his total resources usable for exchange equal R, he does not sit back happily. Rather, he compares his actual capital resources R with those the natives think he has $(R + X)$. Such a comparison leads him to think of himself as almost a pauper, for X is often a variable of immense dimensions. The relative poverty of the anthropologist and its possible misrepresentation is well described by Lundberg: "As a person, however, the western field worker is often perceived as symbolizing incredible wealth and power. Knowing of these symbolic properties can lead the researcher to feelings of powerlessness, ignorance and impecuniousness." (1967; footnote 9.)

Those with the humanistic viewpoint have quite clearly discovered part of the truth: Trust, which lies at the base of their views, is related to risk-taking in a special way. The anthropologist who implicitly or explicitly asks the native to trust him is actually making a rather strange request. The anthropologist wants information, and information (as Norman Whitten very well shows[10]) is power over the informants. Obviously, giving someone power over you involves taking risks, for such power could be used for purposes harmful to you. No amount of verbal manipulation can eliminate this kind of risk as the humanistic definition of trust would have us believe. Differently put, the humanists want informants to magically transform objective risks into the subjective nonrisks they call trust. Informants,

---

[10] Norman Whitten's discussions of how an anthropologist becomes central to a rumor-distributing, power-usurping network radiating from himself runs parallel to the discussions presented in this section (see his conclusions to the Ecuador study, pp. 365–367, to the Nova Scotian study, pp. 394–396, and at the end of his chapter, pp. 396–402.

although often uneducated by formal standards, are rarely stupid by any adequate standard; therefore, they resist being manipulated in this manner. Such resistance is described by the anthropologist as "rapport development problems." If we accept that objective risks cannot be erased by word magic, what really is the meaning of trust? I believe that the word "trust" describes the history of previous transactions which involve risk-taking where the risk-taker received c.n.p. This historical summary is captured in the concept of trust after it has been subjected to coding based on questions such as: What size risks were previously taken? What harmful effects followed such risk-taking—anxiety, gossip, movement of information to "wrong" sources, etc.? What positive effects followed such previous risk-taking behavior—development of friendship, materialistic gains, etc.? Was there a "subjective" net gain or net loss with respect to past risks taken and their costs and rewards? How large was the communications net profit? The trust which N has in A is the sum of a series of bookkeeping entries, balanced for a particular time period and providing predictive information for future transactions. The humanists want trust because they assume that trust *is* rapport. All anthropologists should want trust, since it will probably lead to more rapport: the readiness to take greater risks, to assume more risk units with the anthropologist. However, the mere existence of trust does not mean that rapport will necessarily develop, for the trust may not be great enough: the net profit for risks assumed may be too low to make future interactions profitable. The mere existence of some trust does not ensure rapport. Further, the absence of trust does not necessarily mean the absence of rapport.

In the early days of field work, many informants had no interactional history with the anthropologist, and no transactional credits existed in his account; therefore, relationships with him could not be based on trust. However, relationships develop despite this. At this time the anthropologist's rapport (or the willingness of natives to take risks with him) is based on his image: the community's underwriting of risks which some members may take. Since some rapport can exist in the absence of trust, and since the presence of some trust does not necessarily lead to rapport, it is correct to say that trust is neither a necessary nor a sufficient cause for rapport. How then have the humanists discovered part of the truth in relating rapport to trust? While rapport may exist without trust, any given situation can be described in terms of three related propositions which relate trust (credit balances for previous risky transactions) and rapport (readiness to assume a given number of risk units). First, if N has some trust in A, then A probably has some rapport with N. Second, the more trust N has in A, the more likely it is that N will give A rapport. Finally, the more trust N has in A, the more rapport N is likely to give A.

The Machiavellian engineer of situations and people (i.e., the anthropologist) is not always in the role of research participant-observer. In situations like the work-break game, the anthropologist slides into the role of make-believe native, and at such times he can accomplish little engineering. Further, at times the work-break game ends with the anthropologist temporarily going native, and while in the role of temporary native, engineering strategies are completely given up. In brief, during such times the risk-taking aspects of informational exchanges are covered by the friendliness of the atmosphere. In these kinds of situations, most of the people present try to act *as if* informational exchanges with the anthropologist carried no risks. At such times, therefore, the engineering view of rapport must be combined with the humanistic view. However, it should be noted that the total time than an anthropologist is in some kind of human participant-observer role is relatively small when compared to the total time spent in the field. Therefore, it is the engineering approach to rapport, rather than the humanistic one, with which the anthropologist should be most concerned. In terms of this engineering viewpoint, it is necessary to consider three things: (1) informant behavior involves risk taking; (2) risk-takers can be encouraged to take ever greater risks with the anthropologist; and (3) such "encouragement" comes from the rewards the anthropologist can provide, in terms of the exchange capital brought into the field.

Problem 13: Active Research

When a meaningful, researchable problem has been isolated, and enough rapport exists for the anthropologist to reasonably predict that he will obtain a valid answer, the active research period has begun. Active research involves a variety of related activities, including census-taking, collecting genealogies, administering questionnaires, and giving projective tests. In most research sites census-taking quickly and simply provides the anthropologist with considerable information about the research community, and it provides him with an excuse to meet informants in relatively relaxed conditions. While in their homes, he can invite them to visit his home; he can observe interactions among family members and other intimate details; and he can get a general idea of the types of furnishings and possessions the natives have and how they use them.

Taking a census may require the assistance of a group of

helpers who may have to be taught how to do this work. In Livingston, Nancie González trained three young men to assist her, and among the Oshogbo, William Schwab created a "research organization" that required considerable planning to operate. Although Schwab encountered few problems in running his research team, the inexperienced researcher should be wary of setting up large research teams in the field, for such work requires talents over and above those generally specified for anthropological researchers. Teaching field assistants how to collect data, what data to collect, and checking their work regularly is a time-consuming task requiring patience and tact. Keeping these assistants happy and motivated is a highly sensitive job.

Census-taking is often followed by the collection of kinship information. This work, generally referred to as the genealogical method, selects a given individual (called "Ego") as a reference point and then attempts to relate Ego to a whole variety of consanguineal (blood) and affinal (in-law) kin. By using the genealogical method, the anthropologist obtains data on actual kinship behavior that will permit him to develop the mechanical models that isolate the rules of the system.

The life-history method is also useful in discovering what people do and why they do it. In addition it helps the anthropologist get a good picture of the various types of people in a given system. He gets a perspective on his data and an in-depth view of real people with understandable life styles and personalities who are solving the problems with which their system presents them and dealing with the historical accidents that help shape their lives.

Researchers interested in obtaining data on the psychological states of informants can also collect dreams, administer such standarized tests as the Rorschach test and the Thematic Apperception Test, and give their own field-developed tests, as Maxwell did in Pango Pango.

1. Interviewing. Formal interview approaches are becoming ever more important for anthropological research. They form the foundation of the exciting and valuable new development in anthropological research called "ethnoscience" or the "new ethnography." It is fitting, therefore, to discuss the formal interview from the viewpoint of sociologists, who have made it a critical part of their data-collection procedures, but with special attention to the procedures best suited to anthropological research.

Richardson, *et al.* (1965) distinguish three main types of interviews: the schedule-standardized interview, the nonschedule-standardized interview, and the nonstandardized interview.

The standardized interview is a data-collection strategy in which the same type of information is collected from all respondents. On the nonstandardized interview, however, the interviewer has considerable leeway in what types of information to collect, and the informant is given considerable freedom as to what he discusses. According to Richardson, *et al.* strictly comparable data often is best obtained by use of the schedule-standardized interview:

> To judge by current practices, most investigators believe that standardization is most effectively achieved with the schedule-standardized interview. In this form, the interviewer asks each question in its prescribed sequence and records the response on the schedule—either verbatim or in special precoded spaces. If the respondent does not hear or understand the question, the interviewer is generally instructed to repeat the question without rephrasing it. Because the interviewer's task is to read a set of questions and record the responses, his behavior from one interview to another is partly standardized. His introduction and his statement of purpose are also usually prescribed in detail in order to provide further standardization. (1965:36–37.)

The schedule-standardized interview includes the following four assumptions:

> [That] (1) in any study, the respondents have a sufficiently common vocabulary so that it is possible to formulate questions which have the same meaning for them. . . . [That] (2) a uniform wording for all respondents can be found for any subject matter. . . . [That] (3) if the meaning of each question is to be identical for each respondent, its context must be identical and, since all preceding questions constitute part of its context, the sequence of the questions must be identical. . . . [And that] (4) careful pilot investigations, development and pretesting . . . provide a final schedule of questions that meets the requirements of assumptions (1), (2), and (3). (1965:40–44.)

These assumptions, according to Richardson, are justified "where the respondents have similar personal characteristics—such as education, intelligence, and place of residence—and questionable when the respondents are heterogeneous in the backgrounds and personal characteristics, unless the subject matter is common to all." (1965:44.) Unless *considerable* information exists on the group being studied, the use of the schedule-standardized interview (SSI) is *not justified.*

What is the meaning of the "standardization" most effectively achieved with the schedule-standardized interview? Clearly, it does not mean that similar stimuli are received by all respondents. It means, rather, that attempts are made to program all interviewers to do the same things in an interview.

This interesting conclusion is implicit in a statement by Richardson, *et al.*, about the differences between the schedule-standardized interview and the nonschedule-standardized interview:

> The schedule-standarized interview asks the same questions of each respondent and hopes this will have the same meaning, whereas the nonschedule-standardized interviewer formulates the classes of information he is seeking and hopes he can formulate the questions in such a way that they will have the same meaning for each respondent. (1965:45.)

For most research situations, and especially for cross-cultural research, the schedule-standardized interview has too many problems for effective research if used as *the* major data-collection tool. The nonschedule-standardized interview, on the other hand, is very much in line with anthropological thinking about data collection, as Richardson *et al.*, point out:

> (1) If the meaning of a question is to be standardized, the question must be formulated in words familiar to and habitually used by each respondent. . . . (2) No fixed sequence of questions is satisfactory to all respondents; the most effective sequence for any respondent is determined by his readiness and willingness to take up a topic as it comes up. . . . (3) Through careful study of respondents and selection and training of interviewers, the necessary skills can be achieved to tailor the questions and their sequence so that equivalence of meaning is obtained for all respondents. (1965:46–51.)

The assumptions of the nonschedule-standardized interview coincide with several basic assumptions of anthropological research. First, anthropologists assume that for some data it will be necessary to ask informants the same *kind of question* in order to receive the same class of answers from the whole sample. Second, they assume that the question must be framed in words familiar to and commonly used by informants; thus, before questioning, considerable participant-observation research must be done. Third, they assume that data collectors must be people who—because of past experiences and training, and special training for the current project—can be trusted to make critical judgments in a data-collecting encounter. Fourth, they assume that assistants with inadequate backgrounds in social science must be carefully and regularly coached and supervised by a trained social scientist. Fifth, they assume that the relationship between data collector (researcher) and data giver (informant, respondent) is a critical factor strongly influencing the receiving of valid information. Thus the "readiness and willingness (of an informant) to take up a topic as it comes up" is a critical factor in obtaining valid data. And, sixth, they assume that reciprocity—making the respondent or informant feel good and think it worth his while to give valid information—must somehow be built into the "exchange of information encounters" we call interviews.

One of the prerequisites for the standardized interview is a specification of all items of information sought, before the actual interview. This prerequisite is not required for the nonstandardized interview. The nonstandardized interview thus can be used at all stages of a research project: during its conceptualization when attempts are being made to set boundaries on the types of data that will be collected and near the conclusion when checks may be required on the validity of given types of information already received. It is possible, moreover, to maximize the use of the native as an "informant": someone who has information (some of which may be highly specialized) to provide the researcher, who wants to provide that information, and who, in communicating with the researcher, is also developing some kind of personal relationship with him. In exchange for a degree of involvement in the project, the researcher treats the informant as a junior partner whose view of the project, its goals, and methods are important, rather than as a "respondent," someone who can be programmed to respond to given stimuli, presented in a pre-established way and given in a set order. The informant is asked to help with information about matters with which he is something of an expert; the respondent is used to fill in blank spaces of a certain dimension on a schedule.

The completely open nonstandardized interview, one where anything the informant wishes to communicate gets discussed, can be tightened or slightly structured as the dimensions of the research become clearer and as the problem becomes refined. This can be done by using what Merton and Kendall have called a focused interview: an interview in which questions as such are unspecified, but where the interview is focused on attaining a limited amount of information within specified sociocultural domains.

To more clearly distinguish the focused interview from the nonschedule-standardized interview, I would redefine the focused interview as an encounter with an informant in which the researcher focuses on only one major question and guides the informants' discussions so that they do not wander far from the boundaries set for the quesion. Defined in this manner, the focused interview becomes a subcategory of the nonschedule-standardized interview: a degree of standardization is set by the focus, but, since the focus is only on one subject, the interviewer has considerable leeway in his handling of the interview.

Thus, the focused interview also becomes a sort of midpoint between the nonstandardized interview and the nonschedule-standardized interview.

The utility of the focused interview for anthropological research is considerable, for it allows the anthropologist to get an in-depth understanding of local culture, operational rules, and speculative guides, as well as behavioral patterns, subject by subject. Further, the focused interview facilitates making connections among the various subareas of a system. For example, at a given time the anthropologist may perhaps be focusing his interviews on the question: "What is the proper way to get a wife here?" While allowing the informant considerable freedom to discuss matters of interest to him, the anthropologist guides the interview toward this topic. The somewhat loose structure of the interview will permit the informant to discuss areas which, to the anthropologist, may not appear to be directly related to the subject of marriage, but which in reality are. The focused, one-subject interview can be modified to permit the researcher to dispense with recording instruments (should such a procedure be considered wise). The informal focused interview—conducted as a kind of ordinary conversation—can often gather bits of information not obtainable when the researcher is recording every word of the informant's communication. By limiting himself to one subject in the informal focused interview, the anthropologist facilitates the actual recording procedure used here: his memory.

The focused interview, a one-subject interview where recording instruments are used in the presence of informants, is thus distinguishable from the informal focused interview, a one-subject interview carried on in conversational style without recording instruments. The distinction between recording in front of the informant and recording after the interview has been completed is usefully extended to the nonstandardized interview. That is, an informant can be "interviewed" without the use of paper and pencil and other recording tools and allowed maximal freedom to wander from subject to subject. This *"conversational interview"* has one major drawback: it is difficult to remember all the information provided by an informant. The novice will find it useful to use various mnemonic devices to aid in reconstructing a conversational interview.

The conversational interview and the informal focused interview (Ifi) are data-gathering approaches usable in many settings where the researcher is a participant-observer. Both types can be considered "informal" data-gathering methods, with the conversational interview being informal and unstructured and the informal focused interview being informal and weakly structured. The more information the researcher has on the system being researched, the more it becomes reasonable to structure interviews. The more rapport the researcher gains with his informants, the more likely it is that information that is formally collected (i.e., via a formal interview, where recording instruments are clearly visible) will be valid. Thus, the type of interview that is done at a given stage of research is closely connected with both the rapport level of the researcher and the extent of his knowledge of the system being researched.

In some research situations the researcher might follow a sequence of interview types: (1) the conversational interview; (2) the informal focused interview; (3) the unstructured interview; (4) the focused interview; (5) the nonschedule-standardized interview, and (6) the schedule-standardized interview. This helps him to stay away from formal interviewing until much information on the system has been collected in other ways. Further, it gives him time to develop enough rapport with informants to make formal interviewing meaningful. Finally, this sequence builds up to an efficient data-collecting strategy—the schedule-standardized interview, which is effective if, and only if, the researcher has considerable information on the system being studied. This strategy—holding off from formal interviewing as long as possible—does include a problem; to wit, legitimization of the role researcher. Informants become suspicious when much time passes and the anthropologist continues to "do nothing"; he does not write things down. Some kind of formal work is thus useful early in the research to send the community or tribe the message; "I am really an anthropologist. See, I am working at my trade by writing down things you tell me, and asking you questions about your society."

In some situations, it may be useful to develop various complex interviews: interviews made up of two or more of the types described above. For example, an encounter with an informant may begin as a conversational interview and develop into an informal focused interview, or a complex interview may use certain aspects of the schedule-standardized interview together with some very general questions which allow the informant to "wander around" various topics in the manner of the unstructured interview. The interviewing sequence discussed above is based on the assumption that the less the researcher knows about the subjects being researched, the fewer are the premises and expectations that should be built into the interview situation.

2. Premises and expectations. It is almost impossible to formulate a question that in some way is not connected to and de-

Figure 10 A Typology of Questions

NATURE OF INFORMATION ON WHICH PREMISES ARE BASED	STRENGTH OF PREMISE HELD BY RESEARCHER	
	"STRONG"	"WEAK"
INADEQUATE	*Acultural*	*Probing*
ADEQUATE	*Leading*	*Directing*

pendent on a premise. The premise or assumptional base of the question may be relevant or irrelevant to the question posed. If the question involves a number of premises, some of them may be true and relevant, others true and irrelevant, and others simply false. For example, walking around Anamat, Trinidad, in the early afternoon during a cocoa harvest, I noticed a group of peasants waiting for a "taxi." Our conversaiton went something like this:

MF: "Hi, what's happening?"
Peasant A: "We're off to Arima."
MF: "How come?"
Peasant B: "A's friend is having a féte-for-só today."
(A car pulls up and the peasants get into it.)
MF: "Why are you going to a féte (party; féte-for-só, is a big party) today?"
Peasant C: "Now-for-now, man!"

The car goes off and MF is left in a temporary state of puzzlement.

My first question to the group communicated my surprise that these men were leaving the village and their fields, in the midst of a busy cocoa-harvesting period. My surprise was based on the correct premise that this was a busy time for the peasants, and the premise was relevant to the situation as described: peasants do not usually leave their fields during harvest times unless something very important comes up. My expectation, however, was based on *inadequate information* concerning local culture: I did not understand that a big féte was a "good reason."

As a rule-of-thumb, if the interviewer is unable to categorize his questions according to the rules presented in Figure 10, then it is clear that he does not have enough information on the system to do more than informal focused interviewing. At this time, then, it is wise (1) to use participant-observation as the major data-collection device, (2) to periodically utilize such relatively unstructured interview methods as the informal-focused interview, and (3) to use special or key informants to help him understand the premises and expectations which are proper in terms of the questions the researcher has decided he wishes to ask.

The interview, almost irrespective of its type, appears to have an Achilles heel: the premises and expectations which lie behind many of the questions posed. The consequences of this drawback can be rendered less serious if, before developing any type of interview, the anthropologist asks himself the following questions: (1) What premise or premises guide my questions? (2) What expectations are included in a given question, and are they based on *enough* information on the system being studied to present the question in this form? (3) How strong is my real attachment to these expectations? (4) How can I facilitate the process of clearing my mind (temporarily) of the premises on which my culture of orientation is based?

3. Participation and observation for active research. Participant-observation research, while a main mode of data collecting in the passive-research stage, is but a subsidiary strategy during the active-research period. Once a problem has been clearly identified, and once a battery of interviewing approaches has been developed, the participant-observer role appears almost unnecessary. This, in reality, is not so, for at least four separate reasons.

First, all data collecting requires the researcher to have rapport with the natives; natives must be willing to take risks with the anthropologist. The continued playing of the participant-observer role facilitates rapport maintenance and leads to rapport increases (i.e., increases in the number of risk units an informant is willing to take).

Second, the participant-observer role, even in bull sessions, permits the anthropologist to check on information previously collected in more formal encounters. Respondents (natives who will interact with the anthropologist only in formal situations and with whom he has little rapport), informants, and even friends-in-the-field will, at times, lie to the researcher concerning matters which may be crtical to his research problem. The reasons for such lies may be *personal* (the data-giver wishes to appear wiser, or of higher status, or richer than he actually is), *social* (pressure from the "audience" present in an encounter with the anthropologist), or *cultural* (certain information is not given truthfully in that sociocultural system). False information means that the researcher is being misled as to the nature of the system he is studying. It is wise, therefore, to use the participant-observer role as a data-checking device. Assuming that lies will get into the anthropologist's notebook, irrespective of the level of rapport he achieves, and assuming that it is often very difficult to tell what information is false and what is valid, checks via the participant-observer role are of great value to the project as a whole. The researcher who has systematically planned his participant-observation work during the active research period so that he is able to check on a wide variety of information presented to him through other research techniques, can then return to more formal interviewing in a more aggressive manner. Answers to questions presented which appear false can be *debated* with the informant. Put another way, the more data the anthropologist gets by participant-observation, the more he can debate where he might previously have thought of probing.[11]

Third, some data exist in all social systems that are not obtainable (or not easily obtainable) with methods other than participant-observation. It is rarely possible to get a complete and accurate description of a religious ritual, for example, just by interviewing an informant. Invariably, bits of information are left out by the informant for a variety of reasons: (1) they represent phenomena which the informant thinks "everyone knows" and therefore not worthy of discussion, (2) they represent matters so deeply rooted in the ritual and so often seen by the informant that he actually does not recall them, (3) they relate to things considered too "holy," "personal," or "sensitive" to be discussed, and (4) they relate to matters which the informant cannot discuss, for their discussion presupposes theoretical or methodological skills the informant lacks.

It is foolish to ask an informant to reproduce a given situation by answering such questions as: (1) Who was the instrumental leader of the group? (2) Who was the socioemotional leader? (3) Who most often made statements that created tension? (4) Who most often made statements that evoked opinions from others present? These and related questions can be answered only by someone who has been trained to use Robert Bales's "interaction-process analysis" model (1950). With respect to a variety of problems relating to decision making, interaction-process analysis can be a valuable data-gathering technique for the anthropologist. This kind of work requires the

---

[11] The difference between probing and debating is shown in Perlman's analysis of his fieldwork in Uganda. In his *debates* with his informants he often pointed out inconsistencies in the information they provided.

researcher to reproduce an interactional setting in terms of Bales's categories.[12]

It should be noted that the use of the participant-observer role for such highly specialized data-gathering activities as Bales's interaction-process analysis is predicated on the fact that the anthropologist is in a role conducive to this kind of work. For example, the participant-observer anthropologist who wishes to use Bales's system in an interactional setting (say a village council meeting) must have enough rapport with the group to be able to enter with a large chart and many pencils. He must be given permission to sit through the meeting without participating vocally. His time is completely taken in registering on his chart: (1) the category of statements made; (2) who makes them; and (3) to whom each statement is addressed. Further, this kind of categorization requires a good knowledge of the sociocultural system being investigated and an ability to recognize and name each speaker. Bales's interactional-process analysis can be done only by an anthropologist in the role of marginal native: a role with less rapport would not permit the researcher entry into this situation with his chart and pencils, and a role which includes greater intimacy between researcher and informants would not allow the researcher to use symbols of research.

In brief, obtaining novel data in the role of participant-observer is often possible only if a given subsidiary role (say "marginal native") "belongs" to the anthropologist. It should be quite clear, therefore, that all the logically possible ways of playing participant-observer are not empirically possible. Each role both facilitates certain kinds of behaviors (and their concomitant information-getting possibilities) and makes other kinds of behaviors either impossible or incongruous to the role being played.

---

[12] Sociological researchers can often hire people trained in the Bales system; thus, the sociologist may be able to obtain these kind of data without himself being either a participant-observer or an observer. The anthropologist, however, will generally be unable to hire people to do this kind of work; should the project require very specific data on interactions in small groups, it would be wise for the researcher to make himself expert in gathering these kinds of data. Brief descriptions of Bales's interaction-process analysis can be found in *The Small Group* by Michael S. Olmtead (Random House, New York, 1959), in *Human Groups* by W. J. H. Sprott (Penguin Books, Baltimore, 1958) and in many introductory sociology texts. More complete discussions are found in: Robert F. Bales, *Interaction Process Analysis: A Method for the Study of Small Groups*, Reading, Mass.: Addison-Wesley, 1950, and (for those interested in in-depth discussions of research strategies with small groups), A. Paul Hare, Edgar F. Borgotta and Robert F. Bales, *Small Groups: Studies in Social Interaction*, New York: Knopf, 1955.

Finally, the continued playing of the participant-observer role during the active research period helps the anthropologist to isolate community members who appear to be equipped (in terms of information and time) to assume the role of special or key informant. The use of key informants in anthropological research is both traditional and highly effective for many data-gathering situations. In most field-work situations, the anthropologist faces the problem of finding key informants. It is true that some key informants find the anthropologist rather than being found by them, but such self-selected informants are often marginal men in their system, and the information they possess may be marginal to the anthropologist's interests. Conservatively, I would generalize that *some* key informants must be found by the anthropologist, and a continued use of the participant-observer role facilitates finding them. Discovering key informants in participant-observation situations yields important data not generally discussed in key-informant writings.

In sum, participation and observation remains an important data-gathering technique in active research, since it (1) maintains and/or increases the anthropologist's rapport; (2) provides checks on data collected in other ways; (3) provides novel data not otherwise collectable; and (4) helps to isolate and to type key informants.

4. Biases in field work. One of the major strengths of anthropological field work—the fact that a trained researcher lives with a group, and uses his knowledge, personality, and sensitivity for data-collection purposes—is also a source of major problems in data evaluation: *bias.*

a. Observer bias. Julian Simon, a nonanthropologist, provides us with an objective summary of what observer bias has meant in the history of anthropological field work (1968:88):

> Anthropology has suffered worst and longest from observer bias. Modern anthropologists regard most early anthropological accounts by sea captains and missionaries as almost useless, simply because the authors' perceptions were so warped by their cultural background. Their bias was often that all non-Europeans were heathen, savage, and without law or social organization.

Anthropological field training has, as yet, not managed to rid us of observer biases; indeed an unbiased observer may well be an "uncreatable" phenomenon. Although anthropologists must live with the fact of bias, it is possible to compensate for distortions by understanding the nature and consequences of bias.

Scientific field work must isolate the sources of bias. Among the sources of bias that will be briefly discussed here are culture, personality, visual-memory, and model-use. It is true that the old cultural bias against natives (i.e., that they are savage, etc.) distorted reality, but it is equally true that a new cultural bias in favor of native culture similarly presents an unreal picture of native sociocultural systems. Some anthropologists believe that all cultures are equal, some cultures are more equal (primitive, non-Western, etc.), and some cultures are less equal (the culture of the researcher). This kind of belief system not only distorts native reality by making almost everything appear "good," but develops rationalizations not conducive to scientific development in anthropology. One form such rationalizations take is an overly strong attachment to functional analysis. Once a given sociocultural complex is defined as good, then analyses which show how "the good" functions to maintain the system in equilibrium appears to represent proof of such goodness. Within this framework, anthropologists have been slow in asking such questions as, What conflicts are built into the system being investigated? Is the adaptation here achieved a maximal one, in terms of the goals of the natives? Is the system set up so that some kind of transactional justice is given to the native?

The biases which stem from the personality of the researcher are many and include the selection of a given type of community to study, the selection of given types of community centers for close and frequent observation, and the selection of given types of natives as key informants. Many generalizations concerning the behavior of natives in a given culture, say C, stem from one or two studies of given subgroups of that culture (one or two communities, bands, tribes, communal settlements, etc.). We are then told that the marriage pattern for culture C is m, its settlement pattern is s, and so forth. We are rarely told how representative the group studied is for the total population covered by the term "people of culture C." This information was not provided because generally anthropologists have not done survey research to identify the "universe" in which their research lies. Now, while careful sampling is frequently not practical in anthropological research, it is both practically possible and vital for a good understanding of the data being provided to be told how a particular group was selected for research. It is also important to know something of the personality of the selector: the anthropologist. It should now be simply a matter of good ethnographic procedure to introduce a monograph by a personal history and an honest attempt to present oneself in one's "true colors." An excellent model for such descriptions is Hortense Powdermaker's self-analysis in *Stranger and Friend*.

Once the ethnographer has made clear what type of person

is doing participant-observation research, who is interviewing in various modes, and who is regularly the middle man between reality and ethnography, it is important that he specify the types of informants he was able to attract, in part because of his personality. For each informant not only has differential *amounts* of information to provide the ethnographer (i.e., some informants are more expert on a given subject than others) but he has information of different *types* to provide. Once the informants have been identified by type it is also necessary to describe the relationships which existed between informants and researcher. The myth that good field work implies almost a "love affair" between the anthropologist and his tribe has been completely shattered by the publication of Malinowski's diaries.

How does an anthropologist manage to keep his personality from influencing the sites he selects to observe? Clearly, his personality is a critical variable in such cases where he freely chooses to be at a given center at a given time. For example, while some Anamatians were playing cricket, others were standing around the Junction talking. The fact that I almost invariably ended up in the cricket game says something about me as a person; it also means that I have more data relating to some kinds of interactions (formal games) than others (small-group communications). This ethnographic bias must somehow be accounted for.

Once at a given site for observational and participational work, the researcher's personality is likely to influence reality in terms of at least two kinds of distortions. If the anthropologist is somewhat reserved and sends messages to the natives present far less frequently than normal for that kind of encounter, he may create a *guinea-pig effect:* the people present may feel that they are being put "on stage" to be observed. In such situations, the natives may well provide the anthropologist with a performance, with behavior that is completely atypical. The anthropologist who is outgoing, and extroverted creates a *busy-stranger effect*. Here normal communications and interactions are disrupted by the ethnographer's monopolization of communication channels.

Visual and memory biases are probably related to personality but are more simply treated as separate variables leading to distortions of reality. For a variety of reasons, the researcher may expect to see X, actually be in the presence of Y, and still "see" X.

Visual biases obviously lead to memory distortions: the "wrong" thing is seen; therefore the "right" thing cannot be remembered. Memory distortions exist even when the researcher sees the reality, since various kinds of data (1) are differentially related to the core problem being investigated, (2) have differential emotional meaning to the viewer, and (3) are either immediately recorded, recorded a short time after being observed, or recorded a long time after being observed. When it is not possible to record information immediately, the researcher should be wary not to "forget" data that seem to contradict the aesthetic model he has built to explain the system being investigated. To facilitate the remembering of awkward data, it is important that the researcher make an attempt to state clearly what his hypotheses are concerning the phenomena being researched.

b. Informant bias. Informants provide invalid information for reasons very similar to those that lead to biases in the ethnographer's observations and recordings. That is, informants "see" and "remember" incorrectly for cultural, personality, visual, and memory reasons, and in addition they help to distort an ethnography by providing some data which they knowingly understand to be false. It is not useful to go through each type of distortion an informant (in all honesty) creates, but it is necessary to comment on distortions which may occur because of the researcher's inadequate understanding of differences among his informants.

It is fairly well understood that informants need to be typed, and their information needs to be evaluated, in terms of a number of basic social variables: age and sex, class or caste, race, culture, religion, and their marginality or centrality to the system under study. Not so well understood is the notion that informants must also be distinguished in terms of their life-styles: their typical problem-solving strategies. Three informants may be the same in all the social and demographic variables identified (above) and yet be providing very different kinds of data due to differences in life-styles. One informant (a traditionalist, or *T*) generally follows cultural rules and/or cultural guides. The information the *T*-informant provides is best considered as answers to questions like, What is the proper way to . . . ? The second informant (an operator, or *O*) generally follows operational rules and/or private guides. The information the *O*-informant provides is best considered as answers to questions like, What is the smart way (probably) to . . . ? Finally, the third informant (a speculator, or *S*) follows rules previously described as "suspicions," and/or "rumors." The information the *S*-informant provides is best considered as answers to questions like, What is the smart way (possibly) to . . . ? These three types of informants live in three different subsystems of the sociocultural system being investigated, and the information they provide (coming as it does from three separate systems) cannot be just "added together." Further, when these informants are asked questions of a statistical nature, they will again very likely provide answers that sharply differ.

The anthropologist who works with a few key informants who are very similar in life-style is biasing his data toward one subsystem—perhaps not the most important one—of the society being studied. The situation is even more complex than yet described, for the *V-R* Guidance System includes two propositions: (1) Members of a system are defined as *rational* if they attempt to solve their problems *first* by means of their dominant problem-solving strategy, and if this strategy does not work, by another strategy; (2) Members of the system are defined as irrational if they stay with one problem-solving strategy, despite its failure to solve problems in everyday living.

Of the three basic types of informants that have been identified (*T, O,* and *S*), each may be of two subtypes: irrational (*Ti, Oi, Si*), and rational (*Tr, Or, Sr*). Rational informants are each analyzable respectively in terms of two possible problem-solving strategies: the *Tr* as *TOS* or *TSO;* the *Or* as *OTS* or *OST;* and the *Sr* as *SOT* or *STO.* Thus nine types of informants are identifiable from within this framework.[13] All the types which are *logically* possible, may have no existential referents in a given society. However, it is suggested that ethnographers might usefully consider the life-styles, or problem-solving strategies, of their informants in ways not unlike the model here presented. (See Figure 11.)

5. What to sample: people or information. The discussion of types of informants found in the field is related to two concerns of many anthropologists: (1) How are respondents, general informants, and key informants selected? (2) How many informants does a given researcher need? As anthropology develops scientific rigor in its methodology, it must increasingly pay

---

[13] In other words, given a problem *p*, the irrational traditionalist (*Ti*) will continue using traditional solutions even after it is apparent to any rational native that these kinds of solutions will not solve *p*. Similarly, the irrational operator (*Oi*) and the irrational speculator (*Si*) will continue using their problem-solving strategies even though such strategies do not help the situation.

The rational problem solvers of the system will start with their dominant problem-solving strategy and after finding that it provides no adequate solution will shift to another strategy. For example, the *TOS* will start with traditional approaches, then go on to use operational rules (i.e., try the solution-strategies of operators), and finally try speculative approaches (i.e., try the solution-strategies of speculators). The *TSO* will also begin with traditional approaches; however, when these fail he will first switch to speculative strategies, and finally to the use of operational rules. Similarly, the rational operator (*Or*), and the rational speculator (*Sr*), each has two possible solution-sequences to follow: the *Or, OTS,* and *OST;* the *Sr, SOT,* and *STO.*

attention to questions such as, "How representative was your sample?," and "What type of people were your key informants?" These kinds of questions, according to some scholars, have a simple and satisfactory answer: In anthropological research, the universe to sample is not people (respondents, general informants, key informants), but *information*.

This seductively simple answer is on closer examination neither seductive, simple, nor, indeed, an "answer." First, how is it possible to sample information in anthropological research? To sample means "to take a smaller representation of the larger whole," and in order to do this "the whole" must be known. But when the anthropologist is sampling information, he does not know the whole: he is still struggling to understand the sociocultural system he is studying. What kind of sampling is possible here? Now the sampling of people is a relatively simple procedure; unlike information, people do not have to be "known" for sampling purposes. It is simply necessary to be able to identify them as members of the village, tribe, or settlement being researched to arrive at some adequate sampling procedure. Put another way, no simple procedure exists for the anthropologist to use in identifying the experts who have the type of information required to fill gaps in his data. For (1) What is an informational gap? (2) What kinds of data best fill it? and (3) Who can best provide such data? are all questions which cannot be answered until a good deal of research has been completed.

Second, the well-informed informant approach to ethnogra-

Figure 11   Types of Informants

BASIC TYPES	TRADITIONALIST T	OPERATOR O	SPECULATOR S
GENERAL TYPES	*Ti/Tr*	*Oi/Or*	*Si/Sr*
IRRATIONAL RATIONAL	*Ti* *Tr*	*Oi* *Or*	*Si* *Sr*
RATIONAL SUBTYPES	*TOS* *TSO*	*OST* *OTS*	*SOT* *STO*

phy assumes a simplistic field situation where culture "rules";
I believe that the *V-R* Guidance System (with its six interrelated subsystems) better mirrors the activities that make up
reality. Each of the six boxes can be thought of as inhabited
by a type of informant with a life-style somewhat different
from those living in the other boxes. For the sake of simplicity,
I assumed (above) that only three basic types of informants
need to be indentified: *T*-informants (traditionalists), *O*-in-
formants (operators), and *S*-informants (speculators). By typing these informants according to their "rationality" (their
readiness to use a secondary and tertiary problem-solving strategy), or their "irrationality" (their rigid attachment to only
their primary problem-solving strategy), nine types of informants were identified. Each of these nine types "sees" his sociocultural reality differently. A well-informed informant approach
to ethnography, it seems reasonable to suggest, should attempt
to get at least one of each type of native as an informant. How
is this to be done without a good prior knowledge of the system?
Perhaps in a given society *S*, all of these nine logical types do
not exist, so the anthropologist who keeps looking for them will
be on a wild-goose chase. A random sampling of people in *S*,
however, will probably help in identifying the various types of
strategies used for problem-solving. That is, one can start with
the assumption that random sampling will pick up at least one
of every type of strategist that exists in the system. Is *the*
answer, then, that we should sample people not information?
I do not think so, for it seems quite clear now that we have to
do both. A sampling of people will help identify the kinds of
people who exist in a system, but some of the natives so identified will not be useful as informants or not available for this
type of work. For example, while a *TOS*-strategist may have
been identified by people-sampling and conversational interviewing, this informant may not know enough about subjects where
TOS-strategies are considered important in society *S*, or having
such knowledge, he may not wish to spend much time with the
anthropologist. At this point, it seems reasonable to search for
a *TOS*-informant; to sample information, that is, rather than
people.

In brief, the sampling of people versus the sampling of
information is a false dichotomy; it is necessary for the anthropologist to do both. People-sampling helps in later information-sampling, which may have to be followed by yet more
people-sampling in order to obtain information, as Pearsall says,
on the "pervasiveness, range of variation, and typicality of the
various beliefs and practices." (1965:40.) In other words, al-

though some information-sampling may be necessary, people-sampling must be done to pick up the information that will lead to the construction of statistical models.[14]

Anthropologists, traditionally, have worked with small populations and their studies generally included "everyone"; therefore they have often considered sampling unnecessary. The advice "sample people and information," if followed, may get more anthropologists interested in doing sampling, even if (from a purely methodological point of view) they really don't have to. Stated differently, why should we work with everyone and collect such large amounts of data in each field trip, if the same or even superior results might be achieved by use of a sample? In the words of Goode and Hatt (1952:209), "sampling allows for more adequate scientific work by making the time of the scientific worker count. Instead of spending many hours over the analysis of a mass of material from one point of view, he may use that time to examine a smaller amount of material from many points of view . . . to do a more intensive analysis of fewer cases."

Goode and Hatt talking in terms of sociological research—where senior researchers are often not very involved in data-collection—stress the time saved in data analysis by using sampling procedures. For the anthropologist, however, the time saved includes time in data-collection also, and such time saved can be put to good use. The traditional anthropological fear in field work "I'll never have time to finish," is thus likely to become as outmoded as the semitrained field worker, sent off to "sink or swim."

Researchers may use three sampling techniques: *random sampling, stratified sampling,* or *purposive sampling.* A random sample is used when the researcher lacks a good knowledge of his universe. His best bet here is to let chance decide for him what specific units will be part of the sample. To do this the units of the universe (1) must have a very concrete description, and (2) must be selected by some process that gives "equiprobability of selection to every unit in that universe." (Goode and Hatt, *ibid.:* 214). Once the universe is known and concretely identified, the actual mechanics of the selection process are quite simple. The field worker can just number his units on paper slips, fold them, and throw them into a hat. Since it may well be the case that the population studied does not understand why they were "picked" for a given set

---

[14] My conclusion is supported by Mitchell, who writes: "The starting point in sampling for most statistical work in social anthropology must usually be the individual." (1967:33.)

of interviews, it might be useful to make a ritual out of this selection-by-chance process. Depending on the situation, a headman, shaman, or chief might be asked to pick the bits of paper out of a hat and publicly announce the lucky winners of this game called random sampling.

Stratified sampling assumes considerable knowledge of the universe, particularly the important *strata* therein. Each strata is considered as a subunit that must itself be sampled. For example, if the universe is made up of a disproportionate number of boys and girls aged nine and ten, and if sex and age are considered important in the problem being studied, this universe would be considered as made up of four strata: nine-year-old boys, nine-year-old girls, ten-year-old boys, and ten-year-old girls. Stratified sampling would require that a representative number of *each strata* be included in the final sample.

Purposive sampling is a technique that provides considerable freedom to the interviewer as to who should be in the sample. It is assumed here that a basic knowledge exists of significant characteristics of the universe being sampled with respect to the problem being investigated. This method has been used by Barnes in a study on divorce among the Ngoni. His village selection was not random for reasons he provides (1967:60):

> The sample village should be selected carefully so that it may be representative of the society being studied. Since usually among simple societies very little is known in advance about the population, and since it is usually quite impracticable to select villages at random, this is not easy. What can be done is to compare the village selected with a large number of other villages in respect of criteria which do not require lengthy investigation. Thus we may not be able to repeat a divorce inquiry in many villages in order to see if our first inquiry gave typical results. But we can compare the village in which, for better or worse, the detailed inquiry was made with many others for readily discoverable characteristics such as size, history, kinship structure, apparent wealth, and external contacts, and so verify that in these respects our sample village is typical of its area. In the absence of any better information we then make the assumption that our divorce data are also typical for a larger population.

Methodological purists like Goode and Hatt shake their heads at this, saying, "[Purposive sampling] is not a satisfactory procedure if high precision is desired. . . . Moreover from a statistical point of view this technique is particularly weak, since there is no way of calculating the limits of permissible error, or the required number for the sample, if strict probability sampling is not used." (*Ibid:* 230.) And Mitchell writes: "It is technically incorrect to use statistical measures based on probability theory to make inferences about the population at large from a sample unless that sample is truly a random one . . . and purposive selection of this sort (as done by Barnes) cannot be a substitute for random sampling." (1967:31.)

It should be noted, however, that the question for anthropology is not "if precision is desired" (obviously, it is), but rather "what precision is possible," given the exigencies of field situations; and also that purposive sampling has long been a popular approach for public-opinion pollsters, who despite their few glaring errors, have managed to stay in business.

6. Active research and statistical models. "Statistical models" (Lévi-Strauss, 1953:524–553), as I understand the term, require certain kinds of data. In simplest terms such data can be referred to as "what people do," or behavioral data. An interest in what people do does not preclude an interest in (1) what people say "they ought to do"; and (2) other guidance systems that are less well understood by the native population. An interest in (1) and (2) leads to the development of mechanical models that jointly cause "what people do" to occur. But in order to test the adequacy of our mechanical models to predict and explain actual behavior, we must collect behavioral data and keep them separate from other types of data. This, as I hope to show, is more troublesome than may be obvious. The collection of behavioral data has importance beyond testing already created mechanical models, for behavioral data throw great light on a basic task of cultural anthropology: to understand the nature of man. Thus, for many anthropologists, behavioral data is important in its own right, as it indicates man's attempts to use culture for his own ends, to rebel against it, and to change it—all points long ago made by Malinowski in *Sex and Repression in Savage Society* (1927) and the *Sexual Life of Savages* (1929), and currently being re-emphasized by a number of anthropologists.

Some of the data responsible for discrepancies between beliefs (cultural rules and cultural guides) and behavior do indeed disclose regularities; they are the result of following through the "dictates" of the guidance programs I have labeled operational rules, private guides, rumors, and suspicions. I make this statement as a proposition underlying the *V-R* Guidance System; for Van Velson it is an important hypothesis which goes along with the exciting field-work technique he is developing, the extended case method (1967:129–149). Referring to this method, Max Gluckman has commented (1967:xv-xvi):

[Van Velson's approach] requires taking a series of specific incidents affecting the same persons or groups, through a period of time, and showing how these incidents, these "cases," are related to the development and changes of social relations among these persons and groups, acting within the framework of their social system and culture. My own view is that this kind of approach will greatly alter our view of the working of some institutions, and deepen our understanding of the significance of all custom . . . it will bring to monographic analysis some of the penetration which Freud brought to the study of human personality, and some of the depth that many find in the novel but not in scientific analysis.

Van Velson's extended case method is a strategy of research through which much "noncultural" or "exceptions-data" can be gathered: my *V-R* Guidance System provides a model whereby much of that kind of material can be analyzed and systematically interrelated. Clearly both approaches complement each other; however, in terms of the focus of this section, both approaches require that the anthropologist systematically collect behavioral data.

To better distinguish data usable for statistical models (i.e., behavioral data) from data usable for mechanical models (data referring to system rules and guides), it may be useful to carefully examine the innocent sounding phrase *what people do*. When taken into the field and operationalized, this phrase can be translated in various ways. Including among such I would isolate:

T-1. What people are doing
T-2. What people think people are doing
T-3. What was done at time t_1, t_2, t_3, etc.
T-4. What people think was done at time t_1, t_2, t_3, etc.
T-5. What will be done when . . .
T-6. What people think will be done when . . .
T-7. What would be done if . . .
T-8. What people think would be done if . . .

To get information about *T-1*, the researcher can (1) do participant-observer work; (2) he can hire informants to be participant-observers in given situations; (3) he can ask informants specific questions concerning their own behavior or the behavior of specific neighbors, friends, and kin. The general question "What are people doing about the diseases which are attacking banana plants?" may elicit answers of the *T-2* type, depending on how accurate the informant is in generalizing about behaviors he has personally seen and how good his information sources are with respect to secondary information. Two general principles to keep in mind here are: First, the less summarizing the informant is asked to do, the more likely it is that his statements accurately reflect "what people actually do." Second, the sharper and more measurable the categories given an informant, the more likely it is that actual behavioral patterns are obtained. (See Simon, 1968:85.)

Thus the question "What is Jones doing about his dieseased plants?" is better replaced by a series of questions on the same topic: "Is Jones reading the government pamphlets on how to plant bananas?" "Is Jones using fertilizers to help his bananas to grow without diseases?" Clearly, in order to get "sharp" and meaningful questions on what people do, much needs to be known about the system being researched, further demonstrating the point earlier made that questioning is not very useful until much participant-observation work has been done. To get accurate answers by providing informants with measurable categories also demands a good understanding of the system being studied. For example, in order to get data on land use in Anamat, I asked every peasant farmer what types of trees and plants he had on his land and how many of each he had. After noticing that I was getting very sparse data with this question, I began to ask the peasants to identify by name the trees and plants that I saw. I then talked with a good informant about the information I had collected, and he added much additional data. Once I seemed to have discovered every important item that peasants grow on their land, I was able to question them very specifically concerning trees, plants, shrubs, their numbers, and the yields for given years.

In order to keep informants from generalizing, it is necessary to ask them questions concerning their own experiences. To get these data, it is necessary to question many natives on the same topic. *T-3* questions—what was done at time t_3, for example—are likely to provide data with a number of possible distortions. First, in some systems, the past is thought of as the "good old days," and negative aspects of them are easily forgotten. Second, the informant's memory may not be very accurate, and with all the best intentions he provides false information. Third, the informant may seek to impress the researcher with what he considers the "proper" answer. Finally, the information may be sensitive or secret, and the informants may lie for rapport reasons: the anthropologist has not developed enough rapport to ask such questions, or (from the informant's point of view) such questions require the informant to take more risk units than he is prepared to do.

T-7 questions and their variants generally provide interesting data that the anthropologist finds difficult to decode. This is especially true if conditions are set up which are both novel to the informant and unlikely to occur. For example, I asked my informants what they would do if some kind of mechanical man was invented to do all their work for them. Invariably the peasants found this question hard to answer; however I gathered interesting data on what work means to them, their beliefs about their rights as citizens of Trinidad, and how they felt about leisure time.

T-2, T-4, T-6, and *T-8* questions and questions of the *T-5* types are much more likely to elicit data on the rules of the system (i.e., data that lead to the development of mechanical models) than behavioral data. Data referring to rules, guides, and opinions must be kept apart from behavioral data. That is, rule systems must be identified and interrelated separately, and then the researcher must show (or at times demonstrate) how the rule systems explain the behavior. Clearly, until research methodology becomes more highly developed, both as a science and an art, all the behavioral data will not be explainable. Hopefully, however, it should now be possible to take statistically "normal" behavior for a given population and explain it in terms of the rule systems of the study. It should be noted, at this point, that if the distinction between cultural rules and operational rules (the major distinction of the *V-R* Guidance System) is meaningful, then researchers should often find that their behavioral data falls into bimodal distributions: one statistical norm "caused by" adherence to cultural rules (the proper), and the second "caused by" adherence to operational rules (the smart).[15]

Problem 14: Ethics and Sanity Maintenance

The Society for Applied Anthropology has been discussing the ethical responsibilities of its members for over two decades. In its most recent formal statement on ethics, adopted in 1963, the Society stated the following:

> . . . *To Science* [the anthropologist] has the responsibility of avoiding any actions or recommendations that will impede the advancement of scientific knowledge. In the wake of his own studies he must undertake to leave a hospitable climate for future study. With due regard to his other responsibilities as set forth here, he should undertake to make data and findings available for scientific purposes. He should not represent hypotheses or personal opinions as scientifically validated principles.

---

[15] For those yet unconvinced of the utility of systematically collecting behavioral data in ways that permit statistical analysis, I recommend Clyde Mitchell's essay "On Quantification in Social Anthropology," especially his conclusion that systematic quantification helps the anthropologist to discover regularities: "Means, ratios, and percentages are ways of summarizing the features and relationships in data. Statistical measures based on the theory of probability go beyond the mere quantitative data and use devices to bring out the association between various social facts the observer has collected." (1967:20.)

> *To his fellow men* he owes respect for [their] dignity and
> general well-being. He may not recommend any course of action
> on behalf of his client's interests, when the lives, well-being, dig-
> nity, and self-respect of others are likely to be adversely affected,
> without adequate provisions being made to insure that there will
> be a minimum of such effect and that the net effect will in the
> long run be more beneficial than if no action were taken at all.
> He must take the greatest care to protect his informants, espe-
> cially in the aspects of confidence which his informants may not
> be able to stipulate for themselves.
>
> *To his clients* he must make no promises nor may he en-
> courage any expectations that he cannot reasonably hope to fulfill.
> He must give them the best of his scientific knowledge and skill.
> He must consider their specific goals in the light of their general
> interests and welfare. He must establish a clear understanding
> with each client as to the nature of his responsibilities to his
> client, to science, and to his fellow men.[16]

This statement, which appears to make the anthropologist responsible to science, fellow men, and clients, also outlines his
responsibility to his informants and with the host government,
so that a researcher site is left as a "hospitable climate for
future study." Further, the responsibilities to science include
responsibilities to *all science,* to *anthropology* as a science, and
to *anthropologists* as fellow scientists. This variety of responsibilities thus involves multiple interests, some of which may,
at times, be contradictory. On this point the Ad Hoc Committee
on Ethics (ACE) of the American Anthropological Association
makes the following suggestions (1969:4) :

> In a field of such complex involvements, conflicts are bound to
> arise and create ethical dilemmas. It is a prime responsibility of
> the anthropologists to consider the possibility of such conflicts
> and to plan to resolve them in such a way as to do damage neither
> to those whom he studies, nor to his scholarly community. When
> these conditions cannot be met, the anthropologist would be well
> advised not to pursue the particular piece of research.

Implied here are two important principles: first, that naïveté is
no excuse for unethical conduct in research. A researcher has
the responsibility to gather data prior to undertaking some
research, so that he can predict some possible ethical dilemmas
that he may be forced into. Second, interest in a given piece of
research—a given problem, a given tribe, community, settlement, or whatever—is *secondary* to acting in ways considered
ethical. If an ethical dilemma appears inevitable in a piece of
research, *get another project.*

---

[16] "Statement on Ethics of the Society for Applied Anthropology," *Human
Organization,* 22:237, 1963–1964.

With respect to anthropologists' responsibilities to science, ACE suggests that "there is an obligation not to undertake research where one can anticipate that the results cannot be fully and freely published."

The nature of a scientist's relationships with clients and sponsoring agencies is a subject currently being hotly debated on many university campuses. The ACE report suggests:

> The anthropologist should avoid making claims as to his specific research competence, substantive or methodological, that are inflated or inaccurate . . . he should scrupulously avoid making claims to accomplish more than it is reasonable to believe that his discipline can deliver in the immediate future. Finally, he should not accept sponsorship under conditions where there is a lack of congruence between his own aims and those of his sponsors . . . the sponsorship and the sponsor's purpose should be publicly known—in the case of overseas research to host governments, host organizations, and subjects of field study—and that the results should be freely publishable.

The ACE report does not attempt to cover all ethical questions likely to arise in anthropology. On the contrary, it is emphasized that "the details of standards must grow out of the careful consideration of specific cases and issues as they arise."

The anthropologist who follows the guidelines thus far presented may never do anything describable as morally wrong. However, neither might he do anything describable as morally right. A clue to how to use science in ways to relieve human suffering lies in ACE's negative conclusion: that some research should *not* be done, since it leads to unsolvable moral problems. We might ask, conversely, what research *should be done?* A number of suggestions follow. Kathleen Gough (1968:406–407) suggests that:

> (1) We might examine Frank's [1967] argument, from United Nations figures, that per capita food production in non-Communist Asia, Africa and Latin America has declined in many cases to below pre-war levels since 1960, whereas it has risen above pre-war levels in China and Cuba. . . . (2) We might develop a set of research problems around comparisons of the structure and efficiency of socialist and capitalist foreign aid. . . . (3) We might undertake comparative studies of types of modern inter-societal political and economic dominance which would help us to define and refine such concepts as imperialism, neo-colonialism, etc. . . . (4) We might compare revolutionary and proto-revolutionary movements for what they can teach us on social change.

Gutorm Gjessing (1968:397–402) suggests that we "research" ourselves to discover the unconscious motivations that guide our work, and that we develop theoretical frameworks relevant to the modern world. Such frameworks should include the notions that change and stability are complementary factors; and that a wide sociocultural frame is necessary to understand small community and tribal studies.

Andre Gunder Frank (1968:412–414) suggests that "West European and North American anthropologists can best . . . [do] community studies to analyze the social structure of their own society for a political movement that promotes the necessary social change." Also that Asian, African, and Latin American anthropologists should analyze "how class structure and indeed culture and personality in Asia, Africa, Latin America and also North America are formed and deformed by the world capitalist colonial, neo-colonial and inter-colonial structure" . . . and "how poorly armed guerillas might more effectively resist a brutal and devastating military technology."

Otto von Mering (1968:421) suggests that "the essential scientific obligation is to illuminate for public inspection and redress the functioning (or 'mal-functioning') of a particular social order."

My own suggestion is that anthropologists reexamine a fundamental postulate of cultural anthropology: *cultural relativity,* or the idea that all cultures are equal. I believe that this postulate can be replaced with the proposition *some cultures are inferior.* It is up to the anthropologist to investigate the theoretical problems presented to us by a system such as Nazi Germany. Rules of "proper conduct" were developed under the Hitler regime that today have been almost universally damned. How then can anthropologists continue to talk of the equality of culture?! In truth, it will not be easy to discover the "measuring rods" by which cultural rules are to be evaluated; but this does not mean we cannot try. Culture, it is generally accepted, is a human invention to aid men in adapting to their environments. It would be valuable to develop research projects which help us to identify the kinds of social conditions which lead to what Jules Henry has called "culture against man."[17]

CONCLUSIONS

This chapter has focused on the needs of the novice who has decided to be a cultural anthropologist. Essentially it has attempted to send him (or her) several messages. First, the field has its glories and mysteries, but also involves hard work,

---

[17] Jules Henry, *Culture Against Man,* New York: Random House, 1965.

dedication, and various learnable skills. Second, it is never too early to plan for future adaptations to field-work situations. Third, several early decisions made (for example, what school to go to, whom to "select" as a high-status friend) strongly influence many future critical decisions (for example, place of specialization and type of field-work that will be done). Fourth, many "humanistic" concepts often considered as understandable only through experience, or through analysis provided by existential philosophers, are analyzable within "harder," scientific frameworks.

This chapter asks the experienced anthropologist to try to see the field through the eyes of the novice, and then answer two questions: Do traditional approaches really do an adequate job in preparing the novice for field work? And if not, What modifications can be made to provide superior training?

Anthropology has attracted many people with field-work talents whose creative abilities were rarely dissipated by dull graduate programs, but what "tools" were tranmitted from the experienced anthropologist to the young researcher? More often than not, the novice was sent off with a good knowledge of world ethnography, the names of a few informants, fatherly blessings from mentors, and little else. "Sink or swim," he was told. If the novice sank, then clearly he was not a real anthropologist. If he "swam" and came back with what appeared to be excellent data and intriguing stories about a new ritual, then the training method had proved its value. Robert Merton's "self-fulfilling prophecy" (1957) was a useful ally to much traditional research training in anthropology.

There was, however, a real catch to this idyllic picture, for a good number of researchers neither sank nor swam. They returned with data of dubious value, which anthropology's loose analytic techniques transformed into aesthetic monographs. Anthropologists generally write well and debate brilliantly, so inadequate data were at times disguised in fluent prose and a minimal research design by profound argumentation.

Our mentors' dedicated, honest, and serious attempts at training young anthropologists were hampered by a shortage of detailed first-hand accounts of life in the field, and sophisticated analytical treatments of the problems of field research. First-hand accounts of field work were rarely found for reasons detailed in my introductory essay: history, field-work culture, and the unwillingness of the anthropologist to expose himself in cold print, and analytical treatments of field problems were rarely found because they must be based on the detailed accounts. The essays in this book attempt to supply students with such accounts of life in the field.

A careful reading of the "Social Responsibility Symposium"

(*Current Anthropology*, 1968) will make it very clear that a number of respected anthropologists believe that as a *science* anthropology currently has little to offer toward solving major world problems. Even our widely and loudly acclaimed holistic approach is generally used inadequately, omitting such large variables as international trade agreements and Cold War power politics (Gjessing, 1968).

Are modern anthropologists satisfied to remain middlemen, interpreters between the "hard" sciences and the humanities? Must an interest in human goals—in the reduction of world tensions and in solving the problems of mass starvation and overpopulation—preclude the development of a real scientific methodology? Is it better to cry humanistic tears than to put an adequate anthropological theory in the service of humanity? My answer to all those questions is an emphatic No. We need scientific approaches to such concepts as rapport. Humanism must be saved for where it is really needed: to aid in the isolation of meaningful problems to research and in the development of moral rules for research. We need typologies, but not necessarily those presented in this essay, for typologies are the stepsisters of models, and models are skeleton theories. We need to develop, and systematically use, reproducible methodological procedures. We need field frameworks that give us "level-mobility"—allow us the freedom to move around from cultural to noncultural (social) phenomena and back again—picking up understanding and explanatory powers on the way. Van Velson's "extended case method" and my *V-R* Guidance System are examples of such frameworks. We need to understand the possibilities that quantification methods open up for anthropological research.

Finally, do we in cultural anthropology really have anywhere else to go except toward quantification? Members of our "extended family"—archaeologists, linguists, and physical anthropologists—have already taken the quantification route. The cultural anthropologist, by and large, "plays" with pencil-and-paper approaches and writes literary essays while his "family" is using computers and more and more regularly presenting its findings in the language of science, mathematics.

Cultural anthropologists have many problems to overcome to be able to travel shoulder to shoulder with members of their "extended family." Facts are often described as "dry," especially when presented in statistical and tabular form. Referring to a book filled with facts, Max Gluckman writes "Some reviewers of Van Velson's own recent study of the Lakeside Tonga of Malawi (1964) . . . have found the details of this book burdensome. Heavy demands are indeed made on the reader by this kind of analysis, and I would merely comment that there is no reason why science should be easy reading." (1967:vi.)

Science, particularly the science of man, is not easy to develop and not easy to carry out. Hopefully, this book will stimulate many to make the effort.

APPENDIX: A GUIDE TO PLANNING FIELD WORK

I. Introduction

Knowledge concerning the pragmatics of cross-cultural field work varies greatly. Therefore those who are well versed in such matters as how to (1) select a good graduate program, (2) become a competent researcher, (3) get grants, (4) make travel arrangements, and (5) plan for good health in the field are advised to skip this guide.

II. Selecting a Department for Graduate Studies

The importance of selecting an appropriate department for graduate studies is facilitated by certain pragmatics.

1. Follow news of departments of anthropology in the *Fellow Newsletter*. Available from the American Anthropological Association, Suite 112, 3700 Massachusetts Avenue, N.W., Washington, D.C. 20016 (published monthly and available at a subscription rate of $3 per year).
2. Get the *Guide to Graduate Programs of Anthropology* an annual bulletin of the American Anthropological Association.
3. Attend as many anthropological meetings as funds permit. Information on these annual meetings is also available in the *Fellow Newsletter*. Some of the major annual meetings by months include:
   a. Southern Anthropological Society, February/March
   b. Northeastern Anthropological Association, April
   c. Southwestern Anthropological Association, April
   d. American Association of Physical Anthropologists, April
   e. Society for Applied Anthropology, April
   f. Central States Anthropological Society, May
   g. Society for American Archaeology, May
   h. Canadian Sociology and Anthropology Association, June
   i. International Congress of Anthropological and Ethnological Sciences, September
   j. International Congress of Linguists, August/September
   k. American Anthropological Association, November

4. Once at an anthropological meeting, it may help to become a participant-observer and do focused interviewing. Interview anthropologists on what their departments are like, what studies are considered "in," what parts of the world are best covered in their course offerings, how stable their faculty is (given the "musical chair game" in academia, high faculty turnover is "normal" in many departments), which theoretical approaches are considered "scholarly," and any other related information you can get.
5. Visit the university that you think may best serve your interests before applying. Do participant-observation work with the graduate students; as low-status subordinates in an organization they are likely to give you much useful data.

III. Research Scholars Are Made Not Born

Programming onself for a successful career in field work necessitates planning and self-discipline. The following guides should be useful.

1. Keep a thought notebook. While reading, keep a notebook on problems that appear to exist within the material being digested. This approach serves various purposes: deeper insights are achieved, and problems are thereby "collected" for many purposes. Such a "problem collection" becomes invaluable for a professional career, especially in summarizing understandings achieved via one's problem collection. C. Wright Mills' *The Sociological Imagination* is an excellent guide for the creative use of problem development.

2. Expertise in methodology. A modern anthropologist must beware of being fooled by labels. Field work today often involves the use of quantitative and qualitative statistical analysis, computer programming, and related approaches. It is therefore wise to make oneself expert in all areas of social-science research.

3. Experience in field research. A good way of learning research is by doing research. It is important, therefore, to try to become part of some on-going project. It is also valuable for gaining research experience to find a group with an unusual historical and cultural background and to do participant-observation research.

4. Developing different and new relationships. People whose age, religion, socioeconomic background, culture, experience, interest, and goals are very different from the researcher's provide both an intellectual challenge and useful rapport training.

5. Role-playing. It is valuable to get involved with some kind of theatrical group which puts the researcher on stage in front of an audience. This kind of role-playing is not very different from role-playing in a native community, where the anthropologist is on stage for extensive periods of time.

6. Planning for mental health. The cross-cultural researcher needs mental health. One starts with getting as much psychotherapy as is financially possible. Most universities have free counseling available. In large cities, a variety of facilities are available through numerous mental-health associations.

IV. Guide to Grantsmanship

Most research is funded. It is, therefore, necessary to learn the sources of these funds and the correct procedure for obtaining them. Grant-proposal forms generally follow a predictable pattern modeled after textbook interpretations of scientific method. However, each agency generally has its own peculiar instructions as to how their application for funds is to be filled. Read such instructions carefully. Most grant proposals include the following basic information:

1. Biographical information, including names, dates, addresses, institutions of higher education attended, degrees, and honors received.
2. Formal title of the project
3. Research plan
    (a) Introduction—general background of the research proposed
    (b) Justification—relevance of the problem to on-going research, theory development, etc.
    (c) Methodology—clear statement of the problem to be studied, sampling and data-gathering procedure and techniques, plans for data analysis
    (d) Objectives of the research
4. Total amount requested for the grant and detailed budget
    (a) Salaries—project leader, assistants, clerical aide
    (b) Travel expenses
    (c) Maintenance
    (d) Supplies and services
    (e) Equipment
    (f) Other costs
5. Work schedule and publication plans
6. Other research that the applicant has participated in, his publications, papers, etc.

It is important to pick a fund agency that is suitable for the project. Listed below are eleven different sources for information on the funding of research projects. Additional sources can be obtained from the library. High-status friends are often goldmines of information; an experienced researcher can be of invaluable aid prior to and during the application procedure. The Office of External Research is able to supply a *Directory of Governmental Resources,* which includes information on all agencies, bureaus, and offices of the federal government with available research funds.

1. Office of External Research
   Bureau of Intelligence and Research
   U.S. Department of State
   Washington, D.C.

   Publishes the *Directory of Governmental Resources*

2. American Anthropological Association
   Suite 112
   3700 Massachusetts Avenue, N.W.
   Washington, D.C. 20016

   Publishes *Fellow Newsletter* with information on grants and fellowships.

3. Committee on International Exchange of Persons
   Conference Board of Associated Research Councils
   2102 Constitution Avenue
   Washington, D.C. 20418

4. The Agricultural Development Council
   630 Fifth Avenue
   New York, N.Y. 10020

   Publishes *ADC Newsletter* and *ADC Researcher* containing information on grants and fellowships.

5. Ford Foundation
   320 East 43 Street
   New York, N.Y. 10017

6. American Council of Learned Societies
   345 East 46 Street
   New York, N.Y. 10017

   Publishes *ACLS Newsletter* containing relevant information.

7. American Academy of Arts and Sciences
   280 Newton Street
   Brookline, Massachusetts

8. American Philosophical Society
   104 South Fifth Street
   Philadelphia, Pa.

9. Human Ecology Fund
   201 E. 57 Street
   New York, N.Y.

10. Social Science Research Council
    230 Park Avenue
    New York, N.Y. 10017

11. National Science Foundation
    1520 H Street, N.W.
    Washington, D.C.

V. Natives Beware: Anthropologists Are Coming

After receiving the good news of a successful application for funding, the often agonizing process of completing all the necessary documentation begins. The anthropologist will generally require a passport, visas, health certification, etc.

1. Passport. A United States Passport is a travel document showing the bearer's country of origin and identity, and is issued by the Secretary of State, or under his authority, to persons owing allegiance to the United States, One cannot leave or enter the United States without it (except to Canada, Mexico, or the Bahamas). It is advisable to apply early: it often takes about three weeks to a month's time to process the application.

United States passports are now valid for five years from the date of issue. Renewal can be transacted by mail. While it is possible for members of the same family to travel under one passport (for one fee), be advised against this. In case of emergency, travel separately may be required.

Application for a passport may be made in person to the United States Passport Agency located at:

J.F.K. Building, Boston, Mass.
219 S. Dearborn Street, Chicago, Ill.
51 S.W. First Avenue, Miami, Fla.
Customs House, 423 Canal Street, New Orleans, La.
630 Fifth Avenue, New York, N.Y.
300 N. Los Angeles Street, Los Angeles, Calif.
1410 Fifth Avenue, Seattle, Washington
450 Golden Gate Avenue, San Francisco, Calif.
22nd and E. Street, Washington, D.C.

In other cities, application for a passport may be made before a clerk of a federal or state court that has naturalization jurisdiction.

2. Visas. In most countries where an extended length of stay is planned, a visa will be necessary. A visa is an endorsement on one's passport by a particular country granting entrance into that country. Requirements for a particular country can be obtained from consular representatives located in major cities (especially New York, Washington, D.C., Chicago, San Francisco, Boston). Embassies of most countries are located in Washington, D.C., and addresses of such, or of consuls, may be obtained in the *Congressional Directory*.

It is the responsibility of a traveler to obtain visas, when required, from the appropriate Embassy or consular office. The Department of State, c/o Passport Office, publishes a pamphlet (M-264, 1/68) entitled *Fees Charged by Foreign Countries for the Visa of United States Passports*. It contains information on passports and visas for 170 countries.

3. Health requirements (including vaccinations). Immunization sequences requires much time: start early! To discover the necessary "shots" for the place where research is planned, speak to your physician and write for the following booklets available (for a very nominal fee) from the Superintendent of Documents, Government Printing Office, Washington, D.C. 20402.

Immunization Information for International Travel No. FS2.2: Im 6/2/967–68   40¢

Health Information for Travel In

> *Africa, Including Malagasy Republic and Neighboring Islands,* No. PHS 748 D

> *Europe,* No. PHS 748

> *Asia, Including Japan, Indonesia, Philippines, Australia, and New Zealand,* No. PHS 748 C

> *Mexico, Central and South America, and the Caribbean,* No. PHS 748 B

So You're Going Abroad, No. PHS 748 A

For re-entry into the United States, only an International Certification of Vaccination is necessary. Most foreign countries require such a certificate of entering travelers too.

Although each part of the world is affected by different regulations and suggestions for immunizations, it is generally true that for Africa and South America, yellow-fever shots are essential; for Bolivia, Peru, Ethiopia, and Ecuador, typhus is necessary; East of Suez, cholera immunizations are legally required; and for some areas, an innoculation for plague is recommended. Adequate tetanus and polio boosters are highly recommended, as is gamma globulin (for hepatitis). Typhoid vaccinations are often advisable, especially for tropical areas.

4. Hints for Travel Abroad

(a). *International Student Identification Card.* Information concerning this card may be obtained from:

USNSTA—United States National Student Travel Association
70 Fifth Avenue
New York, N.Y. 10011

or

USNSTA
11753 Wilshire Blvd.
Suite 1
Los Angeles, California 90025

(b). *Youth hostels.* If youth hostels can be of aid, write American Youth Hostels, National Headquarters, 20 West 17 Street, New York, N.Y. 10011

(c). *Character references.* A certificate attesting to one's character is available from the local police in the researcher's home town and is a helpful document.

(d). *Statement of financial responsibility.* A certificate stating one's financial responsibility is an assurance that the anthropologist will not run out of money and become dependent on the host country. Such a statement may simply be a letter from those sources financing the research.

(e). *Photographs.* A number of photographs are necessary in the documentation process. It is suggested that extras be made.

(f). *International driver's license.* An International Driving Permit, recognized in most countries, is available through the American Automobile Association (AAA), or affiliated motor clubs.

(g). *Work permits.* Many countries prohibit archaeological excavations without an official permit. Some countries require permission to do field work or ethnographic studies. It is advisable to check with the embassy or consulate. An application for permission should be made well enough in advance of the planned departure date to avoid last-minute delays and disappointments.

(h). *American Embassy.* Find out where the American Embassy or American Consulate nearest to the researcher's field project is located. It may become very important during the time spent in the field. The American Embassy or Consulate is prepared to assist Americans who may find themselves in any difficulty in any country. It is often advisable that one notify the Embassy upon arrival, indicating place of residence and intended length of stay.

(i). *Luggage and weight allowances.* If one flies overseas on a first-class ticket, he is allowed 66 pounds of luggage; in economy class, 44 pounds. Other luggage may be hand carried on board. Within the United States a traveler is permitted two pieces of luggage for air flights. Excess luggage can be shipped Air Freight, often in the same plane, and at reduced rate.

(j). *Clothing.* It is important that one find out what kind of clothing will be needed for the area in which research will take place.

(k). *Embarkation taxes.* While there is no fee for leaving the U.S.A., there may be fees (head tax, passenger-service tax, embarkation tax, airport-service tax, etc.) upon arrival and departure in many countries. This is easily enough checked with the consul or embassy.

(l). *Customs.* Most countries will allow the traveler to take all personal belongings, duty free, into their territories provided they all leave when the researcher departs. However, before attempting to export anything from an archaeological or ethnographic study, authorization from the proper authorities is generally needed. *Customs Hints for Returning U.S. Residents* is a helpful booklet, available from the Bureau of Customs, Treasury Department, Washington, D.C. 20226.

VI. Survival Skills in the Field

1. Foods and liquids. It is important that the researcher learn the edible and poisonous plants, fish, and animals of the area. It is suggested that one not eat any meat that has not been well cooked. Meat that is freshly killed and completely cooked is generally perfectly safe; as is any fruit that must be peeled and any hot, cooked vegetables.

It is generally wise to avoid prepared milk and milk products. If bottled water is available, one should stick with it completely. If not, the boiling of water or water purification methods are suggested.

The United States Navy prepared a book in 1943 on survival techniques on sea, on land, in tropics, desert, or the Arctic. It is called *Survival On Land and Sea* and was prepared for the United States Navy by the Ethnographic Board and the Staff of the Smithsonian Institute, Office of Naval Intelligence, U.S. Navy, 1943. While the book is not for sale, and is not readily available, it may be worthwhile to try and locate a copy. Some researchers have managed to get this book through interlibrary loan.

2. First-aid skills and supplies. It is important to have first-aid equipment handy and to know how and what and when to use such. The American Red Cross publishes several useful guides.

The following list has been suggested by several anthropologists as *necessary supplies* for anyone going into the field:

a good first-aid kit
snake-bite kit (including antivenom)
hypodermic (disposable) needles and syringes
antidysentery medicines
malarial preventatives
antihistamines (anticold pills)
aspirin
pain medicine
tablets to purify water (halazone tablets)
tissues, toilet paper

It is important to label all medicine by name and use.

3. Drug prescriptions and glasses. If one should wear glasses or contact lenses, try to have an extra pair along, or at least a prescription. If special drugs are needed, or if a medical condition exists, please let others in the area know and have the prescriptions written in generic not commercial terms. Also, if possible, try to locate a physician with western training in the research area.

It is helpful that one keep a small card—such as the following—in one's pocket along with the International Certificate of Vaccination at all times.

Side One

Side Two

Medical Identification

_____

DOCTOR

_____

NAME

_____

_____

NATIONALITY

_____

ADDRESS

_____

_____

_____

_____

_____

_____

ADDRESS

_____

MEDICAL PROBLEMS

_____

_____

_____

_____

CONTACT IN CASE OF EMERGENCY

BLOOD GROUP—Rh FACTOR

4. Travel skills. It is important that one gain skills in the transportational modes used in the part of the world where research is to be carried out. The ability to walk for long distances is a must for field work. Skills in different modes of travel and in sports popular in the culture being researched often help in rapport development.

5. Tools and equipment. Each project requires a different set of tools. The novice is advised to carefully check this out with experienced researchers, particularly those who have worked in the area of the projected study.

6. Field notes. It is important that one have a planned strategy for data collecting and recording and the storing of field notes. It has been suggested that one transcribe and, if possible, type his field notes every day. It is desirable to make a copy of all notes and mail one set home.

To summarize—plan early! All you need is a good education, research experience, funds, mental health, good luck, and a great sense of humor.

REFERENCES

FIELD WORK: AN INTRODUCTION

Berreman, Gerald D.
1962. *Behind Many Masks*. Ithaca, N.Y.: Society for Applied Anthropology, Monograph No. 4.

Boas, Franz
1938. *General Anthropology*. Boston: D.C. Heath.

Chagnon, Napoleon A.
1968. "Yanomamö: The Fierce People." New York: Holt, Rinehart and Winston.

Codrington, R. H.
1891. *The Melanesians: Studies in Their Anthropology and Folk-lore.* Oxford: Clarendon Press.

Evans-Pritchard, E. E.
1964. *Social Anthropology and Other Essays.* New York: Free Press.

Freilich, Morris
1963. "The Natural Experiment, Ecology, and Culture." *Southwestern Journal of Anthropology,* 19:21–39.

1964. "The Natural Triad in Kinship and Complex Systems." *American Sociological Review,* 29:183–200.

1967. "Ecology and Culture: Environmental Determinism and the Ecological Approach in Anthropology." *Anthropological Quarterly,* 40:1:

Freilich, Morris and Peter Hirsch
1967. "Mental Health Culture in Rural Missouri." St. Louis, Mo.: The Social Science Institute, Parts 1, 1A, 2, and 3–8.

Gans, Herbert
1968. "The Participant-Observer as a Human Being." *Institutions and the Person,* eds. H. Becker, B. Geer, D. Riesman, and R. Weiss. Chicago: Aldine, pp. 300–317.

Harris, Marvin
1968. *The Rise of Anthropological Theory: A History of Theories of Culture.* New York: Thomas Y. Crowell.

Junod, H. A.
1913. *The Life of a South African Tribe.* Neuchâtel: Attinger.

Lowie, Robert H.
1937. *The History of Ethnological Theory.* New York: Holt, Rinehart and Winston.

Lubbock, Sir John
1872. *Prehistoric Times as Illustrated by Ancient Remains and the Manners and Customs of Modern Savages.* London: Williams, Norgate.

McGrath, Joseph
1964. "Toward a Theory of Method." *New Perspectives in Organization Research,* ed. W. W. Cooper, *et al.* New York: John Wiley.

Malinowski, Bronislaw
1953. *Argonauts of the Western Pacific*. New York: E. P. Dutton.

1967. *A Diary in the Strict Sense of the Term*. New York: Harcourt, Brace & World.

Mead, Margaret
1949. *Male and Female: A Study of the Sexes in a Changing World*. New York: William Morrow.

Merton, Robert K.
1957. *Social Theory and Social Structure*. New York: Free Press.

Morgan, Lewis H.
1851. *League of the Ho-de-no-saunee, or Iroquois*. New York: Dodd, Mead, 1901.

1871. *Systems of Consanguinity and Affinity of the Human Family*. Washington: Smithsonian Contributions of Knowledge, vol. 17.

Powdermaker, Hortense
1967. *Stranger and Friend*. New York: Norton.

Radcliffe-Brown, A. R.
1922. *The Andamen Islanders*. New York: Free Press.

Rivers, W. H. R.
1906. *The Toda*. London and New York: Macmillan.

1910. "The Genealogical Method of Anthropological Inquiry." *The Sociological Review*, 3:1–12.

Schwartz, Morris S., and Charlotte Green Schwartz
1955. "Problems in Participant Observation." *American Journal of Sociology*, 60:343–354.

Smith, M.
1959. "Boas' 'Natural History' Approach to Field Method." *The Anthropology of Franz Boas*, Memoir 89, ed. W. Goldschmidt. Wisconsin, American Anthropological Association, pp. 46–60.

Spencer, Sir Baldwin, and Gillen, F. J.
1899. *The Native Tribes of Central Australia*. London: Macmillan.

Spencer, Herbert
1873–1880. *Descriptive Sociology*. Vols. I–XV. New York: Appleton.

Tax, Sol
  1955. "From Lafitau to Radcliffe-Browne: A Short History of the Study of Social Organization." *Social Anthropology of North American Tribes,* ed. F. Eggan. Chicago: University of Chicago Press, pp. 445–481.

Tylor, E. B.
  1872. *Primitive Culture.* 2nd ed. New York: Holt, Rinehart and Winston, 1877.

Waitz, Franz Theodor
  1863. *Introduction to Anthropology.* London: Longmans, Green, & Roberts.

Watkins, John G.
  1965. "Psychotherapeutic Methods." *Handbook of Clinical Psychology,* ed. B. B. Wolman. New York: McGraw-Hill, pp. 1143–1167.

Westermarck, E. A.
  1925. The History of Human Marriage, 3 vols., London: S. Ambaras.

Wolpe, Joseph
  1962. "The Experimental Foundations of Some New Psychotherapeutic Methods." *Experimental Foundations of Clinical Psychology,* ed. A. J. Bachrach. New York: Basic Books.

1. FIELD WORK IN TWO NORTHERN CANADIAN COMMUNITIES

Henry, Jules, and Melford E. Spiro
  1953. "Psychological Techniques: Projective Tests in Field Work." *Anthropology Today,* ed. A. L. Kroeber. Chicago: University of Chicago Press.

Honigmann, John J.
  1943–1944. "On the Alaska Highway." *The Dalhousie Review,* 23:400–408.

  1946. "Report on the North" *Canadian Forum,* 25:285–286.

  1947a. "Cultural Dynamics of Sex." *Psychiatry,* 10:37–47.

  1947b. "Witch-Fear in Post-Contact Kaska Society." *American Anthropologist,* 49:222–243.

1949. *Culture and Ethos of Kaska Society.* (Yale University Publications in Anthropology, No. 40.) New Haven: Yale University Press.

1954. *The Kaska Indians: An Ethnographic Reconstruction.* (Yale University Publications in Anthropology, No. 51.) New Haven: Yale University Press.

1958. "Pakistan's Prospects of Development." *Eastern World,* 12:10:16–18.

1960a. "A Case Study of Community Development in Pakistan." *Economic Development and Cultural Change,* 8:288–303.

1960b. "Circumpolar Forest North America as a Modern Culture Area." *Selected Papers of the Fifth International Congress of Anthropological and Ethnological Sciences,* ed. Anthony F. C. Wallace. Philadelphia: University of Pennsylvania Press.

1962. *Social Networks in Great Whale River.* Ottawa: National Museum of Canada, Bulletin No. 178.

1963. *Understanding Culture.* New York: Harper & Row.

1966a. "Education in the Modernization of Cultures: Pakistan and Indian Villages Compared to Eskimo in a Canadian Arctic Town." Paper presented at the International Sociological Association's Sixth World Congress.

1966b. "Social Disintegration in Five Northern Canadian Communities." *Canadian Journal of Sociology and Anthropology,* 2:199–214.

Honigmann, John J., and Irma Honigmann
1944. "Drinking in an Indian-White Community." *Quarterly Journal of Studies on Alcohol,* 5:575–619.

1947. "A Kaska Oracle." *Man,* 47:139–140.

1965a. "Eskimo Learn To Run Their Own Affairs." *The Dalhousie Review,* 45:289–298.

1965b. *Eskimo Townsmen.* Ottawa: Canadian Research Centre for Anthropology.

1965c. "How Baffin Island Eskimo Have Learned To Use Alcohol." *Social Forces,* 44:73–83.

1965d. "Patterns of Eskimo Deviance in a New Eastern Arctic Town." *Research Previews,* 12:1:5–15.

James, Bernard J.
    1961. "Social-Psychological Dimensions of Ojibwa Accul-
    turation." *American Anthropologist,* 63:721–746.

Kluckhohn, Clyde
    1949. *Mirror for Man.* New York: McGraw-Hill.

Leighton, Alexander H.
    1959. *My Name Is Legion.* New York: Basic Books.

Lindzey, Gardner
    1961. *Projective Techniques and Cross-Cultural Research.*
    New York: Appleton-Century-Crofts.

Mead, Margaret
    1956. *New Lives for Old.* New York: William Morrow.

Osgood, Cornelius
    1940. *Ingalik Material Culture.* (Yale University Publica-
    tions in Anthropology, No. 22.) New Haven: Yale Univer-
    sity Press.

Stern, Theodore
    1965. *The Klamath Tribe.* Seattle: University of Washing-
    ton Press.

Swezey, F. Curtiss, and John J. Honigmann
    1962. "American Origins of Community Development."
    Community Development, 10:165–176.

Vanstone, James W.
    1965. *The Changing Culture of the Snowdrift Chipewyan.*
    Ottawa: National Museum of Canada, Bulletin No. 209.

Wilson, Godfrey, and Monica Wilson
    1945. *Analysis of Social Change.* London and New York:
    Cambridge University Press.

Yatsushiro, Toshio
    1960. "The Changing Eskimo Economy." Paper presented
    at the annual meeting of the American Anthropological As-
    sociation.

2. COMPARATIVE FIELD TECHNIQUES IN URBAN RESEARCH IN AFRICA

Kluckhohn, Florence R.
    1940. "The Participant Observer Technique in Small Com-
    munities." *American Journal of Sociology,* vol. 46.

Levy, H.
1947. *The Universe of Science.* Watts.

McEwen, William J.
1963. "Forms and Problems of Validations in Social Anthropology." *Current Anthropology,* 4:2.

Paul, Benjamin D.
1953. "Interview Techniques and Field Relations." *Anthropology Today: An Encyclopedic Inventory,* ed. A. L. Kroeber, *et al.* Chicago University of Chicago Press.

Schwab, William B.
1954. "An Experiment in Methodology in a West African Community." *Human Organization,* 13:1.

1955. "Kinship and Lineage Among the Yoruba." *Africa,* 25.

1961. "Social Stratification in Gwelo." *Social Change in Modern Africa,* ed. Aidan Southall. New York and London: Oxford University Press.

1965. "Oshogbo, An Urban Community." *Urbanization and Migration in West Africa,* ed. Hilda Kuper. Berkeley: University of California Press.

1968. "Differential Urbanization in Gwelo." *Rhodesia,* Ms.

1967. Comments on "Urbanization and Social Change in Africa" by A. L. Epstein. *Current Anthropology,* 290–291.

Stebbing, L. Susan
1948. *Thinking to Some Purpose.* New York: Penguin Books.

Vidich, Arthur J.
1955. "Participant Observation and the Collection and Interpretation of Data." *American Journal of Sociology,* 60:4.

3. VILLAGE AND CITY FIELD WORK IN LEBANON

Ammar, Hamed
1966. *Growing Up in an Egyptian Village.* New York: Octagon.

Antoun, Richard T.
   1965. "Conservatism and Change in the Village Community: A Jordanian Case Study." *Human Organization,* 24:1:4–10.

Ayoub, Victor
   1965. "Conflict Resolution and Social Reorganization in a Lebanese Village." *Human Organization,* 24:1:11–17.

Fernea, Elizabeth W.
   1965. *Guests of the Sheik.* New York: Doubleday.

Fuller, Anne H.
   1961. *Buarij: Portrait of a Lebanese Muslim Village.* Cambridge, Mass.: Harvard University Press.

Gulick, John.
   1949. "The Maronites: A Study of the Indigenous Christians of the Lebanon." Cambridge, Mass.: Harvard College. Unpublished B.A. honors thesis.

   1953. "The Lebanese Village: An Introduction." *American Anthropologist,* 55:3:367–372.

   1954. "Conservatism and Change in a Lebanese Village." *The Middle East Journal,* 8:3:295–307.

   1955. *Social Structure and Culture Change in a Lebanese Village.* (Viking Fund Publications in Anthropology, No. 21.) New York: Viking Press.

   1960. *Cherokees at the Crossroads.* Chapel Hill: Institute for Research in Social Science Monographs.

   1962. "Social Correlates of Urban Growth and Development." *Urban Growth Dynamics,* ed. F. S. Chapin, Jr., and S. F. Weiss. New York: John Wiley, pp. 309–315.

   1963a. "Images of an Arab City." *Journal of the American Institute of Planners,* 29:3:179–198.

   1963b. "Urban Anthropology: Its Present and Future." *Transactions of the New York Academy of Sciences* (Series II), 25:3:445–458.

   1965a. "Old Values and New Institutions in a Lebanese Arab City." *Human Organization,* 24:1:49–52.

   1965b. "The Religious Structure of Lebanese Culture." *Jahrbuch fur Religionssoziologie,* ed. Joachim Matthes. Koln & Opladen: Westdeutscher Verlag, 1:151–187.

1967. *Tripoli: A Modern Arab City*. Cambridge, Mass.: Harvard University Press.

Gulick, John, Charles E. Bowerman, and Kurt W. Back
1962. "Newcomer Enculturation in the City: Attitudes and Participation." *Urban Growth Dynamics*, ed. F. S. Chapin, Jr., and S. F. Weiss. New York: John Wiley, pp. 315–358.

Lutfiyya, Abdulla H.
1966. *Baytin: A Jordanian Village*. New York: Humanities Press.

Nader, Laura
1965. "Communication Between Village and City in the Middle East." *Human Organization*, 24:1:18–24.

Peters, Emrys L.
1963. "Aspects of Rank and Status Among Muslims in a Lebanese Village." *Mediterranean Countrymen*, ed. Julian Pitt-Rivers. New York: Humanities Press, pp. 159–202.

Sweet, Louise E.
1960. *Tell Toqaan: A Syrian Village*. Ann Arbor: University of Michigan Press.

Tannous, Afif I.
1942. "Group Behaviour in the Village Community of Lebanon." *American Journal of Sociology*, 48:2:231–239.

Touma, Toufic
1958. *Un Village de Montagne au Liban* (Hadeth al-Jobbé). The Hague.

Williams, Herbert H., and Judith R. Williams
1965. "The Extended Family as a Vehicle of Culture Change." *Human Organization*, 24:1:59–64.

4. CAKCHIQUELES AND CARIBS: THE SOCIAL CONTEXT OF FIELD WORK

Adams, Richard N.
1957. *Cultural Surveys of Panama-Nicaragua-Guatemala-El Salvador-Honduras*. Washington, D.C.: Pan American Sanitary Bureau, Publication No. 33.

Foster, George M.
1965. "Peasant Society and the Image of Limited Good." *American Anthropologist,* 67:293–315.

González, Nancie L.
1965. "Black Carib Adaptation to a Latin Urban Milieu." *Social and Economic Studies,* 14:3:272:278.

In press. "Obeah and Other Witchcraft Among the Black Carib." *North American Sorcery,* ed. Deward Walker.

Reina, Ruben
1966. *The Law of the Saints.* Indianapolis: Bobbs-Merrill.

Solien, Nancie L.
1959. "West Indian Characteristics of the Black Carib." *Southwestern Journal of Anthropology,* 15:3:300–307.

Tax, Sol
1937. "The Municipios of the Midwest Highlands of Guatemala." *American Anthropologist,* 39:423–444.

1952. *Heritage of Conquest.* Glencoe, Ill.: Free Press.

Taylor, Douglas M.
1951. *The Black Carib of British Honduras.* New York: Viking Fund Publications in Anthropology, No. 17.

Tejada, Carlos, Nancie L. González, and Margarita Sánchez
1965. "El Factor Diego y el Gene de Células Falciformes entre los Caribes de Raza Negra de Livingston, Guatemala." *Revista del Colegio Médico de Guatemala,* 16:2:83–86.

Tumin, Melvin
1952. *Caste in a Peasant Society.* Princeton, N. J.: Princeton University Press.

Wagley, Charles
1949. *The Social and Religious Life of a Guatemalan Village.* American Anthropological Association, Memoir XI.

Young, Frank W., and Ruth C. Young
1961. "Key Informant Reliability in Rural Mexican Villages." *Human Organization,* 20:141–148.

5. MOHAWK HEROES AND TRINIDADIAN PEASANTS

Freilich, Morris
1958. "Culture Persistence Among the Modern Iroquois." *Anthropos* (Fribourg, Switzerland), 53:473–483.

1960. "Cultural Diversity Among Trinidadian Peasants." Doctoral dissertation. New York: Columbia University.

1961. "Serial Polygyny, Negro Peasants, and Model Analysis." *American Anthropologist,* 63:955–975.

1963. "The Natural Experiment, Ecology, and Culture." *Southwestern Journal of Anthropology,* 19:21–39.

1967. "Ecology and Culture: Environmental Determinism and the Ecological Approach in Anthropology." *Anthropological Quarterly,* 40:26–43.

1968. "The Natural Experiment: A Strategy for Anthropological Research." Ms. 90 pp.

Wallace, A. F. C.
1951. "Some Psychological Determinants of Culture Change in an Iroquoian Community." *Symposium on Local Diversity in Iroquois Culture,* W. N. Fenton. Washington, D.C.: Bureau of Ethnology, Bulletin No. 149.

6. RESEARCH IN INDIVIDUALISTIC SOCIETIES

Berde, Stuart J.
1966. "Wild Ricing: The Transformation of an Aboriginal Subsistence Pattern." Unpublished Senior Honors Thesis. Minneapolis: University of Minnesota.

Nickul, Karl
1948. *"The Skolt Lapp Community Suenjelsijd."* Acta Lapponica, 5.

Paredes, J. Anthony
1966a. "The Land and the People: Upper Mississippi Research Project, Preliminary Statistics." Mimeographed.

1966b. "Community Celebrations in Northern Minnesota." Paper presented at the Annual Meeting of the American Anthropological Association.

1969. "Chippewa Townsmen: A Study in Small-scale Urban Adaptation." Unpublished Ph.D. Thesis. University of New Mexico.

Paredes, J. Anthony, and Pertti J. Pelto
1964. "First Annual Report of the Upper Mississippi Research Project." (Unpublished manuscript.)

1965. "Second Annual Report of the Upper Mississippi Research Project." (Unpublished manuscript.)

1967. "Terminal Report of the Upper Mississippi Research Project." (Unpublished manuscript.)

Pelto, Pertti J.
1960. "Innovation in an Individualistic Society." Paper presented at the Annual Meeting of the American Anthropological Association.

1961. "Preliminary Analysis of Skolt Lapp Dreams" (with Ernest Belden). Paper presented at the Annual Meeting of the American Anthropological Association

1962a. *Individualism in Skolt Lapp Society.* Suomen Muinaismuistoyhdistys (Finnish Antiquities Society). Monograph 16. Helsinki.

1962b. "Personality in an Individualistic Society." Paper presented at the Annual Meeting of the American Anthropological Association.

1963a. "Individuaalisuus eli yksilollisyys kolttasaamelaisten yhteiskunnassa." *Kotiseutu* (Helsinki).

1963b. "Alcohol Use and Dyadic Interaction." Paper presented at the Annual Meeting of the Northeastern Anthropological Association.

1968. "The Differences Between 'Tight' and 'Loose' Societies." *Transaction,* 5:37–40.

In press. "The Twilight Zone of Poverty." *The Shadows of Affluence,* ed. Miriam Cohn.

Pelto, Pertti J., Martti Linkola, and Pekka Sammallahti
1968. "The Snowmobile Revolution in Lapland." Helsinki, Journal of The Finno-Ugric Society, 69:1–42.

Roufs, Timothy
1967. "Social Structure and Community Development: An Analysis of a Chippewa Case." Unpublished Master's Thesis. Minneapolis: University of Minnesota.

Rynkiewich, Michael Allen
1968. "Chippewa Pow-Wows." Unpublished Master's Thesis. Minneapolis: University of Minnesota.

Schacter, Jean J.
1967a. "Neighborhood and Family Ethnography in a Northern Minnesota Community." Unpublished Master's Thesis. Minneapolis: University of Minnesota.

1967b. "Family and Neighborhood Ethnography in a Northern Minnesota City." Paper presented at the Annual Meeting of the Central States Anthropological Society.

Schensul, Stephen L.
1965. "Lakewood: An Ethnographic Analysis of a Northern Minnesota Community." Unpublished Master's Thesis. Minneapolis: University of Minnesota.

Schensul, Stephen, J. Anthony Paredes, and Pertti J. Pelto
1968. "The Twilight Zone of Poverty." *Human Organization,* 27:1:30–40.

Simon, Barbara
1967. "Rice Village: An Ethnographic Analysis of a Chippewa Community." Unpublished Master's Thesis. Minneapolis: University of Minnesota.

Stark, Matthew, and Pertti J. Pelto
In press. "The Economic and Social Position of Minnesota Chippewa Indians." *The Shadows of Affluence,* ed. Miriam Cohn.

Whitaker, Gretel H.
1967a. "People and Politics in a Chippewa Community." Unpublished Master's Thesis. Minneapolis: University of Minnesota.

1967b. "Personality Characteristics in a Chippewa Community." Paper presented at the Annual Meeting of the American Anthropological Association.

1968. "Aspects of Personality Among the Rural Poor." Paper presented at the Annual Meeting of the American Anthropological Association.

Symposium: Minnesota Chippewa Indians
1967. The following papers were presented at the Annual Meeting of the Central States Anthropological Society:

Miller, Frank C., "Political Action in a Closed Reservation"

Paredes, J. Anthony, "Indians of North City"

Rokala, Dwight, "Preliminary Report on Genetic Characteristics of Chippewa Indians"

Roufs, Timothy G., "Wicket: A 'Successful' Indian Community"

Rynkiewich, Michael, "Elaboration of Chippewa Pow-Wows"

Simon, Barbara R., "The Structure of Rice Village"

Whitaker, Gretel H., "Indian Politics at James Lake"

7. INTENSIVE FIELD WORK AND SCOPE SAMPLING: METHODS FOR STUDYING THE SAME PROBLEM AT DIFFERENT LEVELS

Buckley, Walter
1967. *Sociology and Modern Systems Theory*. Englewood Cliffs, N.J.: Prentice-Hall.

Driberg, J. H.
1923. *The Lango*. London: T. Fisher Unwin Ltd.

Goldschmidt, Walter
1965. "Theory and Strategy in the Study of Cultural Adaptability." *American Anthropologist*, 67: 2:402–408.

Perlman, Melvin L.
1959. "The Structure of Settlements in Toro." East African Institute of Social Research, Makerere College, Conference Papers, pp. 1–23.

1960a. "Bibliographie analytique" (with M. P. Moal). *Femmes d'Afrique Noire*, ed. Denise Paulme. (Le Monde d'Outre-mer, passé et present, premiere Série Etudes, IX.) Paris: Mouton, pp. 219–278.

1960b. "Property Rights of Women." (Uganda Council of Women, Conference on the Status of Women in Relation to the Marriage Laws.) Appendix IV.

1966. "The Changing Status and Role of Women in Toro (Western Uganda)." *Cahiers d'Etudes Africaines*, 6:4: 564–591.

1969. "Law and the Status of Women in Uganda: A Systematic Comparison Between the Ganda and the Toro." *Tropical Man, Yearbook of the Department of Anthropology of the Royal Tropical Institute*. Amsterdam, vol. 2.

In press. "The Comparative Method: The Single Investigator and the Team Approach." *A Handbook of Method in Cultural Anthropology,* ed. R. Naroll and R. Cohen, Natural History Press.

n.d. *Toro Marriage.*

Riley, Matilda White
1963. *Sociological Research: I, A Case Approach.* New York: Harcourt, Brace & World.

Roscoe, John
1911. *The Baganda.* London: Macmillan.

Southall, A. W.
1960. "On Chastity in Africa." *Uganda Journal,* 24:207–216.

Willer, David
1967. *Scientific Sociology: Theory and Method.* Englewood Cliffs, N.J.: Prentice-Hall.

8. NETWORK ANALYSIS AND PROCESSES
OF ADAPTATION AMONG ECUADORIAN
AND NOVA SCOTIAN NEGROES

Adams, Richard N.
1956. Cultural Components of Central America. *American Anthropologist.* 58:881–907.

Banton, Michael, ed.
1966. *The Social Anthropology of Complex Societies,* A.S.A. Monograph No. 4. New York: Praeger.

Erasmus, Charles J.
1956. "The Occurrence and Disappearance of Reciprocal Farm Labor in Latin America." *Southwestern Journal of Anthropology.* 12:444–469.

Ferdon, Edwin N., Jr.
1950. *Studies in Ecuadorian Geography.* Santa Fe: Monographs of the School of American Research and the University of Southern California, No. 15.

Fergusson, C. B.
1948. *A Documentary Study of the Establishment of the*

Negroes in Nova Scotia Between the War of 1812 and the Winning of Responsible Government. Halifax: Public Archives of Nova Scotia.

Freeman, Frank S.
1955. *Theory and Practice of Psychological Testing.* New York: Holt, Rinehart & Winston.

Foster, George M.
1960. *Culture and Conquest: America's Spanish Heritage.* New York: Viking Fund Publications in Anthropology, No. 27.

Greaves, Ida C.
1931. "The Negro in Canada." *National Problems of Canada.* Montreal: McGill University Economic Studies, No. 16.

Herskovits, Melville J.
1958. *The Myth of the Negro Past.* Boston: Beacon.

1966. *The New World Negro: Selected Papers in Afro-American Studies,* ed. Frances S. Herskovits. Bloomington: Indiana University Press.

Honigmann, John J.
1954. *Culture and Personality.* New York: Harper & Row.

1959. *The World of Man.* New York: Harper & Row.

Hughes, Charles C., *et al.*
1960. *The People of Cove and Woodlot.* New York: Basic Books.

Leach, Edmund R.
1954. *Political Systems of Highland Burma.* Cambridge, Mass.: Harvard University Press.

Leighton, Alexander
1959. *My Name Is Legion.* New York: Basic Books.

Leighton, Dorothea, *et al.*
1963. *The Character of Danger.* New York: Basic Books.

Middleton, John, and Edward H. Winter
1963. *Witchcraft and Sorcery in East Africa.* London: Routledge and Kegan Paul.

Mitchell, J. Clyde
1966. "Theoretical Orientations in African Urban Studies." *The Social Anthropology of Complex Societies,* ed. Michael Banton. New York: Praeger.

Smith, Raymond T.
1963. "Culture and So
Some Recent Work on I
parative Studies of Society an

Smith, T. Watson
1899. *The Slave in Canada*. Collections of t..
Nova Scotia Historical Society for the Years 18.-1898,
vol. 10.

Solien, Nancie L.
1958. "The Consanguineal Household Among the Black
Carib of Central America." Ann Arbor: University of Michigan, Doctoral Thesis, University Microfilms.

Whitten, Norman E., Jr.
1961. "Aspects and Origins of Negro Occultism in Piedmont Village." M.A. Thesis. University of North Carolina
at Chapel Hill.

1962. "Contemporary Patterns of Malign Occultism Among
Negroes in North Carolina." *Journal of American Folklore*,
75:297.

1965. *Class, Kinship, and Power in an Ecuadorian Town:
The Negroes of San Lorenzo*. Stanford: Stanford University
Press.

1967a. "Adaptation and Adaptability as Processes of Microevolutionary Change in New World Negro Communities."
Paper read at the American Anthropological Association
meetings as part of a symposium entitled "Negroes in the
New World: Problems in Theory and Method."

1967b. *Afro-Hispanic Music from Western Colombia and
Ecuador*. Record and accompanying monograph. New York:
Ethnic Folkways, FE 4375.

1967c. "Música y relaciones sociales en las tierras bajas
Colombianas y Ecuatorianas del Pacífico: estudio sobre
microevolución sociocultural." *América Indígena*, 17:4.

1968. "Personal Networks and Musical Contexts in the
Pacific Lowlands of Colombia and Ecuador." Manchester:
*Journal of the Royal Anthropological Institute of Great
Britain and Ireland*, 3:1.

1969. "Strategies of Adaptive Mobility in the Colombian-
Ecuadorian Littoral." *American Anthropologist*, 71:2.

orman E., Jr., and Aurelio Fuentes C.
¡Baile Marimba! Negro Folk Music in Northwest
ador." *Journal of the Folklore Institute*, 3:2. Special
atin American edition.

nitten, Norman E., Jr., and John F. Szwed, eds.
1969. *Afro-American Anthropology: Contemporary Perspectives*. New York: Free Press.

Winks, Robin W.
1964. "The Negro in the Maritimes: An Introductory Survey." Mimeographed ms. in possession of the author.

9. OPEN NETWORKS AND NATIVE FORMALISM: THE MANDAYA AND PITJANDJARA CASES

Basedow, Herbert
1914. *Journal of the Government North-West Expedition*. Adelaide: Royal Geographical Society of Australia, South Australian Branch.

1925. *The Australian Aboriginal*. Adelaide: Preece.

Cole, Fay-Cooper
1913. *The Wild Tribes of Davao District, Mindanao*. Chicago: Field Museum of Natural History, 12:2.

Conklin, Harold C.
1957. *Hanunoo Agriculture*. Rome: United Nations Forestry Development Paper, No. 12.

Elkin, A. P.
1931. "Social Organization of South Australian Tribes." *Oceania*, 2:44–73.

1938–1940. "Kinship in South Australia." *Oceania*, 8:419–452; 9:41–78; 10:196–234; 10:295–349; 10:369–388.

Finlayson, H. H.
1936. *The Red Centre*. Sydney: Angus and Robertson.

Firth, Raymond
1964. *Essays on Social Organization*. London: Athlone Press.

Garvan, John M.
1931. *The Manobos of Mindanao.* (Memoirs of the National Academy of Sciences, Volume 23.) Washington, D.C.: U.S. Government Printing Office.

Hiatt, L. R.
1962. "Local Organization Among the Australian Aborigines." *Oceania,* 32:267–286.

1965. *Kinship and Conflict.* Canberra: The Australian National University.

1966. "The Lost Horde." *Oceania,* 37:81–92.

Leach, E. R.
1950. *Social Science Research in Sarawak.* (Colonial Research Studies No. 1.) London: His Majesty's Stationery Office.

Meggitt, M. J.
1962. *Desert People.* Sydney: Angus and Robertson.

Mountford, Charles P.
1950. *Brown Men and Red Sand.* Sydney: Angus and Robertson.

1965. *Ayers Rock: Its Peoples, Their Beliefs and Their Art.* Sydney: Angus and Robertson.

Pelzer, Karl J.
1945. *Pioneer Settlement in the Asiatic Tropics.* New York: American Geographical Society, Special Publication No. 29.

Radcliffe-Brown, A. R.
1913. "Three Tribes of Western Australia." *Journal of the Royal Anthropological Institute,* 43:143–194.

1918. "Notes on the Social Organization of Australian Tribes." *Journal of the Royal Anthropological Institute,* 48:222–253.

1930. *Social Organization of Australian Tribes.* Oceania Monograph No. 1.

Rose, Frederick G. G.
1960. *Classification of Kin, Age Structure and Marriage Amongst the Groote Eylandt Aborigines.* Berlin: Deutsche Akademie der Wissenschaften.

1965. *The Wind of Change in Central Australia.* Berlin: Deutsche Akademie der Wissenschaften.

Service, Elman R.

1962. *Primitive Social Organization.* New York: Random House.

Stanner, W. E. H.

1965. "Aboriginal Territorial Organization: Estate, Range, Domain and Regime." *Oceania,* 36:1–26.

Steward, Julian H.

1936. "The Economic and Social Basis of Primitive Bands." *Essays in Honor of A. L. Kroeber.* Berkeley: University of California Press.

1955. *Theory of Culture Change.* Urbana: University of Illinois Press.

Tindale, Norman B.

1935. "Initiation among the Pitjandjara Natives of the Mann and Tohkinson Ranges in South Australia." *Oceania,* 6:199–224.

1936. "General Report on the Anthropological Expedition to the Warburton Range, Western Australia, July–September 1935." *Oceania,* 6:481–485.

1959. "Totemic Beliefs in the Western Desert of Australia: Part I, Women Who Became the Pleiades." *Records of the South Australian Museum,* 13:305–332.

1963. "Totemic Beliefs in the Western Desert of Australia: Part II, Musical Rocks and Associated Objects of the Pitjandjara People." *Records of the South Australian Museum,* 14:499–514.

1965. "Stone Implement Making Among the Nakako, Ngadadjara and Pitjandjara of the Great Western Desert." *Records of the South Australian Museum,* 15:131–164.

Yengoyan, Aram A.

1964. *Environment, Shifting Cultivation, and Social Organization Among the Mandaya of Eastern Mindanao, Philippines.* Unpublished Doctoral Dissertation, University of Chicago: Department of Anthropology.

1965. "Aspects of Ecological Succession Among Mandaya Populations in Eastern Davao Province, Philippines." *Papers of the Michigan Academy of Science, Arts, and Letters,* 50:437–443.

1966a. "Baptism and 'Bisayanization' Among the Mandaya of Eastern Mindanao, Philippines." *Asian Studies*, 4:324–327.

1966b. "Marketing Networks and Economic Processes Among the Abaca Cultivating Mandaya of Eastern Mindanao, Philippines." *Selected Readings to Accompany Getting Agriculture Moving*, ed. Raymond E. Burton. New York: Agricultural Development Council, Vol. II, pp. 689–701.

1966c. "Field Report No. 1 on Pitjandjara Fieldwork," to the Australian Institute of Aboriginal Studies. (Doc. 66/491.) December.

1967. "Field Report No. 2 on Pitjandjara Fieldwork" to the Australian Institute of Aboriginal Studies. (Doc. 67/566.) March.

1968. "Demographic and Ecological Influences on Aboriginal Australian Marriage Sections." *Man the Hunter*, ed. Richard B. Lee and Irven DeVore. Chicago: Aldine Press.

In press. "Mandaya Land Tenure." *Land Tenure Systems in the South Pacific*, ed. R. Crocombe.

10. A COMPARISON OF FIELD RESEARCH IN CANADA AND POLYNESIA

Eysenck, H. J.
    1965. *Fact and Fiction in Psychology*. Baltimore: Penguin Books.

Hughes, Charles C., *et al.*
    1960. *The People of Cove and Woodlot*. New York: Basic Books.

Leighton, Alexander H.
    1959. *My Name Is Legion*. New York: Basic Books.

Leighton, Dorothea, *et al.*
    1963. *The Character of Danger*. New York: Basic Books.

Mead, Margaret
    1949. *Coming of Age in Samoa*. New York: Mentor Books.

TOWARD A FORMALIZATION
OF FIELD WORK

Allport, G.W.
1954. "The Historical Background of Modern Social Psychology." *Handbook of Social Psychology*, 2 vols., ed. Gardner Lindzey. Reading, Mass.: Addison-Wesley, pp. 3–56.

Anderson, Nels
1959. *The Urban Community: A World Perspective*. New York: Henry Holt.

Anonymous
1963–64. "Statement on Ethics of the Society for Applied Anthropology." *Human Organization*, 22:237.

Back, K. W.
1956. "The Well-Informed Informant." *Human Organization*, 14:30–33.

Bales, Robert F.
1950. *Interaction Process Analysis: A Method for the Study of Small Groups*. Reading, Mass.: Addison-Wesley.

Barnes, J. A.
1947. "The Collection of Geneologies." *Rhodes-Livingston Journal*, 5:48–55.
1967. "Geneologies." *The Craft of Social Anthropology*, ed. A. L. Epstein. London, New York: Tavistock pp. 101–127.

Beaglehole, Ernest
1949. "Cultural Complexity and Psychological Problems." *A Study of Interpersonal Relations*, ed. P. Mullahy. New York: Hermitage House.

Berreman, Gerald
1968. "Ethnography: Method and Product." *Introduction to Cultural Anthropology: Essays in the Scope and Methods of the Science of Man*, ed. J. A. Clifton. Boston: Houghton-Mifflin Co., pp. 337–373.

Birdwhistell, R. L.
1952. "Field Methods and Techniques, Body Motion Research and Interviewing." *Human Organization*, 11:1.

Bruyn, Severyn T.
1966. *The Human Perspective in Sociology: The Methodology of Participant Observation.* Englewood Cliffs, N.J.: Prentice-Hall.

Buber, Martin
1955. *I and Thou,* trans. Ronald Smith. New York: Scribner.

Chasin, J. B.
1967. *Research Design in Clinical Psychology and Psychiatry.* New York: Appleton-Century-Crofts.

Cicourel, Aaron V.
1964. *Method and Measurement in Sociology.* New York: Free Press.

Colby, B. N.
1966. "Ethnographic Semantics: A Preliminary Survey." *Current Anthropology,* 7:3–32.

Colson, Elizabeth
1967. "The Intensive Study of Small Sample Communities." *The Craft of Social Anthropology,* ed. A. L. Epstein. London, New York: Tavistock, pp. 3–15.

Conklin, H. C.
1964. "Ethnogenealogical Method." *Explorations in Cultural Anthropology: Essays presented in honor of G. P. Murdock,* ed., W. H. Goodenough. New York: McGraw-Hill, pp. 25–55.

Deane, P.
1949. "Problems of Surveying Village Economics." *Rhodes-Livingston Journal,* 8:42–49.

Devereux, George
1956. "Normal and Abnormal: The Key Problem of Psychiatric Anthropology." *Some Uses of Anthropology, Theoretical and Applied.* Washington: Anthropological Society of Washington, pp. 23–48.

Driver, H. E.
1953. "Statistics in Anthropology." *American Anthropologist,* 55:42–59.

Durbin, Marshall
1966. "The Goals of Ethnoscience." *Anthropological Linguistics,* 8:22–41.

Epstein, A. L., ed.
1967. "The Case Method in the Field of Law," *The Craft of Social Anthropology*. London, New York: Tavistock, pp. 205–230.

Evans-Pritchard, E. E.
1964. *Social Anthropology and Other Essays*. New York: Free Press.

Foster, George, M.
1969. *Applied Anthropology*. Boston: Little, Brown.

Frake, Charles
1964. "Notes on Queries in Anthropology." *American Anthropologist*, 66:132–145.

Frank, Andre G.
1968. "Comments in Social Responsibility Symposium." *Current Anthropology*, 9:5:412–414.

Freilich, Morris
(unpublished) "Manufacturing Culture: Man the Scientist."

1963. "Toward an Operational Definition of Community." *Rural Sociology*, 28:117–127.

1964. "The Natural Triad in Kinship and Complex Systems." *American Sociological Review*, 29:183–200.
1969. "Structural Analysis: A Fun Game." Paper presented at 9th Annual Meeting at Northeastern Anthropological Association.

Gans, Herbert
1968. "The Participant-Observer as a Human Being." *Institutions and the Person*, eds. H. Becker, B. Geer, D. Riesman, R. Weiss. Chicago: Aldine, pp. 300–317.

Geertz, Clifford
1967. "Under the Mosquito Net." *New York Review of Books*, September 14, 1967.

Gjessing, Gutrom
1968. "The Social Responsibility of Social Scientists." *Current Anthropology*, 9:5:397–402.

Gluckman, Max
1967. "Introduction." *The Craft of Social Anthropology*, ed. T. S. Epstein. London, New York: Tavistock, pp. xi–xx.

Goode, W. J. and P. K. Hatt.
1952. *Methods in Social Research*. New York: McGraw-Hill.

Gough, Kathleen
1968. "New Proposals for Anthropologists." *Current Anthropology,* 9:5:403–407.

Hallowell, A. Irving
1955. *Culture and Experience.* Philadelphia: University of Pennsylvania Press.

Hare, A. Paul, E. F. Borgatta, and R. F. Bales
1955. *Small Groups: Studies in Social Interaction.* New York: Knopf.

Haring, Douglas, ed.
1956. *Personal Character and Cultural Milieu: A Collection of Readings,* 3d ed. Ithaca: Syracuse University Press.

Hempel, Carl G.
1960. "Operationalism, Observation and Scientific Terms." *Philosophy of Science,* eds. Arthur Danto and Sidney Morgenbesser. New York: Meridian, pp. 101–120.

Henry, Jules
1963. *Culture Against Man.* New York: Random House.

Henry, Jules, and Melford E. Spiro
1953. "Psychological Techniques: Projective Tests in Field Work." *Anthropology Today,* ed. A. L. Kroeber. Chicago: University of Chicago Press, pp. 417–429.

Hilger, Inez
1960. *Field Guide to the Ethnological Study of Child Life.* New Haven: Human Relations Area Files.

Hillery, George A., Jr.
1955. "Definitions of a Community: Areas of Agreement." *Rural Sociology,* 20:111–123.

Hobbs, Nicholas
1965. "Ethics in Clinical Psychology." *Handbook of Clinical Psychology,* ed. Benjamin B. Wolman. New York: McGraw-Hill, pp. 1507–1514.

Honigman, John J.
1963. *Understanding Culture.* New York: Harper & Row.
1968. *Personality in Culture.* New York: Harper & Row.

Hsu, Francis, L. K., ed.
1954. *Aspects of Culture and Personality: A Symposium.* New York: Abelard-Schuman.

Institute of Human Relations
1950. *Outline of Cultural Materials,* 3d ed. New Haven: Yale University Press.

Junker, B. H.
1960. *Fieldwork: An Introduction to the Social Sciences.* Chicago: University of Chicago.

Kaplan, Bert
1957. "Personality and Social Structure." *Review of Sociology: Analysis of a Decade,* ed. J. B. Gittler. New York: Wiley, pp.

Kaufman, Harold F.
1959. "Towards an Interaction Conception of Community." *Social Forces,* 38:8–17.

Kardiner, Abram
1939. *The Individual and His Society.* New York: Columbia University Press.
1945. *The Psychological Frontiers of Society.* New York: Columbia University Press.

Kelly, George A.
1963. *A Theory of Personality.* New York: Norton.

Kerlinger, Fred N.
1964. *Foundations of Behavioral Research.* New York: Holt, Rinehart & Winston.

Kluckhohn, C., H. A. Murray, and D. M. Schneider, eds.
1953. *Personality in Nature, Society and Culture.* 2nd ed. New York: Knopf.

Krech, David, and Richard S. Crutchfield
1968. *Elements of Psychology.* New York: Knopf.

Krech, D., Richard S. Crutchfield, and Egerton L. Ballachey.
1962. *Individual and Society.* New York: McGraw-Hill.

Kroeber, A. L.
1948. *Anthropology.* New York: Harcourt, Brace & World.
1952. *The Nature of Culture.* Chicago: University of Chicago Press.

Kroeber, A. L., and Kluckhohn C.
1952. "Culture, a Critical Review of Concept and Definitions." Papers of Peabody Museum, vol. 42, no. 1. Cambridge: Harvard University Press.

LaBarre, Weston
1958. "The Influence of Freud on Anthropology." *American Image,* 15:275–328.

Langness, L.
1965. *Life History in Anthropological Science*. New York: Holt, Rinehart, and Winston.

Leach, Edmund R.
1954. *"Political Systems of Highland Burma: A Study of Kachin Social Structure*. London: G. Bell (reprinted 1964).

Lévi-Strauss, Claude
1953. "Social Structure." *Anthropology Today*, ed. A. L. Kroeber. Chicago: University of Chicago Press. pp. 524–553.

Linton, Ralph
1936. *The Study of Man*. New York: Appleton-Century-Crofts.
1945. *The Cultural Background of Personality*. New York: Appleton-Century-Crofts.
1956. *Culture and Mental Disorders*, ed. G. Devereux. Springfield, Ill.: Charles C Thomas.

Lundberg, Craig C.
1968. "A Transactional Conception of Fieldwork." *Human Organization*, 27:1:45–49.

Malinowski, B., ed.
1938. *Methods of Study of Culture Contact in Africa*. London: Oxford University Press, pp. 46–59.

Malinowski, B.
1927. *Sex and Repression in Savage Society*. London: Routledge and Kegan Paul.
1929. *Sexual Life of Savages in North-Western Melanesia*. London: Routledge and Kegan Paul.
1967. *A Diary in the Strict Sense of the Term*. New York: Harcourt, Brace & World.

Marwick, M. G.
1956. "An Experiment in Public-Opinion Polling Among Preliterate People." *Africa*, 26:149–159.

Mead, Margaret
1953. "National Character." *Anthropology Today*, ed. A. L. Kroeber. Chicago: University of Chicago Press, pp. 642–667.

Mering, Otto Von
1968. Comments in Social Responsibility Symposium. *Current Anthropology*, 9:5:421.

Merton, R. K., M. Fiske, and P. L. Kendall
1956. *The Focused Interview*. New York: The Free Press.

Merton, Robert K.
1957. *Social Theory and Social Structure.* New York: Free Press.

Mills, C. W.
1959. *The Sociological Imagination.* London: Oxford University Press.

Mitchell, J. C.
1949. "The Collection and Treatment of Family Budgets in Primitive Communities as a Field Problem." *Rhodes-Livingston Journal,* 8:50–56.
1967. "On Quantification in Social Anthropology." *The Craft of Social Anthropology,* ed. T. S. Epstein. London and New York: Tavistock, pp. 17–45.

Murdock, George P.
1949. *Social Structure.* New York: Macmillan.

Myrdal, Gunner
1944. *An American Dilemma.* 2 vols. New York: Harper & Row.

Nadel, S. F.
1951. *The Foundations of Social Anthropology.* New York: Free Press.

Olmstead, Michael S.
1959. *The Small Group.* New York: Random House.

Opler, Marvin and J. L. Singer
1956. "Contrasting Patterns of Fantasy and Mobility in Irish and Italian Schizophrenics." *Journal of Abnormal and Social Psychology,* 53:42–47.

Orwell, George
1946. *Animal Farm.* New York: Harcourt, Brace & World.

Parsons, Talcott
1937. *The Structure of Social Action: A Study in Social Theory with Special Reference to a Group of Recent European Writers.* New York: McGraw-Hill.

Pearsall, Marion
1965. "Participant Observation as Role and Method in Behavioral Research." *Nursing Research,* 14:1:37–42.

Pelto, Perti
1968. "The Differences Between 'Tight' and 'Loose' Societies." *Transaction,* 5:5:37–40.

Powdermaker, Hortense
1966. *Stranger and Friend.* New York: Norton.

Richardson, S. A., B. S. Dohrenwend, and D. Klein
1965. *Interviewing: Its Forms and Functions.* New York: Basic Books.

Rivers, W. H. R.
1910. "The Geneological Method of Anthropological Inquiry." *The Sociological Review,* 3:1–12.

Roberts, John M.
1964. "The Self-Management of Cultures." *Explorations in Cultural Anthropology,* ed. W. H. Goodenough. New York: McGraw-Hill, pp. 433–454.

Rogers, Everret, M.
1969. *Modernization Among Peaseants.* In association with Lynee Svenning. New York: Holt, Rinehart and Winston.

Romney, A. K., and R. C. D'Andrade, eds.
1964. "Transcultural Studies in Cognition" *American Anthropologist,* 66 (3) part 2.

Royal Anthropological Institute of Great Britain and Ireland
1951. *Notes and Queries on Anthropology.* 6th ed. London: Routledge and Kegan Paul.

Sargent, S. Stansfeld, and Marian W. Smith, eds.
1949. *Culture and Personality.* New York: Viking Fund.

Scheler, Max
1954. *The Nature of Sympathy,* trans. Peter Heath. New Haven: Yale.

Selltiz, C., M. Jahoda, M. Deutsch, and S. W. Cook
1959. *Research Methods in Social Relations.* rev. 1 vol. ed. New York: Holt, Rinehart and Winston.

Sheldon, W. H.
1940. *The Varieties of Human Physique: An Introduction to Constitutional Psychology.* New York: Harper & Row.

Shibutani, Tamotsu
1961. *Society and Personality: An Interactionist Approach to Social Psychology.* Englewood Cliffs, N.J.: Prentice-Hall.

Simon, Julian L.
1968. *Basic Research Methods in Social Science: The Art of Empirical Investigation.* New York: Random House.

Smith, Alfred G., ed.
1966. *Communication and Culture: Readings in the Codes of Human Interaction.* New York: Holt, Rinehart and Winston.

Sprott, W. J. H.
1958. *Human Groups.* Baltimore: Penguin.

Steward, Julian
1955. *Theory of Culture Change.* Urbana: University of Illinois Press.

Thompson, Laura
1963. *The Science of Man.* New York: Holt, Rinehart and Winston.

Thompson, Laura
1969. *The Secret of Culture.* New York: Random House.

Valentine, Charles, A.
1968. *Culture of Poverty.* Chicago: University of Chicago Press.

Van Velson, J.
1967. "The Extended-case Method Situational Analysis." *The Craft of Social Anthropology,* ed. A. L. Epstein. London and New York: Tavistock, pp. 129–149.

Vidich, Arthur and Joseph Bensman
1954. "The Validity of Field Data." *Human Organization,* 13:20–27.

Wallace, Anthony F. C.
1961. *Culture and Personality.* New York: Random House.

Wax, Rosalie H.
1962. "Field Methods and Techniques: Reciprocity as a Field Technique." *Human Organization,* 11:3.